FAIRY-TALE FILMS BEYOND DISNEY

The fairy tale has become one of the dominant cultural forms and genres internationally, thanks in large part to its many manifestations on screen. Yet the history and relevance of the fairy-tale film have largely been neglected. In this follow-up to Jack Zipes's award-winning book *The Enchanted Screen* (2011), *Fairy-Tale Films Beyond Disney* offers the first book-length multinational, multidisciplinary exploration of fairy-tale cinema. Bringing together twenty-three of the world's top fairy-tale scholars to analyze the enormous scope of these films, Zipes and colleagues Pauline Greenhill and Kendra Magnus-Johnston present perspectives on film from every part of the globe, from Hayao Miyazaki's *Spirited Away*, to Jan Švankmajer's *Alice*, to the transnational adaptations of *1001 Nights* and Hans Christian Andersen.

Contributors explore filmic traditions in each area not only from their different cultural backgrounds, but from a range of academic fields, including criminal justice studies, education, film studies, folkloristics, gender studies, and literary studies. *Fairy-Tale Films Beyond Disney* offers readers an opportunity to explore the intersections, disparities, historical and national contexts of its subject, and to further appreciate what has become an undeniably global phenomenon.

Jack Zipes is Professor Emeritus of German and comparative literature at the University of Minnesota. In addition to his scholarly work, he is an active storyteller in public schools and has worked with children's theaters in Europe and the United States. Most recently he has published *The Enchanted Screen: The Unknown History of Fairy-Tale Films* (2011), *The Irresistible Fairy Tale: The Cultural and Social History of a Genre* (2012), and *Grimm Legacies: The Magic Power of the Grimms' Folk and Fairy Tales* (2014).

Pauline Greenhill is Professor of Women's and Gender Studies at the University of Winnipeg, Manitoba, Canada. Her recent books are *Channeling Wonder: Fairy Tales on Television* (co-edited with Jill Terry Rudy, 2014); *Unsettling Assumptions: Tradition, Gender, Drag* (co-edited with Diane Tye, 2014); *Transgressive Tales: Queering the Grimms* (co-edited with Kay Turner, 2012); *Fairy Tale Films: Visions of Ambiguity* (co-edited with Sidney Eve Matrix, 2010); and *Make the Night Hideous: Four English Canadian Charivaris, 1881–1940* (2010).

Kendra Magnus-Johnston is an interdisciplinary studies doctoral student at the University of Manitoba. She holds a master's degree in cultural studies and an undergraduate degree in rhetoric and communications from the University of Winnipeg. Apart from recent contributions to edited collections like *Channeling Wonder* and *Unsettling Assumptions*, her research can also be found in journals such as *Marvels & Tales*, *Journal of Folklore Research*, and *Children's Literature Association Quarterly*.

First published 2016
by Routledge
711 Third Avenue, New York, NY 10017

and by Routledge
2 Park Square, Milton Park, Abingdon, Oxon OX14 4RN

Routledge is an imprint of the Taylor & Francis Group, an informa business

© 2016 Taylor & Francis

Library of Congress Cataloging-in-Publication Data
Fairy-tale films beyond Disney : international perspectives / edited by Jack Zipes, Pauline Greenhill, and Kendra Magnus-Johnston.
    pages cm
Includes bibliographical references and index.
Includes filmography.
 1. Fairy tales in motion pictures. I. Zipes, Jack, 1937- editor. II. Greenhill, Pauline, editor. III. Magnus-Johnston, Kendra.
    PN1995.9.F34F33 2015
    791.43′6559—dc23
    2015007822

ISBN: 978-0-415-70929-3 (hbk)
ISBN: 978-0-415-70930-9 (pbk)
ISBN: 978-1-315-88562-9 (ebk)

Typeset in ApexBembo
by Apex CoVantage, LLC

CONTENTS

FIGURES

FOREWORD AND ACKNOWLEDGMENTS

In 2011, after I had finished writing *The Enchanted Screen: The Unknown History of Fairy-Tale Films*, I realized just how much I still did not know about the cinematic adaptation of folktales and fairy tales worldwide, and how much I had not covered in that book. Since I had spent five years working on *The Enchanted Screen*, I had also become fully aware that I would not be able to write a second, more comprehensive, book on the filmic adaptation of folktales and fairy tales by myself. Fortunately, soon after the completion of *The Enchanted Screen* I was invited by Pauline Greenhill to join a research group based at the University of Winnipeg. Indeed, her invitation was a stroke of good luck because I quickly recognized that Pauline, who had recently co-edited *Fairy Tale Films: Visions of Ambiguity* (Greenhill and Matrix 2010), was a dynamo and had gathered together a number of talented scholars of folktales and fairy tales, one of whom was Kendra Magnus-Johnston. After three days of presentations of projects and discussions at the first Winnipeg meeting, I knew I had to act and be opportunistic, not unlike the troubled and fortunate protagonists of fairy tales themselves. I asked Pauline and Kendra if they might join me and develop a second book dealing with fairy-tale films that would cover international developments and focus on cinematic adaptations of folktales and fairy tales in the latter part of the twentieth century and the beginning of the twenty-first. Their welcome response and effective work have led to the production of the present book.

Although there has been an awakening among scholars in the fields of folklore, fairy-tale studies, and cinema studies, who have produced numerous significant essays and a few books about fairy-tale films, this development is still limited to a small group of critics.[1] The relative lack of attention to fairy-tale films is somewhat stunning, given the fact that the production of both Hollywood fairy-tale films, which tend to be global blockbusters, and the wealth of provocative, mainly independent fairy-tale films, have created what I call a cultural tsunami. What is even more astounding is that film critics seem to be puzzled by the attention filmmakers, producers, studios, and TV networks have been paying to fairy tales and folktales when these stories have provided the stuff of which *all* films are made from the 1890s to the present, beginning with the work of Georges Méliès.

I realize that this claim may seem a gross exaggeration; however, the history of folktales and fairy tales demonstrates the degree to which such narratives have pervaded cultural fields including theater, opera, radio plays, painting, vaudeville, musicals, comics, novels, and so on. Indeed, this cultural saturation demands that the motifs, themes, and structures of folktales and fairy tales must be studied if one wants to grasp the complex implications of the works produced in these respective fields. Yet, almost all the books that deal with the history of film and cinematic adaptation of literary works fail to cover or even mention the adaptation and use of folktales and fairy tales. The fairy-tale film seems to be a neglected or abused stepchild, especially in those cultural fields where one would expect better treatment.

In Simone Murray's recent pioneer study *The Adaptation Industry: The Cultural Economy of Contemporary Literary Adaptation* (2012), there is not one word about the adaptation of literary fairy tales or even about the prolific Disney adaptation industry. Murray states:

> *The Adaptation Industry* is designed to showcase a broadly sociological approach to adaptation, foregrounding those issues usually pushed to the margins of adaptation studies work: the industrial structures, interdependent networks of agents, commercial contexts, and legal and policy regimes within which adaptations come to be. This economy-passing adaptation industry both constrains and—crucially—*enables* adaptations in little-analysed ways. In particular, this study posits cultural and commercial concerns not as mutually antithetical or self-cancelling but as complexly interrelated.
>
> (2012, 6)

This is all well and good, and Murray's book lays the groundwork for comprehensive sociological studies of the adaptation of literary works for the cinema. And yet, like other film historians and scholars, she neglects to include and analyze the adaptation of folktales and fairy tales. One would expect at least some remarks about the Disney industry and its socio-economic role in the development of literary adaptation not only in the United States, but in the world. Not a word. One would expect some mention of interrelated studies of fairy-tale films produced by folklorists and literary critics of fairy tales. Not a word.

Though our present book does not cover all the aspects of adaptation that Murray believes need to be addressed in her sociological approach, the writers speak to many facets she mentions and more. In keeping with what Cristina Bacchilega calls "the fairy-tale web" in her highly significant book, *Fairy Tales Transformed? Twenty-First-Century Adaptations and the Politics of Wonder* (2013), our contributors write about the development of fairy-tale films on six continents and discuss the interrelationships between local and global industries and the unique production of fairy-tale films in many different countries. While the essays in this collection examine and analyze films that have sought to transcend Disney's monopolistic network to produce highly experimental and innovative fairy-tale films, at the same time, we acknowledge the ongoing cultural legacies of Disney fairy-tale films as well as the potential that exists beyond them. As a result, I hope that this collaborative book will add to the growing interdisciplinary study of fairy-tale films and prompt more scholars to take fairy tales more seriously than they have in the past.

We all thank the contributors for their perseverance, and the editorial staff at Routledge, especially Erica Wetter, Simon Jacobs, and Emily How for their ongoing support. We gratefully acknowledge funding for the project, Fairy-Tale Films: Exploring Ethnographic Perspectives, from the Social Sciences and Humanities Research Council of Canada [SSHRC] 2011–2015, and for Fairy-Tale Cultures and Media Today, 2014–2018, also from SSHRC, as well as the University of Winnipeg Research Office for a grant. We thank Victoria Brown for copyediting, and Kristy Stewart for doing the index. Once again, I want personally to thank the faerie powers who brought me together with Pauline and Kendra and provided us with the indefatigable Lauren Bosc, who has added a magic touch to our efforts.

Jack Zipes
Minneapolis, January 2015

Note

1 Noteworthy works include Koven (2008); Greenhill and Matrix (2010); Cavallaro (2011); Whitley (2012); Moen (2013); Bacchilega (2013); Greenhill and Rudy (2014); and Short (2014).

PREFACE

Traveling Beyond Disney

Kendra Magnus-Johnston, Pauline Greenhill, and Lauren Bosc

Fairy-Tale Films Beyond Disney: International Perspectives was conceived as a continuation of the conversation developed in Jack Zipes's *The Enchanted Screen* (2011), a work that grapples with the socio-historical development of fairy-tale films with attention devoted mainly—but by no means exclusively—to European and North American cinema and television. While Zipes made considerable efforts to include fairy-tale films from Asia, South America, and Africa, his work—though quite comprehensive in its own right—was not as inclusive as he wished. Thus, the present collection seeks to go not only beyond Disney but also beyond *The Enchanted Screen* itself. The editors wanted to fill some of its gaps, but this project also offered us an opportunity to enrich Zipes's initial assertions, as well as giving international experts a chance to join us in propelling scholarly interest in fairy-tale adaptations beyond Disney. Zipes's own opening "Tsunami" chapter considers several films that have appeared since *The Enchanted Screen*, and underlines again his contention that independent films from outside the Hollywood machine, while by no means uniformly successful or critically and politically cogent, offer significant alternatives to the same old hackneyed clichés.

Predictably, turning to the countless cinematic developments outside Zipes's book has revealed more fissures to explore than it has sealed. Indeed, most contributors found our suggested chapter limit of 8000 words difficult or impossible; many reflected upon research yet to be conducted; and some even commented that they had enough material for a book-length study. This reaction is, of course, good news. We eagerly anticipate much more research and writing on fairy-tale films for years to come. In the meantime, however, we are pleased to offer a collection that provides, at the very least, concerted energy on fairy-tale adaptations in film the world over. Of the twenty chapters, only four focus on majority English-speaking countries. Less than half of the contributors are based at US universities, with the rest residing in Australia, Canada, India, Norway, Poland, South Africa, and the United Kingdom. In addition to insights gathered from different cultural backgrounds, the authors of this collection bring perspectives from criminal justice studies, education, film studies, folkloristics, gender studies, and literary studies, among others.

We judiciously employ as an organizing principle the concept of national cinemas, explicitly in the lower case, in the critical sense as aligned with film theorist, JungBong Choi, who differentiates the term from its potentially nebulous, politically suspect abstraction, "National Cinema," which speaks of nationalisms as "a timeless, space-defying totality" (2011, 177). Instead, the national cinemas referred to here embrace the innate pluralities of production, distribution, reception, and criticism that frame a transnational industry. While nations and nationalisms remain structures of our current world, cinema does not express uniform demarcations of difference that paint a clear mythology about a given nation, nor is outlining national mythologies our intended purpose here. An awareness of geopolitical conditions, however, aids in contextualizing the trajectories from which films are created.[1] The choice to consider fairy-tale film mainly by nation is also a practical one; doing so safeguards from an overwhelming inundation or in Zipes's approximation, a "tsunami" of filmic texts from which to sift meaning. We invite readers to consider the influx of fairy-tale films as pooled by individual contributors and to embrace the reprisals, intersections, and disparities between the films themselves, appreciating the historical moment and national context from which they emerged, and reading across the chapters to appreciate what has become an undeniably global phenomenon.

Our guiding definitions for this volume are drawn from those we prepared for International Fairy-Tale Filmography (IFTF), an online archive launched at the University of Winnipeg in 2014 (Zipes, Greenhill, and Magnus-Johnston n.d.). The fairy-tale films from *The Enchanted Screen*, this volume, and much more, have been incorporated into the IFTF, and we strongly encourage readers to consult it frequently. Fairy-tale films, animated and live-action, short and feature-length, theatrically released, made for television, and direct-to-video, draw on the characters, titles, images, plots, and motifs of wonder tales. Fairy tales can be oral (told by people in different geographical locations and at various historical times up to the present) and/or literary (written by known authors). Fairy tales concern the fantastic, the magical, the dark, the dreamy, the wishful, and the wonderful.

To be clear, the IFTF—like *Fairy-Tale Films Beyond Disney*—is somewhat flexible in its borders. Many contributors use television programming to delineate the trans-mediated climate from which numerous films are produced, such as Napier's examination of Japanese fairy-tale films that includes intermedial franchises like *Sailor Moon* (1992–1997) and *Revolutionary Girl Utena* (1997) which encompass multiple modalities ranging from manga to television to feature films. Lee's chapter on Korean fairy-tale cinema also discusses the diversity of adaptations and uses two made-for-television films to demonstrate variations in adaptations of the "Gumiho" figure from Korean oral tradition. Lee's and Napier's inclusion of television facilitates their making observations about broader trends in fairy-tale adaptation.

Historically, scholars of folklore understood fairy tales as traditional narratives of wonder and magic transmitted not only orally, but also informally, locally, and face-to-face within communities and social groups. As discussed by William Bascom (1965), folklorists distinguish myths and legends from folktales (which include fairy tales) not by their forms but by the *attitudes* of the community toward them. Myths are "both sacred and true . . . core narratives in larger ideological systems. Concerned with ultimate realities, they are often set outside of historical time . . . and frequently concern the actions of divine or semi-divine characters" (Oring 1986, 124). Legends "focus on a single episode . . . which is presented as miraculous, uncanny, bizarre, or sometimes embarrassing. The narration of a legend is, in a sense, the negotiation of the truth of these episodes." This genre, "set in historical time in the world as we know it today . . . often makes reference to real people and places" (125). Folktales, in contrast, "are related and received as fiction or fantasy [and] appear in a variety of forms" (126), one of which is the fairy tale. Most folklorists understand fairy tales as *Märchen*, the wonder tales or "tales of magic" numbered 300–749 in the Aarne-Thompson-Uther classification of international folktales (Uther 2004, vol 1, 174–396). These distinctions, as played out in this collection, have not been employed to limit what contributors could deem relevant to their discussion, but offered instead as principles for judicious consideration and sometimes outright rejection.

We welcomed international scholars to share their interests and create a dialogic space to bring about a novel interdisciplinary conversation; though often speaking to similar issues, there are clear differences in scholarly attentions and even definitional foundations. Wells, for example, offers an essay on fairy-tale films from the United Kingdom, cognizant of the collapse between fairy tales and other narratives that include fairies, and discusses how stories about fairies can be included in his chapter's rubric. In contrast, Napier prefers the term wonder tale because of its (at least superficially) greater accuracy in that many so-called fairy tales actually have no fairy characters in them. In further contrast, Li developed her focus to include an interest in "folktale film," and in doing so, details the shift from legend (specifically, Mulan narratives) *to* fairy tale archetype in Chinese cinema. Such variation speaks to the deliberate ambiguity of our project's parameters and our willingness to indulge in it; the inclusion of such a rich assortment of cinematic adaptations and theoretical underpinnings acknowledges the diversity of scholarly approaches to the subject of fairy-tale film, as well as the unique conditions of production from which films emerge.

Literary fairy tales also concern wonderful and magical events and times but are "written by an individual, usually identifiable author . . . [may] draw upon preexisting published material for some or all of their characters and plot . . . [but] put them together in a new way . . . [and] exist in only one version, fixed in print" (Harries 2008, 579). Thus, fairy tales with known authors like Hans Christian Andersen, Lewis Carroll, Edith (Bland) Nesbit, Carlo Collodi, or Mary Louisa (Stewart) Molesworth derive primarily from an individual writer's creativity. But the actual differences are not always that clear. Oral fairy tales can be found in written forms (such as the works of the Grimm brothers), and most North Americans now encounter all kinds of fairy tales mainly in books—but also in film, television, music, video games, online, and in countless other mediated forms.

Some fairy tales come in both traditional and literary forms. Andersen's "The Princess and the Pea" is based on a traditional folktale type called "The Princess on the Pea" (ATU 704). And the two forms are rarely discrete in the popular imagination; Andersen's "The Little Mermaid" is generally seen as the same kind of story as the traditional "Little Red Riding Hood" (ATU 333). Yet there can be distinguishing characteristics beyond their origins and transmission. Traditional wonder tales usually end happily, while literary tales often do not. Most North Americans expect the main protagonists of all fairy tales to "live happily ever after." But in the tales of Andersen and Oscar Wilde, for example, the conclusion can be sad or depressing. Indeed, in contrast to the Disney film's happy ending, the Andersen version of "The Little Mermaid" concludes with the title character being transformed into sea foam when she fails to marry the prince.

Zipes defines a fairy-tale film as "any kind of cinematic representation recorded on film, on videotape, or in digital form that employs motifs, characters, and plots generally found in the oral and literary genre of the fairy tale, to re-create a known tale or to create and realize cinematically an original screenplay with recognizable features of a fairy tale" (2011, 9). Fairy-tale films do not simply repeat the content of an oral/traditional or literary original; they are adaptations that create new versions in a significant intertextual relationship in which each form informs the other. Our interest in fairy-tale film is not to delineate any alleged origins or trace some perceived progression/regression of narrative adaptations; we are, however, interested in what Linda Hutcheon calls adaptation: "repetition without replication" (2006, 7). The reiteration, then, need not be absolutely faithful to the original; many fairy-tale films transgressively break rules North Americans may associate with the genre.

This process is by no means new, as Jessica Tiffin suggests: "any fairy tale—classic or modern—positions itself intertextually within a complete discourse of fairy tale as cultural artifact, so that any tale becomes a necessary dialogue between its own specific instance and the (unreal) textual expectations of fairy tales in general" (2009, 23). Though his schema is not about film, we find Kevin Paul Smith's description of relations between literature and fairy tale useful. Based on Gérard Genette's (1997a) idea of intertexts, Smith posits eight possible ways for fairy tales to work in literature: authorized (explicit in the title); writerly (implicit in the title); incorporation (explicit in the text); allusion (implicit in the text); re-vision (giving an old tale a new spin); fabulation (creating a new tale); metafiction (discussing fairy tales); and architextual/chronotopic (in a fairy-tale setting/environment) (2007, 10). Contributors were therefore encouraged to include a wide variety of fairy tales—from original fairy-tale fabulations like L. Frank Baum's *Wizard of Oz* or J.M. Barrie's *Peter Pan*, to older tales popularized in European literary tradition, to those from the many non-European oral and written traditions of other continents; but each does so with conscious purpose. Even the definition of fairy-tale author is pressed. Widening her scope from writers only, Magnus-Johnston includes filmmakers like Georges Méliès and Walt Disney as their present-day incarnation. The fairy tales and even the authors considered in the collection are therefore dependent on the contributors' discretion.

Working from these basic notions from the outset, we felt that the best way to ensure that we could produce an exciting and engaging book was to encourage each contributor to bring her/his own background and knowledge. Our work, then, is partial in Donna Haraway's (1988) double sense; the story it tells is necessarily incomplete but reflects the perspectives and enthusiasms of its many authors. In our requests for chapters, we left contributors to their own devices in adjusting the focus of their analytical lens and defining the limits of their inquiry. Apart from the initial chapters that review the international prevalence of cinematic fairy-tales, authorship, and transnational adaptations of "One Thousand and One Nights," the majority of *Fairy-Tale Films Beyond Disney* focuses on cinematic production by country, and how authors interrogate, broaden, or narrow this scope is their own choice.

Thus, for example, as already mentioned, while some chapters focus exclusively on cinematic and feature-length productions, others extend their scope to look at televised fairy-tale adaptations, a choice that depends not only on the author's interests, but also on the particularities of the area they address. The resulting breadth of some chapters, in contrast with the resolute focus of others, provides a complementary balance. It also honors notions regarding nationalism and what constitutes national cinemas in a current context, one that is punctuated by transnational, multinational (often corporate) partnerships. Divergence, of course, is also a realistic outcome of compiling a variety of voices speaking from contexts as varied and particular as the national locations and interdisciplinary perspectives that demarcate the chapters.

A rich diversity of academic concerns and proclivities are reflected throughout the collection. Rather than constrain her discussion to cinematic versions of traditional folktales collected in India, Naithani frames her consideration of Indian films around the fairy-tale elements in Bollywood cinema; her chapter meditates on the mélange or "masala" of commercial cinema. Wells turns his attention to animated fairy-tale films along with other children's films, primarily from England. Given Wells's international renown as an expert in animation studies and Naithani's specialization as a folklorist, their foci provide precise and measured contributions. By no means exhaustive in their coverage of *all* cinematic instances of fairy tales, they offer engaging and pertinent genealogies. Further, research interests of the contributors are also reflected in, for example, Duggan's consideration of satire and queer filmmaking; Balina and Beumers's, Lee's, and Li's of gender issues; and Greenhill and Kohm's of cultural criminology.

In addition to avoiding hamstringing our contributors, giving them considerable leeway has also enabled contributors to be attentive to distinctive cross-cultural but also specifically local and regional manifestations. For example, while the Christmas season has been significant for fairy-tale films and television in North America, the chapter on Poland by Deszcz-Tryhubczak and Oziewicz and the one on Scandinavia by Oxfeldt reveal localized inflections, such as animals being endowed with human speech in Poland or the televised "Christmas calendar" specials in Finland, Sweden, and Norway. Other threads include the emergence in Italian cinema, as outlined by Bacchilega, of the character of Pinocchio, who reappears in Russian film, as observed in the Balina and Beumers chapter, via Tolstoi's character Buratino.

Fairy tales and fairy-tale films alike are paradoxically simultaneously culture-specific and trans-cultural, a characteristic readily observable in the earlier chapters, from Zipes's extensive catalog of adaptations that form his fairy-tale tsunami to Samatar's fascinating international expedition through "One Thousand and One Nights." Magnus-Johnston makes similar observations in the appropriation of fairy-tale authors in film; alongside their creative works, these individuals are rein-vented as (American) global citizens to be consumed by a present-day viewing public. Accordingly, many similar concerns emerge even in otherwise distant and disparate locations. Contributors wrestle with issues that are common to fairy-tale studies in general, including reception-oriented interrogations regarding the value of fairy-tale films and television for child and adult viewers (e.g. Balina and Beumers; Bullen and Sawers; Li); whether or not they can be conceived as serious interventions in cultural, social, and political discourses (e.g. Samatar and Hubner); and ruminations on a Disney-inflected cultural climate—ranging from harmless to hazardous (Bacchilega, Balina and Beumers, Duggan, Hubner, Zipes) but also of other auteurs (e.g. Napier on Hayao Miyazaki in Japan; Duggan on France's Catherine Breillat; Samatar and Zipes "German" on Lotte Reiniger; Hames on the Czech Jan Švankmajer; and Zipes "American" on Tim Burton). Zipes's "Tsunami" and "American" chapters, not surprisingly, consider Disney influence, acknowledging that, particu-larly with *Maleficent* (2014), the corporation may be moving beyond a simplistic compliance with patriarchal norms, even if their capitalist/commercial focus remains unabated.

Fairy-taleness and the relation of film to fairy tale is, not surprisingly, also a concern for many contributors. Zipes's "Tsunami" chapter relates fairy tales to Roland Barthes's idea of myth but also Disney's renditions of fairy tales to Augustin-Eugène Scribe's nineteenth-century "well-made play" structure. Indeed, Balina and Beumers, Deszcz-Tryhubczak and Oziewicz, Hames, and Oxfeldt consider the theme of fairy tales in relation to legend and mythology generally; Li's chapter on fairy-tale films in the Republic of China considers at length the Mulan legend, which she sees as having been rendered fairy-tale-like in part because of its association with the Disney film. Deszcz-Tryhubczak and Oziewicz note that Polish fairy-tale cinema usually either employs international fairy tales from oral tradition or develops narratives that are original to the film, rather than using literary fairy tales. Naithani's discussion of Bollywood films opens the question of whether or not fairy tale can be helpfully understood as a genre of cinema and television. Magnus-Johnston links the shifting representations of fairy-tale authors as a means to showcase the technological innovations of cinema and a frequent site for filmmakers to reflect on their own responsibilities as fairy-tale storytellers. And in his chapter on German fairy-tale cinema, Zipes describes how the Grimm brothers' brilliant legacy of collecting and disseminating oral tradition has paradoxically stymied fairy-tale film production in Germany. He addresses the complex relations of the Grimm collections to German political developments as well as to German fairy-tale films.

The dynamics of colonial appropriation and postcolonial reflexivity are central concerns to those discussing locations with sizable Indigenous populations. Indeed, the relationships between fairy tales, fairy-tale cinema, Indigenous traditions, and settler colonizers can be expressively traced in many national cinemas. The chapters on Africa, Australia, Canada, and Latin America explicitly note the ways in which Indigenous traditions, regardless of their place and significance in their source cultures, have been presumed by White European and North American cultures to be unproblematically homologous to fairy tales; that they are imagined (unlike otherwise similar types of texts like Christian dogma for example) to be entirely fictional.

While the conflation of Indigenous lore with fairy-tale film is explicitly avoided throughout *Fairy-Tale Films Beyond Disney*, the interrogation of racist and colonialist ideologies in postcolonial contexts shapes the treatment of fairy-tale films for many contributors. Bullen and Sawers, for example, note that the ambivalence about homeland, home, and national identity in post-1970s Australian cinema is a result of colonial relationships. Though they decline to detail cinematic works based on Indigenous traditions, their coverage of mainly original Australian fairy-tale films evidences the birth of unique fairy tales shaped by the country's colonial history. Greenhill and Kohm note a few significant works based on Indigenous traditions because of their importance to Canadian cinema and television, but their chapter, for the most part, draws attention to the paradoxes inherent in Canadian cinema—the otherworldly places invoked that are simultaneously in Canada and marvelously elsewhere.

By contrast, Tiffin's chapter on African cinema focuses attention almost exclusively on films of indigenous African traditions, those that are in fact intended as fictional and/or fantastic (as opposed to those which are secret and/or sacred). Tiffin's attention to productions like *Kirikou et la Sorcière* (1998), directed by French filmmaker Michel Ocelot, emphasizes the western colonial gaze (also crucial in Samatar's chapter) that often imposes upon adaptations of West African folktales. Hubner's chapter on Latin American film acknowledges the particular sycretisms of African, Indigenous, and European wonder frames, tropes, and characters, and the political ambiguity of the results. She emphasizes the verisimilitudes of cinema from Latin American countries, including materials and influences from Argentina, Brazil, Colombia, Ecuador, and Guatemala. The films include literary adaptations based on Hans Christian Andersen's "Little Match Girl" to Indigenous Brazilian figures, illustrating the fusion of African-American folklore with the influence of settlers, colonizers, and traders, all framed in a native Latin American folklore that may echo tropes from "One Thousand and One Nights."

The ways in which our contributors take up their subjects is often inflected by the historical trajectories of filmmaking techniques in the context of the region under investigation. For example, Bacchilega and Hubner consider the influence of neorealism as an important thread in Italian and new Latin American cinema (respectively) and both devote considerable attention to live-action film, as a result. Indeed, Hubner's analysis envisions many films as both decolonizing practice and an urgent call for social change; using techniques developed in the cinemas of the French New Wave and Italian neorealism, the films she discusses react against European hegemony and internal social issues. Realism has also strongly affected work in Canada, as discussed by Greenhill and Kohm, as much as for example the financial constraints of government funding for film production. Further, the re-emergence of particular films in multiple chapters conveys the challenge of any nation laying its claim to a specific fairy-tale film, let alone to the fairy tale that inspired it! Duggan's chapter on French fairy-tale film and Tiffin's on African cinema both consider Michel Ocelot's adaptation of West African characters and stories; and Duggan also considers the themes from "One Thousand and One Nights" (Samatar's focus) reflecting colonial relations between France and North Africa.

Another often-cited issue is the place of government involvement in filmmaking and how it has influenced fairy-tale cinema, including by way of funding objectives (as in Canada) and regulation of content (as in India, Germany, Soviet and post-Soviet Russia, Korea, China, and Poland). Political interpretations of films are explicitly linked to nationalism and other ideologies in China, England, Germany, Korea, Poland, and Russia. Indeed, as Zipes's "German" chapter details, the complicated political history of East and West Germany explains to some extent the divergences in their fairy-tale films. Yet though the many joint productions that cross national boundaries are more often initially driven by financial incentives than by a more free-flowing desire for creative and cultural linking, the results can be dynamic and compelling or simply dismal.

Some contributors return to films already discussed in *The Enchanted Screen*, to offer more details and extensive comparative discussion (e.g. Bacchilega on "Pinocchio" films, Hubner on *Pan's Labyrinth*, or Magnus-Johnston on Andersen biopics) or to offer quite different perspectives (e.g. Greenhill and Kohm re-examining Atom Egoyan's *The Sweet Hereafter* as a film about harms against children, a topic also addressed by Hubner). Others, like Lee on Korea, mention important works that Zipes admires and discusses, like Pil-Sung Yim's *Hansel & Gretel*, but choose to detail other films. Yet the vast majority of works discussed here are gathered for the first time under the rubric of fairy-tale film, and many are given serious academic attention for the first time, or for the first time in English. Nevertheless, some lacunae remain. There are certainly fairy-tale films from Finland, Ireland, Israel, New Zealand, the Middle East, and parts of the former Soviet Union other than Russia, for example; work specifically on these areas remains to be undertaken.

The collection begins with three thematic chapters—on the recent global surge of (interest in) fairy tales and fairy-tale cinema and television (Zipes); on Hollywood representations of fairy-tale collectors, authors, and filmmakers (Magnus-Johnston); and on "One Thousand and One Nights" as a transnational source for fairy-tale filmmakers (Samatar). By opening the collection from nowhere and everywhere, we draw attention to the extensive sourcing and reception of fairy-tale cinema across national boundaries. In many ways, Zipes's "Tsunami" chapter provides the *cogito ergo sum* logic underlying the collection; it is necessary because it results from a palpable cultural phenomenon. Whereas Magnus-Johnston's chapter considers English-language Hollywood films, appraising the representation of storytellers and the shifting technological modalities of fairy tales, Samatar traces the genealogy of a tale often used to negotiate the spectacle of Otherness through an exotic and erotic lens. The following seventeen chapters are organized by their national contexts, beginning with European, followed by Asian, and concluding with postcolonial cinemas. European cinema includes Wells, who looks at the UK (mainly England); Duggan at France; Zipes at Germany; Bacchilega at Italy; Oxfeldt at Scandinavia; Balina and Beumers at Russia; Hames at Czech Republic and Slovakia; and Deszcz-Tryhubczak and Oziewicz at Poland. Asian cinema includes Japan (Napier), China (Li), India (Naithani), and Korea (Lee), and is followed by considerations of postcolonial nations: Africa (Tiffin), Australia (Bullen and Sawers), Canada (Greenhill and Kohm), Mexico, Central and South America (Hubner), and the United States (Zipes).

We hope that our readers will make new discoveries and revisit the old with fresh perspectives. Beyond a mere encounter with the familiar and the strange—if such a dichotomous relationship between an audience and the cinema even persists—we hope the familiar will be made strange, and vice versa. This international collection seeks to explore the horizons beyond Disney, yet leave room for future scholarly innovation. Between the good, the bad, and the ugly; the expected and unexpected—and though he is surely still awaiting his wish to curate a gigantic film festival including all the neglected fairy-tale films discovered in his first collection (Zipes 2011, and in the preface)—we trust readers will find this to be a wondrous extension of a project Zipes began with his *Enchanted Screen*.

Note

1 For an extended discussion of national cinemas see Willemen (2006), Nairn (1997), and Hayward (1993).

1

THE GREAT CULTURAL TSUNAMI OF FAIRY-TALE FILMS

Jack Zipes

Fairy-tale films have been swamping big and small screens throughout the world ever since the beginning of the twenty-first century, seeking to overwhelm audiences with innovative and spectacular adaptations in a kind of globalized cultural tsunami. Indeed, journalists and critics often talk about a phenomenal surge or tidal wave of fairy-tale films, and wonder why and how this seemingly perplexing cultural phenomenon originated and spread. Meanwhile, numerous contemporary cinematic fairy-tale films continue to draw attention by shattering and altering the global public's understanding of traditional fairy tales with happy endings. Though many films are frivolous spectacles, an impressive number are fantastic pastiches and explorations of classical tales that stretch the imagination of viewers in unusual ways.

Discussing the web of fairy-tale transformation, circulation, and reception in the twenty-first century, Cristina Bacchilega remarks:

> The contemporary proliferation of fairy-tale transformations in convergence culture does mean that the genre has *multivalent currency*, and we must think of the fairy tale's social uses and effects in increasingly nuanced ways while asking who is reactivating a fairy-tale poetics of wonder and for whom. Even in mainstream fairy-tale cinema today, there is no such thing as *the* fairy tale or one main use of it. This multiplicity of position-takings does not polarize ideological differences, but rather produces complex alignments and alliances in the contemporary fairy-tale web.
>
> (2013, 28)

The more unusual and usual twenty-first-century position-takings in fairy-tale film production come from a variety of directors and countries. The diverse examples offered below will serve to contextualize the critical analysis later in this chapter.

In France, Catherine Breillat produced a new sexually loaded feminist version of "Sleeping Beauty" in 2010 that made her provocative "Bluebeard" film of 2009 appear tame; while Christophe Gans created a spectacular and lavish *Beauty and the Beast* (La Belle et la Bête 2014) in an attempt to supersede Jean Cocteau's great classic, *La Belle et la Bête* (1946). In South Korea, there appears to be a trend to turn fairy-tale films into horror films that led to Kim Jee-woon's terrifying adaptation of a Korean folktale, *A Tale of Two Sisters* (2003); Yong-gyun Kim's transformation of Hans Christian Andersen's "The Red Shoes" into a gory mystery (2005); Man-Dae Bong's

Cinderella (2006) into a scintillating trauma; and Pil-Sung Yim's chilling *Hansel & Gretel* (2007) into a dramatic defense of children.

However, horror is not just reserved for South Korea. British director Iain Softley produced the disturbing *Trap for Cinderella* (2013), about an amnesiac young woman traumatized by a fire that killed her best friend and left her without a sense of her real identity. In another British film, *The Selfish Giant* (2013), directed by Clio Barnard, Oscar Wilde's famous fairy tale is totally transformed into a tragic story about two working-class boys who seek to make themselves rich in a swindling owner's junkyard.

While the fairy-tale films of other countries may yield less horror, the prospects for innovation remain high. After great success with such animated films drawn from West African folklore as *Kirikou and the Sorceress* (1998), *Kirikou and the Wild Beasts* (2006), *Azur and Asmar: The Princes' Quest* (2006), and *Tales of the Night* (2011), the talented French filmmaker Michel Ocelot produced a charming didactic prequel, *Kirikou and the Men and Women*, in 2012. In it, the tiny nude hero once again comes to the rescue of his villagers in five different stories told by his grandfather. Of course, when it comes to animated films, the great Japanese filmmaker Hayao Miyazaki has had a profound influence on directors throughout the world with such works as *Spirited Away* (2001), *Howl's Moving Castle* (2004), and *Ponyo* (2008). Miyazaki's and Ocelot's works demonstrate without deliberate artifice that animated fairy-tale films can stimulate critical reflection, pleasure, and joy by not following a conventional Disney schema.

Miyazaki's direct influence in Japan can be seen in the beautiful and sumptuous hand-drawn film, *The Tale of the Princess Kaguya* (2013), directed by Isao Takahata, which is based on a Japanese folktale, "The Tale of the Bamboo Cutter." There is no happy ending in this film that recounts the struggles of a miniature girl discovered in a bamboo shoot to determine her own destiny, and yet, after Kaguya realizes that she is a moon resident and must return to the moon, one can only admire her true natural nobility when she unwillingly departs for the moon. Moreover, like many of Miyazaki's films, Takahata's story is striking because it uses traditional hand-drawn animation in unconventional ways that go beyond the Disney model.

Indeed, some American "non-conventional" stop-animation films have also gone beyond Disney and suggest that they have been influenced more by Miyazaki than by Disney. For instance, *ParaNorman* (2012), directed by Sam Fell and Chris Butler, explores how Norman, an eleven-year-old boy in the small Massachusetts town of Blithe Hollow, is mocked, bullied, and marginalized because he visualizes and speaks with his dead grandmother and other ghosts victimized by witch hunts of the past. With the help of a book of fairy tales and compassion for the persecuted "witch" Agatha, Norman saves the town from a catastrophe, and the former outcast becomes a hero.

Similarly, in *The Boxtrolls* (2014), directed by Graham Annable and Anthony Stacchi, a young boy by the name of Eggs is treated as a dangerous provocateur, who lives with the monstrous scavengers called boxtrolls. In reality, these creatures are merely peaceful and harmless souls who collect discarded items to build unusual machines in the underground, while the pest exterminator, Archibald Snatcher, is the real monster, who seeks to exterminate the boxtrolls for his own profit. But Eggs exposes him and becomes the town's hero instead of an outsider. In both these films, marginalized young boys dramatically oppose the norms of society, and the digitalized animation that reflects their struggles is innovative, the images, enthralling, and the characterization, extraordinary.

Stop-motion digital animation will probably dominate fairy-tale filmmaking in the years to come and produce such mainstream dreadful films as the American disaster, *Strange Magic* (2015), directed by Gary Rydstrom and produced by George Lucas, which Justin Chang calls "mirthless and derivative" (2015), but they will be contested from the margins of the cultural field by such films as *Jack and the Cuckoo-Clock Heart*. In a review published in *Variety*, Peter Debruge describes the film this way:

> A boy born on the coldest day on Earth survives only by the grace of a magical ticker in "Jack and the Cuckoo-Clock Heart," a Steampunk rock musical reverse-engineered from an album by French band Dionysos and the popular tie-in book written by its frontman, Matthias Malzieu. Co-directed by Malzieu and musicvideo helmer Stephane Berla, this charming yet oddly miscalibrated computer-animated fairy tale combines gothic, Tim Burton-esque elements with a younger-skewing porcelain-doll look, confusing auds as to who's being targeted exactly. The answer; no one in particular, as Malzieu seems to be making this idiosyncratic, overly precious film mostly for himself.
>
> (2014)

Whether this last comment is true, this extraordinary film uses fairy-tale motifs of a frozen heart, noble quests, and the joys of art in such a charming manner that its unique eccentricity can be shared by audiences worldwide and not just enjoyed by Malzieu.

Other directors still rely on more traditional animated techniques to capture such eccentricity. For instance, the fabulous Russian animator Garri Bardin continues to use clay animation and has stunned audiences with his beautiful, politically charged *The Ugly Duckling* (2010), which cleverly transforms Andersen's tale into a parody of pretentious Russian glory and oligarchy, and which satirizes the changes that have supposedly occurred in the "new Russia" (see Figure 1.1). Here a gentle innocent duckling rises above the dilapidated barnyard symbolic of present-day Russia to embrace the freedom of flying on his own.

Turning back to live-action fairy-tale films in our discussion of works that comprise the cultural tsunami, I should like to note some other diverse experiments. For instance, Sheldon Wilson and Catherine Hardwicke, two American directors, introduced werewolves into their versions of "Little Red Riding Hood" in *Red: Werewolf Hunter* (2010) and *Red Riding Hood* (2011), seeking to

FIGURE 1.1 The Ugly Duckling/Swan mocked by real ducks, *The Ugly Duckling* (2010).

titillate audiences with bizarre incidents and contrived plotlines. In contrast, Czech director Maria Procházková's brilliant *Who's Afraid of the Wolf?* (2008) retold the same famous tale from the perspective of an imaginative six-year-old girl, probing the capacity of children to deal imaginatively with family conflict. While not directly adapting "Little Red Riding Hood," Joe Wright's thriller, *Hanna* (2011), constantly alluded to the tale in his pastiche depicting a savvy young girl who learns to take care of herself in a world filled with predators.

Of course, "Little Red Riding Hood" is not the only classical fairy tale which has been cinematically re-envisaged. There has also been a wave of fairy-tale films about "Snow White" such as American productions like Tarsem Singh's *Mirror, Mirror* (2012), Rupert Sanders's *Snow White and the Huntsman* (2012), David DeCoteau's *Snow White: A Deadly Summer* (2012), Rachel Goldberg's *Grimm's Snow White* (2012), Pablo Berger's *Blancanieves* (2012), and Jacco Groen's *Lilet Never Happened* (2012). In addition, "Hansel and Gretel" has received special attention in such diverse films as Mike Nichols's *Bread Crumbs* (2011), Tommy Wirkola's *Hansel & Gretel: Witch Hunters* (2013), David DeCoteau's *Hansel & Gretel: Warriors of Witchcraft* (2013), Duane Journey's *Hansel & Gretel Get Baked* (2013), and Danishka Esterhazy's *H & G* (2013). Adaptations of Andersen's "The Snow Queen" include David Wu's *Snow Queen* (2002), Julian Gibbs's made-for-TV musical *The Snow Queen* (2005), and Chris Buck and Jennifer Lee's well-made film for Disney fans, *Frozen* (2013), which has won many awards for seeming to be an untypical Disney film while once again merely celebrating elitism, the sentimental American musical, and, most importantly, the Disney brand. The other live-action Disney films of this period, Tim Burton's *Alice in Wonderland* (2010) and Robert Stromberg's *Maleficent* (2014), tend to break from the conventional corporate model and may indicate a more serious feminist approach by the Disney studio to traditional fairy tales. Of course, as Burton's *Sleepy Hollow* (1999) and *Corpse Bride* (2005) indicate, his predilection for endorsing weird outsiders will always make his interpretations of fairy tales somewhat unconventional.

Returning to animation, Tomm Moore and Nora Twomey created an unusual Irish fairy-tale film with *The Secret of Kells* (2009), which combines legend with folklore and depicts the struggles of a young apprentice named Brendan to save an illuminated manuscript of the Bible from the invading Vikings during the eighth century. In the course of the action he is aided by a pagan forest spirit whose presence brings out the sacred relationship between religion and nature. In 2014 Moore directed another superb Irish fairy-tale film, *Song of the Sea*, based on tales about the marvelous Selkies, which poignantly portrays a young boy's quest to save his sister and fulfill a promise to his dead mother. But it is not so much the sentimental story that is so compelling in this film, it is its aesthetics. As Carlos Aguilar has written in the *Toronto Review*:

> Resembling rustic watercolor paintings enhanced with movement, there is an artisanal quality to every frame. From the sea, to the city, to the forest and the fantastical underworld, the amount of details employed in every creature and space is breathtaking. Nothing is overlooked. So meticulous is their approach that even transmission towers have a distinct design. Unattainable by solely using computer animation, the film's visual aesthetic feels simultaneously handcrafted and otherworldly. Filled with a classical warmth, "Song of the Sea" should remind everyone why animation, when done as flawlessly as it is here, is such an incredible medium. Color, form, and fluid motion delivered in an unforgettable style that's at the service of a similarly compelling story.
>
> (2014)

In another tender American film, based, this time on folkloric Viking stories, Dean DeBlois and Chris Sanders created a startling film about war and peace that depicts dragons as "the others" in *How to Train Your Dragon* (2010). Unfortunately, DeBlois's sequel, *How to Train Your Dragon 2*, despite some beautiful digital landscaping, is a lamentably sentimental film that borders on glorifying war instead of peace. Following the great success of the first *Shrek* (2001), directed by Andrew Adamson and Vicky Jenson, *Shrek 2* (2004), *Shrek the Third* (2007), and two further "Shrek" films have appeared, *Shrek Forever After* (2010) and the spin-off *Puss in Boots* (2011). The commerical marketing of these mediocre sequels has diminished the poignancy of the original film, which thrived on its hilarious critique of Disney conventionalism. The sequels rendered the "Shrek" narrative predictable and conventional; *Puss in Boots* was irritatingly boring. Fortunately, the animated *Brave* (2012), directed by Mark Andrews and Brenda Chapman, stirred a debate about feminist fairy-tale films just as the live-action trilogy, *The Hobbit: An Unexpected Journey* (2012), *The Hobbit: The Desolation of Smaug* (2013), and *The Hobbit: The Battle of the Five Armies* (2014), directed by Peter Jackson, gave rise to a quarrel about the proper way to adapt J.R.R. Tolkien's fairy-tale novel for the screen. These lavish adaptations demand to be taken seriously, for they draw upon an epic fairy tale that addresses the ravages of war experienced by Tolkien himself. It is, therefore, not by chance that Jackson's three films shed light on the perils of war in our contemporary conflicted world.

In addition to films produced for the big screen, fairy-tale films continue to be created for television, the internet, and iPods. America has at least three concurrent TV fairy-tale series: *Once Upon a Time*, *Grimm*, and *Beauty and the Beast*.[1] Germany has *Sechs auf einen Streich* and *Märchenperlen*, and important series have also appeared in Japan and South Korea. In the United Kingdom, Scotland, and Canada, the BBC *Shoebox* series appealed to large audiences. Significantly, these works are often accompanied by commercials and other peripherals that celebrate the magic qualities of fairy tales and urge us to change our lives by purchasing miraculous products.

Just as Georges Méliès revolutionized the fairy tale at the beginning of the twentieth century and was immediately followed by scores of other European and American filmmakers, numerous directors and artists are now revolutionizing the fairy-tale film, in part due to new technology that enhances cinematic special effects. But again, why such a revolution or tsunami now? Is this twenty-first century wave of fairy-tale films really so startling and new? (Consider the cinematic tsunami of fairy-tale films at the beginning of the twentieth century.) A look at the popularity of fairy-tale films in a historical context offers a more comprehensive perspective on the present.

Plays, operas, and vaudeville shows called *féeries* during the nineteenth century offered early signs that folktales and fairy tales would become a staple of storytelling in the modern mass media throughout the world. But fairy-tale films also stir our minds and emotions as part of our cultural socialization, what Norbert Elias termed the civilizing process.[2] Today, fairy tales inundate homes and schools at all levels; they are also taught at most universities in the UK and North America. They provide advertisements and commercials with narrative plots and characters to sell products. They are found in all walks of life, and to some degree we even try to transform our lives into fairy tales. As the French semiotician Roland Barthes might say, they have become mythic in a negative sense—artificially produced to appear universal and natural versions of the way life should be, all the while concealing their instrumental motives and their basic history and ideology. We are induced to accept fairy tales as part of our lives and as pure amusement without questioning them.

Yet, in my book, *Fairy Tale as Myth/Myth as Fairy Tale* (1994), I remarked that it is impossible to grasp the fairy tale's history and relationship to Barthes's (1973) notion of myth as second nature without considering the basic manner in which they have been adapted, revised, and duplicated either to reinforce or subvert dominant ideologies. Storytelling's memetic nature suggests that cultural memories concerning fairy tales began to form in pre-Christian times. The development of these narratives as a cultural genre has been marked by a process of dialectical appropriation involving storytelling, memorization, duplication, and revision that has set the cultural conditions for its mythicization, institutionalization, and expansion as a mass-mediated form through radio, film, television, and the internet. Indeed, film—animated and live-action, short and feature-length—has been most significant for the fairy tale's great dissemination in the late twentieth and early twenty-first centuries. In my opinion, the fairy tale has become the dominant cultural form of storytelling in our daily lives, thanks in large part to film and other mass-mediated technologies. Consequently, as an accessible and memetic popular genre, the fairy-tale film, along with other adaptations such as literature, drama, opera, cartoon, and so on, purposely brings people together to share relevant stories that speak to common problems. The more bewildering, if not distorted and perverted, our lives become, the more people seek refuge and meaning in fairy tales and other figments of the human imagination like religion. Yet, unlike religion, fairy tales have a secular wondrous appeal geared to help us order our lives and endorse our hope for harmony and peace.

In the twenty-first century, when the world is beset by social and political conflicts that occur with lightning speed, more fairy-tale and fantasy films have been created to address the symptoms that contribute to our present dilemmas. Though many contemporary films are open-ended or tragic, often questioning the possibility of a happy end or harmonious solution to conflicts, they tap into the utopian verve that stamps the fairy-tale tradition in all cultures and countries. And, of course, numerous fairy-tale and fantasy films end in joy. The Méliès and Disney films at the beginning of the twentieth century are exuberant, and their pioneer films, among many others, have fueled the exuberance of brash utopian films of the twenty-first century as can be seen in the Shrek films, Ocelot's Kirikou films, Miyazaki's original Japanese adaptations, and Garri Bardin's Russian interpretations of fairy tales, to name but a few.

More than a hundred different kinds of fairy-tale films produced in the twenty-first century respond, in my opinion, to the utopian longing of audiences who need stories to help them position themselves in relation to the disturbing and relentless changes that continue to occur and threaten to engulf them. Fairy tales are secular and yet seriously spiritual because of their utopianism, because they place faith in humanity, that is, in the human capacity to undo the destruction that humans cause one another and our natural and social environment. Fairy-tale films provide a metaphorical means to step back and, for a brief moment, regard solutions or ways to strategize one's approach to daily existence. And, of course, fairy tales also provide diversion, allegedly pure entertainment, that often apologizes for the unfathomable, dominant ideological forces that pervert our lives. As a result, there is no such thing as a definitive fairy-tale film because there are so many means nowadays to utilize and re-utilize the arsenal of traditional folktales and fairy tales via the medium of film. Consequently, each film which evokes the fairy-tale aura must be understood in the context of its relationship to the socio-economic conditions of the times. The aesthetics and subject matter of each film constitute a position-taking. Fairy-tale films can shed light on human predicaments in a given time, and, at the same time divert our gaze so that we cannot recognize their causes. This socio-cultural function has been part of fairy-tale films from the very beginning, that is, from Méliès's first fabulous *féeries* up to the present blockbusters that use the marvelous to sell themselves and the notion that happiness means belief in the status quo.

Kristian Moen's insightful *Film and Fairy Tales: The Birth of Modern Fantasy*, which examines the origins of fairy-tale films in relationship to modernism, demonstrates that many were produced from the beginning of the twentieth century to the 1930s, and he shows that the basic narrative thread of all kinds of fairy tales formed the narrative structure of all films, live-action and animated. Though the massive early twentieth-century production of fairy-tale films and their offshoots cannot be called a tsunami, one could call it a tidal wave that flooded audiences and certainly laid the basis for the cinematic fairy-tale adaptations that followed. From 1890 to 1940, Moen maintains, the fairy-tale film became popular because it was an outgrowth of modernism. As he remarks:

> [S]ome of the most prominent fairy tale films of the era focused on negotiated modern life through fantasy. Attuned to a world of instability and transformation, cinema fairy tales were

especially conducive to contending with the effects of modernity; while often set in far-off realms of fantasy, they nevertheless helped articulate the ways in which we might see, understand and feel the effects of a changing modern world.

(2013, xvi)

Due to the fast pace of a daily life that included work and leisure time, fairy-tale films reflected through spectacle, wonder, and fantasy how industry and technology affected people's lives in western cultures. However, after the Great Depression beginning in 1929, change was no longer to be glorified but questioned or stabilized, hence the rise of the harmonious, pleasing, and well-made Disney fairy-tale films, which predominated in the second half of the twentieth century.

However, the era of relative stability (1945–1990) in which global capitalism established itself and assumed new forms of control and dominance—despite the Korean and Vietnam wars—came crashing to an end. Technology and politics combined to foster what Zygmunt Bauman (2005) has called a liquid life in which nothing is stable and nothing holds people together because truths have been proven false and traditions revealed as a means to manipulate and limit ordinary citizens' lives. The havoc of our times has, of course, not gone unnoticed by producers of fairy-tale films but has swayed them to forge the current cultural tsunami.

Today, the fairy tale has become a hybrid mode that borrows from other genres and technologies and infuses fairy-tale films with plural meanings and functions. Ultimately, the source of fairy-tale films seems to be a whirlpool of conflicting themes, elements, characters, styles, and ideologies that stir viewers and audiences worldwide. Though the Disney Animation Studio has retained its near monopoly over fairy-tale films, its jurisdiction has become uncertain. With the invention of DVDs, digital art, the internet, and multiplex movie theaters, among others, the Disney Corporation's endeavors to stabilize the fairy-tale film in its name seem outmoded and are openly undermined. Globalization and postmodern technology have provided filmmakers throughout the world with the means to challenge the Disney worldview and conventional narrative. Before turning to these experiments, I want to add a few words about the "well-made" Disney fairy-tale film.

The "Well-Made" Disney Fairy-Tale Film

To my knowledge, nobody has hitherto drawn a connection between the nineteenth century's most influential dramatist, Augustin-Eugène Scribe (1791–1861), and the twentieth century's most popular and successful filmmaker, Walt Disney (1901–1966). To grasp the overwhelming popularity of the Disney fairy-tale films from their inception to the present day, it is helpful to recall Scribe's significance for the development of European drama and how and why he influenced the writing and staging of plays up through the present. Scribe wrote over 400 plays that were translated, adapted, and produced in Europe and North America, and their common structure has come to be known as the "well-made play," or "la pièce bien faite."[3] Though this term is often used derogatively, its prescriptive structure enabled many excellent dramatists of the nineteenth and twentieth centuries such as Henrik Ibsen and George Bernard Shaw to shape their plays with effective plots.

A "well-made" play generally has six elements: (1) A secret is disclosed to the audience but is unknown to the characters of the play; its revelation leads to the climatic scene in which an unfortunate hero is restored to grace. (2) The first scene sets off a pattern of intense action and suspense filled with contrived entrances, unexpected letters, and other devices. (3) The unfortunate hero engages in a series of conflicts with his adversary. (4) The conflict ends with a peripeteia or a sudden fall in the hero's fortunes followed by an obligatory scene in which the adversary learns about the secret. (5) The audience is informed about a central misunderstanding but not the hero and the adversary. (6) Finally, everything is clarified and made plausible to the characters of the play in a logical dénouement. Variations include focus on a woman as heroine, and the six key elements are not a rigid formula. To Scribe's credit, he discovered flexible dramatic functions that were highly effective, appealed to audiences, and influenced numerous playwrights up through the present day including those for the cinema and television, whether they realize it or not.

When Disney began making his first feature-length animated film, he became the Scribe of animated fairy-tale films. He used the storyboard to design a careful and effective structure for *Snow White and the Seven Dwarfs* (1937), and he borrowed elements from the Hollywood and Broadway musicals to add color and to sentimentalize the cinematic stories. Thanks to the enormous success of *Snow White*, he realized that he had found the recipe for a universal appeal, and thereafter he sought to cultivate the taste of family audiences, while simultaneously adjusting the fairy tale's structure and contents to comply with his puritanical and capitalist values. In short, the "well-made" fairy-tale film structure of all Disney studio productions, including those after his death, can be summarized as follows:

1 **Traumatic and Unfortunate Incidents**

An upsetting and often tragic event marks a young woman or man, generally a member of the aristocracy or an extraordinary person, unfortunate and liable to be persecuted. A key ideological function of the Disney "well-made" film is to arouse sympathy for elite characters.

2 **Songs of Woe and Joy**

The hero or heroine sings a melancholy song that indicates her or his desire and/or plight, building audience anticipation for the recovery of lost status. Other songs throughout the movie indicate the protagonists' moods, especially their emotional state and longing for love, security, and happiness.

3 **Banishment and Isolation**

The unfortunate heroine or hero is in danger at home and may be banished or flees. During isolation or travels, she or he must learn how to survive.

4 **Quest, Conflicts, and Comic Relief**

Sometimes a friend undertakes a quest to rescue the unfortunate heroine/hero. Animals, little men, insects, household objects, fairies, snowmen, trolls, or birds help the protagonist to overcome obstacles and provide comic relief. Often more amusing and smarter than the heroine/hero, they make the simplistic storyline palatable. Meanwhile, the evil adversary, frequently a female witch, intensifies her efforts to destroy the likeable protagonists, who often resemble Barbie and Ken dolls.

5 **Peripeteia**

Once it seems that the heroine/hero is safe, his/her fortunes are, however, reversed. Given the crisis, the helpers desperately try to save the heroine/hero who appears to be doomed. The help often includes comic relief through the antics of the helpers.

6 **Miraculous Resolution**

A deus ex machina or miraculous intervention leads to a contrived and predictable happy ending. The resolution often involves the harmonious restoration of the status quo, and the incarceration and/or death of the adversary.

Using this "well-made" flexible structure, Disney and the Disney Studio not only found a dependable means to transform the storylines of every fairy tale they adapted for the screen, using the latest technological inventions to embellish the same plot and message, but they also gradually built audience-standardized tastes and expectations on a global scale. By 2015, the time of this writing, the Disney brand has become a powerful meme. As noun or adjective, when spoken, read, or seen, the term Disney immediately gives rise in the minds of millions of people to predictable notions: the "well-made" fairy-tale film with an appropriate happy and joyful ending; a seemingly utopian theme park of bountiful pleasure where Disney film characters come alive; and clean fun and faith in a father figure who waves a magic wand each time his name is pronounced.

Indeed, Walt Disney is not dead; he has fulfilled his wish for immortality. He and his brother Roy realized that if the Disney animated films were to dominate the fairy-tale film market, they would not only have to find the suitable formula or structure to sell their films successfully, they would also have to create an intricate network that would transform their name into a meme, readily recognizable by the masses in America and now throughout the world. The brand is reinforced through the merchandising of books, films, toys, clothes, gadgets, and food in Disney stores and other venues; attractive and amusing advertisements and commercials in newspapers, journals, billboards, radio, the internet, Amazon, iPhones, and Twitter; theme parks in the United States, France, and Japan; the collaboration and co-option of other film studios such as Pixar and the establishment of a cable TV channel; musicals on Broadway that tour the United States or are performed locally by children's theaters; Disney ice shows; and all kinds of local and cultural events such as the Macy's parade in New York City. In short, there is hardly a medium of communication that has not been infiltrated by the Disney brand. Though the memetic brand may have different connotations for each recipient, the acclamation of the brand name is all that matters for a gigantic corporation that has made culture into commerce. The Disney Studio has established a monopoly over the fairy-tale film without having to announce it, and it plays a massive role in the cultural tsunami.[4]

Its recent production *Frozen* (2013) is a good example of how the "well-made" Disney fairy-tale film manages to create an aura of originality and modernity while actually repeating the same story and embracing the same ideology that Walt Disney fostered in the 1930s. Examining this film's "well-made" structure clearly reveals just how it reproduces its predecessors. The action takes place in a faux-idyllic Nordic realm, for the film is loosely based on Andersen's "The Snow Queen," which the Disney company previously had thought too dark, complicated, and long to adapt for young audiences. The plot had to be simplified and the villainous Snow Queen transformed into a role model, a pliable beautiful Barbie doll, thanks to computer animation. It employs the six functions of the "well-made" fairy-tale film:

1   Traumatic and Unfortunate Incidents

Elsa, princess of Arendelle, is born with the magic capability of turning things into ice and snow, but she is unable to control it, and the capability becomes a curse. She almost kills her young sister Anna. Fortunately, her parents rush Anna to the submissive trolls who heal her. However, from that point onward the children must be separated in the castle until they become teenagers. Tragedy strikes when their parents are drowned at sea.

2   Songs of Woe and Joy

Anna is not told of Elsa's magic powers and sings melodramatic songs of sorrow because she cannot see her beloved sister. Though singing continues throughout the film to denote how a character is feeling, Anna does not learn the truth about her sister through song.

3 Banishment and Isolation

A few years after her parents' death, Elsa is to celebrate her coronation as queen. Anna announces that she intends to marry the handsome Prince Hans of the Southern Isles, whom she has just met. Elsa refuses to give her blessing, and the vivacious and naïve Anna protests. Elsa explodes and cannot control her magic powers, resulting in the petrification of the entire castle and village that will apparently suffer an eternal winter of snow and ice. Elsa, accused of being a witch, escapes to the nearby mountains where she creates an ice palace and feels she can finally be herself. She expresses her sentiments in the film's popular hit song, "Let It Go."

4 Quest, Conflicts, and Comic Relief

Anna, feeling guilty that she caused her sister's rage and its result, decides to search for her. She leaves Prince Hans in charge of the realm and rides off into the mountains where she encounters the helpful and likeable Kristoff, who supplies ice on a sled drawn by an even more likeable reindeer named Sven. They agree to help Anna, and provide comic relief with Olaf, a snowman. Once they reach the ice palace, Anna encounters Elsa, who adamantly refuses to return to Arendelle.

5 Peripeteia

The unfortunate heroine Anna is accidentally struck in her heart by her unfortunate sister, who still cannot control her magic power. She drives Anna and her helpers from the mountain. Kristoff notices that Anna's hair is turning white and that something is wrong. He takes her to the trolls who perform a hilarious song, and then tell him that Anna's heart has been frozen, and unless it is thawed by an act of true love, she will be petrified forever. Anna's condition worsens when Kristoff carries her back to the castle. They discover that Prince Hans is a scoundrel who wants her to die so that he can take over the realm. Moreover, he plans to kill Elsa, whom he has imprisoned in a dungeon.

6 Miraculous Resolution

Kristoff, thanks to his reindeer, realizes that he loves Anna, and vice versa, and rides into Arendelle to show his true love by kissing her. Meanwhile, Anna gathers her strength as she is freezing when she sees Prince Hans about to kill Elsa with his sword. She intervenes, and just as she is frozen solid, Hans's sword breaks on her body. Because of Anna's act of true love, Elsa realizes that she can thaw the realm through true love that modifies her destructive powers. Prince Hans is then sent off in a brig to be punished in his own country. Kristoff is rewarded and will likely marry Anna, who is reconciled with her sister. Arendelle is saved, and the rightful rulers are restored to their proper regal places.

Despite its hackneyed plotline and message that all that is needed to save a person and a realm is true love, *Frozen* has received great praise and achieved extraordinary success. Much of it was due to the hundreds of thousands of dollars invested in the production and publicity. As with most of its big-budget blockbusters, the Disney Studio took great care to hire highly gifted animators, artists, actors, musicians, screenplay writers, producers, and directors. The producers spent huge sums on trailers and other advertisements months in advance of *Frozen*'s release to hype its meaning as *Disney* merchandise, predetermined by paratexts and peripherals. It was the ticket seller Fandango's top advance ticket seller among animated films, and by January 2014, it became the top-selling animated film in the company's history. It also won two Academy Awards, one Golden Globe, and a BAFTA for best animated film of 2013, among many others. Most reviews were enthusiastic.

Frozen set records and has thus far earned well over a billion dollars. Walt Disney Company chair and CEO Bob Iger stated in an interview that *Frozen* has "'franchise' potential" (quoted in Reingold 2014), meaning that the film would be adapted for the stage and other venues, produce more and more dolls, toys and other merchandise, and possibly produce a sequel or two for the cinema or DVD market.

There is no doubt that *Frozen* deserves all these accolades within the current culture industry. As a "well-made" Disney fairy-tale film, its artwork and images are splendid. The computer-generated imagery and hand-drawn animation are perfectly synchronized. The scenes of the ice palace, the mountains, the harbor, the Arendelle castle, and village are drawn with meticulous attention to the slightest detail. Though sisters Elsa and Anna have the same curvaceous figures, bright smiles, vivacity, preternaturally giant eyes, and innocence as all the Barbie-doll Disney heroines, they display winning personalities, especially the younger sister, neglected by the cursed Elsa. Indeed, Anna's dedication and love for her older sister transforms the "well-made" fairy-tale film into a touching melodrama.

Yet, despite all *Frozen*'s winning features, its ideological problems and aesthetic weaknesses manifest themselves only to become merchandise and a franchise. In typical Disney fashion, most characters speak with American accents and a certain denigrating parody appears in the store owner's comic Scandinavian accent to designate his lower-class status. Yet, Kristoff, also a member of the lower class, and none of the other townspeople speak this way. Making fun in the film is often at the expense of the lower classes and Scandinavian folklore. For instance, the trolls are cute little dolls (bound to be sold in Disney stores) that have nothing to do with the profound Scandinavian tradition in which these generally frightening and devious creatures play a significant role. The film's greatest weakness, however, is its celebration of elitism, a mythic given in Barthes's sense of the term. From the first Disney feature to this 2013 production, young and old viewers are expected to be concerned about the destiny of monarchies. If the realms and lives of princes, princesses, kings, and queens are disturbed, we are expected to respond to their urgencies and emergencies. Characters and audiences alike are naturally expected to bow to and help restore challenged monarchies. With the exception of *Pinocchio* (1940) and *Alice in Wonderland* (1951), Disney fairy-tale films do not generally focus on the struggles and lives of members of the lower classes. Though thousands of folktales and fairy tales have plot lines that do not concern upper-class people, the Disney Studio has never chosen one that is not among the classical canon. A "well-made" Disney fairy-tale film seeks to appeal to aspiring lower-class and threatened middle- and upper-class families to retain an appropriate respect for hierarchy and harmony. Perhaps this is the reason why Disney films so dominate these politically tumultuous times and play an essential role in the cultural tsunami. Fortunately, however, numerous fairy-tale films in the global cultural tumult challenge the Disney monopoly's authority.

Marginal and Marginalized Fairy-Tale Films

While Disney fairy-tale products and many other live-action and animated fairy-tale films cry out for stability and the maintenance of current power relations, many more creative and inspiring productions subvert the "well-made" fairy-tale film and delve deeply into the social and political problems that the Disney films avoid. Since the turn of the twenty-first century, well over a hundred unique fairy-tale films that constitute part of the cultural tsunami seek to speak to audiences from the social margins. Many are never promoted, distributed, or noted in the United States, and may even have difficulty finding audiences in the countries in which they were produced. The monopolistic system of film distribution in North America, Europe, and the rest of the world ensures that some of the most extraordinary fairy-tale films of the twenty-first century can only be seen at film festivals or art theaters where runs are short and reviews scarce. Given the questionable monopolistic tendencies of the film industry, I want to draw some of the marginal films into the center of discussion in the balance of this chapter.

In animated fairy-tale films, early signs of subversion or rebellion against the "well-made" fairy-tale films of the Disney Studio started at the beginning of the twenty-first century. *Shrek* (2001), the highly successful computer-animated version of William Steig's picture book *Shrek!* (1990), a delightful parody of "Beauty and the Beast," literally attacked the Disney Studio by drawing parallels to the autocratic manner in which Michael Eisner, head of the Disney Corporation at that time, conducted his business. Lord Farquaad, who controls a sanitized Disney world in perfect symmetry, is a caricature of Eisner. The dictator Farquaad banishes all fairy-tale creatures from his kingdom because he dislikes anything connected to fantasy. Farquaad/Eisner wants to sanitize the world. The frightened fairy-tale characters flee to Shrek's swamp and disturb him so much that he demands that Farquaad take them back. Farquaad agrees if the ugly ogre will rescue the princess Fiona from a dragon. After a number of hilarious escapades, Shrek not only saves Fiona but also wins her heart, and Farquaad is exposed as a petty tyrant. Meanwhile, all the fairy-tale (lower-class, weird, and improper) characters make their home in Shrek's swamp along with Fiona, who will marry him and have his children in sequels. At the end of this film, Shrek, Fiona, and the fairy-tale creatures decide to remain on the margins of society where they are accepted and happy despite their bizarre looks and ways. Ironically, the swamp is their utopia, or at the very least, their refuge from normality.

It is thus from the margins, from the outside, from beneath, that unconventional forces happily create and produce fairy-tale films that compel those who are established in the culture industry to question themselves. They know deep down that they are helpless without the creative artists, thinkers, and workers on the margins. And it is from the margins that unanticipated fairy-tale films are created to challenge the "well-made" positivist cinematic fairy tales that are at the center of the status quo in each society and country of the world. I do not mean to suggest that everything produced on the margins is culturally necessary and valuable for enriching our lives. But, as this book that covers the world intends to show, many strange fairy-tale films have a vitality that sparks our imagination as thinkers and artists in a way that "well-made" fairy-tale films do not. Whether utopian or dystopian, they compel us to confront our social realities and to imagine better worlds and, yes, better human beings. To close this chapter I discuss several marginal examples to demonstrate how filmmakers contest the rigid filmic interpretations of fairy tales that are related to the exceptional films I examined at the end of *The Enchanted Screen*.

As I mentioned above, several bombastic cinematic adaptations of "Snow White" in the past ten years demonized women, stereotyped the fraught relationship between stepmother and stepdaughter, and trivialized some of the tale's key themes. In contrast, Jacco Groen's *Lilet Never Happened* (2012) and Pablo Berger's *Blancanieves* (2012) offer sobering perspectives that provide insights into the particular cultures from which they originate and into universal problems that young women encounter as they reach an age when they must take charge of their own bodies and possible futures.

Despite her talent and intelligence, thirteen-year-old Philippina-American Lilet, who sees herself as Snow White, has no future. She will not become a princess or queen and rule a magnificent realm regardless of how much she tries. As Groen's film commences and the titles flash on the screen, a pretty adolescent girl strides down a brightly lit street, walking gingerly by nightclubs and peddlers. She wears a blouse, jean shorts, and sandals. It is as if she owns the streets, and after she vainly tries to proposition a man, she moves into another district, a shantytown, where an old toothless woman asks, "Snow White, any customers?" The old woman smirks. The girl does not reply but arrives at a place where younger boys are squatting and voraciously eating food. They offer her some, but she declines. They are starving. Then a voiceover in English tells a story. Once upon a time there was a girl in the Philippines named Snow White, who wanted to become an actress. But one day her mother and stepfather made her eat a poisoned apple—we are shown a made-up Lilet being offered as a prostitute to an elderly man by her mother. As she is taken away by the man, the voiceover comments that after eating the poisoned apple, she fell asleep and has been waiting for a long time for someone to kiss her and wake her up.

Groen's disturbing film stems from his experiences in Manila where he met a young prostitute in a mental asylum; she serves as the protagonist in his documentary-like fairy-tale drama based on several years of research. Similar to the German documentary plays of the 1970s and the American political documentary films of the late twentieth century, *Lilet Never Happened* is a fictional account of child prostitution that speaks more potent truths than some allegedly factual documentaries. In *Lilet*, the fairy tale about Snow White is transformed into a scintillating account of a thirteen-year-old girl, who holds on to her dream of becoming a movie star and being rescued by a prince, while she is compelled to work in a nightclub/brothel with other prostitutes symbolically representing the seven dwarfs. A blonde Dutch social worker tries to counter the witch/mother and offer her help, but Lilet is bent on using her street smarts to save herself—an impossible task. While Groen adapts the tale of "Snow White" to speak out against child prostitution, he is never didactic, nor sentimental. He rewrites the story to reveal, in contrast to films like the Indian *Slumdog Millionaire* (2008), that impoverished children will invariably be drained of their potential and will very rarely if ever enjoy the fairy-tale ending. In this respect, Groen's cinematic adaptation undermines the "well-made" fairy-tale film in form and content (see Figure 1.2).

Pablo Berger's *Blancanieves* (2012), a black-and-white silent rendition of "Snow White," also subverts the "well-made" fairy-tale film. It takes place in Seville during the 1920s and can be considered a carnevalesque adaptation of both the Grimms' and Disney's versions of "Snow White." However, unlike Groen's critique of child abuse, there is no explicit political agenda here. Berger's film can be regarded as transgressive more than anything else, and by ironically queering the classical versions of "Snow White," he ridicules their sentimentality and uncovers their happy endings as illusory. The story is quickly told through nostalgic music and grainy black-and-white images. A famous, wealthy bullfighter is gored by a bull and becomes paralyzed. At the same time, his wife dies in childbirth. The bullfighter rejects his newborn daughter whose grandmother becomes her caregiver. Meanwhile, a sinister nurse takes care of the bullfighter, marries him for his money, and connives to dominate the household. Eleven years later, the daughter returns to the family because the grandmother dies, and the bullfighter realizes that the wicked nurse is exploiting him. As he spends time with his daughter Snow White and comes to love her, he teaches her everything he knows about bullfighting. Realizing how much the bullfighter cares about his daughter, the

FIGURE 1.2 Angry Lilet yells at a client, *Lilet Never Happened* (2012).

nurse decides to kill Snow White to prevent her from inheriting her father's money, but she only manages to kill her husband the bullfighter, while Snow White escapes into the woods and is discovered by six dwarfs in a caravan. She joins the members of this troupe, who work in a traveling freak show, and she teaches them about bullfighting. Eventually, they convince her to cross-dress and disguise herself, and she becomes a professional bullfighter in her father's likeness. Soon Snow White becomes famous, and the stepmother discovers who she is and seeks to kill her with a poisoned apple. She succeeds, but the dwarfs pursue her and cause her to be gored to death by a bull. Afterward, they put Snow White into a glass coffin, and she becomes part of the freak show in which spectators must pay to try to wake her. In the final scene the dwarf who loves her the most enters the coffin to sleep with her as he does at the end of each performance. When he does this, a tear trickles down from Snow White's eye along her cheek.

A sad film told through an ironic lens, *Blancanieves* is prevented from becoming a well-made fairy-tale film through estrangement. The film's darkness and subversive twists not only eclipse those offered in the classical Disney film, but also signal that the recent American blockbuster films such as *Mirror, Mirror* and *Snow White and the Huntsman* are nothing but a couple of faint flashes in the pan that should be allowed to flicker out into nothingness. Though *Blancanieves* is no masterpiece, as a marginal work, it offers an alternative to those films that are nothing but bland entertainment. Indeed, *Blancanieves* endeavors to deal with the harsh realities of child abuse and filicide that are also depicted in the American film *Hanna*. In the case of *Blancanieves*, however, the witch's end does not bring a resolution but demands reflection on the part of viewers.

The same could be said about Clio Barnard's 2013 filmic adaptation of Oscar Wilde's "The Selfish Giant." Barnard completely revamps Wilde's sanctimonious religious fairy tale in which the Christ child tempers a mean giant's selfish heart. The giant learns that children can bring him great joy if he allows them to play in his garden, and for his kindness he is rewarded with a trip to heaven. Instead of fostering Wilde's preposterous illusions, Barnard sets her film in the impoverished town of Bradford in northern England where two working-class boys, Arbor and Swifty, spend their days collecting scrap metal and selling it to the monstrous junkyard owner, ironically named Kitten (see Figure 1.3). He has greed written all over him and also wants to make huge sums in harness racing.

FIGURE 1.3 Kitten and the boys in the junkyard, *The Selfish Giant* (2013).

He allows the talented Swifty to train his horse. But when the boys begin to steal scrap metal from Kitten's yard, the "giant" becomes more ruthless and sends them to off to rob a piece of high voltage electric transmission wire to repay him. Unaware of the danger, Swifty is electrocuted while trying to help Arbor to lift the wire. In an unusual gesture of humanity, Kitten accepts the blame for Swifty's death and is sent to prison, while Arbor goes to Swifty's home and persuades the boy's mother to forgive him and to allow him to share her grief.

The Selfish Giant appears on one level as a social realist depiction of a depraved junk owner's destruction of a close friendship between two poverty-ridden teenagers in a region of contemporary England that looks like a devastated war-torn city unfit for human habitation. But the film has greater ramifications, as Will Brooker writes:

> The selfish giant is the system of government that prompts Kitten to run a semi-legal shadow industry, but polices him for his enterprise, keeping him on the edges of official business without safety checks or healthcare. The selfish giant is the society that structures the lives of Arbor, Swifty and their adult equivalents, boxes them into poverty and offers them only limited and risky avenues for escape: the society that keeps them in these desperate, reckless spaces where they run, dodge, swerve, struggle and sometimes die. This ultimately is the power of Barnard's modern fable, that is not a fairy tale, but—in its broader sense if not its specifics—a true story.
>
> (2013)

This is exactly the point that Barnard and other marginal filmmakers want to make: a fairy-tale film today cannot be a "well-made" narrative if it seeks any relevance in our lives.

This perspective can also be seen in the experimental animated fairy-tale films such as the Czech Jiří Barta's *Toys in the Attic* (2009). Commenting on the premiere of the film in New York, Manohla Dargis notes:

> Mr. Barta is more than a decade younger than his compatriot the animator Jan Svankmajer, and less well known, at least in the United States. "Toys in the Attic" isn't as unsettling as Mr. Svankmajer's work, but even in this English-language version, it's scarcely a cute and cuddly family film of the generic type often foisted on American tots. Leaving a screening, a colleague remarked than it may not be right for children, though much depends on the kids. In truth, the movie should be manna for anyone who likes animated fantasies without wisecracks, commercials and overwrought warbling about self-actualization, meaning that it's suitable for those who will grow up either to be the next Tim Burton or simply to enjoy the movies.
>
> (2012)

The plot is simple, while the artwork and politics are intricate. In a forgotten trunk in a musty attic, divided into East and West, a cute antique doll by the name of Buttercup keeps house for a cuddly teddy bear, who is the stationmaster for toy trains, a marionette named Sir Handsome, who resembles Don Quixote, and a clay shape-shifting blob, Laurent, who speaks with a French accent. Every day Buttercup bakes a birthday cake for one of the toys in the attic who roll dice to see whose birthday it will be. This idyllic community in the West is infiltrated by toy spies from the East, and one day Buttercup is kidnapped by secret agents from the East under orders of the bald Head of State of the Land of Evil, who has a human half body, green skin, and smokes cigars. As soon as they are aware of what has happened, Teddy, Sir Handsome, and Laurent set off to rescue Buttercup, joined by a Yiddish-speaking mouse, introduced as inventor Madame Curie. Ironically,

Buttercup does not really need their help, for this modest unassuming housewife-doll turns into a courageous and feisty protagonist, who eventually causes the head of state to collapse, that is, to bring about his own downfall.

The political parable is clear, and though it is enjoyable to view the film as a parody of Eastern European states before and after the fall of the wall in 1989, the art of the stop-motion animation is what makes this film so captivating. Barta, who made a brilliant animated fairy-tale film, *The Pied Piper*, in 1986 with hand-carved wooden puppets and sets that recalled German medieval art and expressionism and dealt with the corruption of totalitarianism, takes a different approach in *Toys in the Attic*. Here every found object that has been cast away or neglected is reincarnated and given new life. It is as though the imagination knows no bounds and must preserve its freedom so that all objects and beings can live with one another in a gentle, but weird, community. Again it is the queering of the fairy tale in which all objects, species, atmospheres, and spaces intermingle, which suggests we can approach the genre and create new narratives in innovative ways. Here the attic becomes a tangible utopia indicating that old worlds can come alive again in new forms.

I see a similar motivation behind Garri Bardin's brilliant claymation animated film, *The Ugly Duckling* (2010), an explicit critique of the authoritarian Russian state. Bardin also produced two superb short parodies, *Grey Wolf and Little Red Riding Hood* (1990) and *Puss in Boots* (1995), which mocked Russian social and cultural policies both before and after 1989. With *The Ugly Duckling*, his first feature-length animated film, he pressed beyond his earlier work in a compassionate portrayal of a bewildered duckling who is constantly stepped upon and marginalized. Moreover, Bardin employs the music of Tchaikovsky and sets the action in a squalid coop in the middle of nowhere, surrounded by majestic lakes and forests that the conformist members of the huge coop can never enjoy. As Richard Scheib remarks:

> Bardin depicts the coop as one modelled along the lines of the classic Communist regime in its heyday. Everybody sings rousing anthems in unison about how great their coop is than any other. There are plentiful parades and dances arranged to show off their glory, even scenes where they come out showing off their production of eggs. Up against this, Bardin clearly favours the downtrodden and pitifully rejected ugly duckling as a voice of non-conformity—the fairytale is broad enough that the ugly duckling can be read as everything from the spirit of individuality to the voice of artistic freedom.
>
> (2012)

Bardin transforms Andersen's tale from a celebration of biological elitism, that is, hereditary rule, to one that depicts the duckling's longing for beauty and freedom. Incidentally, the duckling is not ugly in this film but sweet-looking and forlorn. He tugs at audiences' hearts in his desire to test the limits of his confines and to break out on his own into nature where he is fortunate to join the flying swans, symbols of liberty.

Coda

The five marginal films that I discuss above contest the "well-made" blockbuster fairy-tale films from 2000 to 2015, but are very rarely shown or distributed in English-speaking countries. There are well over 50 other quality fairy-tale films that I could add; some are discussed in other chapters. But they have unfortunately been marginalized by the monopolistic film industry, and this systematic control means that the majority of viewers will not have heard about, nor seen, these films. In addition, they can be difficult to obtain through online stores or services. This unfortunate situation means the cultural tsunami has driven such films to the margins of global cultural production. However, many unconventional fairy-tale films have an impact. Most of the innovative impulses in fairy-tale aesthetics and contents of fairy-tale filmmaking come from the margins of the film industry, and most filmmakers, talented or conventional, are aware of these films. Directors such as Švankmajer, Bardin, Ocelot, Miyazaki, Breillat, Barta, Groen, and others have influenced well-known, successful American and British filmmakers. Yet, given the tendencies of major film studios to put their money into blockbusters or celebrity films and to cater to the lowest possible denominator of viewership, it is debatable whether the unique marginal fairy-tale films will ever enter the mainstream or form a major part of the cultural tsunami. But perhaps it is better this way. Perhaps it is better always.

Notes

1 For critical analyses of these TV series, see Hay and Baxter (2014); Schwabe (2014); and Willsey (2014).
2 See Elias (1978) and my discussion of his work in Zipes (2006b).
3 See Stanton (1957), Taylor (1967), and Cardwell (1983).
4 See the film *Mickey Mouse Monopoly: Disney, Childhood & Corporate Power* (2002).

2

"MY LIFE AS A FAIRY TALE"

The Fairy-Tale Author in Popular Cinema

Kendra Magnus-Johnston

Though somewhat contestable as a self-contained, readily identifiable genre in and of itself, broadly described, a biopic is any film "that depicts the life of a historical person, past or present" (Custen 1992, 5). The biopic "narrates, exhibits, and celebrates the life of a subject," and does so "in order to demonstrate, investigate, or question his or her importance in the world" (Bingham 2010, 10). This chapter focuses on a sampling of live-action biopics that pursue the representation of authors and collectors of the fairy-tale canon. These cinematic portrayals create a paratexual dimension to the fairy tale that exists *across* these films[1] and offer insight into the cultural value of fairy tales themselves and about cinema as a narrative mode. For the sake of continuity and cogency, I treat adaptations author by author. Most films discussed are American, and are a far cry from what could be considered independent or unconventional productions. The chapter concludes by considering the most recent focus on fairy-tale filmmakers, namely, icons Georges Méliès and Walt Disney, and the critical potential offered by depictions from the margins of popular cinema.

Famous Authors and their Function on the Silver Screen

For many, thinking about fairy tales in the present moment invariably calls to mind the famous authors who became mass-mediated tellers, the authorities generally recognized by a modern reading public.[2] For Hans Christian Andersen, Charles Perrault, or the Brothers Grimm (among many others), their names, their lives as historical persons, and their roles as intermediaries have provided considerable fodder for the modern culture industry. But these authors are not alone. Numerous canonical writers have been subjected to fictional resurrections. Fictionalizations have the capacity to rejuvenate the timeworn stiffs into appealing, occasionally errant young men and women,[3] who—through prowess and ingenuity—become successful adult members of society. Especially for fairy-tale authors, these works have the curious habit of recasting the signals of queer[4] tendencies—life-long bachelorhood, unconsummated marriage, and eyebrow-raising relations with children—into family-friendly caricatures whose quirks are attributed to their creative spirit or used for comic effect.

Historical figures depicted in popular film are—like the era in which they lived—unknowable, yet they remain forever tethered to the fictions they created. Michel Foucault positioned the author as an ideological product and identified the "author function" as the cultural and historical assumptions governing the production, classification, and consumption of literature (1979, 159). The discursive fictional identity of popular authors—who I imagine J.M. Barrie *really* was, for example—can be integral to the cultural connotations of their work. In concert with Foucault's argument and in response to Roland Barthes's suggestion to liberate texts with the "death of the author," Kate Douglas explains that "those who now resurrect authors have found similarly specific and empowering functions for them: to sell books, to manipulate the economic power of the celebrity product, and to strengthen the social importance of the arts community and its cultural capital. Authors are useful to consumer culture" (2010, 71). In short, the author is fictionalized and made functional for profit. This arrangement is historically linked to the mass production and consumerism of books as a commercial enterprise. The marketability of the author is not only used to *sell* literature, but their cultural capital is exploited in contemporary popular film.

These claims are especially problematic for authors who cannot contest the terms of their representation. Jack Zipes baldly asks, "is it ethical to produce a film that not only warps Andersen's intentions as a serious writer, but also overshadows his work and his life to such an extent that he and his tales are literally obfuscated and erased?" (2011, 274). While contemporary representation may rejuvenate or modernize artists who have long since died, transparently false autobiographical accounts (biopics) can obscure/deny the legitimacy of the artist's cultural contribution(s). More than debunk these films' historical inaccuracies and anachronisms, exploring the recurring themes and depictions has revelatory potential. For if the appeal of contemporary biopics, as Dennis Bingham argues, "lies in seeing an actual person who did something interesting in life, known mostly in public, transformed into a character" (2010, 10), examining these characterizations can reveal who filmmakers desire these authors to be, or perhaps more intuitively, who filmmakers need them to be when they reflect on their own accountability for contemporary adaptation.

Because traditional fairy tales are retellings and/or adaptations of timeless stories, fairy-tale authors present unique subjectivities for adaptation. When adapting a storyteller's life for a biopic, filmmakers often emphasize the singularity and importance of the stories the figure produced, rather than the details of her/his life; this process becomes manifestly reflexive for filmmakers who identify with their subjects' creative pursuits. Consequently, fairy-tale authors are more than just framed by their cultural production; they are read through it. In other words, the lives of fairy-tale authors are repackaged as fairy tales.

The multiply-mediated conditions of contemporary cultural reception necessitate that scholars recognize the paratextual dimensions that infuse reading practices. The mobilization of authorship as a commodity to be packaged alongside market goods is conspicuous in these biopics as a paratext to their literary productions. To use French literary theorist Gérard Genette's definition of paratext, these films and the characters/stories they relate offer a "threshold," otherwise understood as the "fringe of a printed text" that controls the reading experience (1997b, 2). This threshold is a "zone not only of transition," between the text and off-text, "but also of transaction" because it is a space that structures the public reception of the text (2). Jonathan Gray extends Genette's analysis to consider the proliferation of contemporary mediation. This dimension creates a complex geography of consumption that is generated by industry as well as authors and consumers; Gray argues that paratexts have "considerable power to amplify, reduce, erase, or add meaning" (2010, 46). Authorial identity, however, in the sense that I am implying, cannot be cleanly categorized as something controlled by any single source; it is part of a constellated imaginary reformulated over many years, and in this case, generations.

Hans Christian Andersen: Upbeat Song-Singer, Tale-Spinner, and Downtrodden Day-Dreamer

There have been two live-action American biopics about Hans Christian Andersen.[5] Samuel Goldwyn produced the first in 1952 and the second, an American-British-German co-production with Hallmark Entertainment, was released in 2003. Despite the half-century separating them and the substantial fictionalization of each—one, an extravagant Technicolor musical and the other, a made-for-television melodrama—both films have a remarkably similar plot. Plainly summarized, in them, Andersen, the young, socially obtuse, but ambitious dreamer, departs from his hometown of Odense for Copenhagen, where he faces (mostly) romantic hardship(s), but perseveres. He receives some success publishing his stories and is depicted affably telling them to children; one of his stories is performed by his unrequited romantic interest (a ballerina and an opera singer, respectively) who also appears in his vivid fairy-tale-infused dream sequences. Each film concludes with Andersen as a bachelor on the threshold of his success. Both focus on the fictionalized adventures Andersen undertook en route to becoming a famous author and while both acknowledge his unrequited, somewhat bizarre fixation on inaccessible (exclusively heterosexual) love interests, they invariably underplay the scope of historical Andersen's sexual appetites.[6]

Upon its initial release, *Hans Christian Andersen* (1952) was nominated for six Academy Awards and generated over six million dollars in its initial run (Berg 1990, 465). For Zipes, the film "warps Andersen's intentions as a serious writer" and "overshadows his work and his life to such an extent that he and his tales are literally obfuscated and erased" (2011, 274). Zipes targets the film for its "fraudulent representation" (275) that burned the idea of Andersen as "a happy-go-lucky cobbler" into the imaginations of countless viewers (252).

Anticipating criticism for its inauthenticity, following its ornate introductory credits, the film offers the following declaration: "Once upon a time there lived in Denmark a great storyteller named Hans Christian Andersen. This is not the story of his life, but a fairy tale about this great spinner of fairy tales." Shortly thereafter, the Danish storyteller (Danny Kaye) is depicted entertaining a crowd of schoolchildren with his popular tale "The Emperor's New Clothes." He is an engaging narrator—he sings, performs caricatured voices, and provides animated facial expressions. His stories instruct the children on lessons such as being timely and always keeping one's promises. He even shares worldly observations like "how many kings are queens with moustaches." After the song concludes, the schoolmaster arrives and berates Andersen for distracting the children from their studies. When he objects to the children's Danish history volumes being used to anchor a kite, the storyteller explains, "the history of any country can always stand a little fresh air! Do you know the story of the history book that took a vacation and came back a much better history?"

The confrontation between schoolmaster and storyteller illustrates the film's approach to Andersen as a historical text. In a not-so-subtle nod to Denmark and in stark contrast to Zipes's objection, the defense suggests that manufacturing a "much better history" is as harmless as flying a kite. The scene also introduces the question posed and rather perfunctorily answered in the film about whether or not the "spinner[s] of fairy tales" performs a valuable service. The filmmaker's role is presented in similarly airy fashion, especially as it panders to promoting its own devices with an unabashedly colored perspective (pun intended).

An early trailer for *Hans Christian Andersen* promotes the film as "the romantic life of a storyteller . . . a motion picture of song and dance, love and joy, that's half musical, half miracle" (hdturg 2011). It effuses: "for years, Samuel Goldwyn has been making motion pictures, wonderful pictures, Academy Award-winning pictures, yet never before has he lavished so much time, so many millions, and such magic on any one motion picture" (hdturg 2011). Its transparently schmaltzy message indicates that in contrast to mere Academy Award winners, this film will provide love, joy, miracles, and magic—attributes that a generous producer can apparently buy. The film's promotion hyperbolizes its grandeur and innovation, highlighting its Technicolor production, elaborately emphasized with iridescent pseudo-Danish period costumes.

Hans Christian Andersen presents the most elaborate special effects during Andersen's fairy-tale-themed daydreams. These include an elaborate ballet performance of "The Little Mermaid," a fantasy wedding between Andersen and the ballerina, in an allusion to "The Red Shoes," a disturbing sequence in which Andersen fantasizes about rescuing the ballerina from an abusive marriage. While daydreams might be conventionally understood as spaces for affirmation and whimsical adventure, Andersen's highlight his desire for an orthodox heterosexual relationship (a union described in a duet as "extreme," "hysterical," and "the most unusual on earth"), and invariably point as much to his disconnection with reality as to the film's special effects. In one sequence, the film dramatizes Andersen's otherworldly dream sequence of a ballet instead of filming the ballet actually occurring in the film. Such choices valorize cinema's distinct qualities over live performance.

While being an author is presented as a point of pride and a gateway to notoriety, Andersen's ascendency up the social ladder is marked by considerable cost. The film's titular song, "I'm Hans Christian Andersen," conveys the writer's propensity for wistful tale-spinning, while also distinguishing authorship from trade labor. Equipped with a "pen like a babbling brook," Andersen sings that he has "many a tale to tell" and that he will "mend your shoes . . . when I'm not otherwise occupied as a purple duck, or a mountain side." The nonsensical lyrics conclude with his reasoning that "my pocketbook has an empty look, but if I wish I am a flying fish, or a millionaire with a rocking chair." As Hans Christian Andersen ("that's who," as the song proclaims), he need not toil away as a cobbler, for he can indulge in his fantasies instead. The labor of writing, storytelling, or tale-spinning is not understood as *real* labor, nor apparently is writing a refined practice. When the newspaper editor publishes Andersen's story, rather than legitimize the writer, the editor gives an approximation that he heard indirectly, attributing it to "Hans the Cobbler." Thus Andersen does not pen his first publication. The editor treats "The Ugly Duckling" like a retelling from oral tradition, anonymizing its creator and simultaneously suppressing the identity of the storytellers who came before. He explains to Andersen, "if you write some of those stories down just the way you tell them to the children, I'll print them and pay you for them." The scene swiftly demonstrates the commodification of oral folk narratives and the incumbent prestige associated with literacy, while also short-changing the difference between oral storytelling and mass mediation in literary forms. The event apparently inspires Andersen to call himself a "real writer," imagining his future legitimacy. He sings a new refrain:

> I write myself a note each day,
> and I place it in my hat.
> The wind comes by, the hat blows high
> but that's not the end of that.
> For 'round and 'round the world it goes
> it lands here right behind myself,
> I pick it up, and I read the note,
> which is merely to remind myself
> I'm Hans Christian Andersen,
> Andersen, that's me.

One could argue that given the creative leaps exacted here, actor Danny Kaye may indeed need to remind himself (and his audience) that he is performing as Hans Christian Andersen. Even still, the performance reminds its viewers that authorial names are indeed far removed from the individuals who once owned the rights to their own names and life stories.

The marvel of authorship is diluted in other ways, as well. In a subsequent scene, the camera pans over the signage of "The Little Mermaid" ballet and reveals dozens of artistic contributors with Hans's name at the very bottom. To no one's surprise or dismay, the designation is almost immediately obscured by mud from an oncoming carriage. When Andersen enters the theater, he must introduce himself to the doorman, insisting that he is indeed the ballet's author, asking "don't you read the posters outside your own theater?" The inconvenience of his presence is made abundantly clear when the ballet's director exclaims "Why am I plagued by authors on opening night!?" That he then locks Andersen in a closet from which the ballet's author can only imagine his work's realization, and then forgets about Andersen entirely, speaks volumes to the act of adaptation. However, Hans is not disturbed in the least by this episode. He explains to Doro, the dancer he loves, in an interaction that oscillates between awkward and uneasy, if only because Andersen continues to be so oblivious to her marital bliss: "I knew the story the music was telling. I didn't have to see you dance with my eyes." Evidently, the Andersen conveniently manifested for the film cares not about the distortions and revisions incumbent in adaptation, but is instead devoted to more sentimental aspirations. Upon his exit from the scene, he meekly declares, "I don't think I'll be writing anymore." The film senselessly resolves Andersen's heartbreak, with Peter, his conspicuous boy-helper, explaining that Hans will continue his storytelling because "you're Hans Christian Andersen, that's why." And then with a temporary dissolve, the camera depicts a thick book with the title "Hans Christian Andersen's Fairy Tales" brandished on its cover. The voice of young Peter is heard predicting, "you'll tell stories, you'll write stories, you'll even sing stories over and over and over again."

Significantly, it is actually Danny Kaye who will sing songs from the film "over and over and over again" on recordings like *The Enchanted World of Danny Kaye* (Laws et al. 1960). The film reflexively offers itself as a cinematic substitute for Andersen, literally ventriloquizing his life, as well as his stories. However, *this* version of Andersen does not tell stories to communicate deeper cultural meaning and social critique—or even to promote the innate elitism embedded in tales like "The Ugly Duckling"—but simply does so because of misguided feelings, oh, and because "he's Hans Christian Andersen, that's who."[7]

The other Andersen biopic, *Hans Christian Andersen: My Life as a Fairy Tale* (2003, henceforth *My Life*), begins somewhat less self-consciously with a voiceover from Andersen (Kieren Bew): "Well now, let's begin and when we come to the end of the story we shall know more than we do now. My life as a fairy tale." The arguably delusional protagonist repeats ad nauseam variations on the film's title, assuring others—or perhaps even more, himself—that his life is a fairy tale. The DVD's extra features proclaim, as well, that after watching the "rags to riches" story of Andersen, "you'll believe that fairy tales can come true, too." In contrast to this disclaimer, however, the film concludes with an unexpectedly laconic report from Andersen, who, gazing frankly at the camera, says: "Now my story is done. Life is not always a fairy tale, but I was blessed with a gift to escape into my imagination, to create stories that filled the world with fantasy and wonder, lessons, and love, stories that I hope will live in the hearts of all who read them forever."

The narrative arc is melodramatic at best, and bewildering at worst. While Andersen's so-called imaginative "escapes" are visually stunning and provide a welcome reprieve from Bew's "twitchy and affected performance," which "invokes/evokes the term queer in all its senses" (Greenhill 2015, 120), the conclusion that "life is not always a fairy tale" pays tribute to a popular misconception about fairy tales that insists on conventional standards for what constitutes a happy end. Moreover, the film limits Andersen's critique to social classism and presents his absurd behavior with unflattering gendered implications. While female characters seem accepting of his disturbing, even threatening behavior, countless male characters describe him as "imbalanced." *My Life* seems to convey that women are more understanding, sensitive, and even attracted to eccentric and irrational behavior than their male counterparts. Indeed, when he is not dancing on table-tops, with his mouth agape in childlike transfixation, or abducting his love interests, he bounds around rooms recasting realities in so-called stories, which by any rational measure are more aptly described as compulsive fabrications.

The film's compression of fifty years of historical occurrences into five palatable ones—while absenting all homosexual nuance—offers a jarring and fanciful plot that includes a love triangle between Andersen and two women. The first is his adoring adoptive sister, Jette (a fictionalized rendering drawn from Andersen's real-life relationship with Louise Collin), of whose affections he is apparently utterly oblivious. The other romantic interest is famed opera singer Jenny Lind, whom Andersen appears to pursue, if not stalk, around Europe, despite her obvious lack of reciprocation. Both women reappear in Andersen's daydreams, Lind as the Nightingale and Snow Queen, and Jette as the Little Mermaid and Gerda from "The Snow Queen." Although the film has Jette die tragically at sea, Lind offers a tempered rejection of Andersen, claiming that her public image is but an "illusion," one that acts as a foil to the writer's public image. In a final performance and shortly after receiving a marriage proposal from Andersen, Lind announces her retirement. She stands before the opera house, without accouterment, and announces that "the illusion of Jenny Lind is nothing more than a fairy tale and the spell in the end must be broken. We must not neglect where the path to true happiness lies. The flesh and blood Nightingale might be plain, but her song is more real than that of her gilded imitation." The potentially dissident message to seek "true happiness" and dismiss "gilded imitations" is of course somewhat undercut by Lind's reason for retiring: to devote her life "humbly and gladly" to her future husband, her considerably senior male guardian, who has, incidentally, been ordering her around for the majority of the film. Taken plainly, however, the message could be read that viewers should dismiss popular "gilded imitations" of Andersen's work, seeking instead, as with his projected hope announced at the film's close, to "read them forever," rather than *watch* them on the silver screen.

While the film certainly exposes Andersen's objection to being renowned solely for his fairy-tale publications, it does not entirely reflect the breadth of his work outside the genre, but emphasizes this inclination as a reflection of the writer's self-doubt and miscalculation of their cultural importance. In a heartfelt conversation, his benefactor Jonas Collin explains to Andersen that fairy tales are "more important than you can possibly know. They capture a child's imagination, enclosing it, protecting it, teaching it simple right from simple wrong before life's confusions set in. They tell us good from evil. They are the very heart of all of us and if we do not value them, we all are lost." The conversation concludes with Collin assuring Andersen that "children endure as art endures and you might have both." As with Lind's speech, Collin's counsel is also somewhat weakened by the fact that Andersen neither marries nor procreates and Collin's own daughter dies soon thereafter. However, the message that art transmitted intergenerationally is a more stable form of endurance than biological reproduction is certainly sound in Andersen's case, if not also categorically queer. As a foundational principle supported by repetitious, cross-generational, nostalgia-centered marketing tactics, children's cultural industries continue to prosper (see, for example, Disney's 25-year release cycle on their fairy-tale classics). Envisioning Andersen as aligned with this wellspring for eternal life is compelling, especially when acknowledged as a queer and wildly profitable enterprise that concentrates on the exploitation of children.

The Brothers Grimm: Emancipators, Hucksters, and Peeping Swans

Biopics of the Brothers Grimm—the would-be collectors and editors, and disputable contaminators of fairy tales—present a quality that Jessica Tiffin observes about fairy-tale films in general. She writes that they "tend to flirt superficially and self-consciously with the folk voice" and the three films that follow certainly do just that (2009, 183). Each Grimm biopic teases out its own idea of the importance of fairy-tale traditions and negotiates the Grimms' role in their transmission. Control over storytelling is a running theme whether it is appropriated from female storytellers by the brothers themselves (as in *The Wonderful World of the Brothers Grimm* 1962), challenged by the characters of tales (as in *Once Upon a Brothers Grimm* 1977), or embodied by some mystical property of the folk (as in *The Brothers Grimm* 2005). A continuous thread that runs through them concerns authorial control and accountability for the appropriation of oral traditions.

George Pal's *Wonderful World of the Brothers Grimm* (henceforth *Wonderful*) is the most historically accurate of the three films, not so much from its chronological fidelity, but rather because it situates the story in a realist universe, unlike the fantastic realms of the other two, which indulge in a colorful blend of supernatural enchantment and magical realism. In *Wonderful*, the two brothers are hired by a duke to trace the royal family history, but one of the brothers destroys the project. While one brother (Jacob, performed by Austrian-born actor, Karl Boehm) is a steadfast, rationally minded pragmatist, dedicated to earning an income for his brother's young family, the other (Wilhelm, performed by Lithuanian-born British actor, Laurence Harvey) is preoccupied with collecting the oral folktales of surrounding regions, while ignoring his financial responsibilities. The film conveys three messages: (1) it suggests that cinema is the ideal storytelling technology, (2) it presents literary heritage and the Grimms as emancipators of oral traditions, and (3) it assigns the appropriation and dissemination of fairy tales as a masculine pursuit.

The film's presentation of the cinematic medium as an ideal replacement for oral and literary modes is relatively subtle when it is consumed as a home video. However, given the context of its original marketing, such as its theatrical release on the 150th anniversary of the earliest edition of the Grimm tales, its presentation in three-strip Cinerama, as well as its unique filming methods, its presentation as the next step in fairy-tale technology becomes readily evident. The fairy-tale sequences that interrupt its biographical portions are often visually overwhelming; they include "The Shoes That Were Danced to Pieces," "The Gifts of the Little People," and "The Singing Bone." The inadvertent outcome, reported by *The New York Post*, was that the "episodes water[ed] down the story of the Brothers Grimm" (Lochner 2010, 4). Film scholar David Bordwell has compared the onslaughts of the camera to newer technologies: "the fairy tales give us whirling camera movements, bumpy subjective shots, and frequent assaults on the audience in the manner of 3D" (2012). He draws attention to significant moments such as Pal's stop-motion animation or a coach ride where "the coachman hurls himself to and from the camera," while in another scene, a bumbling servant "slays a dragon in lunging close-up" (Bordwell 2012).

These fairy-tale interruptions occur when Wilhelm purchases or overhears tales told by female storytellers, and when he retells the stories himself. The transmission from oral tales to written, and Wilhelm's insistence on performing this role, casts the act of collection in a heroic, albeit self-righteous and self-congratulatory, light. The film's privileging of literary forms over oral traditions is distressingly unchecked. This slant becomes glaringly clear when Wilhelm chastises an elderly woman for not sharing her stories with a wider public (presumably in a written, mass-mediated form). He not only condemns her interpersonal storytelling technique, whereby she hosts intimate gatherings in her personal home where grown men are not permitted, he charges that "those stories don't just belong to a few children, they belong to children all over the world now and forever after." Although Wilhelm's focus on saving a "priceless literary heritage," that unless documented in writing will "soon be forgotten," is ridiculed by his peers and spurned by his brother, his mission is supported and embraced by the film's conclusion, which features hundreds of children overrunning the Grimms at a train station shouting "We want a story!" Indeed, Wilhelm's consistent, if not afflicting, inability to recall stories he has heard offers a poignant critique of oral traditions. He contemplates, for example, "I just can't seem to remember any. They come and go, slip away. It's a pity there isn't someone to write them down."

Wilhelm's appropriation of the tales and their mass mediation is supported in the film's only supernatural occurrence, which transpires when he has a feverish hallucination. Not entirely unlike the Dickensian Ghost of Christmas Yet To Come, the fairy-tale characters appear in Wilhelm's dream as manifestations of personages yet to be born—fictional creations of the future Grimms.

FIGURE 2.1 The fairy-tale characters hover over Wilhelm's bed, *The Wonderful World of the Brothers Grimm* (1962).

They are figures of the future, but also of the past, since they originate in oral tradition. Fairy-tale characters like Tom Thumb, Little Red Riding Hood, and Rumpelstiltskin surround the bedridden Grimm and implore that their "lives depend on you. If you die, then we'll never be born!" The interaction implies that Wilhelm, presumably with the help of his brother, Jacob, must give birth to fairy-tale offspring to ensure their survival. While the scene depicts authorship as a categorically queer pursuit of male parturition, it also transforms female-centered storytelling into a mission for masculine posterity (see Figure 2.1).

Once Upon a Brothers Grimm (henceforth *Once*) is a live-action made-for-television musical that begins—like countless fairy-tale films—with a gilded storybook.[8] Set in a wholly fictional universe, the film stars American actors: Dean Jones as Jacob and Paul Sand as Wilhelm. The plot involves the Grimm brothers getting lost in an enchanted forest. In sharp contrast to most other fairy-tale author biopics, *Once* does not cover its subjects' humble beginnings; rather, it presents them *after* they have published their fairy-tale collection. Consequently, the film revolves around exploring their roles as authors who have "collected stories by the pound" to "put them all together leather bound" which they sing, reminiscent of Andersen's theme song. However, instead of "I'm Hans Christian Andersen," the duo chime: "Me and him! The Brothers Grimm!" The film is about humbling them into believing that fairy tales are in fact real—and moreover, that the brothers have no authority over the story-world or its inhabitants.

Shortly after the brothers enter the enchanted forest, they lose track of one another; each Grimm ends up apparently randomly inserted into a fairy tale from their recent collection. From "Red Riding Hood," to "The Princess and the Frog," the brothers are mystically cast into various roles. However, they invariably fail to meet the plots' prescriptions. Their inability is perhaps surprising given the fact that the brothers so recently put the stories to print. Instead of controlling the fairy-tale creatures or paternally birthing them (as in *Wonderful*), they find themselves trapped within the fairy-tale realm and utterly ill suited to meet the qualifications for aristocratic male heroism.

In contrast to the intrinsic value attributed to fairy tales and the work of fairy-tale authors in the biopics described so far, *Once*, with its light hearted, occasionally lowbrow, and slapstick humor, imparts to the stories little value beyond escapist entertainment. The brothers finally escape the forest only on the whim of Cinderella's Fairy Godmother. The film ends with the king bestowing a royal honor on them; he declares that because of them "the ancient tales of Germany will now live forever." His statement is, however, undermined by the lack of German characters depicted. Rather, the film actually emphasizes the American appropriation of German folktales and of the Grimms themselves, who amount to little more than failed heroes.

The most recent Grimm biopic is Terry Gilliam's *The Brothers Grimm* (henceforth *Brothers*), which in somewhat unique fashion does not follow the brothers' rise to prominence, but provides a prequel to their lives as scholars and public intellectuals. Set in 1811, one year prior to the publication of the first volume of *Kinder- und Hausmärchen*, the film reinvents its subjects as two conmen traveling the German countryside pretending to vanquish evil spirits. "Will" (Matt Damon) and "Jake" (Heath Ledger) are wayward, morally questionable grifters, with perceptibly ambiguous European, though definitely not German, accents. The pair's lack of fame is one of the primary gags running through the film; where the brothers hope to be recognized for their work, they never seem to accrue the reputation they anticipate. In Gilliam's film, the brothers are presented as anti-heroes, a point that becomes obvious when they are positioned opposite the villain of the film: the wickedly powerful Thüringen Mirror Queen (played by Monica Bellucci), a centuries-old witch who has been kidnapping young girls from the town in order to restore her youthful appearance. Beyond the final sword fight and shattering defeat of the queen, believing in one another is what enables the Grimms to walk out of the final frame of the German countryside in a brotherly embrace "without a bean" to their name.

Rather than interrogate the conventions of film and traditional fairy-tale narratives, in *Brothers* Gilliam mocks the esteem of canonical authors, and further dismantles their nationalist associations. In the film's closing, Jake responds to Will's suggested career path by reaffirming that "this is the real world . . . We are men without country, enemies of the state, and worst of all we haven't a single bean to our name." Will responds, "It's a good name, though, isn't it?" confirmed by Jake with "a damn good name." Making them "men without country," Gilliam, like so many other fairy-tale biopic directors, asserts the universality of fairy tales, as well as the moveable nature of namesakes and the identities of so-called historical figures, which can so easily be manipulated and exploited by entertainment industries.

These closing lines do not interrogate the tenuousness of the Grimms' future as storytellers or the controversies surrounding their transcriptions of oral folktales, but instead simplistically reduce their work to a family name. The authorial seal with which canonical texts are stamped is temporarily broken as audiences are shown the constructedness of authorship. Literary scholar Susan Cahill writes that in staging folk legends that play on the public's fears, while "simultaneously constructing themselves as heroes within this fantasy," the Grimms generate a process not unlike contemporary cinema (2010, 63). Although Gilliam does not seek to revise or subvert the Grimms' work or the conventions of such a fantastic retelling, he is interested in exposing the precariousness of entertainment profiteering. So whereas the brothers say they are "on the verge of an alternative career path; one that uses all [their] new expertise," at the close of *Brothers*, it is only because "there's money to be made in witches." And similarly, as is the case with biopics and the enterprise of fairy-tale publishing, there's also money to be made with the names of famous authors.

J.M. Barrie: Lost [Boy] Between Melodrama and Docudrama

J.M. Barrie was a successful Scottish novelist and playwright; he is perhaps best known today for his authorship of the stage play, *Peter Pan* (1928), the rights of which were famously donated to London's Great Ormond Street Children's Hospital. Despite the notoriety of the curse on anyone who dares pen Barrie's life story, there have been numerous biographies about him.[9] The two biopics focusing on Barrie's life include a three-part BBC dramatic miniseries, *The Lost Boys* (1978), directed by Rodney Bennett, and the family-friendly theatrical feature-length release, *Finding Neverland* (2004), directed by Marc Forster. The former is a strictly fact-driven dramatization, while the latter offers what Jennifer Geer calls the "Miramax treatment" (2007). In contrast to Bennett's work, which was promoted on a platform of historical authenticity, *Finding Neverland* supports a Disney-like ethos that is "child-centered, heavy on fantastic spectacle, and committed to definitions of childhood and fantasy that support utopian wish-fulfillment and exclude unhappiness, death, and social or familial conflict" (Geer 2007, 207).

The BBC series' critical acclaim for its attention to historical detail can be attributed to its screenwriter, Andrew Birkin, who exhaustively investigated the relationship between the Llewelyn Davies family and Barrie, and subsequently made it the docudrama's focus. Given the production's duration—three ninety-minute episodes—the filmmakers furnish an exceptionally thorough account that begins with Barrie's introduction to the boys, includes their parents' deaths, their adoption by Barrie, and their eventual deaths. The attention to historical authenticity is evident throughout, particularly in the film's re-creation of photographs taken during the Llewelyn Davies's stay at Barrie's cottage in the summer of 1901. The cast's staged postures are temporarily recolored in sepia hue, as if perfectly emulating a memory that will later be cherished in a photo album. The series provides some attention to moments of inspiration, as well, whereby Barrie (Ian Holm) jots musings into his notebook accompanied by Holm's contemplative voiceovers; many of the notes are distillations from Barrie's archived notebooks.

Unlike *Finding Neverland*, which offers *Peter Pan* as its central focus, *Lost Boys* is not about the fictional characters, but the Llewelyn Davies boys and Barrie. While the first third follows Barrie being inspired in various ways by the Llewelyn Davies family as communicated by voiceovers and recognizable given some familiarity with the plot of *Peter Pan*, the duration of 180 minutes extends long after the play's production.

The introduction to the screenplay by Louis Marks emphasizes the seriousness with which the screenwriter approached the project: "in the case of Barrie's letters and notebook entries used in the script, some of the text is verbatim, while other parts are invented . . . in other words they are the author's best perception of what the truth might have been, blended with his own dramatic licence" (2004). Marks explains that while the "television trilogy would represent the distillation, the essence of the story told as a dramatic creation" (2004), the wealth of documentary materials— original photographs, personal correspondence, and so on—would appear in Birkin's definitive book (2003). As Marks elaborates, "the book would in fact be the 'documentary', in which the research material would be allowed to speak for itself, while Andrew Birkin the dramatist would express himself through the plays" (2004).

Finding Neverland, in sharp contrast, offers a heavily fictionalized universe that blends fantasy with flexible biographic approximations. Sarah Maier contends that "biomythography," (2007) is a more appropriate term to describe J.M. Barrie's representation in *Finding Neverland*. For Maier, the development of these mythologies accrues in large part from critics and readers interested in the psychological dimension of Barrie's creative inventions. She sees this blend surface in "fantasy sequences clashing with reality" that depict real characters doubled as fictional ones (2007, 151). Indeed, the diegetic universes that exist in Barrie's external and internal self collide in *Finding Neverland*, exposing his affected nature, as well as its potential to be shared. The film's climactic scene, which transpires during the performance of *Peter Pan* delivered in the Llewelyn Davies living room, offers one such collision. After the family has revived Tinker Bell by proclaiming their belief in fairies (a theatrical break in the performance's fourth wall), the fourth wall itself is lifted as though it were a curtain. Peter Pan then floats into the foreground, as the camera moves into the lavish fantasy realm, replete with pirates, mermaids, and fairies prancing through the dewy

FIGURE 2.2 The Llewelyn Davies family enters into the realm of fantasy with Barrie, *Finding Neverland* (2004).

landscape. The Llewelyn Davies family (including the reluctant grandmother) are shown moving closer, as if they are themselves embedded in Barrie's internal fantasy. Conveniently, these scenes also offer considerable space and opportunity to showcase the technological possibilities afforded by the cinematic medium (see Figure 2.2).

In another scene where their mother Sylvia is attempting to prepare the boys for sleep, Barrie imagines the boys taking flight from their bedroom window. Somewhat embarrassed at her inability to calm the children, she explains, "I've grown hopelessly lax in my discipline." Barrie responds approvingly, "Nonsense. Young boys should never be sent to bed." As his gaze darts around the room, in melancholy tone he adds, "they always wake up a day older. And then, before you know it, they're grown." The next shot shifts from over Barrie's shoulder, to a point-of-view from the doorway. The score subtly overtakes the sounds of the boys' laughter, and in reduced speed, one by one, they float into the evening air.

It would be a mistake to conclude that these imaginative intrusions are limited to Barrie's engagement with the Llewelyn Davies family, however. The film depicts the blurring between the writer's material world and that of his imagination as an implicit quirk of being an author. Early in the film, for example, Barrie watches from backstage at his latest play. He imagines a torrential downpour raining over the audience. In another scene, in response to his wife Mary's critique, "surely you don't intend to spend your afternoons with those children do you?" Barrie withdraws into his bedroom, which opens to expose an outdoor paradise. Not unlike the depiction of Andersen in *My Life*, it would seem that Barrie can escape into his imagination. Such departures, evidently, do not amount to standard masculine performance. Barrie's wife leaves him in the film, and while Depp as Barrie and Kate Winslet as Sylvia Llewelyn Davies certainly provide a conventionally attractive heterosexual romantic possibility, there is little in the film to suggest a sexual relationship between them. Like so many other fairy-tale authors, Barrie—even as Johnny Depp—retains a queer presence.[10]

Fairy-Tale Filmmakers: The Next Generation

The interest in fairy-tale filmmakers and their manifestations in cinema is a recent phenomenon that fits into the previous tradition surprisingly well. The two filmmakers who came to my attention were Georges Méliès and Walt Disney; while Méliès has been the central focus of two biopics, Martin Scorsese's *Hugo* and Georges Franju's *Le Grand Méliès*, Disney has recently been featured in three: the independent films *Walt before Mickey* (2014) and *As Dreamers Do* (2014), and Disney Studios' *Saving Mr. Banks* (2013).[11]

French director Georges Franju provides a semi-fictional account of Méliès's life in his short film *Le Grand Méliès*. The writer/director dramatizes Méliès's career as a magician and film-maker—beginning with his death and offering nostalgic reflections on the heights and depths of his tumultuous career. It includes excerpts from some of his short films, while also demonstrating remarkable reflexivity and intertextuality. The casting includes Méliès's own son, Andrew Méliès, as the title character, accompanied by Madame Méliès as herself, with a voiceover by Méliès's grand-daughter (Gladfelder 2013). The film-turned-family-reunion is presented without ostentation; the effect of setting an early scene in Méliès's then-vacated living quarters is surreal and sorrowful. Flashbacks emphasize the cinematic techniques that both inspired and were employed by Méliès himself. Kate Ince provides an example that illustrates the filmic strategies. The sequence includes two juxtaposed point-of-view shots: the first is "a magician's-eye view through a transparent silk handkerchief," which is followed by "keyhole shots through the trick binoculars of a baffled female spectator" (2005, 98). Franju's attention to "seeing, concealing and revealing" in these scenes and throughout the film acts as a tribute to the very "operations that enabled and inspired . . . Méliès's theatrical magic and his fantastic, illusion-based cinema" (98).

In *Hugo*, Scorsese delivers his own tribute to the fairy-tale filmmaker and to the history of cinema. Similarities to Franju's include the meticulous recreation of Méliès's candy-and-toy shop outside the Gare Montparnasse and the inclusion of re-enacted extracts from Méliès's films. But Scorsese's film has a substantially more developed plot, likely due to its basis on Brian Selznick's graphic novel, *The Invention of Hugo Cabret* (2007). *Hugo* as a film (and novel) is unique in the manner in which it fuses apparently competing technologies into an interconnected whole. As Jennifer Clement and Christian B. Long observe, while many popular films "emphasize stories of antagonism, improvement and replacement" between competing media, films like *Hugo*, "deeply concerned with loss, the fragility of art, and the threat of obsolescence, [do] not portray the written word as inferior or lacking in comparison to cinema. Rather, the image and the word are imagined as harmonious collaborators" (2012). While countless fairy-tale author biopics emphasize cinema as replacement of older storytelling traditions, *Hugo* importantly emphasizes that words and images must work together in order to achieve a happy ending for its central characters. And despite substantial critical attention to Scorsese's use of 3D cinema (one reviewer inquired: "Can Martin Scorsese's Hugo save 3D?" [Savage 2011]), the film is just as much about old technologies as new ones.

The film's sequence of mysteries and resolutions are only resolved through a series of missions that incorporate knowledge of books with that of cinema and lived experience. *Hugo* offers its characters their happy endings through the combined efforts of the fictitious film historian René Tabard (who memorably despairs that "happy endings only happen in the movies"), literary afi-cionada Isabelle (who navigates the "Film Academy Library" whose history is organized by books, which prove to print the occasional falsehood), and experienced Hugo (who fixes the automaton that *writes* Méliès's signature) (see also Thomas 2011). It is only through collaboration and embracing, to employ Donald Haase's term, the "hypertextual" nature of remediation, that the characters succeed in their quests, a metaphor that is cleverly exacted in the film's depiction of oral storytelling, live theater, literature, and cinema (2006).

In contrast, exposing both the litigious and sentimental dynamics of contemporary adaptation and remediation, *Saving Mr. Banks* showcases the quandaries of Disney Studios' approach to fairy-tale cooptation, while also exposing the limits of authorial control alongside the consequences of Disney's creative license. The biopic soundly embodies a number of themes evident in so many of the fairy-tale biopics in this chapter. It concerns Walt Disney's (Tom Hanks) manipulation of *Mary Poppins* author P.L. Travers (Emma Thompson) into relinquishing the rights to her fairy-tale invention. Seeking to seduce Travers into creative submission, Disney describes his love for *Mary Poppins* and assures Travers that he is more than "some kind of Hollywood King Midas"; that she would be more than "just another brick in my kingdom." As if in an open letter to all the literary and traditional works Walt Disney has pilfered over the course of building the Disney Studio kingdom (literalized as the "happiest place on earth" in the nostalgic 1960s Los Angeles realized in the film):

> [T]he last thing I would do, the very last thing, is tarnish a story I have cherished. Now the pages of your books are worn to tissue, dog-eared, ripped, torn and falling out because I have pored over them gripped, tormented. Because I love *Mary Poppins* and you have got to share her with me.

Disney echoes the sentiment Wilhelm voices so passionately in *Wonderful*, verbally abusing a female storyteller for not being more generous with her beloved stories. Not unlike the implications of Wilhelm's feverish dream—though the media mogul usurps its queer progenitors—Disney promises to set Mary Poppins free, to "literally fly off the pages of [Travers's] books" because "this movie isn't just going to make my kids happy. It's going to make *all* kids happy, adults too." Doling out the magical properties of cinema, Disney declares, "now imagine! This magical woman who has only lived in your head, you'll be able to meet her, speak to her, you're going to hear her sing" (see Figure 2.3).

FIGURE 2.3 Disney's manipulative tactics include taking P.L. Travers to visit his Disneyland theme park, *Saving Mr. Banks* (2013).

Through this analogy and climactic speech offered near the close of the film, Walt presents cinema's meaningful difference from mere books as a storytelling mode. But rather than, as asserted, permitting the character to "fly from the pages" of Travers's book, in *Saving Mr. Banks*, Mary Poppins becomes a commercial asset of Walt Disney Studios, as well as a fixed embodiment in the popular imagination for "generations to come."[12] In similar fashion, Andersen becomes Danny Kaye; Barrie becomes Johnny Depp; the Grimms, Ledger and Damon; Méliès, Ben Kingsley, and so on.

Rather than escaping into Disney's personal fairy-tale fantasies, the audience receives no insight into his inner workings. The viewer is, however, provided unadulterated passage into Travers's traumatic childhood. Flashbacks convey that her psychological baggage hinders her sharing *Mary Poppins*; the film impresses upon the audience that Disney is either a master of manipulation or the man who cured Travers of her traumatic obsessions. Speaking partly to Travers, partly to the audience, he convinces the writer to consent to allow his team to irrevocably imagineer *Mary Poppins*, and to alter the tale's inflection. According to Disney, "that's what we storytellers do. We restore order with imagination. We instill hope, again and again and again."

As if to hedge their bets on authenticity, the film's credits are accompanied by photographic evidence from Disney's archives—followed by an audio recording of the actual Travers in studio sessions with the Disney team. Viewers are encouraged to accept this proof or at least appreciate the impression of genuineness. Although *Saving Mr. Banks* is not a biopic of Walt Disney, nor, indeed, of P.L. Travers, it provides a compelling historiographical retelling focused on the act of adapting a literary fairy tale to the silver screen. It moreover provides an extremely rare example of a biopic featuring a female fairy-tale author, who though perhaps misremembered in it, is at least recalled. If Walt Disney's storyteller speech is any indication, the film's intention to "restore order to the imagination" will invariably include recasting history at every turn. Doing so is merely a means to an end, or rather, a requirement when the end must be a dogmatically happy one.

When "life is not always a fairy tale": Conclusions and Contrivances

What the major biopics of fairy-tale authors have in common is that they serve as platforms from which to peddle the marvels of the cinematic medium. Danny Kaye provided an opportunity for producer Samuel Goldwyn to showcase cinema as a means to transform historical figures into fairy-tale heroes, to use Technicolor and a live-action musical to harness the popular imagination. *Wonderful* was a vehicle for Cinerama in the way Scorsese's *Hugo* was a vehicle for 3D technologies and hypertextuality.[13] *Saving Mr. Banks* presents cinema as the means to manufacture happiness, recast history, and empower fairy-tale characters to "fly from the pages" of the books that incarcerate them.

Beyond the English-language live-action films covered in this chapter, others like the animated *H.C. Andersen's The Long Shadow* (1998); Denmark's *Young Andersen* (2005); and the Canadian short film *Madame Perrault's Bluebeard* (2011) provide rebellious alternatives to the standard fare. *Young Andersen* exposes a sadistic relationship between a schoolmaster and a young, uneducated artist who must learn to control his "dangerous" imagination, for as explained by his menacing adversary, "danger is related to madness, Mr. Andersen." The film's vivid sequences include one that depicts Andersen escaping his bullies by growing wings and taking flight. It also develops a narrative arc that has Andersen weigh his self-importance and creative genius against the welfare of a young friend. While the imaginative sequences convey Andersen's social anxieties and insecurities, rather than offer senseless digressions (as in so many other fairy-tale author biopics), Andersen's sacrificed friend presents a high cost for creative freedom. In an allusion to Andersen's short story "The Shadow," in Jannik Hastrup's unique animation, the writer exchanges his soul for fame and competes with his shadow for love and social acceptance. In *Madame Perrault's Bluebeard*, Perrault's young wife reads her husband's tale and, visibly unnerved, imagines herself as his character's victim. The short ends with a close-up of Madame Perrault, looking over her shoulder into the camera, fireplace roaring in the background, as she quietly burns the pages of the story. The decorative closing inter-title reads "Charles Perrault published his classic fairy tale 'Bluebeard' twenty years after his wife's death."

Such depictions present authors not as effigies to be destroyed or objects of gratuitous sycophancy, but rather, as unconventional and flawed, but unmistakably human. These films invariably negotiate the costs of fame, whether the tradeoff is the life of a wife or a friend, or the writer's own soul. These authors are presented as dark and as tormented as they might have been in real life; moreover, these films provide a much-needed reprieve from the whimsies offered in popular cinema.

The ways cinematic portrayals have the capacity to retell, but also reformulate the meaning of, storytelling and contemporary authorship, bearing critiques down upon authorial functions and authority, offers an important silver lining to the silver screen. This process is not only limited to the major motion pictures of American cinema—such as Terry Gilliam's playful and idiosyncratic treatment in *Brothers*, which calls attention to the Grimm name as a rhetorical fiction without much material substance or merit—but other, often independent, explicitly non-Hollywood films, which provide a foray into the potential for *new* endings. As is the case with the earliest of the fairy-tale author biopics, *Hans Christian Andersen*, this diverse body provides "a little fresh air" to an otherwise stale creative atmosphere, a welcome challenge to authority which dares to test the power of cinema, as well.

Notes

1 Authorial names are paratextual devices shaped by mediated representation. Elsewhere, I describe how authorial representation affects the seriousness with which a work is viewed in cultural industries, observing that "mediated representations in popular American film act to define, contain, and conflate their identities with specific aspects of their research" (Magnus-Johnston 2013, 66). The American television series *Grimm* plays on similar, but by no means identical, invocations of the name (see Willsey 2014).
2 The trend to label famous authors as authorities is complicated in fairy-tale studies given what Haase has described as their "hypertextual" elements (2006), a topic further explored by Bacchilega, who notes "the existence of competitive authorities and the awareness of multiple traditions" (2013, 27).
3 Despite the conspicuous absence of female fairy-tale authors such as Mrs. Molesworth or Madame Leprince de Beaumont in contemporary biopics, a number of others are dedicated to female authors; such as Jane Austen in *Becoming Jane* (2007) and *Miss Austen Regrets* (2008) or Virginia Woolf in *The Hours* (2002; see Polaschek 2013).
4 My application of the term queer aligns with David Halperin's, who writes, "queer [is] . . . by definition *whatever* is at odds with the normal, the legitimate, the dominant"; it "demarcates not a positivity but a positionality vis-à-vis the normative" (1995, 62; see also Jagose 1996).
5 Jannik Hastrup's animated *H.C. Andersen's The Long Shadow* (H.C. Andersen og den skaeve skygge), 1998; Denmark's made-for-television film, *Young Andersen* (Unge Andersen), 2005; and the Russian short film, *Andersen: A Life without Love* (2006) exemplify the breadth of Andersen biopics (see Staples 2008a, 36–38).
6 Of Andersen's sexual proclivities, Pauline Greenhill cautions against oversimplification, providing an impressive overview of the heteronormative alibis offered by many of his biographers. Writing of Jens Andersen's biographical account, Greenhill observes that it "manifests ambivalence toward heterosexual relationships and decidedly queer heterosocial and homosocial, as well as homosexual, connections" (2015, 116). See also biographical accounts from Bredsdorff (1975), Wullschlager (2000), Zipes (2005), and J. Andersen (2005).
7 Zipes notes that Andersen's *three* autobiographies promoted his belief in intelligent design, attributing that force to his own destiny as a famous writer (2007, 124; 112–13).
8 See for example Bacchilega's nuanced discussion of this trope's use (2013, 73–108).
9 See Birkin's introduction to the revised edition of his *J.M. Barrie & The Lost Boys*, in which he reports that with the untimely death of his son, he felt "somewhat felled by Barrie's curse" (2003, xiv).

10 Given his gendered flexibility on screen, Depp presents an intriguing casting decision. His proclivity for "ambiguously gendered" roles from effete pirates to transvestite film directors highlight what Geer describes as "androgynous, anti-authoritarian elements" (2007, 210; 203). The decision to cast queer suspect Danny Kaye as Hans Christian Andersen marks a similarly conspicuous opportunity for the queer imagination.

11 While I would prefer going *beyond* Disney, the two independent (but saccharine) films are unlikely candidates for a compelling discussion. Both lead up to the creation of Walt Disney Studios. If the trailers are any indication, they appear derivative and contrived, with an undaunted enthusiasm for manifest destiny and the Disney tycoon himself. While *Saving Mr. Banks* is not technically a biopic of the fairy-tale filmmaker Walt Disney, its concentration on Walt, particularly as an adversary to literary fairy-tale author P.L. Travers, is uniquely positioned for this discussion.

12 Jessica Tiffin elaborates on film's distinctive capacity as a visual medium to be "crippling to the kind of imaginative exercise usually required of the reader by almost any magical narrative" (2009, 182).

13 While *Wonderful* attempted to usher in a new technology at the expense of an older one—in its case, oral storytelling for Cinerama—*Hugo* reflects a pluralistic approach that embraces multiple intersecting technologies.

3

SPECTACLE OF THE OTHER

Recreating *A Thousand and One Nights* in Film

Sofia Samatar

> As they watched, the private gate opened, and there emerged as usual the wife of King Shahrayar, walking among twenty slave girls. They made their way under the trees until they stood below the palace window where the two kings sat. Then they took off their women's clothes, and suddenly there were ten slaves, who mounted the ten girls and made love to them. As for the lady, she called "Mas'ud, Mas'ud," and a black slave jumped from the tree to the ground, came to her, and said, "What do you want, you slut? Here is Sa'ad al-Din Mas'ud." She laughed and fell on her back, while the slave mounted her and like the others did his business with her. Then the black slaves got up, washed themselves, and, putting on the same clothes, mingled with the girls.
>
> . . .
>
> When King Shahrayar saw the spectacle of his wife and the slave girls, he went out of his mind.
>
> (Haddawy 2010, 11)

The frame story of *A Thousand and One Nights*, in which tyranny will be defeated by narrative, is activated by a moment of illicit theater. King Shahrayar and his brother King Shahzaman form a hidden audience for the infidelity of Shahrayar's wife, which, unfolding according to a strict choreography, and accompanied by a chorus in black and white, has the air of a stage production. Shahrayar's revenge takes the equally theatrical form of daily executions of a series of brides. To be cured, he must once again become an audience member, but this time for the gifted storyteller Shahrazad, who spins her wonderfully vivid tales in the king's dark bedroom: at once screenwriter, cast, director, and projectionist.

Given the theatricality of these and other scenes in *A Thousand and One Nights* (henceforth, *Nights*), it comes as no surprise that the tales have a long history of adaptation for stage and screen. Even as narrative, the history of these tales is one of performance: they emerged from the narrative traditions of India, Persia, and the Arabic-speaking world, and exhibit features, such as the use of poetry, repetition, and formulaic descriptions, characteristic of oral genres (Müller 2006, 48). As *Nights* traveled it moved across stages as well as booksellers' shelves. In Europe, plays based on *Nights* began appearing in the eighteenth century, following Antoine Galland's 1704–17 translation; in India, nineteenth-century urban theater produced plays based on indigenous versions and others filtered through British theater and pantomime. Drawn from Nagamine Hideki's 1875 translation, the first Japanese stage plays based on the tales were produced in 1906. Only a year later, an early film adaptation was screened in Japan: the Pathé Brothers' *Ali Baba and the Forty Thieves* (Ali Baba et les quarante voleurs 1902). The date of this film, and of others such as Georges Méliès's *The Palace of the Thousand and One Nights* (Le Palais des mille et une nuits 1905), show how closely *Nights* has been intertwined with cinema's history from its beginnings. Moreover, the early screening of *Ali Baba* in Japan points to the way *A Thousand and One Nights*—perhaps the most transportable network of the stories in the world—has accompanied and abetted cinema's global transmission.

Daisuke Miyao traces one fascinating arc of this circulation, in which Paul Leni's German *Waxworks* (Das Wachsfigurenkabinett 1924) inspired Raoul Walsh's American feature *The Thief of Bagdad* (1924), which in turn inspired Ōfuji Noburō's *The Thief of Baghdad Castle* (Baguda-jō no tōzoku 1926). Though the American and Japanese films differ greatly, Miyao argues that both represent their respective nations as modern selves in contrast to exotic and backward others. In so doing, they manifest "the pressures that nationalisms exert on tales that are overtly marked as foreign" (2007, 84). This foreign marking is one of *Nights*' most enduring qualities. In its travels throughout the world, it has carried a particular form of otherness: the exotic.

The exotic, Peter Mason argues, is produced through discovery (1998, 1), a connection that resonates with the Arabic literary genre to which *Nights* belongs: *'ajā'ib*, or wonder tales. *'Ajā'ib* comprise a variety of fantastic types, such as travelers' tales and stories of saints and miracles; their object is to produce wonder and astonishment, a goal often explicitly noted in *Nights*. Emphasizing marvels, the tales have themselves been received as a marvelous discovery outside their areas of origin. Exoticism has been so central to these tales' reception, as they have circulated globally, that they continue to represent foreignness in contexts where they have been familiar for centuries. Through their enduring foreignness, these tales provide space for both constructing the self in opposition to the Other, and donning the mask of the Other to play out fantasies of the self. Thus, while Douglas Fairbanks plays an Arab in *The Thief of Bagdad*, his character's flexibility distinguishes his performance from the fixed stereotypes of the other non-White characters, enabling it to serve a rags-to-riches, primitive-to-civilized drama of Americanization (Miyao 2007, 86). In his bronzed "Eastern" disguise, Fairbanks functions as a masked yet recognizable version of his American audience—as it appears to itself in dreams.

The fantastical nature of the tales of *Nights*, their character as *'ajā'ib*, opens them to this kind of speculative and spectacular play, and their re-creations in the 300 years since Galland's translation have firmly established *Nights*' tales as an expressive vehicle for the exotic. This abiding exoticism depends upon the circulation of *Nights*, in its various tellings, retellings, and reimaginings, as what Philip Kennedy and Marina Warner call "a uniquely accretive cultural bundle," rather than a particular and bounded text (2013, 8).

Works that depart significantly from the source texts may yet be received as part of *Nights*' world by the inclusion of elements belonging to this cultural bundle, such as a name like "Aladdin" or "Scheherazade," or metonymic signifiers of the mysterious East such as turbans, slave girls, and jinn. In the process, while traces of the *'ajā'ib* tradition remain, the emphasis on learning and reflection that characterizes the tales is lost, so that they appeal to the consciousness Abdelfattah Kilito associates with the worst reader of *Nights*: "the one who would see there only the extraordinary stories, the ones that distract and astonish" (2010, 501). Still, if the exotic is a "representational effect" (Mason 1998, 2), intimately linked to sight and spectacle, then the study of film versions of *Nights* presents valuable opportunities for examining the workings of, and the connections between, foreignness, discovery, the marvelous, and visual culture.

The exotic, Mason writes, is "never at home" (1998, 6); if this expresses some truth about the reception of *Nights*, it is also true that these tales are at home everywhere, and have taken more cinematic forms than can be treated in this chapter. I have therefore organized it around three key films: animator Osamu Tezuka's *A Thousand and One Nights* (dir. Eiichi Yamamoto, *Senya ichiya monotagari* 1969), the Indian-Soviet co-production *Alibaba and the Forty Thieves* (Alibaba aur 40 chor/Priklyucheniya Ali-Baby i soroka razboinikov 1980), and *City of Brass* (2002) by Lebanese American filmmaker Hisham Bizri. Each exemplifies an aspect of the relationship between *Nights* and the cinema, and raises issues broadly applicable to the tales' adaptation for the screen. *Senya ichiya monotagari*, an adult animation, draws attention to the symmetries between the exotic and the erotic, a key element of *Nights'* reception and circulation, and dramatizes the voyeurism of both foreign travel and film. *Alibaba aur 40 chor/Priklyucheniya Ali-Baby i soroka razboinikov* is a fascinating transnational production, a drama of illusion and recognition that expresses anxieties about ethno-religious plurality and national culture. The anguished and searching short, *City of Brass*, uses a meta-fictional narrative to meditate on exoticism itself, the power of spectacular images, and the possibility of their subversion and transformation. In the conclusion, I attend to the figure of Shahrazad, her role in feminist thought in the Middle East, and the way the use of her name draws attention to women's voices in performance, television, and film.

Peep Show: Osamu Tezuka's *Senya ichiya monogatari* (1969)

Osamu Tezuka (1928–1989) was a prolific and innovative animator, widely considered the founder of both manga and anime (Lamarre 2009, 52). Tezuka's manga series *Astro Boy* (1952–1968) was adapted into an animated television series (1963–1966), and credited for introducing the style of animation characterized by painterly backgrounds and a limited number of drawings, which would become known worldwide as anime. Though the majority of Tezuka's works are geared toward a young audience, he conceived a trilogy of adult films that he called "animerama": a combination of anime, drama, and cinerama (Power 2009, 137). Tezuka collaborated with director Eiichi Yamamoto on the first two, *Senya ichiya monogatari* (henceforth, *Senya*) and *Cleopatra* (Kureopatora 1970), but was not involved in the production of the third. The "animerama" redefined film animation, Natsu Onoda Power writes, as "a medium capable of eroticism and 'adult' humor," creating a base for today's thriving adult anime industry (2009, 137).

Senya concerns poor but plucky water-seller Aldin (Aladdin), his relationship with slave girl Miriam, and his progression from poverty to riches and back to poverty again. At the film's beginning, Aldin walks into the city of Baghdad alone; at the end, he walks out the same way, after a series of adventures including travel by wooden unicorn, an orgy on an island of snake women, and the rise to become ruler of Baghdad. The story involves scenes of sex and violence, including incest and rape, as well as magical flights of fancy, playful transformations, and humorous dialogue. *Senya* is exuberantly experimental, employing rock music and psychedelic imagery, and combining animation with live-action footage and models.

While the film is undoubtedly stylistically innovative, it also plays on a most conventional curiosity about the sex lives of others. These are always, of course, considered to be abnormal, excessive, and far more exciting than "ours." The history of the global circulation of *Nights* is inseparable from the construction of racial and cultural Others as practitioners of, and therefore potential doorways into, nonnormative, sometimes frightening, but also liberating sex. In *Senya*, sex-as-spectacle is generated through a series of contrasts between interiority and exteriority, and between limitation and abundance, with links to both the text of *Nights* and its travels.

Let us return for a moment to the scene that sets the stories in motion, quoted at the beginning of this chapter. Shahrayar and his brother spy on Shahrayar's wife and slave girls as they cavort with male slaves. This is a moment of discovery, not of an exotic outside, but of an internal betrayal, taking place within Shahrayar's own palace, among his closest intimates. It is also a reverse invasion, in which the Black slaves, captured in lands geographically and culturally removed from Shahrayar's, breach his private territory as symbolized by the female body. By spying on his wife and slaves, Shahrayar peers into the secret life of others: women and people of African descent whom he has considered his own property. The price of gaining knowledge about these Others, of discovering what they *really* think, and what they do when he's not around, is intense humiliation and emotional pain. Readers observing the scene, however, suffer no such pain. Rather, we enjoy both the titillating scene and the king's outrage, as, from our privileged position, we watch the watcher.

In *Senya*, Aldin and Miriam consummate their affections in a scene that moves from a languid dream of penetrative sex to a drama of outrage and humiliation, as the two find themselves the unwilling stars of a peep show. After Aldin rescues Miriam from the slave market, the couple enter a luxurious and apparently empty house, where they spend the night having sex. Although there are images of foreplay, and particularly of Miriam's breasts (which remain exposed throughout the film, until the scene of her death in childbirth), the act of penetration is not directly represented, but suggested through the image of an opening flower. Red and frothy, this flower takes up the entire screen. It draws closer and closer, then invites the audience's gaze to plunge into it, as it evolves into a winding and fleshy scarlet tunnel with a black opening at the bottom. The gaze swirls down the tunnel into the darkness, which is then filled with a field of roses, over which Aldin and Miriam, locked in an embrace, pass on a floating carpet.

The scene creates a magical dream of plenitude, of simultaneous enclosure and freedom, and of a marvelous power to see and be at once inside and outside, above and below. In the morning, however, Aldin and Miriam find themselves locked in the bedroom, while the owner of the house, exhibiting signs of foreignness, effeminacy, and degeneracy in the form of a turban, colored fingernails, and a missing tooth, informs them from his hiding place behind a painting that he has watched them all night. In a mockery of the previous scene's delights, the voyeur peeps through the eyes of a nude Eve; when Aldin, in his fury, tears away the painted face, the image becomes that of a voluptuous female torso, holding an apple, topped with a black peep hole in place of a head. The hole is no longer a tunnel of pleasure but a conduit for invasion by prying eyes. Though it differs from the scene of Shahrayar's discovery in *Nights*, this scene of voyeurism echoes its key themes: abundance within a limited space, the shift from confidence to humiliation, the interplay of interiority and exteriority, and the power of invading eyes.

In western culture, the exotic east has a long history as an imaginative field for playing out fantasies of confinement and freedom. *Nights* provided a powerful vehicle for these fantasies, which often unfolded on the stage: in England, the plays based on the tales that began to appear in the eighteenth century gave new life to an already-existing form of spectacle, the "seraglio drama" (Kuti 2013, 323). Its themes—eastern despotism and decadence, and the erotic prohibitions and excesses surrounding the harem in the European imagination—received a rich new source of inspiration in the *Nights* stories. The preoccupation with polygamy and trapped, secluded women informed and was informed by the Enlightenment interest in faraway lands and the scientific cataloguing of the world's wonders and terrors. This "culture of curiosity," Elizabeth Kuti explains, was distinctly visual: "the discourses of science or pseudoscience, as manifested in the prevalence of the theatrically presented 'curiosity cabinet' or scientific demonstration of wonder, merged with theater as a space for the visual pleasures of curiosity, horror, and wonder" (2013, 324).

Edward Said's statement on the imagined orient reflects the culture of curiosity: "The Orient is a stage on which the whole East is confined" ([1978] 2003, 63). A dazzling multiplicity, limited for the viewer's pleasure, reveals the links between theater, scientific discourse, and voyeurism. Like the voyeur, both the theater-goer and the foreign researcher or collector observe from a position of power while their bodies, their intentions, or both remain invisible to the objects of their gaze. Voyeurism's logic also provides the opportunity for displacement: one can enjoy a peep show without inviting any of the consequences of participation. This reasoning also applies to works marked as foreign, like *Nights*, in which one participates not as oneself, but in the guise of the Other. "In oriental costume," Warner writes, "much could be enjoyed that was otherwise off limits, and the book became a playground for Enlightenment adventurers" (2012, 26).

In *Senya*, the voyeuristic logic of exoticism operates in the same way, but the compass shifts. In Japan, *Nights* was not received as an eastern network of stories, but as a product of western culture. "Adaptations of the *Arabian Nights* on the stage" during the Meiji period of 1868–1912, writes Yuriko Yamanaka, "go hand in hand with the modernization of theater and importation of Western themes into traditional forms of Japanese theater" (2013, 276). In this context, *Nights* "was considered to be part of the Western intellectual repertoire, and not something 'Middle Eastern' or 'Oriental'" (2013, 278). Japanese readers and audiences received *Nights*, arguably quite accurately, as "a constituent part of European civilization" (Nishio 2006, 162), and still regard it as part of English or French literature (2006, 159). In *Senya*, the audience is invited to enjoy a colorful and titillating spectacle not of the exotic east, but of an exotic western fantasy.

The face of Tezuka's Aldin is modeled on that of sexy contemporary film star Jean-Paul Belmondo; his signature song, played during the opening credits and sung by himself later in the film, is a bluesy tune with an English refrain: "Here comes the man called Aldin." Given these visual and musical clues, and the history of *Nights'* reception in Japan, it makes sense to see Aldin's dark skin and fez-like hat, which would constitute signs of easternness in a western film, as signs of westernness: part of a web of associations understood as emblematic of a western imaginary. It is also significant that no character in the film is marked as Japanese, and that Indian and African figures appear as possessions of Aldin and the King of Baghdad when the two stage a competition to see who owns more marvelous treasures. In a vivid demonstration of traveling orientalism, the Japanese film presents a conflict between a western hero and an eastern, Arab villain, in which representatives of various non-western cultures are spectacularly displayed and compared for their market value. The audience's sympathies are meant to rest, of course, entirely with Aldin, reflecting a process of Japanese self-formation in which the western has played a "double role": both imagined other and mirror of the modern self (Nishio 2006, 162).

The transformation of a western fantasy of the east into an eastern fantasy of the west highlights the consistency of the foreignness of *Nights*. For both the eighteenth-century European recipients of the tales, and the nineteenth-century Japanese ones, *Nights* provided a vehicle for Otherness, for the enjoyment of strange and outré sexual fantasies (such as Aldin's orgy with the snake women in the film) and the display of magical wonders framed and distanced so as to be compatible with a modern culture. The voyeurism scene in *Senya* encapsulates an important dynamic, for the audience, after all, have been watching Aldin and Miriam just like the perverse peeper behind the screen, but through an apparently clean voyeurism that is one of the cinema's great pleasures. *Nights'* foreignness manifests this distance in symbolic form.

If it is true, as Warner writes, that the *Nights* tales "place the audience in the position of a child, at the mercy of the future, of life and its plots" (2012, 11), it is also true that they place the audience in the position of the powerful child surveying a kingdom of toys. Distance, which enables a panoramic view, is key to this dynamic of control: to watch from a distance is to see more, to see others as smaller than oneself, to see without being seen. This is the perspective enabled by the flying carpet, the cabinet of curiosities, and the cinema: a vision of simultaneous containment and abundance, of Said's "stage on which the whole East is confined" (2003, 63). *Senya*, with its sexual fantasy, humor, and artistic experimentalism, demonstrates the aptness of the *'ajā'ib* tradition for the screen, on which audiences expect to see displays of technology's modern marvels.

Nights is perfect for the cinema, and film creators have recognized this quality since the medium was developed, producing a vast number of films that emphasize, to a greater or lesser degree, visual wonders, eroticism, and the stereotypical Arab world of the orientalist repertoire. Many are animated: in fact, the first full-length animated film, Lotte Reiniger's *The Adventures of Prince Achmed* (Die Abenteuer des Prinzen Achmed 1926), packed with visual riches and racist caricatures, is based on a tale from *Nights*. *Senya ichiya monogatari* encourages us to recognize the cultural bundle of *Nights*, with its marvels and its misogyny, its racism and its imagination, as emblematic of the promises of motion pictures, and foundational to a modern, global culture of spectacle.

Recognition: *Alibaba aur 40 chor/Priklyucheniya Ali-Baby i soroka razboinikov* (1980)

Senya provides one example of traveling orientalism, in which stereotypical images of certain eastern cultures (Arab and Indian) are reproduced in the creative expression of another (Japanese). This is one version of the process Saree Makdisi and Felicity Nussbaum describe, in which "as the 'Orient' travels through world markets, it reflects its own commodification and participates in its own exoticization to itself and others" (2008, 17). This process takes different forms in regions to which the *Nights* stories are indigenous, and where there is a significant or majority Muslim population and lived experience of cultural practices with recognizable parallels. The 1980 Indian-Soviet co-production *Alibaba aur 40 chor/Priklyucheniya Ali-Baby i soroka razboinikov* (henceforth, *Alibaba*) is a particularly rich example, joining two distinct cinematic traditions, and highlighting the complex cultural exchanges that have characterized the spread of *Nights*. The film is also significant as the creative expression of a practice taking place in both India and the Soviet Union: the attempt to forge a national culture out of disparate ethnic and religious groups. *Alibaba* represents both a utopian yearning for pan-Asian connections, and the distancing, through the tale's exoticizing power, of segments of the nation singled out as foreign, anti-modern, and suspect.

This spectacle of the Other within unfolds simultaneously with another use of *Nights* to generate distance: the adoption of costume drama to express oppositional politics. In places with cinematic traditions that approach *Nights* as part of an indigenous cultural heritage, film and television versions of the tales create an atmosphere of magic and whimsicality that, if it does not depend (as the western and Japanese versions do), on exoticizing a foreign culture, rests on exoticizing the pre-modern past. This magical period can provide a space for dramatizing political aspirations and critiques that are dangerous in the present. With its mix of anti-Muslim stereotypes and social critique, *Alibaba* brings together both Indian and Soviet cinema, both the costuming of the barbaric Other and the costuming of the political self, and both fantasy and social realism.

The history of Soviet-Indian film co-productions begins in 1954, with a declaration, during the first official visit of Indian filmmakers to the USSR, of "friendship and cooperation between the cinemas of the two countries" (Salazkina 2010, 74). This accord involved both encouraging the circulation of films between the two countries, and collaborating to "fuse the cinematic and pictorial traditions of both film industries" (2010, 74). Masha Salazkina analyzes *Alibaba* for insights on the question of "how form can meet . . . complex and multifaceted ideological, geopolitical, and commercial demands within two separate filmgoing cultures" (2010, 77). Considering that no other Soviet-Indian co-production was as successful as *Alibaba* (though the same team produced another film in 1984 with a fairy-tale atmosphere, based on a medieval Punjabi legend), it is likely that the capacious contours of *Nights*, which always has room for one more story, proved a particularly useful vehicle for these requirements. However, as Salazkina also points out, *Alibaba* was made at a time of political convergence, rather than divergence, between India and the Soviet Union. "Seen in its historical context," she writes, "the turn to *The Arabian Nights* as a mythological instance of a pan-Asian culture implicitly affirming the unity between the central Asian Soviet republics and India has sinister overtones in the context of the Soviet invasion of Afghanistan with which the making of the film coincided" (2010, 78). The thieves of *Alibaba* are called *razboiniki* (bandits), the same word used by the Soviet military to describe Afghanistan's mujahedeen during the invasion India supported (2010, 79).

If, as Tetsuo Nishio writes, Europe "discovered her self-identity . . . in the virtual narrative space called Orientalism," this narrative and visual space was also instrumental in Indian and Soviet self-fashionings (2006, 161). Rosie Thomas draws attention to the way "oriental" fantasy films in India, among them several versions of *Nights*, constructed an imaginary, "quasi-Islamicate" orient in the 1920s and 1930s (2013, 364). While this cinematic Islamicate was heavily influenced by Euro-American orientalist fantasy productions, particularly Walsh's *The Thief of Bagdad*, which proved highly popular with Indian audiences, it also drew on indigenous tales and poetry and a history of Mughal courtly culture. These indigenous elements were not, however, represented as fully Indian, but distanced through fantastical representation: "Key to India's oriental fantasy film was its setting within an imaginary world outside India" (Thomas 2013, 364). The distancing and disavowal of images and practices associated with Islam functioned as part of a Hinduizing nationalism contemporary with the surge in orientalist fantasies in Indian cinema. This film history bears on *Alibaba*, which, produced in 1980 on the cusp of a new surge in right-wing Hindu nationalism, reveals anxieties about the coexistence of multiple communities, and represents the formation of national culture as an unfinished project.

For Uzbekistani director Latif Faiziyev, the collaboration's Soviet participant, *Alibaba* was something of a departure, as his earlier films belong to the tradition of Soviet realism. However, even this realist tradition made use of orientalist stereotypes and folkloric plots with ties to fantasy in representing the cultures of the Soviet East, which included the predominantly Muslim Caucasus, Siberia, and Central Asia. The "fanatic clerics" and "despotic beks," which Michael G. Smith describes as typical eastern characters in Bolshevik cinema drawn from fantasy rather than realism, are, as he argues, connected to the deeply ideological fantasies of orientalism and cultural imperialism (1997, 647). The strong postwar Soviet tradition of fairy-tale films would also have been familiar to Faiziyev and his home audience. In addition, *Alibaba* was produced at a moment when Soviet cinema was attempting to maintain and increase its audience by moving away from the realist tradition toward comedies, musicals, and science fiction; Faiziyev's turn to fantasy fits this larger context (Salazkina 2010, 78). In India, as in the Soviet Union, the religion and cultures of Islam were represented as insufficiently incorporated into the nation, and as resistant to full incorporation, through the fantastical world of the *Alibaba* film.

In *Alibaba*, the thieves are stock caricatures of mountain warriors, and unlike other characters, they are not marked by dress as either Indian or Uzbek (Salazkina 2010, 79). They are heavily associated with strangeness and magic from the earliest moments of the film. During the credits, Abu Hassan, the thieves' leader, cries "Open Sesame" to reveal the magic cave, followed by a long shot of the thieves shrieking and hallooing as they dash across a plain on horseback, performing stunts by leaping in and out of the saddle and riding upside down. The equestrian acrobatics of the Caucasus are thus framed by the performance of magic and implicitly placed into the category of supernatural marvels. The thieves are represented as cognizant of and comfortable with magic, and they also use it to understand the world: when they attack a merchant's caravan, the merchant responds with bombs, which the thieves regard as the magic "fire of Satan." Inhabitants of the enchanted world, they are unable to depart from it, even when confronted with demonstrations of modern science.

Costumes serve more than one function in *Alibaba*. If the thieves are set apart as ferociously anti-modern, as superstitious and dangerous outsiders, the other characters' costumes set them apart from their audience's world in a different way: not in space, but in time. Dressed in the costume of a previous era, the characters provide a means to play out contemporary issues, such as concerns about water use. Salazkina calls it an "ironic coincidence" that "a fairy-tale film about the misuse of water was shot in a place and time in which the misuse of water—namely, the water from the

Aral Sea, to irrigate cotton crops in Uzbekistan—was creating one of the greatest environmental scandals and frauds in Soviet history" (2010, 82). Perhaps, however, this conjunction of factors is neither ironic nor coincidental, but an example of masking: dressing contemporary issues in the robes of the past, where the distance between "then" and "now," combined with the fairy tale's otherworldly atmosphere, becomes a way of eluding censure.

The career of Rolan Bykov, who plays the film's villain, is relevant here: before *Alibaba*, he participated in several controversial and banned films, and had a fraught relationship with the state. Salazkina points out the particularly powerful ramifications, given this history, of Bykov's character, the diabolical Abu Hassan, who links the two spaces of the dam and the thieves' cave in "a continuum between robbery, private enterprise, and state corruption" (2010, 85). Abu Hassan is the film's false father, who murders Alibaba's real father and steals his ring. After destroying the dam, Abu Hassan also impersonates the Qazi, the official authority and symbolic father of the village. The layering of false fathers advances a critique of authority, in which the head of the village's ordered society is associated with the lawless and anti-modern bandits. Here, the distance accorded by the fairy tale works as a transparent cloak and the imagined despotism of the past as an allegory for the political climate of the present.

The multiplication of false fathers in the film points to one of its key structures: in *Alibaba*, the false is multiple and the true singular. The most striking demonstration of this structure is the final battle between Alibaba and Abu Hassan in the magic cave, when Abu Hassan creates multiple illusions of himself through sorcery. Alibaba is helpless against this crowd of false enemies, unable to discover the true one, until he sees, on just one figure, his father's stolen ring. The ring possesses the power to reveal the one true enemy; aided by its magic, Alibaba slays his foe. Another case of this same opposition is a trick from the Ali Baba story as related by Galland: when Alibaba and Marjina realize that the thieves have marked their door with an X, they put the same mark on every door on the street.

In *Alibaba*, jewelry has talismanic and symbolic powers. The blue stone in the father's ring relates both to the identification of true and false fathers, and to water, as indicated by a swift cut from a shot of water pouring over the magic cave's mouth to the glittering blue of the stolen ring. The false and true fathers both exert power over water: Alibaba's father built the dam that sustains the village, while Abu Hassan, with his "Open Sesame," magically turns off a waterfall to reveal the cave door. In addition, in his role as the false Qazi, Abu Hassan takes control of the village's water, forcing people to buy it, demonstrating the cruelties of privatization. The name of the village, "Blossoming Garden," emphasizes the centrality of fertility to these symbolic connections. The blue ring represents the father, the blue water his generative power, which—if he is indeed the true father—waters the garden and makes it bloom.

The other significant piece of jewelry in the film is the princess Marjina's anklet. It heralds her arrival in the life of Alibaba, her future husband: it falls on him from a high wall, followed moments later by the princess, who lands in his arms as she flees an unwanted marriage. Later, when Marjina has been recaptured by her wicked suitor, Alibaba arrives disguised as a magician; while the suitor tries to make the princess dance for him, Alibaba assures him that he can make her dance by sorcery. To get Marjina to play along, he displays the anklet; she recognizes it, realizes who he is, and dances, and while the suitor is dazed with lust at the sight, the couple make their escape. If the blue ring relates to fertility, the gold anklet is associated with sex, and particularly with women as both sexual objects and objects of exchange. The gold anklet, with its seductive jingling, makes the link between Marjina the reluctant dancer, objectified and humiliated, and Marjina the hapless slave, put up for auction in the market later in the film. As prospective buyers shout out their bids for her body in gold dinars, Marjina sings of her plight in heartrending tones (see Figure 3.1).

FIGURE 3.1 Marjina on the auction block, *Alibaba aur 40 chor/* Alibaba and the Forty Thieves (1980).

In this film, which fully embraces a gendered binary, the symmetry between the female body and money is the counterpoint to that between the male body and water. It is significant, then, that the film's explicit politics involve a critique of the ownership of water. The idea is represented as base and unnatural, but there is no suggestion that this logic applies to gold. Marjina's weeping on the auction block serves not to critique the ownership of human bodies, but to amplify the emotion of her attachment to Alibaba through the spectacle of her hopeless, utterly submissive, and suggestively undulating body. Indeed, Alibaba's possession of both the thieves' treasure and Marjina is crucial to the film, as it enables the romantic ending. In the final shot of their embrace, Alibaba's role as good leader, suggested by his rebuilding of the dam and recovery of his father's ring, is eclipsed by his role as Marjina's romantic possessor.

In fact, there are two rings, one worn by Alibaba's father and one by Alibaba himself: it is the precise resemblance of these two rings that allows Alibaba to recognize his father's killer. After Abu Hassan's death, Alibaba gives one ring to Marjina. The two embrace beside the magical pool, unified by their twin talismans in the closed circle of the couple: the perfect match. The death of all the other major characters in the film—Abu Hassan, Alibaba's father, his brother, and the spirited Fatima—leaves the couple triumphant. The oppressive overtones of this triumph grow more insistent when we consider that the practice of polygamy, incompatible with the modern, bourgeois couple, is one of the most widely discussed and criticized aspects of Muslim culture, and that Fatima dies with the Muslim profession of faith on her lips, in the film's most explicit reference to Islam. Marjina, on the other hand, whose costume marks her as a "Hindustani princess," survives to be absorbed by Alibaba as his primary treasure and the sign of his victory (Salazkina 2010, 83). The couple's singularity, with their matching rings of truth, and Islam's proximity to death, links the false/true dichotomy in *Alibaba* to the film's treatment of gender and its distancing of the nation's problematic Others.

It is also possible to see, in this association of multiplicity with falsehood, a distrust for the cinematic medium, and a nostalgia for a magical aura of truth and the attendant power of truth-telling that objects have lost in the age of mechanical reproduction. The wicked reproductive sorcery of the false father, Abu Hassan, does after all create a row of identical film-like representations of him, and is directly opposed by the good reproductive powers of the true father, who waters the fields and engenders children. The spirit of the cave, who serves Abu Hassan, floats in the air, a transparent simulacrum, and a ghostly turtle moves on the cave wall as if projected on a screen. These effects belong to a long tradition that recognizes and makes use of the opportunities *Nights* offers for creating spectacular cinematic effects. Yet by linking these cinematic wonders with Abu Hassan's evil magic, *Alibaba* implicitly calls them into question. Film technology's magical powers find expression in the thieves' underground realm. This is the only link drawn between them and the modern world—one that projects them uneasily into the present. The problem of the thieves, and its attendant questions—who are the modern nation's "real" citizens, and what is to be done with Others?—remain unresolved.

Immobility: Hisham Bizri's *City of Brass* (2002)

City of Brass, by the Lebanese American filmmaker Hisham Bizri, draws together two themes mentioned above—captivity and stereotypical images—by interrogating the popular imagination's captivation with them. The 28-minute film draws on the "City of Brass" tale from *Nights*, and in particular on the moment when travelers come upon the eerie, empty city where a mummified princess lies in eternal slumber. The protagonist is not a character from the tales, but their first European translator, Antoine Galland. A letter appears in the film's first moments to tell his story: written by his wife, Adelaide, it describes how the manuscript was offered to him by a mysterious Moor, who proposed, as Galland lacked money to pay for the text, to exchange it for sex with Adelaide. Both lovers accepted the terms, but found themselves drawn progressively further away from one another as the Moor continued to offer new stories. "With each new manuscript we became increasingly lost," writes Adelaide, "Antoine in his translation of 'Madinat al-Nuhas' ['The City of Brass'] and I with my seduction of the Moor." At the end of the letter, Adelaide writes that Antoine has left her for the orient.

Bizri's tale of Antoine and Adelaide reverses the narrative energies of *Nights'* frame story. Instead of bringing a couple together, as with Shahrayar and Shahrazad, the stream of marvelous tales in *City* separates husband and wife. Bizri superimposes the frame story's conflict and resolution on top of one another: the conflict, in which Shahrayar finds his queen making love to a Black slave, reappears in Adelaide's relations with the Moor, but it does not take place before the storytelling that cures the king, as in *Nights*. Instead, access to the stories is made possible by the wife's sexual relationship with a dark interloper. Adelaide's betrayal makes storytelling possible in *City*, and, as the film encourages us to realize, in *Nights* as well. Without the adultery, there is no story. By rearranging the narrative structure thus, Bizri exposes how the wondrous tales of *Nights* depend on racialized and gendered imagery tied to the fears of men in power. Underscoring the frame story's words, Bizri films Antoine writing them in the voice of King Shahrayar: "My wife then called out 'Come, Massood! Come, Massood!' And there came to her a Black slave, who had sex with her multiple times." This moment places the *Nights* text directly against the translator's imagined life, showing how one matches the other, how life imitates art, and how tightly reality is bound to dreams.

Throughout *City*, the filmmaker superimposes in order to expose. Repetition, mirrors, and layering computer-generated images over optical ones reveal the relationships between images in a new way. In an artist's note on the film, Bizri describes his images as "hieroglyphic," possessing "a hidden meaning, symbolical and emblematic" (2003, 7). At times, these hieroglyphs become challenging to read, such as when images fade or blend into one another. The visual layering contributes to the atmosphere of silence and immobility that characterizes *City*, in keeping with its theme of a stalled quest.

City evokes the silent film: the characters write, but never speak. It moves between the spaces of Antoine and Adelaide's home, the desert, and the City of Brass, all of which appear frozen. Snow falls slowly on Antoine and Adelaide's house. The desert dunes lie motionless under the feet of the imaginary travelers, who move with excruciating slowness toward the City of Brass. The city itself, true to its enchanted state, stands empty and silent. Scene after scene of immobility is accompanied by sounds suggesting movement: wind, hoof-beats, the ocean, the cries of birds. The many scenes in the film in which nothing moves, or in which movement is so slight as to be almost undetectable, create a sense of imprisonment intensified by its contrast with the sounds of motion and flight. And if the spaces lack movement, the characters seem turned to stone: the travelers seeking the City of Brass stand petrified in poses of walking, their only movements the flicker of their eyes and the flapping of their clothes in the wind.

Visual and aural elements related to tales of the marvelous—the columns of the City of Brass, the sound of hooves beating toward adventure—are more dynamic and vital than the film's characters. At one point, the image of Antoine at his desk becomes transparent, fading away entirely to the sound of a galloping horse. In another scene, a traveler stands frozen, looking up at the city's columns, gradually fading away as the columns move past him. Representing the move through which Europe came to know itself through the virtual narrative space of the orient, the establishing sequence of Antoine and Adelaide depicts them both engrossed in visual contemplation: Antoine stares at the richly decorated items on his desk, such as a goblet covered with arabesque designs, while Adelaide gazes at her own face in the mirror. The scene expresses the dependence of consciousness on objects and reflects the specifically gendered forms of this dynamic. Antoine defines himself by staring at exotic objects produced by an eastern "Other," while Adelaide defines herself by staring at herself—that is, by encountering her own body as the object of her gaze (see Figure 3.2). Her adoption of the male gaze is underscored in the next scene, when she and Antoine are both looking in the mirror; an instant later, he disappears from it, and is pictured across the room, with his back to her. Adelaide's way of looking at herself originates with Antoine, but persists even in his absence. Like the images of *Nights*, or the oriental objects in Galland's study, Adelaide's reflection encapsulates a narrative that is stronger than Adelaide as a character.

Bizri represents sex as another story in which the images are more powerful than the protagonists. Near the film's end, the traveler lies in the lap of a veiled female figure, gazing up at her bare breast with the same avidity and anguish he turned on the unattainable columns of the City of Brass. Slowly, he reaches for her breast with his tongue, but he fails to touch her. Similarly, the *Nights* tales, as we know from Adelaide's letter, are more powerful than her relationship with Antoine. In two scenes, one member of the couple watches the other sleep, unable to entice the beloved from

FIGURE 3.2 The mirror, from *City of Brass* (2002).

their world of dreams. The final scene, a shot of the ocean, reminds us that Antoine has left his dead marriage with Adelaide for the promise of movement and adventure. Human relationships fade and die in the hall of images, which proves as magical and as enervating as the tomblike City of Brass.

The critique of images, and of the iconography of orientalism in particular, sets *City* apart from *Senya ichiya monogatari*, *Alibaba aur 40 chor/Priklyucheniya Ali-Baby i soroka razboinikov*, and hundreds of other *Nights*-based films designed for mass consumption. In a sense, the task Bizri sets for himself is not only the critique of images, but their redemption. In employing views of deserts, carpets, arches, veils, and so on, he draws attention to the difficulty of re-presenting them in a way that detaches them from, or at least erodes their ties with, the orientalist imaginary that is part of the cultural bundle of *Nights*. His figures' paralysis, his hieroglyphs' spellbound silence, foreground the challenge of attempting to say anything with these images that has not been said before, to move beyond orientalist representation using the images of the *Nights* matrix. Bizri attempts transformation through distortion. His desert does not evoke the usual sense of freedom in a vast romantic landscape; rather, he writes, his "distorted spaces, oblique perspectives and monotone colors" are intended to "allegorically reflect the anguish of the Arab people after the Arab-Israeli wars and the Gulf War and the repressive governments that they continue to endure" (2003, 8). In one of the film's eeriest moments, a group of faceless figures stalks across the desert: these attenuated, roughly textured giants are digital creations based on the sculptures of Alberto Giacometti (Bizri 2003, 10). The ease of their movement shows that they belong to the world of story, rather than the world of human beings; but what are they? Bewitched inhabitants of the City of Brass or grim shadows of Antoine's dream, they pass without speaking, leaving a haunting silence in their wake. Bizri intends the figures "to draw the viewer's attention to the act of seeing itself" (2003, 11); certainly their weird presence interrupts the flow of the desert, preventing its consumption as a typical scene from *Nights*.

The use of digital images in a silent film also superimposes current film technology on a past genre. This move compresses the entire history of film into the space of *City*, emphasizing how *Nights* has been intimately bound up with that history. The shadow figures in the desert recall not only Giacometti's sculpture, but also Lotte Reiniger's shadow puppets for *Die Abenteuer des Prinzen Achmed* (1926). *City* reveals the centrality of *Nights*, with its enduring images of travel and confinement, to the screen dreams of our image-capturing technology. It also represents human beings as prisoners of the images we capture and the stories we tell.

Shahrazad, Tell Me a Story: *A Thousand and One Nights* and Beyond

The 2009 film *Scheherazade, Tell Me a Story* (Eḥkī yā Shahrazād), by Egyptian director Yousry Nasrallah, concerns a talk-show host who turns her television program into a space for women's stories. Set in contemporary Cairo, the film nonetheless uses the central theme of *Nights*: telling a story can save your life—specifically, a woman threatened by male power can save her own life through storytelling. The film also uses a narrative frame (the talk show) and embeds multiple stories within it. Though *Eḥkī* is not a re-creation of *Nights*, the film draws on its tales in important ways. One of the longest and farthest-reaching threads in the *Nights* web is this theme of women's storytelling, which has made Shahrazad a catalyst for feminist thought and expression, especially in the regions where her story first circulated.

These engagements with the figure of Shahrazad are more common in writing than in film. This is not surprising, given the close association of *Nights*' imagery with the objectification of women. As we have seen, commercial film versions usually avoid the frame story altogether, preferring the big-screen possibilities offered by the tales of Aladdin, Ali Baba, or Sinbad; within these films, women generally serve as objects of exchange. Shahrazad, a word artist, has been treated more thoroughly in words than in pictures: Fatema Mernissi's *Dreams of Trespass: Tales of a Harem Girlhood* (1995), Assia Djebar's *A Sister to Scheherazade* ([1987] 1989), and Githa Hariharan's *When Dreams Travel* (1999) are examples of her presence in literary genres such as the novel and memoir.

Shahrazad's story has provided a dynamic starting point for Middle Eastern feminist writing, and its diversity is evidence of the story's power: compare Azar Nafisi's "Imagination as Subversion: Narrative as a Tool of Civic Awareness" (1997), which portrays Shahrazad as a feminist hero, with Joumana Haddad's critique of Shahrazad as complicit with patriarchal structures in her memoir *I Killed Scheherazade: Confessions of an Angry Arab Woman* (2010). These debates around Shahrazad's legacy indicate her significance as a cultural presence, and suggest the network of associations evoked by her name in a film with feminist concerns like *Eḥkī*, or a production designed to appeal to women like the immensely popular Turkish television series *A Thousand and One Nights* (Binbir Gece 2006–2009), a contemporary drama whose main character is named Şehrazat. The voice is key: the orality of Shahrazad's art resonates both with feminist methods of breaking silence and with the lived reality of women, who are less educated and less literate than men globally. An interest in orality, rather than image, inspires Shahrazad's use in Arab-American women's performance: as Somaya Sami Sabry explains, these performers find "the resistance and urgency of the original orality of Sheherazade" useful in conveying their experiences in a post-9/11 world (2011, 215). The voice is also central to Tunisian director Moufida Tlatli's *The Silences of the Palace* (Ṣamt al-Quṣūr 1994), a film that reworks the harem drama familiar from recreations of *Nights* in order to emphasize women's interiority.

Ṣamt opens with a sustained close-up of a young woman's face. Music and the murmur of voices can be heard, but the face, heavily made-up and wearing a blank, fixed expression, is the only visual clue to the scene. The opening of the film both encourages the viewer to dwell on the woman's face, presenting her as a silent form to be contemplated, and emphasizes how little information can be gained from a face. Then the woman begins to sing, and the camera retreats so that the scene of a wedding comes into view. The woman sings a love song, "*Amal Ḥayātī*" ("Hope of My Life") by the iconic Egyptian star Umm Kulthūm, and the central image becomes, not her silent face, but her whole body in expressive tension and motion. In her song, words are repeated several times, opening the way for ambiguity. "Take me in your embrace," the singer concludes, "and leave me to dream. Leave me. Leave me. Leave me." These words bring together the themes we have seen films take up from *Nights*: confinement (in the lover's arms), freedom (to dream), and romance. But the repetitions that conclude the song suggest an emotional shift from romance to rebellion, and the passion of the lone female voice carries a defiant energy. This opening scene relocates attention from an objectified female form, which, as we have seen, has been a key element in the circulation of *Nights* through various patriarchal systems, to a challenging female voice. Who is the singer? What do her words mean—and what does she mean by them? The opening performance's complexity, which distinguishes it from the sexy or pathetic song-and-dance numbers of a film like *Alibaba*, raises questions about women's interior lives.

Like Shahrazad, the young singer Alia is a gifted entertainer, a performance artist; like Shahrazad, she captures the attention of a powerful man. However, Tlatli inverts the fairy tale: Alia's gifts never make her a queen, or even a respectable woman. Her talents can only enable her to earn a precarious living as a musical and sexual entertainer, a captive whose life becomes, she says, "a series of abortions." Significantly, *Ṣamt* contains no fantastical elements, no otherworldly wonders. Its setting is the era of Tunisian independence, and the richly colored paintings in the style of Delacroix that decorate the walls of the palace where Alia serves ironically invoke the lush fantasies of both colonial orientalism and a patriarchal Tunisian postcolony. The film's emphasis on women's speech and song reveals, Suzanne Gauch writes, "how the gaze can only ever partly substitute for the voice of those it takes as its objects" (2007, xv). The film's end layers one female voice on top of another to break the palace's silence: while Alia sings to entertain guests upstairs, her mother, down in the servants' quarters, screams as she dies of a self-induced miscarriage.

The *Nights*-influenced films discussed here that advance cultural critiques—Nasrallah's *Eḥkī*, Tlatli's *Ṣamt*, and Bizri's *City*—break the storytelling conventions of their source, divesting it of either its magic (Nasrallah, Tlatli) or its narrative flow (Bizri). They are exceptions. The vast majority of film versions of *Nights* marshal exoticism and eroticism in the service of mass entertainment, using stereotypes of ethnic and sexual Others as props. It is possible that future filmmakers will attempt significant transformations of *Nights* in film as Hisham Bizri has done. What is certain is that *A Thousand and One Nights* will continue to serve as a magic lamp producing cinematic wonders. As of this writing, Warner Brothers has purchased a script treatment for a seven-part series of films based on the tales, featuring computer-generated imagery—the latest technological marvel (Fleming 2014). Through the cinema, *A Thousand and One Nights* lives on as a powerful generator of visual *'ajā'ib*, and a never-ending spectacle of the Other.

4

BRITISH ANIMATION AND THE FAIRY-TALE TRADITION

Housetraining the Id

Paul Wells

The fairy tale is bound up with virtually every national oral and literary storytelling tradition. Each culture brings variations to common narratives, while adding nuanced local tales of its own. The animated film has been a ready bedfellow of the fairy tale, keen to exploit its rich symbolic and metaphoric principles. As Hilary Mantel reminds us, though, when we read fairy tales today, "the tools of psychoanalysis jump to hand, like the animated dish and spoon in the nursery rhyme. But we mustn't forget the historical reality behind the stories" (2005, 34). This principle guides my chapter's discussion; addressing the British approach to the fairy tale requires a fine analytical line drawn between text, subtext, and context. Crucially, I will also critically engage with the specific ways that animation distinctively mediates the fairy-tale form. This entails addressing how the genre has been defined in Britain; how it functions as a source for British animated shorts; how and why the particular language of animation is deployed; and how this work's aesthetic and conceptual outcomes speak to the dominant paradigms of Britishness, animation, and the fairy tale.[1]

Britishness, like any model of national identity, is notoriously troublesome to identify and define, too often simply reiterating stereotypes and clichés. In this chapter, I determine Britishness in relation to *English* literary culture. British animation has its own issues; its principal influences have been the American cartoon and the Eastern European modernist tradition. Yet it also has its own indigenous approach, especially in regard to its specific styles of wit and visual caricature, but these more dominant classical models in animation vie with traditions of English illustration in representing fairy tales, and often hide or hybridize British tropes. In general, British children's animation has sought to work directly in original illustrators' styles (for example, those of renowned non–fairy-tale children's works like *Rupert the Bear* or *The Tale of Peter Rabbit*). But the fairy tale's British contours are inextricably bound up with folk idioms, literary genres, and vernacular forms. It can be comparatively easy to identify fairy-tale *aspects* in much animation because of storytelling's self-evident artifice, its inherent capacity for metaphor and analogy, and its narratives' underpinning moral and ethical imperatives. It is far more difficult to identify animated films as fairy tales *per se* unless they declare this status by adapting established, popular, largely European fairy tales such as those in anthologies by the Brothers Grimm or Charles Perrault, or written by Hans Christian Andersen, or simply, with the opening line, "Once upon a time." Identifying the British animated fairy tale, however, demands careful tracing of antecedents.

One possible starting place comes in the unlikely guise of Madame Leprince de Beaumont, who wrote "La Belle et la Bête" as a short story for *The Misses' Magazine* in 1758 while working as a governess in England. Her thinly disguised moral tract to encourage young women's complicity in the face of mostly loveless arranged marriages was later described by author Angela Carter as "housetraining the id" (quoted in Warner 2005, 34). This useful observation shows that such stories are readily seen as abstract meditations on unconscious desires and wishes beyond the purview of formal language and expression. The narrative acts as a model by which such desires and wishes might be expressed, but which are ultimately rationalized and contained. Many popular fairy tales address inchoate aspects of familial and social life, and often engage with rituals of justice and punishment accordingly (see Zipes 2011). But the British (animated) fairy tale often pursues other themes, influenced by British faerie—that is, the historical culture of fairies and fairyland—origins. In 1946, Lewis Spence wrote the first historical account of British faerie-legend genesis. Though his perspective largely conflates fairy tale with legend, fable, and folktale, distinctive elements remain.

Spence immediately claims that "fairy" essentially speaks to the "very roots of human belief and primitive methods of reasoning" (1946, vii); tracking the fairy story's emergence across the British Isles shows the evolution of an alternative method of understanding experience, beyond the claims of language and rationality. In this belief system, fairyland is a supernatural world whose governance and influence impact upon human conduct. In its most positive sense, it is a land of quasi-utopian enchantment and magic, informed by powers not fully comprehensible to humankind. But it is also a land of potentially duplicitous illusion and complexity. Faerie is a supernatural presence, almost a spiritual or psychosomatic haunting, populated by (symbolic) elves, goblins, pixies, pechs, fauns, leprechauns, banshees, and indeed, fairies. These embodiments may act as metaphoric mediations of seemingly tacit knowledge and experience outside human agency and certainty. Faerie becomes a method of explaining without wholly rationalizing: creative extrapolation that insists on the maintenance of life outside the rational and known. At once, then, faerie acknowledges that humankind, nature, and lived experience cannot (and should not) be fully comprehended, but also operates as the projection of ideas, issues, and controlling agents that signify less observable, quantifiable, material power and influence.

Crucially, the fairy world is inherently invested with magical qualities to which humankind can only aspire and seek to artificially create or acquire. One of its most important aspects is *transformative* power. As Spence notes:

> By means of this art, or power, the fairies were able to transform places and objects so that they assumed a totally different appearance from that which they naturally possessed. What might appear to the night-bound wayfarer as a lordly castle or a magnificent palace, was found in the light of morning, to be a noisome ditch or a barren rock. Or in the twinkling of an eye, the whole fairy scene might vanish, giving place to moor or wilderness.
>
> (1946, 18)

These qualities give rise to some key popular fairy-tale themes, including the difference between appearance and reality; rapid shifts in status and experience; issues of nature and culture; and power and responsibility outside human agency. But equally, these themes speak to the capacity for animation to achieve seamless metamorphoses; determine the maximum of suggestion in the minimum of imagery; fabricate and choreograph worlds-in-flux; and imply anthropomorphic relevance[2] (see Wells 1998, 68–126). Transformation, or shape-shifting, is not only possible in relation to places and objects, but people and creatures. Protean spirits imbue animals with sentience, or operate with invisibility, their participation merely evidenced in their impact on the material world. Animation has been particularly effective *as* a mode for recounting animal tales, particularly in relation to visual effects in which artifacts and places have a life of their own subject to an invisible hand

(Wells 2009), but it has also been applied to specific aesthetic, narrative, and didactic elements of British faerie.

Faerie in Britain usually relates to the land; simultaneously a rural idyll, an agrarian outlook, a landscape epitomizing the natural world's potency, and ultimately, a burial ground from which spirits might emerge. This was well represented in fairy painting, though the otherworldly concept sat uneasily with the Pre-Raphaelite and Victorian engagement with realism, social observation, and the detailed concern with the everyday. The spirit of faerie seems best epitomized by the literature of Walter Scott, Charles Kingsley, Christina Rosetti, and later, Rudyard Kipling and W.B. Yeats. In contrast, art works by John Lamb and Henry Singleton among others, essentially symbolist in nature, singularly failed to reach the standards of their fairy sources—Shakespeare's *Midsummer Night's Dream* and *The Tempest*—their visual invention limited even in relation to the production design of the period. Yet if faerie fared poorly as part of the early nineteenth century's theatrical imagination, it found better purchase in the color lithographs of children's illustrated books at the century's end. Artists like John Anster Fitzgerald (who specialized in fairy paintings) and Richard Dadd created distinctive works that defined the fairy world in a period when a strong sense remained that such a place might actually exist. Fitzgerald's representations of faerie would readily engage Freudians, playing out lyrical rituals of fairy hierarchies, informed by sexual and violent acts. Dadd, whose mature work was completed in an asylum, painted "The Fairy Feller's Masterstroke," showing the fairy world in the thrall of the moment when a hazelnut is to be cleaved by an axe. This often microscopic world seemed a perverse inflection of the material one, a point taken to its logical extreme in two important later works: Rudyard Kipling's *Puck of Pook's Hill* (1906), a complex mix of English folk rhetoric inflected by Indian exotica, and Estella Canziani's watercolor, "The Piper of Dreams" (1914), reproduced as a hugely popular print, talismanic to First World War soldiers as a representation of the England they believed they were fighting to defend.[3]

The image of a piper summoning fairy spirits, emblematic of the maintenance of dreams, fantasies, and ephemera of the past, seems in accord with a view of England grounded in its formality and ritual, yet driven by flights of fancy and creative desire. This principle seems to be at the heart of faerie and underpins a view of the fairy tale as it emerges in the modern era and becomes a vehicle for the moving image. This model of modernity had seen a greater degree of self-consciousness with the emergence of psychoanalysis and the development of a machine culture predicated on industrialization and new technologies. Spence presents three theories relating to fairy belief:

> 1. that they are the spirits of the human dead; 2. that they are elementary spirits – that is, spirits of nature, the genii of mountain, flood, and forest; 3. that belief in them is due to reminiscences of former peoples or aboriginal races which have been thrust into the more distant and less hospitable parts of a country by the superior weight of an invading stock.
>
> (1946, 53)

Such theories invoke the desire to represent some sense of an imagined England, seemingly lost to the modern world; a key theme of the British animated fairy tale. This idea links to the view that the values, memories, and experiences of the past are inviolate and should imbue present and future conduct.

Some distinct phases emerge in the ways that British animation has used and adapted the fairy tale: first, between 1899 and 1935, the formative period of both animation as an art and the fairy tale in cinema; second, between 1936 and 1967, when the animated fairy tale became a consolidated form and spoke to an imagined community, as Britain sought to advance its own mythologies; and finally, between 1968 and the present day, reflecting the crises of postmodernity. For each phase, I examine the way that faerie has responded to shifting personal, social, and cultural codes.

1899–1935: Even An Englishman Must Move With the Times

Britain produced one of the first animated films, the short *Matches Appeal* (1899), directed by Arthur Melbourne Cooper, advertising matches for Bryant & May, but also raising funds for the Boer War. Maker, photographer, and showman, Cooper was a pioneer of three-dimensional object and puppet animation. Inspired by contemporary British and French magazines, depicting matchstick figures in amusing military poses, Cooper also made playful experiments such as *Animated Matches Playing Volleyball* and *Animated Matches Playing Cricket* (1899) (see Wells 2014). He specialized in a more imaginative engagement with the form, exploiting its freedom to narrate the dreams of toys that have come to life. His *The Enchanted Toymaker* (1904) and *Noah's Ark* (1906) show evidence of the fairy spirit—a model of practice speaking to an alternative parallel world populated by objects playing out seemingly surreal choreographies. This was the stuff of a child's imagination; an inflection of the nursery and children's illustrated literature.

The most notable example of Cooper's work in this style, the short *Dreams of Toyland* (1908), features some forty toy characters, all made at Hamleys toy company, performing comic vignettes. A golly[4] drives a double-decker motor bus (an unusual vehicle at that time); a horse stamps on a male figure; a Chinese man pulls a rickshaw; Dutch dolls walk as a family; a polar bear fights the golly; toys spin and trundle in random patterns on the street; and eventually the bus crashes. The excessive activity engenders a world-in-microcosm that echoes the simultaneity of action in Victorian fairy paintings. This film could represent the unconscious mind of a child in a state of uninhibited imaginative play, but it also clearly speaks to the idea of fairy cultures imbued with modernity. It situates afresh the supernatural fairy-tale ephemera in a new medium not yet certain of its narratives, but remains assured in its assumption of an audience's evolving understanding of, and fascination with, the unseen energies and forms present in the modern world. *Dreams of Toyland* speaks to novelty in a world coming to terms with change, and a fresh understanding of new social forces and material conditions beyond easy comprehension.

This invocation was also observable in the work of silhouette animator, Charles Armstrong, based at the Cumberland Works in Kew, whose *The Sporting Mice* (1909) animated cut out mice performing circus tricks. *Votes for Women: A Caricature* (1909) engaged with a topical subject, proving that animation could embrace social agendas with pertinence and satiric glee. Armstrong, known as "the professor," recognized that animation could *simultaneously* represent alternative, impossible scenarios, while addressing Britain's contemporary political issues. He depicted circus acts in *The Clown and His Donkey* (1910), reflecting the animated film's status as part of the paraphernalia of novelty and marginal entertainment, but making a playful social point, as in *Mr. Asquith and the Clown* (1911). Cooper's toys and Armstrong's circus tricks established their auteurial credentials as well as their technical acumen and sense of Englishness. But crucially, they also spoke to the changing dynamics of faerie as it combined the literary mix of fact and fancy, largely referring to a spirit world—disembodied, environmental, domestic, organic, animal, supernatural—and storytelling's oral traditions, emerging from real-world issues and conflicts. As Spence points out, "fairy belief was developed at more than one period in the past and . . . consisted of various strata, all of which seem to have survived and comingled" (1946, 63).

Modern animation essentially embodied the concept of the spirit world and gave substance to both established and newly emergent storytelling modes, drawing upon the fragmentary and episodic stream of consciousness styles and prose poems of modernist literature and the scene-based attractions of the early narrative cinema (Gunning 1986). As Lev Manovich notes,

> Once the cinema was stabilized as a technology, it cut all references to its origins in artifice. Everything that characterized moving pictures before the twentieth century – the manual

construction of images, loop actions, the discrete nature of space and movement – was delegated to cinema's bastard relative, its supplement and shadow – animation. Twentieth century animation became a depository for nineteenth-century moving image techniques left behind by cinema.

(2001, 298)

Equally, animation and its close relative, the live-action "trick film," created in the spirit of Georges Méliès, became the natural context for faerie and its modernist comic inflection. This affiliation became obvious in the Shakespearian burlesques made by Anson Dyer at Hepworth Picture Plays Ltd. Though only *"Oh" Phelia* (1919) and *Othello* (1920) survive, the promotional material for all six shorts in the series is instructive. B. Reed, writing in *The Bioscope* in 1914, notes that "Mr Dyer exhibits a remarkable mastery of the intricate 'Technique' of the cinema cartoon besides possessing an infinite fund of humour and imagination,"[5] illustrated by his low-rent Ophelia lying in a pond, an image loosely based on John Everett Millais's 1852 painting. In the film, Ophelia falls in the river attempting to pick her favorite flower, and is later revived by 'Amlet, who has learned valuable first aid skills in the scouts. He previously courted her with vegetables instead of flowers, and sought to cut her hair, resulting in the line "to bob or not to bob."

Faerie, then, helps broker the already evolving tensions between popular and high culture. Othello, for example, is presented as a popular blackface minstrel figure who is apparently "not so black as he is painted." This obviously racist gag by contemporary standards nevertheless offers some access to a perhaps distant literary form, if not an alien model of classical theater. Indeed, *The Daily Express*[6] applauds "Mr Anson Dyer [who] breaks new ground with his cartoon burlesque of the 'Merchant of Venice'. It is a grotesquely humourous effort, with just sufficient of the Shakespeare to make it appeal to adults without detracting from its interest for children." Shylock, at the moment in court when he wishes to claim his pound of flesh, for example, is reminded by a local butcher that it costs 2/8d.[7] *The Taming of the Shrew* is also advertised with a visual joke as Petruchio carries off Katherina tied to the back of a motor bike. But in true fairy style, juxtaposition and scale are exposed when his bike cannot pass a snail. 'Amlet features Hamlet's father as a skeletal ghost with boots covered by a transparent sheet. While the fairy tale has never been without (black) humor, the British engagement with faerie essentially inflects quasi-surreal narratives with irony and wit informed by underlying moral codes, often localizing issues and prioritizing joke-making for its own sake.

This aesthetic also informs Dyer's later Kiddie-Graphs series animating *The Three Little Pigs* (1922) and *Red Riding Hood* (1922). These works show how the fairy tale was maintained as a persuasive form of popular storytelling and how related areas of illustration informed the further development of British animated film. Lancelot Speed is a key figure, the main pioneer in the aesthetics and innovation of the British approach. As *The Bioscope* trade magazine remarked as early as 1914, "he is taking this new form of comic pictorial art several steps further forward than it has yet been developed" (quoted in Gifford 1987, 31). He studied at London's Slade School of Art under Alphonse Legros and gained commissions as an illustrator and theater designer (Reed 1914). Speed also became a renowned illustrator of books during the Victorian era, bringing a high degree of authenticity to fairy and mythical environments through their realistic depiction, most notably in Andrew Lang's *The Red Fairy Book* (1890), and much later in his iconographic illustrations for Rupert S. Holland's version of *King Arthur and the Knights of the Round Table* (1919). His work in Mrs. Hugh Bell's (Florence Eveleen Eleanore Olliffe) *Fairy Tale Plays and How To Act Them* (1896) features illustrations that combine the codes and conventions of melodramatic theater and the satiric traits of post-Hogarthian caricature.

Speed translates this visual language in his illustration and theater design—a modification of the symbolic currencies of faerie—into his animated films. For example, *The Emperor's New*

Clothes demonstrates public humiliation; *The Tinder Box*, the iconography of moustachioed, pompous, dismissive leaders; *Bluebeard*, the archetypal villainy of the self-aggrandizing manipulator; and *Rumpelstiltskin*, the empty hypocrisy and indulgence of court life. Anglicizing the popular fairy tale, Speed's films also adapt the idea of faerie to non-fairy contexts and seek to use animation to enhance particular limitations in the English sensibility. As Bell notes, "We in this country labour under an initial disadvantage as far as the successful use of gesture is concerned. The Italians and the French . . . naturally and unconsciously accompany their words with gestures which have come to have an entirely intelligible meaning" (1896, xxvii). Excusing the national observations here, and accepting this limitation in the British theatrical style, Speed innovates by using his illustration and animation to focus on the idea of the symbolic and the gestural.

Speed's short, *Britain's Effort* (1917), for example, depicts the Kaiser as the beast; a vengeful winged creature eager to capture Belgium, configured as a prone and innocent girl. The Kaiser is a sexual aggressor who captures and manacles her, an inhuman/inhumane barbarian. Such characters are common in fairy tales from "Sleeping Beauty" to "Red Riding Hood" to "The Wife of Bath's Tale." The archetypical savior figure arrives in the emblematic British icon, a sleeping John Bull, awoken from his slumbers by Britannia, who points out the Kaiser's villainy, and prompts Britain's response. The Kaiser is also often depicted as a fool, less an idiot than the Shakespearian complex-if-risible-adversary, who may be subjected to humiliation but should never be underestimated. For example, in *The U-Tube* (1917) the Kaiser's intended and highly inventive conquest of Britain is thwarted when his tunneling U-Tube is accidentally re-directed to the North Pole.

Bully Boy (1914) demonstrates Speed's extraordinary artistic skill. The Kaiser is depicted with seriousness and dignity, his pose implying status and power in the long-held convention of pre-Hogarthian British portraiture, only to be undermined in a quietly chilling and subversive way as his helmet metamorphoses into the devil himself. This move ridicules at the same time as it properly acknowledges the scale of the threat. The film's focus is the shelling of Rheims Cathedral, which it calls "The world's greatest gothic work," destroyed by "The work of the world's greatest goth." These visual and linguistic puns play up the idea of a superior wit and integrity, not merely the provenance of the artist, but also the audience's, and by inference, the nation's. One of the most compelling and memorable images, with inevitably Freudian overtones, is a British bulldog devouring a German sausage. *French's Contemptible Little Army* (1914), *Sleepless* (1914), and *Sea Dreams* (1914) all revel in ways of humiliating "the hun" (Germany) and Kaiser Wilhelm is inevitably the butt of the jokes. Speed successfully adapts the typologies and motifs of the fairy tale to the First World War context, the tradition of caricature and satire in Britain, and animation's emergence as an innovative model of expression in advancing illustration and performance.

While elements of faerie appeared in Speed's animated adaptation of A.B. Payne's *Daily Mirror* strip, *Pip, Squeak and Wilfred*, and G.E. Studdy's *Bonzo* cartoons,[8] the spirit of the faerie genre also appears in films by the American Herbert Hoppin and the French Anthony Gross. Gross became one of England's foremost painters and engravers, having attended the Slade, Central School of Art, London, and Academie Julien, Paris. Gross made *Une Journée en Afrique* (1932), *Les Funerailles* (1932), and his most famous work, *Joie de Vivre* (1934), based on his earlier etchings entitled "Sortie d'Usine." Hoppin, a photographer, allied his technical and compositional skills to Gross's graphic flare and distinctive linear design. *Joie de Vivre* featured a floral ballet, in styles made popular by the department store Liberty, and a simple, playful narrative of a boy pursuing two girls with one girl's lost shoe. The film's success led to Gross and Hoppin working at Alexander Korda's London Films, making Korda's first color cartoon, *Fox Hunt* (1936). They worked with a group of Hounslow-based illustrators, including then unknown cartoonist, Carl Giles. Gross became art director at London Films, but returned to Paris to begin work on a full-length color adaptation of Jules Verne's *Around the World in Eighty Days*. Stills from the film were exhibited at the City of Paris Petit Palais exhibition, but production was interrupted by the outbreak of war. Gross became an official war artist, and in the post-war period illustrated literary works (Gross 1992).

The unfinished *Eighty Days* was shown at the Institute of Contemporary Arts, in London, in 1951, prompting resumption of work on it in collaboration with the British Film Institute the following year. An abbreviated version, *An Indian Fantasy* (1951), narrated by Donald Pleasance, was completed in 1955. The film readily combines the tensions between British restraint and heroic irony with a quasi-orientalist impression of the Indian Other, telling how Philias Fogg and Passepartout save Aouda, a young Indian woman, from a Brahmin *sati* sacrifice. After scenes of polite engagement at the Reform Club in London, the film embraces the exotica of the Indian pageant and procession towards the pyre. This sense of the Other and the exotic characterizes a new definition of faerie. When Passepartout takes the place of Aouda's dead husband on the pyre and appears to rise from the dead as the flames begin to engulf the girl, the terrified priests and spectators run away, enabling Fogg and Passepartout to rescue her on a charging elephant. Hoppin and Gross thus embraced the idea of the non-anglicized as the substance of the fairy tale in English imperial culture. *Joie de Vivre*, *Foxhunt*, and *Indian Fantasy* embody Fogg's view that *even* an Englishman must be prepared to move with the times. Their modernist re-engagement with English folk idioms and the *received* ideas about other cultures as expressed in fantasy stories redefined the British animated fairy tale afresh.

1936–1967: A Reet Gradely Show

In the early 1930s, John Grierson's General Post Office film unit changed the terrain of British short filmmaking, by sponsoring animation by major figures like Norman McLaren, Len Lye, and Lotte Reiniger, with impact on experimental films, documentaries, and cartoons. Disney studios had been making *Silly Symphonies* since 1929, perfecting classical animation before making *Snow White and the Seven Dwarfs* (1937). In one sense, the *Symphonies* were experiments, advancing the use of sound, Technicolor, the multi-plane camera, multiple character animation in the "squash 'n' stretch" style (characters as compressible and elongated circles), and numerous other innovations that ultimately defined animation as an art. An alternative experimental tradition emerged in Europe, more affiliated with the fine arts, epitomized by figures like Gross, in films like *Camera Makes Whoopee* (1935), *Hell Unlimited* (1936), *A Colour Box* (1935), *Rainbow Dance* (1936), *The Birth of the Robot* (1936), *Carmen* (1933), *Papageno* (1935), and *The HPO—Heavenly Post Office* (1938). Though Reiniger's work (epitomized in her earlier masterpiece, the full-length feature *The Adventures of Prince Achmed* [1926]), was to foreshadow her later fairy-tale films, the British tradition of faerie sought new directions in the face of these developments in the US and Europe. An acceptance that Disney had colonized both animation and the fairy tale meant that everything in those genres became a response to his achievements. Yet this recognition also afforded an opportunity to create indigenous forms and draw upon localized idioms and mythologies.

Grierson's seemingly radical strategy of usurping commercial contexts for artistic and democratic purposes found direct opposition in the creation of Rank's Gaumont British Animation in 1946. Ex-Disney director, David Hand, who had supervised *Snow White and the Seven Dwarfs*, led the Cookham-based unit in making Disney-styled short films. Rank invested considerable sums of money in recruiting other American cartoon-tradition veterans: Disney studio storyboard artist Ralph Wright, creator of Pluto, and Ray Paterson, animator of *Tom and Jerry*. Initially, Rank wished to adhere to American technical expertise in creating animations of the English literary tradition, touting the possibility of adapting H.G. Wells's *The First Men in the Moon*, Lewis Carroll's *The Hunting of the Snark*, and Kenneth Grahame's *The Wind in the Willows*, each representing a certain vein of Englishness: machine innovation culture, eccentricity, and pastoral whimsy, respectively. Both the cost of such projects and the different levels of expertise in the English animation staff soon thwarted these ambitions. These challenges resulted in two models of postwar British animated fairy tale. The *Animaland* (1946) series was the studio's attempt at Disneyesque fare with anthropomorphized animals, slapstick scenarios, full animation, and a cartoon look. The *Musical Paintbox* (1946) series, far more directed to indigenous sites, topics, and interests, crucially combined montage edits and limited animation. Director Henry Stringer confirms,

> Hand put me to work on a very different style of film because the entertainment cartoons were costing so much. He told me "Make an animated film with very little animation in it, principally a succession of still pictures." Then he ran the "Baby Weems" sequence from a Disney feature, gave me a script entitled *Thames* and sent me off to direct the picture. Well, it was a success, receiving the better notices *and* made at a quarter of the cost of the fully animated films.
>
> (quoted in K. Clark, 1987, 25–27)[9]

The films deployed George Mitchell's BBC choir; composer Henry Reed compiled popular songs to represent the regions on the soundtrack. The new concentration on still imagery drew from artists adhering to postwar Romanticism, epitomized in modernist painters like Paul Nash and Graham Sutherland. The engagement with the indigenous was inspired by folk idioms and vernacular arts and rekindled the British fairy spirit. The films mined every region for local stories and representative art.

In *Sketches of Scotland* (1948), the mythology of Robert Bruce's fear of spiders is revised as a stereotype of the whisky-drinking Scotsman. A drunken Bruce hallucinates the spider as a set of bagpipes, the animation readily facilitating this visual pun, and apparently plays them in an echoing cave, terrorizing the enemy. As the wry narrator concludes, it was "not the story you were expecting." The animation's *reduced* nature and the film's minimalist styling coincidentally chime with some of the *overtly and consciously* modernist principles later championed by United Productions of America, and in Zagreb in the former Yugoslavia, as an *explicit* challenge to Disney. In Britain, such modernity happened by accident through the expediency of costs and labor. G.B. Animation's attempt to be Disney in the guise of the Ginger Nutt cartoons could not succeed because of the banality of its imitation, and its inevitable failure in comparison to the great cartoons produced by the American studios. The *Musical Paintbox* cartoons, though, evolved an aesthetic that was ultimately intrinsically British and inherently faerie in tone and outlook. Crucially, though, faerie now took on a more critical edge in the postwar era.

As Geoffrey Macnab notes,

> the episode, *Canterbury Road* opens with the encouraging injunction "To see your past, Use your imagination," as a pair of doors open and we look into somebody's mind. Then we see a desert with a hole in the ground, a bucket and a placard saying "Beware! Psychoanalyst at work." There are images of such things as pigs on bicycles before we reach the main matter of the short, which is the Canterbury pilgrims and their stories. . . . *Canterbury Road* seems stilted and enervated when compared with the brashness of its American cousins.
>
> (1993, 13)

The approach uses the penetrative qualities of animation to literally visualize an inner state, but having done so, satirizes Freudian psychology's assumptions in supposedly revealing the unconscious mind's motivations and imperatives. The approach in *Canterbury Road* is both a gag and a comment, foregrounding the fairy genre's cynical treatment of modernity, while ironically playing out modernist terms and conditions. Such skepticism also surfaces in *Yorkshire Ditty* (1949), where a woman reacts to a modern artist's abstract interpretation of the landscape by breaking the canvas over his head. This incident is couched within a local romance initially played out to the ditty, "On Ilkla Moor Baht'at" (Yorkshire dialect for "On Ilkley Moor without a hat"). The community goes to the village hall to watch a Magic Lantern show—a convenient way to introduce montage-style animation—and embrace the entertainment as "a reet gradely show" (Yorkshire dialect for "a really excellent show"). With some Disney-style design in flora and fauna, and even a bashfulness in the romanticism, this is a highly localized and determinedly backward-looking fairy tale, which prefers wool homespun direct from a sheep into a household blanket, and the natural appeal of the Yorkshire moor—a bleak snow-laden landscape or a green and pleasant land—to the sophisticated, contemporary, material world.

The preoccupation with the landscape is common to the other sketchbook fantasies, which constitute the *Musical Paintbox* series; however, the challenge and anxiety of modernity remain a parallel aspect in some but conspicuously absent in others. Curiously, the films partially echo the aspirations and outcomes of the 1930s *Shell* guides to various geographical sites, encouraging car owners to travel Britain, in which modern artists were involved. Of Nash's notable *Dorset Shell Guide*, Roger Cardinal writes:

> This popularising work reflects two contrary yet linked values which are integral to Nash's aesthetics: the notion of the modern, embodied in the motor car, emblem of stylish comfort and speed, and the archaic, embodied in the Dorset sites, semi-humanised or entirely wild, to the secrets of which Nash seemed to have privileged access.
>
> (1989, 12)

While the *Musical Paintbox* series may not have aspired to Nash's standard and vision, it is inspired visually by the landscape's associative and symbolic aspects and the romantic tension between modernity and the primal and archaic. *Devon Whey!* (1949), directed by Henry Stringer, implies that glorious Devon is another Eden. The epic grandeur of the landscape is imbued with history; it is the backdrop to progress, epitomized in the voyages of Sir Francis Drake. Folksongs like "The Green Grass Grew All Around" and "Uncle Tom Cobleigh" are modernized through animation. For example, the line-drawn grey mare on its way to Widdecombe Fair is inexplicably pumped up and exploded by its riders for comic effect. The tale of Old Tyler, 97 years old, is recalled in the promotion of Devonshire cider and cream, and in the articulation of distinctiveness and originality.

Wales (1948) also recovers arcane tales like the "Legend of Devon Bridge," featuring Megan, Blodwyn the cow, and the devil himself, which results in Gwilym, Megan's dog, gaining hoofs, tail and horns. "All Through the Night" is sung with typical Welsh pride, and the relationship between the work and family established through coal from the mine in the public house hearth, the belief in community sustained by confidence in the land and its resource. The sense of sustenance offered by the endurance of the land, and the optimism underpinning this picturesque vision of postwar Britain, are part of the neo-Romantic culture prompted and promoted by artists like Nash. But they also appear in filmmakers like Michael Powell and Emeric Pressburger's fairy tales, *A Canterbury Tale* (1944) and *The Red Shoes* (1948). As Cardinal suggests, such work seeks out a view of the landscape as "a continuum," and an address of "fundamental changeless themes," while still operating "as receptacles for subjective impulse" (1989, 7).

In *Cornwall* (1949), this sense of the spiritual and the subjective is recalled in the panorama of harbors, mines beyond the valleys, rainbow-lit vistas, and the tale of "Saint Nyot and the Holy Well," told in the stained glass window of an old church. This reassuring tale of trust, kindness, and forgiveness segues into one of smuggling and piracy played out to the sea shanty "Blow the Man

Down," with the sunset across the rocky shoreline as another reminder of endurance and continuity. These simple, sometimes naïve films, though easily criticized for not fulfilling their initial ambition to emulate Disney, prove engaging in their reflection of an indigenous artistic tradition fundamental to the postwar recovery of a progressive British identity, couched in its culture's deeper primal agendas, and only half-recalled in the neorealist urbanity of much live-action cinema. While ultimately not as successful or enduring as the social realist tradition of British animation, this neo-Romantic fairy work speaks eloquently about a retreat into a folk identity and a parochial wit that signals a deep mistrust of modernity.

John Halas notes that:

> [In the postwar period] animation greatly expanded its position and no longer depended on influences for its ideas. In fact it appears to convey and represent the character of the times more than any other art form in much the same way as the art manifesto did in Paris in 1909. Film animation has expanded in a manner which has brought it closer to the most contemporary form of art and graphics. The point of fusion seems to have been reached in the mid-fifties and is constantly expanding.
>
> (1989, 21)[10]

This "point of fusion" was crucial for simultaneously acknowledging that the animated form could translate into feature-length work, epitomized in Halas and Joy Batchelor's milestone *Animal Farm* (1954), and provide an innovative and unusual vocabulary for the burgeoning advertising industry, keen to fully exploit the potential offered by commercial television's emergence in 1955.

Reiniger returned to London to work in this blossoming environment. She had already made a fairy-tale film, *The King's Breakfast* (1936), in London, sponsored by Grierson, during her first period of artistic success in the 1920s and 1930s. Her flight from Nazism found her settling in London, though, ironically, to make numerous other fairy-tale films for American television during the 1950s, based on the popular stories of the Brothers Grimm and Andersen. Reiniger's demeanor and experience did not make her an innocent translator of common stories, but a gentle satirist attuned to her times. It is easy to be distracted by the lyricism and poise in the movement of Reiniger's silhouette figures, and the aesthetic precision that renders most characters inhabited by different dance styles. These qualities cast the stories as faerie—seemingly ethereal spirits moving through magical landscapes—but the prism of social class is equally relevant, both in relation to British postwar social divisions and the American aspiration to a homogeneous middle class.

A touchstone story in this respect is *The Three Wishes* (1953), featuring Martin, a woodcutter, literally liberating a fairy from a tree, who gives him a magic ring to bequeath him three wishes. Martin seeks the advice of a schoolmaster (seemingly his intellectual and social superior) about what he should wish for, while his wife, Grete, looking after the ring, takes in a neighbor, Kaspar, and accidentally wishes for a bowl of sausages to feed him. Martin is so angry, he insists upon the return of the ring, but also wishes that the sausages fasten to Grete's nose. Failing to chop the sausages off, he is forced to use the final wish to free the sausages from his wife's nose. Yet in the first instance, he fantasizes about having a car, and Grete, fine clothes and accessories, while the headmaster advises that Martin should wish for eternal youth, good health, and untold riches. These aspirant desires speak to postwar reconstruction that in Britain was somewhat undercut by the more prosaic tenets of sausage dinners and petty squabbles. This satiric edge speaks once more to the tension between fairy myth, fantasy, and more basic realities.

This conflict manifests in other ways, too. *Hansel and Gretel* (1953) dispatches the witch in the gingerbread house in an alternative way to the Grimm story, which sees her burned in an oven;

FIGURE 4.1 The Grasshopper speaking with the Ant, *The Grasshopper and the Ant* (1954).

as information emerged about the Holocaust, such imagery was deemed too potentially sensitive and affecting. *The Little Chimney Sweep* (1955), set in eighteenth-century London, and *Jack and the Beanstalk* (1955), a British fairy tale—the first in color by Reiniger's Primrose Productions—both advance the idea of a young working-class underdog given access to middle-to-upper-class culture, and finding unexpected reward for helping neglected and repressed daughters. Reiniger's gentle satire finds best expression, though, in *The Grasshopper and the Ant* (1954), in which she subverts the traditional endorsement of the ant's summer endeavors and the grasshopper's apparently laissez faire attitude by praising the pleasure the latter provides for his community through his music (see Figure 4.1). Despite his rejection by Miss Ant in the depths of winter and his near death from the cold, he still invites her to participate in the dancing that occurs at the house of the mouse and squirrel who saved him. The grasshopper freely deems her enjoyment in the winter months as a reward for her hard work during summer. This outlook readily reflects the egalitarian sense of community in Britain in the postwar period, and the broad endorsement of the view that everyone had something to contribute in an era when rationing was still in existence and the new welfare state was finding its footing. The vindication of the grasshopper was also, of course, a celebration of the contribution of the arts and the traditions of fairy culture as Britain rebuilt its identity.

1967 to the Present: I Smell the Blood of an Englishman . . .

Reiniger's work represents the last moment of thematic coherence in the use of the British fairy tale. Thereafter, the genre becomes a vehicle for personal concerns and a receptacle for the manipulation and parody of typical fairy-tale motifs. *Fairy Tale* (1967) and *Fairy Story* (1968), both written by

Stan Hayward, offer points of comparison. The former treats the fairy tale as inherently imaginary and implausible, and uses the wish-fulfillment model embedded in many such stories to point up the difference between fantasy and reality. In consequence, the short suggests that personal happiness is unattainable. *Fairy Story*, rather than embracing fairy tales, sees them symbolically walloped, a point realized vividly when a fairy is swatted with a newspaper. Perhaps *The Yellow Submarine* (1968), with its edgy drug-fuelled psychedelia and countercultural politics embedded in animation turned cultural phenomenon, rendered the idea of the fairy tale as an innocent and naïve medium of expression obsolete. Seemingly hollowed out of its complex and charged content, and indeed, viewed as a conservative form, such films ensured animation was made radical once more, added to by the *cause celebre* of *Sinderella* (1972), which took the innuendo that characterized the films of Bob Godfrey, like *Kama Sutra Rides Again* (1972), into more explicit sexual realms. *Sinderella*, a pornographic animated version of "Cinderella," fell afoul of American law, and was ultimately banned from exhibition and distribution.

As the New York District Court's "1083 Memorandum of Decision" (1972)[11] reported, "While the narrator recites the script with the tonal wonderment of a fairy tale free from vulgarity, the film depicts sexual organs and sexual acts." The adult content normally metaphorically subsumed within the fairy tale as an exploration of psychological and emotional issues is physically and materially explicit. In *Sinderella*, the title character has sex with a range of fairy-tale characters including the three bears. Ostensibly, the humor emerges from the incongruity between the supposed neutrality and innocence of the storytelling and the exaggerated depiction of masturbation and intercourse. The court's verdict is in part based on the report of three professors, Charles Winick (responsible for a report about cartoons for the National Association of Broadcasters insisting that animation should be funny and family-friendly), Frank Hoffman, and Richard Brown, who all found merit in the film. They felt that the film matched a newly liberated sexual climate (one that embraced *Fritz the Cat* [1972]), especially if it was awarded an X certificate. The judge, however, insisting that animation should be viewed in the same way as any other form, and calling upon the verdicts for *I am Curious (Yellow)* (1967) and *Language of Love* (1969), found only prurience in the film's engagement with sex, and no redeeming social value. As the judge ascertained in the report, "Incongruity alone, devoid of underlying intellectual or ideological content, is a mere gimmick, it does not infuse the cartoon with enough social value to retrieve it from the trash can."

Subsequently, the British animated fairy tale lost its ideological agenda, evidenced, for example, in an innocuous animated version of Charles Kingsley's 1862 novel, *The Waterbabies, A Fairy Tale for a Land Baby*, produced as *The Waterbabies* (1978). This feature film diluted the original's pro-Darwinist themes and critique of child labor, offering instead an underwater tale including a shark and a kraken, not present in the original story. Though Kingsley's novel became less popular with increasing realization of its racist themes, its approach to modern social issues was significant. The absence of the novel's critical potential in the film reflects the animated film industry's preference for innocuous storytelling, privileging the dynamic action of animation and illustrative forms for their own sake. Arguably, this aesthetic was echoed in the emotionally charged adaptation of Raymond Briggs's *The Snowman* (1982), which might be viewed as British animation's most notable fairy tale. The film features a snowman that comes to life at Christmas and transports a young boy on a magical flight across London, to the song "Walking in the Air," before melting the next day. On the one hand, the film is inspirational and uplifting; on the other, it movingly meditates on inevitable loss and disappointment, a key theme in Briggs's works. The film indicates that British animated narratives could recall the transformative spirit of traditional faerie, once more redefining the landscape in the service of magical revelation. This concept also becomes fundamental to Sir Paul McCartney's animated adaptations of Mary Tourtel and Alfred Bestall's Rupert the Bear stories in *Rupert and the Frog Song* (1982) and David Wiesner's *Tuesday*, winner of the Caldecott

FIGURE 4.2 The Unnameable Little Broom, *The Unnameable Little Broom* (1985).

Medal for Illustration, filmed with the same title in 2001, featuring flying frogs and pigs, in rejuvenated pastoral idylls.[12]

These ever-evolving landscapes shifted again after *The Unnameable Little Broom* (1985) (see Figure 4.2). Its distilled symbolic interpretation of the first tablet of "The Epic of Gilgamesh" casts the hero in a floating mechanistic box pitched against a winged harpy, Enkidu, who dwells in a dark forest. The spirits of faerie cast a site of sexual tension and violent intent differing from earlier works. If these films reclaimed a visual tradition for the British fairy tale, their more Gothic and psychosomatic imperatives were re-engaged by the Quay Brothers and their embrace of an Eastern European sensibility. The American-born Quays, admirers of filmmakers like Walerian Borowczyk, Jan Lenica, and Jan Švankmajer and writers like Bruno Schulz and Franz Kafka, returned the British fairy tale to a sense of otherness. Their mode of address offered insight about the darker aspects of the human condition, and crucially, those desires and feelings often beyond the breadth of literary genres. If the chant of the giant in "Jack and the Beanstalk," "I smell the blood of an Englishman," propelled a literal chase, then such words also serve as a metaphor for the ways in which the Quays engaged with essences, the unobserved fairy energies and spirits in objects, detritus, and sound.

The Quay brothers effectively re-invented the British pastoral fairy tale as a return to a distillation of the organic and a deep engagement with primal knowledge. In films like *Street of Crocodiles* (1986), *Rehearsals for Extinct Anatomies* (1987), *The Comb* (1990), and the *Stille Nacht* series (1988–2001), they use animation to penetrate the invisible, not as a trite fairyland, but as an entry into other-worldliness. The brothers use the fairy tale as a vehicle to express a deeper sensuality allied to the animator's hands-on technique and also to existence attuned to unspeakable or inarticulate feeling. *In Abstentia* (2000) offers a relentless and intense study of a woman's deep psychological trauma in an asylum, haunted by an animated figure in constant torment; *The Phantom Museum* (2003) gives an oblique and sexualized interpretation of the medical paraphernalia collected by Henry Wellcome; and *Maska* (2010) is an expressionist encounter with Stanislaw Lem's short story of the same name, inverting the idea of Maria, the female robot in *Metropolis* (1927). These three films engage with an enigmatic poetry of memory and use the modern fairy tale as a site of repression, suppression, and oppression. The animation dramatizes interiority; the fairy primal-scene is an irrational space, sometimes beyond comprehension, requiring empathy and attention in the viewer. But arguably, the imagery deliberately seeks to be beyond orthodox representation, and speaks to a different register of fantasy, closer to phantasmagoria. Indeed, the Quays' fairy-tale films speak not to the omission of modernity in search of a more primal or pre-linguistic world, but to the collision of science, technology, solipsism, and metaphysical change that is the consequence of modernism. As Marina Warner notes, "the characteristic material of the phantasmagoria . . . occupies a transitional zone between the sublime and the Gothic, between the solemn and the comic, and between seriously intended fears and sly mockery of such beliefs" (2006, 153). Thus in *The Phantom Museum*, medical equipment of various types and vintages moves from implied functionality to a fetishised sensual suggestibility. The objects are shot and animated to simultaneously embody threat and absurdity; technological progress and basic tool; utopian cure and dystopian weapon. This kind of image-making prioritizes the re-staging of objects in processes of transubstantiation that re-configure afresh both the object's materiality and its meaning.

Even though the Quays create this phantasmagoric space as a primal scene, a number of British feminist filmmakers most explicitly use the fairy tale to explore this complex terrain. Karen Watson's *Daddy's Little Bit of Dresden China* (1988) introduces the filmmaker's story of child molestation by her father with a re-telling of "Snow White" to explore the predatory exploitation of innocence. In works like *Dresden*, Watson restores the intimidation and sense of foreboding in the fairy tale as a conduit for the darker machinations of human experience hidden from public gaze. The invocation of fairy-tale horror is most explicit in Marjut Rimmenen and Christine Roche's *The Stain* (1992), which features the nightmarish implications of familial rape and incest. As Karen Beckman remarks,

> On one level, *The Stain* in the feminist tradition of Angela Carter and Jeanette Winterson, uses the suspended and ahistorical time of the fairy tale to take the narrative beyond the experience of an individual subject in order to explore the ubiquity rather than the uniqueness of the "dark side of life" that [feminist filmmaker Michelle] Citron sees as excluded from the sanctioned images of the home movie genre.
>
> (2012, 189)

The implied conservatism of amateur live-action footage that Citron envisages records the affirming occasions of family life rather than its more everyday dysfunctional events. The unusual incidents, usually accidents, recontextualised as comedy in many clips programs, are countered with the radicalism of the animated faerie.

The spirits in *The Stain* are the memories of unspeakable acts of abuse and violence between father and daughter, and between twin brothers and their sister; the murder of a baby; neurotic, compulsive and suicidal tendencies; and the contradictory notions of self-destructive desire and suffering that make domestic power relations ambiguous and beyond dichotomies of abuser and victim. *The Stain* essentially works as a re-configuration of fairy-tale structures and an explicit rendering of themes and perspectives sometimes only implied or alluded to within them. If the traditional fairy tale embeds its complexities in symbolic action and metaphoric suggestion, *The Stain* uses the same tropes to expose, reveal, and make explicit. Such an approach renders the faerie as a perverse landscape and transformation as private transgression. As Warner concludes:

> Spirits are still alive, if not in the sense that a believer in Marlowe's audience or a participant in a spiritualist séance would have meant. Angels and spectres have changed character, and meaning and impact, but they are viable and powerful through entertainment media in ways that cohere with their past appearances. . . . They wrap us in illusions, and have installed a new supernatural at the heart of the personal and social imagination.
>
> (2005, 335)

The animation offers insight and impact not about a fairyland but concerning an everyday world made surreal and perverse—a neverland—by its difference from personal, social, and legal *public* orthodoxies. The British animated fairy tale in all its forms, therefore, has a profoundly interrogative and recuperative agenda. Constantly recalling lost utopian thought, repressed or oppressed desires and ideas, alternative liberating fantasies, and simpler humanitarian principles, it operates as a defense from inappropriate, ill-fitting, or imposed notions of modernity in the British context. The versatility of animation facilitates the visualization of the shifting parameters of faerie in ways that preserve the deep Romanticism in British culture set against the orthodoxies of the social realist and naturalist traditions of representation. Consequently, the fantastical and the phantasmagoric serve to reconfigure landscape as both a psychological and physical site, equipping each terrain with a spiritual and political dimension. The British animated fairy-tale film depicts these landscapes, and as such, conserves British idiosyncrasies and heritage, animation as a bona fide historically charged art form, and the fairy tale as one of the most potent forms in literary, visual, and popular culture.

Notes

1 The abundance of live-action British fairy-tale films includes Michael Powell and Emeric Pressburger's *The Red Shoes* (1948), Neil Jordan's *The Company of Wolves* (1984), and Jim Henson's *Labyrinth* (1986), but this chapter deals exclusively with animated shorts and features, and features including animated special effects.

2 Much animation is predicated on the ways animals might embody human traits and characteristics, and consequently may speak to taboo themes and issues which might not necessarily be directly addressed through human representations. Animation filmmakers, when seeking to adapt established stories, may interrogate them for anthropomorphic relevancy.

3 Charles Sturridge's *FairyTale: A True Story* (1997) epitomizes this conjunction. Loosely based on the supposed discovery of the "Cottingley fairies" by schoolgirls Elsie Wright and Frances Griffiths in 1917, it juxtaposes the latter with changing contingencies and agency in the modern world including World War I's onset, Harry Houdini's emergence as one of the world's foremost illusionists and stunt artists, and a theater production of J.M. Barrie's *Peter Pan*.

4 A golliwog, popular in many short stories by Enid Blyton, and manufactured as a toy, is a blackface doll now critically perceived as a racist representation.

5 This and further promotional material was drawn from the Animation Academy Collection, Loughborough University, UK.

6 This quotation is cited on the promotional material.

7 Shillings and pence was a pre-decimal model of currency in Britain; two shillings and eight pence approximates to 30 pence in English currency or 25 cents in American currency.

8 These popular newspaper and comic strips were important popular ephemera seeking to capture the cultural zeitgeist. Such strips were sometimes collated into annual publications or retrospective collections.

9 Stringer's reference to Baby Weems alludes to the sequence in the Disney part live-action, part animated feature, *The Reluctant Dragon* (1941). This simplistic and sometimes fallacious behind-the-scenes view of the Disney studio is a delicious satire of the short-term fads and the destructiveness of consumer society, but it is notable primarily for the way it is animated. Rather than the rich, full Disney animation to which audiences had become accustomed, it uses a form of partial animation, which is incredibly effective.

Essentially, what the viewer is shown are (at least in theory) the working drawings taken from the story-board of a cartoon in preparation; fairly often, there is a degree of animation within what are otherwise still sketches (Grant 1993).

10 Halas recalls the Manifesto Figaro, in which artists, led by Filippo Marinetti, presaged the emergence of Futurism and Cubism.

11 "1083 Memorandum of Decision." 1972. 369 F.Supp. 1082: United States v ONE REEL OF 35mm COLOR MOTION PICTURE F, December 29.

12 See the film *Inside the Green Book: The Life and Films of Geoff Dunbar* (2011) for more information on the making of these films.

5

THE FAIRY-TALE FILM IN FRANCE

Postwar Reimaginings

Anne E. Duggan

The French have been making fairy-tale films since the birth of cinema. A pioneer in the genre, Georges Méliès began producing films in 1896, many of which included magical or supernatural elements. His first full-fledged fairy-tale film was *Cinderella* (Cendrillon 1899), followed by adaptations of "Little Red Riding Hood" (1901), "Bluebeard" (1901), *Arabian Nights* (1905), and numerous other films with folk and fairy-tale motifs.[1] Méliès met with strong competition from Pathé-Frères, which also competed successfully on the American market.[2] In 1902 Pathé-Frères produced *Ali Baba and the Forty Thieves* (Ali Baba et les quarante voleurs), followed a year later by *Puss-in-Boots* (Le Chat botté) and versions of "Aladdin" (1906), "Cinderella" (1908), and "Snow White" (1910), along with many more related to the fairy-tale genre.[3] The early history of French fairy-tale films was vibrant, path breaking, and globally influential, with the pioneering work of directors and animators like Méliès, Albert Capellani, Emile Cohl (the inventor of animation), and the Russian-born stop-motion animator, Ladislas Starewitch.[4]

With respect to the history of French animation, Donald Crafton remarks: "The battle against American domination was lost by the mid-twenties" (1990, 208). Disney, of course, was at the forefront, leading film critic Pascal Vimenet to ponder: "How does one escape Disney? This is the question that French directors have been asking and continue to ask. Disney animation remains a reference, positive or negative" (1985, 46).[5] While Crafton and Vimenet struggle with how French directors can overcome Disney's impact on animation, the same could be asked about the company's effect on fairy-tale film, whether live-action or animated. Disney's *Snow White and the Seven Dwarfs* (1937), *Cinderella* (1950), and *Sleeping Beauty* (1959), have dominated and continue to dominate fairy-tale cinema in France, as elsewhere.

Direct and indirect challenges to Disney's fairy-tale hegemony have taken many forms in France, from artistic experimentation and parody to the development of queer revisionings of classical tales. Animators like Paul Grimault, Jean-François Laguionie, and Michel Ocelot have contested the Disney model through an artisanal mode of production, sophisticated storylines, a painterly animation style, and an integration of important political and social questions. Within the domain of more mainstream animation, Pascal Hérold's *Cinderella 3D* (Cinderella au Far West 2012) explicitly pokes fun at Disney's *Cinderella*. In *Beauty and the Beast* (La Belle et la Bête 1946, which influenced Disney's version), Jean Cocteau produced a surreal and queer fairy-tale film that indicated how the marvelous could be used to represent non-normative forms of sexuality.[6] Such a move appealed to later queer and feminist filmmakers, including Jacques Demy, François Ozon, and Catherine

Breillat. These directors explicitly challenge Disney films' normative sexuality, while they generate new, liberating fairy-tale forms.

Particularly important in France are live-action and animated film adaptations of tales from the *Arabian Nights*. At least two reasons explain their relative prevalence. Not only was the French orientalist Antoine Galland largely responsible for the proliferation of the *Arabian Nights* in Europe, but also France has had a long—and problematic—history with Arab and Berber North Africa. The French began colonizing North Africa in 1830, and today North Africans make up the country's largest ethnic minority. Given the close contact between France and the Maghreb, the orient in French filmic renditions of the *Arabian Nights* bears a distinctly North African flavor. While some adaptations display typical orientalizing motifs also found in American filmic versions, directors like Pierre Aknine and the innovative animator Francine Miailhe negotiate between orient and occident and display a deep appreciation for North African culture.

Although the French fairy-tale film declined in popularity in the 1920s, the genre began a slow comeback from 1946 onwards, establishing new models and trends. My chapter traces these postwar reimaginings, focusing in particular on reworkings of the classical fairy-tale in the tradition of Charles Perrault, the Brothers Grimm, and Disney; the oriental tale in the tradition of the *Arabian Nights*; and the genre itself, with a focus on non-canonical and original fairy-tale films. The first section centers on politicized, subversive, and queer revisionings of classical tales. For the most part, such films use taken-for-granted knowledge about source tales to introduce twists and turns, deviations and subversions of well-known stories like "Little Thumbling," "Bluebeard," and "Sleeping Beauty." The second section explores the *Arabian Nights*, considering how adaptations engage questions of gender, race, sexuality, and representations of the orient. The last section considers films by Grimault, Laguionie, and Ocelot, who draw from non-canonical texts to create new and original tales within a painterly animation tradition.

Reimaginings of the Classical Fairy Tale

Postwar reimaginings of the classical fairy tale follow a somewhat predictable evolution when it comes to gender and sexuality. Filmic adaptations of "Little Thumbling" ("Petit Poucet"), for example, move from centering on a little boy's actions to creating positive female characters who share in the hero's exploits. The sadistic hero of Charles Perrault's "Bluebeard" becomes a somewhat emasculated, gentle, even desirable monster. Cocteau's 1946 *Beauty and the Beast* suggested a queer reworking of the source tale, but fairy-tale queer potential was not explored again until Jacques Demy's *Donkey Skin* (Peau d'âne 1970), followed nearly twenty years later by François Ozon's *Criminal Lovers* (Les amants criminels 1999), and Breillat's arguably queer rendition of "Sleeping Beauty" in 2010.

"Little Thumbling"

Jack Zipes's discussion of the Grimm brothers' "Hansel and Gretel" notes that the tale can be related to the culture of late eighteenth-century peasants faced with war and famine. Child abandonment was a means for parents to survive: "the tale can be interpreted as a rationalization of such abuse" (Zipes 2002, 38). French peasants of Perrault's period also persevered in a culture of war and famine. Animator Jean Image and directors Michel Boisrond and Olivier Dahan deal with the challenges of adapting an early modern tale to twentieth-century realities in different ways, transforming it into a boy scout fantasy, a family drama, and a story dealing with the realities of war.

In 1950 the Hungarian-born Jean Image released *Johnny the Giant Killer* (Jeannot l'intrépide), championed as "France's first color, feature-length cartoon" (Neupert 2011, 111). Image takes the story of Perrault's "Little Thumbling" as a point of departure for a new story. The film opens with a group of boy scouts camping in the woods. The little redhead Jeannot reads "Little Thumbling" to his friends. He decides they need to hunt down the ogre, and leads them through the forest to the ogre's castle. Part vampire, part ghoul, the ogre shrinks the boys and plans to eat them. Jeannot escapes and ends up at the hive of a beautiful queen bee. When the hive comes under attack by hornets, the film plays on tropes from the swashbuckler film, a popular genre of the period.[7] Bee and hornet stingers serve as swords, and Jeannot turns out to be a bold and skilled fighter. After saving the queen bee—his romantic love interest—Jeannot goes to save his friends from the ogre, with the assistance of the bees and other insects, who function as his animal helpers. Although young Jeannot does not ride off into the sunset with the queen bee—he is, after all, a little boy—he leads his friends back to the campground, bringing the shrunken ogre in a cage. Perrault's tale becomes a pretext for boys' play, and the film avoids the problem of child abandonment by using the source tale simply as a point of departure, feeding the adventurous imagination of Jeannot, who reads the tale through the lens of the swashbuckler genre.

First suggested by Image, the tradition of the love interest in French versions of "Little Thumbling" continues in the live-action films of Boisrond and Dahan. Boisrond's adaptation brings back the theme of parental abandonment and introduces that of the overprotected child. Well before the parents abandon their children, Little Thumbling falls in love with Rosemonde, a princess locked inside the castle by her overprotective parents. Both Rosemonde, separated from the rest of the world, and Little Thumbling, marginalized within his family, find themselves very much alone, but when Little Thumbling manages to capture Rosemonde's runaway kite and return it to her, the two bond. Then famine arrives, and Little Thumbling's parents abandon him and his siblings in the forest. As in Perrault, Little Thumbling defeats the ogre and saves his brothers; Boisrond has the king reward him with the hand of the princess for having saved the kingdom from the ogre. The film ends by invoking the writer of the source tale; as the story spreads throughout the kingdom, it eventually reaches the ears of Charles Perrault. The last scene is that of a man with a feather quill writing "Once upon a time . . . "

The film redeploys the tale to examine different types of problematic relations between parents and children. While Little Thumbling is neglected and abandoned by his parents, Rosemonde is smothered by hers. The film also presents a fairly traditional representation of gender. Women are either passive, helpless damsels in distress, like the princess or the ogre's wife, or they are demonized—as in the traditional tale—in the form of the ogre's daughters.

For his 2001 film, Dahan reworks Perrault's tale and Boisrond's film to create a sophisticated and politicized adaptation of "Little Thumbling." Dahan exaggerates Little Thumbling's marginalization within his family by making the explicitly patriarchal father complicit in it. His marginalization leads him to wander in the woods, where he meets Rose, one of the ogre's daughters; she likewise is marginalized within her family. Drawing from Boisrond's Rosemonde, Dahan makes his Rose a much more active character. She is instrumental in the children's escape from the ogre's house and in Little Thumbling's acquisition of the seven-league boots.[8] Indeed, Rose is a sort of double of Little Thumbling. Despite the fact that she takes a traditional place next to her husband in the film's epilogue, she proves to be a thoroughly active character throughout the narrative, while Little Thumbling models a non-normative masculinity that nevertheless leads to success.

Dahan situates the story within the context of war, and introduces the one-eyed, iron-legged soldier into the plot, a double of the figure of the ogre. In the film, war is the immediate cause of starvation: the iron-legged soldier and his men pillage the food supplies of Little Thumbling's family, shortly followed by the soldiers of the crown taking any remaining food. War constantly looms in the background: as the children make their way towards the ogre's home, they pass a field of dead soldiers. Interested in abandonment in his previous films, Dahan connects this theme to war in *Little Thumbling*:

> When I wrote the script, I was watching every day on television the children of Kosovo and their families thrown into the streets. The notion of war, of famine. Today, I see the children of Afghanistan. The notion of war, of famine. The tale of "Little Thumbling" is pertinent through the ages. It treats universal and very real subject matter.
>
> (quoted in Bradfer 2001, 26)

Dahan's *Little Thumbling* is as much about marginalization and abandonment as it is about war, and how war affects children. Particularly striking is the parallel Dahan creates between the ogre, who wears a martial mask, and the iron-legged soldier: both are killers, devourers, of men. The iron-legged soldier has one eye, recalling the Cyclops of mythology, who also consumes men like an ogre. Just as the hero is doubled in Little Thumbling/Rose, so is the villain in the ogre/iron-legged soldier. Through such parallels, Dahan suggests that the existence of ogres and their threat to children is very real indeed. The ogre becomes a figure for war, and the tale becomes one about war's consequences for children.

"Bluebeard"

Bluebeard represents another type of ogre-figure, a devourer of wives instead of children. Several films made in France deal with the character, and I focus here on those versions that draw from the Perrault rather than the Landru tradition of Bluebeard tales.[9] In films by Christian-Jaque and Breillat, Bluebeard develops a special relationship to his last wife, a detail absent from Perrault's tale, and the last wife turns out to be, in each case, particularly spunky.[10] Proposing a more active female character, who has some affection for her potential tormenter, Christian-Jaque's film sets the precedent for Breillat's 2009 period piece.

Christian-Jaque is indeed familiar with different Bluebeard traditions. His count Amédée de Salfère (Pierre Brasseur) visually resembles Walter Crane's rather Henry VIII-looking Bluebeard. When the count tells Aline (Cécile Aubry), his new wife, about his previous wives, the film draws from Anatole France's "Seven Wives of Bluebeard" (1909), in which the narrator gains his readers' sympathy by relating his "real life" and his eccentric and insupportable wives. In both story and tale, this narrative strategy means we lose sympathy for the wives, but they are not simply passive victims.

Aline proves to be a complex character. At the film's beginning, when the count's men trample through his subjects' town to announce that he will be taking a new bride and eligible girls must attend a ball, everyone flees in fear except Aline. Moreover, unlike the heroine of Perrault's tale, she does not sacrifice herself for the sake of her family's economic security: Aline's father is very much alive, running an inn. Fascinated by the nobility's wealth and by Bluebeard, and proving fearless at his mention, Aline takes the place of a noble girl who fears being married to the notorious man. In some ways, Aline plays a Scheherazade-like role in her willingness to give herself over to an apparent brute in place of other women, but she does so out of naïvety and playfulness rather than wisdom. After Aline marries Bluebeard, Giglio, her previous suitor, and her sister Anne wish to help her flee the castle, but Aline does not understand why: she needs no saving, at least not at this point of the film. And indeed she has nothing to fear, for the big secret Aline uncovers is that Bluebeard's wives are in fact alive and well. Ironically, her discovery of the living wives pushes the count and his Majordomo to consider killing Aline in order to maintain the legend they had spent years cultivating.

For Susan Hayward, the postwar 1950s period represented a crisis in masculinity, which plays out in different ways in French film. In one trend, the swashbuckler, nostalgic forms of an apparently unproblematic masculinity can be foregrounded. But in *Bluebeard* we see instead strong female characters in what ultimately proves to be a very vulnerable patriarchal structure. Hayward notes "the truth about Bluebeard's tyranny: it is all a bluff. . . . Supposedly, the blue beard is a sign of his cruelty and homicidal nature; instead, it is pure masquerade. Masculinity is exposed here as pure construction" (2010, 92). The scene immediately preceding the count's demise demonstrates this artifice. The count calls upon Perrault to write his "history . . . a bloody life . . . and worthy of inspiring a man of your talent." Comically, the film suggests that Perrault's tale is propaganda issuing from Bluebeard himself.

In some respects, Christian-Jaque's film has affinities with more sexually experimental films like Cocteau's *Beauty and the Beast* and Breillat's *Bluebeard* in the affection shared between a non-normative male character (his masculinity was a fraud) whose legend makes him into a monster, and an assertive, fearless female character. Indeed, Aline seems to regret that she will not remain with Bluebeard and will marry an appropriate suitor, Giglio, who displays more conventionally masculine qualities, including his desire to "save" the supposed damsel in distress. Breillat, "the *first* female filmmaker ever to adapt 'Bluebeard' for the screen" (Zipes 2012, 50), takes some of her cues from Christian-Jaque's comic rendition.

Breillat creates a double narrative juxtaposing two sisters who read "Bluebeard" in the 1950s and the two sisters who live out the story in the seventeenth century. Like Christian-Jaque's Aline, the historical drama's Marie-Catherine (Lola Créton) does not fear Bluebeard, and in fact bonds with him. Breillat emphasizes the age difference and size of the two characters; Lola Créton was about fifteen when she played Marie-Catherine (compared with a more mature Cécile Aubry, twenty-two when she incarnated Aline), and looks even younger next to Dominique Thomas, playing Bluebeard, who physically dwarfs her.

This Bluebeard is more beast than tyrannical count, and Breillat's Beauty proves to be somewhat beastly herself. When Marie-Catherine first meets Bluebeard, he tells her that he is a "monster," "a sort of ogre," which does not faze her. Later in the 1950s narrative, Catherine—Marie-Catherine's modern counterpart—embellishes Perrault's tale by saying that Bluebeard cooks little children, then imagines that he will marry a beautiful ogress. Just before Bluebeard is about to confront Marie-Catherine about the soiled key, the couple share a leg of lamb and consume it like two animals—or ogres. Marie-Catherine's "becoming ogress" culminates in the final scene, in which she caresses Bluebeard's severed head on a plate. The scene recalls paintings of Judith and Holofernes and Salomé and John the Baptist, but the head's positioning also suggests that Marie-Catherine indeed has become an ogress, preparing to devour her beloved Bluebeard.

As Cristina Bacchilega has argued, the feminist aspect of Breillat's film plays out in several ways. First, the historical drama emphasizes much more than the tale the economic and social despair into which the death of a father can plunge a family in the early modern period. Second, with respect to the 1950s plot, the opposition between the two sisters relates different reading strategies that foreground how the sisters resist or submit to the original, patriarchal tale. Finally, Breillat's "focus is not on Bluebeard as the starting point or on the heroine's brothers in the final rescue scene, but on the two girls throughout" (2013, 89). In Breillat's hands, "Bluebeard" becomes a story about women and their relationships more than one about a notorious serial murderer.

Queer Tales

In these different renditions of "Bluebeard," the traditional heroine is empowered and loves in ways that challenge conventional gender roles and heteronormativity. Aline and Marie-Catherine display singular behavior that marginalizes them in ways that bring them closer to the mysterious figure of Bluebeard, whose complexity makes him a more sympathetic character in the film than in Perrault. Within French fairy-tale cinema, Cocteau, Demy, and Ozon represent a genealogy of queer directors who draw from the fairy-tale genre to explore queer forms of sexuality. Although Breillat is not considered a queer director, her films constantly challenge normative forms of sexuality, and her version of "Sleeping Beauty" can be read as a queer film. Just as explorations of gender become more and more pronounced moving from the 1950s to the 2000s, so Cocteau and Demy's queer reworkings of sexuality in classical tales are more subtle and indirect, whereas Ozon and Breillat take it on more directly.

Much has been written on Cocteau's monumental *Beauty and the Beast*, which has become a common point of reference when discussing the tale within fairy-tale studies.[11] For Irène Eynat-Confino, the beast in Cocteau's works serves as a figure for "monstrous" forms of sexuality: "by using the monster as a trope or a concrete supernatural being . . . he was giving voice to an ordeal that he shared with the many whose sexuality was nonnormative and condemned as such by society" (2008, 93). The "unnatural" union of human and beast comes to signify what 1940s French society considered another type of unnatural union—bonding between two men.

This association between beast and queer sexuality is further emphasized in the relation between director and star: Jean Marais, who played the Beast, was Cocteau's longtime partner. Given this extra-textual relation between director and actor, Daniel Fischlin argues:

> The Beast . . . is thus an ambiguous sexual construct, a queer, especially in a reading that incorporates Cocteau's directorial eye into the context of the gaze constructing the beast as an object of desire. From that perspective the film's camera-work becomes a sensuous point of contact between Cocteau and his lover, a way of constructing their queer relationship in a visual code driven by the passion of the lover's gaze. At that level of signification the Beast becomes the very signifier of queer presence in the film.
>
> (1998, 80)

Here, the Beast is positioned as the object of desire, not only from the director's perspective, but also from Belle's. As critics like Hayward have remarked, Belle is "disappointed at the end of the film when the Beast—*la Bête*, whom she now realises she loves, transforms into Prince Charming" (1996, 47). Indeed, Beauty fell in love with the Beast, not the prince. The closure Jeanne-Marie Leprince de Beaumont offers at her tale's end, in which Beauty wonders where the Beast went upon his transformation, but is "agreeably surprised" and lives out her life in "perfect happiness" (1758, 82–83), is disrupted in Cocteau by Beauty's disappointment. Cocteau's film, then, hints at the idea that the perfect heteronormative conclusion may not be perfectly satisfactory, a notion that returns in Demy's work.

Demy maintained a longstanding interest in both the fairy tale and the work of Cocteau throughout his career.[12] His early short, *The Handsome Indifferent One* (Le Bel Indifférent 1957), was based on a Cocteau play. Jean Marais played the incestuous king in Demy's *Donkey Skin* and later made an appearance in *Parking* (1982), a modern version of Orpheus, a story Cocteau also treated in 1950. Folk and fairy-tale motifs pervade most of Demy's oeuvre.[13] In *Donkey Skin*, however, we can best view the connections he makes between Cocteau's *Beauty and the Beast* and queerness, as well as Demy's interest in Disney.

Perrault's tale about father–daughter incest takes on queer dimensions in Demy's film. Whereas in the source tale, the king desires his daughter who has no wish to marry him, in Demy the princess (Catherine Deneuve) desires her father as well. The film's Lilac Fairy (Delphine Seyrig) informs the princess that she cannot marry her father for reasons "of culture and legislature," not out of any deep-seated moral principles; the Fairy is also the princess's rival for her father's love. By focusing on incest's illegality as opposed to immorality, the film denaturalizes the taboo. That the incestuous father is played by Marais, Cocteau's Beast, foregrounds the film's queer coding. Ultimately, beastly and incestuous desire represent non-heteronormative forms of love standing in for a queer desire rejected by society. Just as Beauty appears disappointed at the Beast's transformation at the end of Cocteau's film, so the princess appears disappointed when she prepares to marry the tale's prince, evident when the Lilac Fairy announces: "Oh, darling! I'm marrying your father. Try to look pleased."

Demy enjoys destabilizing the traditional tale's universe. The world of "once upon a time" is perturbed by multiple intrusions of modernity, associated with the Lilac Fairy, whose 1930s style contrasts significantly with the film's overall early modern look. She gives to the king poetry from the future (by Cocteau and Guillaume Apollinaire), mentioning modern conveniences such as gaslights and telephones. Rather than traveling in a beautiful coach or magical mode of transformation, the Fairy arrives at the princess's wedding in a helicopter. When princess/Donkey Skin bakes the love cake for the lovesick prince, Demy playfully takes aim at Disney. Alluding to the scenes of domesticity in Disney's *Snow White*, Demy has the princess carry out domestic work in an exquisite ball gown, which feels just as incongruous as a helicopter in a fairy tale.

Demy's experiments in queer and fairy-tale filmmaking paved the way for the work of Ozon. Like Demy and Cocteau before him, Ozon draws on the marvelous to denaturalize normative gender and sexuality. His 1998 *Sitcom* blends elements from Franz Kafka's *Metamorphosis* (2009 [1915]) and Pier Paolo Pasolini's *Teorema* (1968) to completely destabilize the heteronormative bourgeois family. A year later, his *Criminal Lovers* gives a queer twist to "Hansel and Gretel." The film's first part concerns Luc and Alice's murder of their North African classmate Saïd, to whom both are attracted. Their murder cannot be separated from their "fear of desiring the Other (another race)," and in Luc's case, his fear of "desiring the same (homosexuality)" (Hain 2007, 286). In the second part, "the narrative turns into a queer variation of a Hansel and Gretel-like fairy tale" (Schilt 2011, 51). The duo get lost in a forest where they bury Saïd's body; they make their way to the home of a cannibalistic "ogre" (a large, foreign-accented man), who holds them prisoner, and awakens Luc to his queer sexuality.

Indeed, the film teases out the source tale's queer potential. Lack of food drives "Hansel and Gretel," leading to the parents' crime of abandonment; hungry, the children arrive at the home of the "Other," the witch/ogress; she desires to eat them, but thanks to Gretel they defeat her, cross the river, and reunite with their father. Ozon complicates and queers the plot, but draws on some of the gender play in the Grimms' tale, wherein Hansel is the active principal in the first part of the tale, leaving pebbles then bread to mark their trail home, whereas Gretel dominates in the second half, killing the witch. In *Criminal Lovers*, Alice dominates the crime story, taking the lead in the murder of Saïd, whereas Luc, literally playing the role of Gretel (he carries out domestic chores for the ogre), ends up orchestrating their escape. Although the lack of food remains a theme, it is paired with sexual lack: Luc cannot have an erection or orgasm with Alice. Only after he is sexually "devoured" by the ogre can Luc access his own sexuality and make love to Alice in the woods near a waterfall when they escape.[14] This scene renders pornographic a typical Disney moment in which a virginal heroine and her prince encounter each other in the woods, surrounded by innocent woodland creatures. In Ozon's film, real woodland creatures, including a deer, a fox, a hedgehog, and a dove, voyeuristically gaze upon the naked couple as they make love. Throughout the film, as predator becomes prey (the ogre refers to Luc as "my little rabbit"), binaries opposing human and animal, masculine and feminine, straight and queer, same and Other, constantly break down.

As does Ozon in *Criminal Lovers*, Breillat shakes up gender roles and normative forms of sexuality in *The Sleeping Beauty* (La belle endormie 2010). Like Ozon's Luc, Breillat's heroine is initiated into sexuality through a same-sex experience: the Romany woman, not Prince Charming, awakens her sexuality. And like Ozon's criminal couple, Breillat's Anastasia and Peter/Johan switch back and forth between playing traditionally masculine and feminine roles.

In turning the story of a passive princess who waits to be saved by a prince into a queer feminist tale, Breillat frames the film with "Sleeping Beauty" into which is folded Hans Christian Andersen's "Snow Queen," setting up a dialectic between the two tales. Anastasia, a six-year-old, spirited girl who pretends to be the knight Vladimir, is cursed like Perrault's heroine to sleep for one hundred years; she awakens as a sixteen-year-old. Taking a cue from Perrault, Breillat's fairies grant Anastasia many adventures while she sleeps. Here Breillat interpolates the Snow Queen. Anastasia meets Peter in her dream-world journey; he similarly but more figuratively sleeps and is led away by the Snow Queen. Anastasia spends her dreamtime on a quest to find Peter, encountering, among others, a Romany girl, the only character from her dream world to return as an adult in the frame narrative. Just as six-year-old Anastasia is about to complete her quest, sixteen-year-old Anastasia awakens to find Johan, Peter's grandson, in her bedroom. However, her (re)union with Peter/Johan turns out to be less than ideal, and the film ends with a modern, pregnant Anastasia disenchanted with her Prince Charming.

Breillat ignores the quest narrative of the prince who comes to save (wake) the sleeping princess and instead focuses on the quest narrative of young Anastasia, who independently moves from adventure to adventure to find Peter. As Maria Garcia argues, "Breillat consistently re-imagines the much-celebrated rites of passage often reserved, in literature and cinema, for boys" (2011, 32). She also challenges normative sexuality in the film: "Breillat sets out to overturn the male fantasy that forms the subtext of nearly all the romantic fairy tales upon which young girls are weaned—that men awaken the virgin to her sexuality and, by extension, to her identity" (Garcia 2011, 32). Challenging binaries such as male/female, active/passive, straight/queer, the film depicts the source tale's heteronormativity as unsatisfactory, while opening up a space for liberating, queer possibilities.[15]

Reimaginings of Tales from the *Arabian Nights*

French directors taking on classical tales find various ways to contest the Disney paradigm, challenging in particular its representations of gender and sexuality.[16] One domain where Disney has *not* exercised global fairy-tale film influence is in *Arabian Nights* adaptations. As noted earlier, Galland launched the European oriental-tale trend, and he could be considered the author of the popular tales "Aladdin" and "Ali Baba."[17] Just as progressive rethinking of gender and sexuality manifests in filmic adaptations of classic tales since the 1940s and 1950s, so, for the most part, does a progressive rethinking of the relationship to the ethnic Other in films from the *Arabian Nights*.

Jacques Becker's *Ali Baba and the Forty Thieves* (Ali Baba et les quarante voleurs 1954), came to define the tale for generations of French people. The association between the celebrated comedy actor Fernandel and the character Ali Baba persisted some forty years later, evidenced in the cartoon version of the tale appearing in the animated television series *Thousand and One Nights* (Mille et une nuits 1993), conceived by Marie-France Brière, in which Ali Baba resembles the Marseillais actor.[18] Becker initially chose the Martiniquan singer and actor Henri Salvador for the role, which would have significantly changed the racial dynamics of a film that includes only one non-French actor.[19] Becker had wanted to make a film about Morocco, and chose the area of Taroudant to film the exteriors. According to Valérie Vignaux, this desire influenced the filming of *Ali Baba*: "The camera lingers on the faces and manners of the [Moroccan] extras to give us the tones of another culture" (2000, 167).

Nevertheless, story modifications and the often exoticizing ambiance only strengthen problematic images of the Arab world. In this version, an unmarried Ali Baba is the servant, not the brother, of Cassim (Henri Vilbert). Whereas in Galland, Morgiane, a clever slave, is rewarded for her courageous actions by Ali Baba, who marries her to his son, in Becker's film Morgiane is a slave woman whom Ali Baba purchases for his master, and she becomes Ali Baba's love interest. Besides her belly dancing, Morgiane is quite passive. Played by the Egyptian actress and dancer Samia Gamal, Morgiane represents, in Insaf's Ouhiba words, "the archetype of the Oriental woman subject to the whims of a man" (2012, 76).[20]

As the film progresses, Ali Baba ends up fighting two enemies—Cassim and his men, and the forty thieves—who end up annihilating each other at Ali Baba's wedding to Morgiane. In the conclusion, Ali Baba opens the cavern up to the whole city, giving the stolen riches to the people. Such an ending recalls the American western, wherein the White man frees natives from other natives, bringing justice and a happy ending. (Though Fernandel was supposed to be Arab, his renown as a French actor ultimately makes him a French character.) Filmed the year Morocco gained independence from France, and punctuated by traditional Moroccan music, cuisine, and costume, the film never quite manages to overcome its colonial impulses.

Filmed in Ouarzazate, Morocco, Pierre Aknine's 2007 two-part television film *Ali Baba and the Forty Thieves* (Ali Baba et les quarante voleurs) presents a telling contrast to Becker's film. Aknine includes an integrated cast of French and French North African actors, speaking to France's increased acknowledgement of people of North African descent, as well as a more sensitive approach to Arab culture. The film's themes challenge some cultural norms of both western and eastern societies and bridge the gap between them, and it restores the central role of women found in the source tale.

The film opens with a grandfather, who turns out to be Ali Baba (Gérard Jugnot), recounting his story to his granddaughter Kenza (Florella Campanella). Aknine situates the story within the context of political tensions between Charlemagne and the caliph (Amidou). The caliph sends ambassadors to Charlemagne with gifts, and Charlemagne reciprocates with a gem-studded cross his ambassador Séraphin (Ken Duken) brings the caliph. The idea for the setting may have come from Pierre Gaspard-Huit's 1963 film *Shéhérazade*, starring Anna Karina, in which an envoy of Charlemagne, the knight Renaud, falls in love with Shéhérazade, intended for the caliph Haroun-al-Rashid.[21] In Aknine's film, unbeknownst to the caliph, his wife the calipha plots with the vizier to undermine his reign by pushing him to war against the Christians. As Ali Baba remarks, perhaps in a wink to the popular *Arabian Nights*-inspired comic *Iznogoud*, "every vizier wants to overturn every caliph!"[22] The forty thieves, who raid the caravan and kill the caliph's ambassadors, are led by Malik (Thomas Trabacchi), the calipha's son. But Charlemagne's devout ambassador Séraphin manages to escape, dressed as a female slave, thanks to the help of Morgiane (Leïla Bekhti). The story becomes even more complex with the internal family drama of forced marriage. Ali Baba wants to marry his son Slimane (Marc Ruchmann) to the apothecary's rather ugly daughter, but Slimane has fallen in love with Morgiane. After Cassim is killed, Ali Baba prepares to marry his brother's wife, Ouria (Saïda Jawad), but his wife Yasmina (Michèle Bernier) becomes jealous.

While the film challenges the practice of forced marriage within Arab culture, it also questions Christianity's condemnation of sexuality and magic. Séraphin, the film's only western character, is a seriously devout man whose piety is frequently mocked. When Ali Baba uses the magical lamp, Séraphin condemns it as witchcraft, but Ali Baba insists: "We are in the Orient, Séraphin, the land of tales and enchantment." When a flying carpet is used to retrieve the stolen cross Charlemagne sent to the caliph, Séraphin declares: "it's . . . it's a miracle!" Ali Baba retorts: "Here we just call that magic." The most humorous moments are when Yasmina and Ouria accidentally give Séraphin a virility potion, which torments the poor Christian and leads to his union with Ouria, whose name sounds like "houri," a beautiful celestial maiden of Muslim paradise, while "Seraphin" signifies a Christian angel. That the film concludes with their union could be read as a reconciliation of the two cultures, mirrored at the political level when the caliph receives Charlemagne's gift and peace between the two peoples is maintained.

While both Ali Baba and Aladdin[23] have been the focus of French directors of live-action and animated films, Shéhérazade has also made it to the screen, incarnated by Anna Karina in 1963, and by Catherine Zeta Jones in 1990 in Philippe de Broca's *1001 Nights* (1001 Nuits). Filmed in Morocco, Tunisia, and France, de Broca's film for the most part is focalized through Shéhérazade, who is asked by several children to recount her life as she prepares for her execution. In this *Arabian Nights* version, Shéhérazade not only is the narrator but also the main character of her stories. A slave girl presented to King Shariar (Thierry Lhermite) by the grand vizier (Roger Carel) in lieu of the vizier's own daughter, Shéhérazade initially manages to evade her fate not through storytelling, but through ruses worthy of Little Thumbling. A swashbuckling heroine, she comes across, among other characters, Sinbad (Vittorio Gassman), who reveals that he cannot sail and invented all of his stories.

When she first escapes the king's men, she encounters the thief Aladdin (Stéphane Freiss), with whom she finds the magical lamp. Jimmy the Genie (Gérard Jugnot) emerges from the lamp looking like a twentieth-century Brit with his bowler and cane. The film actually opens with Allah sending Jimmy to live in England, "the land of eternal rain," where over the course of the years he takes on many English mannerisms. The magic Jimmy offers Shéhérazade turns out to be twentieth-century machines, including a motorcycle, plane, and helicopter. De Broca was likely familiar with Demy's *Donkey Skin*; they collaborated in different capacities.[24] Like Demy before him, but in a more farcical manner, de Broca uses the intrusion of twentieth-century culture to destabilize the tale's universe.

A much more artful representation of Shéhérazade occurs in the hands of animator Francine Miailhe. Her 1995 *Shéhérazade* proves unique in its style: Miailhe uses paint on glass, which emphasizes the sense of morphing and metamorphosing in the stories she tells. For *Shéhérazade*, Miailhe draws from the styles of Paul Cézanne and especially Georges Rouault, evident in her stained-glass and image-framing (see Figure 5.1). She foregrounds North African culture, including a henna ritual before the wedding and the soundtrack of North African music and instruments.

FIGURE 5.1 A Rouault-like shot of Shahzaman gazing upon the orgy in Miailhe's *Shéhérazade* (1995).

Miailhe emphasizes both the violence and the sensuality of the *Arabian Nights*. The dramatic representation of Shariar abducting and murdering woman after woman is striking. Miailhe depicts their deaths as genocide, with piled up naked corpses. Her representation of the sultana's orgy is mature and somewhat explicit, with naked bodies melting together in a sort of dance. At the film's conclusion, three boys appear at dawn after the 1001st night. Dinarzade narrates: "Shéhérazade had transformed the ogre into a man, then the man into a father, slowly, and by the sole power of words, she brought Shariar to love and returned the world to the order of life." The morphing bodies throughout the film complement the overall narrative in which Shéhérazade transforms the sultan, and consequently, the world around her.

Generic Reimaginings: Animators Move Away from the Canon

Both Aknine and Miailhe draw from the tradition of the *Arabian Nights* to find common ground between cultures, an idealist objective also found in the work of Laguionie and Ocelot, both of whom were influenced by Grimault. For the most part, these directors work outside the Disney large-scale studio production in a more artisanal style, creating animated films within a painterly tradition. The least painterly of the group, Grimault was instrumental in supporting Laguionie, helping him produce his first animated short. In turn, Laguionie set up a small-scale animation studio called La Fabrique, where his friend Ocelot made "a series of cut-paper short films" (Neupert 2011, 127). Most of their corpus consists of lesser-known tales or their own original stories, and often their films bear political and philosophical messages.

Perhaps best known for *The King and the Mockingbird* (Le roi et l'oiseau 1980), Grimault collaborated with the poet Jacques Prévert, with whom he worked on several animated films. The film has its origins in Grimault and Prévert's unfinished adaptation of Andersen's "The Shepherdess and the Chimney Sweep," which nevertheless was released in 1952 by Grimault's business partner, André Sarrut.[25] By 1947 Grimault and Prévert had already adapted Andersen's "The Steadfast Tin Soldier," which concerns a toy—an acrobat conscripted into the army in Grimault and Prévert—in love with a doll, who is pursued by an evil jack-in-the-box. Neupert remarks: "*The Little Soldier* is exemplary of Grimault's themes as well as his consistent visual style. Though it is ostensibly a children's story, the implications of a handsome young man sent into a battle he does not understand, while the powerful male figure stays home, forcibly seducing the female, hold the mood in a relentlessly serious level" (2011, 103). This scenario anticipates the very similar rivalry in *The King and the Mockingbird* over the shepherdess between the king, a powerful older man, and the chimney sweep, his social inferior. Grimault integrates Andersen's story about two porcelain figurines—two characters from two different paintings in the film—into the larger frame of the conflict between the megalomaniac King Charles and the clever bird, the tale's narrator.

The film opens with a tiny bird in a cage being used for target practice by the cruel and inept king; it turns out to be the narrator's child. The king's palace is an immense high-rise with elevators. Quite modern, it also resembles Versailles, with its gold trimmings and prolific images of the king; not surprisingly, a portrait of Louis XIV looms in the background (see Figure 5.2). The king is Ubuesque, using trap doors to eliminate anyone who crosses him or does not fulfill his orders, including painting him without depicting his crossed eyes. The king's portrait is as cruel and ambitious as its model: it eliminates the real king in a trap door and pursues the shepherdess, with whom the chimney sweep runs off. In their escape, the chimney sweep saves the title bird's child—who again gets caught in a trap set by the king—and befriends the bird. They all run into the lower city, populated by the poor who cannot see the sun. Police wearing bowlers and loudspeakers activate surveillance, calling for the capture of the shepherdess and the chimney sweep. The birds, the chimney sweep and the shepherdess, the caged lions, and the poor unite against the king, his Bobbies, and

FIGURE 5.2 Hyacinthe Rigaud's famous portrait of Louis XIV looms in the background of *The King and the Mockingbird* (1980).

his giant robot. The palace is destroyed, the king shot into space, and the film's final image shows the robot's fist—controlled by the bird—crushing the cage used to trap its child.

Grimault's fairyland is far from utopian, a surveillance society dominated by a modern king whose despotism makes us question our idealization of fairy kingdoms. Indeed, the king uses the fairy-tale genre, particularly Perrault, to legitimate his claims on the shepherdess. His robot repeats, mechanically: "It is written in the books, kings marry shepherdesses."[26] Initially conceived of just after World War II, the film also treats the subject of forced labor, ironically referred to as "voluntary work." From February 1943 to the end of the war the Vichy government conscripted some 600,000 Frenchmen into forced labor and sent them to Germany (Granet-Abisset 2010, 113–14). The king's fascistic ways certainly could be read as a figure for the authoritarian Maréchal Pétain. That one of Pétain's advisers remarked in 1941 that the maréchal "now had more power than any French leader since Louis XIV" (Jackson 2001, 133) and Grimault's inclusion of the famous portrait of the Sun King strengthens such a reading.

Of course, the film's meaning goes beyond a World War II allegory, evident in the acclaim it gained when released in 1980. The film valorizes artistic and political freedom, symbolized by the liberation of the bird, a recurring figure in Grimault and Prévert. In their animated short *The Scarecrow* (L'Epouvantail 1942), the title character protects two little birds from a slick cat's claws. In the 1946 *The Magical Flute* (La flûte magique), a castle lord forbids a boy-minstrel from playing his lute, which the lord crushes; a kind bird transforms into a flute, which magically makes people dance when they hear the music.[27] *The King and the Mockingbird* is also a call to solidarity among the marginalized; those locked in figurative or real cages bond to free themselves. However, as

Neupert observes, "Grimault's characters struggle to escape repression, often through creativity, but they never really manage to improve the world around them. There are no Disney endings with a celebration of a new social order" (2011, 101).

Although Grimault was an important influence on him, Laguionie's animation style is more experimental, yet maintains his predecessor's political and philosophical impulse. While *Gwen, or the Book of Sand* (Gwen, ou le livre de sable 1985) is a post-apocalyptic tale that invokes the oral story-telling tradition, *A Monkey's Tale* (Château des singes 1999) reads like an animal fable. *The Painting* (Le Tableau 2011) best illustrates the affiliations between Laguionie and Grimault, and foregrounds the painterly tradition in French animation.

Gwen bears affinities with René Laloux's science fiction *Fantastic Planet* (La Planète sauvage 1973), both stylistically and thematically. Laguionie also inscribes orality within the film, represented by the 173-year-old narrator, the nomad Rosaline. Situated in different spaces within a world destroyed by consumer society, the film opposes two peoples. The nomads live in the desert's open space, created by ecological disaster. They live on legends, very much outside the consumer culture of the inhabitants of "land of the dead," who worship store catalogs, and chant product descriptions as if they were passages from a religious text. The plot follows a quest structure: when the young Gwen's companion is taken away by the monstrous "macou," which dumps consumer waste in the desert, Gwen and Rosaline journey to the land of the dead to retrieve the boy. In an interview, Laguionie explains that Gwen's quest draws upon that of Orpheus: both seek to save a beloved from the land of the dead.[28] Laguionie's animation is striking: giant objects are scattered throughout the desert, the density of which increases as one approaches the land of the dead. The desert nomads walk and hunt on stilts, which creates beautiful yet bleak scenes of movement.

Whereas *Gwen* stages an insurmountable divide between two peoples, *A Monkey's Tale* works to bring two peoples (back) together. This animated film relates the story of two tribes of monkeys that used to be one before a legendary earthquake. Those who live in the jungle canopy are called the Woonkos, and those who live on the jungle floor are the Laankos. Over time, each group developed prejudices against the other, and a Woonko named Kom begins to challenge these beliefs, upheld by the elder Korkonak, who insists: "there are no questions!" Kom ends up falling to the jungle floor, and is taken in by Master Flavius and Gina, the servant of the princess Ida, whose illness makes her bedridden. The king's chancellor is having Ida poisoned in order to take power; he plans to force the king to abdicate and to rule in lieu of the practically comatose princess.

Those of the jungle floor consider Kom's people barbaric and uncivilized, but Gina and Master Flavius recognize that the Woonkos and the Laankos are not that different. Kom learns about Laankos society, which is hierarchical, reflected in one's position (lower or upper) in the castle domains, whereas Woonkos society is much more egalitarian. Kom eventually uses the knowledge of the Woonkos to heal the princess—no longer a "sleeping beauty," as Gina suggests—but rather than marry the princess, Kom returns to the canopy with Gina. The hero rescues the princess, but lives happily ever after with her servant, a conclusion that challenges conventional fairy-tale plots and their implicit class prejudices.

In *The Painting*, Laguionie foregrounds the problematics of racial or ethnic difference and social hierarchy. Like *A Monkey's Tale*, it moves towards social harmony. The character Lola, a Pafini, relates the story, which takes up elements from Laguionie's previous films as well as Grimault's *The King and the Mockingbird*. It concerns the characters of a painting who are divided into three groups: the Toutpins ("tout peints" or "all-painted"), the Pafinis ("pas finis" or "not finished") and the Reufs, who are basically sketches. The Toutpins reside in the beautiful castle, supported by the enslaved Reufs, while the Pafinis live hidden in the forest below. These two spaces—the castle and the lower woods—reflect a class and racial hierarchy that is destabilized over the course of the film. The labyrinthine stairways that lead down to where the Pafinis live are reminiscent of those in

The King and the Mockingbird, which also spatializes social hierarchies and has characters magically emerge from paintings.

Drawing from the artistic styles of Monet, Picasso, and Matisse, among others, this stunningly animated film shapes the racial and class conflict around the love story between Ramo, a Toutpin, and Claire, a Pafini.[29] The Pafini Lola, the Toutpin Ramo, and the Reuf Plume set out on a quest to locate the painter of their painting, whom they hope will complete the work and thus resolve the characters' socio-racial conflict. On their way they pass through a beautiful enchanted forest, encounter the drummer boy Magenta from another painting, and end up in a third painting to enjoy carnival in Venice. Although they only encounter the painter's portrait, they manage to locate paint, which they bring back and share with the Reufs and the Pafinis. A utopian order is ultimately achieved with the abolition of ethnic or racial hierarchy while upholding the principle of individual creativity, exemplified in the characters who paint themselves in marvelous colors.

Laguionie's friend and colleague, Ocelot also deals with questions related to marginalization and ethnic and racial difference in his animated films, and draws from different artistic—specifically national—traditions.[30] However, his treatment of gender is not as progressive as Laguoinie's. His films often concern active heroes who save damsels in distress, even when they have a powerful heroine like *Kirikou and the Sorceress* (Kirikou et la sorcière 1998), Ocelot's first feature.

The hero of this African tale, Kirikou, is a Tom Thumb figure, born with the ability to speak and run. Wondering where all the men of his tribe are, Kirikou is informed that the sorceress Karaba devoured them. Kirikou continually asks: why is Karaba so mean? He learns that she does not devour the men; she turns them into fetishes that she controls. Like Christian-Jaque's Bluebeard, she allows the people to believe the legend in order to maintain her control over them. Kirikou also discovers that the sorceress is mean because of a painful thorn in her spine, the source of her magic. When Kirkou removes the thorn, Karaba transforms into a kind woman, and Kirikou metamorphoses into an adult man; the fetishes turn back into the village men, and unity is reestablished. This theme returns in "The Witch" ("La sorcière"), one of the shorts included in *Princes et princesses* (2000). In both films, the hero defies common knowledge about the nature of the witch marginalized by the community, and reintegrates her into it.

Ocelot's second animated feature, *Azur et Asmar* (2006), is largely about border-crossing, touching on the filmmaker's own position as a Frenchman who spent much of his youth in Africa (Apostolou 2009, 102). Azur, a Christian prince, grows up with Asmar, a Saracen, whose mother Jénane is Azur's wet nurse and nanny. The boys are raised as brothers by Jénane, who tells them stories about the djinn fairy, imprisoned in a glass cage, whom both boys dream of saving. Azur's intolerant father chases Jénane and Asmar away, but as soon as Azur reaches adulthood, he travels to the land of his adoptive mother, seeking to save the djinn fairy. Azur reaches an orient that bears specifically North African traits, evident in its cuisine and music, as well as in Jénane's tattoos.[31] Ocelot also draws on the Arab mosaic tradition for his decors. Fotoni Apostolou remarks that Ocelot "reverses the roles of Self and Other to make the young man from the Occident become an immigrant in the Orient, perceived as a threat and permanently excluded from the host community" (2009, 103). Although initially hostile towards his adoptive brother, Asmar comes to embrace him as the two pursue their quest to save the djinn fairy. Ethnic or racial blending is foregrounded at the film's end: Azur is united with the North African djinn fairy, while Azmar is paired with the European elf fairy.

In his two collections of short films comprising tales from different traditions, *Princes et princesses* and *Tales of the Night* (Contes de la nuit 2011), Ocelot draws from the silhouette-style animation of Lotte Reiniger. *Princes et princesses* includes stories from or set in Europe, Egypt, and Japan, and *Tales of the Night* from the Caribbean, Mexico, and Africa. Ocelot's visual style in his use of cutout silhouettes is striking but also self-reflexive. Before each tale, three characters—the boy, the girl, and the technician—generate ideas and assemble costumes and plots that they will then perform. By focusing on performative aspects of presenting a tale to an audience, Ocelot connects his work back to the oral tradition; his characters appropriate and create tale variants through (staged) spontaneity.

Concluding Remarks

The fairy-tale film in France is characterized by a strong tradition of artistic experimentation, particularly evident in the painterly animation styles of Laguionie, Ocelot, and Miailhe. Drawing from surrealism and psychedelic culture respectively, Cocteau and Demy further challenge canonical tales from the perspective of sexuality, a tendency continued in the work of Ozon and Breillat. From parodies to queer reimaginings, French directors directly and indirectly challenge Disney's hegemony over the global fairy-tale film market. They also counter conservative, bourgeois ideology infused in Perrault and Grimm tales such as "Snow White," "Cinderella," and "Sleeping Beauty," which have become canonical in Europe and North America since the early twentieth century.

French fairy-tale film from the postwar period to the present demonstrates a shift in which female characters and the figure of the Other—ethnic, racial, or social—increasingly are given voice and more active roles, and their marginalization challenged. In versions of "Little Thumbling," a central female character gets integrated into the story, and takes on a more significant role as we move from Image and Boisrond to Dahan. Bluebeard no longer completely dominates his wives; he can fall victim to them, and even fall in love with them. Ocelot's sorceresses find true love, as does Dahan's ogress Rose. Moving away from the stereotypical representations of the orient that we see in Becker's work, Aknine demonstrates a more sensitive approach to representing the Arab Other than previous directors. Through their filmic tales, Aknine, Laguionie, and Ocelot all challenge racial and ethnic prejudices in various ways, promoting mutual understanding and cultural appreciation at a time when the French government has banned the wearing of the Muslim hijab in public institutions, and when the anti-immigrant far-right party, the National Front, maintains a very comfortable position within the French political landscape. The recent release of Christophe Gans's *Beauty and the Beast* (La Belle et la Bête 2014), starring Vincent Cassel, which plays on the cute woodland creatures found in Disney only to undermine the class message of the tale at the film's conclusion, and Breillat's plan to top off her two fairy-tale films with a third,[32] also a version of "Beauty and the Beast," suggests that French directors will continue to reimagine the fairy tale in ways that challenge Disney hegemony, as well as their own society.

Notes

1 See Malthête's filmography of Méliès's films (2002, 242–66). For short descriptions of Méliès's films, see Frazer (1979, 59–222); see also Moen (2013, 39–74).
2 Richard Abel demonstrates that Pathé was able to successfully compete against Thomas Edison and had wide distribution in the US (1999, 24–25).
3 See Abel (1998, 434–62) for a filmography for Pathé-Frères.
4 In 1906 Capellani directed four fairy-tale films for Pathé-Frères. On Cohl, see Crafton (1990). On Starewitch, see Martin (2003).
5 All translations from the French are mine.
6 Disney drew the character Gaston from Cocteau's Avenant; both serve as doubles and rivals of the Beast, albeit in different ways. See Cummins (1995, 27).
7 On the swashbuckler in Hollywood and France in the 1930s to 1950s, see Hayward (2010, 137).
8 See Thirard's remarks on gender in the film (2008, 84).
9 Henri Landru was a French serial killer who became known as a modern Bluebeard. In France, Claude Chabrol (1963) and Pierre Boutron (2005) made films on the subject (see Tatar 2004, 132–33 and 151, and Zipes 2011, 168–71).
10 This is also the case of Bubnov's animated short *Bluebeard's Last Wife* (La dernière femme de Barbe-bleue, 1996), whose title character turns out to be Medusa.

11 On questions of sexuality in Cocteau's work, see Eynat-Confino (2008); on *Beauty and the Beast*, see Hearne (1989 esp. 79–89), Hayward (1996), Fischlin (1998), and Sheaffer-Jones (2002); on Cocteau and Angela Carter's renditions of the tale, see Bryant (1989).

12 For studies of Demy's films and biography, see Berthomé (1996) and Taboulay (1996).

13 For a more in-depth study of Demy's fairy-tale films and their relation to a queer sensibility, see my *Queer Enchantments* (2013).

14 For a more extensive analysis of the queer underpinnings of Ozon's film, see my forthcoming "Binary Outlaws."

15 For a more in-depth reading of Breillat's *Sleeping Beauty*, see my forthcoming "Binary Outlaws."

16 See also films by Sussfeld and Picha, which parody the morality and puritanical representation of sexuality in Disney.

17 On Galland's authorship, see Chraïbi (2004) and Larzul (2004).

18 A producer and artistic director for French television, Marie-Claire Brière conceived of two animated television series aimed at children that drew from the *Arabian Nights*. In 1996 she oversaw the creation of *Thousand and One Nights*, with thirteen episodes based on different tales. That same year she also created *Princesse Shéhérazade*, with fifty-two episodes.

19 On Becker's preference for Salvador, see Vignaux (2000, 165).

20 Hayward also remarks that her appearance would have been titillating for western audiences because she had become "something of a persona non grata in Egypt" with Nasser's rise to power (2010, 96).

21 Unfortunately, I have been unable to locate Gaspard-Huit's *Shéhérazade*. Its influence can be seen as well in Philippe de Broca's *1001 Nuits* (1990).

22 *Iznogoud* (2005) is based on the comic book series and animated series created by René Goscinny and Jean Tabary, centering on the vizier Iznogoud's desire to become "caliph in place of the caliph."

23 Jean Image also did a version, *Aladdin and the Magical Lamp* (Aladdin et la lampe magique 1970).

24 Both Demy and de Broca directed parts of *The Seven Deadly Sins* (Les Sept péchés capitaux, 1962) and later de Broca completed *Louisiana* (Louisiane, 1984), a film Demy had started to shoot. See Rège (2010, 307).

25 On the "Affair of the Shepherdess and the Chimney Sweep," see Roffat (2014, 55).

26 Although not exactly a fairy tale, "Grisélidis," published with Perrault's classic tales, concerns a prince who marries a shepherdess.

27 *The Turning Table* (La Table tournante) contains several Grimault shorter films, including those discussed here.

28 See the interview with Laguionie included in the DVD.

29 In an interview included in the DVD, scriptwriter Anik le Ray remarks that she had conceived of the Toupins in the style of Monet, les Reufs in that of Picasso, and the nude Garance in that of Matisse.

30 For *Kirikou*, for instance, Ocelot was inspired by a sculpture from Benin to design the grandfather's head-dress; the sorceress's hut is modeled on a Conigui hut from Guinea, while the sorceress's headdress draws on that of an actual princess from Dahomey. Work grounded in national and period art forms is characteristic of each of his films.

31 Algerian singer and musician Souad Massi, who contributed to the soundtrack, herself crosses between North African and European traditions.

32 Breillat has mentioned this intention in several interviews.

6

THE CHECKERED RECEPTION OF FAIRY-TALE FILMS IN THE GERMANY OF THE BROTHERS GRIMM

Jack Zipes

The Early Years of Fairy-Tale Films in Germany (1895–1933)

As in most western European nations, the development of the fairy-tale film began during the 1890s, but German filmmakers were faced with a problem that other countries did not have to confront. Ironically, their greatest heritage, the Brothers Grimm and their folktales and fairy tales, caused difficulties. By the end of the nineteenth century, the Grimms' tales had become so identified with the alleged naturalness and purity of German culture that it was considered almost a crime to modify, change, or adapt them in a way that might make the tales inauthentic—including the production of fairy-tale films. As a result, there was a kind of moral imperative implicit in the making of Grimms' fairy-tale films, mainly for young audiences: to remain as faithful as possible to the original texts, to suffuse the films with Germanic elements, and to emphasize the fairy tales' charming "folkloric" aspects.

Horst Heidtmann's talk on media adaptations of folktales elucidates just how dependent Germans in general became on the Grimms' tales: "The *Children's and Household Tales* (*Kinder-und Hausmärchen*) advanced as the prototype of children's literature, by which not only all other fairy-tale collections were to be measured, but children's literature overall. The image of children's literature was dominated so strongly by fairy-tale books that in 1918 Charlotte Bühler [a prominent German psychologist] created the term 'fairy-tale age' for a phase in middle childhood" (2000 n.p., see also 2007). As this chapter demonstrates, this ideological faux-nationalist[1] and psychological attitude toward the Grimms and other German authors of fairy tales such as Wilhelm Hauff and Ludwig Bechstein, not to mention the German Romantics, has continued with some variation up to the present. But first, let us consider the beginning of this development.

In a significant study of silent fairy-tale films at the end of the nineteenth century and beginning of the twentieth century, Willi Höfig provides a succinct account of the German production of silent fairy-tale films, largely based on the Grimms' tales. By focusing on different "Hansel and Gretel" adaptations beginning with a 1907 version and ending with a discussion of Hanns Walter Kornblum's production in 1921, he comes to some unusual conclusions that offer insight into the trajectory of fairy-tale film production in Germany. Characteristic in this early period is that "there is a simplicity in the portrayal of the course of the incidents—no parallel plot lines and motivations are made recognizable as elements of the incidents. In short: realistic, concrete storytelling" (Höfig 2008, 92). Höfig goes on to add that the early silent fairy-tale films tend to be "un-fairy-tale-like" (*unmärchenhaft*) and more like realistic period pieces in which the characters obey conventional laws of action that accord with the Grimms' texts.

Whether live-action or animated, the films and their magical and miraculous transformations were intended to have a natural and realistic veneer of authentic German lore. Generally speaking, these early films are "unfairy-tale-like" because they rarely move spectators to a fairyland or other world; instead, they tend to take place in a realistic German environment. In addition, by the 1920s, fairy-tale silent films—also a few with sound—were produced for pedagogical purposes and were the subject of debates about morals. For the most part the fantastic elements in films produced between 1917 and 1933 were minimized in classical fairy-tale cinema such as Paul Leni's *Briar Rose*,[2] (*Dornröschen* 1917), Paul Wegener's *Hans Trutz in the Land of Cockaigne* (*Hans Trutz im Schlaraffenland* 1917), and Alf Zengerling's *Snow White* (*Schneewittchen* 1928) and *Cinderella* (*Aschenputtel* 1931). Indeed, there was little experimentation in the production of fairy-tale films whereas expressionist horror films and mysteries, often based on legends, were much more innovative.[3]

Fairy-tale experimentation materialized in the realm of adult cinema. For instance, Paul Wegener directed three interesting short films, *Rübezahl's Wedding* (*Rübezahls Hochzeit* 1916), *The Pied Piper* (*Der Rattenfänger* 1919), and *The Lost Shadow* (*Der verlorene Schatten* 1920); Ernst Lubitsch adapted E.T.A. Hoffmann's "The Sandman" ("Der Sandmann"), in a short live-action film with the title *The Doll* (*Die Puppe* 1919) and also a tale from "The Thousand and One Nights," which he called *Sumurun* (1920); Fritz Lang created *Tired Death* (*Der müde Tod* 1921), which included three tales within a framework that resembles ballads; Ludwig Berger directed the feature-length *The Lost Shoe* (*Der verlorene Schuh*), a humorous version of "Cinderella," in 1923; and Leni produced his magnificent horror and fairy-tale film, *Waxworks* (*Das Wachsfigurenkabinett* 1924), which included an exotic adaptation of a tale from "The Thousand and One Nights."

And, of course, there was the unusual animated fairy-tale work of Lotte Reiniger that commenced in the 1920s and ended in the 1950s. In *Masters of Animation*, John Grant writes:

> Lotte Reiniger pioneered the art of silhouette animation; this art might not seem very important to the history of animation, but even today the earliest of Reiniger's animations possesses a beauty and fascination that far transcends anything on offer from most animators of that era, who were largely concerned with churning out productions of mind-numbing mediocrity that were just good enough to stop the audience from walking out. Reiniger's animations, by contrast, are touched by a love for the form and by a joy in the very act of creation, ensuring that they are today as magical as they ever are.
>
> (2001, 78)

This is certainly true of her artwork, but she was not particularly inventive about questioning or changing fairy-tale narratives, mainly the Grimms' tales, which she adapted with her silhouette cutouts. The narratives are almost all linear and realistic. To be sure, she emphasized aspects of fairy tales that suited her ideological inclinations or changed the tales to make them more succinct. For the most part, however, she tended to be conventional if not conservative in her interpretations. Altogether she produced approximately 18 fairy-tale films from 1922 to 1961, all in the same elegant and subtle style that sought to enhance the features and struggles of oppressed characters, while leaving content and plot unchanged. Her jointed cutout figures were designed to move smoothly, and her protagonists were given special attention and were displayed in unique ways—at times through contrast with white backgrounds or through telescoping. Interestingly, Reiniger's greatest achievement was not a German narrative, but an adaptation of a fairy tale from "The Thousand and One Nights."

Never before did any artist create an animated feature-length fairy tale with such refinement and invention as Reiniger did in *The Adventures of Prince Achmed* in 1926, and never after did she produce such an imaginative and original film with her silhouettes. Perhaps because the subject matter was so foreign, she proved a most imaginative and impressive storyteller, taking substantial poetic license and weaving strands of fairy tales from "The Arabian Nights" into a brilliant technical and ideological re-creation. Her film is a kaleidoscopic voyage into another world, an imagined orient, filled with dreamlike, erotic and weird images and characters that constantly shape-shift into new constellations. This kind of experimentation with animated fairy tales was rarely produced in German cinema at that time, and it was not pursued in the years to come.

The Seamless Transition of German Fairy-Tale Films in the Nazi Era, 1933–1945

The majority of the German fairy-tale films up until 1933 were intended to enhance German cultural belief systems through realistic action, enthralling forest settings with cute cottages and majestic castles, traditional peasant dress and costumes; and to imply that the Grimms' tales or any fairy tale, for that matter, emanated from German soil. Given this Germanic conceit, it was relatively easy for the films to comply with Nazi ideology of Aryanism.

For instance, filmmakers Ferdinand, Hermann, and Paul Diehl used clay animation during the 1930s and 1940s to make a series of successful stop-motion animation fairy-tale films and produced seven adaptations of the Grimms' tales: *The Bremen Town Musicians* (1935), *The Boy Who Went Out to Learn about Fear* (1935), *Table Be Covered* (1936), *The Seven Ravens* (1937), *The Wolf and the Seven Kids* (1939), *Puss in Boots* (1940), and *Sleeping Beauty* (see *Briar Rose* 1943). These films were produced in association with the Reich's ministry of education and tended to stress German customs, traits, and settings.[4] Experts in the development of clay animation, the Diehls followed in Reiniger's footsteps by paying attention to realistic details and closely adhering to the Grimm tales' original contents and plots. The characters are dressed meticulously to befit their occupations. The backgrounds and settings are naturalistic. Some of the villains, such as the innkeeper in *Table be Covered*, or the sorcerer in *Puss in Boots*, have Semitic features, but for the most part, the Diehls did not transform the tales into anti-Semitic Aryan propaganda. Their short films always included a voiceover, and their faithful interpretations demonstrated their great skills in the use of clay figures to enact the fairy tales as literally as possible.

Even while the Diehls were somewhat apolitical, the implications of their emphasis on the wholesomeness of Germanic qualities—and this was true in the overwhelming majority of the fairy-tale films produced during the Nazi era—still helped enable the National Socialists to manipulate and utilize films' content to celebrate a mythic German heritage. Other major fairy-tale producers and directors such as Hubert Schonger, Alf Zengerling, Alfred Stöger, Herbert Fredersdorf, Eric Kobler, Fritz Genschow, and Franz Fiedler rose to the fore to produce fairy-tale films that clearly supported the National Socialist ideology in cinemas and schools.[5] As Heidtmann remarks, "The fairy-tale films were distributed most of all as 'instructional' films through state agencies. The National Socialists gladly promoted the production of fairy-tale films because their educators saw that sturdiness (Bodenständigkeit), devotion to the home country, and the 'German soul of the folk' were articulated in the folk and fairy tales" (2000). Although Genschow made a disturbing Nazi adaptation, *Little Red Cap and the Wolf*, in 1937, most of the aforementioned directors and producers were not strident National Socialists. If anything, they were opportunists who collaborated with the Nazis by following the pattern of realistic natural fairy tales that evoked nostalgia for a German idyllic past.[6]

In addition, as Cornelia Endler comments, their films only had to emphasize so-called Germanic virtues to serve the National Socialist cause. "In particular the most entertaining fairy tales that were seemingly free of ideology," Endler writes, "rose in the Third Reich to become models of German and especially folk virtues." She goes on to explain that, "the qualities of the characters, which the heroes of the fairy tales embodied, coincided with those of the Nazi educational ideals. Above all the fairy tales of the Brothers Grimm were highly esteemed by the National Socialists because they offered great potential and possibilities to be ideologically interpreted" (2006, 12). The potential for ideological exploitation can be seen in Zengerling's *Puss in Boots* (1935), *Briar Rose* (1936), *The Enchanted Princess* (1940), and *The Frog King* (1940); Schonger's *Snow White and Rose Red* (1938), *The Star Coins* (1940), and *The Brave Little Tailor* (1941); Franz Frieder's *Little Muck* (1944); and other fairy-tale films by Genschow, Robert Herlth, Walter Röhrig, and Erich Dautert, who either directed or acted in Nazi films during this period. The prevalent themes concerned handsome and righteous kings, who saved realms from dark villains and intruders, and virtuous steadfast women, who were industrious and willing to sacrifice themselves for their country and wait for princes to come and rescue them. Many of these ideological motifs were already embedded in the Grimms' tales, so it did not take much to filter them through films that appeared innocent and natural.

Divisive Approaches to the Fairy-Tale Film in West and East Germany, 1945–1990

No sooner did World War II come to a close than explanations were urgently sought to explain why the Germans had committed such atrocious acts. After all, Germany had always been regarded as one of the more enlightened and humanistic European nations since the early nineteenth century, when the Grimms, along with many other great Romantic writers, supported the movement to unify the German principalities and bring about a constitutional monarchy. Given the importance that fairy tales—particularly those of the Grimms—played in the German socialization process, it was almost inevitable that the occupation forces, led by the British, briefly banned the publication of the Grimms' fairy tales in 1945 (Bastian 1981, 186). According to the military authorities, the brutality in the fairy tales was partially responsible for generating attitudes that led to the acceptance of the Nazis and their monstrous crimes. Allegedly, the tales gave children a false impression of the world that made them susceptible to lies and irrationalism.

The foolish decision by the occupation forces had, nonetheless, a positive side, for it led the Germans themselves to debate the value of fairy tales.[7] Recall that the Grimms' tales were practically synonymous with the *Märchen* (folktale or fairy tale) and that their collection, especially during the Nazi regime, was seen as identical with a German national tradition and character. Unless a distinction indicated otherwise, it was understood that discussions about fairy tales and folktales after 1945 referred to the Grimms' work. Indeed, the Grimms ruled the realm of this genre, and for this reason they were also held partially responsible for what transpired during the German Reich.

Although the ban against publishing the Grimms' fairy tales was lifted by 1946, the discussion about their brutality and connection to Nazism continued into the early 1950s in both East and West Germany. There were two general arguments in this debate: either the Grimms' tales had conditioned German children to accept savage acts and prepare them for a ruthless regime, or the tales had nothing to do with the barbarism of the Nazis; rather, the tales' cruelty had to be understood in light of traditional German authoritarianism and socio-economic factors. The controversy over the Grimms' tales was never resolved, largely because the viewpoints expressed could not be tested and because very little research had been done about the effects of fairy tales on children and adults. However, the debate about the Grimms' tales set the tone for their reception in both Germanies, where there were, once upon a time, two distinctive Grimm traditions in the Federal Republic of Germany (FRG, West Germany) and the German Democratic Republic (GDR, East Germany) from 1948 to 1989.

In fact, the overall reception of the Grimms' tales and fairy-tale films in the postwar period is a complex issue. Factors that must be taken into consideration include the German people's attitude toward the Grimms' tales as part of their cultural legacy; the policies of publishers and the government; the use of the Grimms' tales at home and in schools, libraries, and the mass media; the influence of scholarly and critical works on the Grimms by academics, psychologists, and folklorists; the differences in the reception of the Grimms' tales based on age, gender, and other demographic variables; and the influence of different media formats such as the references to the Grimms' tales appearing in advertisements, commercials, feature films, and cartoons.

In West Germany there was almost an immediate restoration of the production of traditional fairy-tale films for children that consciously or unconsciously perpetuated Aryan and patriarchal attitudes. All the key producers and directors who had been active during the Nazi period—Schonger, Genschow, Kobler, Fredersdorf, Walter Janssen—became important players in the development of fairy-tale films for children from 1947 to 1960, when these films formed about 10 percent of the market. For instance, Schonger directed *Mother Holle* (1947), *The Enchanted Little Cloth* (1948), *Little Brother and Little Sister* (1953), and *The Golden Goose* (1953); Kobler, *Snow White and Rose Red* (1955) and *Snow White* (1955); Fredersdorf, *The Princess and the Swineherd* (1953), *King Thrushbeard* (1954), *Rumpelstiltskin* (1955), and *Puss in Boots* (1955); Genschow, *Little Red Riding Hood* (see *Little Red Cap* 1953), *Cinderella* (1955), *Briar Rose* (1955), *Table Be Covered* (1956), and *Snow White* (1959). All of these films were live-action and produced primarily for the cinema with the same artificial acting, folksy music with songs often performed by children, with slapstick humor, obvious and predictable events closely connected to the original texts, paternalistic voiceovers by male narrators, use of child actors to sweeten the plots, idyllic forest settings and majestic castles, and traditional costumes from the eighteenth and nineteenth centuries.

Three German films from 1953 and 1954 illustrate the style of kitschy, artificial nationalist pandering that I describe above. In Janssen's *Little Red Cap*, produced by Schonger, viewers are introduced to a polite, helpful, and industrious girl, living in a cottage that resembles the witch's candy cottage from "Hansel and Gretel." She lives there with her widowed mother and five adorable clumsy brothers and has a diligent huntsman, dressed in an official park ranger uniform, as her best friend. The raggedy wolf who encounters her in the woods and eats her and grandma looks more like a harmless stuffed toy than an animal. The dainty Red Riding Hood is easily rescued by the huntsman and her brothers, and everyone dances around the dead wolf at the end of the film.

In Genschow's *Snow White and Rose Red* (1954), the storyline is altered to include two brotherly princes to ensure that the pious and demure sisters, Snow White and Rose Red, have suitors to happily wed at its end. Again there is a charming simple cottage in the woods where a widowed mother raises her daughters to be honest and virtuous for their future princely husbands. The villain of the film—a wicked dwarf—is more comic than threatening, and there is no sense that this foreign, Other figure may have a claim against the brothers who trespass in his realm.

Alf Zengerling's *The Princess on the Pea* (1953) introduces children into the plot, including one in blackface makeup and dressed as a servant, who runs all kinds of errands for the king, a likeable widower. Andersen's fairy tale is transformed into a fatuous story for infants; it is just as "un-fairy-tale-like" as all the films from the 1950s and 1960s. Children are worried about the fortunes of a cute cat, charged with eating the king's favorite mouse, while the king's son, who looks more like a jester than a prince, keeps seeking the right princess, who feels the tiny pea under her mattresses. By no surprise to anyone, he finds her and weds her in a teenage marriage ceremony.

Most of these films were produced for the cinema until 1957; subsequently, the federal government passed a law for the protection of children that prevented anyone younger than age six from attending the cinema. At this point, the production of fairy-tale films was no longer profitable; however, many were produced for television audiences later on. Otherwise, the Disney animated fairy-tale films filled a gap in the postwar years, and they still play a major role in Germany. Among works for adults, one might consider the profound development of "Heimat" films from 1950 through the 1970s as fairy tales. This term indicates a love for home or the fatherland expressed in an emotional and sentimental fashion. The majority of these films were set in small country communities and involved common people—generally farmers or townspeople—with familial problems and romantic conflicts that were always happily resolved. These films exhibited an unabashed love for the fatherland and played on the deep desires on the part of the German people to recover a harmonious past while moving forward, overcoming an ugly recent history, and creating a so-called economic miracle.

Aside from the Heimat films were works with clear fairy-tale motifs, such as *The Tin Drum* (1979), based on Günter Grass's picaresque novel, and *The Neverending Story* (1984) and *Momo* (1986), based on Michael Ende's fairy-tale novels. However, these adaptations were never socially or culturally associated with a fairy-tale film tradition in West Germany, where the film industry remained unproductive and uncreative in adapting fairy-tale narratives.

In contrast to the Federal Republic of Germany, in the German Democratic Republic, the postwar debate about the harmful effects of the Grimms' tales was always tied to *political* questions about the cultural heritage. That is, once the communists solidified their power in 1949, all literature considered bourgeois was to be evaluated and appropriated in a dialectical sense to further the nation's progress toward genuine socialism and eventually communism.[8] The Grimms' tales were rather easy to appropriate because they were considered part of the oral folk tradition and thus depicted how people from the lower classes overcame oppression and fought to improve their lot.

Scholarly works by Gerhard Kahlo (1954) and Waltraut Woeller (1955) elaborated this position to show the folktale's connection to the historical reality of peasant life experience. Kahlo and Woeller argued that the Grimms' tales and other German folktales contained positive elements of the class struggle and were part of a grand European tradition that corresponded with the internationalist aspect of communism. Moreover, the tales were considered helpful in developing young peoples' moral character, a fundamental educational principle in the Soviet Union and Czechoslovakia. As Anneliese Kocialek stated:

> The moral and aesthetic education of pupils through folktales in the primary levels of the schools in the German Democratic Republic are inseparably connected with one another. The special attributes of the artistic fairy-tale forms make the children more receptive to the moral content and simultaneously provide aesthetic pleasure. The tales of our own people are superbly suited to maintain in our children a love for their homeland, and the tales of other peoples waken in them a respect for their cultural achievements.
>
> (1955, 183)

Since the state and party leadership stringently set specific criteria for the moral and political development of the people in the GDR, the Grimms' tales came under close scrutiny, and beginning in 1952, the early editions of their tales underwent revision so they conformed to the state's value system. Racist and religious elements were eliminated; violence and brutality were diminished; and moral statements were added. It was not until 1955 that the first unabridged complete edition of the Grimms' tales was published, but even afterward, the censorship and/or revision of the Grimms' tales continued. The result was a de-historization of the Grimms' tales due to an endeavor to transform them into pure folktales that could be used for the moral and political elevation of the people. From 1952 to 1975, 48 different editions of the Grimms' tales were published in the GDR[9] with very little criticism of possible regressive elements and with changes based on a one-dimensional view of folktales. The Grimms' tales were considered sacrosanct in East Germany, but for different reasons than in West Germany. The tales were regarded as perfect for the moral upbringing of children and for making adults aware of the class struggle. It was, in fact, during this period that the most exceptional contributions to the Grimm legacy in East Germany began.

One of the best-kept secrets of the Cold War was East Germany's production of marvelous fairy-tale films for children.[10] Fortunately, since the fall of the Berlin Wall, the secret is out, and it is now easy to gain access to these cinematic treasures created by DEFA (Deutsche Film Aktiengesellschaft), the state film company of the former East Germany. More than 25 fairy-tale films, produced from 1950 until 1989, emphasize the profound humanitarian aspects of the fairy tales of the Brothers Grimm and other writers such as Gisela von Arnim and Wilhelm Hauff, who enriched the European fairy-tale tradition with original works. In addition, DEFA adapted Mongolian, Ugurian, and Arabian fairy tales for the screen in an effort to extend beyond the European tradition and introduce children to other cultures with traditional stories about the valorous deeds of common people.

The DEFA films, which are now shown on television and are distributed through videos and DVDs in Europe and America, use live characters in realistic settings that recall the historical background of the fairy tales. This realism quickly becomes fantastic and magical, and the films, which vary in directorial style, blend imaginative plots with messages that stimulate young viewers to think about social issues involving greed, vanity, envy, tyranny, racism, sexism, exploitation, and hypocrisy. Incidentally, this cinematic fairy-tale project was organized before any similar work in West Germany, not to mention other western countries and the USA—and similar projects were common in other East European bloc countries.

Originally, East German cultural authorities considered the DEFA films with measured skepticism because they did not believe fairy tales were the proper means to convey and promote socialist ideas and morals. However, filmmakers soon proved the government wrong by transforming the tales and changing them into dramatic allegorical depictions of moral dilemmas. Films like *The Singing Ringing Tree* (1957), *The Tinderbox* (1959), *Snow White* (1961), *Little Red Cap* (1962), *How Six Made their Way through the World* (1972), and *Iron Jack* (1988) stress the need for cooperation and mutual respect to defeat evil tyrants and predators.

The focus in most of the fairy tales is on the little hero or the oppressed heroine so that young viewers can better identify with the protagonists. Thus, the diminutive young man in *The Brave Little Tailor* (1956), directed by Helmut Spieß, shows how a small person can use his wits to succeed in life. Here success is not defined by a royal marriage and the acquisition of money. In fact, the tailor chooses a servant as his bride after the king and his haughty daughter leave the kingdom. In *How to Marry a King* (1969), directed by Rainer Simon and based on the Grimms' "The Clever Peasant's Daughter," the young protagonist Marie demonstrates her cunning in original ways so that she not only weds a king but also teaches him a lesson in social justice (see Figure 6.1).

In *Who's Afraid of the Devil?* (1977) directed by Egon Schlegel, a peasant boy named Jacob avoids the king's death sentence and then uses his wits to disguise himself, outsmart the devil, and win the king's daughter for his bride. Finally, in *Gritta von Rattenzuhausebeiuns* (1985), based on a fairy tale written by the Grimms' friends Bettina and Gisela von Arnim, a plucky young girl of thirteen prevents a kingdom's overthrow by a ruthless governor and also helps her father, a misfit inventor, get his feet on the ground.

All these films are filled with learning processes that stimulate critical thinking in young viewers without being overly didactic. *The Blue Light* (1976), directed by Iris Gusner, and *Bearskin* (1986), directed by Walter Beck, depict the ways young men are mistreated by kings after they have served their countries in war. The discharged soldiers seek their revenge by making pacts with demonic characters, but learn that friendship, kindness, and generosity are more important than revenge and money. Other characters also come to realize that greed for material wealth can turn them into

FIGURE 6.1 The tricked king leads his wife back to the palace, *How to Marry a King* (1969).

callous people. For example, in *Rumpelstiltskin* (1960), directed by Christoph Engel, the king who only thinks about gold spun into straw by the miller's daughter realizes that his newborn son is more important to him than all the money in the world.

The lessons in the DEFA fairy-tale films are not overly preachy. They arise almost magically and often comically from the stories themselves that the screenwriters and directors have retold and altered in innovative ways. With nearly no graphic violence, the films also include an implicit message that any human being is capable of changing for the better. All these positive ideological values, however, are tempered by kitsch aesthetics and stereotypical characterization. Some films also lack humor and the zest for joy, more apparent in the Czech fairy-tale films. Even still, it is difficult to generalize about the DEFA films because they evolved considerably over time, were created by different directors, and were often responding to political censorship in subversive ways.

Commenting on the rise and fall of DEFA in East Germany from 1946 to 1989, Detlef Kannapin has written:

> It is doubtless the case that DEFA did not follow a monolithic aesthetic formula. It is also beyond question that the contents of DEFA films set new standards in the German cinema landscape both with their tradition of antifascist films and with the tendency to observe attentively the lives of the lower and middle strata of society. DEFA productions were also of great substance as logistical and technical undertakings. But in terms of film aesthetics I can see no specific studio style in evidence. That is, unless one tries to paste together a make-shift DEFA aesthetic out of such traits as the use in conventional films of dream sequences

in the style of poetic realism, or the wordiness of rather many DEFA works, or pathos in film—which surely is inadvisable. On the other hand, it should be objectively stated that the aesthetic innovations in the 1960s were hardly able to carry over in the films of the 70s and 80s.

(2002, 16–17)

While Kannapin's remarks are true—there was no governing DEFA aesthetic—all the films in the former East Germany were subject to great scrutiny and censorship, and the filmmakers were obliged to abide by principles laid down by the state and Communist party. These entailed an adherence to anti-fascism, social realism, positive depiction of workers and farmers (that is, the common people as heroes), a socialist appropriation of German history and culture, and basic support of current political policies without any criticism.

The Return to Conservatism: The Commercialized Fairy-Tale Film in Unified Germany, 1989 to the Present

The strong political and moral adaptation of fairy tales for the cinema in East Germany had to end with the reunification of Germany. Whether this type of experimentation with the Grimms' tales for the cinema will ever return remains to be seen. However, reunification allowed all the East German DEFA, Czech, and Russian fairy-tale films to be marketed in the west. As Sebastian Heiduschke points out:

> [B]y transforming the films from intangible products into commodity items that could be purchased and owned by individuals, [the distribution company] Icestorm established DEFA as a unique German brand name, allowing former GDR citizens to claim them as part of their identities. Initially, the company selected titles for release based on the input from previous customers to determine the most successful DEFA film genres in the GDR and therefore the most promising products for commercialization on home video. Thus the first wave of VHS releases saw fairy-tale films such as Wolfgang Staudte's *Die Geschichte vom kleinen Muck* (*The Story of Little Mook*, 1953) that had enchanted children and adults alike in the GDR and now targeted parents who wanted their children to grow up with these movies from their childhood.
>
> (2013, 65)

Most are live-action films, although numerous excellent animated fairy-tale films were also created in Eastern Europe from 1945 to 1990.[11]

What is interesting today is that, while DEFA sought to demonstrate how the Grimms' tales were part and parcel of a German socialist heritage, the films as DVDs circulate in a reunified capitalist Germany and must compete with other German series of fairy-tale films that are ideologically closer in keeping with patriarchal and capitalist ideals. For instance, Greenlight Media introduced the animated series *SimsalaGrimm* in 1999 and produced 52 episodes up until 2010, based largely on the Grimms' tales and several tales from Hauff, Andersen, and Joseph Jacobs. The format of each 25-minute episode calls for two charming characters, zany mischief-maker Yo Yo and the more serious and studious Doc Cro, to become involved in a revised tale geared primarily toward amusing audiences. The major function of these figures is to provide comic relief as they intervene to help the good characters.

For the most part, the directors of these skits have simplified the tales to provide commercially digestible amusement for children between the ages of four and ten. Shows like *SimsalaGrimm* fail to question the ideology of the original Grimm texts in order to address political conflicts as the DEFA films always did. The focus tends to be on Yo Yo and Doc Cro, rather than on exploring the Grimms' tales in any critical or creative depth. For this reason, despite the good reception of *SimsalaGrimm* by young viewers, two important societies, the Europäische Märchengesellschaft and the Märchen-Stiftung Walter Kahn, along with numerous independent storytellers, educators, and film critics, initiated a controversial debate in 2000 about the denigration of the Grimms' legacy that continues up to the present day. According to Daniel Drascek, the critics of *SimsalaGrimm* (and also other fairy-tale TV series) accuse its producers of falsifying the folklore tradition of the Brothers Grimm, commercializing the tales irresponsibly, and harming the imagination of children by visualizing tales that were created to be told by oral storytellers (2001, 79–89).

Diverse opinions represented in the book *Märchen—Kinder—Medien* (Fairy Tales—Children—Media), edited by Kurt Franz and Walter Kahn (2000), reveal how critics are seriously concerned about the Grimms' legacy of folktales and fairy tales and how differently they assess filmic adaptations. Some, such as Christoph Schmitt, Joachim Giera, and Lutz Röhrich, suggest that the questionable or so-called inauthentic fairy-tale films keep the Grimms' tradition alive—that it will remain resilient no matter how it is interpreted or transformed. Despite, or perhaps because of, the critical reception, the *SimsalaGrimm* series continues to enjoy popular success; it is well funded, widely disseminated internationally, and accompanied by toys, puzzles, coloring books, games, and other merchandise. Its success has spawned two live-action fairy-tale series for television, *Märchen-perlen* (2005) and *Sechs auf einen Streich* (2008). Both are modernized interpretations of the Grimms' tales intended for children and families. They are shown primarily on Sunday afternoons and around Christmas. Thus far, the 20+ adaptations draw large audiences, in spite of their uneven quality. As a result, thorny problems in the Grimms' tales are avoided, showing a return to the harmonious "un-fairy-tale-like" aesthetics and contents of fairy-tale films that originated at the beginning of the twentieth century. While the producers of the series tend to draw contemporary meanings from these tales and at the same time preserve their supposed original messages in high-quality productions, it is clear that the films are bound by the demands and ideologies of German television codes and prescriptions.

It seems as though the popular success of these conventional made-for-TV fairy-tale films has discouraged filmmakers from producing innovative films for the cinema. Aside from co-productions, there have been relatively few feature-length fairy-tale films produced by German companies in the last 25 years. Two are noteworthy for their high kitsch quality: *7 Dwarfs—Men Alone in the Woods* (7 Zwerge—Männer allein im Wald 2004) and the sequel *7 Dwarfs—The Woods Are Not Enough* (7 Zwerge—Der Wald ist nicht genug 2006), two live-action films with great box-office success, both directed by Sven Unterwaldt. These comedies are loosely based on the Grimms' "Snow White" and depict the absurd adventures of seven men named Brummboss, Sunny, Cloudy, Tschakko, Cookie, Bubi, and Speedy, who have decided to live deep in a forest without women because they have all had mishaps with the female sex. Indeed, they are all misfits, and when Red Riding Hood and Snow White wander into the forest, the blundering men are at first flustered but eventually save the latter from the evil queen. In the sequel, they rescue her once again, this time from Rumpelstiltskin.

Both films are insipid; the gags are infantile and offensive; the slapstick acting is worse than that of the Three Stooges; the pandering director simply wants to feed unthinking audiences accustomed to trivial fun more junk food to go along with their popcorn. Although these two films have been successful in Germany, they were not dubbed or subtitled for distribution elsewhere. Yet the German producers believed that if they made a computer-animated 3D version in German and English, they would obtain the success they desired on the international market. Consequently, *The Seventh Dwarf* (Der siebte Zwerg) appeared in late September 2014, to a mixed reception in

Germany because it dumbed down what was already a dumb interpretation of the seven dwarfs to attract family audiences worldwide. In this film, the youngest dwarf named Bubi makes a foolish mistake and causes a wicked ice fairy named Dellamorta to freeze a beautiful princess named Rose, along with everyone in the Castle Fantabularasa. But the dwarfs manage to escape and eventually find the young cook's assistant, Jack, who kisses and saves the frozen sleeping princess. Aside from some cute gags and clever special effects, this film repeats conservative Disney messages along with recognizable stereotypes and a conventionally boring plot.

Although *The Fairy Tale about the Princess, Who Absolutely Wanted to Appear in a Fairy Tale* (Das Märchen von der Prinzessin, die unbedingt in einem Märchen vorkommen wollte 2013) is also trivial, it offers a good example of the typical filmic adaptations of sentimental literary fairy tales published for young readers in contemporary Germany. This story concerns a charming princess named Clara, who can never do anything in a proper fashion.[12] Consequently, she is always mocked by her older cynical sister and criticized by her finicky father. Set in the nineteenth century and filmed in a medieval castle and forest in southern Tirol, the film shows Clara already in a fairy-tale world, but she ironically wants to be like a princess in a fairy tale to be happy. She discovers a book of Grimms' fairy tales and then tries to act out several stories in her world. Though in comic incidents she bumbles her chances to be a proper fairy-tale princess, she eventually finds a prince who accepts her as she is. Together with the court jester, a horse, wolf, and some frogs, they set out into the wide world to find happiness. Intended for young audiences, the film wants to be as cute as the princess. It is well-crafted but harkens back to the silent fairy-tale films of the early twentieth century by treating the fairy tale as if it must always end happily—even though the original story by Susanne Straßer challenges the notion of conventional fairy-tale plots. In this respect the film avoids taking itself or its source seriously.

Three other twenty-first century films, Christoph Hochhäusler's *In This Very Moment* (Milch-wald 2003), Doris Dörrie's *The Fisherman and his Wife* (Der Fischer und seine Frau 2005), and Marco Kreuzpaintner's *Krabat* (2008) should be taken much more seriously. In a clear reference to the Grimms' "Hansel and Gretel," Hochhäusler's bleak but brilliant film concerns the accidental abandonment of two children, Lea and Konstantin, and parents' incapacity in our post-industrialist world to provide the young with the nurture and care they need. The plot is simple and straight-forward: young Sylvia has become a stepmother by marrying an older widower named Joseph, who has two children, Lea and Konstantin (Konsti). They are clearly well-to-do and have recently moved into a suburban house in the midst of renovations in the former East Germany, which itself is in need of renovation. Everything is white, sterile, and unfinished inside the house; Sylvia has not adjusted to the house or to mothering the two stepchildren who resent her. The house's undergo-ing renovations combined with the unprepared young wife who has married a rich professional can easily be interpreted as an allegory of contemporary East Germany after the fall of the wall in 1989. The young stepmother is not up to the task of raising these children. In the film's establishing sequence, she picks them up from school and drives them to do some shopping in Poland, where it is cheaper than in Germany. However, she has an argument with Lea and temporarily abandons both children on the road to the shopping center. The children wander into a forest and become lost and eventually are taken to a Polish city by a worker who delivers cleaning fluid to different hotels in the region. At first he wants a reward for finding them, but he eventually abandons them on a highway because they cause him so much trouble.

There is no happy ending, for the family has degenerated and cannot hold itself together in an apathetic world. The children are left to their own devices because anxiety and alienation cannot create bonds of support for the young. The film reflects how misunderstanding is the way people communicate—whether in the former East Germany or Poland—and certainly the language and cultural misunderstandings contribute to the conflicts concerning the children. Silence, alienation, and repression are also contributing factors to the family's dilemma. Evidently, the children are not willfully abandoned in this film, but they have been psychologically forsaken. Though they head for home at the end, it is questionable whether they can find home in a world replete with lies and miscommunication.

Such is Hochhäusler's pessimistic comment on fairy-tale happiness. Dörrie is much more optimistic even if she is somewhat one-dimensional and reactionary with *The Fisherman and his Wife*. She argues for a simple anti-capitalist life while reacting to the feminist movement by presenting women as weak and more drawn to glamour and money than men. Her film is a comedy based on the Grimms' dialect tale, "The Fisherman and his Wife." It begins in Japan where a young German fish veterinarian, Otto, meets a lovely young fashion designer, Ida, who is on vacation in Japan. They fall in love and marry almost immediately. When they return to Germany, they live in a shabby caravan where Otto makes a living curing and dealing in exotic fish. Ida designs unusual scarves and dresses. As they begin to prosper, Ida insists on moving to more comfortable and luxurious places—an apartment, a condominium, a huge mansion with servants—and she also changes her looks to become more stylish and fashionable. Her ambition leads to marital strife and separation until Ida and Otto lose all their money and wealth. Most of the blame is placed on Ida, as with the fisherman's wife in the Grimms' tale. Gradually, she realizes how much happier she was with Otto when they were living in a caravan and struggling. Consequently, she returns to him in a grand, sentimental gesture of reconciliation.

The film is framed by two animated talking fish, Otto's pets, who comment on his relationship with Ida. They appear to be humans living under a curse who will be released from the spell if Otto and Ida stay together three years. Ironically, they are then transformed into frogs; supposedly this is Dörrie's lighthearted joke about the Grimms' tale and fairy-tale expectations. But it is not a joke to depict a young contemporary woman punished because she is too ambitious while her tender young husband tries to preserve the integrity of their marriage. While not as banal as the "Snow White" filmic adaptations, Dörrie's film is a superficial interpretation of the Grimms' tale with a stereotypical Hollywood touch.

In contrast, Kreuzpaintner's *Krabat* is a more thoughtful interpretation of Otfried Preußler's important fairy-tale novel of the same name. Some background information supports the significance of this filmic adaptation. Preußler's novel has deep roots in a Sorbian legend about a mysterious magician, Colonel Schadowitz of Särchen. It can be traced back to the sixteenth century in a region that borders on Germany, Czechoslovakia, and Poland. By the beginning of the twentieth century, the legend had been transformed into a hybrid fairy tale concerning a poor young man apprenticed to a demonic sorcerer, who works with black magic in a mysterious place. The apprentice must surpass the magical knowledge and skill of the sorcerer and use it to free himself, as well as his companions (if there are any). The most famous adaptation consists of novels written by Jurij Brězan, *Krabat oder Die Verwandlung der Welt* (Krabat or the Transformation of the World, 1976) and *Krabat oder Die Bewahrung der Welt* (Krabat or The Preservation of the World, 1993). The most significant reworking for young adult readers is Anthea Bell's translation of Preußler's novel into English in 1972, *The Satanic Mill*. It was adapted for the cinema (as *Krabat* or *The Sorcerer's Apprentice*) in 1978 by the brilliant Czech animator Karel Zeman.

Kreuzpaintner's stark realistic film follows Preußler's novel closely and covers the three years of Kabat's adolescence narrated at times by a voiceover, an older Krabat, who reflects about the trauma of his youth. Krabat, a fourteen-year-old Sorbian/Wendian orphan, whose parents died from a great plague, travels about begging in the countryside of Lusatia with other young men. He dreams about black ravens that lure him to the Black Mill, where he becomes apprenticed to the tyrannical Master, a sorcerer of black arts, who promises to teach Krabat magic and compensate him for his hard work at a mill that resembles a dungeon. Krabat agrees, and meets eleven other apprentices who are all afraid to tell him about the slave-like conditions. At the end of several months, Krabat learns enough magic from the Master's Koraltor, the black book, to change himself into a raven. He also befriends the head apprentice, Tonda, on whom he can depend. During Easter in a nearby village, Krabat hears the singer Kantorka, and is enchanted by her voice. Tonda warns him never to reveal her name because he had once loved a maiden from the village, and she had been mysteriously killed. Toward the end of the year on New Year's Eve, Tonda himself is also mysteriously murdered.

The following year, Krabat befriends a youngster named Juro. Once again Krabat is drawn to the maiden Kantorka and performs astral projection to be in her presence in the village. He almost commits a grave error, but Juro saves him so that the sorcerer does not notice anything. When New Year's Eve arrives, another apprentice is mysteriously killed, and it becomes clear that the Master is the murderer. In the third year, Krabat cannot get Kantorka out of his mind and constantly dreams about her. He uses magic to contact her, and since she, too, has dreams about him, they meet and declare their love for one another. However, Juro realizes that Krabat is ill-equipped in the art of magic and as a result is endangering Kantorka's life, as well as his own. So Juro, who has secretly committed all the sorcerer's magic knowledge to memory, begins to teach Krabat. To protect Kantorka, Krabat decides to break contact with her and arranges a meeting with her to inform her that, if she loves him, she should come to the mill on New Year's Eve and ask for his freedom. At the same time she is forced to identify him among the other apprentices when she is blindfolded. She agrees, and when Krabat returns to the mill, it is clear that the sorcerer plans to kill him. When Kantorka comes to the mill that evening and demands Krabat's freedom, the master blindfolds her and leads her to the apprentices. To his dismay, she identifies Krabat because of her love for him; this means the sorcerer must die at midnight when the mill is to be destroyed by flames. Meanwhile, Krabat leaves with Kantorka and the apprentices, who celebrate their freedom (see Figure 6.2).

A good part of this story was filmed in the rugged countryside of Romania, and it develops into a chronicle of the times, the Thirty Years War, 1618–48, that makes the shapeshifting and magic appear credible. Magic is part of seventeenth-century quotidian life. Magic is knowledge that equals power, and the narrator tells the story matter-of-factly. He reports succinctly and bluntly because he seeks to grasp and depict the reality of poor abused apprentices during a period of war when they are at the mercy of not only the sorcerer but also the prince and an anonymous character

FIGURE 6.2 Krabat and friends after freedom gazing at the burning satanic mill, Kreuzpaintner's *Krabat* (2008).

who makes money from the apprentices' work at the mill. The film's entire atmosphere and lighting are gloomy, the opposite of spectacular American or lighthearted German fairy-tale films. The mill in which Krabat and the apprentices work is depicted as a prison or concentration camp. The work is drudgery. The village nearby is impoverished. The landscape is withered. Kreuzpaintner draws parallels with the Nazi era—the Master is a ruthless dictator—and of course, parallels can be drawn with other historical figures and periods. Kreuzpaintner's fairy-tale film significantly breaks with a tradition of happy endings. The narrator remarks that he and the apprentices felt after all that happened that they could determine their own futures without magic, for they had gained freedom. Then they are pictured trudging into a forlorn wilderness. They move on with bitter hope.

Of course, in the real contemporary Germany and in its film industry, hope is not bitter, but it is also not all that bright; contemporary German filmmakers (with the exception of Hochhäusler and Kreuzpaintner) have not produced remarkable fairy-tale films for the cinema. For the most part, they have returned to their earlier twentieth-century tradition of making "un-fairy-tale-like" films that seek to remain faithful to the Brothers Grimm. Though the Grimms' tales have been adapted and tweaked to appeal to family audiences and some contemporary issues, the TV and DVD fairy-tale films are brimful of faithful adaptations to the Grimms' texts that can be soaked up by viewers on Sunday afternoons and over the Christmas holidays. Hope for a different approach to fairy-tale film, it would seem, can only come from beyond the borders of the Germany of the Brothers Grimm.

Notes

1 Interestingly, the Grimms never thought of their collection as purely German, which was one of the reasons they never called their collection *German* children's and household tales. By the time the last edition was published in 1857, the footnotes, written primarily by Wilhelm Grimm, demonstrated that the collection was basically European, and Wilhelm included many sources and citations from European tales (see Wardetzky 2014).
2 The German title for "Sleeping Beauty" is "Dornröschen" or "Briar Rose," which I use here.
3 For an excellent, comprehensive account of this period, see Jörg (1994).
4 See Endler (2006, 227–41). In addition, for a useful account of the Nazi regulation of animated films see Giesen and Storm (2012).
5 For an insightful study of this period, see Schlesinger (2010).
6 For more information, see Zipes (1982).
7 Cf. Langfeldt (1940); Gong (1947); Boettger (1948); Lenartz (1948); and Petzet (1947).
8 See Steinitz (1951).
9 Cf. Bennung (1975, 292), and Bastian (1981, 225).
10 See König, Wiedemann, and Wolf (1998).
11 For a full discussion of these films, see "Between Slave Language and Utopian Optimism: Neglected Fairy-Tale Films of Central and Eastern Europe" (Zipes 2011, 321–48). See also the excellent comprehensive study written by Qinna Shen (2015).
12 The film is based on Susanne Straßer's *Das Märchen von der Prinzessin, die unbedingt in einem Märchen vorkommen wollte* (2010). Some of her delightful illustrations run through the film. There have been numerous filmic adaptations of fairy-tale books by such authors as Janosch, Preußler, and Christine Nöstlinger.

7

FAIRY-TALE FILMS IN ITALY

Cristina Bacchilega

Pinocchio—one of only four feature films produced and distributed in Italy in 1911—was the first screen adaptation of Carlo Collodi's 1883 fairy-tale novel that Walt Disney's animation would subsequently bring to a global audience's attention in 1940. Directed by Giulio Antamoro, *Pinocchio* stands out among Italian silent black-and-white films of the era—from *The Taking of Rome* (La presa di Roma 1905), *Last Days of Pompeii* (Gli ultimi giorni di Pompei 1908), and *Romeo and Juliet* (Romeo e Giulietta 1908) to *Dante's Inferno* (Inferno 1911), *Cabiria* (1914), *Maciste* (1915), and *Gerusalem Delivered* (Gerusalemme Liberata 1918)—that were characterized by a focus on epic history, high literature, or mythological prowess.

Fairy tale and fantasy are not key words in the best-known or authoritative histories of Italian film. This is due in part to the scarce attention that film critics and theorists globally have paid to films that adapt or evoke fairy tales, as Jack Zipes observes (2011). But also taking into account historical and culture-specific reasons better contextualizes a discussion of fairy-tale films in Italy.

First, in the Italian silent-film era, many feature films relied "upon recognized literary or operatic classics," which "fulfilled two functions: this use of canonical works provided familiar plots to Italian audiences and helped to elevate the cinema above the fairground associations that accompanied its first decade of life" (Bondanella 2009, 6), when "itinerant cinema" (*cinema ambulante*) was presented as popular country-fair entertainment. Second, with historical epic and costume drama as the most popular silent-film genres at home and for export, the scope of literary adaptation at this time of most exuberant Italian filmic production was apparently unparalleled in other filmic traditions.[1] A great many Italian films in the 1905–1920 period drew on "the newly forged (or emerging) Italian library, an ideal library in which poetic, narrative and theatrical classics were mixed in with feuilletons, abridged libretti, and biographies of famous men" (Brunetta 2003, 30). Their grandiose retellings of Homer, Dante Alighieri, Shakespeare, Alexandre Dumas, and Gabriele d'Annunzio served to consolidate a sense of Italian modernity and culture strongly rooted visually in the Renaissance and ideologically in nationalism.

Third, regardless of its early and plentiful production, Italian cinema's reputation with the public as well as critics rests overall on post-World War II neorealism and auteur films. Discussing Italian cinema almost automatically means referring to Roberto Rossellini's *Rome, Open City* (1945), Vittorio De Sica's *The Bicycle Thief* (1948), or Luchino Visconti's *The Earth Trembles* (1948) as foundational and pointing to how neorealism's legacy informs subsequent significant Italian films. Based on anti-Hollywood aesthetics, filmic neorealism centered on foregrounding its documentary function and anti-fascist activism.[2] The critically consistent positioning of "neorealism as the ethical and aesthetic centre of Italian cinema" has resulted, on the one hand, in a strong scholarly focus on Italian film as "mirror" of the nation and, on the other hand, in Italian film studies' categorical dismissal of genre films and their popularity (see O'Leary and O'Rawe 2011). While Peter Bondanella (2009) works to undo this ideological and aesthetic hegemony of neorealism, his discussion of genre films foregrounds the Italian *peplum* or "sword and sandal epic," horror, comedy or *commedia all'italiana*, spaghetti western, the Italian thriller (*giallo*), and political or detective film (*poliziesco*)—genres operating primarily in a mimetic tradition of storytelling. Starting in the 1970s, it became increasingly clear that Italian-style comedy as well as *gialli* and *polizieschi* intervened in contemporary debates (about divorce and terrorism, for instance) and were deployed as social critique during especially difficult times. But fantasy remained politically suspicious.[3]

Fourth, after the first couple of decades, Italian film production declined in Italy, and with few exceptions the post-World War II market has been dominated by Hollywood.[4] With the development of new audiences between 1950 and 1975, filmmaking in Italy boomed, but statistics on moviegoers (e.g. 350 million before the war and 800 million in 1955, Sorlin 1995) must be understood in the context of import-export ratios. For instance, during the 1951–1955 period, when some 200 films were made in Italy every year, approximately 220 overall were exported to the USA, while over 1,000 Hollywood films were shown in Italy (Bondanella 2009, 66). By the end of the 1970s, Italian cinema faced yet another economic crisis, as television became increasingly competitive and influential directors like De Sica, Pier Paolo Pasolini, and Visconti were no longer active. Since then, movie-ticket sales have gone up, but non-Italian films continue to earn more than two thirds of total revenues; the most popular films are American ones with expensive special effects (Bondanella 2009, 497–98); and in the first decade of the twenty-first century the ratio of imports to domestic releases has consistently been 2–3 to 1 (Holdaway 2012, 279). The Walt Disney Company Italia S.r.I was founded as Creazioni Walt Disney S.A.I in 1938, the same year in which *Snow White and the Seven Dwarfs* was released in Italy. Consequently, Disney's animated films, television channels, comics, and other merchandise have been part of Italian children's fairy-tale experiences for generations.

What is the place of fairy-tale film, then, within Italy's cinematic production and reception? Many, scholars and viewers alike, might say it doesn't have one, but such a verdict depends implicitly on the tendency to associate Italian film with traditions of high culture, celebration of patriotic ideals, and predominantly mimetic conventions. As with any other hegemony, this image of Italian cinema is built on the dismissal of other possible narratives, and a focus on fairy-tale films may begin to tell a different tale about Italian cinema's history, nationalism, consumption, and poetics—a minority tale, but one that delineates distinctive features of this national fairy-tale film tradition and also contributes to a more multifaceted understanding of cinema in Italy.

In what follows, I discuss Italian films which fit varied definitions of "fairy-tale film," whether they adapt fairy tales for the screen, invoke wonder and fairy-tale symbolism to disturb mimetic narrative styles, or elicit hope by making the impossible possible for those who suffer social injustices (Greenhill and Matrix 2010). And I map how these films have been an integral, if not highly acclaimed, part of Italian cinema all along, inhabiting a complex relationship with the nation as imagined community, playing out their tropes in a range of genre mixes, and contending with a highbrow disdain for entertainment that appeals to women and children as audiences.

Pinocchio's Makeovers

Published by Carlo Lorenzini, under the pseudonym of Carlo Collodi, in the early 1880s, barely a decade after the unification of Italy as a nation, *The Adventures of Pinocchio. The Tale of a Puppet* (Le avventure di Pinocchio. Storia di un burattino) begins tongue-in-cheek with the narrator announcing that "once upon a time" there was not a king, as children reading it may have expected, but "a piece of wood" (Collodi 2002, 3).[5] This log's transformations into puppet, rascal, makeshift watchdog, elementary-school pupil, donkey, worker, and finally child were meant to delight and instruct Italian children as well as to educate and satirize the newly formed nation where corruption, ignorance, and poverty were proving to be great challenges. A tale about how to become citizens of a respectable nation (see Stewart-Steinberg 2007) that deploys the local language, traditions, and customs of Collodi's Tuscany, *Pinocchio* is also about the human in relation to the animal world and the land; an individual's liminal state in an "eat-or-be-eaten" world; and childhood, as the puppet-child's struggle to balance obedience and independence is resolved only when he becomes the model son ready to take on adult responsibilities. While Pinocchio's curiosity and innocence have charmed audiences all over the world, Collodi's *Bildungsroman* is rooted in specific Italian debates concerning parental and government expectations of what children should and should not do that resulted in late-nineteenth-century education and labor laws.[6] As lower elementary education was first legally required in 1877, Collodi's novel illustrated "in dramatic terms the dangers of not going to school" (Ipsen 2006, 14), which included laboring for itinerant entertainers, going to prison as a child vagabond, and being sold to work in foreign factories. In its fantastic exploration of socialization and the "human disposition . . . to transform the world and make it more adaptable to human needs, while we try to change and make ourselves fit for the world" (Zipes 2012, 2), Collodi's *The Adventures of Pinocchio* turned out to be a fairy tale with global appeal, as well as strong roots in Italy's national growing pains.

By the time Antamoro, under the pseudonym Conte Gant, first adapted Collodi's novel for the screen, it had already experienced several makeovers at the hands of illustrators—including Attilio Mussino also in 1911—and writers of sequels and spinoffs such as *Lucignolo, l'amico di Pinocchio* (Lamp-Wick, Pinocchio's Friend 1900, see De Berti [2004] and Marchese [1983]) and *Le strabilianti avventure di Pinocchio poliziotto* (The Astonishing Adventures of Pinocchio Policeman 1910, see De Berti [2004] and Marchese [1983]).[7] That Collodi's novel had already been translated into English and was well known in Italy to children and adults of all social backgrounds made it prime cinematic material. In contrast to the grandiose costume-drama or epic cinematic adaptations of the time, Antamoro's *Pinocchio* built on the *commedia dell'arte* and the *féerie*, Italian homegrown roots of cinematography, as well as on the early Lumière cinematic tradition of making a magic spectacle of the everyday. In doing so, the film offered an adventure-filled and somewhat melodramatic comedy that took full advantage of the children's novel's popularity as well as of that of comic actor Ferdinand Guillaume, known as Polidor.[8]

Antamoro's *Pinocchio* was more an adventure story and a slapstick comedy than a fairy tale, but some of its transformations identify hotspots in the novel that later adapters continued to contend with. The very first scene sets the stage for the film's reliance on the famous comic's antics as well as the director's amplification of Geppetto's and Pinocchio's relationship. In this paratextual preamble, Polidor appears on a theatrical stage, and following not his first but his second somersault—a gesture to how new the magic of film must have felt—he turns into Pinocchio, thanks to one of George Méliès's first technical innovations, the stop-motion trick. As Pinocchio, Polidor then brings forth Geppetto, and the two mime their son–father affectionate relationship. When they retire behind the curtain, Polidor invites the audience to follow them, and an inter-title introduces the storyworld and Pinocchio's "birth" as Geppetto carves him out of a large piece of wood. We see, first, that the film's magic has less to do with Pinocchio's transformations in the story than with cinematography itself, Polidor's transformation from actor to character, and the audience's suspension of disbelief as the adult actor impersonates both puppet and child. Thanks to this lack of verisimilitude as well as to the presence of the Fairy, Antamoro's comic film retains a fairy-tale-like quality. Second, the film is framed as a theatrical performance, where inter-titles guide viewers from one episode to the next—all the more important to viewers who know Collodi because the order of Pinocchio's adventures differs from the novel. And third, from his inception, Pinocchio—just as in Collodi's novel—acts mischievously with his father, and in a chase scene that other films will restage, wreaks havoc in the village, but with no malice. He continues to get himself into trouble, but there is no emphasis on the talking cricket or the didacticism that characterize Walt Disney's *Pinocchio*. Antamoro's film instead privileges the adventurous, Jack-like aspect of the character and tale to the point of adding a rather long, completely new episode.

In chapter 23 of the novel, a talking pigeon reassures Pinocchio that Geppetto is alive and in search of him: "now he's got it into his mind to search for you in the far-off lands of the New World" (Collodi 2002, 108). This is Collodi's only mention of the New World, but of course Italians' emigration to the Americas would bring major social change in the next few years. In the 1911 film, Pinocchio swims across the ocean to flee from prison, is swallowed by a whale (in whose belly he is reunited with Geppetto), and eventually some Native Americans attack the whale and capture father and son. Impressed that Pinocchio is made of wood, the Native Americans decide to make him their new chief, but also prepare to roast and eat his ordinary father. It is at this point, rather than in the Disneyfied escape from the sea monster's belly, that Pinocchio's newly found sense of responsibility towards his father shines: he uses his authority to order that Geppetto be released and then, having escaped himself, he enlists Canadian soldiers to defeat the "savage" Native Americans. Following the battle, the Canadians fire a cannon, and Pinocchio flies home to Geppetto riding the cannonball. This is not the film's end, but it is much more dramatic a scene than Pinocchio's final transformation into a boy, marked visually by his bourgeois clothes and surroundings rather than by action. This episode in North America is filled with stereotypical tropes from other mass-culture genres, like the western and fantastic-travel fiction. But was Antamoro also extrapolating from the novel's fairy-tale symbolism and its rootedness in the contemporary social problems in Italy, when he added an episode that suggests how emigrating Italian youth needed to support aging parents and return home? The film, like the fairy-tale novel, couched its moral and social message in comedy and fantasy.

Mostly shot in the open, Antamoro's *Pinocchio* is filled with village-life and countryside scenes that depict Italian people and farmlands in the early twentieth century. Within this world, as in Collodi's novel, a child's imagination and independent action bring havoc, even danger, to others as well as to himself, but in the city—represented by Playland and symbolic of modernity—the puppet-child or human-in-progress is most threatened. Also featuring many sequences shot outdoors, Luigi Comencini's *The Adventures of Pinocchio* (Le Avventure di Pinocchio 1972) sought to portray a turn-of-the-twentieth-century Tuscan peasant and village culture that in 1972 could only be the product of nostalgic reconstruction. Three other factors contextualize a reading, however brief, of Comencini's adaptation: Walt Disney's animated feature film, *Pinocchio*, had since 1940 not only monopolized the image of Collodi's puppet, but also Americanized his character and quest (Zipes 1996); Italian cinema of the time had to contend not only with American imports, but television; and the 1960s were marked by youth movements and social unrest in Europe and the USA, with the 1970s leading only to increased economic and political crisis in Italy.

In stark contrast to Disney's Technicolor classic animation film that won an Academy Award for the hopeful song "When You Wish Upon a Star," Comencini's *The Adventures of Pinocchio* has a much humbler profile. First produced as a mini-series for Italian television, it begins with the arrival of a wagon in a hill village during a cold and dark winter, and with Fox and Cat's announcement that, before leaving for the faraway Americas, Fire Eater is bringing his "famous" puppet show to the villagers. These are clearly hardworking people who lead harsh lives; among them Geppetto, the poorer of two carpenters, is presented as particularly destitute and frugal. In his one-room dwelling, we see a detail that Collodi thus described in the novel: "a fireplace with the fire burning, but the fire was painted, and near the fire there was painted a pot that boiled cheerfully and sent forth a cloud of steam that looked just like real steam" (Collodi 2002, 11). Deep sepia tones dominate both outdoor and indoor scenes. The walnut log that has yet to become Pinocchio speaks, just as in the novel, and his first words suggest his vulnerable naïvety and playful potential: to Master Cherry, the well-off carpenter who starts to saw and hammer at "him" to make a table leg, the sentient log says "Don't hurt me" and "You are tickling me!"

When Geppetto takes the log and carves himself a puppet so as to feel less lonely, the newly named Pinocchio does not speak, but mischievously moves his painted eyes and pointy limbs to shock and hit his "father." Comencini effectively combined a somewhat surreal animation à la Jan Švankmajer with live action, featuring beloved Italian celebrities Nino Manfredi (Geppetto) and Gina Lollobrigida (the Fairy), slapstick comics Ciccio Ingrassia and Franco Franchi (Fox and Cat), and cinematic icon Vittorio De Sica (the Judge) as well as the child actor, Andrea Balestri (Pinocchio). The very next day after his "birth" as a puppet, Pinocchio materializes in the flesh thanks to the magic of the Fairy, the spirit of Geppetto's dead wife, who wants to fulfill his wish for a real child. She demands that Pinocchio be an obedient child, go to school, work hard, and support his father—or else she will turn him back into a puppet.

The Fairy's conditional magic is key to this film's thematic and visual power. In the course of his adventures, in addition to being fully transformed into a donkey in Playland and then made to work in the circus, Pinocchio the child reverts to being a puppet three times. The child's clothes may suggest his progress in the world—he goes from wearing a brown-sack tunic and running barefoot, to donning the flower-print paper suit Geppetto makes him, to sporting a well-made school uniform and shoes when he is at his best behavior with the Fairy. However, Pinocchio's never-ending hunger and lack of control over his bodily transformations are clear signs of his ongoing liminality. In contrast to the novel, where the puppet transforms into a real child only after holding two jobs to support ailing Geppetto and also studying in the evening for five months, Pinocchio in Comencini's film keeps going back and forth between independence and conformity, reforming himself and then transgressing several times over—until the puppet and his father are reunited in the sea monster's belly, and Geppetto pleads with the Fairy to put a stop to this carrot-and-stick pedagogy and calls her a witch.

As a result of parental negotiation rather than Pinocchio's maturity, the puppet becomes lifeless and Geppetto gains a real child. Zipes comments, "Pinocchio as a self-indulged boy remains spoiled and the apple of his father's eye. There is something about this indulgence that has nothing to do with boyhood in nineteenth-century Italy but more to do with late-twentieth-century attitudes towards boys, especially in Italy" (2012, 311). While I agree that the father–son dyad is privileged in Italian culture and cinematic representations of family (Günsberg 2005), I would complicate this judgment. First, Comencini's Pinocchio is goodhearted but weak, more than spoiled; and second, once he accepts Pinocchio as flawed and thus human, Geppetto is capable of learning from his son's zest for life and hope, enabling them both to leave the sea monster's belly that the old man had experienced as a refuge, and return to life in the world.[9]

Comencini's *The Adventures of Pinocchio* ends with father and son making it safely to shore on Tuna's back (see Figure 7.1) and with Geppetto running after Pinocchio on the beach. The child shouts that he is hungry and hopes someone will feed them. He has the final word, "Don't be afraid. I am here now!" Neither child nor adult has gained that bourgeois state of wellbeing in Collodi's ending and Antamoro's film. The fairy-tale quest for home as "a utopian struggle to know oneself and what it takes to move forward to a just society" (Zipes 2011, 285) finds no resolution in this *Bildungsroman interruptus*, a bittersweet 1970s commentary on Italians and Italy as a nation. The director spoke of Collodi's novel as a tale expressive of peasant culture ("un storia contadina") that, as I see it, the film nostalgically evokes but also affectionately critiques for its

FIGURE 7.1 Geppetto and Pinocchio riding the Tuna to shore, *The Adventures of Pinocchio* (1972).

proverbial conservatism and lack of social action. Much effort in the storyworld is spent on making Pinocchio conform and behave properly, while nothing is really done about institutional corruption, exploitation of workers, and poverty. That Pinocchio spends so much time on the move is a double-edged sign: movement is necessary for social change, but running towards a more just future can be confused with running away from one's problems. Some 60 years after Antamoro's *Pinocchio*, emigration to the distant Americas is clearly demythologized by Comencini as a solution to Italy's economic crisis, but there is no suggestion of a political alternative to corruption and injustice, other than an indulgence of youthful rebellion and a sentimental retreat to patriarchal, homosocial family romance.

Other Italian filmic adaptations of Collodi's fairy-tale novel range from Giannetto Guardone's film, which closely followed the novel's plot and even reproduced some of its illustrations (1947), to Alberto Sironi's film for TV that included Carlo Collodi as a character (2008). But I focus here only on one more live-action film, *Pinocchio* (2002), directed by Roberto Benigni who also starred as the puppet-child. While Benigni's *Life Is Beautiful* (La vita è bella 1997) won three Academy Awards in 1999, including best actor in a leading role, *Pinocchio* received mixed reviews in Italy and was a dismal failure in the USA, where it won the Razzle Award in 2003 for Benigni as worst actor. Accompanied by great fanfare, this *Pinocchio* cost 45 million euros—making it the most expensive Italian production to date—but thanks to its constellation of merchandise, massive distribution by Medusa, and Berlusconi's television advertising, the film generated some 20 million euros during opening week alone (Manai 2009, 155). How does it retell Collodi's novel and its fairy-tale core?

The makeover in this case is visually dazzling and an homage, especially in the vivid Playland scenes, to the Italian director Federico Fellini, who, the year he died, had been discussing with Benigni a *Pinocchio* remake. Because Benigni's is also filled with references to other *Pinocchio* films, it gains from being read intertextually rather than simply as an eccentric one-man show.

Like Comencini's, Benigni's *Pinocchio* begins with a vehicle entering a dark village, but it is a fairy-tale carriage pulled by myriad white mice, driven by the aging Medoro who holds on to his childhood and stuffed animals, and transporting the Blue Fairy (Nicoletta Braschi, Benigni's partner in life and on screen). Once the carriage stops, the two engage in a philosophical conversation about death, life, and beauty that is occasioned by the appearance of a blue and clearly mechanical butterfly. As the Fairy brings more light to their surroundings and the carriage leaves, the camera follows the butterfly into the village, no longer deserted but filled with people in motion. With both the mice and the butterfly as unmistakably artificial "special effects," this preamble sets the tone for the mix of fantasy and realism that the film sustains throughout.

The framing device (along with the magically driven carriage) also recalls the complex and glittery fairy tales by the French *conteuses* of the late seventeenth and early eighteenth centuries, which Collodi had translated into Italian shortly before writing his own fairy-tale novel. Finally, this narrative framing of the puppet's adventures gestures back to Antamoro's film, which had been restored in the 1990s. While these are not the only Italian adaptations in which an adult plays the puppet-child, once Benigni comes onto the scene as Pinocchio, links between his and Polidor's slapstick are strong.[10] And, as in Comencini's film, not only the setting, but the actors' language is emphatically Tuscan, something completely lost in the English dubbed version.

Follow the fantastic butterfly, ephemeral avatar of transformation, and meet the unpromising hero. In the midst of a crowded lane, a log falls off a cart; it rolls and rolls bringing trouble wherever it goes, until it knocks on Geppetto's door. This incipit is one plot change that Benigni's film makes, emphasizing the reciprocal choosing of son and father, as the carpenter greets the log with pleasure and immediately thinks of making himself a puppet that will support him in his old age. A few other significant changes demonstrate how Benigni's film adapts Collodi.

First, though the talking cricket appears more than in the novel, the significance of school and work as ethical foundations and character-building experiences is toned down. School is more for socialization—bullying and prejudice characterize Pinocchio's experiences there; and work becomes not so much a site for redemption as exploitation. In one of the final scenes between Geppetto (Carlo Giuffrè) and Pinocchio, the puppet is exhausted from all-day physical labor, but Geppetto, now accustomed to his support, urges him to stay awake and weave baskets for sale. The irony is palpable, especially since the Fairy then comes to transform Pinocchio into a real boy but, immediately after, leaves him for good and tells Medoro, somewhat nostalgically, that Pinocchio had been such a lovely puppet.

Second, in contrast to the disturbing aspect of Pinocchio and Geppetto's symbiotic rapport, the friendship that Pinocchio develops with Lampwick (Kim Rossi Stuart) assumes a more positive valence. They first meet in prison, where neither deserves to be, and they share a lollipop of "the best kind" in Lampwick's judgment, tangerine flavor. When Lampwick, the unrepentant rascal, is missing at the party the Fairy organizes to celebrate the puppet's progress in school, even she approves that Pinocchio goes looking for his friend. This homosocial relation rests on reciprocity, and while doomed, it is celebrated in Benigni's film: just before Lampwick—who has been overworked as a donkey by the same farmer who hired Pinocchio—dies, his friend shares the best-kind lollipop with him.

Third, while the novel's puppet is adamant about not wanting to go to school or to work, he is not petulant and shrill the way Benigni's Pinocchio is; even compared to Comencini's child actor, Benigni as Pinocchio cries a lot and uses language manipulatively to ingratiate himself with the

Fairy. This change results in a less naïve and more trickster-like Pinocchio and also in an infantilization of the character that is at odds with the actor's size and age, and especially impacts the protagonist's relationship to the Fairy, the only significant woman figure in his life.

Fourth, the Fairy's power is at odds with Collodi's didacticism. Braschi's diaphanous beauty and dress make her a supernatural presence, at times enchanting and at others Madonna-like. But though she delivers Pinocchio's final transformation, she seems from the first frame to the last incapable of believing that it really matters, that Pinocchio's life will be better. She is a melancholic, even disenchanted Fairy. If Benigni's film offers a comic representation of Italian masculinity, then, maternal women are idealized for indulging infantile, needy men who eventually grow up when they accept life in a homosocial exploitative world. Whether the film ideologically deplores this sad state of being, or celebrates the momentary indulgence of Pinocchio as symbol of escape, is hard to tell in a film so openly narcissistic. In the final scene, Pinocchio, the real boy, enters the school building, but his puppet-looking shadow goes chasing after the butterfly, and the camera settles on the beautiful Tuscan hills in a tourist-brochure-like shot. Benigni's interpretation of Collodi's novel, though faithful as far as retaining the plot's full episode arc, is also symptomatic of a disturbing self-indulgence that inescapably extends beyond the protagonist's representation.

These three *Pinocchio* adaptations as fairy-tale films confirm that Collodi's marvelous puppet-child and his transformations continue to hold the Italian imagination, but also show that the novel's ambition to sustain the making of a modern nation was, on screen, however affectionately, discredited as comedic, contradictory, or unfulfilled fantasy. These films speak to Italians and of Italy, but not for Italy as an imagined community. They also show both an emotional attachment to this iconic character and an investment in fairy-tale symbolism's roots in the struggles of the precarious everyday rather than in the expectation of an unequivocal happy ending. If the magic of *Pinocchio* still has cultural capital as specifically Italian, these films tell us it is to be found in zest for life and trickster inventiveness rather than lasting transformation; local rather than national culture; male-centered nostalgia for unchallenged patriarchy or an amused giving in to it; disillusion with promises of justice and corruption-free institutions; and most of all commitment to a tradition of artful filmic illusion in realistic settings.

Animation and Fairy Tales for All, Children and Adults

Such artful illusion often instigates fairy-tale suspension of disbelief in animated films, but their production in Italy is quite small. The stakes are high since, while animation is not for children only, Disney has definitely dominated the Italian children's cinema market. I discuss different examples of fairy-tale animation in Italy to highlight their high quality as well as their distinctiveness in response to, and in the context of, global fairy-tale Disneyfication.

The first Italian color feature, *The Singing Princess* (La rosa di Bagdad 1949), was also the country's first animated feature film. It premiered at the Festival of Venice in 1949, did quite well at the box office, and was released in English in 1952 with seventeen-year-old Julie Andrews lending her voice to Princess Zeila. Directed by Anton Gino Domeneghini, this remarkable film is clearly influenced by Disney—Princess Zeila's grace and singing voice are reminiscent of Snow White's, and the three bumbling old sages are lookalikes of the well-meaning dwarves—but also by *The Thief of Bagdad* (1940) in its characterization of Jafar, the villain Sheikh, and of Zeila's father, caliph Omar III. The simple story is beautifully told through animation and voiceover.

"Once upon a time" when the happy, hardworking people of Baghdad were ruled by the good, naïve Omar, messengers were sent out to invite the princes of the lands flanking the river Tigris as the time had come for Princess Zeila to choose her suitor. But aided by his magician Burk, whose cape enables him to fly, the power-hungry Jafar is the only suitor to arrive and ask for the princess

FIGURE 7.2 Disenchantment: the three Sages, turned into babies, start to age, *The Singing Princess* (1949).

in marriage. A struggle ensues between the villains and young Amin, a generous and talented musician who is Zeila's teacher and friend, aided by his brave magpie Kalinà. In this moral struggle, magic plays a major role: when Zeila wears Jafar's enchanted ring she believes she loves him; Burk kidnaps Amin and, to ensure that nobody will recognize him, transforms him into a Moor (*moretto*); and Amin cuts off some of Burk's magic cape to fly away. In a more parodic mode, thanks to Burk's powers, the three old sages are entreated by a Black beauty to drink from the spring of youth, which they do so enthusiastically as to become babies.

Eventually, Fatima—a beggar who benefited from Amin's generosity and reveals herself as a supernatural being similar to Pinocchio's fairy or *fata*—gives Amin "Aladdin's magic lamp," and its genie becomes not Amin's servant but his strategist. Thanks to the genie's advice, Amin defeats the evil magician, and all the harmful transformations he had caused are undone (see Figure 7.2). Fair-skinned once more, Amin returns to Zeila, and by playing his flute charms Jafar and his large Black thug to dance right into the river where they meet their demise. This scene echoes the queen's punishment in the Grimms' "Snow White" tale, but rather than gruesome, it is lightheart-edly magical thanks to the genie's orchestration of it and Riccardo Pick Mangiagalli's music. When Zeila calls Amin her "hero," it becomes clear to all that they are in love and should marry; great celebrations with fireworks ensue.

Financed at first by the fascist Ministry of Popular Culture, this film took over a decade to complete, requiring Domeneghini to seek personal loans, move his creative team during World War II to the northern Italian countryside to escape bombings, and take the film to London for its Technicolor processing. An admirer of early Walt Disney, Domeneghini emulated his visual style and animation techniques, and in *Silly Symphonies*-style relied heavily on music to enhance his film. However, Domeneghini was no mere Disney follower. By setting the story in Baghdad, Domeneghini was pursuing a long-standing creative interest in the orient and the *Arabian Nights*. Thanks to the talented illustrator Libico Maraja, who headed production design, sets are not only vibrant but painterly; Zeila sings not only while fantasizing about her Prince Charming, but in public events for her people, who applaud her soprano voice as if they were at the opera; and the love between Zeila and Amin is based on their long-term friendship and shared passion for music. Like the presence of operatic performance, other details point to a specific cultural framework for the film: when Amin's mother is told that his marriage to Zeila will elevate her socially as well, she responds, "a mother is more than a queen," reinforcing Italian *mammismo*; and the film's overall disparaging representation of Blacks or Moors is symptomatic of the recent fascist colonial ventures in North Africa. Disney's techniques are thus deployed to support and enhance Domeneghini's Italian vision of animation and magic in *The Singing Princess*.

Also inspired by opera, as well as fairy tales and Italian folklore (especially the irreverent Pulcinella, stock Neapolitan character from the *commedia dell'arte*), internationally acclaimed illustrator, painter, stage and set designer, and animator Emanuele Luzzati enjoyed a long artistic career that included animated TV commercials for Barilla pasta (1959) in *Carosello* (see Bacchilega and Rieder 2014) and Academy Award nominations for two of his animated shorts. With Giulio Gianini, Luzzati directed *The Magic Flute* (Flauto magico 1978), a delightful shortened adaptation for children of Wolfgang Amadeus Mozart's fairy-tale opera. Papageno is both the live narrator (Marcello Bartoli) and the comic character with whom the audience is invited to identify. In a kaleidoscopically colorful animated storyworld, human and monstrous silhouettes, surreal landscapes, and enchanting birds alternate with geometrical compositions to visually convey the magic and emotional vibrations of Mozart's arias. Simpler and Chagall-like are the drawings in Gianini and Luzzati's *Pulcinella* [Punch] *and the Magic Fish* (Pulcinella e il pesce magico 1981), a lighthearted retelling of the "Fisherman and His Wife," in which the escalation and subsequent crumbling of their wishes turn out to be part of a dream the hapless Pulcinella had while fishing for their dinner. Luzzati's art—which continues to educate and entertain children, as seen in a recent DVD that groups several of his fairy-tale shorts as part of a Propp-like game for children only—also galvanized other talented Italian animators such as Pino Zac, whose delightful adaptation of Italo Calvino's fairy-tale novel, *The Nonexistent Knight* (Il cavaliere inesistente 1959), innovatively mixed live action and animation in 1969; Bruno Bozzetto, whose *Allegro non troppo* (1976) parodied Disney's *Fantasia*; and Enzo D'Alò.

In *Pinocchio* (2012), director D'Alò explicitly posed his animated film in answer to Disney's corruption of a work many perceive as quintessentially Italian. D'Alò's film also dialogues with other Italian adaptations of Collodi, including the 1972 feature-length cartoon directed by Giuliano Cenci, which pictured a Pinocchio modeled on Attilio Mussini's illustrations and an adult, motherly Blue Fairy in medieval-looking garb; popular comic actor and songwriter Renato Rascel provided voiceover narration and sang some of the songs.[11] Concentrating on the loving and playful relationship between Geppetto and Pinocchio, D'Alò's film is dedicated to his father and all dads in the world ("al mio babbo e a tutti i babbi babbini del mondo"), with "babbini" as a Collodi-derived endearing diminutive of "babbi" (daddies) that somewhat infantilizes the parent in its assonance with "bambini" (children).

D'Alò's opening scene in muted grey tones shows a very young Geppetto flying his bird-shaped kite that eventually escapes his hold, and wishing he could fly like it. As the titles announce Pinocchio's story, bright colors and magic flood the screen. The same kite flies purposefully into the window of a small cottage where Geppetto, now an old and lonely man, is first rudely awoken by the noise and then delighted to embrace the kite and the memories it brings back. In the havoc that the wind and kite wreak, a log of wood falls from the carpenter's shelf and cries out first in pain and then in child-like laughter. Intrigued by the log's potential and wishing to end his loneliness, Geppetto immediately starts to carve a puppet. But the exuberant Pinocchio runs away the moment he is finished, and Geppetto must chase after him. The film follows the usual developmental narrative, but accentuates reciprocity in the father-son relationship and parallels the puppet's transformation into a "real boy" with Geppetto's becoming happier and more playful. The film's final scene shows the two dancing, singing, then running outside to play in a vibrantly sunlit Tuscan landscape.

Gone is any didacticism, as D'Alò suggests there is a Pinocchio in each of us, and embracing him will make us more human. Pinocchio errs—he is taken in by the Fox and Cat, gets drunk at the inn with them, and goes to Playland, a psychedelic funhouse kept running by children-turned-donkeys in the underground workhouse—but also earns Geppetto's and the Blue Fairy's affection. This child-like puppet never works, but runs, plays, eats, and dreams. He lies about a tummy ache the very first day he is supposed to go to school, but shows his good heart by offering to sacrifice his life to save Arlecchino, the dog Alidoro, and his father. Rather than being educated and disciplined, his task is to figure out who his true friends are; tongue-in-cheek, he refers to the Fairy, who is his age, as his girlfriend. Pinocchio's joie de vivre remains unfettered throughout and proves contagious in the end as Geppetto appears rejuvenated and the final song invites viewers to identify with Pinocchio's humor and imagination. "I am Pinocchio" ("Sono Pinocchio"), sings Lucio Dalla, beloved Italian songwriter and musician who died unexpectedly after completing the film's upbeat and captivating musical score, which—inspired by Rossini's opera *Cinderella*—includes waltz, clarinet solos, and jazzy melodies.[12] While D'Alò does not eschew Collodi's darker elements, presenting for instance the Fairy's death as part of Pinocchio's nightmare, the film as a whole is characterized by its verve, as the whimsical episode with the Green Fisherman (dubbed by Dalla) dipping Pinocchio into flour to fry him with his other fish confirms.

First conceived in 2000 but shelved because of Benigni's forthcoming film, D'Alò's *Pinocchio* relies on classic 2D and 3D animation that, in contrast to Disney's sharp focus on characters, immerses Pinocchio—whose features are more rounded than in any other cartoon—into the unrealistically swirly hills of a recognizably Tuscan backdrop (masterfully designed by Lorenzo Mattotti) and, in turn, immerses viewers into the dreamlike, worry-free atmosphere of his picaresque adventures. Playful sounds, a festive color palette, and the drawings' organic lines all contribute to conveying the experience of Pinocchio's and Geppetto's easy-going life and loving relationship. If Pinocchio's fairy tale is symptomatic of an Italian mindset, D'Alò presents escapist optimism, especially unabashed in the face of high unemployment rates and a lack of opportunities for youth in twenty-first-century Italy. It also offers a radically new image of Geppetto as dreamer and Pinocchio's playmate, and an enchantingly immersive visual fairy-tale experience that, like Domeneghini's and Luzzati's animation, provides a stylistic alternative to Disney's classic and computer-animated models, but cannot compete with them at the box office.[13]

Fairy-Tale Tropes and Genre Mixing

How do live-action Italian films that evoke fairy tales and address general audiences contend with the codes of realism? While titles clearly indicate that adapting individual tales is part of the Italian tradition, few films present themselves as fairy tale, preferring different genres. *A Modern Cinderella* (Cenerentola 1913) documents silent-film production and modernity; *Sleeping Beauty* (La bella addormentata 1942) tells of seduction and trauma in a small Sicilian town, ending with its female protagonist's death; a horror and psychological thriller filmed in English, *Bluebeard* (1972) features Richard Burton as a rich German baron with a Nazi past, fixated on his dead mother; *Snow White & Co.* (Biancaneve & Co. 1982) is soft-porn comedy; and Roberto Cimini's *Red Riding Hood* (2003) is a black comedy set in Rome where a young girl and her "imaginary" wolfish friend go on killing rampages that she sees as serving justice. This consistent turning away from magic and wonder in live-action films whose titles declare their fairy-tale associations is striking in comparison to French and American film histories. I see this trend as, on the one hand, participating in the extensive production of genre films that has historically undergirded the acclaimed high-culture cinematic traditions in Italy and, on the other hand, symptomatic of an avoidance of the fairy tale for fear of limiting one's audience to children in an already small market.

As in recent American fairy-tale films, fairy-tale tropes and themes in Italian genre films are most often adapted to produce comedy and horror, and only rarely do they effectively harness the fairy tale's potential for social critique or psychological depth to achieve high-quality cinematic artistry. A comedic sequel to the traditional tale, *Princess Cinderella* (Cenerentola e il signor Bonaventura 1941) is filled with irony and the grotesque, and written and directed by satirist Sergio Tofano. Cinderella's stepsisters conspire to have her kicked out of the palace, leaving Prince Charming desolate. Signor Bonaventura (played by Paolo Stoppa), Tofano's comic-strip character in the children's serial publication *il Corriere dei Piccoli* who is famous for his "misadventures" (*disavventure*), is the unlikely hero. After meeting many challenges—including two ogres, one vegetarian, the other carnivorous—with the help of his hapless friends and a fairy, he returns Cinderella to the royal court. Like the text for Tofano's comics, the dialog is in rhyming verse.

Fantasy and horror film *Suspiria* (1977) tells of a young American dancer in a prestigious German ballet school: she witnesses murders, drinks magic potions, and eventually destroys the witches who secretly control the school. Director Dario Argento and cinematographer Luciano Tovoli explicitly linked the highly charged atmosphere, music, and color palette of this internationally successful cult film to German expressionism, fairy-tale magic, and psychoanalysis. Tovoli studied Disney's *Snow White and the Seven Dwarfs* (1937) for color and chose Technicolor, the expensive technology that Hollywood had just discontinued, to convey the symbolism of female initiation and the unconscious (Bondanella 2009, 324).

Otherwise, on the whole, fairy-tale fantasy is suspect in Italian film, unless it is cast as romance that targets women in particular and models gender relations that may run counter to Hollywood but are nevertheless conservative, if not sexist. Extremely popular at the Italian box office were *Bread, Love, and Dreams* (Pane, amore e fantasia 1953) and *Scandal in Sorrento* (Pane, amore e . . . 1955), "Cinderella" tales that greatly contributed to rival divas Gina Lollobrigida's and Sophia Loren's celebrity while offering, in the style of a romance-centered or "rosy" neorealism, a placebo to the public in the face of stark socio-economic inequalities in post-World War II Italy. In *More than a Miracle* (C'era una volta 1967)—directed by Francesco Rosi and featuring Mario Piccioni's captivating musical score—a beautiful and spirited Neapolitan peasant-scullery maid (Sophia Loren) competes with seven princesses in a dishwashing contest to marry an arrogant but good-hearted Spanish prince (Omar Sharif). Lamberto Bava's predictable films for television (e.g. *The Dragon Ring* [1994] and *The Princess and the Pauper* [1997]) are tales of mistaken identity, sibling rivalry, sorcerers, and dragons, and they foreground the princess's marriage plot in enchanted medieval-like kingdoms. Shot in Val Borbera, Italy, and initially released in Scandinavia, *The Italian Key* (2011) is a multinational production directed by Indie filmmaker Rosa Karo, a modern-day feel-good romance featuring a girl who did not at first believe in fairy tales. There is to date no Italian fairy-tale romance film substantially indebted to feminism, not even the second-wave gender-politics of *Ever After: A Cinderella Story* (1998).[14]

More intriguing and memorable in the Italian tradition are high-production-value films shot in mimetic genre traditions that, somewhat jarringly, demand their viewers' suspension of disbelief. This combination, which also pertains to live-action *Pinocchios*, has powerful and mixed effects in films that fictionalize historical events and communities. For instance, the fairy-tale tropes (princess, prince on a white horse, and evil monster) and feel of Benigni's Oscar-winning Holocaust film,

Life Is Beautiful (1997), gave rise to controversy. The initial voiceover announces a simple tale, filled with wonder, joy, and sorrow. When the voiceover returns at the end, the audience realizes it is the protagonist's son speaking as an adult survivor of the concentration camp where much of the action was set; thus, the story of their imprisonment as Italian Jews and of the father's fantastic tales to shield his son from realizing the horrors around them is centered around a child's experience. For some, the film's fairy-tale aspects work because they symbolize childlike innocence and encourage hope in the face of unspeakable evils. However, for others, by deploying make believe as its key survival strategy and by presenting the child not as indicting witness of social horror but as spectator of a one-man improvisation show, *Life Is Beautiful* infantilizes its audiences and gratuitously confirms "the life-affirming, democratic and humanitarian values of post-war Italians" (Lichtner 2012, 197). Considering the complex real-life uses that children themselves made of fairy tales to survive the Holocaust (Haase 1998), the one-on-one emotional equivalence of fairy tale and innocence and the positing of fairy tale as dream (see Bullaro 2003) are also problematic.

Blending realism and wonder was not new to Italian film, and De Sica's *Miracle in Milan* (Miracolo a Milano 1951) is a prime example of magical realism *ante litteram*. Having shifted away from his earlier neorealism, De Sica relies on the supernatural—a wish-granting dove that the protagonist's dead mother brings him—to provide a community evicted from its shantytown with escape from the police. In the movie's final scene, as they fly on broomsticks into the faraway clouds, the escape is shown to be both utopian and illusory. The representation of the rich developers and of the protagonist's naïve romance is just as powerful as the unsentimental wish-granting scenes, which recall the greed and waste in "The Fisherman and His Wife" tale. Overall the film's fairy-tale elements show that a good heart and individual wish fulfillment are no substitute for organized class struggle, while at the same time suggesting that creativity and optimism also play a part in transforming social relations; *Miracle in Milan* is provocative and magical, but the balance between hard facts and fantasy remains up in the air.

Pasolini's 1974 *The Flower of the Arabian Nights* (Il fiore delle mille e una notte), also known as *Arabian Nights*, provides a different and more poetic mix of the mundane and supernatural. Shot in Eritrea, Iran, Nepal, and Yemen, it features markets, deserts, gardens, and palaces in scenes that flirt with orientalist imagery, but refrain from the more common cinematic tropes of magic carpet, larger-than-life genie, and evil woman. Rather than centering on the adventures of a popular *Arabian Nights* hero (e.g. *Ali Baba and the Sacred Crown* [1962] and *Ali Baba and the Seven Saracens* [1964]), the film samples some of the collection's less known "flowers," interlocking tales where love, sex, false identities, and betrayal lead to varied outcomes. The frame tale of the naïve Nûr al-Dîn and the beautiful trickster, Zumurrud—adapted primarily from "Alî Shâr and Zumurrud"—surrounds stories including "The Adventures of the Poet Abû Nuwâs," "The Porter and the Three Ladies," "Tâj al-Mulûk and Dunyâ," and "Aziz and Aziza." While in some cases love brings sorrow and death, in the frame tale the two young lovers happily find each other again in a different city where Zumurrud, disguised as a man, has been made king. While the last lines are Nûr al-Dîn's, "The beginning was bitter but the end is sweet," the film's epigraph from the *Arabian Nights* reads, "The truth is to be found not in one dream, but in many dreams," and the tales reward characters who do not interpret dreams at the expense of everyday experience.

Part of Pasolini's *Trilogy of Life*, following *The Decameron* (1971) and *The Canterbury Tales* (1972), this unique adaptation of the *Thousand and One Nights* celebrates uninhibited sexuality regardless of its orientation, "challenging notions of order, gender, [and] political hierarchy" (Lundell 2013, 122). With feminist writer Dacia Maraini collaborating on the script, this *Arabian Nights* presents smart, loving, and active heroines; and, rather than staged as heteronormative spectacle, male and female nudity is often accompanied by laughter and playfulness. Pasolini later disavowed the subversive and anti-hierarchical power of sexuality as having been coopted by consumer capitalism, but this film remains a beautiful homage to the wonders of laughter, sexuality, and storytelling in the everyday—albeit of exotic dream-like worlds.

Focusing on fairy-tale films shows they have had a significant part in cinematic production and reception in Italy, offering alternatives to the Disneyfication of *Pinocchio* and animation; adapting fairy-tale tropes to other film genres; and providing a sense of wonder with mixed effects in a tradition where neorealism, comedy, and thrillers are most acclaimed. It is also clear that the gender politics of fairy-tale films in Italy has largely been conservative if not regressive, and that the genre has received minimal attention, with the exception of Rosa Karo, by women directors. And, while the restorative powers of transformation in fairy tales have applied to the representation of family, class conflict, and trauma, its full potential has hardly been tapped. In such a context, *Chlorophyll From the Blue Sky* (Clorofilla dal cielo blu), drawn from Bianca Pitzorno's innovative novel for children, stands out as an animated ecological-fantasy film (1984). The plot centers on a baby plant from another planet and the transformations that caring for her bring about in a grumpy botanist, the children who unexpectedly come into his life, the Dahl-like "witches" who hate children and cats, and the super-polluted city of Milan.

Finally, it is notable that, beyond the adaptation of Collodi's *Pinocchio*, Italian films have not drawn on the homegrown oral and literary traditions of folk and fairy tale. As I write this chapter, the English-language film, *The Tale of Tales*, is in production. Starring Salma Hayek and Vincent Cassel, it is directed by award-winning Matteo Garrone, and adapts three tales from Giambattista Basile's seventeenth-century Neapolitan collection of fairy tales, *Lo cunto de li cunti* or *Pentamerone* (see Nancy Canepa's translation 2007). Famous for his political satire (*Gomorra* 2008; *Reality* 2012), Garrone has already offered spirited representations of contemporary Naples and is attracted to the combination of ordinary, grotesque, and magic in Basile's collection (Vivarelli 2014). Will he meet its cinematic challenge in a refreshing way?

Notes

1 Italy embraced the new industry and art: Bondanella estimates that "between the birth of the cinema in Italy and 1930, some 9,816 films of various lengths were made. Of these, some 1,500 have survived, among them only several hundred feature films" (2009, 3). In 1912 alone, more than 1,000 films were produced in Milan, Rome, and Turin; and by 1914, Italy was the third largest exporter of moving pictures in the world, with great success in the United States (Brunetta 2003).

2 As Millicent Marcus argued, neorealism was "the via maestra [the master road] of Italian film, . . . the point of departure for all serious cinematic post-war practice" (1986, xvii, her translation).

3 O'Leary and O'Rawe polemically conclude that, in Italian film studies, "realist cinema more broadly inherits the connotations of anti-fascist, democratic, critical and even civilized per se; all that is not realist is somewhat pernicious and *uncivilized*, *qualunquista* when not reactionary" (2011, 111).

4 Italian cinema faced its first crisis largely because of World War I, and in the early 1930s Italy was producing no more than ten films a year. In the 1937–1947 period, thanks to the Italian government's substantial support, national film production grew again and became competitive abroad, but by 1948 Hollywood had re-conquered two thirds of the market.

5 Pinocchio's story was first published serially between July 1881 and January 1883 in the *Giornale per i bambini*, appearing as a volume only in February 1883. Collodi had intended to end the story with Pinocchio's death by hanging in Chapter 15, but fan letters to the newspapers as well as the writer's precarious finances convinced him after a hiatus to revive Pinocchio and the publication. Over a few decades, the novel was translated into several European languages, and its multimedial adaptations continue to ensure Pinocchio's extraordinary popularity as a character.

6 According to Italy's first labor law (1886), "children under the age of 9 could not work in industrial factories, quarries, or mines. . . . A maximum workday of 8 hours was established for children between the age of 9 and 12. A second law, which covered both women and children, came in 1902. The minimum working age was raised to 12, and the building trade was added to those covered. . . . The maximum

workday was set at 11 hours for 12–15 year olds and 12 hours for women over 15" (Ipsen 2006, 97). Often orphans and abandoned children worked in the mines; labor laws did not account for the great many children working on farms, or performing as wandering child musicians—the kinds of child labor *Pinocchio* represents.

7 These publications show how *Pinocchio*'s cultural capital was quickly and serially exploited in mass culture, with the famous puppet appearing in travel and fantastic novels—such as the 1910 *Little Pinocchio at the North Pole* (Pinocchietto al Polo Nord) and the 1911 *Pinocchio on the Moon* (Pinocchio nella luna)—genres popularized by Emilio Salgari and Jules Verne respectively. The titles of these spinoffs are cited by De Berti (2004) and based on Pasquale Marchese's (1983) *Bibliografia pinocchiesca*.

8 Guillaume, who started his career in the circus, made several comic films with Antamoro; his wife, Lea Giunchi, partnered with him and played the Fairy in *Pinocchio*. Guillaume's appearance as a clown in *La dolce vita* was Federico Fellini's homage to the comic's talent and popularity in early film.

9 Notably, in all of these films, whether it is called a shark (as in Collodi's novel) or a whale, the sea monster looks whale-like. Antamoro's early film portrayal of a whale (*balena*) indicates that the associative power of Job's story with this Pinocchio episode was active well before Disney.

10 Perhaps the long tradition of live-action *Pinocchio* films in Italy and the memory of other adult actors cast as child-puppets contribute to the Italian public's readiness, compared to American reviewers' refusal, to suspend disbelief in Benigni's performance.

11 The animated film *Le Avventure di Pinocchio* directed by Umberto Spano in 1936, is now lost except for a few images.

12 Cenci's 1972 animated feature film also capitalized on a well-known celebrity at the time, comic actor and songwriter Renato Rascel who provided voiceover narration and songs.

13 D'Alò's most successful animated fantasy film, *La gabbianella e il gatto* (1998), had record sales with 1.5 million spectators and won several awards; *Pinocchio* (2012) grossed €1,259,000 in its first six months, while *Snow White and the Huntsman* made €8,850,000 in Italy in 2012.

14 This problem does not apply to Italian fairy-tale films only. Danielle Hipkins points to "the dominance of popular Italian contemporary films that insistently continue to suture Italian history and the male gaze, whilst female protagonists (often contested by two men in a typical Oedipal structure) remain firmly entrenched within the private sphere, and the critical acceptance of this tendency" (2008, 213).

8

THE FAIRY-TALE FILM IN SCANDINAVIA

Elisabeth Oxfeldt

In Scandinavian countries, the written fairy-tale tradition has endured since the nation-building years of the nineteenth century. Folktales were collected, literary fairy tales were penned by some of Scandinavia's most renowned authors, and in more recent years, children's fantasy literature, adapting folktale elements, has gained enormous popularity. In Norway, Peter Christen Asbjørnsen (1812–1885) and Jørgen Moe (1813–1882) collected and published folktales during the 1800s in the tradition of the Brothers Grimm, which are still widely distributed and read. Most children, for instance, are likely to receive a richly illustrated collection at the celebration of their baptism and will later read the tales in school, learning about their various subgenres. The trolls of the folktales have become a national symbol and favorite tourist souvenir.

In Denmark, Hans Christian Andersen (1805–1875) famously developed the genre of the literary fairy tale, and his works, too, serve as popular gifts for children, bedtime reading, and part of the school curriculum. Andersen's tales have also resulted in the establishment of a national icon and a tourist attraction in the form of a statue of the Little Mermaid, located at Copenhagen harbor. In Sweden, Selma Lagerlöf (1858–1940) used the fairy-tale genre to write Sweden's best-known geography series *The Wonderful Adventures of Nils* (Nils Holgerssons underbara resa genom Sverige 1906–1907)—about the boy Nils who is magically made tiny and ends up surveying all of Sweden from the back of a migrating goose. The image of Nils has also become a national icon and figures, for instance, on the Swedish 20-crown bill. In the second half of the twentieth century, Astrid Lindgren (1907–2002) developed several literary universes based on children's adventures and encounters with folktale figures. All of these are literary tales that are—to varying degrees— known in all the Scandinavian countries, and they are, not too surprisingly, often adapted into fairy-tale films.

Thus, in Scandinavian countries, the fairy-tale film is firmly grounded in particular "national" authorships.[1] In Denmark, the legacy of Andersen remains vibrant; in Norway, the fairy-tale collectors Asbjørnsen and Moe provide seemingly endless sources of inspiration for new adaptations; and in Sweden, the fairy-tale entertainment industry is strongly influenced by Lagerlöf and Lindgren. In addition, there is a strong Scandinavian tradition that combines Christmas and Christian customs with folklore elements, especially elves. This has resulted in an abundance of cultural and commercial Christmas fairy-tale adaptations for theater, film, and television. Successful tales often cross various media and in the process of doing so occasionally cross national boundaries within Scandinavia, as well.

One unique Scandinavian phenomenon is the televised "Christmas calendar" (*julekalender* or *adventskalender*). The concept originated in Sweden in the late 1950s (on radio) and in the early 1960s (on TV). In recent years, successful television calendars have been adapted as fairy-tale Christmas films. This phenomenon illustrates the way revisionists use isolated fairy-tale and folktale elements to interrogate contemporary social and environmental issues. In this chapter, I trace the fairy-tale traditions based on particular popular authorships and Christmas entertainment traditions in each of the three Scandinavian countries: Denmark, Norway, and Sweden.

Denmark

For more than a century, Hans Christian Andersen has been a great source of inspiration for Danish film. Denmark's first feature-length animated film was Svend Methling's *The Tinderbox* (Fyrtøjet 1946), an adaptation of Andersen's tale by the same title (Schepelern 2004, 5). Already in 1939, the Danish film director, Carl Theodor Dreyer, regarded Andersen's fairy tales as a national treasure trove and suggested that the Danes build an entire film industry to animate his tales. He was convinced that the Danes could outperform Walt Disney, who was considered a capable artisan, but no true artist:

> With Hans Christian Andersen's fairy tales we Danes possess one of the greatest literary archives in the world. We also possess a series of significant artists who draw and paint and who have the advantage over all other artists and painters because they originate from the same background and absorb the same spirit as Hans Christian Andersen did.
>
> (Dreyer 1964, 54)[2]

Three quarters of a century later, Andersen's fairy tales are constantly adapted worldwide, including Disney's *The Little Mermaid* (1989), arguably one of the most widely recognized animated films inspired by an Andersen tale. Nonetheless, the Danes continue to adapt Andersen's tales, too, and I shall discuss three significant filmmakers: Jørgen Lerdam, Mihail Badica, and Queen Margrethe II.

The Fairytaler *(2004) Hans Christian Andersen Series*

During the 200th anniversary of his birth in 2005, there was a revival of interest in Andersen and his works, as well as high aspirations that Danish Andersen productions would reach international audiences. Jørgen Lerdam directed *The Fairytaler* (Der var engang . . . 2004), which consisted of 30 animated films made for children's television and distributed on DVD in five different languages (Danish, Norwegian, Finnish, Swedish, and English). Aesthetically, the *Fairytaler* films appear to be more inspired by Japanese than American animation. The mermaids in *The Little Mermaid* (Den lille havfrue 2004), for instance, look more like Hello-Kitty figures than Disney's cross between ballerinas and Barbie dolls. With wide, heart-shaped faces and solid fish tails, they appear stylized, childlike, and asexual.

The Fairytaler films maintain a high level of fidelity in adapting Andersen's tales. They are, however, modified in three major ways. First, aimed at young children, they contain less violence and ambiguity than Andersen's texts. In *The Little Mermaid* (2004), for instance, the witch does not cut out the mermaid's tongue, but rather plucks it out. Also, the family is depicted as a safe haven in *The Ugly Duckling* (Den grimme ælling 2004) when the duck-turned-swan seeks and is reunited with his mother at the end of the film. Andersen's duckling, on the other hand, never seems to give her a second thought after he is adopted by swans. Second, Christian and neo-platonic ideals are replaced with welfare-state ideals pertaining to social equality. In *The Little Mermaid* (2004), the prince nearly drowns, not because of the storm per se, but because he is willing to sacrifice his own life and throw himself into the ocean in an attempt to save the life of an ordinary sailor. The life of royalty has no greater value than that of a commoner. The same point is made in *Clod Hans* (Klods-Hans 2004) where *The Fairytaler* adds the twist that Hans falls in love with the princess without realizing she is royalty. Third, the *Fairytaler* series strengthens the status of girls. Here, girls, too, may be heroines—and not just *suffering* ones. For instance, the child pointing out that the emperor is naked at the end of *The Emperor's New Clothes* (Kejserens nye klæder 2004), is a girl—breaking with a long tradition of assuming that Andersen's candid child is male.[3] *The Fairytaler* has had a relatively strong cultural impact, at least in the Scandinavian countries where it has been a part of children's programming on national TV stations.

Mihail Badica's Hans Christian Andersen Adaptations

Romanian-born Mihail Badica has made two puppet and clay animated films based on Andersen's tales, *The Tinderbox* (Fyrtøjet 1993) and *Clod Hans* (Klods Hans 1999).[4] Both films are extremely energetic, colorful, burlesque, and self-reflective—full of gags, vulgarities, physical humor, play, and medial experimentation. In addition, Badica's figures express themselves not only orally, but also through a subtle sign language. It is probably no accident that Badica's films are based on those of Andersen's tales which are most closely linked to folktales rather than literary fairy tales.[5] One might furthermore say that Badica sees through Andersen's art of refinement and reworks it within a folktale tradition.

Badica constantly experiments with his medium, using elaborate framing techniques to introduce his fairy-tale adaptations. *The Tinderbox* is introduced by a sequence of paper cuts, starting with Andersen's own paper cuts and slowly evolving into war scenes with soldiers made of silk paper.[6] The viewer is thus given an impression of the background of the main character, the soldier, and when Andersen's tale actually begins *in medias res*, the medium changes from paper cuts to three-dimensional puppets. *Clod Hans* is similarly placed within a double frame. An audience drawn in front of an outdoor theater comes to life as they evolve into three-dimensional puppets, waiting anxiously for a puppet show to begin. Here, Andersen is subtly referenced as the theater is decorated with Danish flags and the year 1855 (*Clod Hans*' year of publication). As the performance of the tale ends and Badica zooms out on the theater and the audience, Andersen's face is fleetingly superimposed upon that of the moon. Badica's productions are art films that are imbued with intertextual borrowing, fictional and medial layering, as well as romantic irony. Hence, Badica's works lend themselves to family audiences allowing both children and adults to enjoy different aspects of the films.

Royal Hans Christian Andersen Adaptations

While Badica's films show an interest in the folksy hero, those film adaptations inspired by Queen Margrethe II (henceforth, Queen Margrethe) focus on young, self-sacrificing girls confronted by threatening antagonistic queens. Queen Margrethe explains that these are tales that fascinated her when she was a child.[7] In the early 1990s, producer Jacob Jørgensen saw Queen Margrethe's decoupage art and suggested they collaborate on a film project. The result was *The Snow Queen* (Snedronningen 2000). Jørgensen and Queen Margrethe then decided to collaborate once more on *The Wild Swans* (De vilde svaner 2009), a film project for which Queen Margrethe not only provided the decoupage art, but also was in charge of costumes, scenography, and screenplay.

The Snow Queen (Snedronningen 2000) is a 30-minute, live-action made-for-television production. All live-action scenes are filmed with composited visuals (i.e. using a blue screen), with

FIGURE 8.1 Eliza and Fata Morgana, *The Wild Swans* (2009).

inserted digital backgrounds. The backgrounds consist of Queen Margrethe's decoupage art (also published in book form as an illustrated version of Andersen's tale [Snedronningen 2000]). Pictures are cut from old art catalogs, auction catalogs (e.g. Sotheby's), and other magazines featuring painterly and photographic images of old furniture, jewelry, flowers, nature, etc. The fragments are pieced together in imaginative ways, suggesting a refined fairy-tale-like dream universe through which the actors exist. Constantly rotated, they contribute to the creation of a fluid rather than a static theatrical story world, and there is always something intriguing for the eye to explore. The story is narrated in a voiceover by Queen Margrethe herself, with the actors presenting the scenes in pantomime. Overall, the film combines new technology with nostalgia for Denmark's national romantic Golden Age. The film was well received: film critic Kim Skotte, for instance, deems it a successful visual fairy tale, emphasizing Queen Margrethe's elegant and imaginative art as well as her pleasant narrating voice (Skotte 2000).

The Wild Swans (De vilde svaner 2009) is an even more elaborate film adaptation carried out in the same style (see Figure 8.1). This time, Queen Margrethe not only produced the decoupage art used in the film (again also published in book form as an illustrated version of Andersen's tale [De vilde svaner 2009]), but she is also, as indicated above, credited with costume design, scenography, and screenplay. In addition she figures in a frame-tale introduction and makes a cameo appearance as a grimy, old woman within the film's diegetic universe in one of its final scenes. This 60-minute digital-theater film combines voiceover (provided by renowned actress Ghita Nørby rather than Queen Margrethe) with dialogue (not just pantomime). Though clearly a national prestige production, it was a box office failure with only 4,000 tickets sold (Körner 2009). Most reviewers agreed that the most successful aspect of the film was the design consisting of the Queen's decoupage art. Those who disliked it were often critical of the performance style and further evaluated some episodes as too frightening for children, specifically the episode featuring the wicked stepmother queen transforming her eleven stepsons into swans, and the episode featuring their sister, Eliza, visiting a graveyard to fetch nettles while nocturnal ghouls feed on cadavers.

TV Christmas Calendars

There is no strong connection between the Andersen adaptations and the Danish TV Christmas calendars. Yet, as Gunhild Agger (2013) has pointed out, the very popular Danish Christmas calendar went through a mythic and cultural-historical turn in the mid-1990s. We may therefore regard contemporary Danish TV calendars as combining the traditions of the almanac, folklore (sometimes incorporating Christian traditions), myth, and cultural history.

As I mentioned above, the TV Christmas calendar concept originated in Sweden. In 1957 the Swedish Radio (SR) broadcast their first 24-episode Christmas calendar. Aired between December 1 and December 24, the program lasted five minutes each day. During each episode, an adult host and a group of children would discuss Christmas and Christmas traditions, sing Christmas songs, and open a door to reveal a surprise picture each day in a double-layer, printed cardboard Christmas calendar. Listeners were provided with a similar cardboard calendar. The concept was transferred to Swedish television (SVT) in 1960. Denmark's Radio (DR) reproduced the idea in 1962 and immediately paired the idea with educational programs about developing countries. The children could buy a cardboard calendar in their local bank and the revenue would support projects in developing countries. Norway's National Broadcast (NRK) finally adopted the concept in 1979. The TV calendar programs have developed over time, mainly from shorter to longer programs, from more episodic frame tales to continuous 24-episode storylines, and from puppet shows to live-action programs. Today they constitute prime time entertainment and are viewed not only by children, but by the entire family.

In Denmark, the Christmas calendar series changed its name in 1977 due to accusations of unfair competition. Other producers of printed Christmas cardboard calendars complained that DR used its monopoly to advertise for its own calendar, making it difficult to sell other calendars. The solution became DR's downplaying of the Christmas motifs and their foregrounding of the support for developing countries. DR renamed their programs and calendars "The Children's Calendar for Developing Countries" (*Børnenes U-landskalender*). The cardboard calendars featured images of children in various parts of the world rather than figures associated with Christmas, such as elves (*nisser*) (Mikkelsen 2014).

In 1986, however, the sanction was revoked, and that year DR featured what was to become an extremely popular new series: *Christmas at the Castle* (Jul på slottet 1986, with reruns in 1991, 1998, and 2013). When it first aired, *Christmas at the Castle*, a costume drama that was filmed at Rosenholm Castle over six months, was the most expensive calendar produced by Denmark's Radio (DR) to date. As Agger argues, *Christmas at the Castle* exemplifies a new trend, as it turns to tradition and cultural heritage, combining Danish history with a prince-and-princess romance as well as the folkloristic tale of a parallel—and intersecting—world of elves.

In this series, a king is tricked by an evil count (his advisor) into participating in a war that ruins him. As the drama begins, the count informs the king that at this point he can establish peace with his rival kingdom by paying them his weight in gold before Christmas. This leads to silly dieting and attempts at gold-making. Meanwhile, a mysterious hunter, Valentine, shows up and offers to work without compensation in the king's barn. Inside the castle's walls and in the attic, a small family of elves wakes up after a season of hibernation. Since the king's daughter, Princess Miamaja, believes in elves and leaves them food, they help and support her and her family.

By the middle of the series, an enemy baron shows up and threatens that, if the king cannot pay his weight in gold, he has to marry off Princess Miamaja to the unknown prince of the rival kingdom. Since this is a Christmas fairy-tale series, Christmas and winter, too, end up threatened. First, the king decides on a game of rhetoric. Since he has "until Christmas" to pay the enemy, he simply exercises his royal power and calls off Christmas—to the detriment of his subjects, the elves, and the members of the royal family themselves. At the same time, the youngest of the elves tries to make gold to help the king, but accidentally makes a concoction that turns winter into summer (since this is filmed on location, it becomes evident that it is filmed over several seasons). In the end, catastrophes on all levels are warded off. The king's lost riches are found and returned by the elves. Princess Miamaja and Prince Valentine get married after a few spats; winter returns as the elves undo their concoction; and everybody can celebrate Christmas at the Castle. It is worth noting that there are no religious motifs in this series, and that dialogue is based on a pastiche language, imitating older Danish, that is not easily accessible to children, but rather indicative of the series being general family entertainment. *Christmas at the Castle* has survived since 1986, not only through television syndication and on aftermarket VHS and DVD release, but also through theater adaptations and through the songs made for the series, which have been released on separate CDs, which continue to be popular. It is a good example of a contemporary Christmas fairy-tale TV series both because of its popularity and because of the way in which it combines Christmas, folklore, cultural history, and romance.

Norway

In Norway we find that the folktales collected by Asbjørnsen and Moe during the nineteenth century continue to be adapted, most notably by Ivo Caprino (1920–2001), Ola Solum (1943–1996), and Nils Gaup (1955–).

Ivo Caprino's Puppet Films

Film director and writer Ivo Caprino is best known for his stop-motion puppet films, which include his well-renowned feature-length film, *Pinchcliff Grand Prix* (Flåklypa Grand Prix 1975), Norway's most popular film of all time. Caprino also made a series of 15-minute shorts based on the folktales that Asbjørnsen and Moe collected and published in *Norwegian Folk Tales* (Norske folkeeventyr 1841–1844). These films, made in the 1950s and 1960s, include: *Little Frick and the Fiddle* (Veslefrikk med fela 1952), *The Ashlad and His Good Helpers* (Askeladden og de gode hjelperne 1961), *The Fox's Widow* (Reveenka 1962), *The Seventh Master of the House* (Sjuende far i huset 1966), and *The Ashlad and the Hungry Troll* (Gutten som kappåt med trollet 1967). Caprino intended to make a feature film about Asbjørnsen's travels around Norway collecting folktales. The frame tale was to be live action whereas the stop-motion puppet sequences were to be inserted to illustrate the collected folktales.[8] Funding was never secured for this project, but the short fairy-tale sequences enjoyed their own independent release. *Little Frick and the Fiddle*, for instance, is still charming as a purified, non-violent musical adaptation of the folktale. The story is narrated through a combination of voiceover, diegetic dialogue, and singing (in folksong style) against elaborate sets. In Caprino's film, the country policeman who has tried to get Little Frick executed is finally tied to a tree and forced to dance while Little Frick plays his magic fiddle. The policeman's arms and legs bounce up and down, and he nearly dies laughing, we are told. His fate is significantly less comical in Asbjørnsen and Moe's version where his enchanted dancing results in "big pieces of [the policeman's] back scraping off against the tree."[9]

Most recently, Caprino's puppet films were reissued in remastered versions in the four-disc DVD set, *Caprino's Wonderful World* (Caprinos eventyrlige verden 2005). This compilation also includes several of his other puppet films—most notably his Andersen and Thorbjørn Egner adaptations. On the occasion of Andersen's 150th anniversary, Caprino made *The Steadfast Tin Soldier* (Den standhaftige tinnsoldat 1955), which premiered at an Andersen celebration in Odense, Denmark. In addition, Caprino is also well known for his puppet film *Karius and Baktus* (Karius og Baktus

1954) based on Norwegian author Egner's story about two trolls living in little Jens' teeth, hoping Jens will supply them with lots of sugar, so they can build fancy homes with doors, windows, and balconies in his teeth. Jens finally learns to brush his teeth, and Karius and Baktus are flushed down the drain.

Ola Solum's The Polar Bear King

The first feature-length live-action adaptation of a Norwegian folktale was Ola Solum's *The Polar Bear King* (Kvitebjørn og kong Valemon 1991). It was an international endeavor aimed at an international market and produced by the newly established Northern Lights Film and Television Production (Northern Lights film og TVproduksjon A/S), comprised of five producers: two Norwegian, two Swedish, and one British. The Norwegian producer, Erik Borge, wrote the manuscript based on the folktale from Asbjørnsen and Moe's collections. This is a beast bridegroom tale in which King Valemon is turned into a bear after he refuses to marry a witch. The cast included Norwegian, Swedish, and German actors, with seventeen-year-old Norwegian Maria Bonnevie starring as the princess. The animatronic bear featured in the film was made in England, at Jim Henson's Creature Shop. The film was shot in Norway and Sweden, and it was recorded in both a Norwegian-language and an English-language version.

As an adaptation, *The Polar Bear King* turns Asbjørnsen and Moe's folktale into a sentimental fairy-tale romance with two creatures falling in love and having to overcome a series of obstacles before they can marry. The love story is constructed around a North–South binary that is absent from Asbjørnsen and Moe's version. In addition, the English voiceover engenders a less folksy and more bombastic tone, one perhaps associated with international fairy-tale films as a genre. Asbjørnsen and Moe's conversational "Well, then, once upon a time, as might be, there was a king"[10] is turned into an unequivocal: "Once upon a time" completed by a final ". . . and they lived happily ever after." Throughout the film, the voiceover explains the characters' motives and actions. While there is no direct mention of love in the folktale, the voiceover elaborates on the dilemma experienced by King Valemon once the witch has cast her spell: "No one can live without love, especially a prince under an evil spell." Transformed into a polar bear, he "turned to Winterland searching for someone who could love and understand a polar bear." Meanwhile the princess of the North longs for the blossoming apple trees of the South. The two meet, fall in love, and the princess insists on following the bear to the South: "She knew this was the place she had been searching for all her life."

In addition to introducing a North–South binary, the film adds the character of the Devil himself (played memorably by Helge Jordal), thus establishing an unambiguous plot device demarcating good versus evil. The witch claims to be Valemon's evil side and that together they will become the perfect human being. Yet, the Devil warns that "too much evil destroys evil." This principle allows the princess to trick all the evil trolls, witches, and devils who attend the decadent wedding feast. Sneaking into the witch's laboratory, the princess creates a concoction containing "a lot of evil" (although the laboratory scenes are not part of Asbjørnsen and Moe's tale, their inclusion results in dramatic special effects). The princess pours her "special brew" into every cup, except King Valemon's. The Devil—as the master of ceremonies—raises his cup for a toast: "We are gathered here tonight to marry good and evil. As long as good and evil exist side by side we maintain a reasonable balance. And there'll always be a need for us and our services." After everyone drinks they consequently combust. King Valemon and the princess marry and journey northward to visit her family.

The dichotomies around North vs. South and good vs. evil may be viewed as replacing the gender dichotomy upon which the original tale is constructed. In Asbjørnsen and Moe's version, the princess goes to live with King Valemon. In order to break the spell, she has to accept that he turns into a human at night without witnessing the transformation first-hand. On a journey home, her mother gives her a candle and urges her to light it and find out what her lover looks like. Although both kings—her father and King Valemon—explicitly warn her not to listen to the advice of her mother, the princess is unable to resist the temptation. King Valemon is utterly distraught when—with only one month of the seven-year spell remaining—he wakes to candle wax dripping upon his face and as punishment, must marry the witch. In bear form, he plans to set out for the witch's kingdom the very next morning; however, the princess throws herself on top of him, grabbing on to his fur. Here a tale of suffering, endurance, magic, and cunning begins. Together, they eventually find their way to the witch's castle, and King Valemon comes up with a method to kill the witch. In Asbjørnsen and Moe's version then, the moral is that a woman should heed the advice of patriarchs. When the princess finally succeeds, it is because she is good, generous, willing to endure suffering, and evidently has learned her lesson. In the film, however, gender roles are modernized; by (1) introducing the male devil as complementary to the evil female witch, (2) having the princess cross-dress and orchestrate the death of evil herself, and (3) changing maternal roles into something positive, the film presents more evenly balanced gender performances. Overall, *The Polar Bear King* is a visually impressive film that features beautiful landscapes, elaborate wedding feasts, and entertaining special effects tied to the making of the evil potion.

Ola Solum's Journey to the Christmas Star *(1976)*

Ola Solum directed the extremely popular *Journey to the Christmas Star* (Reisen til julestjernen 1976). This pastiche fairy-tale film is loosely based on Sverre Brandt's 1924 drama of the same name. The National Theatre in Oslo commissioned Brandt to create a Christmas drama that would rescue the theater from economic ruin; as it turned out, they could not have made a better decision. Staged every year, the play has been the most performed show at the theater (with more than 500 performances in total). In 1976, Ola Solum created a film adaptation, which has been similarly successful, and since 1996 NRK has aired it every Christmas Eve (Antunes 2013, 242). It has become an ingrained part of Norwegian Christmas traditions.

Solum's film is about a king, a queen, and their young daughter, Princess Golden Top (Gulltopp). As the family decorates for Christmas, Golden Top wants her parents to place the real, celestial Christmas star on top of the tree. Her mother explains that this cannot be done and gives her a golden heart on a chain. An evil count—the king's brother—lures Golden Top to venture into the forest at night in order to fetch the real star. She passes out in a storm and is found by a group of market entertainers who raise her as their own child, calling her Sonya. These entertainers also function as the story's narrators, with the film containing several play-within-a-play sequences. With Golden Top gone, the king curses the Christmas star, which subsequently extinguishes. A guilt-ridden queen goes out to find Golden Top, and she, too, disappears. Many years pass and the market performers arrive at the castle with Sonya, who is now a young woman. They stage a play before the king and his court, indicating in a manner reminiscent of Hamlet's play-within-a-play that they know about the evil count—who is also watching. The count and the king interrupt the play, and the artists are thrown out. Sonya, however, gains an opportunity to talk to the king about his grief. Unaware that she herself is Golden Top, she decides to go out into the forest and find the Christmas star so that everyone may once again find happiness.

On her quest, an old woman with magic powers helps Sonya. The old woman sells sheaves of grain (typically used to feed the birds in Norway at Christmas time), and Sonya agrees to pay her with the golden heart necklace. When the count finds out about her mission, he pursues her, but Sonya evades him with the help of little elves (*smånisser*) and Santa Claus himself. Santa Claus delivers the message that the Christmas star has been in the sky all along; one only has to wish strongly enough for it to shine. Sonya wishes passionately, and sure enough, it begins to shine again. When the count finally catches Sonya, he throws her into a dungeon and claims to have returned the Christmas star himself. He then offers to find the princess and asks that in return, he may marry her in order to inherit half the kingdom. The king acquiesces, but then the old woman who had earlier sold sheaves of grain to Sonya arrives to unmask the evil count. She proves her version of the story because she has Sonya's golden heart necklace. As it turns out, the old woman is the queen, and in the end, the family is happily reunited. This story appears to combine a Christian Christmas message with magic and folklore, and core nuclear family values.

Nils Gaup's Journey to the Christmas Star (2012)

Oscar-nominated Nils Gaup directed a new version of this classic film in the new millenium, premiering in 2012.[11] This, to a certain extent, was a risky venture because so many Norwegians harbored a strong nostalgic attachment to Solum's film with Hanne Krogh playing the adult Sonya, singing what has become a very popular Christmas song, "Sonya's Song to the Christmas Star" (*Sonjas sang til julestjernen*). The adaptation is based on Brandt's original play rather than Solum's film. Thus, the figure of an evil witch is revived, with her colluding with the count against the royal family. Vilde Zeiner stars as 12-year-old Sonya, returning to her father's castle and then departing on a quest for the Christmas star. Other roles are played by some of Norway's rising-star actors, with Agnes Kittelsen playing a beautiful, Gothic witch with a spiteful, superficial teenage daughter (serving as a foil to Sonya); Anders Basmo playing the king; and Jakob Oftebro playing a kitchen boy. Gaup also chose to exploit modern technology and special effects in order to create a more action-oriented adventure. The filming took place in Norway and the Czech Republic, combining Norway's remarkable winter landscapes with scenes from a thirteenth-century Czech castle.

Scriptwriter Kamilla Krogsveen eliminates not only the young Golden Top but also her mother, the queen, by summarizing their story in an introductory tale, narrated in a voiceover accompanying colorful book illustrations. By the time the live-action film begins, Sonya is twelve, her mother has died of grief, her father has cursed the Christmas star, and he has been given ten years to find it again. Rather than being adopted by caring market entertainers, Sonya is kept hostage by a family of exploitative thieves who make her life miserable. Thus, we recognize an added Cinderella motif as well as motifs from the robber girl scene in Andersen's "The Snow Queen" (a motif further developed in Astrid Lindgren's *Ronia the Robber's Daughter* [Ronja Rövardotter 1981], adapted to film by Tage Danielsson in 1984).

Good and evil are set against each other with the witch and the count plotting against the king from the outset. Good people are blonde, and evil people are dark and Goth-looking, appearing in elaborate, black costumes. In the opening scene, Sonya tries to escape from the family of thieves. She refuses to become one of them, and ends up in the castle kitchen where the thieves catch up with her and urge her to help them steal food. The kitchen boy sees how Sonya refuses to steal and chases the others while Sonya runs into a great hall where she tries to hide. The king enters with his dog Bruno, who quickly uncovers Sonya's hiding place. Without realizing it the king is briefly reunited with his daughter, until Sonya decides to embark on a quest to find the Christmas star for the king.

Instead of meeting her mother disguised as an old woman, Sonya encounters an owl that helps guide her in the right direction. Along her journey, she also rescues a little bog elf (*mosenisse*) from a bird trap. In return, the elf blows magic elf dust on her, which causes her to shrink and enables her to escape from the count. Climbing inside a tree with the bog elf, Sonya meets the elf's family and asks for their help. A bed-ridden elf grandfather advises Sonya to seek help from Santa Claus (*julemannen*). She must awaken a hibernating bear and ride it to the North Wind. The scenes with Sonya clinging to the bear are reminiscent of *The Polar Bear King*. Rather than showing a girl clinging to a white polar bear in a summer landscape, this film shows Sonya clinging to a brown bear in a snow-covered winter landscape.

The religious motifs become more significant as the North Wind demands an act of faith (rather than passionate wishing, as in Solum's film). Sonya has to throw herself off the mountaintop and trust that the North Wind will catch her and bring her to Santa Claus. Meanwhile, the witch has supplied the count with a broom and a chase begins. Filmed with a bluescreen, Sonya and the count whirl through the air, Sonya trusting the wind (in a flying pose, with her arms outstretched before her) and the count riding his broom so recklessly that he eventually loses control and drops to the ground. Sonya arrives safely at Santa Claus and his helpers' workshop on Christmas Eve. Santa Claus knows who is good and who is bad as his workshop is surrounded by fir trees that represent the soul of each living human being (this is a Christian motif that is related to Andersen's "The Story of a Mother" [*Historien om en Moder*, 1848]). The count's tree has withered entirely, illustrating how rotten he is. The king's tree has begun to wither after he cursed the Christmas star. Sonya's tree is bright green. Santa Claus explains that the shining Christmas star is a matter of faith. If Sonya's faith is strong enough it will light up. Sonya closes her eyes in a passionate act of faith, and her gold heart lights up, which is said to prove that she will be able to return the glowing Christmas star to the king.

As Sonya heads home, the witch appears and traps her within the branches of a tree. The witch has been watching Sonya's adventures through a crystal ball. The witch then steals Sonya's golden heart and gives it to her own daughter; she enchants her daughter's hair, turning it blonde so that she might pose as Golden Top. The count, the witch, and her daughter introduce "Golden Top," who is wearing the golden heart necklace. The king is just about to sign a contract that allegedly promises that he will never curse the Christmas star again; in reality, he is about to sign over his kingdom. In the nick of time, the bog elf (Mose) arrives to liberate Sonya with his magic shrinking dust.

Sonya runs to the castle and reaches the king just as he is about to complete his signature. The dog recognizes Sonya, and she is furthermore able to prove her purity and origins since in *her* hands, the golden heart begins to glow. In a final tableau, the king and Sonya are shown eating dinner in front of their decorated Christmas tree. Sonya's mother never appears, but in an act of grandiosity and justice, the king invites the kitchen boy and his sweetheart to join them at the table. Thus, the reunited nuclear family of the 1976 version is supplanted by a socially progressive gesture allowing for substitute family members, and a leveling of social classes. The film's message is partly social democratic and partly Christian as Sonya has proven her faith through a journey of suffering, faith, and endurance. Sonya has a golden heart, not just literally but also figuratively.

Gaup's *Journey to the Christmas Star* (2012) has been sold to at least 74 countries and has been distributed by the Walt Disney Corporation. It has been a commercial success with spin-off merchandise, yet the critical acclaim has varied with reviewers disagreeing as to whether the combination of a classical, solemn fairy-tale narrative style and modern dramaturgy supported by digital effects works. Reviewers have regarded it as the 1976 version "Disneyfied" and "having met *Harry Potter*" (Kielland 2012; Aalen 2012). To some it is too Disneyfied and Americanized meaning that it appears generic (Kielland 2012); to others it is not Americanized enough in the sense that recent Hollywood family films have led audiences to expect more scenes and cultural references aimed at entertaining adult viewers (Lismoen 2012). Some critics like the special effects (Sæverås 2012; Steinkjer 2012); some find them half-baked and embarrassing (Kulås 2012). Finally, some embrace the purely good, self-sacrificing and brave Sonya while others demand a modern heroine who more actively and individualistically sets out to realize her own potential and achieve her own goals

(Lismoen 2012; Kulås 2012). This type of heroine manifests in my next example: Christmas films and TV calendars featuring the Blue Mountain (*Blåfjell*).

Gudny Ingebjørg Hagen's Blue Mountain and Blue Elves

In 2008, NRK experienced enormous success with their Christmas calendar series *Christmas in Blue Mountain* (Jul i Blåfjell 1999—shown in reruns in 2001, 2004, 2008, and 2011). The series was based on author Gudny Ingebjørg Hagen's ideas and manuscript and quickly traveled to the stage as well. Many regarded *Christmas in Blue Mountain* as a fierce competitor—on stage, screen, and television—to *Journey to the Christmas Star* (1976). This was to be *the* new Norwegian family Christmas show. The producers quickly decided to make a film version called *Christmas Eve in Blue Mountain* (Julenatt i Blåfjell), produced by Storm Rosenberg and directed jointly by horror-film director Roar Uthaug and Katarina Launing who is known for working with child actors.

For the feature film, scriptwriter Hagen set the plot one century prior to the other Christmas calendar series. The film introduces Queen Mountain Rose (Dronning Fjellrose) as a timid child princess, who has to venture out of her comfort zone—Blue Mountain—in order to save her ailing father's life. Fourteen-year-old Ane Viola Andreassen Semb plays the princess, and fifteen-year-old Johan Tinus Austad Lindgren plays Dreng Dronningssøn, who becomes her companion and helper. Hagen has a clear political agenda as she designs the blue elves as a modernized version of the traditional elf wearing a red hat. By creating a universe initially resembling a form of apartheid with blue elves not allowing red elves into their mountain, Hagen makes a point about multicultural and multiethnic values. In addition, the story delivers an ecological message as the blue elves are in charge of resources whose mismanagement would have ruinous consequences. In the end, Princess Mountain Rose succeeds in saving her father *and* the world as she cooperates with the red elves, letting go of traditional social fears and prejudice. The film is thus a good example of fairy-tale narratives used to promote social integration and environmental stewardship. In 2009, these seemed to be popular messages as the film broke box office records with 74,618 tickets sold during the premiere weekend. This was the highest number of tickets sold to a Norwegian children's film during its premiere weekend to date ("Fakta—Blånissene" 2009).

André Øvredal's The Troll Hunter (2010)

I close my discussion of Norwegian fairy-tale films with enormous cult success, *The Troll Hunter* (Trolljegeren 2010)—a mockumentary directed by André Øvredal about a contemporary operative secretly working for the Norwegian Police Security Service. The film is full of references—explicit and implicit—to Asbjørnsen and Moe's collected folktales. Having allowed a couple of student journalists to follow him on a troll hunt, the troll hunter tells them to forget about folktales; they are "just for kids." When one of the students asks him what to do if a troll should engage him in an eating contest, the hunter replies: "An eating competition? Asbjørnsen and Moe don't exactly correspond to reality." As a satire, the film pokes fun at folklore as well as the contemporary Norwegian welfare state. As Ellen Rees argues, *The Troll Hunter* may be regarded as "a cautionary tale about government bureaucracy that loses sight of its mission and gets caught up in a self aggrandizing and exploitative conspiracy that serves the state rather than the citizens" (2011, 61).

Sweden

In Swedish fairy-tale films, the legacies of Selma Lagerlöf (1858–1940) and Astrid Lindgren (1907–2002) endure.

Selma Lagerlöf and Dirk Regel's The Wonderful Adventures of Nils *(2011)*

Selma Lagerlöf, the first female writer to win the Nobel Prize in Literature, is most widely known for her pedagogical novel *The Wonderful Adventures of Nils* (Nils Holgerssons underbara resa genom Sverige 1906–1907). She composed it on a commission from the National Teachers Association to write a geography reader for the public schools. Lagerlöf put great effort into studying the flora, fauna, and natural resources of Sweden's various regions and created an exciting pedagogical text by linking geography lessons to the tale of naughty farm boy Nils. Nils does not treat the farm animals with respect, but rather delights in hurting them. One day he catches an elf (*tomte*) in a net, and when he refuses to let it go, it turns Nils into a Lilliputian (*pyssling*). As a Lilliputian, Nils is able to communicate with animals. When migrating wild geese fly over the farm, one of the farm geese wants to join them and Nils, trying to hold it back by tugging on a piece of rope tied around its neck, ends up attached to it as it flies off. Now begins a journey over all regions of Sweden—an educational trip in terms of both geography and personal development. At the end, Nils has learned his lesson and is turned back into a human being.

The Wonderful Adventures of Nils is a national and nation-building story, but it also carries a broader appeal as a story about nature and ecology. As Christopher Oscarson argues, it is "marked with a distinctive environmental bent" (2009, 101). Lending itself to splendid nature shots, the story has been adapted several times, in both live-action and animated film versions. Most recently it was adapted as a Swedish-German 230-minute co-production directed by German Dirk Regel in 2011. This version uses an impressive mix of real animals, puppets, and computer-generated imagery (CGI). Selma Lagerlöf (played by Cecilia Ljung) figures in a frame tale, writing the story; yet scenes with her writing are interspersed throughout the film until the two universes are brought together with Lagerlöf's encountering her character and giving him a ride, helping him on his journey. Nils, in turn, gives her permission to use his story for her schoolbook.

The film adaptation furthermore emerges as a romance as Nils is turned into a fourteen-year-old farm boy in love with the pharmacist's daughter, Åsa. Nils and Åsa have to overcome a series of obstacles until they are finally united at the end. The first obstacle is that of class prejudice as Åsa's father does not consider Nils good enough for his daughter. The second obstacle is Nils's bad treatment of animals, which infuriates Åsa. The final obstacle is the main event of Nils's being turned into a Lilliputian and disappearing with a group of geese. This journey, however, also becomes the solution as it teaches Nils how to behave with respect and loyalty towards fellow beings, and finally become a "real human being" and "big," both literally and figuratively. The film is a pleasant entertainment because of its plot, but also because of the beautiful aerial photography covering Skåne in the south to Lappland in the north. The facial close-ups, too, are very enjoyable, not least those of the animals, and the overall combination of human thought and voices and animal footage is very entertaining.

Olle Hellbom's The Brothers Lionheart *(1977)*

Astrid Lindgren is best known for her Pippi Longstocking series, but she has also created children's fantasy books more closely tied to folklore and adventure, such as *The Brothers Lionheart* (Bröderna Lejonhjärta 1973) and *Ronia the Robber's Daughter* (Ronja Rövardotter 1981). In both cases she also adapted her own novels for the screen. Both are live-action feature films.

The Brothers Lionheart is a story about two brothers, the younger of whom, nine-year-old Karl, suffers from tuberculosis and is about to die. His older brother, thirteen-year-old Jonathan, comforts him by telling him about the campfires, adventures, and fairy tales awaiting them both in the afterlife. The place they will meet again is called Nangijala and it is a site where good fights against evil, ultimately in the shape of a fire-breathing dragon. The plot takes a surprising turn, however, as a fire breaks out in the brothers' apartment building. Jonathan risks his life to save Karl, jumping out from a window with Karl on his back—and dies. As Karl starts losing faith in the existence of Nangijala, a white dove shows up on his windowsill. Karl takes this to be a message from Jonathan. That night, as he falls asleep, he enters a feverish dream about Nangijala. The life-on-earth section is captured in a frame tale told from Karl's perspective and rendered in sepia tones in an urban setting in the early twentieth century.

The main part of the film, released in 1977, is in color and starts with Karl arriving in Nangijala. Here, the boy is drawn into a medieval universe where Jonathan is a courageous fighter against evil. The story turns into a coming-of-age story with Karl finally proving himself just as courageous as his older brother. In the end, Jonathan slays the fire-spouting dragon to save Karl and all other innocent people. Yet, Jonathan is injured by the dragon's fire and loses the ability to move his legs. He tells Karl that people who die in Nangijala move on to a new site of adventure called Nangilima. Karl now offers to take Jonathan on his back and jump off a cliff so they will arrive in Nangilima together. Hence, the theme of the frame tale is repeated while the roles of the brothers are reversed. The camera subsequently focuses on their campfire, while we hear Karl exclaiming that he "sees the light." Adult viewers, at least, understand that Karl's seeing the light captures his moment of real-life expiration.

The film is relatively slow-paced and quite poetic. It contains beautiful nature scenes with the boys on horseback. Most of the scenes are filmed in Sweden and Denmark while the landscape used when the boys arrive at the land of evil and ultimately slay the dragon, Katla, is a magnificent Iceland, characterized by black lava. As it is suggested that a new adventure will take place after Karl and Jonathan die in Nangijala, we return to the sepia-toned realistic frame tale. Here we see a tombstone decorated with a white dove, commemorating the brothers, and we assume this to be the source of inspiration for Lindgren's bittersweet adventure tale and film.

Tage Danielsson's Ronia the Robber's Daughter *(1984)*

This film (Ronja Rövardotter 1984) is an upbeat adventure that continues to appeal to children and adults alike, with impressive acting, scenography, nature scenes, and special effects. This Lindgren story is also set in medieval times and is structured around two feuding clans of robbers who constantly fight and consider each other evil. Each robber chieftain has a child, a girl Ronia and a boy Birk. Ronia and Birk secretly become best friends and refuse to carry on the feud between clans. In addition, they refuse to live as robbers who take what is not rightfully theirs. The film is in many ways a coming-of-age story with Ronia and Birk going off into the woods for days, weeks, and months on end (see Figure 8.2). In beautiful surroundings they ride on horseback, go swimming, and fend for themselves while also watching out for rump-gnomes (*rumpnissar*), grey dwarfs (*grådvärgar*), harpies (*vildvittror*), and the "unearthly ones" (*de underjordiska*). The film was developed over several seasons, adding to the variety of the natural environments. Illustrating the passage of seasons, one shot, for instance, shows a splashing waterfall during summer quickly morphing into a frozen, icy waterfall through what comes across as fast-forwarding. The special effects used to represent the supernatural beings are also quite impressive. The harpies, for instance, are captivating, screeching, raven-like birds with human lower faces and chests, modeled on slender, curvy, nude women.

While Ronia and Birk were played by unknown child actors Hanna Zetterberg and Dan Håfström, the adult roles were played by famous actors such as Per Oscarsson (starring in *Hunger* [1966]), Lena Nyman, and Börje Ahlstedt (both starring in *I am Curious (Blue)* [1967] and *I am Curious (Yellow)* [1968]). The adults have exuberant roles that are enjoyable to watch—and they

FIGURE 8.2 Birk and Ronia, *Ronia the Robber's Daughter* (1984).

come across as having been fun to perform—as the actors imitate merry medieval life with lots of feasting, dancing, singing, fighting, and naked frolicking in the snow. *Ronia the Robber's Daughter* was a major success in 1984 and has remained a popular family adventure film in Scandinavia since. It won a Silver Bear for outstanding artistic contribution at the 1985 Berlin International Film Festival.

Conclusion

In Denmark, Norway and Sweden, fairy tales are alive and well in books, on stage, and on the screen. Film productions tend to be tied to national cultural heritage with the Norwegians adapting Asbjørnsen and Moe's collected folktales, the Danes adapting Andersen's romantic literary tales, and the Swedes adapting tales written by Selma Lagerlöf and Astrid Lindgren. In addition, during the past twenty-five years, the tradition of national televised Christmas calendars has led to many new and original fairy-tale films, allowing the producers, on the one hand, to revel in elves, romance, myth, and cultural history and, on the other hand, to use elf universes for more didactic purposes based on a moral of cultural tolerance and environmentalism.

Notes

1 I define *Scandinavian* fairy-tale films as works directed or produced by Scandinavians. I exclude international adaptations of Scandinavian fairy tales. Volumes could, for instance, be written about international Andersen adaptations alone.

2 "*Vi danske ejer i H.C. Andersens eventyr et af de største litterære aktiver i verden. Vi ejer også en række betydelige tegnende og malende kunstnere, der har det forud for alle andre tegnere og malere i verden, at de er rundne af den samme*

jord og har indsuget de samme stemninger som H.C. Andersen." (Unless otherwise indicated, all translations are my own.)

3 See Oxfeldt (2006) for an analysis of *The Fairytaler*'s *The Little Mermaid* (compared to Disney's version and an Australian version) and Oxfeldt (2009) for comparative analyses of *The Little Mermaid* and *Clod-Hans* (*The Fairytaler*'s version compared to Mihail Badica's).

4 Klods-Hans is also known in English as Jack the Fool, Jack the Dullard, Blockhead Hans, Silly Hans, Clumsy Hans, and Hans the Clopper.

5 In the fairy-tale part of his literary production, Andersen started out rewriting folktales he had heard as a child, but eventually moved beyond this point of departure as he developed his own style, genre, and stories. His later tales and stories contain folktale *elements*, but cannot be considered rewritings or adaptations of particular tales. Of his 156 tales and stories, approximately ten are considered rewritings of particular folktales, including "Clod Hans," "The Tinderbox," "The Wild Swans," and "The Princess and the Pea" (Mortensen 2003, 17–18).

6 Andersen was a productive and talented paper cutter. His paper cuts are on exhibit at Odense City Museums: <http://hca.museum.odense.dk/klip/billedstart.asp?language=en>.

7 She recalls having *The Wild Swans* read to her when she was about eight years old and being fascinated and frightened at once (Queen Margrethe 2009).

8 *The Wonderful World of the Brothers Grimm* (1962) uses live-action sequences for the fairy-tale retellings of "The Gifts of the Little People" (ATU 503) and "The Singing Bone" (ATU 780).

9 "*Danset og skurte store stykker av ryggen sin på den.*"

10 "*Så var det en gang, som vel kunne være, en konge.*"

11 Gaup's *Pathfinder* (Ofelaš; Veiviseren 1987) was nominated for an Academy Award within the category of Best Foreign Language Film in 1988.

9

"TO CATCH UP AND OVERTAKE DISNEY?"

Soviet and Post-Soviet Fairy-Tale Films

Marina Balina and Birgit Beumers

Introduction: The Soviet Fairy Tale, After Folk and Before Film

In 1929, Petr Bogatyrev and Roman Jakobson argued that "a fairy tale fulfills the role of a social utopia" (1966, 10). The dream of a better life, the very essence of folktales, became the focus for many Soviet-period fairy tales, suggesting that the present had improved, and the future would be even greater. Yet the genre did not easily fit the new Soviet literary requirements; it went through a period of harsh battles and rigorous ideological debates. Literary critic and educator Esfir' Ianovskaia's article "Does the Proletarian Child Need the Fairy Tale?" (1926), included in a volume edited by the proponents of the new educational science, pedology (Sokolianskii, Popov, and Zaluzhnyi 1928, 91; see also Hellman 2013, 354–62), vehemently rejected the need for fairy tales.[1] Trying to create standards and apply measurements to every child's activity, the pedologists attempted to establish rules and regulations for children's literature, which was viewed as a utilitarian tool rather than as a means to influence young peoples' imagination generally.

The pedologists enlisted strong support among party leaders and government institutions. According to folklore scholar Felix J. Oinas, in the early 1920s "the belief that folklore reflected the ideology of the ruling classes gave rise to a strongly negative attitude toward it. . . . A special Children's Proletkul't sought to eradicate folktales on the basis that they glorified tsars and tsarevichs, corrupted and instigated sickly fantasies in children, developed the kulak [rich landowner's] attitude, and strengthened bourgeois ideals" (1978, 77). Among the fairy tale's chief opponents was the powerful Nadezhda Krupskaia, Lenin's widow and a leading authority on education and library science in the new Soviet state. In 1924, as chair of the Committee of Political Education, she was instrumental in putting together an influential manual that led to fairy tales' exclusion from library shelves (Dobrenko 1997, 176), including the folktale collections by Aleksander Afanas'ev, the famous "Scarlet Flower" by Sergei Aksakov, collections by Vasil'ev (pseud.) and Klavdiia Lukashevich, "Fairy Tales in Verse" by Onegin (pseud.), and "Russian Fairy Tales for the Little Ones" by Ol'ga Rogova.

The manual labeled both folktales and literary fairy tales as works that "badly influenced the yet-to-be developed conscience of children" and destroyed "their ability to comprehend materialistic images of the world" (quoted in Dobrenko 1997, 175). In the 1920s, the fairy tale was thus stripped of its function of "socialization of children" (Zipes 1997, 3). Considered fundamentally "bourgeois," with form and structure standing "in direct opposition to the task of fostering communist values," the fairy tale was not to be used in children's education "even if it did contain revolutionary content" (Rybnikov 1928, 12). Fairy-tale elements such as magic, fantasy, animism, and anthropomorphism were labeled idealistic.

Nevertheless, the fairy tale returned in the 1930s. Its historical and ideological rehabilitation started with Maksim Gorkii's speech at the First Soviet Congress of the Writers' Union in August 1934. Oinas writes: "Gorkii's insistence that folklore belonged, first of all, to working people had far-reaching implications. As if by magic, it opened the eyes of the party leaders to the possibilities that folklore would have for the advancement of communism. And from that time on, we can follow the conscious use of folklore for social and political use" (1978, 78). Gorkii's position was supported by Samuil Marshak, a leading writer of the new Soviet children's literature. Marshak straightforwardly and unrestrictively used "fairy tale" (*skazka*), a word that had acquired negative connotations in the debates of the late 1920s and early 1930s. It is then no surprise that few fairy-tale films—animated or live-action—appeared before the mid-1930s. Though the creation of films specifically for children was debated in the late 1920s, it was not until 1936 that a studio for children's films (Soiuzdetfil'm) and one for animation (Soiuzmul'tfil'm) were established (see Beumers, Izvolov, Miloserdova, and Ryabchikova 2009).

At about the same time, Disney studios' cartoons reached Soviet screens. Some early animated examples were shown in 1933 at a festival of American animation. Then in 1935, the First International Moscow Film Festival screened the shorts *Three Little Pigs* (1933), *Peculiar Penguins* (1934), and *The Band Concert* (1935); they remained in distribution after the event. The celebrated *Snow White and the Seven Dwarfs* (1937) reached Soviet screens only after the war, as a trophy film brought back from the front, and it was in distribution from 1955 to 1959. In the meantime, filmmakers who had visited the United States in the 1930s, including Grigorii Aleksandrov and Sergei Eisenstein, became acquainted with Disney's works. What particularly impressed audiences and filmmakers were the conveyer-belt production methods using animation celluloid, rarely employed in Soviet animation prior to 1936, and Disney's style and aesthetics, characterized by fast-moving plots. Eisenstein saw in Disney's cartoons the perfect embodiment of his ideas on totemism (see Leyda 1986)—equating man with animals and merging the features of both identities—as shown in his montage in *The Strike* (Stachka 1924), where he used animal images to highlight his human characters' features: the fox for slyness, the owl for cleverness, the monkey for drunkenness, and so on. Animation lent itself especially well not only to the creation of magic worlds but also to translations of an unspeakable (Soviet, Stalinist) reality through Aesopian language, transferring social comment onto the animal world.

Paradoxically, then, the fairy tale was reborn as a literary genre at the height of Stalinism, changing its features under the ideological pressures of the time, strongly influenced by Stalinist cultural aesthetics. Some major tropes were imposed on folkloric plots, modifying folktales significantly as well as singling out those that fit the new paradigm, usually ones which celebrated the juxtaposition of poor vs. rich with the former's subsequent victory. New literary tales were written with these tropes in mind. Defining the totalitarian culture of the Stalin era were: the protagonist as exclusive carrier of a positive and didactic message; a surrogate family with ideological rather than blood ties; and the oppositional war trope, which juxtaposed native vs. foreign and upper vs. lower class. The plot dynamics were motivated by party consciousness.

Central to the projected ideal family was an attempt to create a unified national identity, one of the most important tasks for the USSR as a multinational state. As a rule, a female character (implicitly a substitute for Russia) needed rescue by the protagonist, who defended her against the enemy, thus instilling in viewers a sense of patriotism. Within the war trope, the traditional good vs. evil opposition gained a distinctly class-based character as the underdog protagonist fought against upper-class hegemony. This conflict often involved casting the enemy as a foreign power, outside the native purity of essential goodness that is wrongly oppressed.[2] This chapter explores some paradigms of fairy-tale films of the Stalinist era, including the 1930s, before moving on to the postwar period.

The Fairy Tale Meets the Silver Screen

Despite the dearth of fairy-tale films in Soviet Russia of the 1920s, only a few animated films were made specifically for children, largely illustrating contemporary Soviet tales. Thus, *Senka, the African Boy* (Sen'ka Afrikanets 1927), directed by animators Iurii Merkulov, Daniil Cherkes, and Ivan Ivanov-Vano, was based on Kornei Chukovskii's well-known story "The Crocodile." The film deploys animation to illustrate the journey into a child's imagination. It opens with live-action footage of a boy visiting the zoo, where he finds a book about African animals. He is transported by its illustrations and travels in a dream to the foreign land, only to wake up in his own bed. This framing device became typical for many Soviet cartoons and the live-action works of such filmmakers as Aleksandr Rou, Aleksandr Ptushko, and Nadezhda Kosheverova, but it was also a staple of Disney features (Zipes 2011, 88). It repeats one of the key elements of classical fairy-tale structure—the journey to another land from which the hero returns, having gained experience and reached adulthood (Propp 1968). In Soviet animation this journey is initiated (and guided) by book illustrations, and the viewer/listener/reader has no doubt that it is imaginary. Responsibility for the process of maturation is thus not left to imagination and magic, but is determined by a book—published by the Soviet State publishing house and thus imbued with Party-approved ideological content.

By the mid 1930s, thanks to the impact of Gorkii's speech, but also to advances of film technology, more sophisticated creations of the fairy tale's magical realm were possible. Here, Ptushko's work played a major role. On the one hand, he experimented with drawn and puppet animation, introducing color and advancing Soviet animation in the direction of Disney, whose Technicolor feature *Snow White and the Seven Dwarfs* remained a highly-esteemed film for Soviet animators. On the other hand, Ptushko and his cinematographer Nikolai Renkov experimented with the composite shot, using live-action footage in the same frame as puppet animation to great effect in their adaptation of Jonathan Swift's famous novel—with a special, Soviet twist to the plot, whereby Gulliver frees the land of Lilliput from (capitalist) exploitation—under the title *The New Gulliver* (Novyi Gulliver 1935).

The combination of realism and utopia required in the ideological realm was well matched by the use of animated tricks within live-action footage. Ptushko's work at Mosfilm on the creation of fairy-tale cartoons with a three-strip color film, pioneered by the inventor Pavel Mershin, had a huge impact on Soviet animation. These films have been disregarded by scholarship due to their inaccessibility.[3] They include a number of classical fairy tales—a first for Soviet animation—such as Sarra Mokil's puppet animation *The Wolf and the Seven Goats* (Volk i semero kozliat 1938). Ptushko's color version of *The Fisherman and the Fish* (Skazka o rybake i rybke 1937) (see Figure 9.1) provides a fine example of the narrative-framing device: a book opens, the pages turn, and the images come to life. At the film's end, the book closes again, sealing the fairy-tale realm and confining it to another diegetic space. Moreover, the film sets a unique precedent for collaboration with the miniature artists at Palekh, a school of lacquer-box painting, which had been forced to abandon its fairy-tale themes of Baba Yaga, Ivan the Fool, and the Firebird, in favor of images of workers and peasants.

Many of Ptushko's live-action films[4] are classical renderings of folktales and fairy tales and are infused with his substantial experience in animation. In *The New Gulliver*, the Land of Lilliput is presented as the dream place of the young pioneer Petia Konstantinov, who helps the Lilliputian workers overthrow their evil, cruel king. Combining human actors and clay puppets, Ptushko created two separate narrative layers: one depicting Petia's dream in which he leads the Lilliputians

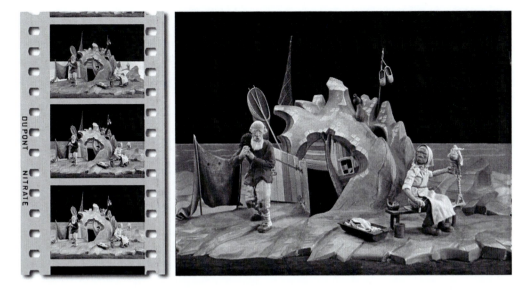

FIGURE 9.1 Left: the three-strip nitrate film; right: the restored color image, Ptushko's *The Tale of the Fisherman and the Fish* (1937). Courtesy of Nikolai Mayorov.

to a successful proletarian revolution; and another plane of everyday Soviet school reality. Carlo Collodi's *The Adventures of Pinocchio* (1883) proved a popular text, rendered first in Aleksei Tolstoi's celebrated fairy tale *The Golden Key* or *The Adventures of Buratino* (Zolotoi kliuchik, ili prikliucheniia Buratino 1936[1960]),[5] and turned into a film by Ptushko, who unites two different sets of characters, human actors, and marionettes, within a magic space that stands in for (Soviet) reality. Tolstoi himself provided the screen adaptation and created a different ending, wherein a flying ship comes to rescue the puppets and take them to a wonderful, free land. The rescuer, resembling an Arctic explorer, denies the villain Karabas entrance into this beautiful world of the future, hits him in the face, and throws him into a puddle.

A remarkable addition to the film was the song, written by Mikhail Froman, bearing a compelling resemblance to the famous song "Somewhere Over the Rainbow" from Hollywood's *The Wizard of Oz* (1939). Although in both, the beautiful land where the dreams "that you dare to dream really do come true" appears as a utopian landscape without any specific geographical locators, the song from *The Golden Key* has many recognizable spatial references. The mythical land "beyond the sea" was coded for its viewers as Soviet Russia with its mythologized mission to find a better tomorrow.[6]

Tolstoi's story created a class-conscious world. The Doctor of Puppetry, Signor Karabas Barabas, is a villain who amassed huge sums of money by exploiting poor little dolls that fear him and never resist. The class struggle generates a longing for a strong leader who will inspire everyone to unite behind a just cause—happiness for the poor and the end of exploitation. To turn Buratino into a leader, Tolstoi empowers him with the special knowledge of a secret door, and the story develops around Buratino's search for a golden key that opens the door into the land of universal happiness. An intriguing feature of the Soviet version is the permanent presence of Buratino's long nose. While Pinocchio's nose lengthens only when the puppet lies, his Soviet counterpart is born with a long nose, and all of Papa Carlo's attempts to adjust its size fail. This strengthens the message of a possible imperfection in a potential leader.[7] In order to succeed, Buratino needs others' help, thus introducing the obligatory socialist message that emphasizes the power of collective struggle.

Collodi's Pinocchio searches for self-centered solutions, while Buratino aims at achieving universal happiness. Magic power (in Collodi's narrative, the Blue Fairy) is replaced by the power of the organized collective, capable of bringing out an individual's best virtues. Almost forty years later, Leonid Nechaev offered a new interpretation, *The Adventures of Buratino* (Prikliucheniia Buratino 1976), which represents the change of the zeitgeist in two different epochs of Soviet history, and is discussed below.

The shift towards realism after the 1934 Writers' Union Congress explains the increased production of live-action fairy-tale films by both Ptushko and his colleague Rou. They made children's versions of musical fairy tales for adults as created by Grigorii Aleksandrov and Ivan Pyr'ev, following the Stalinist slogan "we were born to make fairy tales come true."[8] In his overview of Rou's films, Peter Rollberg states that one of the filmmaker's major achievements was his preservation of the "stylistic, mythical and moral integrity of the fairy tale" (2009, 592). Indeed, Rou's dedication to the genre was remarkable from his very first fairy-tale film, *On the Pike's Command* (Po shchuch'emu veleniiu 1938). Rollberg also stresses Rou's ability "to prove that fairy tales were elastic enough to adapt to a variety of circumstances" (Rollberg 2009, 591). This elasticity remained a major trademark of Rou's fairy-tale films and enabled him to adapt to the socialist realist discourse. His knowledge and appreciation of the folkloric tradition did not impede his ability to freely move across accepted plotlines and borrow characters from vastly different sources. Creating his own narrative from folktale building blocks, he crafted works that could engage with the politics of his time and pass the restrictive censorship of Stalin's Russia. The hybridity of his live-action films was quite different from Ptushko's; while the latter relied on special effects and mixed actors with puppets, Rou experimented with the very essence of the fairy-tale fabric, its characters and plots. This approach allowed him to provide his audience with a very specific, didactic message. The magic tricks that were supposed to shock and impress Ptushko's viewers were standardized by Rou and became part of the everyday human existence of his fairy-tale characters.

On the Pike's Command was the first live-action film based on the newly rehabilitated fairy-tale genre and the first in which Rou began to formulate his artistic principles. Loosely following Elizaveta Tarakhovskaia's play (1965),[9] he merged two folktales ("On the Pike's Command" and "The Princess Who Never Laughs") to create a true celebration of magical transformation as an everyday reality. In this world, buckets of water walk uphill and a sleigh moves without a horse. Rou's protagonist Emelya is quite different from his folktale counterpart—a lazy, comical character whose luck (catching a magic pike) was simply a random occurrence.[10] By contrast, the film's main character embodies the Stalinist prototype of a positive hero in the form of a poor, but inventive, hard-working victim of social injustice who deeply deserves happiness. The streetwise Emelya's juxtaposition with the degenerate Tsar Gorokh (the first of many roles featuring one of Rou's favorite actors, Georgii Milliar) perfectly illustrates the newly established socialist realist requirement of *narodnost*—the demand to create literary works that reflect the common people's needs and aspirations. However, even this plot element did not protect Rou from censorship attacks; he was accused of making his film purely entertaining, void of substantial social critique.

In the 1930s, the very act of creating a film based on a Russian fairy tale was courageous, since the genre had only recently returned to the arsenal of literary works approved by Soviet censorship. The film's overwhelming success was in part due to its enthusiastic audience, which played an important role in the direction of cultural consumption. Richard Stites suggests that "the 'ruralisation' or 'rustification' of Soviet cities in the 1930s affected the economy and culture of Soviet civilization. . . . The general influx of poorly educated masses led to an overall narrowing of culture, and to a spread of 'irrational and obscurantist tendencies' in the workplace and in all walks of life. Peasants were unable to leave their values behind in the villages" (1990, 82). The fairy tale was the perfect vehicle to convey new alleged miracles promoted by the Soviet system, in the realms of rapid industrialization under Stalin's Five-Year Plans or the social engineering of a New Man/Woman. Thus, *On the Pike's Command* integrated magic into everyday life; moving household items or bringing about weather changes at the simpleton's demand were on par with technological advances, which were often treated as enchanted objects.[11]

Only a year later, Rou produced *Beautiful Vasilisa* (Vasilisa prekrasnaia 1939). The merging of different fairy-tale plots had already become his aesthetic signature, and *Vasilisa* incorporated several versions of "The Frog Princess" tale, featuring a female protagonist without royal status. Rou's Vasilisa is a peasant girl, depicted in sharp contrast to the two other female characters: Malan'ia, the merchant's daughter, and Belendrissa, the nobleman's daughter. Together they represent a variety of vices: they gossip, they are lazy, they envy each other, and they are impatient. Vasilisa embodies patriarchal Russian values, while simultaneously serving as a symbol of new Soviet beauty. As a traditional female fairy-tale character she is hard working, polite, trustworthy, and devoted to her man. Most importantly, she needs to be rescued. At the same time, she conforms to the physical features promoted by Stalinist culture. As Oksana Bulgakova (2002) writes, the 1930s brought new standards of Soviet beauty: strong legs, broad shoulders, and obvious physical strength.[12] Notably, Vasilisa's feminine beauty leads to her capture and forced marriage at the hands of the dragon.

The focus on achieving personal happiness that lies at the core of this tale's war trope distinguishes it from the earlier search for universal happiness. Another cinematic twist is the frequent intertextual citations. In the scene where Ivan obtains his magic sword, when he finally looks at himself in the mirror, he is transformed into a Russian warrior reminiscent of those featured in Sergei Eisenstein's *Alexander Nevsky* (1938). Viewers are thus invited to draw a parallel and read Ivan as a fighter for a larger cause, just as Vasilisa figures as Mother Russia who must be saved from evil invaders. This metaphorical construct foreshadowed Rou's next film, *Kashchei the Immortal* (Kashchei Bessmertnyi 1944), which became a metaphor for World War II, or the Great Patriotic War, 1941–1945.

Actor Milliar stated that Rou created *Kashchei* as a parody of Fritz Lang's *Die Nibelungen* (1924) (Sirivlia 1997). Indeed, the imagery of Rou's fairy tale resembles Lang's film. Much has been written about visual quotes from Lang being used by Eisenstein in the image of the Teutonic knights in *Alexander Nevsky*. Film critic Natal'ia Sirivlia sees a similar practice in Rou's film and illustrates the resemblance between the protagonists, Nikita Kozhemiaka and Siegfried. Also, Kriemhild and Mar'ia Morevna are both noble maidens with long braids. Sirivlia also finds similarities in the depiction of landscapes in the two films when nature foreshadows important and tragic events. In *Kashchei*, Rou combined different fairy tales with the Russian epic, the *bylina*, the source for the character Kozhemiaka. In Rou's patriotic tale, victory over the evil Kashchei is an allusion to Russia's victory over the German forces.

Rou's work at Soiuzdetfil'm (later reorganized into the Gorkii Film Studio for Children's and Youth Films) reveals the impact of production facilities on creativity as much as the fairy tale's return to the Soviet cultural repertoire. Ptushko experimented with color film in the 1930s; Rou also contributed to technological advancement with his stereoscopic (3D) film *May Night* (Maiskaia noch' 1952), based on Nikolai Gogol's story. Meanwhile, at Soiuzmul'tfil'm, established animators continued to make fairy-tale films. Ol'ga Khodataeva animated (with Zinaida and Valentina Brumberg, and her brother Nikolai) one of the first Soviet folktales *The Samoyed Boy* (Samoedskii mal'chik 1928), loosely based on a narrative about a child who travels to Leningrad to gain an education. Khodataeva also created the New-Year's tale *Father Frost and the Grey Wolf* (Ded moroz i sery volk 1937), while the Brumberg sisters continued their work with the classical tales *Red Riding Hood* (Krasnaia shapochka 1937), *Ivashka and Baba Yaga* (1938), and *The Tale of the Tsar Saltan* (Skazka o tsare Saltane 1943). However, the Soviet Union had yet to produce a full-length animated feature.

During the war, Soiuzmul'tfil'm was evacuated to Samarkand, where the lack of facilities almost halted the production of cartoons. Back in Moscow, animators actively began work on Russian and foreign fairy tales for feature-length cartoons, seeking to make box-office profits, as the US industry had achieved with Disney's *Snow White*. The fairy tale suited propaganda purposes. It was connected to the national heritage and thus allowed for the integration of ethnic minorities into the all-embracing Soviet society (a feature also pertinent in the twenty-first century with the project "Mountain of Gems" [*Gora samotsvetov*], discussed below). It could also show a child's maturation with a socialist revision; the protagonist makes a journey into the realm of imagination, gains experience, and eventually becomes a proper adult member of Soviet society. As Semen Ginzburg comments: "The magic in the Russian folktale is almost always realistically motivated; it is a special fairy and metaphorical form of the reflection of reality" (1957, 15). The fairy-tale world also functioned as a means of escape from the unpleasant reality of Stalin's tyranny, offering happy endings and, if not victories over unjust rulers, then a new generation taking over the kingdom. Moreover, the fairy-tale hero answers for his actions, and is granted magic help as a reward for a good deed. This system offers recompense unavailable in socialist society; equal measures of punishment and reward only exist in the magic world.

How Soiuzmul'tfil'm Did Not Overtake Disney

After World War II, animators helped create the reputation of Soviet animation with their fairy-tale renderings. They included Zinaida and Valentina Brumberg's *The Magic Little Bell* (Chudesnyi kolokol'chik 1949); Aleksandra Snezhko-Blotskaia's *Geese-Swans* (Gusi-lebedi 1949); Ol'ga Khodataeva's *Sister Alenushka and Brother Ivanushka* (Sestritsa Alenushka i brats Ivanushka 1953); and former Leningrad book illustrator Mikhail Tsekhanovskii's *The Post* (Pochta 1929), based on Marshak's story about a letter traveling the world and the efficiency of the postal services.

Yet Ivanov-Vano became the master of the fairy-tale genre and the creator of the USSR's first feature-length animated film, *The Humpbacked Horse* (Konek-Gorbunok 1947, remake 1975). Based on the 1834 tale by Petr Ershov about a peasant boy and his unintentional rise to tsar-dom, the plot adapted well to the Soviet context, accomplished masterfully by satirists Nikolai Erdman and Mikhail Vol'pin.[13] The plain, Ivan-the-Fool character, transported from his village, receives a little humpbacked horse (*konek*), which turns out to be a clever, resourceful, and witty companion, offering good advice in all situations. The boy goes to the capital, a two-dimensional medieval town created in woodcut style (a reference to the ancient Russian folk art of the *lubok*), where he becomes the tsar's stable boy. The jealous stable-master instills in the king a variety of desires, which Ivan must satisfy. He manages all the tasks with the horse's magical assistance, which includes flying across Russia with sparks of magic. The simpleton boy is a model of behavior; obedient and meek, he is rewarded for complying with the most absurd tasks, while the king and stable-master are punished for their excessive demands. The tale emphasizes the need to fulfill the king's commands, thus pleading for non-rebellion against the social order. Justice is established by pure magic. In Stalin's Russia, this message invests the magic animals with the roles of guardian angels at times when demands (from kings or parents) are nonsensical. Thus, the film cradles the young Soviet spectator in the security of children's magic where nothing is impossible. As Zipes argues, the film "harbor[s] utopian notions of an anticipatory illumination – the wish image of eliminating a dictator, [focusing] on the struggles of a happy and honest young peasant to survive the machinations of a corrupt court" (2011, 93).

Ivanov-Vano excelled with his adaptations of Aleksandr Pushkin's *Tale of the Dead Princess and the Seven Knights* (Skazka o mertvoi tsarevne i semi bogatyriakh, scripted with Iurii Olesha, 1951); of Aleksandr Ostrovskii's play rendition of *Snow White* (Snegurochka 1952); and of Marshak's fairy tale *Twelve Months* (Dvenadtsat' mesiatsev 1956). He also animated *Once Upon a Time . . .* (V nekotorom tsarstve 1957) and the feature-length comedy based on Russian fairy tales *Go There, Don't Know Where* (Podi tuda, ne znaiu kuda 1966), both scripted by Erdman. Indeed, Erdman and Vol'pin as scriptwriters enhance their films' attractiveness to children: the immediacy and the often sharp-edged verbal exchanges give the dialogue a humorous tone, allowing for laughter and contemporary appeal.

In *Once Upon a Time . . .* , based on the folktale "Emelya the Simpleton," village life is drawn in the plain, coarse style of Russian woodcuts, while the court is depicted in elaborate, detailed drawings. The source tale has been modified to accommodate a foreign prince, caricatured in the anti-western climate of the Cold War with its drive against dandyism as embodied by the *stiliaga* (the Soviet version of the "dandy," who is obsessed with appearance) of the 1950s. The lazy Emelya catches a pike, which, in return for its release, fulfills all of his wishes. Resting on his oven while the magically animated broom, sledge, and axe do his work, Emelya wins the heart of the princess and marries her. Peasant traditions are victorious over the artificial court style. Chaos ensues when Emelya's rule commences: the tsar is forgotten, the crown lost, and the (useless and authoritative) tsar leaves his kingdom. With its grotesque portrayal of monarchs—Russian and foreign—and Erdman's pointed dialogue, the cartoon promotes simple life and rural wisdom rather than social manners and monarchical rule, with all the allegories to Stalin that may arise. *Once Upon a Time . . .* is pedagogically subversive in condoning and rewarding Emelya's laziness. However, it is politically correct for its scathing view of the foreign prince and grotesque portrayal of the royal battle for power as a fight between tin soldiers. Instead of revering magic, the story challenges it; the use of animation undermines magic and presents it as a parable for contemporary society in an open way typical of the Thaw, marked by the relaxed restrictions commonly associated with Nikita Khrushchev's Secret Speech at the Twentieth Party Congress in February 1956.

Fairy-tale cartoons thematically enhanced a strong Russian character with the moral value of humility, while stylistically remaining conventional and realistic, using rotoscoping—filming real actors and copying their movement onto celluloid—for characters and their movements. The combination of a conventional visual style and satirical texts allowed the cartoons to remain ambivalent and appeal to adults and children alike. Soviet cartoons could mock a kingdom, in another space and time, demarcating it as "Other." If Disney created a "totalizing spectacle that basically glorifies how technology can be used to aestheticize social and political relations according to the dominant mode of production and ruling groups that entertain a public spectatorship" (Zipes 2011, 23), Soviet cartoons stuck to moral values of meekness and self-sacrifice, as well as aesthetic traditions that ranged from Palekh lacquer-box techniques over the paintings of Viktor Vasnetsov to the book illustrations of Ivan Bilibin. Soviet animated fairy tales challenge less through their visual style, falling in that sense into Zipes's "conservative" category (2011, 53), than via the subversive social order they present, which allowed class mobility, women's emancipation and empowerment, and the toppling of rulers.

Cartoons reflect the political and social shifts in the Soviet Union of the 1950s. We examine two films by Tsekhanovskii made before the Thaw and towards the end of Khrushchev's rule in October 1964 respectively, to assess the shifts in the social order that informed these cartoons' settings. In the animated film *The Frog Princess* (Tsarevna-Liagushka 1954), scriptwriter Vol'pin merged the classical Russian story with the recurrent fairy-tale plot whereby the beloved princess is sought and rescued from her captor, Kashchei the Immortal. Tsekhanovskii's characters' movements are almost life-like, making them not grotesque or comic, but somewhat sad, a result of the "éclair" (rotoscope) technique. (Disney, who developed this method, used it to stylize movement rather than emulate the motion of actual people and objects.)

The tale reinforces the existing social order. The prince remains among the imperial order, with grace and beauty relegated to the fairy-tale realm. Plump, harsh women of former merchant and noble classes, their appearances degraded to common socialist workers, occupy the present society. This critical portrayal of women under socialism contrasts with Rou's live-action version of the same story, wherein Vasilisa is presented as a new kind of Soviet beauty. The fairy tale asserts matriarchal over patriarchal structures in Soviet society, ruled by Stalin as "father of the nation," thus providing subtle subversive commentary. At the same time, the conventional pattern of a reward for the completion of a series of tasks remains contained within the conventions of the fairy tale. As Zipes astutely notices, the task of animators was "to impart a strong sense of Russian nationalism through the characters, designs, and background of their films, to focus on the collective rather than the individual hero, and to depict young characters who demonstrated proper ethical behavior that all good young Soviet citizens were to imitate" (2011, 90).

In the feature-length *Wild Swans* (Dikie lebedi 1962), Tsekhanovskii (assisted by his wife Vera) sets Hans Christian Andersen's tale in medieval times for the witch-hunt of princess Elisa, whose brothers have been turned into swans by the evil stepmother brought home by an imbecilic but sweet father. By the same witchcraft, Elisa saves her brothers from their predicament and returns them to their human form. The cartoon is conventionally drawn and simple movements are rotoscoped. The characters' appearance reveals whether they are good or bad. The visual techniques are quite conservative, certainly in contrast to Tsekhanovskii's legendary, albeit incomplete, cutout masterpiece *The Tale of the Pope and His Worker Balda* (Skazka o pope i ego rabotnike Balde 1936) based on Pushkin's fairy tale in verse and set to Dmitri Shostakovich's score.

What is noteworthy about *Wild Swans* is its emphasis on individual action. The eleven princes may cherish their sister and transport her in a net to the shore and the king may love and fight for her, but she alone must weave the eleven shirts from nettle in complete silence to save her brothers. Her vow nearly costs her both love and life; the king is about to leave for a hunt and she is about to be burnt at the stake for witchcraft. Yet the classical Russian values of endurance and self-sacrifice to save others are rewarded. Elisa has matured and is ready to become queen, while her brothers and husband remain rather infantile. With the gradual Thaw of the 1950s, the emphasis on the collective gave way to the individual in live-action feature films about the war[14] as much as in fairy tales. The foregrounded individual often appears as title character, and children can actually be wiser than parents. Most important, however, is the stress on intrinsically Russian moral values of self-sacrifice, humility, and meekness to achieve a victory over evil forces. Matriarchal rule is consolidated, while male rulers (father, the young king) are ridiculed.

Andersen proved particularly appealing in the Soviet context, partly thanks to his concern with the social inequality that he, not unlike Gorkii, often blamed for his child characters' misery, thus offering a perfect fit for a socialist reading (see Bagrov 2005). Thus, Vladimir Degtiarev's *The Ugly Duckling* (Gadkii utenok 1956), Leonid Amalrik's *Thumbelina* (Diuimovochka 1964), and Ivan Aksenchuk's *The Little Mermaid* (Rusalochka 1968) became Soviet animation classics, alongside Tsekhanovskii's *Wild Swans*. Andersen's tales also often served as the basis for live-action films, adapted by the playwright Evgenii Shvarts. Many classical Russian fairy tales were animated,[15] but mostly as short films, and generally in drawn animation techniques or cutouts rather than puppets, which were mostly used for tales involving animals or invented creatures, such as the famous cartoon character Cheburashka.

By the mid-1970s, television had reached large portions of the population. While cinema admissions were gradually declining, it also became clear that Soviet animation could not compete with Disney. Nevertheless, the late 1960s brought to the fore a new generation of talented artists who would turn to animation. Indeed, Soviet animation could do better than Disney; it would focus on short films rather than features, and would develop auteur animation (see Pontieri 2012). Iurii

FIGURE 9.2 Nechaev's *The Adventures of Buratino* (1976).

Norshtein's adaptations of Vladimir Dal's tales *The Heron and the Crane* (Tsaplia i zhuravl' 1974) and *The Fox and the Hare* (Lisa i zaiats 1973) established him as one of the world's leading animators. He created a rich poetic universe with animal characters that inhabited a world possessing depth (unlike the flat drawings in Disney style), using paper and celluloid cutouts on a rig with several levels of glass panels and a camera mounted on the top (see Kitson 2005).

Television became a second lifeline for fairy-tale films, both animated and live-action. In the first half of the 1970s, a special television program was launched, entitled *Visiting the Fairy Tale* (V gostiakh u skazki), which lasted until 1995 and was extremely popular among children and adults. Moreover, fairy-tale films were regularly shown on television and often specially commissioned. A fine example of the latter is Leonid Nechaev's 1976 musical version of *The Adventures of Buratino* (see Figure 9.2). If Ptushko's 1939 version of *The Golden Key* was a highly charged ideological production that celebrated Stalinist cultural values, Nechaev employed Tolstoi's famous fairy tale to critique the stagnant atmosphere of Brezhnev's 1970s, which was marked by the country's deep disillusionment with utopian socialist values. The de-Stalinization Thaw process that began with the Twentieth Party Congress in 1956 and the cultural reforms of the early 1960s had been short-lived.[16] Party control soon extended into all areas of cultural production and often resulted in the imprisonment and persecution of members of the creative intelligentsia.[17] In this ideologically stagnant atmosphere, children's literature and films became a viable, even vibrant, outlet for creative freedom, providing artists, writers, and filmmakers with an opportunity to experiment, explore new themes and employ new creative devices. The fairy tale, in both literary and cinematic versions, offered a basis for the use of Aesopian language to reflect upon social and political realities.

The omission of the "golden key" from the title *The Adventures of Buratino* immediately shifted the narrative away from Tolstoi's story and Ptushko's film version. This story was *not* about the search for the key to universal happiness, but instead focused on the hilarious adventures of the wooden doll Buratino and his friends. The allusion to reality in Nechaev's film about marionettes from the puppet theater of Signore Karabas Barabas was established through the director's choice of casting real children instead of puppets. Moreover, the film started with a preview composed of a set of children's drawings depicting different episodes from the original book, ensuring an address directed to the child-viewer. Nechaev seemed to establish a direct link between his musical and the book rather than Ptushko's well-known film. The stylized, hilarious fight between Papa Carlo and his friend Giuseppe, and the jumping and laughing tree-log from which Buratino would be carved were aligned with the conventions of the fairy-tale genre. From the very beginning, every scene closely follows the popular book; Buratino's transformation from a simple piece of wood into a mischievous boy full of good intentions appeared as a miracle, and his coming of age is full of references to everyday life.

Yet the voice of reason is present in the film through the only marionette, the Cricket, who acts as a mechanism to deliver didactic messages. By posing as the messenger of a universal conscience, the Cricket mirrors some of the Soviet social mores of the day. The Cricket constantly tries to teach the impatient boy common wisdom of proper behavior, but spectators easily detect the strings that make this puppet move and talk. The already subversive image of the conscience as something that can be easily manipulated and pulled into different directions from above is only the first of many demonstrations of the social critique embedded in the film. In order to truly free himself, Buratino must get rid of this obtrusive construct, so he jumps into the streets to embrace his new adventures. The first scene that the newly freed character confronts—a theater caravan with prison-like bars on the windows slowly moving through the city—shocked audiences of all ages.

The appearance of a caravan full of children—actors playing the roles of marionette characters—was accompanied by dance music (the legendary "Butterfly Polka," adopted from Ptushko's version). However, the light and playful polka had been changed completely. Composer Aleksei Rybnikov deliberately incorporated heavy percussion and brass instruments into his musical arrangement so the polka resembled a funeral march. The child actors were completely over-powered by the huge figure of Karabas Barabas, the puppet theater owner and—as he cynically calls himself—"the total master of happy marionettes and their indisputable theater director." Karabas's total domination both visually and acoustically is strengthened by the refrain of a musical number performed by the chorus of his puppets—the children who, with their thin voices, obediently reply to their master's self-glorifying song: "Glory to our master, the daring Karabas, / We happily live under the protection of his beard, / And he is not our torturer at all, / But rather our leader and teacher."

The double meaning of this song, composed by the famous Russian bard Bulat Okudzhava, could have been easily decoded even without its politically daring refrain. The parallel between Karabas and the Soviet leadership was obvious because the titles of "teachers and leaders" were applied without exception to all of them, from Lenin to Brezhnev. Here the fairy tale offered a critique of the totalitarian society that the viewers inhabited.

Another important element of Nechaev's film is the absence of the golden key, which was supposed to open the door to the glorious socialist future. In Tolstoi's story, the old swamp turtle, Tortila, gives the key to Buratino out of pity after the two villains, the Cat Basilio and the Fox Alisa, have thrown him into the water. In Ptushko's version, by contrast, Buratino saves one of Tortila's children taken away by the story's crook Duremar, by selling his primer to buy the baby turtle's freedom. In the musical, Tortila cannot even remember the magic door, but can only reminisce about the good old times and lament the cruel new world order. The film's ending stresses the overall feeling of disappointment with reality; the main characters turn away from the theater audience that had greeted them. They return to the pages of the gigantic book (the very same one from Ptushko's version, in which a magic ship emerges to save the puppets and take them to the land of absolute happiness), to step back into the imaginary world that is preferable to reality.

The fairy-tale films of the Stagnation era emphasize the fairy-tale genre as a vehicle for social critique, evident in on-screen versions of Soviet fairy tales by satirists such as Shvarts or Olesha.[18] These tales' subversive nature made them suitable for both children and adult audiences. While young viewers followed the dynamic plots, their parents enjoyed the sharp critical remarks and utterances full of hidden meanings, which reflected life in a totalitarian society, recreated within the boundaries of the magic world. Fairy-tale films became truly protean in their ability to move across the worlds of magic and interweave fantasy and reality. Screen adaptations of plays based on fairy-tale plots were a major trend in both film and television productions of the late 1970s and 1980s.[19]

No Fairies but Heroes: Post-Soviet Stories

Few fairy-tale films—animated or live-action—were made in the socially and politically tumultuous years of perestroika (1986–1991) and in the 1990s, largely because of the film industry's crisis (see Beumers 1999). In live-action film, Anna Melikian's *The Mermaid* (Rusalka 2007) borrows thematic elements from Andersen's fairy tale, while the story is set in contemporary Moscow and explores the solitude and isolation of a teenager who longs for her childhood home at the seaside. For Melikian, the structural element of the journey undertaken by a teenage protagonist into another (new, unknown) world, endows films with a fairy-tale atmosphere, yet the process often ends in tragedy rather than a happy ending. Two major trends concerning animated fairy tales need consideration here: first, animated features have been distributed since the 2000s, and they have—after a slow start—conquered the market; second, the project "The Mountain of Gems" has created a platform for a new generation of animators. In a sense, both wish to revive Russian folk heritage through the medium of cinema.

The first animated features were based on classical tales—the German writer Wilhelm Hauff's *Little Long-Nose* (Karlik nos 2003) and a remake of Tchaikovsky's *The Nutcracker* (Shchelkunchik 2003); both had little success at the box office in a still ailing Russian film market, which picked up in 2004. Then followed Valerii Ugarov's *Babka Ezhka and Others* (Babka Ezhka i drugie 2007; sequel *New Adventures of Babka Ezhka* [Novye prikliucheniia Babki Ezhki], directed by Nikolai Titov and Oktiabrina Potapova 2007), which mix characters from Russian fairy tales and myths to create adventure stories. Babka Ezhka is a little Baba Yaga—a little girl dropped by a lost stork in the midst of the forest. She is raised by mythological creatures ranging from the real Baba Yaga and Kashchei the Immortal, to the wood spirit Leshii, the water spirit Vodianoi, and Kikimora, thus acquainting young audiences with the main characters of Russian legends and fairy tales, albeit in a somewhat muddled arrangement (see Morris 2009). Georgii Gitis's *The Adventures of Alenushka and Erema* (Prikliucheniia Alenushki i Eremy 2008) turns the fairy story of Alena who falls in love with Erema into a gripping adventure.

Turning to postmodernist practices of parodying Soviet culture—specifically the tradition of the Stalinist musical—in *The Ugly Duckling* (Gadkii utenok 2010), Garri Bardin transforms the Andersen tale into a musical set to melodies from Tchaikovsky's *Swan Lake* and *The Nutcracker* that form the backdrop for the perfectly choreographed movement of the chickens who refuse to accept the duckling in their midst. Stylistically, Bardin mocks the Soviet obsession with high-brow classical art through numerous references to popular culture; thematically, the film reflects Bardin's preoccupation with social isolation and discrimination, which makes it appealing to a broad audience: "The parody of a closed society that lives secluded in a little fenced world with a freedom-revolutionary-flag raised every morning, with pompous parades and a religious devotion to a useless leader, is vividly felt by an audience accustomed to Soviet times" (Pontieri Hlavacek 2011).

Above all, though, the Petersburg studio Mel'nitsa (The Mill), founded in 1992 by Aleksandr Boiarskii and the composer Vladimir Vasenkov, has played an active role in the process of reviving animation, largely co-producing with Sergei Sel'ianov's CTB independent studio, one of the most successful in Russia. In 2004, Mel'nitsa and CTB produced a feature-length film based on the Russian folk legend *Alesha Popovich and Tugarin the Serpent* (Alesha Popovich i Tugarin zmei 2004), followed by *Dobrynia Nikitich and Gorynych the Dragon* (Dobrynia Nikitich i zmei Gorynych 2006), and *Ilya Muromets and Robber-Nightingale* (Il'ia Muromets i Solovei-razboinik 2007). These films, which became known as the "heroic blockbusters," not only revived Russian legends, but also brought full-length animation back into the market; the second and third films made significant profits in national distribution. This is largely achieved through witty dialogue that makes the tales palatable for the contemporary viewer (see Beumers 2014). Following this commercial success, other animated films loosely based on fairy-tale themes were made,[20] including the box-office hit, *Prince Ivan and the Grey Wolf* (Ivan tsarevich and seryi volk, dir. Toropchin 2011, sequel in 2013), which—with a budget of $3 million—grossed over $24 million in Russia, compared to $33 million box office receipts for Disney's *Frozen* (with a budget of $150 million) after its release in Russia on 12 December 2013.

"The Mountain of Gems" (*Gora samotsvetov*) is a development of the studio Pilot, founded in 1988 by Aleksandr Tatarskii. In 2004, he launched this series of short cartoons based on the fairy tales and legends of the peoples of Russia, underlining a concern with stories that encompass a range of ethnic groups and regions in an attempt to forge a new, post-Soviet national identity for the Russian Federation. This project has helped establish young animators who experiment with the short form and reach an audience through the series' sale to television and DVD release; five parts were released as "Mountain of Gems"—Ruby, Emerald, Amethyst, Amber, and Sapphire—and further DVDs followed suit.

A strong patriotic tone looms over the series as it apparently seeks to re-appropriate the heritage of the multinational Soviet state. Yet it should also be clear that popularizing fairy tales of the regions and peoples in the Russian Federation is laudable, whether or not an Armenian, Ukrainian, or Belorussian narrative belongs to the Russian tradition. A short trailer with the slogan "Multi-Russia" (Mul'ti-Rossiia) accompanies each film, highlighting aspects of life in various regions. In this respect, the project is concerned with national identities, highlighting regional and ethnic differences as an aspect that enriches Russian culture rather than suggesting a unified national identity. The trailers may seem overly patriotic, although they introduce each region or ethnic community: "We live in Russia. The coat of arms is the double-headed eagle, and the emblem is decorated by Saint George, the dragon-slayer. The Russian flag is tricolor—red, white, and blue. The capital is Moscow. The country is multinational and there is this region . . . ."

From the regions, the project included Konstantin Bronzit's *Tomcat and Fox* (Kot i lisa 2004), based on a Russian fairy tale from Vologda; Oleg Uzhinov's *Zhikharka* (2006), based on a fairy tale from the Urals; Mikhail Aldashin's *About Ivan the Fool* (Pro Ivana-duraka 2003), based on a tale from Yaroslavl; and Tatarskii's own *The Big Cockerel* (Bol'shoi petukh 2004) from the Pskov region. The tales share a concern with characters who are duped by others. Aldashin's is the most classical, a version of a Russian fairy tale about the youngest and dumbest brother, kind and unassuming, but lucky all the way along. *Tomcat and Fox* is made in cutout animation; the fox cheats the other forest animals and makes them work for her and the lazy cat, posing as an important person. The social overtones are clear—poor folk are exploited when they fall for appearance alone. Similarly, appearances matter for the little girl Zhikharka, who lives with a blacksmith and a crow. When she is alone, the fox tries to catch her, eventually masquerading as a hare. Yet Zhikharka, a clever girl, resorts to the fairy tales she knows and puts the fox into the oven (a fate normally associated with Baba Yaga). *The Big Cockerel* also sees social justice established in the end, when the cockerel retrieves items that have been illegally appropriated by the landowner. On the whole, little creatures fend for themselves—and they can win.

"The Mountain of Gems" also includes tales of the Nanai, Nenets, Nivkh, Dargwa, Hutsul, Itelmen, Moksha, Evenki, Kalmyk, Uighur, Udmurtian, Erzya, Tat, Ossetian, Tatar, and Karelian people. The variety of geographical areas offers much scope for visual and musical approaches. The Karelian tale *About a Sheep and a Goat* (Pro barana i kozla 2004) was directed by Natal'ia Berezovaia and Elena Komarova. The witty dialogue includes: "Once upon a time there lived, well, a sheep, and that . . . what d'you call it, I forgot, a goat . . . ," imitating the speech of the region's people. The farmer holds a feast and is about to slaughter a sheep, when the goat tells it to run. Scared, the sheep and the goat get to the dark forest and settle peacefully there, possessing a cow's skull that is capable of frightening predators. The story's dim-witted creatures master their lives through luck and chance. They do not actively seek their fortune, but gain happiness without material riches through the typically Russian feature of passivity. Similarly, the Hutsul tale about the poltergeist *zlydni*—*Meanies* (Zlydni 2005)—is rendered by Stepan Koval' and Tatarskii through plasticine animation. Thrice, a hard-working family man gets rid of the meanies of the title (*zlydni*) but they return; thrice, he rebuilds his entire household. When the jealous neighbors deliberately bring back the meanies, the little poltergeists remain with the neighbors instead. Human endurance with fate is ultimately rewarded, while meddling is punished. Once again, passivity has the upper hand. Andrei Kuznetsov's *Mergen* (2013), a computer-animated film based on a Nanai story, concerns a child, Mergen, raised by animals after his parents have been snatched away by a black monster. One day, Mergen saves a girl who knows the monster. Mergen conquers the beast on his own and frees the taiga and its inhabitants. Endurance and suffering are rewarded.

Thus, the project curiously seems to empower the little creatures of Russian fairy tales, who successfully rebel against their oppressors, while characters in tales from ethnic minorities tend to remain passive and be rewarded for their endurance. Animation, feature-length and short, allows animators to hark back to Russia's rich cultural heritage by drawing on folk legends and fairy tales, while also incorporating regional cultures into the mainstream, equipping Russia's national identity with diversity and depth by encompassing both past and periphery. The social order appears to be both confirmed and challenged in these tales, depending on their geographic origin.

In a sense, with the patriotic twist of the commercial blockbuster cartoons of Putin-era cinema and the "Mountain of Gems" project, the fairy tale on screen offers less of an opportunity for escapism than an outlet for criticism and laughter, indirectly and metaphorically challenging the political and social situation, making fairy tales part of entertainment and—at least in animation—social criticism. Ultimately, though, a film such as Maksim Sveshnikov and Vladlen Barbe's *Snow Queen* (Snezhnaia koroleva 2012) cannot quite compete with Disney's *Frozen* (2013), and certainly not yet on an international market.

Notes

1 Pedology later experienced a complete defeat in the Soviet Union. The Central Committee of the Communist Party special decree of 4 July 1936 "On pedological perversions in Soviet educational institutions" condemned pedology as an "anti-Marxist, reactionary, and false science about children" primarily for its focus on the influence of milieu and heredity.

2 This feature also changed during the Thaw when protagonists internalized warfare as a private struggle against their own shortcomings.

3 Ptushko helped develop the three-strip color film method at Mosfil'm. Similar searches for color processes at Lenfil'm led to a slightly different technique that focused on drawn animation. The (nitrate) films have been preserved at Gosfil'mofond (Russian State Film Archive) but could not be projected due

to shrinkage and the impossibility of running two nitrate strips through a projector. They were digitally restored between 2011–2014 by Nikolai Mayorov and Vladimir Kotovskii and copies are now preserved at Gosfil'mofond (see Mayorov 2012).

4 Ptushko adapted literary fairy tales throughout his career, but puppet animation disappeared from his live-action films, marked by an abundance of special effects, including *The Golden Key* (Zolotoi kliuchik 1939), *The Stone Flower* (Kamennyi tsvetok 1946), *Sadko* (1952), *Ilya Muromets* (1956), *Sampo* (1959), as well as adaptations of Aleksandr Pushkin's *The Tale of Tsar Saltan* (Skazka o tsare Saltane 1966) and *Ruslan and Ludmila* (1972).

5 On the creation of Tolstoi's story, see Lipovetsky (2010, 125–145).

6 On different film versions of Buratino, see Prokhorov (2008) and Balina (2009, 183–199).

7 Tolstaia (1997, 38) and Lipovetskii (2003, 252) offer different explanations about this plot twist based on adult polemics over the aesthetics of the literature and arts of the early 20th century called "the Silver Age."

8 The first line from the so-called Aviators' March ("Even Higher"), music by Iulii Khait and lyrics by Pavel German, 1920. For a translation see van Geldern and Stites (1995, 257–258).

9 Tarakhovskaia participated in the scriptwriting, but Rou replaced several parts of the play with his own material (see Paramonova 1979).

10 All but one of the three versions of the "Emelya" tale in Afanas'ev describe the main character as lazy; the same plot about a sluggish peasant was also reworked in Tolstoi's retelling of Russian folktales, first published in 1913 (see 1984).

11 For example, in everyday parlance the new Moscow metro (1935) was referred to as "miracle-staircase" (*lestnitsa-chudesnitsa*), and its underground stations as "palaces of marvel."

12 Vasilisa's physiognomy stands in contrast to the other two female characters, one obese, the other extremely thin.

13 In the 1920s, Vol'pin and Erdman wrote satirical sketches for the Moscow Satire Theatre, including the opening review, *Moscow from a Point of View* (Moskva s tochki zreniia, 1924). Along with their co-writer Vladimir Mass, they were arrested in 1933. Both worked at Soiuzmul'tfil'm after the war and received the Stalin Prize in 1951. For a discussion of Erdman's scripts for fairy-tale films, see Kovalova (2012).

14 For example, Mikhail Kalatozov's *The Cranes are Flying* (Letiat' zhuravli 1957) or Grigorii Chukhrai's *Ballad of a Soldier* (Ballada o soldate 1959).

15 For example, the fairy tales of Aleksandr Pushkin: *Tale of the Golden Cockerel* (Skazka o zolotom petushke 1967), *The Tale of the Fisherman and the Fish* (Skazka o rybake i rybke 1950, also Ptushko, 3-strip-color, 1937), and *Tsar Saltan* (Skazka o tsare Saltane 1943; 1984).

16 The might of the Soviet Bloc was shaken internationally through the uprisings in Poland and Hungary in 1956; the construction of the Berlin Wall in 1961; the Cuban Missile Crisis of 1962; and the Soviet invasion of Czechoslovakia to crush the "Prague Spring" in 1968.

17 For example, the 1958 campaign against Nobel Prize-winner Boris Pasternak; the incarceration of poet Joseph Brodsky in 1964; and the arrest of writers Andrei Siniavskii and Iulii Daniel in 1966.

18 For example, *Cain the 18th* (Kain XVIII 1963) by Nadezhda Kosheverova and Mikhail Shapiro; Kosheverova's *The Shadow* (Ten' 1971); Aleksei Batalov's *Three Fat Men* (Tri tolstiaka 1966).

19 For example, Mark Zakharov's *The Everyday Miracle* (Obyknovennoe chudo 1978), *That Very Münchausen* (Tot samyi Miunkhgauzen 1973), and *The House, That Was Built by Swift* (Dom, kotoryi postroil Swift 1982).

20 *Three Knights and the Queen of Shamakhan* (Tri bogatyria i Shamakhanskaia tsaritsa 2010); *Three Knights on Distant Shores* (Tri bogatyria na dal'nikh beregakh 2012); *How to Catch the Firebird's Feather* (Kak poimat' pero zhar-ptitsy 2013).

10

THE CZECH AND SLOVAK FAIRY-TALE FILM

Peter Hames

It hardly needs stating that folktales and fairy tales do not respect geographical and ethnic boundaries. Yet the tradition of the fairy-tale film in Czechoslovakia and the Czech and Slovak Republics is distinctive, particularly for such small countries. Regular production since World War II continued throughout the period of the nationalized industry (1945–1993) and, in the case of the Czech Republic, has survived the onset of privatization. Production has been frequent and fairy-tale films clearly reflect an audience expectation.[1] Apart from films based on the work of Czech writers and collectors, there have been adaptations from the Brothers Grimm and Hans Christian Andersen. Tales of princesses, princes, and kings are frequent, and the word "princess" often appears in Czech and Slovak titles.

Interest in folktales and fairy tales obviously extends beyond the film industry and derives from similar concerns in the literature and music of the Czech revival in the nineteenth century. Among the nineteenth-century founders of modern Czech literature, both Božena Němcová and Karel Jaromír Erben were collectors of Czech and Slovak folktales, and their influence is readily apparent in both Němcová's seminal novel *Babička* (Grandmother 1855) and Erben's collection of poetic ballads, *Kytice* (A Bouquet 1853 and 1861). Erben's work was in essence part of his career as an archivist, and his collection of folksongs and rhymes published in 1864 included over 2,000 songs, providing an essential resource for Czech folklore study. Alois Jirásek's *Staré pověsti české* (Old Czech Legends 1894), aimed at children, should also be mentioned.

Czech composer Antonín Dvořák's opera *Čert a Káča* (The Devil and Kate 1899) was inspired by Němcová, and *Rusalka* (1900), although nominally based on Friedrich de la Motte Fouqué's *Undine* (1811), was according to its librettist, Jaroslav Kvapil, primarily influenced by the mood of Erben's *A Bouquet*. The latter also inspired four of Dvořák's tone poems, including *Vodník* (The Water Goblin 1896) and *Zlatý kolovrat* (The Golden Spinning Wheel 1896), as well as his oratorio *Svatební košile* (The Wedding Shirt aka The Spectre's Bride 1884). Josef Suk's *Pohádka* (A Fairy Tale 1901) was based on the music he wrote for Julius Zeyer's play *Radúz a Mahulena* (Radúz and Mahulena 1898), inspired by the Slovak fairy tale. Both *Rusalka* and *Radúz and Mahulena* subsequently formed the basis for feature films, notably Petr Weigl's *Radúz and Mahulena* (1970) and *Rusalka* (1977).

Other collectors of folktales included Jakub Malý, who published *Národní české pohádky a pověsti* (Czech National Folktales and Legends) as early as 1838, and Jiří Polívka who, together with Johannes Bolte, published the four-volume *Anmerkungen zu den Kinder- und Hausmärchen der Brüder*

Grimm (Notes to the Tales of the Brothers Grimm 1913–1932). In the twentieth century, a number of leading writers produced collections of fairy stories, including Karel Čapek (*Devatero pohádek/ Nine Fairy Stories* 1932), Josef Lada (*Nezbedné pohádky/*Topsy-turvy Tales 1939), Jan Drda (*České pohádky/*Czech Fairy Tales 1958), František Hrubín (*Špalíček pohádek/*A Bundle of Tales 1960), and Jan Werich (*Fimfárum* 1960). Many of these works have been adapted to film. Other names regularly associated with fairy-tale films have included creative writers such as Miloš Macourek, František Pavlíček, and Ota Hofman. While the works of Němcová and Erben were adapted between the two world wars, the impulse to produce work in the fairy-tale genre was initially rooted in animated film. The history of the Czech animated film dates from the mid 1920s. These early animations were mainly short advertising films but they often contained fairy-tale elements.

In the post-World War II period, the key names were Jiří Trnka and Karel Zeman. Trnka, also an illustrator, painter, and set designer, illustrated many collections of fairy stories—among them the Brothers Grimm, Andersen, Charles Perrault, Jean de La Fontaine, Erben, Drda, Werich, and the Czech surrealist, Vitězslav Nezval. Bettina Hürlimann describes his work as possessing a vitality that virtually bursts the borders of the pictures "with the kind of life that is taken on by old and long familiar toys like dolls and teddy-bears" (1967, 226). The breadth of his illustration indicates something of the wider cultural background and there is little essential difference in visual form between his film adaptation of Andersen's *The Emperor's Nightingale* (Císařův slavík 1948) and his feature-length puppet films such as his versions of Jirásek's *Old Czech Legends* (Staré pověsti české 1953) and Shakespeare's *A Midsummer Night's Dream* (Sen noci svatojánské 1959).

Zeman, who worked in France in the 1930s as a poster designer and window dresser, made his first film, *A Christmas Dream* (Vánoční sen), in 1945. He drew his subject matter from both folktales (*King Lávra/*Král Lávra [1950], *1001 Nights/*Pohádky tisíce a jedné noci [1974], and *The Sorcerer's Apprentice/*Čarodějův učeň aka Krabat [1978]) and fantastic literature (Jules Verne's *An Invention for Destruction/*Vynález skázy [1958], and Gottfried Bürger's *Baron Münchhausen/*Baron Prášil [1961]). His importance and influence has been acknowledged by contemporary English-language directors such as Terry Gilliam and Tim Burton. The work of Trnka and Zeman was highlighted as a major achievement as early as 1949 and went on to international success in the 1950s.[2]

Bořivoj Zeman directed the first two live-action fairy-tale films—*The Proud Princess* (Pyšná princezna 1952) and *Once Upon a Time There Was a King . . .* (Byl jednou jeden král . . . 1954)—both adapted from Němcová. These were followed by *Stick, Start Beating!* (Obušku, z pytle ven!, dir. Jaromír Pleskot, 1955) from Erben; *The Princess with the Golden Star* (Princezna se zlatou hvězdou, dir. Martin Frič, 1959) from Němcová; *The Three Golden Hairs of Old Man Know-All* (Tři zlaté vlasy děda Vševěda, dir. Jan Valášek, 1963) from Erben; *The Golden Fern* (Zlaté kapradí, dir. Jiří Weiss, 1963), from Drda; and *The Incredibly Sad Princess* (Šíleně smutná princezna, dir. B. Zeman, 1968). These early films often exhibited a charm and simplicity at variance with political realities, and in many ways provided a model for the later films of directors such as Václav Vorlíček and Zdeněk Troška.

Animated film was central to the postwar development of the fairy-tale genre, extending from the late 1940s through to the present, despite the funding crises of the 1990s. The early work of Trnka, K. Zeman, Břetislav Pojar, and Stanislav Latal has been followed by Viktor Kubal (in Slovakia), Vlasta Pospíšilová, Jan Švankmajer, Jiří Barta, and more recently, Aurel Klimt and Jan Balej. The three *Fimfárum* films (2002, 2006, 2011) have successfully maintained the animated fairy-tale tradition.

While a number of live-action fairy-tale features were produced between 1950 and 1970, the genre developed more extensively in the 1970s and 1980s. This expansion in production could well have been related to the aftermath of the Soviet invasion in 1968. The cumulative banning of over 100 of the Czechoslovak New Wave films of the 1960s ushered in a new era in which films were to be positive, uplifting, entertaining, and, above all, harmless in the eyes of the Soviet-installed government. Fairy tales could present precisely this kind of apparently innocuous material.

The directors of the Czechoslovak New Wave of the 1960s—the first generation to make an international impact—made no substantial contribution to the fairy-tale genre until the 1970s. However, one film from the New Wave era does deserve consideration—Jaromil Jireš's *Valerie and Her Week of Wonders* (Valerie a týden divů 1970), which had been prepared the previous year. Based on a Gothic novel by the surrealist poet Vitězslav Nezval, it has become something of an international cult movie in recent years and was a clear precursor to the Neil Jordan/Angela Carter adaptation *The Company of Wolves* (1984). Carter, in fact, had been impressed by Jireš's film and both films directly chart their heroines' rite of passage into sexuality.

In some ways a straightforward adaptation of Nezval's original, the film tells of Valerie's "week of wonders," the week in which she begins to menstruate. Possibly the first film to directly address the subject, it focuses on her changing experience of the world and, in particular, her view on competing sexual realities and fantasies. The film makes no clear division between reality and fantasy, but Valerie appears to be living with her grandmother in a provincial village. She is threatened by a sinister vampire known as Tchoř (Polecat), who also doubles as a bishop, a father figure, and her grandmother's lover. Her closest friend is the poet and musician, Orlík (Eaglet), who features as both brother and boyfriend (and Tchoř's assistant), rescuing her from frightening situations. Grandmother also appears as a mysterious second cousin and as her mother. This Freudian potpourri, of course, has many links with the standard characters in fairy tales. Valerie escapes from crisis to crisis with the aid of her magic earrings, much like the transitions to alternate realities in *Alice in Wonderland*.

This is clearly a male fantasy, in Jonathan Rosenbaum's words, "spurred by guiltless and polysexual eroticism" (2008), but Valerie maintains her innocence, immunity, and humor throughout. The screenplay was co-written by the director, writer, and designer Ester Krumbachová, best known for her collaborations with the overtly feminist Věra Chytilová. Krumbachová undoubtedly exerted an influence, and, in the film's promotion, both she and Jireš expressed their intention to make a film that was ultimately reassuring (Jireš 1970, 9).

The Nezval/surrealist connection leads directly to the work of the surrealist animator, Jan Švankmajer, the one major talent to produce uncompromised work during the years of "normalization" (1970–1989) in Czechoslovakia. While he made two key live-action, stop-motion animated fairy-tale features, *Alice* aka *Something from Alice* (Něco z Alenky 1988) and *Little Otik* (Otesánek 2000), he has never been a director for children. Two short films that were to prove significant forerunners of these features were the animated *Jabberwocky* (Žvahlav aneb šatičky Slaměného Huberta 1971) and the predominantly live-action *Down to the Cellar* (Do pivnice aka Do sklepa 1982) (see Figure 10.1). The full title of the first is *Jabberwocky or Straw Hubert's Clothes*, referring to both Lewis Carroll (a favorite of the surrealists, of course) and Nezval's story for children. In *Jabberwocky*, Švankmajer, who has always described his work as a dialogue with his childhood, evokes the world of children's toys. Small dolls, a kitchen stove, dancing clothes, paper boats, a waltzing penknife, children's bricks, and a real cat all combine in what Vratislav Effenberger describes as "a variety show from the playfulness of a child's imagination" (1972 [2008], 159). But in a film that begins with a hand slapping a baby's backside, it is not the sanitized imagination of a Walt Disney. Here the toys are destroyed and reconstructed, the dolls cooked and eaten, and the knife draws blood from its own haft. The animation was by Pospíšilová, who had also worked with Trnka.

In *Down to the Cellar*, a little girl goes to the cellar to fetch potatoes, where she meets a chest that takes on a life of its own, a terrifying cat, animated shoes, a strange old woman, and a would-be child molester. Based on Švankmajer's own childhood memories of being sent to the cellar, it was part of the Czech surrealist group's collective project on "Fear." The little girl is a precursor of the child heroines of *Alice* and *Little Otik*.

FIGURE 10.1 *Down to the Cellar*, Švankmajer (1982). Courtesy of Athanor Film.

While *Alice* is surprisingly close to Carroll's original, it differs from conventional versions of the book, featuring grotesque animals created from bones and skulls, and far-from-lovable re-creations of the White Rabbit, the March Hare, and the Mad Hatter. Carter, who dedicated her story "Alice in Prague or The Curious Room" to Švankmajer, described the film as "a tribute of one master of invasive dreaming to another . . . grotesque, funny, insidious, beautiful, a wonder itself" (1988).

While Alice is played by a real little girl, the world of her imagination is represented in stop-motion animation by puppets and animated figures. Her transformations in size, achieved through changing from human to doll, could suggest the instability of her identity. Yet the intermittent close-ups of her lips introducing the episodes suggest that she has ultimate control of these imaginings. At the film's end, when she has been condemned to death and the White Rabbit, armed with a pair of scissors, appears as an actual executioner, she announces in retaliation: "Perhaps I'll cut *his* head off."

The first director to specialize almost exclusively in the fairy-tale genre was Vorlíček, who made the enormously successful *Three Nuts for Cinderella* (Tři oříšky pro Popelku 1973), scripted by Pavlíček from Němcová's original. A co-production with the East German DEFA company, it enjoyed both national and international success, becoming a staple ingredient of Christmas television post-1989. Jack Zipes discusses Vorlíček's work at some length in *The Enchanted Screen* (2011). The films' often conventional approaches to form are frequently counterbalanced by the inventive screenplays of writers such as Pavlíček and Macourek.[3] The success of *Three Nuts for Cinderella* probably sparked the sequence of co-productions between the Slovak industry and the West German Omnia Film in the 1980s, which drew on some of the most talented Slovak directors.

The first of these was Martin Holly's *Salt More than Gold* (Soľ nad zlato 1983). Although the story differs somewhat from Němcová's version (the basis for *Once Upon a Time There Was a King*), its main premise is unchanged. A king has three daughters who are asked to profess their love. The two older daughters tell him that they love him more than silver and gold while his favored younger daughter, Maruška, says that she loves him more than salt. As we know from other versions, salt is the most valuable commodity, and Maruška is ultimately vindicated.

The film opens with a knightly tournament, in which eligible suitors fight for the hands of the princesses. The two elder sisters marry their champions, who subsequently plot to depose the king. Maruška, in the meantime, is in love with a "gardener," who leaves her with a salt rose. In reality, he is heir to his father, the King of the Underground's kingdom of salt. His father, who distrusts all contact with humans, turns his son into a pillar of salt, but he is saved by Maruška. She is directed to the kingdom by fairies, consults a wise woman spinning in the woods, fulfills a test in which she fills a bottomless well, and passes over three valleys and three mountain ranges in search of the water of life that will resuscitate him. The costumes by the painter and costume designer Theodor Pištěk (who won an Oscar for *Amadeus* two years later) are striking, but the overall tone of the film is understated, with a simple and relaxed storytelling that clearly has its young audience in mind.

Miloslav Luther's *King Blackbird* (Kráľ Drozdia brada 1984) was the first of his feature films and, like his third, *Mahuliena: The Golden Princess* (Mahuliena, zlatá panna 1986), was adapted from stories collected by the Brothers Grimm. Both are striking and original works, while, like *Salt More Than Gold*, maintaining their focus on storytelling. *King Blackbird* is based on the story better known as *King Thrushbeard* (the basis for *The Proud Princess*), about the beautiful but spoilt Princess Anna, who rejects King Michal when he pays suit to her, disobeying her father, King Matúš, and declaring that she does not want to get married. Her father vows to give her to the first beggar who comes to the gate.

Michal duly disguises himself as a beggar and Anna is transported across the river. Initially, she refuses to work for him, but eventually learns to tread clay and work as a potter. When the "beggar" is ill, she goes to market with the pots to sell them, but they are destroyed by a passing carriage. Returning to his house, she discovers that the beggar is being transported to jail. At this stage, Michal's identity is revealed to the audience (but not to Anna). She follows him to the castle, where she does exemplary work in the kitchens and gets the job of taking food to the "beggar" in the dungeon. This is all part of Michal's deception—and he observes that Anna has to learn that "people are happy when they love someone." In a beautifully realized scene at the end of the film, Anna walks to the top of the castle in the snow accompanied by the sound of a flute, and releases a caged blackbird that has been blamed for "his sorrows."

When Michal reveals that he only acted the role of the beggar, Anna tells him that it was the "beggar" who was real for her and that she will wait for him, for it is he that she has come to love. They are reconciled when he rejoins her at the house, still in the guise of the beggar. In the role of Anna, Adriana Tarábková makes a persuasive transition from spoilt princess to the woman who has fallen in love—an evolution shown through mise-en-scène rather than dialogue. The music score by the virtuoso flautist Jiří Stivín affects period atmosphere and varied timbre to great effect (he also was the sound of the piper in Jiří Barta's animated feature *The Pied Piper*/Krysař [1986]).

Mahuliena: The Golden Princess is set in the Middle Ages, beginning in a king's fortress or camp, but without the visual costumes and pageantry typical of the genre. The sense of an encampment on the banks of the Danube is convincingly portrayed. A prince and his mentor Ján are sent on a journey to avoid witnessing the tribute of gold that has to be paid annually at the summer solstice to the legendary Zlatovlad (Lordogold). Ján, who the king describes as being "like his own son," is entrusted with the task of safeguarding the prince and given an old magic crown that has been in the tribe "since ancient times." However, if he reveals its magic properties, he will be turned to stone and can only be saved through a great sacrifice. Zlatovlad's power is said to reside in the full-size statue of Mahuliena, the river maiden.

The film takes the shape of an epic quest, reminiscent of J.R.R. Tolkien's *Lord of the Rings*. The crown's magic resides in its ability to predict what is about to happen. The heroes escape from danger three times before Ján recognizes the nature of its power. They reach the spring of the golden river, entering an underground cavern where all the people are blind, behaving like the living dead. Finally, they encounter Zlatovlad and the figure of "the golden maiden," Mahuliena. She can belong to anyone "strong enough to behold her beauty."

They begin the journey home with the now humanized Mahuliena, but a rift is created between Ján and the prince, who believes that Ján wants to supplant him and marry Mahuliena. The prince departs with Mahuliena on a raft, with Ján abandoned and chasing after them. The flowers in her hair turn into a water snake that bites her on the lips before swimming away. Ján swims to the raft and kisses her on the lips in an attempt to extract the poison. The prince misunderstands, accuses him of being in league with Zlatovlad, and tries to drown him in order to find the truth about his hidden motivation. When Ján reveals the secret of the crown—that it was entrusted to him until the prince became wise—he turns to stone and falls to the river bottom. He is finally rescued by the joint efforts and "great sacrifice" of both the prince and Mahuliena.

This striking film combines many mythological elements—the goddess of the river, beauty that cannot be beheld, figures turning to stone, and a story imbued with pervasive supernatural and fantastic elements. It also makes effective use of the Slovak landscape and scenery—a landscape of which animals are a constituent part. In an early scene, a lizard crawls across a hand, presaging the later episode with the snake. The imagery is both original and mystical.

Juraj Jakubisko, one of the most radical Slovak directors of the late 1960s, had all his early work banned or stopped during production and was unable to return to feature direction until 1979. His main contribution to Slovak fairy-tale films was *Lady Winter* (Perinbaba 1985), adapted from the Grimms' *Mother Hölle*. Developed on a number of levels, the narrative basically juxtaposes the supernatural world of Perinbaba with reality. The real world is that of the little girl, Alžbeta, whose mother dies, and whose father marries again, introducing Alžbeta to a stepmother and her daughter, Dora. In constant interaction with the real world is the figure of Death, in this case in the character of an old woman. Indeed, much of the film has to do with thwarting the approach of Death.

At the beginning, a group of travelers is overcome by an avalanche, leaving a little boy, Jakub, in a cradle. When Death (who can change momentarily from young to old) approaches, he tweaks her nose. Perinbaba, who controls the seasons, watches the events in a crystal ball. She has never seen anyone react in this way and takes Jakub to her kingdom. Rather than underground as in the Grimms' version, Perinbaba's kingdom is inside a mountain, enabling her to look down on the real world. Despite this terrestrial modification, when Alžbeta is thrown down a well by her stepmother, she reaches Perinbaba via an underground stream. It seems Perinbaba inhabits a world, which—above or below—is apart from that of reality.

Perinbaba adopts Jakub as her apprentice. She twirls around to make snow while he creates frost on the window. "We'll cover forests and fields and the world will rest and (be able) to give bread to the people," she says. Perinbaba's magic eiderdown supplies the feathers for the snow and also possesses magic properties that allow the film's protagonists to fly. When Perinbaba decides to waken nature, they see Alžbeta playing her pipe. Jakub is attracted to her and decides to re-enter the real world—but by so doing, he again becomes human and subject to aging and death.

As in "Cinderella," Alžbeta works for her stepmother after her father's remarriage. With the help of Perinbaba's eiderdown, Jakub escapes to reality, growing into a young man during his flight, and helps Alžbeta with her chores. When they go fishing on the ice, Death engineers an unsuccessful attack by wolves. The parents decide that Jakub is a useful servant and would make a good son-in-law. However, the stepmother wants him to marry *her* daughter, Dora, and plans to kill Alžbeta.

FIGURE 10.2 *Perinbaba*/Lady Winter, Jakubisko (1985). Photograph by Václav Polák © Slovak Film Institute Photoarchive.

In a complex dénouement, the stepmother and Dora throw Alžbeta down a well, where she ends up in the world of Perinbaba. Jakub is held responsible and condemned to be hanged. He can escape only if a virgin promises to marry him. Dora volunteers. Alžbeta can return to earth again "with love in her heart." While all ends with happiness and a wedding, the stepmother and her daughter fly away in Perinbaba's sheets, falling into a lake of pitch (echoing the original story) (see Figure 10.2).

Quite apart from the additional complexities of the story, this is very much a Jakubisko film, set against the Slovak mountains and villages, and full of folk customs and traditions. Magic, birds (doves and peacocks), the ever-present sound of the flute, a circus, and the positive acceptance of folk characters are all part of his world. Jakubisko, sometimes referred to as "the Slovak Fellini," here confirms the connection by casting Giulietta Masina—Fellini's Gelsomina—as Perinbaba. She is a friendly and witty fairy while Death, if not exactly affable, is something of a comic figure to be both accepted and laughed at.

The other Slovak-German collaborations were Juraj Herz's *The Galoshes of Happiness* (Galoše šťastia 1986), from Andersen,[4] and Dušan Trančik's adaptations of Andersen's *Mikola and Mikolko* (1988) and the Grimms' *Seven With One Blow* (Sedem jednou ranou 1989).

The two feature animations by Viktor Kubal can be included as part of the fairy-tale genre, although both are based on popular Slovak legends and actual historical characters. *Jurko the Brigand*

(*Zbojník Jurko* 1967) tells the best-known story about the legendary bandit, Jánošík. In the film, the baby Jurko's mother is arrested and he is suckled by a fairy spirit, who revisits him at key points in the story to provide him with the magic belt that gives him almost superhuman powers, ensuring his final escape to an apparently eternal life in the mountains. Kubal, who went to school in Jánošík's hometown, imbues his characters with simple and flowing lines, which combine with the story's emphasis on pastoral beauty and child-like animals to create a mood of enchantment. The folk-inspired music of Juraj Lexmann adds to the film's elegance and simplicity.

Kubal adopts a similar approach to his film about Erszebét Báthory, the legendary "Bloody Countess," who allegedly maintained her youth by bathing in the blood of virgins—also the subject of Peter Sasdy's *Countess Dracula* (1970) and Jakubisko's *Báthory* (2008). While he does not eliminate the blood, Kubal's *The Bloody Lady* (*Krvavá pani* 1980) tells the story of an innocent and affectionate young woman who is nursed back to health by a woodsman after contracting a fever in a thunderstorm. She falls in love and literally leaves him with her heart. Her character changes immediately and she begins to treat her favorite animals with cruelty, eventually whitening her skin with the blood of maidens. The legend takes its course, and she spurns the return of her heart (although it is eventually restored). The complexities of the story range from lyricism to expressionism, with small gestures that are both humorous and critical of its protagonists. Again, Kubal's simple and minimalist style gives the film a peculiar force.

In the post-communist era, the fairy-tale film has survived despite the problems frequently experienced in other areas of production. Vorlíček continues to work regularly. Another director to become a regular of the genre is Troška. He first attracted attention with an inventive adaptation of Jirásek's *The Treasure of Count Chamaré* (*Poklad hraběte Chamaré* 1984) and has subsequently pursued a resolutely commercial course, specializing in down-market comedies. He has also directed seven fairy tales, three adapted from Drda and one from Němcová.

Zipes (2011, especially 339–40) discusses a number of Vorlíček's later films, notably *Queen of the Lake* (*Jezerní královna* 1998). In addition, Vorlíček directed *Thomas the Falconer* (*Sokoliar Tomáš* 2000), which was filmed in Slovakia and adapted from a 1932 novel by Jozef Ciger-Hronský, perhaps the outstanding Slovak inter-war novelist. *Thomas the Falconer* was a Slovak-Polish-French-Hungarian-Czech-German co-production, and was scripted by Ondrej Šulaj, one of Slovakia's major screenwriters. The film is set in the fifteenth century when Slovakia was part of the Kingdom of Hungary.

It centers on the legend of "the King of the Falcons," who saved King Mathias Corvinus of Hungary when he was lost. As a result, the bird was freed; it wears a medallion around its neck. At the beginning of the film Lord Balador announces that he would give his castle on the Danube in exchange for the St. Matthew falcon. Tomáš has grown up in the mountains and appears to have a magical rapport with animals, understanding their speech. He pulls a thorn from a horse's hoof, hides a polecat in his shirt, and scares off a crow approaching a falcon's nest. When wolves surround his family's smallholding one evening, he is able to scare them off with a howl. In spite of Tomáš's ability to deceive the predators, the wolves nevertheless kill his father and he is left in his grandfather's care.

The main thrust of the plot lies in the relationship between Tomáš and Princess Formina, Balador's daughter, born a day before Tomáš. Balador plans to marry Formina to Count Ostrík, but when his entourage arrives at the castle bringing gifts, he cannot persuade the princess to dance. Tomáš, the commoner, appears by accident before the princess, and dances with her at her request. He is granted a bequest of land as a result of a trick in which Formina colludes.

Alongside this apparently orthodox fairy-tale romance is the story of Vagan, the former head falconer, who has been sacked in disgrace. His home now shelters others whose faces do not fit at the castle—a dwarf whose tongue was cut out, a refugee who had been pursued by Balador, and

Tomáš himself. Labeled outlaws, their reassertion of justice and their life in the mountains as vic-tims of a corrupt aristocracy is not far removed from the traditional legends centering on Jánošík.[5] With the help of the King of the Falcons, all is eventually resolved.

The film is directed effectively, with an involving and dramatic story that contrasts the free life of the rebel with the corrupt world of the aristocracy. While Balador is not depicted as evil per se, his opponents and inferiors are routinely whipped and hunted (Formina tells Tomáš that he wouldn't survive the whipping ordered by her father)—and torture chambers are not a routine ingredient of most fairy-tale films. The open depiction of the death of animals is also unusual. In one sequence, Balador's dog hunts a rabbit and, in another, the trained falcon preys upon a rabid fox and a rabbit; although the killings are not shown, the camera does reveal the animals' corpses. In a sense, this is a continuation of the presence of death, which began with the loss of his father. The poetic center of the film, however, lies with the circling flight of the falcon.

In *Helluva Good Luck* (Z pekla štěstí 1999), adapted from Drda's *Czech Honza*, Troška tells the story of Jan (Honza), who loves Markytka, stepdaughter of a local farmer. Unfortunately, the farm-er's biological daughter, Dorota, wants Jan for herself to ensure her inheritance of her father's farm; she is determined that Markytka should inherit nothing. Dorota arranges for a recruiting gang to take Jan to the army, despite the fact that he is not eligible because of his sick mother.

Jan escapes through the woods where he comes upon a house inhabited by (rather comical) devils. They have a magic briefcase from which soldiers can materialize to defend them, a magic napkin capable of producing whatever meal is imagined, and a cloak that can make the wearer invisible. The film then illustrates the truth of the saying, "Whoever makes devils his friends has good luck." A complex story develops in which Jan defeats the three-headed dragon, Buciphal, rescues Markytka from execution, defeats corruption in the royal palace, and the romantic couple eventually become king and queen. Troška's approach, with its special effects (including CGI) and comic interludes, resembles the western fairy-tale tradition or even the English pantomime.

In *The Loveliest Riddle* (Nekrásnější hádanka 2008), also adapted from Drda, Troška continues to make effective use of landscape and castles. Matěj is working in the fields, harvesting, when he rescues a dove from attack by a hawk. He is also an inveterate teller of riddles and has a riddle for his girlfriend, Majdalena. As an orphan, Matěj has limited prospects, and Majdalena's father intends to marry her to the handsome Jakub. The dove speaks to Matěj, while geese comment on the couple and their love for each other. Matěj hitches a lift on a carriage taking a suitor to the Princess Rozmarý.

The princess is Matěj's obverse. She asks riddles of her suitors, who repeatedly fail her tests and lose an ear or part of a nose as forfeit. Matěj intervenes, answers her riddle, and sets her one that she cannot answer. He gets a kiss in exchange and the lady courtiers faint at the sight. The next day, the members of the court think up riddles to trick him, but they fail and Matěj earns money from the king in lieu of the princess. Subsequently, he becomes involved with a gang of outlaws and is sentenced to death. In the end, he marries Majdalena, rescuing her from marriage to Jakub, and the princess also finds a worthy match. While its pantomime-style villains are all over-the-top and non-threatening, the film is nonetheless presented with a light touch.

In general, Troška's films conform to conventional themes and are in no way subversive—a young hero leaves an idyllic countryside but eventually returns to its security and his true love. In the meantime, he triumphs over corrupt courts and aristocrats, is helped by animals and assisted by comic devils and water sprites. While frequently directed with skill, his films never approach the wonder of Trnka and Zeman, still less the unpredictable depths of a Švankmajer.[6]

The years 2000–2001 saw two very different films inspired by Erben's work: F.A. Brabec's *A Bouquet* or *Wild Flowers* (Kytice 2000) and Švankmajer's *Little Otík*. Švankmajer's work was highly individual while Brabec aimed at a broader commercial appeal.

Based on Erben's *A Bouquet*, Brabec's film adapts seven of Erben's original thirteen poems. Ultimately, the director faces the impossible task of finding a visual equivalent to Erben's highly distinctive verse and vision. While the film has been criticized for its linguistic adaptation, the verse is used sparingly, with the film concentrating primarily on visual re-creation. This was the second feature directed by Brabec, an established cinematographer, and it won him a Czech Lion for cinematography. The film was made for the company set up by Jakubisko following the division of Czechoslovakia into the Czech and Slovak Republics in 1993. He has a credit for "artistic supervision," and many of *A Bouquet*'s folk-style elements could easily be from one of Jakubisko's own films. The seven stories are often quite elliptical (in Hollywood terms) with implied rather than reinforced dénouements. Nonetheless, Brabec's approach reinforces romantic-lyrical stereotypes, a tendency more obvious in his unfortunate adaptation of Mácha's *May* (Máj 2008). In *A Bouquet*, however, he is constrained by using Miloš Macourek's adaptation, and also by the discipline of Erben's original.

The seven sections vary in length, with three developed more thoroughly than the others, one of medium length, and the remainder featured as little more than episodes. In the first major section, *The Water Goblin* (aka *The Water Sprite*), Brabec tells the tragic story of a young girl taken as his wife by a water sprite. She gives birth to his child, but asks for permission to return to the human world to see her mother. He agrees, provided the child is left with him. However, when it is time to go back, her mother locks her in. The water sprite demands her return to the accompaniment of storm, thunder, and water rushing under the door. The dead baby is left on the doorstep, we assume killed by the sprite (although we are spared the sight of the original poem's headless corpse). The section is notable for its underwater scenes with much use of balletic slow motion, and its striking use of color—the green of the underwater world, the red scarf that she drops into the river, is grasped by the water sprite, and returned in the final scene.

In the second major story, *Wedding Shirts*, a young woman prays to the Virgin for the return of her man, "who left for foreign lands." In apparent response to her prayer, the ghost of a soldier knocks at the window and persuades her to fly off with him. She asks what news of his father and mother? But on nights like this, they say the dead rise from the ground. She is forced to remove the rosary and the cross as he takes her to his "castle" (the graveyard). She seeks refuge in a mortuary, where the devilish ghost resurrects a corpse to let him in. But the latter crumbles with the dawn and the girl's hair has turned white. The flying couple are effectively filmed, and the ghost reveals his true nature in a sinister progression.

The medium-length story is *The Noonday Witch* (Polednice), in which the arrival of the noonday witch parallels a woman's attempts to cook food for her husband, returning from the fields, and her attempts to pacify a crying child. As she works, she turns over tarot cards on the kitchen table. In desperation, she calls the witch to come and fetch her child, and the wind blows over one of the cards to reveal death. The witch is both sinister and comical (she is chastised by children on the road). In the final scene, we see the child's body under a white drape.

An old man tells the third major story, *The Golden Spinning Wheel*, to a young boy. A lord riding through the woods sees a beautiful maiden, Dora, washing naked under a waterfall and falls in love. He approaches the house where she lives with her stepmother in the woods. The mother and the biological daughter, who is almost identical to her stepsister, murder Dora with a knife and an axe, dismembering the body and burying it. They go to the castle where the lord assumes that he is receiving the object of his love. However, when a golden spinning wheel is delivered to the castle, it gradually reveals the truth. It demands two legs, two eyes, and other parts from the dismembered corpse. Dora is resurrected. The mother and her daughter receive a similar fate to their victim, says the old man, when they are attacked and devoured by wolves.

The three shorter episodes serve as introductory and concluding sequences of the film. In the opening, *A Bouquet*, children attend the death of their mother and follow the procession at her funeral, tending the grave where heather now grows. The final two sequences comprise *A Daughter's Curse* (Dceřina kletba) and *Christmas Eve* (Štědrý den). In the first, a daughter reveals that she has killed an innocent dove (her own child). She is condemned to death and, as she approaches the gallows, her image is intercut with the cross. Her final message to her mother is a curse for giving her to the husband who was untrue to her. In *Christmas Eve*, two girls spin with their grandmother. They go out into the snow-covered landscape where they chop through the ice to discover the names and appearance of their future lovers.

While purists may object to Brabec's ornamental approach, the film remains disturbing by conventional standards and has the advantage of making a classic into something lively and accessible. Švankmajer's *Little Otik*, in contrast, is much closer to Erben's dark visions, in using them as a springboard for his own deeper imaginings. The film began as a project for an animated film by Švankmajer's wife, the painter and designer Eva Švankmajerová, which was published separately as a fold-out book. The animation survives as a film within a film as the little girl, Alzbětka, reads the story of Otesánek, inter-relating it with its re-enactment in the world around her. *Little Otik* tells the story of a childless couple who desperately want a baby. Mr. Horák digs up a tree root vaguely resembling a child, trims it, and presents it to his wife. Mrs. Horáková, much to his dismay, proves only too willing to treat it as real and is soon powdering its bottom, changing its nappies, and cutting its nails. Otik turns into a living creature with a cannibalistic appetite and grows progressively out of control, with the family cat, a postman, and a social worker sacrificed to his voracious appetite. Alzbětka, who lives in an adjacent flat, through reading the story, begins to understand what is happening in the neighboring apartment (previously she had been reading *Sexual Dysfunction and Sterility* under the dust jacket of Erben's *Fairy Tales*). She attempts to feed and protect the creature, who is seen mainly in fragments—mouth and hands, living demands rather than a complete identity. Besides its resemblance to a horror film, *Little Otik* is also an extremely witty take on family life with a fine eye and ear for the banalities of domestic situation and conversation.

Who's Afraid of the Wolf? (Kdopak by se vlka bál 2008) is a second feature film by Maria Procházková, a filmmaker who began as an animator, and focuses on a child's view of reality. As with Švankmajer, the fairy-tale world interacts with the real world. The film begins with a camera searching through the woods, images of a child and a wood, and little Terezka waking from her dream. The early dialogue in the film addresses the subject: How real are dreams? If you think really hard about something, can it become reality? In an unpleasant invasion by the real world, her father reads an item from the newspaper about a lost girl.

Unlike Švankmajer's film, in which the folk world consumes the real one, *Who's Afraid of the Wolf?* is about how Terezka makes sense of the adult world. The film thus echoes what Bruno Bettelheim referred to as "the uses of enchantment" in his 1976 book of the same name. Terezka's mother is a former opera singer whose husband works in airport security. Her daughter is the child of a previous relationship with Patrik, a famous cellist, who is unaware of her existence. Terezka's maternal grandmother, who has maintained contact with Patrik and actively supports a return to the previous relationship, complicates the situation. The threat to Terezka's world lies in the break-up of the existing family unit. The situation, however, is unclear and largely restricted to what Terezka can see and overhear.

The child's world contains different explanations and realities. Her mother reads Terezka her favorite story about Little Red Riding Hood and images and ideas from the story interpenetrate the film. She feels sorry for the wolf at the zoo, imagines herself in a cot in the country, confronts the wolf, and plans to go to a party as Little Red Riding Hood (while others go as princes and vampires).

Terezka already believes that she is not her mother's child (because they don't look alike) and has picked up the idea that she may have been swapped at birth. One of her friends tells her about a friend's parents who are getting divorced—but also about a scary movie on television about aliens. On a school trip to Karlštejn castle, one of the children sees a ghost and Terezka concludes that her mother is an alien "from another planet." Terezka also believes Patrik to be an alien, albeit only an "average" one.

The adult story and the fairy tale about Little Red Riding Hood develop parallels as Terezka and her mother visit her grandmother with a basket of presents on her name day. It is the grandmother who reveals the truth to Terezka about her parentage, leading to the crisis in which her stepfather rescues her and takes her to his workplace at the airport. Terezka believes that her mother would have stayed if Terezka had not discovered that she was an alien. At the end of the film, when Terezka runs away, shared concern brings mother and stepfather together again, and Patrik demonstrates his preoccupation with himself. The film's happy ending reveals that the mother is singing again and the stepfather is spending more time with the family. Images from the beginning of the film also appear at the end. Initially, in Terezka's fantasy, her stepfather had saved her and killed the wolf.

The overall style of the film seeks to immerse viewers in the world of children, where they stealthily watch forbidden television and overhear adult conversations whilst hiding in a cupboard or under a table. Their imaginative world is the product of both traditional and contemporary culture—aliens, jigsaws of Cinderella, princesses, vampires, and robots. There is also an obsession with origins, new babies, and conversations at night that may be dreams. Procházková also reveals her animation background with line drawings on the photographic images (scribbled lines on Patrik's arm when he is described as an alien, a red cross on the mouth of a man who mentions divorce).

Overall, the film is an imaginative investigation in which the wolf represents a threat to Terezka's childhood stability, but also reappears as the dog that rescues her. The adult conflicts—of love, ambition, envy, status, and work—are explained through the child's dreams and imaginative world, with the threats of the real world embodied in fantasy. Procházková maintains that she intended the film to be seen by adults and children together, and it is one of the few films to suggest an interaction between the real world and that of the fairy tale. *Who's Afraid of the Wolf?* retains a mood that is both reassuring and playful.

It is perhaps appropriate to return, in conclusion, to the Czech tradition in puppet animation, which has undergone something of a rebirth. Feature animation virtually died with the termination of the nationalized industry and animation as such struggled to survive. However, the strategy of combining a number of stories as a single feature was adopted, one of the first being the adaptation from Jan Werich's stories, *Jan Werich's Fimfárum* (Fimfárum Jana Wericha 2002). The film combined a number of stories already made by Pospíšilová (in 1987, 1991, and 2000)—together with two new episodes by the young animator, Aurel Klimt. Two further films followed, *Fimfárum 2* (2006), with two episodes by the veterans Pojar and Pospíšilová, and one each by Klimt and Jan Balej, and *Fimfárum—Third Time Lucky* (Fimfárum do třetice všeho dobrého 3D 2011), in which Pospíšilová was joined by Kristina Dufková and David Súkup.

Between World Wars I and II, Werich, a revered figure in Czech culture, established the legendary Osvobozené divadlo (the Liberated Theatre) in which, together with his colleague Jiří Voskovec (who after the war emigrated to the USA, acting on Broadway as George Voskovec), he created a unique form of political comedy-musical. Remaining in Czechoslovakia after 1948, Werich appeared in a number of films, including Zeman's *Baron Münchhausen* and as the storyteller and magician in Vojtěch Jasný's *Cassandra Cat* (Až přijde kocour 1963), a film in which a cat can see people's true nature through the use of magic glasses.

Based on Werich's recorded readings (he died in 1980), the films dramatize his stories. Primarily moral tales set in a traditional village setting peopled by farmers, innkeepers, teachers, and blacksmiths, they in some respects recall the prewar drawings of Josef Lada. While Pospíšilová's approach is traditional, that of Klimt and Balej verges much more on the grotesque. In the first of the series, Klimt's *Fearless Franta* (Franta nebojsa), a boy who does not understand fear, is exposed to a night in a local pub where spirits from the graveyard take over in visions that almost echo George Grosz. In the title episode, *Fimfárum*, a blacksmith is required to perform a range of impossible tasks by a local nobleman on pain of death. In defense, he enlists the help of the devil and a water sprite. Klimt's frequently incontinent one-eyed nobleman would have found no place in the world of Jiří Trnka. In *Fimfárum 2*, Klimt contributed the story of "The Three Hunchbacks of Damascus" (Hrbáči z damasku), an Arabian Nights-style tale about three hunchback swordsmen, all of them blind in the left eye, and lame in the right leg.

Another multi-story puppet film was the adaptation of Jiří Marek's *Car Fairy Tales* (Autopo-hádky 2011), in which a princess learns to laugh when confronted by a disreputable mechanic, an accountant meets a fairy who is only interested in fast cars, and a magic fish supplies new parts for a battered old banger. It was the last film to feature the work of Břetislav Pojar. Jiří Barta, director of the remarkable *The Pied Piper*,[7] having failed to complete a version of *The Golem*, finally made a second feature, *In the Attic—Who Has a Birthday Today* (Na půdě aneb Kdo má dneska narozeniny 2009), a remarkable evocation of a dream-world concocted from the contents of a childhood attic. Jan Balej also completed his second full-length puppet animation, *Little from the Fish Shop* (Mála z rybárny 2015), inspired by Andersen's *The Little Mermaid*.

While television provides a market for the fairy-tale film, it is clear that the fairy-tale tradition is deeply embedded in Czech and Slovak culture. Jan Svěrák, best known for his Oscar-winning *Kolya* (Kolja 1996), recently directed *Kooky* (Kuky se vrací 2010), about the adventures of an abandoned teddy bear, using toy-objects made of cast-off materials, and followed with *Three Brothers* (Tři bratři 2014), about three brothers who leave home to see the world and find themselves involved in classical fairy tales. Alice Nellis has also adapted Němcová's *Seven Ravens* (Sedmero krkavců).

Why should fairy stories have proved so popular? Answers are necessarily speculative. One reason could be that the work of Němcová and Erben, given its links to the Czech Revival, is not only admired but also linked to the expression of national identities. Further, the tradition of puppet and "trick" films, associated with the work of Trnka and Karel Zeman, corresponds to a tradition of puppet and experimental theater. In addition, the commitment to producing films for youth (including fairy tales) had become sufficiently well established during the communist era to survive it. This unique combination of factors contributes to the distinctiveness of Czech and Slovak fairy-tale films.

Notes

1 While distinctions can be drawn between fairy tales and folktales, there are frequent overlaps between them in the world of film production, and also with fantasy and other genres.

2 The work of Trnka and Karel Zeman would merit book-length studies. I have not discussed them in detail here as Zipes (2011) has provided extended analysis of many of them.

3 Vorlíček's fairy-tale films include *Girl on a Broom* (Dívka na koštěti 1971), *How to Wake Up a Princess* (Jak se budí princezny 1977), *The Prince and the Evening Star* (Princ a Večernice 1978), *The Magic Book* (Kouzelný měšec 1996), *The Firebird* (Pták Ohnivák 1997), *Queen of the Lake* (Jezerni královna 1998), *Saxana and the Lexikon* (Saxana a Lexikon kouzel 2011), *and Princess Goldenhair* (Zlatovláska forthcoming).

4 Zipes (2011, 337–39) discusses *The Galoshes of Happiness* as well as a number of other films by Herz including *Beauty and the Beast* (Panna a netvor 1978) and *The Frog King* (Žabí král 1990).

5 Juraj Jánošík, who was executed for highway robbery in 1713, became the focus for many legends and stories about outlaw life in the Carpathian Mountains in what is now present-day Slovakia and in Poland. A Robin Hood-type image has prevailed and he has been identified with the Slovak national cause. He has been the subject of six feature films and a Polish television serial (see Hames 2014).

6 Troška's other fairy stories are *Princess Jasna and the Flying Cobbler* (O princezně Jasněnce a létajícím ševci 1987), *Princess from the Mill* (Princezna ze mlejna 1994), *Princess from the Mill 2* (Princezna ze mlejna 2 2000), *Helluva Good Luck 2* (Z pekla štěstí 2 2001), and *The Devil's Bride* (Čertova nevěsta 2011), from Němcová.

7 Discussed by Zipes (2011, 213–15).

11

POLISH FAIRY-TALE FILM

130 Years of Innovation and Counting

Justyna Deszcz-Tryhubczak and Marek Oziewicz

Introduction

The invention of the kinetoscope by Thomas Edison in 1888 was a milestone in the transition from pre-cinematography of peep media to modern motion cinema. A similar passion for projected entertainments was pursued by inventors elsewhere, including Europe and Poland, which was partitioned at that time. In the years 1893–1896, the first attempt at devising a Polish cinematograph was made by Kazimierz Prószyński. In 1894, a year before the Lumière brothers' famous screenings, Prószyński built a Pleograph, his own cinematograph, which was a projector and a camera in one. Then, in 1909, he invented the Aeroscope, the world's first light hand-held camera. Mass-produced, the Aeroscope was used by newsreel camera operators on all continents for another twenty years. Prószyński is only one among several pioneers of Polish animation and feature film, although much less known worldwide than, for example, Georges Méliès.

Commenting on Polish cinematography, animated-film expert Giannalberto Bendazzi maintains that Polish films are marked by exceptional emotional depth, stemming from an ongoing commitment to the exploration of human nature (2008, 7). Bendazzi links this striking quality of Polish films to the historical turbulences experienced by Poles in the twentieth century and to their realization that intellectual, spiritual, and artistic freedoms must never be taken for granted. The other source of appeal of Polish cinema, however, is its creative vitality marked by huge doses of humor, optimism, and hope. It is our contention that Polish fairy-tale films partake in both trends, relying on wonder and magical estrangement to illuminate complex issues of real life.

The fairy-tale film, as we understand it in this chapter, is a sprawling category that includes, but is not limited to, adaptations of literary or oral fairy tales as well as original works. Neither adaptations nor original works are airtight terms; we acknowledge that, as Christine Wilkie puts it, "the situation of fairy tales in contemporary culture is analogous to Barthes's notion of 'lost codes'. The tales are intelligible because they build already embedded discourses which happened elsewhere and at another time" (1999, 132). Adaptations—or Wilkie's "texts of quotation" and "texts of imitation"—are often innovative and do more than simply allude to an authoritative pre-text, which is usually hard to identify other than as a hall of mirrors without a singular ur-text. Original fairy tales, by contrast, can be thought of as original only because they are "genre texts"—narratives that draw on "identifiable, shared clusters of codes and literary conventions"—which makes it possible to theorize them as new adaptations of these recognizable patterns (132). For all this overlap, a taxonomy based on a division between adaptations and original fairy tales is useful, and we take adaptation in its broadest sense as a cluster of "creative transformative processes . . . such as appropriation, expropriation, translation, concretization, amplification, extrapolation, and reaccentuation" (Zipes 2011, 10) that cue the audience to a specific or generic fairy-tale hypotext as a structuring pattern onto which the film is mapped. The line between specific and generic fairy-tale intertextualities is blurred, but as our discussion illustrates, the division has its practical uses. Our working definition of original works refers to films that (1) employ the poetics of the fairy tale to achieve a sort of otherworldliness associated with the genre and (2) establish it as an implied interpretative framework.

When applied to Polish fairy-tale films, the above taxonomy must be qualified. First, although Polish fairy-tale films have a long tradition reaching back to 1911, only a small portion of the European fairy-tale canon has made it into film in Poland. In some cases versions of these tales were available in foreign film adaptations and so there was no incentive to produce a Polish one. In other cases, their absence from Polish canon could be attributed to political pressures blocking them during the communist era or simply a cultural preference for other tales. Whatever the reason, the bulk of Polish fairy-tale films comprise adaptations of Polish fairy tales and original fairy-tale films. Second, given that film making and distribution occur in an institutionalized context involving political decisions concerning access to technologies and resources, Polish fairy-tale films since 1945 have developed under two very different sets of circumstances: the restrictive and centrally planned cultural policies of the communist era until 1989; and since 1990, the financially strapped though culturally more liberal conditions in democratic Poland. Each of these political environments has set different opportunities and restrictions that are intertwined in the texture of Polish fairy-tale films. In recent years new technologies have changed the film landscape so that Tomasz Bagiński could achieve otherworldly effects in his computer-animated film, *The Cathedral* (2002), or so that Jan Komasa could re-create the 63-day rebellion of the 1944 Polish resistance against the Nazis in his pioneer documentary drama, *The Warsaw Uprising* (2014), composed entirely out of archival material shot during the period.

Inasmuch as fairy-tale films can be categorized in various ways—on the basis of specific cinematic techniques, format, or intended audience—for the purpose of an overview, we have organized this chapter in two sections, each with three subsections. Films discussed in section one include a range of productions for children, adults, and cross-over audiences—cartoons, short animated films, TV series, and feature movies—based on animation or mixed media. Section two, also spanning different audience ages, explores live-action feature films and TV series. Additionally, each section discusses three sub-categories: adaptations of Polish folk and fairy tales, adaptations of international fairy tales, and original fairy-tale films. Although we are selective, the examples we have chosen are notable and representative of what we see as larger trends in the development of Polish fairy-tale films.

Animated Fairy-Tale Films and TV Series

When Poland emerged from the wreckage of World War II, it already had a strong tradition of animated fairy-tale films to look back on. In 1910, Władysław Starewicz, a Polish caricaturist and stop-motion animator working in Russia and France, directed a nature film called *Lucanus Cervus* about a species of stag beetle. As the live beetles refused to adapt to the conditions of the film studio, Starewicz made plasticine models of the insects and animated their bodies with wires (Giżycki 2008a, 13). Starewicz's first dramatized beetle puppet film was *Beautiful Lukanida* (1912), an adaptation of the story of Paris and Helen, which blended mythology with Aesopica in a light hearted fairy-tale format. Starewicz followed this interest throughout his career, adapting fairy tales or developing his own stories with a fairy-tale generic framework. Starewicz's most ambitious venture, released eight months before Disney's *Snow White*, was a feature-length film with stop-motion animated puppets, *The Tale of the Fox* (1930). An exceptional highlight of this pioneering production is its extradiegetic level: a human hand introduces the ape narrator, who in turn discusses La Fontaine's characters as they step out of the book until the eponymous fox appears. While the fox closes the book and is framed within the cinema screen, the ape operates a cinematograph. A human hand subsequently removes the ape to finish the film, thereby alerting the viewer to the experience of watching an adaptation of a fairy tale.

Starewicz also made three silent adaptations of La Fontaine's *Fables*, reworked Hans Christian Andersen's "The Steadfast Tin Soldier" into an original scenario for a film, *The Little Parade* (1928), and animated his own stories, which incorporated sequences with real actors. The most successful among those, *The Voice of the Nightingale* (1923), was a variation on Andersen's fairy tale starring Starewicz's daughter Nina Star, for which he received the 1925 Hugo Riesenfeld Gold Medal for best Fiction Short Film (Giżycki 2008a, 14). The 13-minute-long film depicts a young girl who catches a nightingale, dreams about the bird and its mate, and realizes that birds should be free. In return for its freedom, the nightingale loans her its voice during the day, which explains why nightingales only sing at night. Following the release of this film, Starewicz was offered a filmmaking job in the US, which he rejected fearing the loss of creative independence he had enjoyed in France.

Throughout the communist era since 1945, fairy-tale inspirations remained an important aesthetic element of Polish films, yet in many cases they also acquired a salient ideological significance. The politically approved mode of artistic production was social realism, and so non-mimetic themes and genres were discouraged. Nevertheless, filmmakers sought to escape the formal and thematic monotony either by resorting to readymade fairy-tale patterns or by inventing their own stories. One way to win the censors' approval for fairy-tale animations was to present them as material suitable for educating children about the national lore and showcasing the indomitable spirit of the Polish people. Such was the case with the earliest postwar fairy-tale adaptation, Zenon Wasilewski's *In Times of King Krakus* (1947).

Based on Wasilewski's war-lost project, it retells the legend about the Vavel Dragon, killed not by a knight in a spectacular combat but by a smart shoemaker's apprentice, who feeds the dragon a poisoned decoy sheep. This was the first Polish animated film to gain recognition at international festivals and it earned Wasilewski close scrutiny on the part of communist authorities. Despite delivering a message of survival through common people's ingenuity and of the ultimate defeat of a supposedly unbeatable foe—both themes that appealed to the Polish audience after the war—Wasilewski's interest in non-realist themes was also understood to reflect his opposition to the poetics of social realism (Giżycki 2008b, 30).

Another early animated rendering of the Polish folklore material was Jerzy Zitzman's cutout film *Bulandra and the Devil* (1959). A loose adaptation of a literary legend from Silesia, it tells how the coal miner Bulandra wins golden ducats from a magical creature inhabiting the mine, and how the devil seeks to steal Bulandra's sudden wealth. The world of the tale is populated by magical creatures from Silesian folklore, including little black devils that guard robbers' money and water demons that drown people in ponds. Also the visual design of the setting and the cutout characters were inspired by the Polish tradition of decorative handmade cutouts. Other elements of Silesian culture also appear in Wacław Kondek's *Ondraszek* (1959), based on a folksong about a robber. Among later productions influenced by the Polish folk tradition are the children's series *Let's Love Monsters* (1970), by several directors, including Stefan Szwakopf, Alina Maliszewska, and Zofia Oraczewska, as well as Piotr Paweł Lutczyn's *Pyza's Travels* (1977–1983)—a film based on Hanna Januszewska's folklore-inspired *Pyza on Polish Trails* (1956). The traditional Polish belief that on Christmas Eve animals may use human speech is the focus of Stanisław Lenartowicz's live-action/ animated *Christmas Eve in the Forest* (1996).

FIGURE 11.1 Forever changed, the young protagonist returns from his visit to the legendary submerged town, *The Lost Town of Świteź* (2010).

The most recent examples of the symbiosis between the animated film and Polish lore are the 26 short films in *Polish Fairy Tales and Folk Stories* (two series: 2002–2005 and 2007–2009) as well as such stand-alone productions as Kamil Polak's award-winning *The Lost Town of Świteź* (2010) (see Figure 11.1). Each film in the *Polish Fairy Tales* series has a different director and offers a unique interpretation of a given tale, including its own graphic style, which ranges across diverse animation techniques. Polak's *Świteź* is a visually stunning CG adaptation in 3D that engages in a unique conversation with the folklore material. On the one hand, through the recreation of a Gothic atmosphere of the journey to a mysterious past that cannot be forgotten, *Świteź* is a loose rendering of Adam Mickiewicz's 1822 Romantic ballad of the same name. On the other, it is a highly original take on the legend about a sunken medieval town, recreated in image and sound, but also through computer graphics enriched by specially commissioned oil paintings modeled on nineteenth-century Polish realist masters and medieval icons. The choral and orchestral score by Irina Bogdanovich enhances the emotional impact of the film as a story about patriotism, courage, sacrifice, and faith.

An important source of inspiration in Polish animation has also been myth. Early examples of such adaptations include Edward Sturlis's puppet masterpieces *Damon* (1958), *Bellerofon* (1959), *Orpheus and Eurydice* (1961), and *Danae* (1969). In Krzysztof Raynoch's humorous *Prometheus* (1985) the protagonist not only steals fire from the gods but is also a utopian social reformer. The most notable adaptation of mythical stories in Polish animation, however, is Lenartowicz's *Kalevala*—a trilogy consisting of *Aino* (1983), *Ilmarinen* (1985), and *A Quest for the Gold Mill* (1986). The films employ a painterly combination of animation with a voiceover commentary by Polish poet Ernest Bryll.

Among other inspirations for animated adaptations, Polish literary fairy tales have been by far the dominant source, with many films and series becoming exceptional cultural phenomena on their own. Such is the case with the animated television series, *The Strange Adventures of Matołek the Billy-Goat* (1969–1971), based on one of the earliest Polish comic books for children written by Kornel Makuszyński and illustrated by Marian Walentynowicz. First published in 1932, the Matołek comics have been popular well into the present and represent perhaps the best Polish example of the oral tradition of "Jack tales" (Zipes 1996, 12). In each episode of the televised series, the bungling folk protagonist travels in search of Pacanów, a town where goats are shod. Matołek's naïvety and gullibility always distract him from his goal, but are also a blessing that enables him to survive all dangers. Another of Makuszyński's children's classics, *The Two Who Stole the Moon* (1928)—first made into a full feature movie in 1962—was also adapted by Leszek Gałysz in his *Jacek and Placek*; an animated TV series (1984–1989) and then an animated feature movie (1992). Both have enjoyed a nearly cult status. Jacek and Placek, prankster twins from a poor village, leave their caring mother to search for a land of plenty where there would be no need for work. As the quest proves unsuccessful, the boys decide to steal the moon. This turns out to be equally futile. Finally, they return home and accept that happiness comes from hard work. Despite the overtly didactic message, the films captivated audiences with their distillation of an ideal world, enhanced by the abundance of magical places and characters. The appeal of the series partly derives from the almost psychedelic colors of the animation and the original score composed by Lady Punk, one of the most popular Polish rock bands of the 1980s. The feature film based on the series received the Best Animation Feature Award at Santa Clarita Valley International Film Festival in 1994.

Other successful adaptations of Polish literary fairy-tale classics include *The Kidnapping of Baltazar Gąbka* series (1969–1970), followed by *The Expedition of Professor Gąbka* (1978–1980), based on Stanisław Pagaczewski's 1966 children's fantasy novel under the same title; Zdzisław Kudła's *Kidnapping in Tiutiurlistan* (1986), based on Wojciech Żukrowski's anti-war novel under the same title (1946); and Krzysztof Gradowski's *Mr. Blot's Triumph* (2001), a live action/animation film, based on Jan Brzechwa's 1965 novel of the same title. In 2002 Andrzej Bogusz directed 52 episodes of *King Matt the First* series, based on Janusz Korczak's 1922 novel, which served as material for the animated feature film made in 2007. Similarly, a collection of philosophical tales by Polish philosopher Leszek Kołakowski were also adapted using animation in *Fourteen Fairy Tales from the Kingdom of Lailonia of Leszek Kołakowski* (1963). Such directors as Krzysztof Kiwerski, Zbigniew Kotecki and Maciej Wojtyszko made the films between 1997 and 2011. They employ a range of techniques, from classical celluloid animation, through cutout and puppet animation, to live action/animated film. The series has a cross-generational appeal and encourages its audience to see the world with a more discerning eye.

Another strand of Polish fairy-tale film—adaptations of international fairy-tale lore—took much longer to take off than adaptations of national classics. Perhaps the first such project was the children's black-and-white series *Jack in the Land of Fairy Tales* (1964), a joint endeavor by several Polish directors in which a boy who is an avid reader leaves the modern reality to safeguard the happy endings of various fairy-tale plots. This formula of allegedly improving the classic tales later evolved into parody and grotesque, noticeable especially in retellings of the European tradition. Black humor emanates from Zofia Oraczewska's *The Adventures of Hansel and Gretel* (1983) and *The Adventures of the Little Red Riding Hood* (1983), as well as from Alina Maliszewska's *New Robin Hood* (1983).

A more recent example of the satirical take on the fairy tale is Andrzej Czeczot's animated film *Eden* (2002), in which the everyman Youzeck journeys across Hell, Purgatory, and Heaven. The three realms do not differ much from each other, and while the heavenly New York City is presented as the epitome of success, the film overtly debunks this status. Moving from one realm to another, the pipe-playing Pole encounters historical, mythical, and fairy-tale characters, such as the legendary Polish highlander outlaw Yanoshek, Neptune, Sisyphus, God, Bill Clinton with Monica Lewinsky, and Chopin. The sheer abundance of sources points to the fairy tale as just one taproot of pop culture, while the interactions among real and imaginary characters create a hyperrealist ambience. Drawn in black-and-white, unlike other characters, Youzeck is a passive observer of the life going on before his eyes, becoming active only when he senses an opportunity for sex. Marked by the postmodern poetics of excess and jouissance, the film contains no dialogue or CGI effects, with the episodic narrative being propelled by the jazz-folk-classical score composed by Polish jazz musician and composer Michał Urbaniak.

One of the most unconventional renderings of the European fairy-tale material is Piotr Dumała's black-and-white short film *Little Black Riding Hood* (1983), a production made by engraving images on gypsum panels. The protagonist is a clumsy girl wearing a black hood. On the way to visit her grandmother, the girl is overwhelmed by an inexplicable fury and eats everything she encounters, including the wolf. The girl is then shot by the hunter, upon which the wolf leaves her belly, eats the hunter, and runs to Grandma's house, where a woman wearing a Samurai kimono kills him. The hunter escapes from the wolf's belly, returns to the forest, and the story begins again, this time with the wolf developing an erotic relationship with the grandma. Although Dumała's tale appears to be a surrealist joke drawn by a child's hand, the animation gradually matures in form and content until it becomes a reflection on a naive perception of the world filtered through traditional, deeply internalized fairy-tale scenarios. Another instance of a subversive take on the fairy tale is Leszek Komorowski's *Baba Yaga from 8 a.m. to 3 p.m.* (1984), in which popular fairy-tale characters are deported to a theme park.

Polish animators have also adapted international literary fairy tales. A particularly interesting example is Tadeusz Wilkosz's *Colargol*, an adaptation that included both a stop-motion TV series (1968–1974) and feature films. Known in the US as Barnaby, the genial bear cub was created by French author Olga Pouchine in the 1950s. In 1957 the French TV producer Albert Barillé secured sufficient funding to employ Wilkosz, the best Polish animator of the period, to design the puppets and set up a production team. Wilkosz's cooperation with a foreign party was unprecedented in Poland at that time. Despite numerous obstacles, up to 1974, 53 episodes of *The Adventures of Colargol* series had been created. The material from the series was used in three feature films: *Colargol in the Wild West* (1976), *Colargol Conquers Outer Space* (1978), and *Colargol and the Magic Suitcase* (1979). The popularity of *Colargol* was partly due to its offering the audience a refuge from everyday reality. *Colargol and the Magic Suitcase*, for example, features the bear crossing borders with the help of a suitcase that can change into an airplane. Communist censors saw that magical freedom of movement as a form of sedition against highly restrictive state regulations about traveling abroad, especially to the west (Armata 2008, 83).

Another widely acclaimed Polish adaptation of international literary fairy tales was Lucjan Dembiński's *The Moomin Stories* series (1977–1982). Based on Tove Jansson's work, the series is a semi-flat stop-motion puppet animation with the narrator's voiceover instead of characters' dialogue. The characters are made of felt and the setting is composed of textures and fabrics: sand, flowers, buttons, feathers, corduroy, and wool. Several episodes served as material for Dembiński's feature films: *Happy Days of the Moomins* (1983), *Winter in Moominland* (1986), *The Moomins' Summer* (2008), and *Moomins and the Comet Chase* (2010). Although supposedly too scary for young viewers, the series is true to Jansson's stories and "the melancholy spirit" of her artwork (Sheridan 2004, 167). Equally successful was Janusz Galewicz's artistically savvy puppet TV series *In the Land of Oz the Wizard* (1983–1989), based on L. Frank Baum's Oz tales.

Among the most recent examples of adaptations of the international fairy-tale canon is Joanna Jasińska-Koronkiewicz's *The Flax* (2005), a painted animation based on Andersen's tale and released to commemorate the 200th anniversary of his birth. The flow of the paintings depicts the metamorphoses of flax into linen, paper, and sparks, while at the same time conveying the reassuring message that as long as one believes in oneself, it is possible to find self-fulfillment. A current fairy-tale project testifying to the continuous interest in the literary fairy-tale tradition is Jasińska-Koronkiewicz's

Paint Me a Fairy Tale series (in production). Based on oil painting filmed process, the series is to include adaptations of Andersen's "It's Quite True!" "Little Ida's Flowers," "What the Old Man Does is Always Right," and "Ole-Lukoie."

Just as traditional tales gave rise to the development of a literary genre, they also inspired the creation of original fairy-tale films. One of the earliest such productions in the postwar period was Wasilewski's animated fairy-tale film *Mr. Feather Dreams* (1949), in which an elderly clerk dreams about sailing over the town in his bed. He lands in his office, where he traps his boss in a drawer, announces that he is the new boss, and introduces new rules. In the end, it turns out that Mr. Feather overslept and is late for work. This barely disguised critique of state bureaucracy was censored however, and the film was shelved indefinitely (Giżycki 2008b, 31). Also noteworthy is Wasilewski's *Michałkowice Tale* (1954), a technologically advanced 30-minute color production about a poor peasant boy falling in love with a princess. Wasilewski's later original fairy-tale films include *Magical Gifts* (1956), *Once Upon a Time There Was a Little Pig* (1960), and *The Wooden Rider* (1964). Other directors of that period also made original fairytales, such as Władysław Nehrebecki's *Kimsobo the Traveler* (1953) and Ryszard Kuziemski's *A Fairy Tale* (1968).

It was in animations for young audiences, especially TV series done in the 1960s, that original fairy tales were particularly abundant. The earliest examples include Lechosław Marszałek's, Władysław Nehrebecki's, and Kudła's episodes in *The Adventures of the Blue Knight* (1963–1965) and Bogdan Nowicki's *Fairy Tales and Fairy Quarrels* (1964), both of which follow conventions of the chivalric romance. Other popular series launched in the 1960s included the 114-episode puppet animation *Teddy Floppy Ear* (1975–1987), which depicts a small community of anthropomorphized animals; *Reksio* (1967–1990), whose dog protagonist assumes various professional and social roles; *The Enchanted Pencil* (1963–1977), in which a boy overcomes problems using a pencil that transforms drawings into real objects; the charming and still very popular Filemon the Cat series—*The Strange World of Filemon the Cat* (1972–1981) and *The Adventures of Filemon the Cat* (1977–1981); and a detective series, Wojtyszko's *The Secret of the Marabut's Code* (1976–1979). Original animated fairy-tale series, such as Romuald Kłys's *Fox Leon* series (1981–1993) and Krzysztof Kowalski's animated movie *The Fairy Tale about Three Dragons* (1987), as well as Aleksandra Magnuszewska-Oczko's *Ventures into Fairy Tales* (1989–1993), were especially successful in the 1980s. Perhaps the greatest hit of the 1980s and early 1990s was Wiesław Zięba's three seasons of the Wicker Bay chronicles—*The Secrets of the Wicker Bay* (1984–1988), *The Return to the Wicker Bay* (1995), and *Winter in the Wicker Bay* (1998)—that recounted the adventures of anthropomorphized animals inhabiting the bay's ecosystem.

The first decade of the twenty-first century saw the release of several original fairy-tale animated feature films. Using protagonists from Henryk Jerzy Chmielewski's longest-published Polish comic series *Tytus, Romek and A'Tomek* (1957–2009), Gałysz's *Tytus, Romek and A'Tomek Among Dream Thieves* (2002) tells a story based on an original script by Małgorzata Sikorska-Miszczuk. On planet Transformation, Prince Saligia buys people's dreams and turns them into commercials. When he tries to steal Titus's dream of becoming a human being, Titus and friends—aided by fairy-tale characters including the Little Prince and the Frog Princess—defeat Saligia and free everyone's dreams. The story suggests that one cannot exchange dreams for material goods and that dreams are the most efficient weapon against ideological oppression. Another original work is Wilkosz's puppet fairy-tale animation *The Mystery of the Fern* (2004); on St. John's Eve, when the magical fern flower blooms, several kindergarten toys are accidentally taken away by thieves who abandon them in a forest. The toys survive thanks to animals' help and the story—without CGI effects or catchy songs—successfully conveys an important ecological message. Wojciech Gierłowski's live-action/animated film *The Wet Fairy Tale* (2006), in turn, draws attention to the Polish Easter tradition of Wet Monday, an occasion where young people splash each other with water.

Original animated fairy-tale films have also been used as vehicles for visual poetry. One of such renderings is Witold Giersz's *The Star* (1984), an animated painterly fairy tale based on Bryll's lyrics. In a northern country Santa Claus and his helpers watch the blazing star that heralds the coming of Christmas. The star is long unnoticed in a metropolis where a group of powerful men control the population and its dreams. Yet, when the star arrives, the citizens shake off oppression and follow the star to new freedom. A distinct poetic quality also marks Daniel Szczechura's *Bedtime Story* (1997) which he acknowledges is based on Jan Wołek's poem and Lithuanian painter Statys Eidrigevičius's drawings. An oneiric tale about a restless bunny searching for a safe home in a dangerous world, the film blends the animal's dream and its real-life experiences in recurring configurations, suggesting that the quest for happiness has no conclusive happy ending. Equally concise and thought provoking are painterly depictions of the liberating and dangerous powers of imagination: Jasińska-Koronkiewicz's *Milenka* (2001) and *Dunia: There and Back* (2003), whose female protagonists are torn between reality and the world of their dreams. The potential of imagination is also the focus of Wojtek Wawszczyk's *Splinter* (2006): a painterly 3D story about a wooden bench that falls in love with a girl who sometimes happens to sit on it. The bench's affection is so strong that it manages to free its legs and run along the streets. When it realizes that the girl has a boyfriend, it begins to enjoy bringing pleasure to those who visit the park.

Live-Action Fairy-Tale Films and TV Series

Just as there was a 20-year lapse between the first animated adaptations of Polish fairy tales and adaptations of international lore, so too there was a significant lag between the rise of animated and then live-action fairy-tale films. With the country in ruins after World War II and the new communist regime in place, Polish cinematography, especially in its live-action films, focused on themes related to what has been called "the Cause": large historical, political, or social issues that dwarfed individuals and ignored children as the audience or characters (Kornacki 2012, 152). Additionally, because the fairy-tale live-action format clashed with the requirements of socialist realism, it was not a high priority for the government-subsidized national film industry. As a result, the first live-action fairy-tale film for children premiered only in 1957; the first fairy-tale production addressed to adults came a decade later.

The slow rise of the feature fairy-tale film began with adaptations of Polish literary classics, such as Korczak's *King Matt The First* (1922) and Makuszyński's *The Two Who Stole The Moon* (1928). Given Korczak's stature as an educator before World War II, as well as his heroic death in the gas chamber, Korczak was the most fitting symbol of Polish, Jewish, and child martyrdom. The first fairy-tale feature film released after 1945 was thus the adaptation of his novel. A metaphorical tale about ten-year-old Matt's failed attempt to achieve a just society, Wanda Jakubowska's *King Matt the First* (1957) was noted for its brilliant scenography and paid tribute to Dr. Korczak. Jan Batory's *The Two Who Stole the Moon* (1962) was more explicitly educational. As an adaptation of Makuszyński's facetious fairy tale about lazy twins, the film was marked by artistic experimentation and heart-warming tone. Jacek and Placek, who set out on a quest to steal the moon, end up with another treasure: an appreciation of work and sacrifices people make for one another. The fact that the film stars the Kaczyński brothers—Poland's political leaders in the mid-2000s—added an additional twist to its recent renewed popularity.

The trends first seen in those two films were representative of a host of other adaptations released in the 1960s and 1970s. When the fairy-tale poetics began infiltrating production for young adults, it first emerged, interestingly, in the genre of war movies. Konrad Nałęcki's TV series *Four Tank-Men and a Dog* (21 episodes, 1966–1970), which recounts a story of a Polish tank crew during the last two years of World War II, has since enjoyed a cult status in Poland and across the Eastern

Bloc largely because it was "created as a fairy-tale narrative" (Leszenko and Zaszyński 1971, 278). Although the series was an adaptation of Janusz Przymanowski's 1964 pro-Soviet novel of the same title, its propagandist aspects have been completely ignored by the audience enchanted by what amounts to a fairy-tale narrative about a good-natured boy torn away from his father and homeland, tossed far into the Siberian taiga, only to return home in triumph. Accompanied by a band of trusted and colorful companions, facing numerous trials and tribulations, Yanek finds his true love—a Russian nurse Marooshya played by one of the most beautiful Polish actresses of the period, Pola Raksa. He then goes on to crush the enemy, free the people, and reunite with his family. Audiences who were tired of the tragic tone that dominated war-themed movies thus far welcomed this upbeat though not comedic view of World War II as a fairy-tale adventure. The change, of course, came at the price of trivializing the reality of fighting on the eastern front and ignoring the uneven and mostly oppressive character of Polish–Soviet relations during and after the war. While *The Four Tank-Men* series was not intended to be seen as a fairy tale, by adding the element of the improbable, yet possible, it drew on the fairy-tale schemata to create wry yet optimistic narratives about hope and the triumph of goodness—a message best suited to the fairy-tale convention and especially resonant against the political hopelessness that followed the crushing of the Prague Spring in 1968.

The Four Tank-Men series was an exception though.[1] Until the mid-1980s, fairy-tale feature films were addressed primarily to children and made up only a small percentage of productions for this age group. Among several works completed at this time, noteworthy titles include Jerzy Szeski and Konrad Paradowski's *Mary and the Gnomes* (1960) and Halina Bielińska's *The Hour of the Crimson Rose* (1963)—an adaptation of Maria Krüger's 1960 teen novel of the same title. The former—an adaptation of Maria Konopnicka's classic *Little Orphan Mary and the Gnomes* (1896)—pioneered the use of mixed techniques by combining live-action and puppet gnomes. Bielińska's comedy, in turn, used the device of time travel to whisk a modern teenage girl to the 1880s Warsaw where, like Cinderella, the protagonist Anna finds her "prince" and true love.

Perhaps the most successful film adaptation of the Polish fairy tale in the twentieth century, however, was a series of movies about Mr. Blot (see Figure 11.2). Directed by Gradowski,

FIGURE 11.2 Fairy-tale visitors, *Mr. Blot's Academy* (1983).

Mr. Blot's Academy (1983, in two parts), *Mr. Blot's Voyages* (1985), *Mr. Blot in Space* (1988), and *Mr. Blot's Triumph* (2001)—the latter in mixed media—were adaptations of Jan Brzechwa's extremely popular fairy-tale trilogy *Mr Blot's Academy* (1946), *Mr Blot's Voyages* (1961), and *Mr Blot's Triumph* (1965). *Academy*, which was closer to Brzechwa's original than the sequels, is a story of ten-year-old Adam, a freshman in the magical academy headed by the eccentric Prof. Ambrose Blot. It recounts how students and Mr. Blot resist attempts to destroy the academy and the world of wonder and magic. Shot during the last months of Polish Martial Law (1981–1983), *Academy* was an explosion of color, song, and imaginative exuberance at the time of severe economic recession and general gloom. With the score composed and performed by the most popular rock bands in Poland, well-constructed plot, awe-inspiring decorations and locations—in Poland and the USSR—and with phenomenal acting, especially by Piotr Fronczewski who played Mr. Blot, the film took everyone by surprise.

Although a success that drew an audience of over 12 million people—one third of Poland's population (Kursor 1988, 15)—*Academy* was also a source of endless trouble for the state-owned producer. For example, the screenings that packed audiences into public theaters lasted for three years because the national distributor lacked funds to commission more copies. At the same time, another government agency lowered the ticket price for this film to one fourth of the ordinary theater admission, making this potentially top-grossing Polish movie earn just about half of its production cost. If this was not enough, the same agency then refused, on financial grounds, Gradowski's request for a few thousand meters of color tape that would be necessary to produce a version of the movie for international distribution. *Mr. Blot's Voyages*, *Mr. Blot in Space*, and *Mr. Blot's Triumph* were not as successful, but all four productions feature one or another version of the conflict between technology and imagination, with power- and control-obsessed science represented by barber Philip's mechanical android and the creative, magical science embodied in the imaginative teacher Mr. Blot.

Two other important fairy-tale adaptations since the Blot films include *Jolly Devil's Friend* (1986) and *Master Twardowski* (1995). Jerzy Łukaszewicz's *Jolly Devil's Friend*, an adaptation of Makuszyński's novel *Jolly Devil's Friend* (1930), is a story about a young orphan's quest to confront the Spirit of Darkness and regain eyesight for his adopted father. In the course of his travels, the boy befriends a creature from elsewhere, little devil Piper, who is not yet marked by good or evil and so can be drawn toward the Light side of the conflict. Although visually stunning, the film was less successful than its literary original. Łukaszewicz was an experienced camera operator at the time of the film's production and he debuted with this film as writer and director. Another ambitious adaptation, this time of J.I. Kraszewski's 1840 novelistic retelling of a Polish legend, was Gradowski's *Master Twardowski* (1995). Being the third filmic adaptation—after Wiktor Biegański's 1921 and Henryk Szaro's 1936 versions—Gradowski's film tells a Polish Faustian legend about a sixteenth-century magician who repeatedly eludes hell's snares and eventually escapes to the moon, riding a rooster. While *Twardowski* was one of the first films in Poland to use CGI, it failed to repeat the success of the Blot films.

Unlike in animated films, feature adaptations of international fairy tales have not been numerous in Polish cinematography. The first such production was Bielińska's *The Nutcracker* (1967), a watered-down rendition of E.T.A. Hoffman's 1816 novella, but with the same ending, where Mary's devotion to the underdog Nutcracker breaks the evil spell and turns him into a human again. Despite its message of love redeemed, the film was nowhere near as successful as Bielińska's earlier *The Hour of the Crimson Rose*. Much better received was Jerzy Gruza's *The Ring and the Rose* (1986), a creative musical-like adaptation of W.M. Thackeray's 1854 *The Rose and the Ring*. The film starred some of the most famed Polish actors of the time and was shot in picturesque Polish castles. Its original script stood out, among other things, by using hilariously domesticated translations of characters' names. The extended version of the film was released the same year as a five-episode TV series.

Somewhat more ambitious, though more loosely based on its source—Andersen's 1847 "The Story of a Mother"—is Mariusz Grzegorzek's *Conversation with a Man from the Wardrobe* (1993). Grzegorzek flips Andersen's story from a mother's tale to that of a son who fell victim to his mother's possessive love. Born after his father's death, Karl becomes his mother's sole obsession, which alienates him from the outside world. When his mother eventually rejects her disoriented adolescent son, Karl is sent to a special education center and ends with a job he hates. Unlike Andersen's mother, who accepts her child's death as God's better choice, Grzegorzek's Karl cannot accept his mother's rejection. He starts and ends in a clothes cabinet, his sole refuge, wishing for the childhood he never had. The themes of bullying and extreme insecurity that arose with the economic transformation following the collapse of communism were well received. However, the film has come to be seen as a solipsistic psychological drama about the personal trauma of being unprepared for the real world, a trend that pervaded new Polish cinema of the 1990s (Kornacki 2012, 148).

When it comes to more widely known fairy tales, only one classic was made into a film since 1990—albeit with an ambiguous result. Łukaszewicz's 56-episode TV series *Cinderella* (two seasons, 2006–2007) tells a story of eighteen-year-old Blanca, who discovers that she was adopted. Although her foster family is a loving one, with no evil stepsisters or abusive stepmother, Blanca runs away to find her biological parents. Assisted by a magical purse given to her by a nun, Blanca follows the clues that lead her to another city, where she finds her parents and her sweetheart Max. She also receives support from her foster parents, with whom she reconciles, but the happy ending is delayed as the last episode ends with a cliffhanger about Blanca's mother's death.

Perhaps the most interesting facet of Polish fairy-tale feature movies and TV series have been original works predicated on "the narrative structure and patterns of different types of fairy tales" (Zipes 2011, 14). Embodying themes or moods that evoke the fairy-tale exploration of the human experience through condensation, distortion, or selective focus on specific themes, these films deal with challenges that emerge in the process of identity formation and with the significance of human relations. The range of these original fairy-tale films is broad, with some of them addressed to young and some to adult audiences, each category participating in the fairy-tale discourse in unique ways.

The first modern fairy-tale film for adults produced in Poland was Witold Leszczyński's award-winning debut *The Life of Matthew* (1967). Although technically an adaptation of Norwegian Tarjei Vesaas's *The Birds* (1957), the film tweaked the novel's story to Polish circumstances and adapted the elsewhere setting so as to make it into a fairy-tale parable. The protagonist is 40-year-old child Matthew who develops a magical relationship with the natural world, but remains a misfit in the human world—a world populated only by his sister Olga. When she finds a husband, a stranger from far away, nature tells Matthew that his world has ended: his bird friend is shot, his namesake tree is struck by lightning, and his sleep is filled with nightmares. Feeling abandoned, Matthew commits suicide.

Fairy-tale family movies offer significantly more hopeful storylines, such as Maria Kaniewska's *Duchess Anna's Ring* (1970) and *The Magic Playground* (1974). Both films employed shape-shifting curses and time travel to enable modern protagonists to visit the past and interact with historical as well as fairy-tale characters. Productions for adults, however—especially those by Piotr Szulkin and Leszczyński—retained their dark and dystopian mood. Szulkin's dystopian science fiction films— *The Golem* (1979), *The War of the Worlds: Next Century* (1981), dedicated to H.G. Wells but sharing with it only the title, *O-bi, O-ba: The End of Civilization* (1984) and even *King Ubu* (2003)—are all futuristic versions of oppressive socializing processes and fit the definition of dark, fractured fairy tales for adults. *The Golem* draws on elements from the rabbinical tradition, *Frankenstein*, and Andersen's story "The Shadow." *The War* and *Obi-Oba* are indebted to "Bluebeard" and the biblical Apocalypse, whereas *King Ubu* reworks motifs from Andersen's "The Emperor's New Clothes" and from the Grimms' "The Fisherman and His Wife."

Leszczyński's two later films—*Konopielka* (1981) and *Requiem* (2001)—are also dominated by fairy-tale themes. Like Szulkin's, Leszczyński's films are marked by resistance to larger social pressures. However, the clash between tradition and progress is played out not in the future but in materially and culturally anachronistic villages. When the world of their traditional beliefs crumbles, Leszczyński's protagonists in each movie undertake a heroic attempt to show their communities that the passing away of their simple worlds, although unavoidable, is a tragic loss. No amount of progress can ever replace tradition, and without tradition people are stripped of belief, dignity, and a sense of purpose. These, Leszczyński gloomily suggests, can only be found in a fairy tale for which the modern world has no time anymore.

Some of this pessimism was lifted at the time of communism's collapse and in the first decade of Poland's democracy, making the late 1980s and the 1990s a golden age of Polish fairy-tale film. Juliusz Machulski's blockbuster *Kingsize* premiered in 1987. A political satire on late-communist reality, the film depicted how power and access to privilege are used to control society but, as the fairy tale demands, are ultimately doomed to fail. Probably the only Polish fairy-tale film to use "slave language"—a language of "dissent through complicity" used by artists contending with censorship (Zipes 2011, 322–23)—*Kingsize* tells a story of a totalitarian gnome society, where the dream of freedom can be realized by drinking a magic potion and moving to Kingsize, the world of ordinary humans, choices, technology, and women. The gnome society is kept in check by secret police headed by Dinky Colonel Munchy-Crunchy, but his control is challenged by the gnome resistance that seeks to make Kingsize available to everyone in Drawerland. The hilariously entertaining and profoundly political story of gnome resistance made *Kingsize* an instant classic and to some extent mediated expectations about the collapse of communism in 1989.[2]

While the fairy-taleness of *Kingsize* was widely noted, the fairy-tale feature film for adults exploded in the 1990s most notably in a series of films by Jan Jakub Kolski: *The Burial of a Potato* (1990), *The Posthumous Boy* (1992), *Johnnie the Aquarius* (1993), *Miraculous Place* (1994), *The Sabre from the Commander* (1995), *The Plate Player* (1995), and *The History of Cinema Theater in Popielavy* (1998). Kolski's films depict the lives of down-to-earth characters and take place in a fairy-tale location dubbed by critics as "a place apart and full of wonder, somewhat terrifying and mysterious, and somewhat silly and puerile, but always sought for and precious" (Wajda 2004, 198). Each protagonist deals with the demands of the ubiquitous supernatural within worlds limited to the immediate vicinity of their villages and understandable through folk wisdom.

Johnnie the Aquarius is quintessentially representative of Kolski's fairy-tale poetics and his mythologizing of rural communities. When village philosopher Johnnie discovers that he can miraculously control water, he leaves his pregnant young wife and sets out to mend the world. Quick fame leads to arrogance; despite the miracles he performs, Johnnie fails to return in time for his wife's delivery. In a barn, alone, Veronka gives birth to a baby with a tail. Trusting in her husband's healing powers, Veronka seeks him out, but Johnnie is unable to heal his own son. His gift is gone. Johnnie then tries, and fails, to reverse time to undo the damage he has done, but Veronka forgives him and the couple find peace through acceptance. A tale of temptation and of hard-learned lessons of humility, *Johnnie* is both a fairy tale and parable.

In films for young audiences, no one has done more to infuse the fairy tale into modern life than Andrzej Maleszka, whose filmography is best described as a blend of fairy tale and fantasy. In the 1990s Maleszka pioneered the creation of several original Polish fantasy TV series. His 12-episode *The Transformation Machine* (two seasons, 1995–1996) was soon followed by Łukaszewicz's *The*

Mystery of Sagala (1996, 14 episodes) and *Spear of the Sun* (1999, 13 episodes). In each series, teenage protagonists come into possession of a magical object—a transformation machine, the Sagala stone, or an ancient Incan spearhead—which they first use to manipulate reality, and then, when they realize unforeseen consequences that such transformations entail, they destroy or return the magical object to its rightful owner. The three series are generic hybrids, with individual episodes drawing from science fiction, fantasy, and fairy tales.

Maleszka's greatest achievement came with the *Magic Tree* TV series (7 episodes, 2003–2006). Like Kolski for adults, Maleszka for young audiences affirms that extraordinary things can happen to ordinary people. Each episode in the series forms an independent whole, involves different characters, and is preceded by the same introduction about how a thunderstorm clear-cut an ancient oak in the Varta River Valley, how people took it to a sawmill, not realizing it was a magic tree, and how its timber was used to produce hundreds of ordinary objects, which retained some of the tree's magical powers. After the objects are shipped to stores, extraordinary things begin to happen. The TV series won a number of awards, including a 2007 International Emmy Award. The feature film *The Magic Tree: The Red Chair* (2009) also garnered glowing reviews and received several awards including the 2009 Rights of the Child Award at the Chicago International Children's Film Festival. In all of these works, specific Polish settings and protagonists reflect local culture and modern circumstances, suggesting that magic is not limited to Harry Potter's Britain or Percy Jackson's America, but can also be found in contemporary Poland.[3]

Part of the message of *The Magic Tree* films centers on shifting from extraordinary events to an ordinary world, thus making the ordinary enchanted. This hopeful theme also informs a host of original fairy-tale feature films for adults produced in the first decade of the twenty-first century such as Jerzy Stuhr's *The Big Animal* (2000), Kolski's *Jasminum* (2006), and Marta Filipiak's *Saturday Mountain* (2012). Stuhr's one-of-a-kind film is a modern fairy tale about a small-town clerk in provincial Poland who adopts a Bactrian camel abandoned by a traveling circus. This ruins the protagonist's respectability in his closed community, making him the epitome of otherness but also a flag bearer for all those resisting routine and uniformity. The camel becomes a statement about the freedom to be different. When it suddenly disappears, the dream will live on—as suggested by a small boy who, in the final scene, winks at the protagonist and shows him a camel figurine that he carries in his pocket.

Kolski's *Jasminum*, in turn, draws on the trope of unusual place rather than unusual situation. As another modern fairy tale, it is a story of a miracle in a backwater monastery, charmingly narrated by a five-year-old girl who visits it while accompanying her art-restoration specialist mother. Perhaps the most unabashedly fairy-tale feature film of the recent years, however, is Filipiak's *Saturday Mountain*. Shot in black-and-white, with a beautiful soundtrack and title cards in lieu of dialogue, the film recounts how three unnamed brothers search for the water of life to revive their ailing mother. The first and second brothers are turned to stone, but the third reaches Saturday Mountain, receives the water, and returns home. On the way home he lifts the curse from his two brothers. When the mother awakens from her deathly slumber, the three brothers and the community meet for a joyous feast. Like in Maleszka's and Kolski's films, the dominant fairy-tale theme here is the appreciation of the ordinary things in life.

Conclusion

Given the number and diversity of fairy-tale films we have discussed in this chapter, many of them technically innovative and artistically refined, it appears that the fairy tale has long been a substantial component of Polish cinema. Fairy-tale hypotexts and features such as magic, the fantastic, animism, anthropomorphism, and the happy end have been used in numerous films for young and adult audiences. At the same time, reference sources such as Marek Haltof's *Polish National Cinema* (2002) and *Historical Dictionary of Polish Cinema* (2007) do not recognize the fairy-tale film as a separate genre, especially as a category of films for adults. This may eventually change, as fairy-tale inspirations will likely remain significant features in modern Polish cinema just as they have been since its emergence in the early 1900s. There is much to look forward to in the future. For example, in 2007 Studio ORKA and the National Audiovisual Institute launched a joint project, *The Canon of Polish Fairy Tales*, aimed at creating a 26-episode animated 3D series. The project involves major Polish directors and screenwriters and its goal is to produce film versions of Polish fairy tales, many among which—like "The Basilisk," "The Legend of Kunigunde, the Evil Princess," "The Last of the Giant Family," or "Torun Gingerbread Boy"—have never been adapted to film. This and other ongoing projects suggest that the fairy tale continues to inspire Polish directors. As it did to earlier generations, the fairy tale in its narrative and filmic forms offers both creators and audiences a means to challenge and comment on contemporary social reality, which is often grasped with deeper clarity when seen through the lens of "once upon a time."

Notes

1 The other exception, in productions for adults, was Tadeusz Chmielewski's three-part movie *How I Unleashed World War II* (1969). Recounted from the point of view of a rank-and-file protagonist, this unique film was the first and the most successful Polish comedy yet about World War II. It offered a farcical account of such traumatic events as the German invasion of Poland, life in a POW camp, and fighting against the Nazis in different war theaters. The film showed these events as experienced by a well-meaning but goofy Frank Dolas, whose earnestness and ineptness—although not philosophical distance—put him in the same category as Hašek's Švejk. The movie starts with an episode when the private Frank, riding a train to his assigned post, falls asleep and ends up in a car on the German side of the border just minutes before the Nazi attack begins. Going for a pee, he sees a German general; trying to capture him, Frank fires in the air. The German cannonade follows immediately and throughout the movie Frank struggles with a terrible sense of guilt that his single shot unleashed World War II.
2 For an extended discussion of this film, see Oziewicz (2011).
3 For an extended discussion of Maleszka's *Magic Tree* TV series and feature film, see Oziewicz (2012).

12

NOT ALWAYS HAPPILY EVER AFTER

Japanese Fairy Tales in Cinema and Animation

Susan Napier

Japanese culture has a distinct and deeply rooted fantasy tradition, ranging from the supernatural encounters depicted in the tenth-century classic *The Tale of Genji* (Shikibu 1978), through an incredible variety of medieval folktales of the common people, to the spirit-pervaded Noh drama of the samurai class. Unsurprisingly, this tradition has inspired such modern narrative arts as Japanese cinema, animation, television, and video games. Although prewar live-action films tend to be *shomingeki* (movies about the common people) or *jidaigeki* genres (period films involving samurai), since World War II, Japan has produced a remarkable number of major works that draw on the supernatural, the magical, and the miraculous. These include such live-action masterpieces as the eerie 1950s classic *Ugetsu* (dir. Kenzo Mizoguchi, 1953) or Kurosawa's elegiac celebration of folkloric magic in *Dreams* (1990). In the 1990s and early 2000s a spate of live-action supernatural films gained international attention in the form of "J [Japanese] horror."[1]

Undoubtedly, the animated medium has proved the most active in mining the rich trove of Japanese folktales, myths, and fairy tales. This is hardly unique. In the west as well, many of the most important fantasy movies have been animated, with Walt Disney Studios, in particular, drawing from the European fairy-tale tradition. Animation, which essentially draws from the imagination rather than reality, is a medium particularly suited to fantasy.[2] The flexibility of its imagery, reaching even more easily into the oneiric and unconscious than live-action film, makes it ideal for expressing states of wonderment and magic. Perhaps equally important, especially in relation to Japanese fantasy, is animation's consistent fascination with metamorphosis. Paul Wells has described metamorphosis as perhaps the "constituent core of animation itself" (1998, 69). From the Fleischer brothers' parodic fairy tales of the 1930s to contemporary avant-garde animation, transforming bodies, or simply transformation itself, has supported and propelled many fantasy narratives.

This chapter explores Japanese fairy-tale (or, as I prefer to call them, "wonder tale") films, in both live action and animated media. By the 1970s, Japanese live-action cinema was entering a decline in quality and production and many of the industry's most imaginative and creative talents were turning towards television, animation, and video games. Particularly in the last several decades of the twentieth century, the animation art form known as anime has been impressively prolific in production and international popularity. While live-action film has substantially recovered in Japan, animation studios continue to produce the most successful fantasy genres. This is particularly true in the case of the extraordinary Studio Ghibli, a small Tokyo company internationally acclaimed for its animated fantasies, especially those of its major director, Hayao Miyazaki. Although Miyazaki's partner, Isao Takahata, directed the production company's most recent Ghibli fantasy masterpiece, *The Tale of the Princess Kaguya* (*Kaguyahime monogatari* 2013), Miyazaki remains a central figure in the industry, despite the announcement of his retirement in 2014.

Before turning to specific films, however, it is worth noting some of the major differences and similarities between Japanese wonder tales and those of the west. As Jack Zipes describes it, the wonder tale "seek[s] to awaken our regard for the miraculous condition of life and to evoke profound feelings of awe and respect for life as a miraculous process, which can be altered or changed to compensate for the lack of power, wealth and pleasure that most people experience" (2011, 22). Japanese fantasy fulfills the first half of these conditions quite effectively, but the question of whether it fulfills the second is somewhat problematic. Fantasy in Japan, while it certainly has wish fulfilling and wondrous aspects, also engages with darker and more complex human conditions, such as loss, grief, and bittersweet melancholy. The realms of Japanese fantasy are rarely the lands of "happily ever after"; rather, tales do not necessarily end in compensatory power, wealth, or pleasure. As Japanese psychoanalyst and fairy-tale scholar Hayao Kawai explains, Japanese fairy tales often end in what has been described as a "situation of nothing" (1996, 20). This so-called nothing does not mean that nothing happens in Japanese tales, but it proposes that the endings do not provide an unambiguous, upbeat conclusion where all plot twists are neatly fastened, evil is punished, good is rewarded, and very frequently, the de-facto "happily-ever-after" is preceded by a man and woman being wed.

Not only do Japanese wonder tales often lack happy endings, they also frequently lack the typical quest/adventure structure that characterizes countless western fairy tales. Hayao Kawai recounts the experience of a western scholar who, while reading the classical Japanese story of the fisherman Urashima Taro who goes beneath the sea for a sojourn at the Dragon King's palace to his young son, was interrupted by his son asking disappointedly, "When does he [Urashima] fight?" (1996, 13). While the scholar's son expected a violent battle between a heroic human and an evil dragon, "Urashima Taro" in fact, ends with the rather passive protagonist's return to his home village where he discovers that what had appeared to be three years in the palace of the Dragon King was actually three hundred. Depressed and lonely, he opens a magic box given to him by the king's daughter. Does he find treasure and jewels or a magical talisman to return him to the undersea palace? No. Black smoke wafts out of the box, aging Urashima beyond recognition to the point where he dies of a sudden onslaught of old age. In this bittersweet rendition of a Rip Van Winkle story, the protagonist, unlike Rip, does not get to return home to live out his happily ever after, but instead must confront his own mortality and pay the price for his three years of pleasure.

The frequent lack of a quest motif and the complex, but subtle range of emotional experiences in Japanese wonder tales may be related to the fact that, in comparison to traditional western tales, many protagonists in Japanese folklore and fantasy are women. Indeed, so prominent is the female element in Japanese tales that Kawai has suggested, "the essence of Japanese fairy tales can be seen through 'female eyes' rather than 'male eyes'" (1996, 26).[3] Although women in Japanese tales can, like their western counterparts, appear vulnerable and in need of rescue, it is more likely that female characters will appear pro-active, passionate, and even menacing. Of course some are witches, as in the west, but to a remarkable degree female characters often figure as active agents, noblewomen who successfully reject male advances, such as in the "Tale of the Bamboo Cutter," recently made into the aforementioned *The Tale of the Princess Kaguya*, in which the princess refuses five noble suitors and finally rejects the emperor himself. At other times, they are the active agents of seduction or even entrapment. In the previously mentioned "Urashima Taro," the King's daughter, metamorphosed into a turtle, invites the protagonist down to the Dragon Palace. More sinisterly, in *Ugetsu* (1953), a movie based on the eighteenth-century collection *Tales of Moonlight and Rain* (Ueda 2008), the ghost of a former aristocrat and her serving woman lure the hapless hero to a ghostly mansion.

These last two examples bring up another distinctive element of Japanese wonder tales: the prevalence of supernatural entities known generally as *yokai*. Michael Foster suggests that the term can be translated variously as "monster, spirit, goblin, ghost, demon, phantom, specter, fantastic being, lower order deity, or, more amorphously, as any unexplainable experience or numinous occurrence" (2009, 2). Japan has a rich and multifarious tradition of *yokai* who manifest themselves in folktales, paintings, and woodblock prints. Representations of *yokai* range from mischievous and relatively benign to terrifying remnants of a pre-modern world in which the supernatural had not yet been repressed. The first cinematic appearance of the *yokai* occurred in the 1935 animated short *Danemon Ban-The Monster Exterminator*, today, they are ubiquitous in the arts of contemporary Japan. From live-action films, such as *The Great Yokai War* (2005), to animations such as the blockbuster television and film series *Inuyasha* (2000–2004), Mamoru Oshii's uncanny fantasy *Urusei Yatsura: Beautiful Dreamer* (1984), or the highly original *yokai*-esque creatures in Studio Ghibli's *My Neighbor Totoro* (1988) and *Spirited Away* (2001), the *yokai* have colonized the contemporary Japanese imagination.

I would argue that the *yokai*'s popularity is strongly linked to their deep associations with traditional Japan. While in Japan's early modernization period in the late nineteenth century, traditional folklore was perceived as old-fashioned, even deterring the national priority to catch up (technologically) with the west, the country has recently moved towards re-embracing its allegedly threatened local traditions. It is probably no accident that as urbanization and its attendant social ills—alienation, materialist consumption, and generational isolation—have increased, a fascination with the occult and supernatural elements have intensified in Japanese popular culture. As Gerald Figal (1999), Marilyn Ivy (1995), and I (Napier 1996) have shown,[4] the supernatural in Japan acts not only as a bridge to wonder or horror but also as a means to subvert modernity and westernization, offering tantalizing visions of alterity. In recent years, as Japan has become the poster child for the post-industrial society, the fantastic has become a mode for critiquing the excesses of modernity but also a sometimes problematic pathway to embodied nostalgia. At the same time as tradition "vanishes," to use Ivy's term, the Japanese are trying to catch hold of it, reawakening to their rich tradition of animism which suggests that the numinous pervades our ordinary world, in the form of revenant spirits, the sublimity of nature, and a sense of the permeability of boundaries between this world and others.

For example, in Japanese folklore, animals often have considerable agency. In contrast to western archetypes, where the animal is often an enchanted human as in "The Frog Prince" or "Beauty and the Beast," Japanese animals/*yokai* frequently turn of their own accord into humans for purposes of mischief, play, or seduction. One particularly frequent and tragic motif is that of a female beast or bird—often a fox or a crane—who transforms into a beautiful woman and marries a human, usually bearing him children. Almost always, however, the man chances to see her in her animal form and this causes her to leave her family and never return. This type of story emblemizes what Kawai calls the "situation of nothing" (1996, 20) since very little has changed for the primary protagonists at the end of the story; however, as in the Celtic Selkie tradition, there are children left behind. In Japanese folklore, the vision of a vanishing woman who leaves without a trace is deeply connected to the single most important concept in Japanese aesthetics, *mono no aware*—the "sadness of things." First named by an eighteenth-century scholar, Motoori Norinaga, *aware* refers to the beauty of life, love, and nature, and their inevitable end. But it is in the dying of beauty that Japanese culture finds real beauty, not because it worships death, but rather because death makes humans love and appreciate life in all its fragile evanescence. The enchanting vanishing woman thus becomes a symbol of the cycle of life and enhances our sense of the beauty and preciousness of life and the world around us.

I turn now to a more detailed discussion of Japanese fairy-tale films. While I will deal mainly with recent movies from the past few decades, it is useful to give some historical context in order to understand their development. As mentioned above, most prewar Japanese live-action films were realistic domestic dramas and comedies or high adventure samurai period pieces. Not surprisingly, given animation's flexibility, it is in that medium that we find the first filmic interpretations of fairy tales. In fact, one of the very first animated films in Japan was based on the famous folktale of "Urashima Taro," also discussed above. Although no complete version of this film has been preserved, a nine-minute animation called *Chinkoroheibei and the Treasure Box* was indeed created by the famous early animator Noburo Ofuji in 1936. The work takes many liberties with the original story, however, turning Urashima into a mouse with suspiciously Mickey Mouse-esque ears, and having him chase a turtle to an undersea palace, ruled by what looks to be a giant flounder, and ending with Urashima being turned into an adorable dog rather than dying of sudden old age.

During World War II, Japanese animators made cute animals and classical fairy tales into overt vehicles of propaganda, as in *Momotaro's Sea Eagle* (*Momotaro no umiwashi* 1942) and *Momotaro's Divine Warriors of the Sea* (*Momotaro no umi no shimpei* 1945). They are based on one of the most popular Japanese fairy tales of all time, the story of Momotaro, or "Peach Boy," who was found in a giant peach. Once he turns into a big and strong young man, Momotaro decides to go off and invade "Demon Island," populated by horned monsters who capture innocent victims and do not respect the Japanese emperor. Along the way, Momotaro teams up with a dog, a monkey, and a pheasant, who quarrel among themselves until he imposes harmony on the group. Working together, they destroy the demons and rescue their pathetic captives.

It is ironic that director Mitsuyo Seo applied this particular fairy tale's more conventionally western structure of quest and reward and used it for memorable pieces of anti-western propaganda. Made for children, the films mix cute animal characters with images of aerial warfare to represent the Japanese as all-powerful conquerors. In *Momotaro's Sea Eagle*, Seo re-interprets the attack on Pearl Harbor in fairy-tale terms. Modernizing the traditional storyline, the movie depicts Momotaro and his crew of animal comrades planning and then attacking "Demon Island," i.e. Pearl Harbor. Momotaro is shown as a handsome matinee idol, but his comrades and the soldiers they command are all animals. The demons are represented as beefy Americans with horns on their heads, including an obvious homage to the character Bluto in the *Popeye* comic strips who, in rather un-demonic fashion, cries and blubbers as the navy ships explode around him.

The film is a strange and memorable mixture of charming fantasy and vivid, though bloodless, military violence. Using the recently adopted multi-plane camera to create vivid scenes of flying and aerial bombing (in some cases using actual newsreel footage), the film concentrates much more on the animal soldiers than on Momotaro himself, who appears only occasionally to cheer on his troops. The animals pilot the planes and press the bombing levers, creating a truly disconcerting impression that aligns cuteness with violence. As in the original story, Momotaro's followers in the film are fewer and weaker than the well-equipped demons, but they nevertheless triumph over the larger, technologically advanced enemy.

Momotaro's Divine Warriors is less clearly based on the original tale but is a fascinating depiction of a specifically Japanese style of imperialism that may have been inspired by the original story's recounting of how the boy and his animal comrades free the demons' innocent victims. In this later film, once the western demons are subjugated, the colonial animals happily cooperate with Momotaro to bring victory and peace to a tropical homeland that strongly resembles Southeast Asia.

Thomas Lamarre has suggested that the filmmaker used different animal species in an attempt to engage with the perplexing reality of Japanese imperialism during the war through fantasy. Under the concept of the Greater East Asian Co-Prosperity Sphere, the Japanese military embraced a vision of a united East and Southeast Asia from which the western colonizers are ejected so that the disparate Asian nations can join in harmony under the protective wing of Japanese militarism. Lamarre explains that the colonial peoples "appear as cute and friendly animals that fairly cry out for nurture" (2008, 78). This contention is supported by the fact that one of the main tenets of the original fairy tale was the harmony that Momotaro enforces among his animal followers.[5]

Japan's utter defeat in World War II brought immense changes. A once militaristic and imperialistic nation that had believed in fighting until the end now turned in on itself to examine its wounds and search for a new pacifist direction. Out of this complicated and painful postwar world arose some of the greatest cinematic works in Japanese history, specifically the films of Akira Kurosawa, Yasujiro Ozu, and Kenzo Mizoguchi. While Ozu continued his prewar representations of the lives of ordinary Japanese, Kurosawa and Mizoguchi experimented with fantasy and the supernatural to explore some of the thornier political and moral issues of the time. Kurosawa's famous *Rashomon* (1950) was based on two tenth-century folktales from the *Konjaku Monogatari* collection (Ury 1993). The film delved into the nature of truth and memory in a society where corrupt leaders and war criminal trials had made these concepts highly problematic. With its brooding vision of a devastated city gate and a murdered character who speaks from beyond the grave to tell his version of events, *Rashomon* is hardly a conventional fairy tale full of supernatural characters, but the film is pervaded with the feeling of the numinous around us, in nature and even potentially in human beings.

Mizoguchi's classic *Ugetsu* is very much part of the wonder-tale tradition and, like *Rashomon*, is considered one of the masterpieces of the Japanese cinema. Released in 1953, the film is an intense indictment of war, overweening ambition, and human greed that also manages to create an exquisite sense of melancholy that can justifiably be described with the term *aware*. Revolving around the fleeting nature of love and worldly success, the movie creates a bittersweet portrait of human foibles. It is also stunningly beautiful, using light, shadows, and water, plus an eerie blend of Noh theater chants,[6] Japanese flutes, and western harmonies to create an uncanny atmosphere in which the marvelous or the dreadful seem to lurk around every corner (see Figure 12.1).

The movie is based on two stories from the eighteenth-century collection of supernatural tales known as *Tales of Moonlight and Rain* compiled by the scholar Ueda Akinari from Chinese and Japanese ghost stories. The first story, "The House Amid the Thickets," tells of an ambitious man who leaves his wife at home for seven years while he goes off to profit from war. Upon his return, he rejoices to find her waiting for him, only to learn the next morning that she had been killed during the war and had returned in spirit to him for a single night. The second tale, "The Lust of the White Serpent," recounts how a beautiful woman tricks a young man who discovers that she is actually an evil snake.

Mizoguchi combined the two stories to create a portrait of different kinds of lusts and the terrible consequences they bring. *Ugetsu* features two brothers: Genjuro, who hopes to make money from pots he sells during wartime, and Tobei, who dreams of becoming a samurai. In classic moralistic fashion, both achieve their ends only to realize that their sacrifices were too great. Genjuro the pot maker is invited by a beautiful woman to show his wares at her mansion and becomes enthralled by her, forgetting his wife and child. Tobei, the would-be samurai, becomes a warrior through trickery and then discovers that the wife he abandoned has become a prostitute. It is really the female characters who are the most intriguing, however, such as Genjuro's beautiful young seductress, who, it turns out, is a ghost who has died before ever "experiencing love." Far from being the original story's evil snake, however, the young woman in the film is a "very sad and gentle ghost" (Sato 2008, 115). While the scene in which she seduces Genjuro is appropriately eerie, with clear overtones of Noh plays in its staging, music, and use of mask-like countenances, Mizoguchi extracts compassion rather than terror in his portrayal of this lonely spirit, who ultimately is forced to give up Genjuro due to the imprecations of a Buddhist priest.

Even more memorable is Genjuro's long-suffering wife, Miyagi, who desperately tries to keep him at home and safe from the depredations of war. This part of the story conforms more closely

FIGURE 12.1 The family crosses a mysterious river on the way to a new life, *Ugetsu* (1953).

to its original source in that Genjuro also comes home to find his wife alive and welcoming, only to discover at dawn that she died in the war and he has slept with her spirit. Rather than being played for horror as in a later version in the 1964 movie *Kwaidan*, Genjuro's loss and Miyagi's sacrifice come across as tragic reminders of how war can warp and destroy even decent and sensible people. The movie ends with a twist on the absent-woman motif. The final scene focuses on the two brothers, the surviving wife, and Miyagi and Genjuro's little son working near their kiln. As Sato points out, "[through the camera's focus] the audience seems to have become Miyagi, the ghost" (2008, 116), gazing with satisfaction at her now redeemed family. We hear her voiceover telling Genjuro, "I am always at your side," and complimenting him on the beautiful pots he is making. Finally she gently laments her own death and ends with the resigned words "But that is the way of the world I suppose." If not quite "happily ever after" in the conventional western sense, a bitter-sweet harmony has been restored through the traces of a vanished woman.

The 1960s brought radical politics to Japan and some directors felt disenchanted by what they saw as Kurosawa's and Mizoguchi's old-fashioned humanism. Members of the Japanese cinema's New Wave tended to create more violent and nihilistic visions than those of their predecessors, and some major filmmakers experimented with fantasy. Although not quite magical, Hiroshi Teshigahara's famous *Woman in the Dunes* (1964) created a village and a beautiful and seductive woman hidden in the dunes of Western Japan that became an allegory for such characteristic issues of modern life as surveillance, existential alienation, and the perversion of tradition. The eponymous and mysterious woman of the story recalls the ghost in *Ugetsu* in her complex combination of seductress and victim.

More overtly fantastic but also containing some memorable female characters is the 1964 film *Kwaidan* by Masaki Kobayashi. An anthology of short tales based on Japanese stories collected by the American writer and folklorist Lafcadio Hearn (2004), the movie uses vivid colors to create supernatural effects that are in their own way as memorable as the black-and-whites of Mizoguchi and Kurosawa. This is especially the case in the "Yukionna" (snow woman) section of the movie. An archetypal *yokai*, this woman of snow appears to stranded travelers in snowy landscapes and uses her cold breath to freeze them to death. In Hearn's story and in the film, however, the *yukionna* takes pity on a handsome young man and tells him that he may go, as long as he never tells anyone about his experience. Sometime later, the young man meets a mysterious and beautiful woman whom he marries. Years after, he mentions his snowbound experience to her and it transpires that his wife is actually the snow woman who this time shows him no mercy. A dark version of the traditional *yokai*-as-wife paradigm, Kobayashi's adept handling of the whirling snow scenes and the occasional surreal glimpse of what look like gigantic female eyes render the story even more magical.

In "Black Hair," *Kwaidan*'s more nihilistic version of the Miyagi/Genjuro story in *Ugetsu*, a selfish wastrel returns home to find his wife waiting for him faithfully, as in the earlier movie. But in this case, when the man wakes up he finds himself sleeping with a corpse and entangled in spider-web-like long black hair that seems to enmesh him like a living thing. Kobayashi uses only a few colors, mainly a rich and dense black, to create a vision of a lost and confused man. Less *aware* than sheer terror, "Black Hair" suggests a turning away from the lyrical and strangely hopeful nostalgia of *Ugetsu* towards a sense of the world as a complex and frightening place.

An even more visually stunning fantasy movie appeared at the end of the 1980s, Kurosawa's late work *Dreams* (1990). The film is famous for its use of color to create a dazzling world that is, ironically, less dreamlike and more akin to highly colored "*tableaux vivants*," as Terrence Rafferty in a largely critical review describes it (1994, 218). A compendium of eight vignettes, the movie uses both traditional folklore and Kurosawa's own imagination to create a series of eco-fables that ultimately provide a vision of loss and transcendence that, while overlaid with didacticism, still offers moments of profound beauty and wonder.

I agree with Rafferty that the movie contains more than its fair share of "feeble sermonizing" (1994, 221), especially in the overtly moralistic second half, which largely dwells on apocalyptic visions linked to nuclear warfare. In contrast, the film ends with the more lyrical (albeit obviously didactic) "Waterwheels" segment, envisioning a pastoral community that celebrates the cycle of life and death through the image of the village's ubiquitous waterwheels. Despite the critiques, the film's visual magic occasionally succeeds in taking the viewer across boundaries into a densely realized transformed world, such as in the "Waterwheels" segment or, more sinisterly, in the "Blizzard" sequence, which contains another chilling vision of the *yukionna* featured in *Kwaidan*.

But perhaps the most successful vision of boundary crossing, in this case quite literally, is the beautiful and surreal opening sequence. In this striking vignette, a child in the prewar period transgresses his mother's prohibition and goes into a forest on a rainy day. Once there, he witnesses a fox wedding, an event based on the atmospheric conditions involved in a sun shower that pre-modern Japanese folklore interpreted as lights from a wedding procession of foxes. Kurosawa literalizes the foxes into a slow-moving parade whose stylized movements and masked faces, combined with eerie and powerful music,[7] create the kind of uncanny atmosphere associated with the Noh drama. Aside from the eerie beauty of the procession scene, the episode's end is particularly interesting; the boy returns home only to have his angry mother tell him that the foxes knew he was spying on them and have left him a sword with which to commit suicide. If he can find them, and they accept his apology, he will live, but he must first leave home in order to find them. The episode ends with a vision of a rainbow arching across a magnificent valley, presumably a sign that the boy has indeed been forgiven.

In many ways the episode resonates surprisingly well with western archetypes in that the boy (and note that it is a boy—this film focuses on masculine protagonists) first performs a prohibited act that leads him to see marvelous and forbidden things. He is then punished by exile and forced to seek adventure and redemption in the world outside. This westernized paradigm is perhaps not surprising, given that Kurosawa is seen by many critics in Japan as one of their more western filmmakers in his use of structure and characterization.[8] But the vignette's overall impact places it in the more fluid and borderless world of Japanese animism, as Rafferty, despite his criticism, seems to agree. His description of the sequence as offering a "wholly original sense of the rapturous fear and awe we feel when we first come upon the natural world" (1994, 220) encapsulates Zipes's definition of the wonder tale, although the emphasis on nature is perhaps more specifically Japanese.[9]

Reverence for nature and fear of a looming apocalypse are important themes in *Dreams*, although rather tritely presented. But these themes become even more important in the wonder-tale movies of the 1990s and 2000s. For this period, we turn almost exclusively to animation. Indeed, the anime boom that started in the late 1980s and continues to this day is the source for the most memorable visions of magic and the supernatural.

The 1980s and 1990s animation included the rise of animated television. Major fantasy series included such hugely popular female-centered series as *Sailor Moon* (*Seera Muun* 1992–1997) and *Revolutionary Girl Utena (Shojo kakumei Utena* 1997) (see Lezubski 2014). *Sailor Moon* appealed to and even inspired young girl viewers who were fascinated by the (for that time) groundbreaking notion of girl superheroes fighting for justice. The series went on for many episodes and sometimes used classic western fairy tales (such as Hans Christian Andersen's "The Snow Queen") for inspiration. *Revolutionary Girl Utena* (1997) was even more innovative. It took on the fairy-tale cliché of the knight rescuing the princess and turned it upside down, creating a beautiful heroine with strong protective instincts and sword expertise, elements that would traditionally be coded as masculine. The series also feature themes of incest, apocalypse, and homoeroticism, and developed a strong following in the lesbian, gay, bisexual, transgender (LGBT) community abroad.

Sailor Moon (1992–1997) and *Revolutionary Girl Utena* (1997) were made into feature films. Viewers who had grown accustomed to watching and re-watching their favorite animated series on videotape clamored for full-length film versions. While many were science fiction, the market for fantasy was expanding and included stand-alone films. The films produced by Studio Ghibli were the most prominent, but I begin by taking note of one film from another major animation director first. Mamoru Oshii created *Urusei Yatsura: Beautiful Dreamer* in 1984; he would go on to become internationally famous as the director of *Ghost in the Shell* (1995) and *Ghost in the Shell II: Innocence* (2004).[10] While these eerie, challenging, and beautiful films are essentially cyberpunk science fiction, *Beautiful Dreamer* is an extraordinary fantasy film. Mixing elements of traditional Japanese folklore with apocalyptic visions and zany humor, the film is a fantasy *tour de force* that is also a stimulating meditation on dreams and reality.

Beautiful Dreamer is based on the immensely popular and long-running animated series *Urusei Yatsura* (TV), which was in turn based on the manga series of the same name by the prolific and imaginative female manga writer Rumiko Takahashi. More than any other artist in this period she is responsible for bringing *yokai* back into public consciousness. Her art is largely television-oriented with some filmic realizations. Her most popular series, *Ranma ½* (1989–1992), *Urusei Yatsura* (1981–1986), and *Inuyasha* (2000–2004), freely mix an incredible array of *yokai* from folklore and mythology and sometimes her own inventions to create worlds in which (sometimes hapless) humans come up against supernatural situations of a dizzyingly wide variety.

The *Urusei Yatsura* (TV) series actually blends science fiction with folklore in its basic premise; a group of Oni demons (the same ones we encountered in the Momotaro propaganda films) come from outer space to take over Earth. They give the planet one chance to survive; a teenage boy named Ataru, known for his stunning fecklessness and lecherousness, must defeat the Oni leader's beautiful daughter, Lum, in a physical competition. Through last-minute trickery Ataru triumphs and saves Earth; in the meantime, Lum falls in love with him and decides to stay on Earth with the boy and his long-suffering parents.

The ideal representation of what the Japanese refer to as their "bubble period," a time of unrestrained economic growth leading to an emphasis on consumption and play, *Urusei Yatsura* (TV) offers wonder tales for a new age, mixing carnivalesque satire with magical events and characters. Oshii's *Beautiful Dreamer* film is a tribute to the series; it continues the carnivalesque and the supernatural but also brings in deeper and more disturbing themes. *Beautiful Dreamer* plays off the legend of Urashima Taro and his voyage through time and space to create a meditation on youth, desire, and the ultimate evanescence of the material world.

Set on the night before a high school festival in which Lum, Ataru, and their friends enthusiastically participate, the film's action soon spirals into the uncanny in a combination of apocalypse meets *Groundhog Day* (1993). The friends realize that not only are they repeating the same actions over and over, but they are also unable to leave the area around the high school except to go to Ataru's house, the only one which is still occupied and still has electricity and running water. Surprised but not frightened, they eventually discover that their entire community has been broken off from the world and now rides through space on the back of a giant tortoise (see Figure 12.2), just as Urashima had ridden on his way to the underwater palace of the Dragon King. Like Urashima, they lose all sense of time and space, happily enmeshed in an endless adolescent summer.

At the film's climax, they discover that they have all become part of the dream of Lum. Her Oni powers have combined with those of another *yokai*, Mujaki, a weaver of dreams, to keep them forever in a world of innocent teenage joys, playing and consuming material goods in the apocalyptic wasteland of their former town. At the end of the film, another *yokai* appears, Baku the dream eater, who is a prominent figure from Japanese folklore. After a number of surreal sequences, which play on the porous boundary between reality and dream, the teenagers are released from Lum's oneiric world back to reality. *Beautiful Dreamer* presents some highly original changes on the classical Urashima legend, but it ultimately remains faithful to a vision of the world in which pleasure, dreams, and reality can become mixed together in a way that is exacting but strangely appealing nonetheless.

FIGURE 12.2 The protagonists discover that their town is being carried on the back of a giant turtle, *Urusei Yatsura: Beautiful Dreamer* (1984).

Boundary crossing, apocalyptic visions, and the nature of dream and reality all play important roles in the works of Studio Ghibli, arguably the greatest producer of fantasy animation since Walt Disney Studios. But whereas Disney has been harshly criticized for its formulaic stories, regressive patriarchal agenda, and relentless pandering to audiences looking for "feel good" entertainment, Ghibli is internationally recognized for its remarkably original narratives, strong and independent young heroines, and a moral agenda which, while utopian in its message of hope against painful odds, is also deeply rooted in an awareness of the darkness and complexity of the world from which it springs.

One element on which Disney and Ghibli concur is in their dazzling use of animation to create stunning and memorable visual images that suggest a world of wonder. In the case of Ghibli, however, this world of wonder is not always restricted to a conventional fairy-tale setting in an alternative narrative space. Instead, in such works as *Porco Rosso* (1992), about a flyer who has transformed into a pig after World War I, or in the 1995 love story *Whisper of the Heart*, which begins with its young heroine following a cat, wonder drifts in and out of the ordinary world.

This is especially true of one of the studio's early masterpieces, *My Neighbor Totoro* (*Tonari no Totoro* 1988). Acclaimed as one of the greatest animated films of all time, *Totoro* is a deceptively simple tale of two young sisters who move to the country while their mother is sick and encounter a magical woodland spirit that the younger girl calls a "totoro." Interestingly, this made-up word derives from European fairy tales about trolls ("toruru" in Japanese); however, Totoro is far from troll-like.

A large fuzzy creature who seems to be a mixture of owl, cat, and badger, Totoro embodies a particularly benign form of nostalgic animism, appearing when the children are lonely or in need and associated with such natural elements as the wind, the earth, and plants. Japanese audiences saw in it a vision of a lost and highly nostalgic recent past but when the film was first released in America, movie reviewer Roger Ebert in an otherwise ecstatic review felt the need to warn his audience that the film contains "no villains, no evil adults, no fight scenes . . . no scary monsters" (Ebert 1993). Indeed, very little action happens except for a poignant and painful scene where Mei, the younger sister, gets lost, and her older sister turns to Totoro for help. Very much a wonder tale, *Totoro*'s miracles are gentle and often almost literally organic—a garden grows during a single night, Totoro takes the girls flying on the wind, and a pair of headlights on a rainy night metamorphose into a giant "cat bus." *Totoro* concludes in a vision of restoration rather than change, an invocation of Kawai's "situation of nothing." But it leaves behind an enchanting yet subtle vision of the wonders of the natural environment and a world still unsullied by economic and industrial development.

Two more Ghibli fantasies take on, in a far more aggressive way, the issues of a lost past and a devastated environment, while using traditional *yokai* in a highly original fashion.[11] These are *Pon-poko* (*Heisei tannuki gassen ponpoko* 1994) directed by Isao Takahata and Miyazaki's 2001 masterpiece *Spirited Away* (*Sen to Chihiro no kamikakushi*). While Miyazaki's film is far better known (winning an Academy Award for best animated feature), the two have some distinctive elements in common. Both are adventurous but bittersweet explorations of a lost Japan, embodied in the form of a rich variety of fantasy creatures and spaces. While *Ponpoko* draws from folklore, *Spirited Away* draws from both folklore and the director's vivid imagination.

Spirited Away creates a marvelous fantasy space for its creatures—a gigantic version of a traditional Japanese bathhouse, whose tired and soiled clients are gods in need of rest and relaxation. A richly detailed reminder of a lost pre-modern Japan, the bathhouse both emblemizes the richness of traditional Japanese culture and also its fragility, as much of the film's action concerns the site's vulnerability to invasion by impure and transgressive creatures. They include a young human girl, Sen, who must find work in the bathhouse in order to save her parents who have been transformed into pigs by the bathhouse's owner, the witchlike Yubaba. More than many of the films I have discussed so far, *Spirited Away* does contain some traditional fairy-tale elements, most obviously the parents' curse by a witch and the young protagonist's quest to rescue them. There is also an enormous emphasis on food and consumption, evoking associations to "Hansel and Gretel."

As is typical with Miyazaki, however, he plays innovatively with these familiar elements to create a memorably original film. The young protagonist is a girl rather then a plucky male hero, and her quest is not for fame and fortune but simply for restoration, to remove the curse on her parents and to return to the real world. Even Yubaba, the witchlike figure, is not presented as evil but rather as a harassed business owner who must deal with annoying interruptions like humans wandering into her bathhouse. The original conception of the film had been more conventionally western-structured, with Miyazaki planning for Sen and her friend the handsome river spirit Haku to overthrow Yubaba and liberate her parents through force. Time and monetary considerations sent the film in a different and far more interesting direction. Latching onto a *yokai* character fleetingly glimpsed in an early scene in the film, Miyazaki made this character, now known as "No Face," into a central figure in the film. While it is based on a traditional and terrifying *yokai*—a creature that literally has no face, Miyazaki makes the character into a force of chaos, impurity, and gluttonous consumption, creating in the film's second half a transgressive and carnivalesque vision of a world threatened from within and without.

Ultimately it is left to Sen to control No Face and rid the bathhouse of his presence, a very different quest from her original one. Far from the traditional hero who gains worldly goods and prestige, Sen instead grows in maturity and emotional complexity, becoming one of the most appealing and memorable protagonists of any recent fantasy film. The rich and vibrant world of the bathhouse will stand the test of time as a reminder of what human beings lose when they turn their backs on wonder.

Ponpoko lacks a human protagonist like Sen and its "fantasy space" is actually the real world of nature, a forest outside of Tokyo, just before developers set out to turn it into condominiums. The forest is populated by *tanuki*, Japanese raccoon dogs, famous in folklore for their ability to shape-shift. The director Takahata dramatizes this ability, imagining a war between the *tanuki* and the developers. Poignantly, the *tanuki* come close to winning, by virtue of their ability to turn into everything from more frightening versions of *yokai* to earth-moving equipment and even into humans, creating a dizzying and delightful array of onscreen transformations culminating in a visually stunning *yokai* parade.

Ultimately, this Japanese eco-fable cannot deliver the fairy-tale happy ending. In a brilliant self-reflective twist, the humans witnessing the parade decide that it was simply an advertisement for a new Wonderland theme park to be built near the site of the former forest. The film's saddest scene is its penultimate one in which two tired-looking business-suited executives (called "salarymen" in Japan) drinking energy drinks look at each other and suddenly see that each is a transformed *tanuki*. Combining many distinctive elements of the Japanese wonder tale—beasts who are more or less on par with humans, a privileging of metamorphosis, a love of nature, and a bittersweet, even elegiac ending—*Ponpoko* creates a very personal form of apocalypse seen from the point of view of the nonhuman.

The last film I discuss, Takahata's *The Tale of the Princess Kaguya* (*Kaguyahime monogatari* 2013), is a fitting one to end this chapter. Not only is it one of the most beautiful and moving fairy-tale films ever made in Japan, but it also may be seen as a fascinating combination of conventional European folktale elements within a quintessentially Japanese structure redolent of *aware*, in its melancholic celebration of the transient beauty of love and life. *Kaguya* is based on the ancient "Tale of the Bamboo Cutter," which, more than most Japanese stories, contains such typical European elements as a court, a princess, noble suitors, and not just one but five quests.

The story begins with a marvelous incident, common to many fairy tales worldwide, of an elderly childless couple, who discover a charming baby and raise the child as their own. In this case she is a baby girl, known as Kaguya (Shining) for her radiant beauty. She is found in a stalk of bamboo, and the old couple who find her are soon graced with gold and jewels as well. Eventually they become so wealthy that they move to the capital, where rumor of Kaguya's beauty and charm moves five noble suitors and finally even the emperor to contend for her hand. But Kaguya has no intention of marrying. Consequently, she sets each of the five clearly impossible tasks, and the men inevitably fail in disastrous and humiliating ways. Even the emperor ends up disappointed.

It turns out that Kaguya is actually a princess from the moon, sent to earth for some unspecified transgression.[12] She initially forgets her earlier life but eventually recovers her memory and realizes that her people will soon come down from the moon to take her back. Despite all the best military efforts of the emperor, who gathers an army around her house on the night of her forcible departure, it ends with the surreally beautiful scene of the princess ascending to the moon, dressed in a feather robe and accompanied by attendants playing heavenly music. In the story's coda, the emperor burns the elixir of life that the princess left for him, along with her letters and, according to the story, the smoke from the burning can still be seen in Fuji's volcanic activity. The ultimate vanishing woman story, the "Tale of the Bamboo Cutter," is also one that addresses elements of national pride (Fuji as the symbol of Japan) and the culture's deep connection with nature, since Kaguya can be seen not only as a moon princess but also as related to mountain and volcano deities.

Takahata retains most of the basic elements of the story, but he also adds a great deal from his own imagination to create a work of exquisite lyricism that has already been acclaimed as a masterpiece in Japan. His most significant addition is his vision of Kaguya growing up, which takes place in a mountain village far from the capital. Framed by transcendentally beautiful nature scenes that run the gamut of the seasons, Kaguya plays with insects, animals, and the other mountain youths, including a handsome elder brother figure, Sutemaru, a character created by Takahata. Kaguya maintains her love of nature even when she goes to the capital, building a miniature forest in her palace's back garden. But she is unable to import her childhood friends to the capital and, in one particularly haunting sequence, reality mixes with dream as she hallucinates returning to the mountains only to find a vast snow-filled wasteland. Lying prostrate on the snow, she mutters, "I've seen this place before," indicating the beginning of recovered memories of the moon.

While Takahata does not add a happy ending, he does provide viewers with one dreamlike sequence in which Kaguya and Sutemaru fly through the clouds in an allegory of lovemaking. But Sutemaru must return to his own family, and the princess must abandon the world that she has grown to love. Takahata intensifies the poignancy of the original tale by envisioning Kaguya's wrenching leave-taking from her elderly parents, an eerie and mystical scene of the moon people's descent, which is augmented by adding otherworldly music and having the moon people closely resemble Boddhisatvas from traditional religious paintings.

The Tale of the Princess Kaguya (2013) is a universally accessible tale of love and wonder, but there is no denying its distinctively Japanese elements. To a post-earthquake and tsunami Japan, the film offers a profoundly beautiful vision of the natural cycle of birth, growth, and death, and then, perhaps, rebirth.[13] One of the film's haunting songs, "Warabe no uta," centers around the image of a spinning waterwheel that brings "Spring, summer, winter, fall" and "insects, birds, animals and grass." The simple image and lyrics suggest the cycle of life without any of the overblown didacticism of the waterwheel image in *Dreams*.

Similar to *Ponpoko* and *Spirited Away*, *Kaguya* comments on the loss of natural habitat but in a subtle and oblique form, such as when the princess, frustrated with life at the capital, calls her miniature garden woodland "a fake." *Kaguya* also indirectly addresses a major concern of Japanese society—the question of an aging population. Two of its most prominent characters are Kaguya's elderly mother and father. Indeed, several critics have commented on a memorable early scene in which the old woman's breasts suddenly enlarge and fill with milk, a vision not so much of restored youth as of restored vitality and hope for the future. The challenges of love are also expressed, both in Kaguya's lingering affection for her childhood friend Sutemaru and, even more movingly, in her pain-filled parting from her elderly parents.

Like Urashima Taro, who returns from a world of wonder back to reality, Kaguya must regain her memory and return to the place of her birth. The difference, of course, is that the world of wonder she is leaving is our world in all its complex, challenging, and yet still enchanting beauty. Japanese fairy-tale films remind us that wonder is not necessarily "once upon a time" or "happily ever after," but may also lurk just around the corner or behind a tree, where a Totoro rests enjoying the evening breezes.

Notes

1 "J Horror" has produced brilliant and memorable works (see McRoy 2005), but the genre centers on ghosts rather than folktales or fairy tales per se, so I will not include those films in my discussion.

2 Whereas live-action film, even at its most avant-garde, relates at some level to an objective reality, animation comes from inside the animator's head and can therefore be more imaginative and unrestrained. For further discussion see Napier (2005, 4).

3 The question of why women in Japanese fairy tales are both ubiquitous and psychologically important is intriguing. Although I have found no substantive research on this point, I would point to the similar trends found in Japanese mythology and would also allude to the well-known historical fact that female

writers penned a significant amount of early court fiction (795–1185). Indeed, Japanese mythology is heavily imbricated with the feminine, starting with the Sun Goddess Ameterasu, the progenitrix of the Japanese imperial household, and including the goddess Izanami who, with her husband/brother, brings forth the Japanese islands and is an extremely powerful and controlling deity in her own right. Written in the tenth century but still widely read today, *The Tale of Genji* combines realism and the supernatural to create a chilling psychological portrait of Lady Rokujo, an aristocratic woman whose jealousy is so strong that it causes her spirit to leave her body and attack several of Genji's lovers.

4 As Figal suggests, many Japanese fantasists dedicated themselves to the "other world" because they harbored a "critical nostalgia in relation to the present world" (1999, 220).

5 John Dower argues that the studio and navy that commissioned the films "drew together here many of the assumptions concerning themselves and the enemy that had emerged as central as the war unfolded. Apart from the obvious pitting of good against evil, these included the divine origin and righteous mission of the Yamato race, the 'proper place' and assigned tasks of all good-hearted Japanese, the lower status and menial functions of the less civilized peoples of the rest of Asia, and the demonic and craven nature of the white enemy" (1986, 255).

6 The Noh theater was created in the fourteenth century for the aristocratic and samurai classes. Its plays revolve heavily around the supernatural, especially gods and demons, whose supernatural appearance is underlined by brilliant costumes, strange masks, and eerie music and chanting.

7 Mitsuhiro Yoshimoto notes Kurosawa's brilliant use of sound in this film, "articulating a kind of cinematic space" that adds to the intensity of the best episodes (2000, 361).

8 The episode also suggests an autobiographical element since Kurosawa's decision to become a filmmaker in the 1930s was an unusual and adventurous commitment for that time and place.

9 For an exploration of the importance of nature in Japanese culture see Shirane (2013).

10 Oshii also produced the eerie alternative history film *Jin-Roh: The Wolf Brigade* (1999). Directed by Hiroyuki Okiura, it plays disturbingly on the tale of "Little Red Riding Hood" to imagine an alternative post-World War II world in which Germany has conquered Japan and secret guerilla fighters, including a mysterious girl in a red hood, work to destroy the military police (see Greenhill and Kohm 2013).

11 Tomoko Shimizu suggests that the monsters (*yokai*) in Ghibli movies are "in a certain way the surplus of modernity, the things that have been lost or made extinct by the modernization process" (2001, 110–15). In other words, the spirits in Ghibli films are the (dis)embodied memories of the Japanese past, and in *Spirited Away* we find them alienated from their natural world and forced into leisure activities at the bathhouse.

12 The question of what constituted Kaguya's transgression has preoccupied many Japanese scholars and critics but so far there has been no consensus. For more on this question see the discussion between Isao Takahata and Shoehi Chujo (Chujo 2013). Nevertheless, her transgression-exile-redemption cycle expresses a major Japanese folkloric archetype, the so-called *kishuryuritan* or "legend of the exiled young noble," according to Haruhiko Oita (2014, 75). This popular theme is found even in *The Tale of Genji* but the *woman* is the exiled nobility in this case.

13 Saeko Kimura explicitly links the film to the events of Fukushima and afterwards, saying that "the idea of the world as polluted is taken from the original story [but now] we think of the earthquake or the pollution of nuclear energy" (2013, 104).

13

THE LOVE STORY, FEMALE IMAGES, AND GENDER POLITICS

Folktale Films in the People's Republic of China (PRC)[1]

Jing Li

"There is scarcely an adult or child born in the twentieth century, who, in the Western world, has not been exposed to a Disney fairy-tale film or artifact" (Zipes 2011, 17). The Disney Corporation's almost monopolistic mediation of oral and literary fairy-tale traditions through cinematic technology has not only standardized and institutionalized fairy-tale films as a genre (Zipes 1996, 20–21) but also geared much scholarship towards critically reflecting on Disney's "mode of conformity" (Zipes 2010, xi) as well as analyzing competing alternatives that question the spectacularized happy world that Disney has invented within capitalist socioeconomic structures (Greenhill and Matrix 2010).

Yet, fairy-tale film production remains a culture-specific phenomenon. In the Chinese context, fairy-tale films' inception and development took place within a century of turbulent history, during which China transformed from an imperial empire to a nation-state; from facing invasions by western colonial powers to the chaos of its own civil war; and, more recently, from an extremely politicized communist hegemony to a socialist market economy that embraces consumerism and globalization. These radically and rapidly shifting political-social conditions, in which the nation-state often has a strong presence, have been the most decisive forces to shape not only the fairy-tale film's growth but also the entire landscape of Chinese cinema.

Oral and literary tales (especially those from traditional theater) inspired the earliest Chinese filmmakers. Fairy-tale film has survived political-social changes throughout the history of Chinese cinema, illustrating its incredible vitality. The folk associations and traditionalism of Chinese fairy-tale films function quite effectively to engage audiences in the high tides of commercialism and ideological propaganda alike. These films may not always be noteworthy for their cinematic art, which is a possible reason for their currently overlooked status in the historiography of Chinese cinema. But their liveliness, particular sources, and changes made for cinematic re-packaging enable these films to speak to each particular era in their own way. Exploring their ideological interrelationships with other mainstream or avant-garde film genres shows that, as Zhang Yingjin argues, while official Chinese film history "looks incredibly homogenous and monolithic" (2011, 18) and its "microhistories or minor stories" have been "marginalized by a grand history of national development," the complexity and multiplicity offered by these films' "alterity" "constitute fissures and fragments that refuse or exceed totalization" (2011, 20).

After a historical review of fairy-tale films' development against the larger backdrop of Chinese cinema, this chapter focuses on questions of complexity and multiplicity through the lens of the love story—central to cinematic adaptations of traditional tales as well as other film genres. The interconnected core issues are the textual and historical transformations of female images and gender politics in the cinematic re-tellings of these traditional tales in post-1949 China; and how the reflected discourses of gender, womanhood, and love converse with those in state-promoted films, among others of the time. The chapter closes with some thoughts on these films' ideological conservatism, echoing that of Disney's fairy-tale films in the American context.

The English "fairy tale" has a readily translated term, "*tonghua*," meaning "children's story." However, *tonghua* is usually associated with classical works in European fairy-tale traditions, such as those of the Brothers Grimm and Hans Christian Andersen. Here, I use the more inclusive "folktale," *minjian gushi* (*minjian* meaning "among the folk" and *gushi* meaning "tale"), to refer to the incredibly rich and vast repertoire of storytelling traditions indigenous to Chinese culture. Given the long history of cross-fertilization between orality and literacy in storytelling traditions in China (J. Li, 2008), Chinese folklorists use "folktale" for narratives of both oral and written origin that have been widely circulated and passed down from generation to generation.

The tales adapted to Chinese cinema have three main sources: orally disseminated narratives that may have written documentation or exist in traditional theaters (e.g. regional operas); stories originally from classical literary works, but widely diffused by professional storytelling and traditional theaters; and classical literary works based on oral storytelling traditions. These tales may contain elements of magic or the formulaic structure of a hero/heroine's journey as Max Lüthi (1982/1986) or Vladimir Propp (1968) defined for the European fairy tale, and many correspond to ATU tale types. The folktale films discussed here include feature-length animated films for a target audience of children and young adolescents almost exclusively, and live-action films produced in mainland China.[2]

Entertainment (*yule*) or Vehicle of Ethics and Social Responsibility (*zaidao*): 1911–1949

Soon after the Lumière brothers held their first public screening of short films in Paris in 1895, film was introduced to China as a novel western technological attraction. On August 11, 1896, a French showman dazzled a Shanghai audience with the *xiyang yingxi* (*xiyang* meaning "western" and *yingxi* "shadowplay") amidst variety shows. In 1905, the first Chinese film, *Conquering the Jun Mountain* (Ding Junshan, three reels, a segment of a Peking opera stage performance), was made by Ren Jingtai, owner of Beijing's Fengtai Photography Shop (Fengtai Zhaoxiangguan). In the following two decades, Chinese cinema experienced its first growth spurt, evolving from "a leisure attraction to a narrative art" (Zhang 2004, 13–14) characterized by the founding of numerous film production companies, the establishment of acting schools, and the publication of film journals.

This first developmental stage strongly conveyed Chinese cinema's hybrid nature, despite imported western technological elements. Especially in the mid- and late 1920s, films of opera stage performances and costume dramas, with scripts originating from the vast repertoires of regional storytelling traditions and vernacular novels, became a dominant genre for early filmmakers' experimentation (Zhang 2004, 38). These tales' salient presence as well as their deep roots in China's folk narrative heritage[3] signaled the first golden age of folktale films. In Shanghai, the Tianyi studio founded by the Shaw brothers in 1925 was the major producer of folktale films, some of which achieved phenomenal success even in Southeast Asian markets (ZDZ 1996). Tianyi's popularity resulted from its films' entertaining function, yet also from its conscious efforts to use widely circulated traditional tales to create something distinctively Chinese to resist the dominant status of imported western (especially Hollywood) films at that time (Tan 1995, 18–19). As Zhu Ying points out, both nationalism and pragmatism (i.e. market competition) gave legitimacy to the cultivation of domestic entertainment pictures (2003, 182). Between 1927 and 1928 over two-thirds of domestic films were costume dramas, the majority modeled on the narrative formulas of traditional scholar-beauty (*caizi jiaren*) romances, and tales of woman warriors or of immortals and demons.

Folktale films' popularity in the late 1920s also related to the harsh political climate. Not long after the Republican Revolution ended the Qing dynasty and founded the Republic of China in 1911, China entered another turbulent era (1916–1928) during which political factions and regional warlords fought to control the nation-state, with much bloodshed. Throughout the late 1910s and 1920s, the Nationalist Party (Kuomintang, KMT), led by Sun Zhongshan (Sun Yat-sen) and his successor Jiang Jieshi (Chiang Kai-shek), initiated a series of political and military actions to consolidate the Republic. These included working with the Chinese Communist Party (CCP) to fight against warlords, and organizing the Northern Expedition in 1926 to (at least nominally) re-unify China under the KMT regime. Yet the KMT soon divided into left- and right-wing factions and the CCP suffered a violent crackdown in the Shanghai Massacre of 1927. To avoid potential persecution during Chiang's political terrorism, many filmmakers steered away from social realist efforts and looked for inspiration in allegedly apolitical folk traditions or literary classics.

Some film critics of the time disapproved of these early folktale films' apolitical and commercial tendencies and their sentimental dispositions, arguing that filmmakers must re-evaluate traditional materials and choose sources with "motion" and "energy" over syrupy romances (Qin 2012, 370). On the national level, the KMT state condemned many costume films as feudal and "generally unsavory, especially in their influence on the uneducated masses" (Berry and Farquhar 2006, 58). By 1931, the Republican state banned the production of films that focused on sorcery, mystery, or phantasmagoria. However, a few folktale films contrastively advocated cinema's function as a vehicle of ethics and social responsibility, engaging with the political-cultural discourses of the time. For example, in 1927, scriptwriter and director Hou Yao adapted *The Romance of West Chamber* (Xixiangji), a play written by Wang Shifu (1250–1307?), endeavoring to craft a plot conveying the "modern" spirit that valued sacred love, individualism, and human rights (ZDZ 1996).

The integration of commerce and politics in the making of folktale films continued during the following two decades, though the genre itself remained largely on the cinematic margins. From Japan's invasion of northern China in 1931 to the founding of PRC by the CCP in 1949, the country was engulfed by the anti-Japanese war (1937–1945) and the civil war between the KMT and the CCP (1945–1949). This distinctive historical context engendered a flourishing leftist film movement and the prominence of political melodrama. Regardless of the filmmakers' affiliations and artistic models, their films were generally characterized by realistic representations, willingness to expose social problems and reach out to the masses, the urgency of national salvation, and a yearning for national empowerment (Pang 2011).

Against this politicized mainstream, folktale films, produced mainly by the Xinhua studio, founded in 1934 in Shanghai, experienced considerable ideological pressure. *Mulan Joins the Army* (Mulan Congjun 1939), immensely popular in Japanese-occupied Shanghai, can be seen as the studio's response to the cause of national resistance (Fu 1998). The formula of mixing romance with patriotism satisfied the need to balance commercial imperatives with political demands. Another successful film, *Princess Iron Fan* (Tieshan Gongzhu 1941), a well-known episode from the classical novel, *Journey to the West* (Xiyouji, see Wu 1980),[4] was deeply influenced by American cartoon style and the success of Disney's *Snow White and the Seven Dwarfs* (1937). The Wan brothers—Wan Laiming and Wan Guchan—adapted this tale into China's first feature-length animated film with the intention of producing a story "based purely on real Chinese traditions." They noted: "it was clear to us that we had to arouse the national spirit of the public by stressing the need for resistance.

The end of the shooting occurred just at the time of the invasion of the foreign concessions [in Shanghai] by the Japanese, so, when the prints came out, we had to cut in a song for Zhu Bajie, the pig, with the lyric 'People Rise and Fight Until Victory'" (Wan 1981, 20). Thus, the Buffalo monster's defeat at the film's end was achieved only after the villagers were mobilized and unified, differing from the oral and written versions' victory assisted by the Jade Emperor's celestial troop. Despite their commercial and entertaining character, these folktale films contested political and social waves and, to some extent, this engagement worked reciprocally with their market success. As Laikwan Pang asserts of 1930s Shanghai films, nationalism sells (2011, 59).

From State Hegemony to Humanism and Globalization: 1949 to the Present

In his review on 1930s and 1940s Chinese cinema, Zhang Yingjin concludes with the following reflection:

> It must be admitted that the "golden age" period appears "golden" only in retrospect and that its achievements can be fully assessed only with historical hindsight. After decades of political repression and ideological brainwashing in mainland China and Taiwan during the 1950s and 1960s, the period looks attractive because it has been marked by the flexibility of multiple political affiliations and the possibility of alternative aesthetics and artistic models. . . . [E]verything was as yet unsettled, and opportunities, albeit often short-lived, were still obtainable.
>
> (2004, 112)

Zhang's view summarizes the key force that singlehandedly shaped Chinese cinema in the decades after the founding of PRC in 1949. The socialist state finished nationalizing China's film studios in 1952 and subsequently gained unchallenged hegemony over filmmaking, administratively and ideologically.[5] This deepened state-level practice reflects the central tenet of Mao Zedong's 1942 Yan'an talk on the instrumentalization of literature and art for political ends; creative works needed to be accessible to workers, peasants, and soldiers, and serve class struggle-centered socialist ideologies. In addition, by 1953, to further improve film's efficiency as a propaganda tool, millions of mobile projection units were set up to better spread Party policies and state ideologies to remote areas.

Perhaps not surprisingly, folktale films entered their second golden age in this extremely politicized climate. Between 1949 and 1966, at least 121 opera films were produced, some of which are still honored as cinematic masterpieces (Li 2006, 156–157). Judith Zeitlin points out that "the Party's cultural policy during this period was open to folklore as an expression of the common people and as a way to appeal to their sensibilities" (2010, 220). The state saw folktale films, adopting familiar artistic forms and contents, as a powerful channel to accomplish its project of nation-building and to "inculcate the new ideology of socialism" on the grassroots level (Teo 2013, 215). Repackaging and transforming fairies or historical heroes into socialist characters was embraced as a common strategy to realize the films' political function.

For example, *The Lady in the Painting* (Hua Zhong Ren 1958) was based on a popular Chinese tale group. In many orally transmitted versions, a poor young farmer buys a painting containing the image of a beautiful lady. She is a fairy or animal spirit and admires his diligence and kindness. She emerges from the painting to do household work when he labors in the fields, and eventually marries him. But she often disappears or leaves in the end. However, the fantasy atmosphere of a fairy–human love story is much diluted by the class ideology in the film, foregrounding a class-struggle theme. The fairy is instead a village girl, who hid in the painting to avoid being forced to become the vicious emperor's concubine. The film ends with the destruction of the emperor's palace and a victory song condemning feudal society as well as the emperor's atrocities against the common people. This cinematic adaptation reflects the aesthetics of socialist realism that most films in this era faithfully pursued: to depict class-consciousness, heroic characters, and the triumph of the public over private interests. Yet, as will be discussed later, when juxtaposed with this revolutionized trend, some folktale films also showed a certain luxury to "pursue certain cinematic arts theoretically justifiable as national styles" (Zhang 2004, 209). These films experimented with portraying the lively ordinary life of commoners, characters of relative ambivalence, and even personal feelings like romantic love.

This high point for folktale films and the film industry came to a halt when Mao launched the Proletarian Cultural Revolution in 1966. The Beijing Film Academy was shut down in the same year. Well-received and artistically mature folktale films like *Third Sister Liu* (1960) were criticized by the central government as the "poisonous weed" of bourgeois ideologies. Chinese cinema's "spring" did not arrive until 1978 when Mao's era ended and China initiated open-door and reform policies. In this so-called "second Hundred Flowers" (Clark 1991) period, not only did filmmaking resume, it also represented a dramatically different landscape of decentralization and de-politicization.

From the 1980s to the mid-1990s, Chinese cinema witnessed the emergence of new wave (avant-garde) films that broke away from ideological orthodoxies and started to enhance its international profile. These films were made by fourth-and fifth-generation directors, the first graduates of the Beijing Film Academy after its re-opening in 1978. They endeavored to re-assess ideology-centered socialist film traditions and re-introduce moral, psychological, and political complexity and ambiguity for in-depth cultural critique (Rayns 1991). Artistically and intellectually, these films opened a groundbreaking chapter in Chinese cinematic history. However, as Zhang points out, their insistence on "showing" rather than "telling" challenged viewers "to take up a subject position," increasing the level of difficulty in film appreciation (2004, 236). Consequently, these films did not appeal to the majority.

In contrast, folktale films of this era tended to be much more conventional thematically and artistically. The adaptation of traditional love stories continued to be the majority in this genre, in tune with the larger context of rising cinematic humanism and the revival of commercial films at this time. According to Paul Clark, the end of Mao's era transformed cinema from an ideological medium to "a part of Chinese cultural life" that could more directly reflect societal changes (1991, 58). The beginning years of this "spring" saw the flourishing of otherwise suppressed films featuring love stories, personal feelings, and human relations. In addition, in the mid- and late 1980s, the re-recognition of cinema's commercial potential also contributed to the vibrancy of folktale films. Due to the emergence of other entertainment means (e.g. TV and karaoke bars), film attendance declined in urban and rural areas at an alarming rate (Braester 2011). A series of top-down reforms also changed the industry's institutional and fiscal structures. Self-reliance and greater autonomy for local studios and distribution centers replaced the state system of guaranteed purchases, forcing those involved to consider box-office success before production. The popular journal *Contemporary Cinema* hosted several roundtable discussions and critical forums from 1984 to 1989, examining and eventually justifying "entertainment films" (Li 2007, 424–31). According to ZDYYZ (China Film Art Research Center), entertainment films accounted for 60 percent of productions in 1988 and 75 percent in 1989 (ZDYYZ 1995, 428).

Against this background came the attention-drawing surge of 1980s ghost/spirit-romance-horror films. They were largely adapted from a seventeenth-century classical tale collection titled *Strange Tales from a Scholar's Studio* (Liaozhai Zhiyi, hereafter *Liaozhai*) and written by Pu Songling (1640–1715). Encompassing a broad array of oral and written traditions (Luo 2009), its supernatural romance tales, especially of ghosts and fox spirits, have inspired continuous cinematic adaptations in history and seem to have spoken particularly well to the post-1980 humanistic and commercial trend.

Chinese cinema in the late 1990s and the new millennium became more diversified and multi-faceted (Lim and Ward 2011). Avant-garde films continued to develop on the industry's margins. State power retreated further, while the Ministry of Radio, Film and Television (MRFT) officially promoted and supported so-called "main melody" (*zhuxuanlu*) films, to "invigorate national spirit and pride" (Braester 2011, 181). Yet what makes this era distinctive is the re-entry of Hollywood films into China after almost half a century's restriction. Hoping to stimulate and revitalize domestic film production, MRFT opened the market in 1994 to ten foreign "megafilm" (*dapian*) a year (Rosen 2002). China's joining the WTO in 2001 greatly accelerated its cinema's integration into the global market. A more systematically established commercial mainstream emerged, modeled largely after Hollywood, including genre films with relatively high production values, increasing transnational investment, growing emphasis on box-office success, as well as "incorporating Chinese audience[s] into the monological Hollywood audience" (Zhu 2003, 71).

In this globalized climate, folktale films tend to go back to prominent tales that have been adapted many times in Chinese cinema's history. In the new century, the legacy of *Liaozhai* films is still very much alive, including re-makings of *Painted Skin* (Hua Pi 2008) and *A Chinese Fairy Story* (Qian Nü You Hun 2011). With a transnational film crew, Hong Kong director Ma Chucheng repackaged the Mulan ballad into the sentimental blockbuster *Hua Mulan* in 2009. Further, in 1999, the Shanghai Animation Film Studio released the fifth feature-length animation film in the history of PRC to celebrate the State's fiftieth anniversary. Titled *The Magic Lotus Lantern* (Bao Lian Deng), it was adapted from a tale of filial piety that has circulated in oral and written forms for more than a thousand years (Li 2010). Its great box-office success stimulated the making of *The Magic Aster* (Malan Hua 2009) and *Finding the Milu King: The Magic Reel* (Milu Wang 2009), based on a children's ballad and a mythological animal tale respectively.

The traditionalism of these folktale films, especially in terms of their stories' origins, enables them to retain "Chinese cinema's cultural relevance or identity" (Zhu 2003, 170). Yet they also tend to pursue the western megaproduction model with big budgets, celebrity stars, and advanced technology as well as commercially viable narrative formulas. For example, *The Magic Aster*'s director, Yao Guanghua, notes that the source tale group often centers on Xiao Lan and Ma Lang's married life and morality. But his film re-focuses on how they fall in love and ends with their marriage, making it a sentimental love drama. Yao particularly cited Disney's *Sleeping Beauty* and *Cinderella* as models for this change (2009).

Film critics lament that these films' characters are stereotyped to resemble those of Japanese and/or Disney animations, such as the prince, princess, and humorous sidekick (Zhu 2007; Bao and Ma 2009). For example, Ma Lang in *The Magic Aster* swings among the forest vines, recalling Disney's *Tarzan* more than a farming peasant in northern China (Wang 2009). Thematically, these films also tend to deviate from traditional morality to embrace transnationally-shared themes such as self-realization (e.g. *The Magic Lotus Lantern*), the war between justice and darkness, and the harmonious co-existence among humans, animals, and nature (e.g. *Finding the Milu King: The Magic Reel*). These trends raise concerns about the erosion of Chinese characteristics (Yang 2009).

The Love Story, Female Image, and Gender Politics

Folktale films of the 1950s, 1980s, and 2000s—three important developmental stages of this genre in PRC—show that love stories have been central even in prohibitive socialist times. Their consistency and vitality renders them an effective window through which to view female images and gender politics in dramatically different socio-political climates, along with their historical trans-formations. Such films also prompt questions about how discourses of gender, womanhood, and love in this distinctive genre of traditionalism converse with those of other dominant or mainstream films of their times, and thus offer a more multifaceted understanding of the ever-shifting landscape of Chinese cinema.

The mid-1950s to the mid-1960s: Love and Politics

As indicated above, folktale films in this period were recognized as an effective propaganda tool to cultivate ideologies among the masses. Yet they also created a unique discursive space to cooperate with but simultaneously resist politicized cinematic narrations of gender and love. Previous schol-arship has noted that the mainstream films rarely presented love as their core narrative framework (Han 2012). When they did, the grand narratives or social construction eclipsed any sentimen-tal narratives about love. One representative example is *The Red Detachment of Women* (Hongse Niangzijun 1960), in which Wu Qionghua is enlightened by Party member Hong Changqing and transformed from an oppressed slave to a revolutionary soldier. In the original script, Hong's diary, discovered after his death, reveals his love for Wu. However, the film erased this detail and replaced it with Wu's application letter to join the Party (Zhang Jiyue 2014, 70–71), changing the image of Hong from Wu's possible lover to her spiritual father (Chen 2004, 77). This change indicates that Wu's emancipation can be complete only after she erases her own sexuality and embraces her sole viable identity as a revolutionary. With the disappearance of individuality, emotion, and gen-der difference, Wu becomes a univocal symbol for the oppressed class. Thus, Zhang Jiyue argues that though women gain seemingly equal status to participate in revolution, they cannot do so without first expunging their gender. This alienated identity unavoidably leads to films adopting male perspectives, the ideologically correct relationship between husband and wife, and the politi-cized (non-sexual) representation of female bodies (2014, 50–99). Even in the few movies that more explicitly focus on love stories, such as *The Story of Liu Bao Village* (Liu Bao de Gushi 1957), the female character's choice of lover is ultimately determined by his political achievements. The film powerfully tells the audience that, "without the liberation of the people, personal happiness is not possible" (Chen 1989, 142). Love must be merged into revolutionary discourses (Rao et al. 2013, 337).

Compared to these classic red films, folktale films exhibit more ambiguity, though they hardly escape the omnipresent state hegemony and socialist class ideology. Like the re-packaged revolution-ary messages in *The Lady in the Painting* mentioned above, *Third Sister Liu* (1960), an award-winning cinematic adaptation of a popular folktale from Guangxi province, illustrates how to integrate "his-torical legends with the need of modern revolution" according to Zheng Tianjian, a leading member of the script-writing group (1960, 92). Zheng mentioned that Third Sister Liu, commonly called "folksong fairy," has different identities in written and oral traditions, as "a talented female scholar who excelled at love songs" and "a village girl of a poor peasant family," respectively. To "enrich the educational value of this film about the reality," the film deliberately chose the latter to portray Third Sister Liu (1960, 93). One powerful plot element that showed Liu's class-consciousness, the confrontation between the villagers led by her and the landlord who forbade them to sing, was also "transplanted" from elsewhere (Zheng 1960, 93). Consequently, the landlord's hatred of Liu due to her rejection of his love pursuit in the tale traditions is changed to class struggle (Yang 1986). In the heated scene of Liu's singing followed by that of the villagers, the close-up of her determined facial expressions shows her heroic fight against the evil landlord (see Figure 13.1).

Though its political messages greatly overshadow the love theme in the tale traditions, the film still creates a space of flexibility and ambiguity in representing a female image and her love interest.

FIGURE 13.1 Repackaged class ideology and revolutionary heroism, *Third Sister Liu* (1960).

Rather than alienating or rejecting her femininity and sexuality, the film's close-ups show Liu's beautiful appearance, sweet voice, shyness in front of her lover, and their emotional exchange of a pouch as a love token, as well as the final scene of rowing away to eternal happiness. It is true that Liu's songs are ideologically colored, but her body is not hijacked by revolutionary demands. The candid display of her love avoids obliterating her gendered identity. Clark argues that together with the picturesque landscape, melodious music, and colorful ethnic costumes, the film creates a spectacular audiovisual treat unthinkable in an overly politicized, Han-majority setting (P. Clark, 1987).

This ambiguity also manifests in other earlier folktale films when the political climate was still relatively relaxed, such as *The Heavenly Match* (Tianxian Pei 1955) and *Liang Shanbo and Zhu Yingtai* (1953), as well as in *Ashima* (1964), which was made much later but banned. These films follow socialist ideologies to condemn the patriarchal feudal order that suppresses the freedom of love (i.e. the old society vs. the new society founded by the CCP). Yet by no means do they remove, politicize, or subordinate the love theme. Their emotional scenes show the romance of falling in love, the touching promises or joy-filled married life the couple share, their heart-wrenching separation, and the spiritually inspiring imagination of the couple's happiness in another world. More importantly, the courageous pursuit of love is represented as more than a mere response to ideological pressure.

For example, in *The Heavenly Match*, the seventh fairy cannot stand the loveless life of Heaven. She marries Dong Yong, a poor peasant who sells himself into servitude to give his deceased father a proper burial. Director Shi Hui admitted that originally, he and his team disliked the portrayal of the fairy in the local *huangmei* opera version. She takes the initiative and "forcefully" pursues Dong's companionship during her planned "encounter" on the road. However, after watching many opera performances during his script-writing process, Shi found that the audience wholeheartedly loved her (1957). Their emotional reactions eventually persuaded him to restore this unconventionally daring image and, similarly, to focus on the idealized woman-weaving-and-man-ploughing married life that, though not quite revolutionary, is strongly valued in traditional self-sufficient rural economies.

The flexibility and ambiguity that folktale films enjoy in this era offer a counterbalance to the political weight of doctrinaire propaganda. As Pickowicz argues,

> bipolar conceptions of absolute good and evil . . . are already deeply embedded in the consciousness of viewers who love traditional stage conventions. The result is that the censor is satisfied, while many in the audience believe they are viewing something old and familiar. The political message is thus overwhelmed and finally submerged in a sea of breathtaking landscapes and traditional artistry.
>
> (2012, 220)

Yet, as the other side of the token, as Zhang Jing (2014, 25) argues, blending humanistic love (*renxing ai*), personal affection (*renqing ai*), and love for all the ethnic nationalities (*minzu ai*) with the belief system of the Party creates "the cultural soil" for forming and strengthening political ideologies and identification.

Liaozhai *Films in the 1980s (and early 1990s): Love and Moral Codes*

When the Cultural Revolution ended in 1976, love stories began to emerge from the ideological shadows. In the refreshing tide of cinematic humanism, *Love Story on Lushan Mountain* (Lushan Lian 1980)—one of the earliest productions of its kind—enchanted domestic audiences with its conspicuous foregrounding of romance but also with one of the first onscreen kissing scenes in almost 30 years of socialist rule. Yet the love story did not deviate from the polarized narrative mode that has been more or less practiced throughout the history of Chinese cinema, which plays out the tension and/or conflict between the pursuit of freedom in love and the restraint of social systems and regulations (e.g. arranged marriage, concubinage, social status/class gap, or political commitment) (Wu 2008).

In the first decade or so after Mao's era ended, this narrative mode continued to strongly shape the depiction of love, sexuality, and marriage in Chinese cinema. But the difference is that these films structured their stories more critically within this mode. For example, *Love Story on Lushan Mountain*, still heavily colored by political messages about national unification and patriotism, also featured an open, positive portrayal of the younger generation's passionate affection. Romance was privileged as a powerful force to thaw political differences with the parent generations who fought for the CCP and the KMT during China's civil war. In *The Herdsman* (Mu Ma Ren 1982) and *Hibiscus Town* (Furong Zhen 1986), individual fates during the turmoil of the Cultural Revolution became a window to reflect on the suppression of humanity and the resilience of love. In *Good Woman* (Liangjia Funü 1985) and *A Girl from Hunan* (Xiangnü Xiaoxiao 1986), filmmakers turned their lenses on women's helpless positions vis-à-vis sexuality, love, and marriage in China's rural patriarchal society (Zhang 2004, 232–33). However, these filmmakers' in-depth cultural critique often concluded with unfortunate endings, revealing the unshakable power of entrenched traditions. In a telling contrast, female director Huang Shuqin explored similar issues from a gendered perspective. *Woman Demon Human* (Ren Gui Qing 1987), using religious tales about folk ghost-exorcist Zhong Kui as a narrative backdrop and intertextual allegory, tells the identity-searching journey of female opera performer, Qiuyun, who takes the role of Zhong Kui and other male martial characters on stage (Cui 2003, 219–38). Qiuyun excels at her art, but her choice to perform masculine roles expresses her revolt against her mother, who was a charming but "shameless" opera performer who committed adultery and abandoned her daughter. When a married man finally rouses Qiuyun's sexuality and desire, this forbidden relationship is persecuted by social norms. Zhong Kui, a powerful, ruthless demon, who in the legend cares for his sister so deeply that he determines to marry her well, eventually becomes a medium for Qiuyun's identity search. The final scene dramatizes this tale with a conversation between Zhong Kui and Qiuyun's inner self. She ends her quest for the answer to the question "who am I?" with the claim that she is happily married to the stage.

Dai Jinghua points out that, despite Qiuyun's stage success, this film is about the permanent loss of her female identity. But Qiuyun is far from a determined rebel waging feminist battles against male-centered society. This character is more about encouraging the audience to see her experiences from a female perspective. As the director Huang explains, "I want to open a window on the wall of a room that usually has only north and southward windows. Through this new window a different view might be seen" (quoted in Dai 2004, 253). By focusing on "the texture of femininity" rather than the feminist critique on women's hopeless fates (Zhang 2004, 233), this film unfolds a gendered perspective on the *process* of female consciousness.

Compared to these films, *Liaozhai*-based romance-horror films in this era such as *Ghost Sisters* (Gui Mei 1985), *The Fox Spirit Romance* (Hu Yuan 1986), and *Inside an Old Grave* (Gu Mu Huang Zhai 1991) depict a different scenario. Set in pre-modern times, these romances often take place in a deserted or haunted place where a scholar encounters a female ghost or fox/flower spirit. These women's gentle care, sensuous bodies, and poetic talents weave a passionate companionship. In the end, they usually revive and/or enter the human world as wives, living happily ever after or disappearing after protecting or rescuing their husbands.

Undoubtedly the highly-charged, sentimental love-and-death romances and their mixture of sexuality and horror appealed to domestic audiences. Yet emotional stimulation and sensory excitement did not prevent these films from exploring the tension/conflict between the freedom of love and the constraints of social forces. In addition to the need to overcome the boundary between the human and ghost/spirit worlds in the original stories, these films intentionally created social obstacles to the couple's happiness, such as the father's disapproval of the marriage due to the scholar's poverty or lower social status (i.e. *Inside an Old Grave*) or official corruption (i.e. *Ghost Sisters* and *The Fox Spirit Romance*). However, unlike their contemporaries' cultural critique of political hegemony or gender mentioned above, these *Liaozhai* films also shift the focus onto corrupted morality and social injustice.

Liaozhai films heavily intertwine romance with the construction of the idealized social order, moral codes (Fu and Huang 2004), and gender norms that return women to the patriarchal system (Ma 2000; Xu 2003). For example, by sanitizing male protagonists' behaviors (e.g. overdrinking, visiting prostitutes, or practicing concubinage) in the original tales, the films reconstruct them as romantic and faithful companions. The movies' now morally superior characters are incorruptible gentlemen who refuse sexual or monetary temptations, risking their lives to fight social injustice against women, the weak, and the poor. For example, in *Ghost Sisters*, the scholar Wang jeopardizes his own safety when he represents the victims of malicious gentry families in the corrupt court. With an admiring yet authoritative tone of moral preaching, the sisters praise his honorable deeds: "It would be wonderful if all the people in the world were as incorruptible as you"; "There would be no evil in the human world if all the people were as good-hearted and benevolent as you." Scholar Wang's image becomes that of a model citizen upholding an idealized social order.

Female images were also glorified, but geared towards patriarchal gender roles; the original tales' often highly sexualized, seductive ghost or fox spirits were neutralized and changed to purified mutual affection. These supernatural "aliens" (Barr 1989) willingly offer their tender, nurturing, beautiful bodies, artistic talents, and economic expertise, seeking nothing in return except for entry into the human world as loving wives. These hyper-feminine characters (Zeitlin 1997), like Lian Suo and other female spirits in *Inside an Old Grave*, usually do not transgress gender boundaries into the public sphere, though they actively encourage and assist their (future) husbands' pursuit of political success. In *The Fox Spirit Romance*, the exceptionally strong title character offers her husband moral guidance and petitions the emperor when the corrupt local court sentences her husband to death. Given that she takes no such action when other villagers suffer similar fates, her heroic act serves to keep her family and thus her social role intact, rather than to fight social injustice as these films' male protagonists do. She pretends to be a courtesan to get the emperor's attention and, in return for rescuing her husband, agrees to be the emperor's concubine. She returns to the spirit world to avoid further harm to her just-released husband. This ending differs from Pu's, in which the fox spirit leaves because her husband repeatedly fails to take her advice; in the cinematic adaptation, she does so in order to maintain her fidelity, an example of championing womanhood's moral foundation.

Of course, female images in Pu's *Liaozhai* were far from homogeneous in representing male-centered discourses on femininity, sexuality, and gender (He 2004). Filmic adaptations in the 1980s and early 1990s reinforced more passive representations, especially compared to the female protagonist in *Woman Demon Human*.

Painted Skin *(2008) and* Hua Mulan *(2009): Love Myth and Gender in the New Century*

The love story has diversified in unprecedented ways in the post-1990s landscape of Chinese cinema. As Wu Rongsheng insightfully analyzes, obstacles to love come less from external political or social forces than from the protagonists' own inner worlds, especially their inability to communicate and understand each other in the rapidly modernized yet flattened, commercialized urban context (2008, 139). While some films still produce idealized stories of pure love, like *The Road Home* (Wode Fuqin Muqin 1999), the majority deconsecrate psychological processes of love, either returning it to trivial daily life or portraying its fragmentation or distrust (Deng 2011, 100; Du 2011; Sun 2014; Wang 2014). The cinematic adaptations of folktales in this era, not prolific but often commercially successful, also echo the trend of shifting to the ontological questions of love in romance films, such as *Painted Skin* (2008) and *Hua Mulan* (2009). Given both tales inspired numerous cinematic adaptations, the new re-writings provide a telling conversation with their predecessors on issues of love and gender.

In *Painted Skin*, a moral preaching tale in Pu's *Liaozhai*, a scholar meets a beautiful woman on the road and takes her home. A ghost, she wears a piece of beautifully painted human hide. Despite his wife's objection, the scholar insists on keeping the woman until a Daoist priest advises him not to do so, but this counsel arrives too late. The ghost kills him by ripping out his heart. To revive her husband, the wife follows the priest's instruction to find a beggar. She allows him to beat her and forces herself to eat his phlegm. The ghost thus eliminated, the wife vomits out a clot—her husband's heart. In his commentary, Pu clearly states that this story warns of the danger of lust and the need to see through deceptive appearances. However, considering that the deconstructive force in this and many other *Liaozhi* tales comes from female seduction and the scholar's helpless attraction to it, Pu's commentary conveys a male perspective on the threat of unregulated female sexuality and its praise of self-sacrificing wifely virtues.

This view is faithfully presented and reinforced in the influential 1965 cinematic adaptation. The film added plot elements to further contrast the two women's behaviors, and firmly reinforced polarized female social roles—the demonized whore, who must be banished from the family, and the virtuous wife, reviving and maintaining idealized gender norms and social order.

However, in the 2008 adaptation, director Chen Jiashang seemed to re-write this tale warning against lust into a love myth for China's contemporary urban audiences. Courting box-office success, the film skillfully repackages the scholar into a macho but sentimental general and the inhumane ghost into a fox-spirit who changes from wanting to eat his heart to seeking his heart as a lover. The general painfully struggles between fidelity to his wife and affection for the fox-spirit without knowing that she eats human hearts to maintain her beautiful human appearance. When the wife discovers the truth, the fox-spirit threatens to kill the general and everyone else unless the wife claims that she is the demon. Of course, she sacrifices herself to protect her beloved husband. When he tells his dying wife that he loves her whether she is human or demon and kills himself to be with her forever, the fox-spirit loses her hope of winning his heart but is simultaneously enlightened about what love means. She uses her magical lozenge to revive the couple, giving the audience a happy ending.

Unlike the previous films' nonnegotiable battle between good and evil, morality and immorality, the 2008 version depicts love as a purification journey, a self-improvement process for all except the wife—always portrayed as a saint. The husband learns responsibility and sacrifice to maintain the purity of love and the family. The demon, rather than being condemned and eliminated, redeems herself with compassion to make a grand love story possible. The film's exploration of the struggles between love and responsibility speaks well to the love lives of China's contemporary inhabitants, rapidly spinning away from traditional values and desperately needing an ethical core in the face of too many temptations (Li Chunfang 2008). Yet, we must also dwell on how this love myth is told and how gender plays a role in constructing its sacredness.

The firmly established moral dichotomy between two female images is faithfully re-presented and reinforced. The demon's dangerous nature and her unregulated female sexuality are enhanced through multiple exposures of her sensuous, irresistible, near-naked body, along with the general's sexual dreams and affection towards her. Further, the film not only has the wife perform her womanly virtues and die for her husband, it elevates her to saintliness by allowing her no struggle when facing another man's affection. In contrast, not only does her husband admit his sexual desire for another woman, the film sympathetically describes his psychological struggle. His final lofty act—choosing to return to his wife after confessing his love to the fox-spirit—makes his character even more likeable and sympathetic. Yet women's immoral desire must be eliminated or tamed; the demon eventually learns compassion and transforms herself into a wifely image. Both women desperately love the man, and their fates depend on his acceptance and approval. The wife dies happily because her husband chooses to die with her and the fox-spirit finds purpose after he confesses affection for her. Viewed in this light, the sacredness of the love myth hinges on the husband, who in numerous retellings never escapes temptation. And his commitment and loyalty determine whether the women's absolute devotion to him can be realized. Thus, scarcely different from previous adaptations of *Painted Skin* or the 1980s *Liaozhai* films, the 2008 re-telling is still shaped by authoritative male discourses on love and gender (Tian 2009).

If women's patience, devotion, and sacrifice in *Painted Skin* eventually transform their man and win his love, what could be the fate of a fearless woman warrior's romance in current cinematic storytelling? A year after *Painted Skin*'s release, Hong Kong director Ma Chucheng presented his romance-war film *Hua Mulan* (2009). Adding romance to Mulan legends is not new in Chinese cinema as shown in the first adaptations by Tianyi Studio (1927) and Minxin Studio (1928). But the 2009 version distinctively shows Ma's intention to let Hua Mulan tell her own story—not as deified hero but as an emotional individual and as a *woman*.

It follows the common storyline. Hua Mulan starts her journey as an intelligent daughter with great martial-arts skills. Thus, her learning or coping with military competence is never the film's focus. Further, she joins the army to fight for the Wei State more as a daughter's filial deed than as a conscious or explicit act of patriotism or loyalty. When a theft leads to body-searches of all the soldiers, Hua Mulan admits to a crime she did not commit to avoid exposing her female identity, although this choice means she will get the death penalty. Her choice confirms her friend Wen Tai's

FIGURE 13.2 The blood-stained wooden name-tag of Wen Tai and the rising of a warrior, *Hua Mulan* (2009).

suspicion about her sex. She asks him to burn her body after her death so that the secret is kept forever. Neither filial nor patriotic duties, not even her own life, are as important as her chastity.

Wen Tai rescues her, but does not immediately reveal his identity as prince of the Wei State. Hua Mulan fights alongside him, but as they achieve military victories, she finds herself washing more and more dead soldiers' blood-stained wooden nametags. Her sole positive feeling on the battlefield, her love for Wen Tai, is also brutally rejected. He fears she will make military misjudgments due to her personal feelings, which actually do lead to the loss of lives. Hua Mulan becomes depressed to the point of neglecting her military duty until Wen Tai, severely wounded, fakes his own death to revive her zeal (see Figure 13.2).

Hua Mulan does not disappoint him. She learns to put the victory of the army and the security of her country first, even when watching her childhood friend and other fellow soldiers die. Now a mature and invincible warrior, she infiltrates the enemy camp, saves Wen Tai, and ends the war. Even more incomparable, she assists the enemy state's princess, who wants to marry Wen Tai to ensure long-lasting peace between their countries. Hua Mulan sacrifices her own love for peace and returns home alone. When Wen Tai comes back for her, she confesses her love but refuses to run away with him for the greater good of peace.

Superficially, the 2009 film depicts a journey of self-growth similar to Disney's *Mulan* (1998), but its theme dramatically differs. Rather than depicting self-approval or finding her own value, it offers Hua Mulan an emotional journey to experience war, fame, love, death, and loss, through which she eventually *chooses* to be a warrior for her country not for her love interest. The plot draws her clear trajectory from a girl who practices filial piety, defends her chastity, and falls in love, to being a woman warrior who learns that her country is more important than her own happiness and makes and accepts this choice.

This transformative course breaks an unspoken rule of Hua Mulan tale traditions in the Chinese context. Pre-modern theater or fiction may praise Hua Mulan's military and literary competence, but mainly depicted her as an ideal representing two fundamental Confucianism-centered moral principles of filial piety and loyalty (*zhong*). Her temporary transgression of gender boundaries and destabilization of gender norms were justified by the Confucian patriarchal society as she performed these duties in disguise and in support of men. Therefore, as Joseph Allen concludes, the core of the Hua Mulan tales is always the return home to marriage, restoring her traditional female identity and position (1996).

Hua Mulan's loyalty, not her filial piety or marriage, carried the greatest weight in the period approaching the Late Qing, when China faced imperialist invasions. In 1899, reformist intellectual Liang Qichao advocated replacing the concept of "the subordinates of the emperor" (*chenmin*) with that of "the people of a nation-state" (*guomin*) to foster China's self-strengthening (quoted in Ke 2012, 13). With her glorious military deeds, Hua Mulan offered an ideal image of *guomin*, elevated from a daughter showing filial piety and loyalty to a cultural symbol of nationalism and patriotism. Cinematic adaptations reflected and further reinforced this transformation, always corresponding with national crises. The 1927 and 1928 versions were released during the Northern Expedition that eventually ended the warlords' control and re-united China. Leftist screenwriter Ouyang Yuqian explained his 1939 version as a response to the 1930s Japanese invasion. In socialist China, the 1956 Henan opera adaptation was made in the context of the Korean War.

Except for the latter version, which completely absented romance, the patriotic and nationalistic Hua Mulan still enjoyed either a sweet romance on the battlefield or happy marriage upon her return. The 1927 and 1928 versions postponed her wedding due to the outbreak of war. This plot not only glorifies her sense of responsibility but also ensures her joining the army with a marriage to which she could return. The 1939 film even allowed Hua Mulan to choose her own husband, revealing a modern sense of romance. The 2009 adaptation breaks intentionally from this conventional ending. Hua Mulan returns home not for her wedding but for the long-lasting peace of two countries. How do we understand this film's loss of romance or marriage and its overshadowing of individuality in the face of the state? Does this go against the director Ma's intention of letting Hua Mulan tell her story as a woman?

This question can be related to scholarly discussions on the issue of women and the nation-state in Chinese cinema. Chris Berry and Mary Farquhar point out that womanhood in Chinese cinema is often constructed around "the narrative model of the daughter myth" (2006, 113). The images of Hua Mulan and her sisters embody "a national and anti-imperialist discourse" and indicate a "*metaphorical* relation" of woman "to an essential and ahistorical national identity" (italics added). Tani Barlow (1994), Lydia Liu (1991), and Dai Jinghua (1994), in different contexts, also argue that throughout Chinese modernity, the specificity of women's interests are often subsumed under the nationalist agenda and the construction of woman always occurs within the nation-state's discourses. In 1950s and 1960s socialist films, including the 1956 *Hua Mulan* opera, femininity, womanhood, and romance are suppressed and transplanted by political passion for Party-State ideologies and causes. In these cinematic narratives, women lack discursive autonomy and cannot narrate their love interests or experiences as gendered individuals. Their screen performances become a sociopolitical signifier for narratives of the Party and nation-state.

Most Chinese-language scholarship on the 2009 film shares the viewpoint that, when her love is put on her country's altar as a sacrifice, Hua Mulan as an individual disappears. Her halo as a patriotic and nationalistic symbol becomes even more sacred as she chooses this path. But unlike feminist perspectives that criticize her loss of romance and individuality, some argue that this ultimate daughter myth reflects the political consciousness of contemporary Chinese women, and their feminist desire and initiative for being visible and active in both the public and domestic spheres (Peng 2010; Jiang 2010). Peng points out that, compared to the enemy state's princess whose marriage renders her a mere pawn, Hua Mulan shows active political agency with her intelligence, skill, and courage. Peng argues, "She [Mulan] is irreplaceable: it is not that she needs men [to love]. Rather it is men who need her. It is not that she needs her country [to be a heroine]. Rather it is her country that needs her. It is she who chooses her country, not the other way around" (Peng 2010, 35).

The contrast presented here concerns the differences between western feminist perspectives and their Chinese counterparts' open-ended textual interpretations (Cui 2003), which is beyond this chapter's scope. But what needs to be noticed is that, despite its similarity to the 1956 opera version's ending, the 2009 film makes a breakthrough in Hua Mulan cinematic traditions by privileging her perspective as a woman. Director Ma Chucheng ensures not only romance but also a sentimental love story to the point that the film is criticized for the over-flowing of love and tears and the fact that the camera lens always follows Hua Mulan's eyes (Niü 2010). During the filmmaking, Ma also invited female scriptwriters to talk about how Hua Mulan as a woman would respond to war: "I really want to know how Hua Mulan would think at that moment. This is the biggest difference between men and women. Men may not give it much thought, but women may develop doubts on why we have war" (San 2009). Thus, no matter how we interpret her transformative trajectory and concluding saintly image, we cannot deny there is always a female-centered impulse that poses questions about war, life, love, and the state.

As Kristine Harris (2012, 327) reminds us to attend to the "sensory impact" of Hua Mulan's temporary but dazzling battlefield images rather than just the ending of the film, this female-centered impulse provides a different perspective, as does Huang Shuqin in her film *Woman Demon Human* (1987). Even when Hua Mulan bids her closing farewell to Wen Tai, her voiceover offers a contested statement about what she has accomplished for her country: "If one dies on the battlefield, life is melted into earth without any trace like rain. However, if one falls in love at this moment, hope re-blossoms from earth and passionately embraces life." Here, love is stated as a magical force that gives lost life meaning that would otherwise disappear without a trace. In this sense, director Ma actually narrates another love myth for his contemporary audience that blends with "the daughter myth," but still grows its own root to enable Hua Mulan to have it all.

Ideological Conservatism in Folktale Films in the PRC

Through the lens of the love story, we can see how folktale films are strongly shaped by the specific socio-political climates of different historical times. The eternal question of love has transformed in the past decades from a revolutionary quest to a humanistic moral reflection and to an ontological search. But this chapter also indicates that the retellings of folktale films speak with distinctive voices when compared to their contemporaries. Whether standing as artistic masterpieces in an extremely ideological time, being overlooked as mediocre commercial films during the new wave of experimental cinema, or flirting with both neo-nationalism and commercialism in mega-production mode, these folktale films may not offer the most radical or reflexive positions on discourses on gender, womanhood, and love. For example, though Third Sister Liu's character is heavily painted with revolutionary colors, her charming femininity and unfettered emotional expression make her escape genderless, collectivized heroine images in the cinema of socialist realism. Yet, when Huang Shuqin opens a new window to view female consciousness, the beautiful and talented fox spirits and ghosts in *Liaozhai* films return to their domestic sphere to reinforce traditional womanly virtues of total devotion and sacrifice. Even the newly reformed image of Hua Mulan, given the privilege to narrate a female-centered story, must surrender her romance to the centuries-old daughter myth so that her onscreen character better matches popular expectations and renders her authentically Chinese. Thus, folktale films maintain a discursive distance from both politicized mainstream themes and the critical edge of experimental films, more or less counterbalancing ideological extremes. This gulf denotes not only these films' slower pace in discursive change but also their tendency to respond directly to popular sentiments and conventional values.

This feature recalls a major critique of Disney's cinematic instrumentalization of the fairy tale and its deeply conservative approach to prevailing conventions, especially on gender and power relations. Jack Zipes points out that this ideological conservatism appeals to "our craving for regularity and security in our lives" (2010, xii) and, because of this, pacifies "the rebellious instincts of audiences" (1994, 140). He sees Disney's productions as a less progressive force that discourages reflection and social transformation. To a great extent, this perspective speaks well to folktale films in the PRC, as this chapter shows. Yet, in contexts like the extremely politicized communist rule of the 1950s and 1960s in China, the ideological conservatism of folktale films functions as a counter-balancing force through which the glow of humanity could still survive. In the case of Hua Mulan, the issue becomes even more complicated because of the unusually long-term cultural weight she must shoulder in particular historical contexts. Her 2009 incarnation remains an unresolved controversy. While the image irritates some western feminist critics, it is applauded by their Chinese peers for the same reason—the disappearance of her gendered individuality.

In this sense, the Chinese context is better served by viewing conservatism in folktale films as a tendency to maintain discursive distance from ideological extremes and thus a way to understand popular expectations. This perspective contextualizes folktale film discourse as one of many alternatives, and the core question also shifts to how these various forces communicate with each other and contribute to discursive scenarios of gender, womanhood, and love. As in the North American context, especially towards the end of the twentieth century and later, while "the Disney paratext" (Greenhill and Matrix 2010, 5–8) continues to be produced and transformed, more fairy-tale films return to "the roots of folklore's darker elements" with much sexual and moral ambiguity (2010, 10) that enable more refreshing conversations. In the Chinese context, Hua Mulan may add shades of grey to the landscape of folktale films, but it also suggests something more exciting yet to happen.

Notes

1 I thank this volume's editors for inviting me to participate in this project, and Gettysburg College for generously supporting my research trip to Beijing in summer 2014. All transcriptions of Mandarin Chinese follow the standard *pinyin* Romanization system. I also follow the Chinese convention of listing surname before given name.

2 Although understandings of Chinese cinema increasingly diversify, this chapter's scope is limited to films produced in mainland China, especially before the twenty-first century, because the political-social climate for filmmaking varies in different Chinese-language regions. In the new century, with the globalization of Chinese cinema, China's film market has become transnational, though the mainland/Hong Kong/Taiwan market remains its major target, as exemplified in *Painted Skin* (2008) and *Hua Mulan* (2009).

3 These films revealed inseparable aesthetic connections to traditional opera theater. Filmmakers preferred pictorial stability over mobility, symbolic props over realistic settings, and flat character archetypes representing moral values over complex individuals. They also tended to adopt the opera stage's spatial framework, positioning characters according to their social statuses (Hu 1996). Hou Jue and other film critics in the 1920s, who first theorized the newly imported art form of "shadowplay," also consciously validated "play" or "theater" as the essence of cinematic practice, considering the camera more recorder than participant (Zhu 2003, 42).

4 Being one of the four most celebrated works of classical fiction in China, *Journey to the West* has inspired dozens of filmic and TV adaptations in China since the Wan brothers produced *Princess Iron Fan* in 1941. For further readings, see Chen (2012) and Magnus-Johnston (forthcoming).

5 From 1949 to 1966, in the eve of the Proletarian Cultural Revolution (1966–1976), brief times of what Paul Pickowicz calls "cultural thaw" appeared when state control was loosened to allow more nuanced views. However, Pickowicz points out that by no means was the CCP's domination questioned. Rather, filmmakers "had to legitimize their ideas by making it clear that the goal was to strengthen, not weaken" the state machine (2012, 12).

14

"IT'S ALL A FAIRY TALE"

A Folklorist's Reflection on Storytelling in Popular Hindi Cinema

Sadhana Naithani

In 2006, I had an unusual invitation: to deliver a keynote lecture at the First All India Screen Writers' Conference at the Film and Television Institute of India, Pune. I decided to take the opportunity to open a discussion as to why so few Hindi films are based on folktales and fairy tales. During the conference, I happened to sit next to the renowned teacher of film studies, Satish Bahadur.[1] Before the session began, we exchanged a few words of introduction. I knew of him through many of his former students, but I introduced myself by saying that I study folktales and fairy tales. At this Professor Bahadur smiled, pointed at the stage where celebrities of popular Hindi films (Bollywood films)[2] were gathering, and said "These films. . . . it's all a fairy tale."

I guessed he meant Bollywood films, but wondered what fairy tale meant for him: a popular genre of storytelling that is formulaic, fantastic, and non-serious in its social commentary, or wondrous stories with deeper meaning? I had no chance of inquiring further as the Bollywood session began, and I did not meet him again (he died in 2010). His comment, however, has remained with me to this day, and I have often reflected on it in different contexts, as a way to understand popular Hindi films in general.

Only two Indian films are clearly based on traditional folktales: *Bhavni Bhavai* (*The Tale of the Life* 1980, originally in Gujarati) and *Paheli* (*The Riddle* 2005). *Bhavni Bhavai* narrates in the performance genre of Bhavai the old story of a king who wanted to make a human sacrifice to his newly constructed stepwell, in the contemporary setting of a group of lower caste people migrating to the city. *Paheli* is based on a folktale from Rajasthan about a woman whose newlywed husband goes away for trade. A ghost falls in love with her and comes to her looking like her husband. Films on mythological-religious stories, like *Jai Santoshi Maa*,[3] form a very different category—that of religious films. Clearly, traditional narratives and fairy tales have not been important to popular Hindi cinema. Yet Indian films are well known for their fantasy-dominated stories, and are often seen as escapist[4]—characteristics and value judgments that have been leveled at the fairy tale also. But does that make popular Hindi films fairy tales?

The cultural and theoretical aspects of exploring popular Hindi films as fairy tales pertain to cinema's place as popular culture and its relationship with this pre-modern form of storytelling. Questions about the relationship between fairy tales and popular Hindi films gain significance when the latter's mass appeal in India is taken into consideration. Are such Bollywood films only, as Theodor Adorno (2002) might argue, products of a culture industry that manipulates the masses? The issue gains other dimensions because the expanding international appeal of these films has made their differences from Hollywood apparent. Can "difference" as a concept in contemporary cultural theory whereby variation between two cultures is not explained hierarchically, but accepted without value judgment, be used to understand something about each of these phenomena (Hetzel 2004, 240)?[5] Connecting popular films with fairy tales also requires us to consider theoretical approaches that treat fairy tale as socially, historically, and culturally rooted narrative (see Röhrich 1956; Zipes 2006a) with liberatory potential (see Bacchilega 2013). In this chapter, I explore popular Hindi cinema in India with reference to the fairy tale as a fantastic story with deeper meanings.

The available scholarship considers these films with reference to social and historical realities and seems unconcerned with the art of storytelling;[6] rather, Bollywood is itself considered a genre of storytelling. The growing international scholarship on popular Hindi cinema tends to take its form as given, rather than analyzing storytelling as an aesthetic category. Films are often categorized with reference to genres like action, romance, family drama, and comedy, which anticipate storylines and audience expectation. Such classifications are not equally useful in varying cultural contexts. For example, Bollywood does not separate the genres; rather, it offers a mix. Though Bollywood films seem like fairy tales, they are neither based on fairy tales, nor do they identify themselves as fairy tales. Yet the audio-visual language of these films relates to the historically older form of storytelling in complex ways. Popular Hindi films can be usefully compared with the fairy-tale genre, not least because the latter is primarily an aesthetic identification of an artistic form and the elements that make it. As a concept, genre does not depend on the specific narratives that are classified within it; rather, new texts may continue to emerge, the identifying elements of which match with those of an existing form (see e.g. Frow 2013).

Genres: Fairy Tale and Bollywood Film Story

The works of Max Lüthi (1976), Lutz Röhrich (1991), Jack Zipes (2006a), and Cristina Bacchilega (2013) describe the fairy tale as a form of storytelling identified by its use of fantasy, wonder, and magic. Traditional Indo-European fairy tales often employ a formulaic beginning, "once upon a time," that takes the recipient to another time and space, where magic and wonder become believable. With more fantasy than reality and an apparent disregard for rational perception, the plot typically involves the attainment of a beloved or marriage. The central theme unfolds through good and evil characters, but the victory of good over evil, achieved through fantastic means, is certain. Generally a happy ending brings the recipient to a formulaic conclusion in which all the good characters of the story live "happily ever after," despite their earlier conflicts and troubles. The events may themselves be beautiful visions or brutal actions, but they are fantastic and rarely depend on everyday logic. And yet, this fantastic tale can touch the deepest corners of human emotion and psyche, conscious and unconscious.

The process can be displayed within the fairy tale. While tales do not always cure real people, a frame narrative could reflect a teller's belief that stories can heal disturbed minds, enlighten souls, and thus change reality (see Frank 2010). For example, in "One Thousand and One Nights," the tales that the heroine, Scheherazade, narrates not only save her life but also heal the mentally disturbed king. The apparently normal reality at the beginning of a fairy tale is disturbed soon after, but the trouble is always resolved, usually with a beneficial transformation. The happy ending restores harmony. The fairy tale narrates hope in the possibility that evil can be vanquished and a better future attainable.

Debates about the genre concern possible interpretations of this storytelling form, and the main question can be glossed as: how realistic are fairy tales? Are they dependable, though fictional, sources to understanding the realities of the societies in which they are told? Some scholars argue that the fairy tale is too fantastic to be reliable, that it has traveled from place to place, and that one cannot even ascertain whether fairy tales belong to the places where they have been narrated and collected, let alone analyzing how they relate to specific social realities.[7] Those who disagree point to storytelling's metaphorical nature and have developed ways of decoding metaphors to conclude that underneath a superficially simple fairy tale's surface lies a powerful liberating narrative against injustices common to human experience across linguistic and cultural boundaries (see Radner 1993; Turner and Greenhill 2012). They point to fairy tales' continued popularity across changes in historical conditions, technological inventions for cultural communication, as well as generations of tellers and recipients. Feminists have similarly occupied a variety of positions. While some argue that the fairy tale endorses patriarchal social values, others contend that these stories reveal the predicament of women in patriarchal societies, but that this depiction is aimed at changing the situation, as it does in the story itself (see Haase 2004). These divisions bring to the fore aspects of storytelling that go beyond the fairy tale's structural replications.

The same questions about realism are often applied to Bollywood. Most scholars and audiences do not consider these films realistic. But again, ideas vary, from considering the works as cultural and sometimes literal trash, which has no place in academic discourse, to nuanced examinations of its significance by those in the humanities (such as cultural studies) and the social sciences (King 2012; Mehta and Pandharipande 2011). Hindi cinema's popularity not only within India, but across its borders, has meant that neighboring countries have been avid viewers regardless of their current or historical political relations with India. For example, in Pakistan, Bollywood films are just as popular as they are in India; people watch these movies whether or not public authorities sanction them. The same holds true for Afghanistan, Sri Lanka, Bangladesh, and Nepal. When these countries have film industries of their own, they occupy very little space compared to Bollywood films. Beyond South Asia, Bollywood films have been popular all across west Asia and Africa, as well as socialist Russia and communist China.[8]

These films' audiences have expanded in Europe and North America since the beginning of the twenty-first century, not only because of these countries' large expatriate communities, but also because Bollywood represents one of the few alternatives to the imperialism of Hollywood cinema. Indeed, Bollywood's strong appeal to local audiences has limited Hollywood's space for targeting the Indian market. Since India liberalized its economy in 1991, cultural media have become far more international. This process has been further expanded by new media technologies. The cultural impact of these technologies is widely visible, but Hollywood only shares space with the popularity of Bollywood as a very minor partner.[9] Throughout its history, Indian cinema's social, economic, and political contexts have changed several times, accompanied by technological and cultural changes. From its beginning in 1913 with *Raja Harishchandra* (discussed below), when the colonial government in British India was not favorable to Hindi cinema, the film industry in Mumbai, the capital city of the Indian state of Maharashtra, has gone through many phases, which has radically transformed its function. For example, the increasing corporatization that has replaced more family-based companies has reshaped the cinematic production process.[10] In spite of change within and outside popular Hindi cinema, the Bollywood film has been identified as a genre with a distinct mode of cinematic storytelling. Its language is very different from Hollywood's. This difference has created market space by virtue of the genre's ability to indirectly compete with Hollywood without impeding the latter's market share. Although Bollywood has influenced Hollywood, the reverse is also true.[11] Bollywood's point of difference defends against the far superior technological achievements of Hollywood. Cultural theories of the late twentieth and early twenty-first centuries celebrate a cultural phenomenon for its difference particularly from the dominant and canonized forms. In other words, one may not explain divergence between Bollywood and Hollywood as the former lacking in comparison with the latter, but as "difference" where they hold equal value (Hetzel 2004, 240). Thus Bollywood's significant place in international markets is echoed in its crucial location in the academic world. Rather than evaluating the cinema as better or worse than other forms, this research explores it as the choice of millions of people.

Considering popular Indian film's connection with one of the oldest forms of storytelling—the fairy tale—is particularly relevant because India has been a formative location in fairy-tale studies, as one of the oldest producers of stories. The question is not how many fairy tales have been made into films, but how the fairy tale forms part of cinematic storytelling techniques. It could be framed thus: how do popular Hindi films reflect a consciousness about fairy tales? To understand the relationship between storytelling in popular Hindi cinema and the fairy tale, I explore the structural and interpretational aspects of these films. My concern is particularly the form that defines the majority of popular Hindi films, locally called *masala*[12] and *formula* films, entertaining movies with predictable story lines. These often turn out to be blockbusters, watched by millions, thereby mounting record commercial success.[13] Such films have become very popular in the western world, particularly over the last two decades.

The scholarship is still taking shape.[14] Social scientists and cultural analysts examine popular Hindi cinema to discuss representations of history, politics, economics, postcoloniality, and gender (see "South and Southeast Asian Cinema" 1996), but in all these studies the form of storytelling is taken as a given, and the discussion builds its edifice on the basis of the plot. In the latter area—the specifics of their stories—these films do not look like fairy tales! The characters are contemporary or in definite historical settings and the issues around which the stories are woven are those of current society, polity, economy, and culture. In contrast, the fairy tale is famous for its pre-modern characters and settings, and unless there is a conscious attempt to change it, it is usually located in a fictional, but pre-modern world.

The structure of popular Bollywood films has remained rather constant over several decades, although the themes of their stories have changed in the light of alterations in social and political conditions. For example, the post-independence hope for the future is expressed in films like *Hum Hindustani* (1960), individual criminality in an overall unjust social system as in the cult film *Deewaar* (1975), communal violence in *Bombay* (1995), and terrorism as in *Fanaa* (2006). Rather than analyzing particular Bollywood masala films, I am concerned here with their stable structure, which is one of the reasons for the attention they have gained in the international context. This stable structure can be compared with that of the fairy tale.

Structural Comparison: Fairy Tale and Bollywood Film Story

Generalizing about Bollywood, the basic structure of the popular Hindi film allows it to tell a social story, that is one concerning family ties and emotional bonds, involving a fairly large number of characters and never seriously critical of society. The protagonists—male or female—are themselves deeply rooted in the structure of family, friendship, and community solidarity. The male protagonist is a dutiful son, loving brother, loyal lover, and honest citizen (often a soldier). He is brave and willing to die for his words, nation, or cause. The female protagonist, generally playing second fiddle to her male counterpart, is attractive, amiable, somewhat naive, and ready for marriage. Their class is very important, as are other social markers like urban or rural, illiterate or literate, powerful or powerless, wise or otherwise, and so on. All are clearly identified and play crucial roles in the story. The poor, weak, and powerless are generally the positive characters, but the rich, strong, and powerful may sometimes be kind, generous, and just. This description of the protagonists matches those of many well-known fairy tales, like "Cinderella" or "Snow White."

At the plot's center is the romantic love story of the male and female protagonists and the trials and tribulations they must experience that end in a socially acceptable marriage (see Dwyer 2004). The specific form of these obstacles differs somewhat from one story to another. Each forms a specific theme in the love story, such as love vs. nation; love vs. caste, class, and religious identities; love vs. social pressures; or love vs. criminals. When the story is about love vs. nation, for example, the male protagonist is likely to be a soldier or military officer, for whom the call of duty takes precedence over passionate love. The film certainly proves the value of this hierarchy, even though he invariably gets the love that he seeks at the end of the story. If the theme is love vs. caste, class, and religious identities, a difference of status between the lovers leads to great difficulties in their pairing, but finally love triumphs over all social pressures. If the theme is love vs. criminals, violence ensues as the lovers try to save their love and society from criminals, terrorists, smugglers, and the like. If one lover is a criminal then the audience will learn how social injustice and the protagonists' childhood circumstances made them so. The centrality of this boy-meets-girl theme resembles fairy-tale characters' searches for love and a spouse, and the conflicts they must endure to achieve them.

Good, sympathetic characters and villains complicate the plot's central theme of love. Positive characters are friends, family members, particularly elders, but sometimes strangers. Negative characters and foes are the protagonists' social inverses or others. They are rarely female. Male villains are ugly, have anti-social economic attitudes, and are licentious, womanizers, or drug addicts. But because they are portrayed as grotesque, they generate laughter in the audience instead of fear. When they are cruel, they are justifiably and brutally punished by the protagonists. Clearly their treatment resembles that of fairy-tale villains. For example, in "The Juniper Tree," the murderous stepmother gets a millstone dropped on her and Cinderella's stepsisters have their eyes pecked out by birds.

The fight between good and evil forces is obviously tilted in favor of the villain in the beginning of the story, but as the plot unfolds, this tilt moves in the opposite direction. Good finds support from unlikely locations, including animal and divine sources, and finally wins. The process and its outcome is predictable and pre-determined by the genre itself, even though the specifics of each story differ. This is also a quintessential characteristic of the fairy tale (see Propp 1968). The progression to the end, however, is not fraught with dangers alone. There may be family events, social gatherings, good times, sad times, times of religious fervor, periods of idealism, and depiction of a great variety of human relationships or even human–animal relationships, that lead to the ultimate conflict with the villains and triumph of the hero. There may be many tragic sacrifices along the way. The latter are often the stuff of stories, but in Hindi cinema they occur in every film.

One feature that remains present is song and dance,[15] dispersed throughout the story. In many films, almost every situation has its own song, and some also include dance. Song-and-dance sequences have become the distinguishing marks of popular Hindi cinema—indeed, of all Indian cinema. Actual experiences in human life and society, from childbirth to puberty to marriage to death, are frequently celebrated with music, but Bollywood has created several new situations and locations for song: law courts, hospitals, airports and airstrips, cruises, and streets, among others. There is a song for every situation. The characters may start singing with music inexplicably present in the background, or they may begin dancing with a group of fifty who have emerged from nowhere and disappear as suddenly (see e.g. Gopal and Moorti 2008). This feature connects Bollywood to oral forms of storytelling and folk theatrical performances of epics, called *leela*, both of which combine narrative, lyrical, and musical texts. In oral storytelling as well as in performance, narrators or actors narrate, sing, and play music. In the early days of cinema with sound and before playback recording, one of the main qualifications for an actor was training in singing, as was the case for female actors and singers such as Noor Jahan (1926–2000), Geeta Dutt (1930–1942), and Suraiya (1929–2004), and male actors and singers such as K.L. Saigal (1904–1947) and Kishore Kumar (1929–1987). These song-and-dance sequences are crucial to the story. They mark turning points and give expression to all kinds of issues. For example, the song "Holi ke din" brings the conflict between the heroes and villains to a pitched battle in the film *Sholay* (1975), and the song "Jab pyar kiya to darna kya" from *Mughal-e-Azam* (1960) was the courtesan's defiant response to the emperor's opposition to her love affair with the crown prince.

International audiences may see these musical sequences as the particular aspect of Hindi film storytelling which differentiates it from other, particularly European and American, cinematic forms. Songs, dances, and music from Hindi cinema have become *the* musical culture of contemporary India. They are not only loved and enjoyed, but are also played and performed at occasions in daily life, particularly marriages. Through song-and-dance sequences these films narrate their stories in genres of romance and action, generally separated in Hollywood films but usually combined in Hindi cinema. Love and action are a favorite combination in fairy tales: even when action is not woven around romance, it still ends in the attainment of love, marriage, or wealth.

In its structure and elements, popular Hindi cinema resembles the fairy tale; both are formulaic, and their structure well-known to the audience. From "once upon a time" to "happily ever after," every formal element is, to a large extent, predetermined by the genre. Various stories are narrated within this formation, and compliance to the structure itself justifies the narrative being classified in the genre. Structurally then, Bollywood films can be called fairy tales. But does this cinematic form, like its fairy-tale counterparts, reliably reflect social reality?

Interpretational Value: Fairy Tale and Bollywood Film Story

The themes of Bollywood films over the decades reflect the striking social, political, and economic concerns of the filmmakers. The first film made in India depicted the most famous story of the sub-continent. *Raja Harishchandra* (1913) concerns a king so generous and charitable that he gives away his entire kingdom and every bit of personal wealth. Consequently, he is reduced to working as the man who lights the funeral pyre (the lowest position in the caste structure). At the end of this extreme story where the king not only becomes the poorest man, but even sells his wife and child as domestic slaves, comes the formulaic divine intervention; the entire experience was a test of the king's virtues. Nonetheless, Harishchandra is the proverbial honest ruler in Indian lore. The film was made in colonial India with the freedom struggle against British colonial rule gaining momentum. In the following decades, Hindi cinema supported the freedom struggle through inspiring stories and songs, which are still aired on public radio on Independence Day and Republic Day (for example, *Anand Math* 1952, *Shaheed* 1965). After independence in 1947, Hindi cinema has reflected many themes that have been important for Indian society, state, and the pluralistic public sphere, like *Mother India* (1957), which thematises feudal exploitation of farmers by money lenders and landlords, *Aandhi* (1975), which thematises political corruption, or *Border* (1997), which thematises the war with Pakistan. The years 1944–1960 have been termed the Golden Age of Hindi cinema, when several films, including *Awaara* (1951), achieved popularity and high artistic quality, and won international acclaim at film festivals (Chakravarty 1993).

Scholars have talked about the hopeful movies of the 1950s (Vasudevan 2000), romantic movies in the 1960s, social upheavals of the 1970s, the glamorization of criminals in the 1980s, and liberalization and globalization since the 1990s (Mehta and Pandharipande 2011; Srinivas 2005). So impressive are the details of this list that one might assume the industry is not only socially aware but also socially responsible, but this is very far from the case when we analyze the stories in detail and find their treatment of social issues simplistic. Simultaneously, it cannot be denied that Bollywood, especially in cult films, has often narrated stories of the downtrodden. However, a formula for hit films emerged in the 1960s with romance at its center, and made all other issues nothing more than props to support the romantic story.

A comparison with fairy tales helps to illuminate how realistic these film stories are, how reliable their social commentary, and what symbolic value their characters hold. However, asking how to understand India through its popular Hindi cinema requires a note about some significant differences between fairy tales and films. First, the oral fairy tale cannot really be dated—the moment in which it is told and/or recorded is only a single snapshot of its ongoing history. In contrast, films are registered and their time and place of origin is clear. Second, the oral fairy tale not only has an indeterminable origin, but also most scholars agree that the genre is associated with the lower social orders, particularly in terms of class and gender. The fantastic imagination about good and bad kings and queens; brave, intelligent commoners and wise fools; and free interaction with other worlds underwater and in the skies shows at one level the narrators' distance from power centers, and at another level their quest for liberation from reality and a change of system. Conversely, professionals and fame-seekers create commercial Hindi films, though they are realized in large teams. The results are subject to many market-oriented considerations. And finally, in order to be released in India, they need a certificate from the Central Board of Film Certification.[16]

Despite repeated allegations of vulgarity and violence in films,[17] the Central Board of Film Certification permits not only sex and violence, but also sexist, feudal, and conservative perspectives.[18] Though board members come from a variety of backgrounds, every film must be cleared by this organization of the state. The oral fairy tale submits to no such apparatus. It originates at the margins of the public sphere and recognizes no law. Its own language of metaphors is so highly evolved that it can slip through the crevices of power and be performed on a royal stage while narrating the stories of tyrants brought to their end by ordinary mortals. Different collectors and writers of the oral fairy tale, like the Brothers Grimm, have tried to play down its anti-authoritarian nature according to their own ideological considerations. Literary authors like Angela Carter, Salman Rushdie, and Günter Grass have used the fairy tale subversively to challenge normative narratives of gender and history. Their style has been identified as magical realism, rooted in the genre. These authors are conscious of their politics and aesthetics, but so are some scriptwriters of popular Hindi cinema such as Gulzar and Khwaja Ahmad Abbas. The poet, lyricist, scriptwriter, and director Gulzar is known for films like *Bandini* (1963), *Maachis* (1996), and *Aandhi* (1975). More recently his song "Jai Ho!" from *Slumdog Millionaire* (2008) won an Oscar. Khwaja Ahmad Abbas (1914–1987) wrote cult films like *Awaara* (1951), *Shree 420* (1955), and *Bobby* (1973). One of his first films, *Neecha Nagar* (1946), won the Palme d'Or at the Cannes Film Festival.

And yet, no matter how radical the story seeks to be, the fact that a film must obtain a censor certificate before being released means that it must observe ideals enshrined in the Indian Constitution, for example adherence to the principles of secularism and equality of all before law. No matter how justified the hero may be in murdering the villain, she or he must face the law, and perhaps spend a term in prison before the final happy ending. After a film narrates stories of official corruption, apathy, inefficiency, and collaboration with anti-social elements, it will finally show the law taking its course and setting everything right. The mockery expressed in a popular and oft repeated phrase, "*Kanoon ke hath bahut lambe hain*" (the arms of law are very long) implies that the law will catch up with the criminal sooner or later. Alternatively, the judge in the film may reprimand the hero in yet another famous expression, "*Kanoon ko apne hath mein mat lo*" (don't take the law in your own hands).

Despite the parallel presence of repeated formulaic phrases in them, no fairy tale's hero ever goes through these particular indignities. His victory over the villain is immediately rewarded with a princess-wife and the possibility of a good life. The authority may actually bow down to the hero's achievement. The fairy tale is very clear on which side of the conflict it stands and waits only for logic to judge the situation. The Bollywood hero may have a free run while fighting villains, but must finally be contained within the so-called democratic society. The rare anti-hero, in films like *Mother India* (1957), *Ganga Jumna* (1961), *Deewaar* (1975), or *Khal Nayak* (1993), generally driven by social and personal circumstances to a life in the underworld, must die at the end. The more conventional Bollywood film, epitomized in movies like *Kashmir ki Kali* (1964), *Betaab* (1983), *Chandni* (1989), *Main Hoon Na* (2004), *Chennai Express* (2013), and so on is a story of boy meets girl, ending in marriage. In films like *Gangs of Waseypur*[19] (2012) and *Queen*[20] (2014), love and marriage remain the pivotal points in the story.

The fairy tale has existed across time and space. Its characters are not merely iconic, they are archetypal. They are bigger than themselves because they symbolize particular kinds of human beings and their attributes. They are part of a people's cultural consciousness, in most cases across cultures and languages. But while Cinderella is embedded in international cultural consciousness, characters like Raja Harishchandra are part of cultural consciousness of a very pluralistic South Asian society. Harishchandra symbolizes a selfless monarch, who instead of revelling in his wealth gives it away. He is the antithesis of the common logic of power and presents an imagination of a non-normative rule. But he is a legendary figure, related to Hindu religion. Such characters appear in Indian folktales and fairy tales, but as already indicated, they do not become the subjects of films. Absent from Bollywood are the innumerable nameless fairy-tale kings who are willing to see the logic of justice or who go out wandering at night to get to know their people, or the proverbial wise and stupid learned man, the naive and the intelligent women, and so on. Bollywood has not only failed to make films based on Indian oral tales of wonder and magic, it also has not learned their art and craft of storytelling. Instead, it has merely copied the most superficial elements of the fairy tale's structure. Perhaps, therefore, its structural similarities with fairy tale do not match the levels of depth in their meaning.

Characters in popular Hindi films are based on an identifiable social reality in India, but they transform real occurrences and situations into imagined ones. Thus, period films like *Mughal-e-Azam* (1960), *1942: A Love Story* (1994), and *Mangal Pandey: The Rising* (2005), set in very definite historical situations, have stories with little or no historical basis. The peak of success achieved by *Mughal-e-Azam* was linked to the popular perception of that period of history, which in turn was widely influenced by the film. There is no historical evidence of Emperor Akbar having had to oppose the love affair of his son and crown prince with a courtesan, as the movie would have it. Yet the film made the story so believable! The archetypal images of the fairy tale—a king as father, a son as rebel and a helpless beauty in between—made historical validity irrelevant.

Entertainment drives the culture industry of Bollywood, and even justifies what it otherwise cannot, for example the use of explicitly sexist lyrics and dance performances called "item numbers" by female artists. What is entertainment? It appears that Bollywood filmmakers perceive it as a form of pleasure which can be bought and sold; it engages the buyer briefly but does not bother her or him with thoughts and dilemmas later on. In other words, forms of art created primarily for entertainment are consciously non-serious, though certainly not without ideological perspective (see Prasad 1998). The distinction between commercial cinema and art cinema is relevant.[21] Commercial cinema serves entertainment, not realistic social commentary. It may touch reality to exploit it for its own purposes: poverty looks beautiful; extreme violence does not result in pain but simply in more action, and so on. History and politics may provide the beginnings of a good masala, but to make it spicier, a healthy dose of fiction is required. There is commerce involved at every stage, and the social reality that the film reflects is the reality of the culture industry itself. Once a successful combination of masala has been achieved, innumerable copies inevitably follow. Further, over the last few decades, Bollywood has openly and covertly copied Hollywood films and Indianized the content.[22]

Bollywood is unimaginable without its actors, those who can attract huge audiences and deliver one hit film after another. The industry is actually plagued by their stardom, which leaves very little room for public attention to directors, cinematographers, editors, and sound engineers behind hit films. The scholarship on Hindi films too includes large numbers of monographs about individual actors (see Desai 2005; Pinto 2006). Yet their periods of stardom have become much shorter than in the 1980s, when some stars ruled the industry for a decade or more. Their names and influence on fashion may be remembered, but too often the characters they played on screen are forgettable. Perhaps a few villains remain, but they lack symbolic value that could exist outside of the narrative, as the figure of Bluebeard can stand for misogynist, homicidal husbands in general.

Contrast this with fairy-tale characters like the Pied Piper of Hamelin, Scheherazade, Red Riding Hood, or Cinderella. Across time and space, they create a sense of identification in their listeners. The power of the music of the Pied Piper to teach a lesson to those denying him his wages, or Scheherazade telling stories to save her life, or the temptation experienced by Red Riding Hood in the forest, or the glass shoe of Cinderella are ideas embedded in an international cultural consciousness. To quote Zipes, that is why fairy tales stick (2006a). No character of popular Hindi cinema has such power. They are copied by—at best—a generation and then replaced by others, because they no longer inspire the imagination. Popular Hindi cinema stories have a finite life, not a symbolic one that transcends time and space. Not every narrative must be timeless, but Bollywood contrasts with the fairy tale's symbolic value.

Fairy tales may not provide direct social commentary, but they do reflect on human nature as expressed in various roles that people play throughout their lives. The characteristics, dilemmas, and situations that the fairy tale presents seem fantastic, but they are realistic on a deeper level that speaks to the subconscious, and once inserted, they remain embedded. These abstractions can be carried across time and manifest in varying forms in different places. The fairy tale may focus on the micro—sometimes literally in the form of the smallest possible character like Tom Thumb—but its aggregate exists everywhere in the macro reality, like the proverbial drop containing the entire ocean.

Popular Hindi films do not lead to the emergence of abstractions as symbols. Their plots offer a sequence of events that resolve a situation of crisis. There is no moral to be derived at the end, apart from the words inscribed in the emblem of India, "*Satyamev jayate*" (Truth shall win). The saying was so literally realized in the films of the 1970s that it became a joke. These cinematic stories maintain ideological positions that can be outright conservative; at best they criticize some aspect of society that is already under attack in the public sphere, like caste oppression, women's empowerment or exploitation, national integrity, and so on. Their critical perspective is finely balanced so as not to disturb any section of the society. Criticism becomes furthermore diluted because of the multi-religious and multi-lingual nature of Indian society. While popular Hindi cinema propagates or even invents certain biases, such as obesity as funny, Pakistan as enemy state, Himalayan people as exotic, or a fair complexion as necessary for beauty, its commercial interest is best served when it does not raise serious controversies. So, for example, films sympathetic to women will advocate for women's rights on moral grounds, but not challenge the patriarchal order in itself; in their essential attributes gender roles remain normative. The same applies to representation of other social and political realities (Kishore, Sarwal, and Patra 2014).

Commercial Hindi cinema operates in a highly complex social and cultural context. Social, economic, and other disparities offer a situation where old, new, and futuristic coexist, leading to diverse expectations. Popular Hindi cinema is watched by people of different classes, by literate and illiterate, by urban and rural, and cuts across the linguistic divisions. It is watched, with or without subtitles, in non-Hindi language zones, even when anti-Hindi movements dominated their local politics. All social issues are so fantastic in their representation that they qualify for the disclaimer: "The characters and events in this story are purely fictional. Any resemblance to persons living or dead is coincidental."

The fairy tale, too, hides the realistic identities of its characters and events behind fantasy. It achieves this effect so rigorously that it can be difficult to find any resemblance to reality. But in so doing, it reaches the truth behind empirical experience and expresses it through metaphor. For example, the tale about the goose that laid one golden egg each day, until the human owner kills it to get all the eggs at once, is not about the individual's stupidity, but about common human greed and avarice to acquire as much as possible in the shortest possible time, even at the cost of another's life. There is no need to search for the historical identity of this man because he potentially exists in everyone. Popular Hindi cinema rarely achieves such abstraction. It hides reality to make the grim seem glamorous (as in *Company* [2002]) or to avoid legal problems due to possible identification with real people and events (as in *Aandhi* [1975]). Their diverging relationships with reality create huge differences in the interpretational value of fairy tales and popular Hindi films. While Bollywood masala films are only about the characters in their narrative, fairy tales are not about the figures through which they tell a story, but about characters inside us.

Is it All a Fairy Tale?

Popular Hindi cinema is structurally a fairy tale, probably due to the predominance of orality in the cultural expression of the sub-continent. Regardless of their education, people learn from oral stories. In the context of Indian oral narratives, tales of wonder and magic exist not only in the Indo-European classic fairy tale, but also in ancient texts like the fables of the *Panchatantra* or the Buddhist *Jataka* stories. They remain in popular culture and influence a broad sense of social morality. Similarly, epic narrative and performative traditions, *katha vachan* (stylized oral narration of religious stories) and *leela* (performance of epics in folk theater as song–dance–drama) respectively, are also experienced by all in some form or another. If the urban populace has been separated from the face-to-face tradition, they still experience the epics through television where the performances ape the *leela* paradigm, that is song–dance–drama. The makers of Bollywood films are similarly exposed to them in some form or another, and therefore, many fairy-tale elements are present in their manner of storytelling: fantasy, magic, wonder, and a world of its own.

And yet, popular Hindi films differ from fairy tales because their stories vacillate between realistic and fantastic elements rather aimlessly. While fairy tales can be connected to a *Weltanschauung* in general where good is good, and bad is bad, any generalization regarding Bollywood's ideology is difficult. It is so not because every individual film lacks ideology, but because there is no ideological commitment on an overall level, only adherence to legally defined ideas. The Bollywood film does not aim to have a philosophical theme, just a topical one. Professor Bahadur's observation may point to an important connection of Bollywood films to fairy tales, but on further examination the complexity of this relationship becomes visible.

Notes

1 Professor Bahadur taught film appreciation at the Film and Television Institute of India, Pune, from 1963 to 1986, and introduced film studies to several educational institutions across India. See Bahadur and Vanarase (2011).

2 For an introduction to Bollywood, see Joshi (2002), Das Gupta (1991), and Kaur and Sinha (2005).

3 The story is about the benefits gained from worshipping the goddess Santoshi. It revolves around a married woman who undertakes to fast on sixteen Fridays, as prescribed, and leads her family to prosperity and happiness.

4 On the escapist properties of Indian cinema, see Brook (2011) and Salam (2013).

5 In his study of the theoretical perspectives on *difference* Hetzel discusses what the concept means in a globalizing world order. His assertion that in the study of cultural phenomena, acceptance of *difference* enables us to see the irreducible uniqueness of an individual phenomenon within the large concept of culture (2004, 240), has significant implication with reference to the international reception of Bollywood films.

6 See, for example, "South and Southeast Asian Cinema" (1996), a comprehensive online archive of relevant literary and videographic resources.

7 Lutz Röhrich summarizes many such views in the first paragraph of his seminal work *Folktales and Reality* (1991, 1).
8 Several websites show Bollywood's spread across the globe. For more information, see Bukker (2011), Sanghi (2012), PTI (2013), Rehman (2014), Chowdhury (2008), and Prabhakar (2012).
9 As Young and Gallo (1996) argue, "the cultural distance between India and most American films again kept US market penetration in India to 1.5 percent in 1995. Hit Indian films are 3-hour musical comedy/drama/thrillers, and even worldwide hits like 'Jurassic Park' making scarcely a dent in India" (169).
10 For a thorough discussion on the subject, see Ganti (2012) and Punathambekar (2013).
11 A good example of such generic influences is the Bollywood sequence that closes Tarsem Singh's Hollywood blockbuster *Mirror, Mirror* (2012), based on the story of Snow White.
12 "Masala" literally means a combination of spices for a certain preparation of food. Masala film implies a combination of emotion, action, comedy, song, and dance. The concept is used popularly and in scholarship; for instance David Martin-Jones defines the film *Nina's Heavenly Delights* as a "masala" of Scottish-Indian identity (2009, 86).
13 Wikipedia provides lists of these films for every year since the 1930s ("List of Bollywood Films"). See particularly lists for the 1960s, 1970s, 1980s, and 1990s and check those listed under "Highest Grossing," implying commercial success and popularity, to see how themes within the overall paradigm of song-dance-drama have changed. In the 2000s, a few off-beat films, like *Bheja Fry* (2007) and *Kahani* (2012), offer different narratives. For example, *Kahani* is about a married, pregnant woman of Indian origin, resident of England, who comes to India in search of her missing husband.
14 Fareed Kazmi is of the opinion that "No matter how staggered they [scholars of Indian films] might be, they have developed useful tools to understand the grammar and language of Indian films, map out their terrain, locate their source, mark out its boundaries and goalposts, grasp its sensitivities and inner logic, make visible its interpellating (sic) processes and demystify its ideology" (2010, ii).
15 For detailed discussion of this theme, see Morcom (2007).
16 Central Board of Film Certification (CBFC) is a Statutory body under Ministry of Information and Broadcasting, regulating the public exhibition of films under the provisions of the Cinematograph Act 1952.
17 Mazzarella (2010) and AFP (2013) give an impression of the public perception of obscenity in Bollywood.
18 For more details on censorship of Hindi films, see Bose (2005).
19 The story is about three generations of a small-town mafia family. Their fascination with Bollywood is a sub-theme in the narrative.
20 This film starts with the preparation of the female protagonist's wedding, but soon the groom decides not to go ahead with the marriage. The heroine goes on her planned honeymoon alone. As a middle-class Indian girl she has no experience of traveling solo, and her trip to Europe becomes a journey of self realization.
21 On the subject of popular and art cinema, see Bahadur (2014).
22 For an exhaustive list of Bollywood adaptations of Hollywood films, see Pranshu (2014).

15

THE FAIRY-TALE FILM IN KOREA

Sung-Ae Lee

There are three broad currents in the development of the fairy-tale film in Korea. The first, and oldest, involves film adaptations of Korean folktales and legends. The earliest of these were made during the period of Japanese colonization of the Korean peninsula and imparted various cultural and political messages. A silent film adaptation of the folktale "Chunhyangjeon" by Japanese director Hayakawa Matsujiro marks the first in 1923. As Lee Hyangjin observes, the folktale expresses a desire for a utopian society through its story of forbidden love between the daughter of a *gisaeng* (courtesan) and a *yangban* (aristocrat) (Lee 2005, 63).[1] The themes of the breakdown of class barriers and the destruction of corrupt power represent such a recurrent desire in Korean society that the tale has been adapted to film at least twenty times since Hayakawa's silent film. Indeed, the first Korean film with sound was an adaptation of "Chunhyangjeon" by Korean director, Lee Myeong-U in 1935.

The Korean film industry languished between 1937 and 1955: with Japan's invasion of China, Korean language films were banned and replaced by propaganda films in Japanese; the American occupation and puppet dictatorship after World War II was not conducive to a film industry; and what industry infrastructure that survived was destroyed during the Korean War (1950–1953). Another adaptation of "Chunhyangjeon," directed by Lee Gyu-Hwan in 1955, is credited with inspiring a boom in film production after the mid-1950s (Lee and Choe 1998, 111). This film has unfortunately not survived but, according to Lee Young-Il and Choe Young-Chol (1998, 112–13), in its year of release it was viewed by more than a tenth of Seoul's population. Two adaptations were made in 1961, Hong Seong-Gi's *Chunhyang* and Shin Sang-Ok's *Seong Chunhyang*. The most remarkable version, to be discussed below, was directed by Im Kwon-Taek in 2000. Most recently, the tale has been adapted to a television drama about modern teenagers, *Delightful Girl Chunhyang* (Koegeol Chunhyang 2005). Several other well-known tales have been adapted or modernized for film, again often in multiple versions, such as "Arang"; "Fool Ondal and Princess Pyeonggang"; "Gumiho" (The Fox with Nine Tails); "Janghwa Hongryeonjeon" (The Story of Janghwa and Hongryeon 1962); "Oseam"; "Shimcheongjeon"; "The Weaver Girl and the Cowherd" (aka "Gyeonu and Jiknyeo"—a Korean analogue of the well-known Chinese tale), to name a few.

The folktales circulate in numerous variants and multimodal forms, and are not associated with household names such as the Grimms or Hans Christian Andersen, but rather known by the tale's title. Hence a film adaptation cannot be traced to a particular printed text, but stems from what cognitive narratologists call a "script." A script in everyday life is a stereotyped sequence of actions that is part of a person's knowledge about the world. Scripts encompass ordinary behavior such as the process involved in catching a train from one place to another (arriving at the station; obtaining a ticket; identifying the correct platform; and so on). The pre-stored knowledge representations that we use at a train station are comparable to the stereotypic plot structures that readers call upon to anticipate the unfolding story logic of creative works (Herman 2002, 89–91; Stephens 2011, 14). However, the retelling of a familiar narrative prototype, such as the suffering and triumph of an innocent persecuted heroine, will involve a choice amongst possible variants of a familiar story, and the coexistence of multiple possibilities creates a script (Lee Sung-Ae 2014, 276). As Jack Zipes observes about the related concept of a fairy-tale hypotext (a pre-existing text upon which an adaptation is purported to be based), "the hypotext is more a notion than anything else" because its sources are flexible and fluid and it may draw upon several variants of a tale type (2011, 8). This understanding of hypotext roughly corresponds with the notion of script employed in cognitive narratology, although a script may also blend different tales. A script may be represented by a pattern of action sequences, as in the case of the innocent persecuted heroine, or by a single action sequence within a larger pattern (for instance, how people are shown to respond when confronted by a monster). Korean film adaptations of folktales are adaptations of a script, not a specific text, and this practice carries over to the second source of film adaptations, western fairy tales.

The second current consists of a relatively small group of western fairy tales which have been adapted for the Korean cinema from the Grimms, Charles Perrault, or Andersen. These adaptations are usually at some remove from the western tales, which circulate as scripts rather than the European originals. The Perrault and Grimm tales include "Cinderella," "Beauty and the Beast," "Snow White," and "Hansel and Gretel." The Andersen tales comprise those which perhaps have the widest circulation in East Asia more generally: "The Little Mermaid," "The Little Match Girl," "The Ugly Duckling," and "The Red Shoes." Western fairy tales are normally adapted to local genres—historical drama, horror, romantic comedy—and occasionally (more often in TV drama) different western sources may be blended through homologies or common script elements, as, for example, blendings of "Cinderella" and "The Little Mermaid."

The first adaptation of a western script to a local genre was *Princess Snow White* (Baekseol Gongju 1964). In this film, the ruler of the Madal kingdom cherishes his only daughter, Princess Snow White. But the princess has to flee the palace because her stepmother, the second queen, is conspiring with an evil government official to seize the kingdom and hence kill the princess. The Vice-Minister puts down the conspiracy, and Princess Snow White returns to the palace to help her father rule wisely. The western script's emphasis on rivalry over personal beauty has been replaced by the theme of a struggle for power within the palace, which at the time was emerging in Korean cinema as a major allegory for current affairs. Shin Sang-Ok's *Prince Yeonsan* (1961) and *Yeonsan the Tyrant* (1962) were leading historical films of the early 1960s, and their accounts of internecine feuding within the royal palace and a consequent coup d'état are inspirational for the historical analogue blended with fairy tale in *Princess Snow White*.

The third current blends tales from the two traditions—Korean and European. Although this cross-cultural phenomenon is quite rare in film, it is common in television drama. The most obvious possibilities lie in the blending of eastern and western analogues of the same tale type. An example is the formulation of a new script by blending a "Cinderella" script with one derived from the tale of "Kongjwi and Patjwi," the Korean variant of the East Asian persecuted heroine tale that spread westward in a truncated form to emerge as the European "Cinderella."

Western fairy tales are much less likely to be adapted for the screen than are local folktales, whose familiarity is assured by dissemination in other media. For example, recent picture book versions have been published of: *Princess Bari* (2006), *Story of the Wise Princess Pyeonggang and the Brave Ondal the Fool* (2012), *Shimcheongjeon* (2010), and *Gyeonu and Jiknyeo* (2009). This dissemination also keeps a tale available as an intertextual resource, so while there has not been a dedicated film adaptation of "Fool Ondal and Princess Pyeonggang" since Lee Gyu-Ung's 1961 version, this popular tale has remained familiar through childhood and other retellings and is recognizable when incorporated thematically or structurally in a film about something else. The highly popular television variety show *Running Man* built one of its episodes on the script of a Princess training an "Idiot" ("Ondals and the Three Princesses," Episode 137, 2013). There was also a modern retelling of the tale in a 2009 TV series, *Invincible Lee Pyeonggang* (Cheonhamujeok I Pyeonggang). Embedded so deeply in the culture, such folktale scripts are readily recognizable whether in imaginative retellings, as in *Chunhyang* (2000), contemporary analogues, as in the crime thriller *Arang* (2006), or oblique blendings, as when "Gyeonu and Jiknyeo" and "Pyeonggang and Ondal" are fused in *My Sassy Girl* (Yeopgijeogin Geunyeo, "The Bizarre Girl" 2001).

The two main functions of folktale films in Korea have been cultural conservation and sociopolitical allegory, which is hardly surprising given Korea's turbulent history through the twentieth century. Im Kwon-Taek's *Chunhyang* (2000) achieves both of these aims. The film's most dramatic strategy is to frame the narrative as performed by a *pansori* singer, which imparts a strong sense of cultural context. In fact, the *pansori* performance by Cho Sang-Hyun, one of the greatest modern exponents of the form, was constructed from a combination of the vocal line from a 1976 recording and the visuals from a 1995 performance. *Pansori* is a unique Korean narrative genre, whose most distinguishing characteristic is that "one *sorikkun* (singer) sings a long dramatic song that lasts for about three to four hours, and sometimes up to eight hours, relying solely on the accompaniment of a single *gosu* (drummer)" (Han 2007, 91).

The genre developed in the seventeenth century and flourished in the nineteenth. Five *pansori* cycles have survived, the oldest of which is *The Tale of Chunhyang* (Lee 2005, 70), which perhaps also best exemplifies the transition from a lower-class genre to an upper-class entertainment. At its core, *The Tale of Chunhyang* contains a wish that a talented individual could escape the rigid class stratification of the Joseon Dynasty (1392–1910) by ascending to a higher class. However, the Joseon Dynasty was a neo-Confucian state, and Confucian precepts determined both governance of the populace and of the individual body, so when *yangban* (aristocratic) society became interested in *pansori* in the nineteenth century, the "Chunhyang" script increasingly absorbed the Confucian values of that class, notably "a highly centralized state hegemony and hierarchy (bureaucracy) and the precedence of politics over economy and society" (Han 2013, 6). The *pansori* version of *The Tale of Chunhyang*, with which Im Kwon-Taek worked to develop his film, presented him with a deep social contradiction between rigid hierarchy and personal development that to a great extent is still visible in modern Korean society.

The film opens by reproducing the breach of hierarchy on which the tale pivots: the forbidden, secret marriage between Mongryong, son of the provincial governor, and Chunhyang, daughter of a courtesan. While taking a break from his studies for the civil service examination to enjoy the Dano festival (fifth day of the fifth month of the lunar calendar), Mongryong sees Chunhyang playing on a swing, a traditional women's pastime at Dano. Her action is significant in two ways. First, her assumed status is marked by her higher-class dress and accompanying servant woman, but she openly breaches decorum by displaying herself in a society where only lower-class or serving women are readily visible. When Mongryong sends his servant, Bangja, to bring Chunhyang to him, Bangja tells her that she has behaved inappropriately: "in this open field, you flaunt your bare ankles, tease us with your raised dress, pretty smile, and giddy laugh. No wonder he fell for you." Her behavior is indicative of her independent mind and readiness to defy convention.

Second, her physical activity introduces the film's visual and ideational focus on her material, corporeal body, an emphasis underlined by a visual reference in the film to Shin Yoon-Bok's famous painting, *Dano Scenes* (see Figure 15.1), which viewers reconstruct from fragmented close-ups

FIGURE 15.1 Left: Shin Yoon-Bok's *Dano Scenes* (1805–1810). Right: two close-ups where Chunhyang mounts the swing, *Chunhyang* (2000).

which reveal that both the posture and the style and color of the clothing are identical. As the eye moves across the painting from the red dress of the woman at the swing to the lower left-hand corner, it lights upon four half-naked *gisaeng* bathing, their status evident in their hairstyles. This painting is the first in Korean art to depict female nudity, and the film's allusion to it thus borrows its emphasis on female corporeality.[2]

Chunhyang initially rejects Mongryong's advances by sending him a poem. Though she is also expert in Chinese calligraphy, and an excellent performer on the *geomungo* (a traditional Korean stringed instrument of the zither family), it is her body—desired, loved, and tortured—that finally matters. When Bangja informs Mongryong that Chunhyang has spurned all men who have approached her, he responds, "The world's precious beauties are destined to have an owner," but instead contracts a secret marriage with her. Their wedding night captures the mind-body conflict, as the seduction of the shy, reluctant bride is played out against the backdrop of a screen display-ing poetry and images of peach and plum blossom, familiar symbols of evanescence. Chunhyang subsequently becomes sensual and physically playful, but their joy is short-lived. Because neo-Confucianism was maintained as the state ideology and social norm, behavior that deviated from neo-Confucian orthodoxy was vilified as "despoiling the Way" (Kim 2014, 400). Mongryong cannot tell his stern patriarchal father about his morganatic marriage, which disrupts family con-tinuance, so when the family moves to Seoul, Mongryong can only promise Chunhyang to return as soon as he has passed the civil service examination.

In the event, it is three years before Mongryong returns, now incognito as a Royal Inspector of local government. During his absence, the new Governor Byun Hak-Do demands sexual service from Chunhyang, and orders her to be publicly tortured when she refuses. In contrast to the earlier intimate and private bedroom scenes, Chunhyang's body now becomes a public spectacle, a site upon which is staged the struggle between Chunhyang and the tyrannical Governor. Torture scenes are familiar in Korean historical films and dramas, but are seldom represented as such a formally staged mise-en-scène. The episode is divided in two: the first half depicts the torture, while the second shows *pansori* singer Cho Sang-Hyun describing the event to a very responsive audience. The effect is to metacinematically emphasize the theatricality of the production. The first half is filmed from behind Chunhyang, with only two frontal close-ups, so that visual stress falls on the staging and Byun's roles of both plaintiff and judge. When at some points the camera is behind Cho there is a suggestion of visual isomorphism, which further foregrounds the theatricality of the structure. The process of dispute again pivots on neo-Confucianism: Chunhyang's citation of and determination to observe the second of the three ways a woman must follow throughout her entire life—to follow her husband, once married—and the Governor's legal assertion that her social status as a courtesan's daughter has precedence over her marital status. Indeed, that none of the extant *pansori* texts challenges the Governor's perspective reflects the power wielded by Confucian scholars within the state. When Mongryong returns, endowed with the power to dismiss the provincial government, he is in time to save Chunhyang from being beaten to death to celebrate the Governor's birthday. The *pansori* all include a carnivalesque routing of dishonest bureaucrats but only one mentions the Governor, who is merely advised to govern more wisely in future. In contrast, Im's film adds a brief scene in which Mongryong visits the now-deposed Governor in his temporary prison, where their conversation includes the following exchange:

Mongryong: Adoring a pretty woman is natural. But don't you think what you did to Chunhyang was too harsh?

Byun: Class has a definite order. A daughter of a courtesan becomes one naturally. She didn't disobey just me . . . but she disgraced the law, and committed treason.

Mongryong: It wasn't injustice . . . it was her will to be a human being.

The elevation of moral justice over a ruling class's self-regarding legal structure rebalances the script's internal conflict such that female transgression encapsulates both class and gender confrontation with neo-Confucian patriarchy, as the tale is returned to what may have been its original emphasis.

The problematic, rebellious or abjected female has been a frequent figure in Korean folktale films. Another area where she plays a role is in tales concerning fox spirits. Probably originating in China about a millennium ago, folktales about fox spirits circulate in several traditions in East Asia, but evolved in a unique way in Korea so that the tales generally concern only female foxes whose behavior is usually demonic. This representation appears in both historical and contemporary, popular culture settings, in both of which retellings of fox stories follow two main scripts (see Lee 2011, for an extended discussion). On the one hand, the fox perceives its difference from humans as inferiority, and aspires to better itself by becoming a human being or rising to heaven. This aspiration is structurally comparable to the neo-Confucian model of elevated subjectivity, wherein the self is first subsumed into the family, then into the community and finally into the universe. In the androcentric subjectivity espoused by neo-Confucianism, women (and non-humans) were not considered full subjects and hence the gumiho (fox with nine tails) is what Kim Taeyon aptly calls a "subjectless" body (2003, 101), denied such elevation.[3] The other principal difference is that the gumiho requires the death of one or more humans to implement her transformation, which commonly depends on eating the victim's liver. The second script type portrays the gumiho as more predatory: because she is a shape changer, she can replace a daughter of a family and devour the family's livestock and eventually most of the family, until a monk teaches a son of the family how to defeat her. The two scripts may merge, since their common ground concerns human victims, and the motive for the impersonation in script two may be to gain the liver(s) necessary for the fox to become human.

The first of six film adaptations of the gumiho script was Shin Sang-Ok's *The Thousand-Year-Old Fox* (Cheonnyeonho 1969). Shin's decision to set the film in the *Silla* dynasty (668–935 CE) and to represent the gumiho as a malevolent spirit that possessed a human woman's body, locates the narrative within a traditional folktale script. The second adaptation, Park Heon-Su's *Gumiho*

(1994), is set in a contemporary context and marks a shift from cultural conservation to an often comedic popular culture context. Park's film has influenced most subsequent representations: two more films, two made-for-television short features, and five TV drama series, beginning in 2004. Park created the first gumiho with whom audiences could empathize, although his film nevertheless requires that her desire to become human is eventually thwarted by her development of altruistic feelings towards her target victim and her decision to choose her own death instead. The gumiho's aspiration to become "a human being" is a greater deviation from social order than that attributed to Chunhyang, not least because the gumiho derives from a belief system older and less rational than Confucianism. A comic sub-plot in which the heroine is pursued by a demon sent from hell to rid the world of its last gumiho suggests that threats to social order must be purged by destroying what is alien and Other. Though the traditional gumiho uses sexual allure to capture her victims, the film's fox-spirit Hara develops a genuine love for her potential victim Hyuk. Viewers are frequently reminded, however, that her attractive body and the expensive house she lives in are illusions of transformation; such superficialities are a regular tactic of the gumiho who can cast a glamor upon her victims. The less elegant parts of the house, the cellars and yard, which contain the cadavers and hens she devours raw, remind viewers of the beast-form she seeks to leave behind. Yet the film suggests that her house's duality reflects the social evils of the society she strives to join; she is as much victim as perpetrator. By the film's close, Hara and Hyuk are caught in a situation that must cause the death of one of them, and each struggles to keep the other alive. The concept of a shared cross-species humanity articulated here establishes ground for subverting the traditional story's patriarchal metanarrative and re-signifying the fox's otherness to reflect society's ethnic others, such as immigrants, and thence challenges social classification of people according to their otherness (Lee 2011, 141–42). Thus the parallel between the fox and the ethnic Other appears as the principal theme of both the 2007 animated film *Yeoubi, the Five-Tailed Fox* and the most highly acclaimed of the TV drama series, *My Girlfriend is a Gumiho* (2010).

Two made-for-TV films were produced for Korean Broadcasting System's series "Hometown of Legends." *Return of the Gumiho* (2008, dir. Kwak Jung-Hwan) is an homage to Shin's 1969 *The Thousand-Year-Old Fox*, depicting a vengeful and violent gumiho. *Gumiho* (2009, dir. Shin Hyun-Soo), on the other hand, demonstrates the enduring influence of Park's 1994 film, with a pleasant, amiable woman forced to hide from gumiho-hunters in a human village. Alison Peirse and James Byrne suggest that because both films deliberately look back at the folktale origins of the tales, they offer "traditional representations of the *gumiho* as a creature of horror, much in the same way as Shin's Silla-set *The Thousand Year Old Fox* depicts the *gumiho* as a malevolent female spirit" (2013, 45). This partial reading, however, overlooks the films' common construction of the gumiho as a victim of male violence and duplicity. Kwak's film reverses human and gumiho functions, so that human males murder female relatives with gumiho genes to eat their livers and absorb their life force. The gumiho who discovers this understandably attempts to slaughter the men involved, but the practice continues because she shows mercy.

In Shin Hyun-Soo's film the gumiho-script has been substantially modified by combination with an unrelated script that blends "Gyeonu and Jiknyeo" with "Fool Ondal and Princess Pyeong-gang." In order to become human the gumiho marries a poor and inept young man and manages his life so that he becomes prosperous and successful. After 1,000 days she will become human, but her husband lacks Ondal's character and, having squandered his newfound wealth, betrays her to the hunters, who intend to sell her body parts for medicinal purposes. She overcomes her foes, but must spend the rest of her life in the solitude which is the lot of the gumiho. The explicit moral with which the film closes—"This legend shows how human desire can be much more destructive than any other animal or malignant spirit"—suggests that identification of society's others is a product of self-interest.

Recent gumiho texts indicate that Peirse and Byrne fall short of the point in asserting that, "Despite the increasingly disparate depictions of the *gumiho*, a single thread endures: the connections between the fox and the unruly female body, an idea that can be traced back to its folkloric origins" (2013, 45). Rather, "the unruly female body" no longer demands to be contained, but has in popular culture become an appropriate female resistance to enduring masculinist Confucian ideology. By 2013, the 149th episode of *Running Man* assumes a general familiarity with the gumiho-script and its adaptations, sustaining a running joke about the physical attractiveness of the gumiho and making visual and verbal references to *Return of the Gumiho* (2008) and to *My Girlfriend is a Gumiho* (2010). What it seems to be arguing is that a modern society requires a modern conception of female sexuality, such that antiquated gender assumptions must give way to "the unruly female body."

One of the most successful of recent folktale adaptations that involve an unruly female protagonist has been *My Sassy Girl* (2001). While it tells its own story, this film is a mash-up of folktales and other genres, which it deploys, along with a self-reflexive use of cinematic techniques, in ways that make it the most metacinematic of Korean folktale films. Set in contemporary Seoul, it depicts an unstable, off–on, unconsummated relationship between Gyeonu, an engineering student, and an unnamed young woman ("The Girl"). It is not an overt adaptation of a folktale, but its narrative arc parallels that of "Gyeonu and Jiknyeo" while drawing on versions of "The Heavenly Maiden and the Woodcutter" (Korea) and "The Buffalo Boy and the Weaving Maiden" (China).[4] Audiences are cued to look for connections from the beginning of the film because the male protagonist has the same name as the Korean folktale character and in an opening vignette from his childhood his mother is shown dragging him into a public bath-house with the title "Weaver Girl Bath-house" (*Jiknyeo tang*) over the door. The bath motif is not found in "Gyeonu and Jiknyeo," however, but has been taken from "The Heavenly Maiden and the Woodcutter." The film thus works with a recognizable script, but embraces multiple intertextual folktale referents.[5]

The character here named "Gyeonu" is a narrative schema: a poor member of an underclass, such as a buffalo boy, a cowherd, or a woodcutter (the characters have other names, or are unnamed, in the analogues). In the Chinese "Legend of Dong Yang and the Weaving Maiden" he appears as a poor but diligent student. Jiknyeo, like her counterparts in the analogues, is a daughter of the heavenly king and is renowned for her weaving ability. The script includes three causes for their marriage. First, the heavenly king wishes to reward Gyeonu for his diligence and honesty; second, Gyeonu steals Jiknyeo's clothes while she bathes in a mountain pool, so she must become his wife ("The Heavenly Maiden and the Woodcutter"); or third (in modern retellings), Jiknyeo sees Gyeonu and falls in love with him. The couple live a life of prosperity because of Gyeonu's diligence and Jiknyeo's weaving. They have (usually) three children. The motif of socio-economic advancement is also the core motif of "Fool Ondal and Princess Pyeonggang," so the two folktales have a propensity to overlap or blend at this point. The couple is eventually forced to separate, for one of three reasons: after the third child is born Jiknyeo regains her heavenly clothes and returns home; or the heavenly king decrees that a time limit had been set on the marriage; or within a few months of the wedding, the heavenly king concludes they are failing in their duty of diligence (the usual Korean version).[6] They are permitted to meet on the seventh day of the seventh month of each year (in the lunar calendar), but because they are separated by the Milky Way crows and magpies work together to form a bridge for the couple.

My Sassy Girl transforms and modernizes the script in several ways. Gyeonu is an indifferent university student from a comfortable middle-class family. The Girl, also a student, one year younger than Gyeonu, is from an indeterminate higher socio-economic group. She aspires to write film scripts and is thus a weaver of stories, three of which are embedded in the film and form part of its metacinematic fabric. These stories are self-reflexive, since their genre conventionality comments back on the film's cinematic processes, and in the visual presentations she herself plays the heroine and Gyeonu is cast as either villain or victim. The dualism in these metacinematic insets, together with Gyeonu's reluctance as their first reader to disclose how bad they are, emphasizes their status as constructed texts and draws attention to the overall constructedness of *My Sassy Girl*.

The couple's first meeting lacks the portentousness of the folktale script, but is merely a chance encounter on a railway platform. The Girl is extremely drunk and at risk of falling in front of an oncoming train, so Gyeonu pulls her out of the way. He then reluctantly takes responsibility for her when she passes out and the other passengers assume she is his girlfriend. Both then and subsequently her behavior is very unruly. She is overbearing towards Gyeonu and her dealings with strangers are often aggressive. Gyeonu tolerates her behavior because he recognizes she is affected by an unrevealed trauma—later disclosed to be the suicide of her fiancé—and he wants to help. A schema based on the education of "Fool Ondal" is evoked here. In the folktale, the Princess guides and educates Ondal, transforming him from an ignorant beggar to a great military leader. In a more modern scenario, Gyeonu becomes wiser through tolerance of The Girl's misguidance, as his capacity for empathy and compassion is enhanced by his experience. Film and TV drama frequently identify an incapability for altruism as a social problem amongst South Koreans. Gyeonu is consistently altruistic, at times to his own disadvantage; the Girl's unruliness towards strangers usually involves sudden interventions in social situations (in one example she attacks a group of businessmen who are paying schoolgirls for sex—another prevalent social problem in South Korea). Gyeonu's informal education further develops after the two break up; he strives to deal with his incompetence in physical activities (kendo, squash, and swimming), and he writes stories about the Girl on an internet blog, which leads to a film contract and a new career direction—and, of course, *this* film. A further image developed from the folktale is the bridge, which takes several metaphorical guises over the last part of the film. The Girl organizes that they bury a time capsule containing letters to each other (that is, one kind of "bridge") beneath a special tree, and then she breaks off the relationship. They make a pact to meet again after two years, but the Girl doesn't appear and they no longer have any means of contact, until they are accidentally reunited and finally become a couple in a romantic ending that departs from all versions of the folktale.

The film's adaptations and blendings of recognizable folktale scripts to produce new meanings is part of the metacinematic effect in pointing to the instability of images and their signification. For instance, in the folktale, Gyeonu and Jiknyeo are separated because, too engrossed in their love for one another, they have become a narcissistic dyad and neglect the social responsibilities inherent in their names and functions (*Gyeonu*, "herder of cattle"; *Jiknyeo*, "woman who weaves cloth"). At their first yearly meeting afterwards, they remain divided by the Milky Way—they shout each other's names from opposite sides, but neither can see nor hear the other because of the vast distance. The birds decide to make themselves into a bridge on the next and subsequent meeting days, not because of compassion but because the lovers' tears cause severe storms and rain on Earth.

The folktale script and the film adaptation depict different versions of emotional turbulence because they presuppose valuations of different bases for love. The film will inevitably place a higher value on romantic love because that is an expected convention in a majority of contemporary cultures. It interrogates its own assumption at various times, however. Thus when Gyeonu complains that the Girl's "action movie" sketch should end with the leading characters kissing, she dismisses the suggestion as "melodramatic." The film also questions the coincidence of its ending. *My Sassy Girl* reproduces the folktale's image of an expansive gulf at the moment the Girl and Gyeonu begin to break up, when she sends him on an obviously futile journey from one mountain peak to another opposite to find out if they can hear each other over that distance. When he appears on the other mountain she shouts an apology for her emotional inadequacy, as a shot–reverse shot sequence creates the illusion that the river below flows between them like the bridgeless Milky Way. The scene is more than a clever game with the folktale image, however—it is a metacinematic comment on the power of narrative to create, deceive and transform.

The cinema audience is invited to identify connections and misconnections and to enjoy the jokes. The inversions and disparities suggest that the folktales function to give some shape to the story, but their relevance may also be primarily as a source of humor because contemporary society is disinclined to treat older values seriously. The reason the heavenly maiden must marry the wood-cutter when he steals her clothes is that he has seen her naked body, which only a husband should see. As Kim Taeyon observes, however, "Women are no longer ruled by the Neo-Confucian com-mand to be invisible, to protect their bodies from both sight and touch. . . . Women have become extraordinarily visible in Korea, free to be observed and appreciated in any public space" (2003, 103). The old rule is thus inverted in *My Sassy Girl* when Gyeonu carries the drunk, unconscious Girl to a motel, and then takes a shower there to wash off her vomit and his own sweat. While he is naked, two young female police officers burst in and arrest him, presumably on a charge of abduc-tion and attempted rape. It is a comic scene which culminates in Gyeonu's attempt to cover his genitals with his hands, and an armed police-woman's instruction, "Hands up!" If there's a serious point here, it is that folktales are apt to treat sexual duress as a matter of course.

The viewing audience will also enjoy being part of the film's deliberate deceptions, especially as these concatenate in the closing sequences. After the couple bury their time capsule at a trysting tree and separate, and the Girl fails to keep their appointment to meet there after two years, the passing of time is signified by a sequence of dissolves that show Gyeonu moving to and fro as the seasons change. Finally, a long shot shows a figure walking up the hill to the tree and sitting against its trunk. The camera zooms in on the tree's canopy, and then tracks down to the seated figure, who is an old man. We assume that time has continued to pass, since this is a principal function of the cinematic dissolve, and Gyeonu has now become old. In terms of cinema conventions this is a reasonable expectation. The scene feels rather like an homage to the work of Georges Méliès, in its heavy use of dissolve (a technique developed by Méliès) and narrative focus on a favorite Méliès figure, the optimistic dreamer who clings to his vision (Zipes 2011, 48). But we have been cleverly deceived. A moment later the Girl walks up to the tree. She is exactly one year late, and the old man returns us to "Gyeonu and Jiknyeo" by declaring that the Girl is so beautiful he thought an angel had arrived. In their ensuing conversation, he advises her to search for Gyeonu rather than leaving things to chance, because Fate is "building a bridge of chance for someone you love."

Minutes later the film repeats the dissolve convention, and the director is almost mocking his audience as we again fall for the trick. The Girl stands on a train platform, in a reprise of the time she and Gyeonu first met. She is pensive and sad, as she has been searching for Gyeonu without success. She boards the train, and as the door closes Gyeonu runs up but is unable to get on. He sees the Girl, but her back is towards him, and the train moves away, implying an image of star-crossed lovers forever apart (see Figure 15.2, frame 1).

The film could have ended at this point, producing the kind of bitter-sweet closure reminis-cent of "The Shower," Korea's most famous short story, in which childhood puppy-love is cut off by death. "The Shower" elsewhere plays a metafictive role when the Girl rewrites its ending as one of her adaptations, so the audience is being cued to interrogate the concept of closure. At this point, the camera instead moves into a dissolve shot from the Girl to a pensive, middle-aged woman (see Figure 15.2), and an audience will again assume that 20–25 years have passed and the Girl has grown older. The illusion is once more dispelled when the Girl, dressed as on the train, enters the room and greets the older woman. This woman is, at last, the bridge, as by melodramatic coincidence both the Girl and Gyeonu were coming to meet her: she is both the mother of the Girl's dead fiancé and Gyeonu's aunt, and she had invited them to meet in the hope they would go out together. In its continued foregrounding of cinematic conventions, the film dismisses the sad

FIGURE 15.2 *My Sassy Girl* (2001) dissolve shot.

sentimentality of modern retellings of the close of "Gyeonu and Jiknyeo" and replaces it with a sentimental romantic ending whereby the couple can finally be together. As they discreetly hold hands beneath the table, Gyeonu's voiceover directs the audience to the contrivances of narrative and the problem of endings: "Is this too coincidental?"

The romantic ending segues into an epilogue vignette, in which the couple, dressed in school uniform, wave their ID cards as they enter a club. The film thus closes by returning to the carnivalesque unruliness of earlier sequences, perhaps gesturing towards the playfulness denied to Gyeonu and Jiknyeo, but in any case tempering the romantic close. The carnivalesque use of uniform has a complexity beyond simple control of children's behavior. As a consequence of Japanese colonization, Korean school uniform is a variation of Japanese uniform, in turn based on Prussian military uniform. As a visual code, even more than half a century after liberation, the uniform connotes discipline and authority, and the concept of proper hierarchy which the Girl's unruliness has consistently challenged. Although she has finally come back to the sphere of normative heterosexual coupling, the couple show a willingness to make choices that continue to challenge the social conformity that condemned Gyeonu and Jiknyeo to blighted lives.

Instead of hand-holding and mischief, the 2008 American remake of *My Sassy Girl* substitutes the romance cliché of the sustained, passionate kiss. The change is indicative of a continued ambivalence in Korea about Hollywood genres, since one of the many games played with the close is to evoke and dismantle romance genre. Such ambivalence is also evident in Korean appropriations of western fairy tales. Korean children grow up familiar with the classic western tales, which are made available through picture books and short TV animations, and of course in mainstream cinemas. In 2014, for example, *Frozen* ranked second in the South Korean box office (albeit earning only 60 percent of the gross gained by the local hit, the historical drama *Battle of Myung-Ryang* [Lee Hyo-Won 2014]). Western fairy tales have proved to be a useful cinematic resource for films involved in social critique—for example, films that depict unusual female roles in conflict with the neo-Confucian ideology that continues to underlie Korean gender roles, as Kim Taeyon has eloquently argued. A woman is no longer valued as a potential bearer of sons or a domestic laborer but for a physical beauty necessary to make a good marriage or progress in a career. According to Kim, the apparent change is in practice a continuation of "the techniques of Neo-Confucian governmentality which maintain that women are subjectless bodies whose primary means of improvement are through the body" (2003, 108). Korean cinema has not cultivated simple transposition of familiar western fairy tales to screen, but develops homologous narrative forms. The films' titles cue audiences to recognize a possible homology, although they may signal only a loose analogy. The short made-for-TV film *Brother and Ugly Duck* (2013) has numerous parallels with Andersen's original tale and overarching structure, whereas the feature, *The Ugly Duckling* (2012), directed by Kwak Kyung-Taek, a story of a misfit in the army, achieves more by visual allusion than narrative. *Brother and Ugly Duck* is a useful vantage point from which to consider Korean adaptations of western fairy tale both because its narrative form is more transparent than most and because it resonates with a continuing intervention in culture expressed in the themes of Andersen's tale; that nobility resides in sensitivity rather than birth, and that all of us have the capacity to transform ourselves positively (Tatar in Andersen 2007, 70, 99). A secondary theme is that of child abandonment and the grounding of a family bond on love rather than blood relationships.

While "The Ugly Duckling" is a single identifiable source, Andersen's tales—like folktales—are mediated through translation and retelling. They are widely popular throughout East Asia generally; translations and adaptations of individual tales into Korean have appeared at least once each year from 2001 to 2010. This output, which includes several summary paraphrases in picture books, is symptomatic of how the notion of "malleable beauty" pervades modern Korean culture. Because of the conditions of production, reference will again be to a script rather than to Andersen's original, but this script will normally include the following schemas: an adopted orphan; abandonment and physical hardship; persecution by peers because of apparent difference; persecution by an older woman; a helper; a sojourn in the wilderness; malleable beauty; personal transformation or development. All of these schemas are present in *Brother and Ugly Duck*, which depicts the struggle of Eunguk, a young man orphaned in his late teens, to deal with the teen rebelliousness of his younger stepsister, Eunsu, who he has been raising for ten years. Like the swan egg in Andersen's tale, Eunsu has been interpolated into the family; she is the daughter of the second wife of Eunguk's father, who took her into the family after her mother ran off and abandoned her. Eunsu only discovers late in the film that she has no blood relationship with Eunguk, and this knowledge sparks what Naomi Wood identifies in Andersen's tales as "the terrors of childhood: terrors of isolation, abandonment, extinction" (2006, 93). Because Confucianism is grounded in the notion of family, a Confucian society such as Korea has a poor record on domestic adoption. Throughout the film, Eunguk's aunt reiterates that he should simply abandon Eunsu because there is no blood relationship, even though she has been his "sister" for most of her life.

The film's reflections of the script function as a criticism of Korean social behavior and its differential criteria for male and female success. First, the ugly duckling role has been doubled. Eunguk grew up as a swan, talented and handsome, but his affection for and commitment to Eunsu has gradually transformed him into an ugly duck. He failed to complete his university studies and consequently works in a menial post office job, and at the beginning of the film faces rejection by his long-term girlfriend because of his ever-diminishing agency and sense of self. As I noted above, film and TV drama frequently identify an incapability for altruism as a social problem amongst South Koreans, so it is significant that the film invites audiences to empathize with Eunguk rather than dismissing him for his failed masculinity. On the other hand, although Eunsu is a pretty young woman, she is an ugly duckling because of her brattish behavior towards Eunguk and her peers. Further, although her desire for improvement involves only minor physical change, local audiences will recognize the ugly duckling to swan discourse used with reference to cosmetic surgery. With 20 percent of Koreans resorting to some form of cosmetic surgery procedure, the idea that "beauty is malleable" (Burkley et al. 2014, 467) seems to be deeply ingrained. The film makes a further allusion to this discourse through Eunsu's desire to be a pop singer and her continual attempts at beautification before auditions; it is widely assumed that the *hallyu* (Korean wave) success in pop culture and especially the dominance of pop idols in the pop music industry has fuelled the cosmetic surgery industry. The film, I suggest, offers an analogy between an unattainable career (long lines of girls queue for auditions) and unattainable beauty images.

Eunguk's paternal aunt frequently expresses hatred and resentment towards Eunsu, asserting that she herself should have the money spent on Eunsu's upbringing. Her insistence that Eunsu be either sent to her mother or simply abandoned reflects the kind of entrenched self-interest that is a recurrent focus of criticism in contemporary Korean films. Eunsu's fantasy of transformation is to become a pop idol, which results in her persistent absence from school to attend auditions and stealing money from Eunguk to spend on hairstyling. Auditions are a site of rejection, of course, and analogous with the swan's experience with the cat and the hen, but the greatest rejection occurs when Eunsu tracks down her mother, only to find that she denies Eunsu's existence. At this point of lowest abjection, Eunguk finds her and affirms that affection and mutual support are far more important than blood relationship, and takes her back home. Eunsu now realizes she must help Eunguk to become a swan again.

The western fairy tale most often adapted in Korea to explore the malleability of beauty is "Cinderella," although the title appears in only one notable film, directed by Bong Man-Dae in 2006. A horror genre piece that satirizes the Korean obsession with cosmetic surgery, the film is more like a response to cultural-historical processes than an adaptation of a "Cinderella" script. It involves a cosmetic surgeon's mistreatment of her stepdaughter, a young girl she has kidnapped, by transplanting her face to replace the horribly scarred face of her daughter. Given the social view that a pretty face is a girl's greatest economic asset, the parallel with the maltreatment of Cinderella becomes clearer. There is no prince, kiss, or otherwise happy ending here, however, as the nameless, faceless girl hangs herself and begins to haunt the surgeon's patients, driving them to suicide. Bong's *Cinderella* is a female-focused narrative; there is less pressure on males to embody beauty, so it seems inevitable that a story focusing on male appearance, like "Beauty and the Beast," would be adapted less often than "Cinderella," or that local beast-groom tales, such as "The Toad-Bridegroom" (Zŏng 1982, Tale 76), are retold but seldom adapted or developed as complex narratives.

The theme of malleable beauty may become a source of comedy when the protagonist is male. Also satirizing cosmetic surgery, *The Beast and the Beauty* (2005) is a lighthearted romantic comedy with a predictable story line: a beautiful young woman, Jang Hae-Ju, blind since childhood, mistakes Gu Dong-Geon's car for a taxi and gets in, and they develop an affection for one another in subsequent meetings. The film is not obviously adapted from any retelling of Madame Leprince de Beaumont's "Beauty and the Beast," but instead has some parallels with Cocteau's *La Belle et la Bête* (1946) and *Shrek* (2001). There is a handsome rival for the Beauty's attention (as in Cocteau), and the significance of perception is emphasized by the technique of scene repetition: "Beauty" appears in repeated scenes with the same setting and action, but now with one man, now the other. The ogre Shrek is generically evoked when the male protagonist, Gu Dong-Geon, meets the Beauty's family, and they recoil in melodramatic, overstated fear (see Figure 15.3). Though protagonist Dong-Geon, a voice actor performing the role of "the Space Beast," thinks of himself as particularly ugly, the traditional framing structure of a merchant losing his fortune, stumbling into the Beast's castle, and exchanging his daughter for his life is absent. The only physical transformation the Beast undergoes is a worsening of appearance.

The film is of particular interest as an adaptation because once a Korean audience recognizes that Hae-Ju is a "heavenly maiden" it can perceive that the western fairy tale has been lightly blended with both "Gyeonu and Jiknyeo" and "Fool Ondal and Princess Pyeonggang." The

FIGURE 15.3 Hae-Ju's family recoils melodramatically at the sight of the monster, Dong-Geon, *The Beast and the Beauty* (2005).

Korean folktales are themselves restructured so that they acquire quite different narrative emphases: Hae-Ju and Dong-Geon bring happiness and playfulness to one another's lives, but their separation occurs early and is the catalyst for the story. Trouble arises when Hae-Ju regains her sight after a corneal transplant and Dong-Geon pretends to have taken a temporary job in Hawaii so that he won't be seen until he has dealt with the problem of his ugliness. The actual problem, as defined by Leprince de Beaumont, is that the Beauty must "prefer virtue before either wit or beauty" (Tatar 1999, 41–42), which she does when Dong-Geon finally comes out of hiding. His attempts to hide from Hae-Ju and get cosmetic surgery, while trying to impede the advances of his rival, the handsome prosecutor Ju-Ha, are "fool" behavior and sustained until their eventual reconciliation when "Princess Hae-Ju" corrects his behavior and he recognizes his "Ondal" role. In its contrast between constructive surgery (the corneal transplant that restored Hae-Ju's sight) and its carnivalesque representation of the unnecessary surgery to remove the scar from Dong-Geon's forehead (the surgeon instead removes his eyebrow), the film proposes the simple message that the drive for physical conformity is like a sci-fi nightmare. People should instead stay true to their natural bodies.

The Beast and the Beauty is not a deep film, but the structural parallel with the western fairy tale, emphasized by the transposition within the title, prompts audiences to search for connections and then to consider the cultural and ideological functions of adaptation. A similar principle is followed in, for example, Yim Pil-Sung's *Hansel & Gretel*. Grounded in the despotism that emerged in the South after the Korean War, the adaptation shares with much contemporary Korean cinema an assumption that self-interest is a core defect in Korean society (see Lee Sung-Ae 2014, 285–87). Contemporary adaptations of Korean folktales also follow the principle of loose structural parallels, notably Ahn Sang-Hoon's *Arang* (2006), a contemporary detective story homologous with the eponymous folktale, and Kim Jee-Woon's *A Tale of Two Sisters* (2003). The English title of *A Tale of Two Sisters* unfortunately obscures the film's status as a folktale adaptation: it is the sixth film released under the title of a well-known folktale, "Janghwa, Hongryun" (Rose Flower, Red Lotus). As Coralline Dupuy (2007) observes, the story would be familiar to Korean audiences from folktale retellings or from the older films, but would not be familiar to western viewers. Nevertheless, to recast a tale of family disintegration as a modern psychological horror film functions as a commentary on the moral perspectives of the society in which it is retold.

The examination of a society's moral perspectives in a period of great social and political change is the function that overarches Korean folktale films. They interrogate the relationships between power and justice and the immutability of social hierarchies; they ask whether talented individuals can find social advancement, and whether neo-Confucianism still determines family relationships and gendered behavior; and contend that altruism can become a social principle to rival self-interest. That film adaptations keep critiquing these issues may be a sign of hope, but may equally be a sign of despair.

Notes

1 All Korean names appear as family name followed by given name. There are several systems for romanizing Korean words. I have generally followed the Revised Romanization of Korean (RR).

2 Shin Yoon-Bok's pen-name was Hye-Won. *Dano Scenes* is included in his album, *Transmission of the Spirit of Hye-Won* (Hye-Won Jeonsincheop), a collection of 30 paintings housed at the Gansong Art Museum. The album has been designated National Treasure No. 135. Shin's real-life scenes "sought to highlight the nobility's hypocrisy and debauchery" (Cho 2008, 52).

3 For the gumiho, these aspirations are different possibilities, rather than a rising sequence. The TV series *My Girlfriend is a Gumiho* (2010) incorporates all three as repeatedly refused statuses. In the opening episode, a back story about the gumiho's first attempt to enter the human world, as a bride, functions as a mise-en-abyme for the series; she is denied a family, then a community, and finally the grandmother spirit imprisons her in perpetuity within a painted screen.

4 There are also playful references to other folktales, which are perhaps no more than a game with the audience. For example, when Gyeonu opens the time capsule he and the Girl have buried, there is a toad inside. This is evidently an allusion to the folktale "Dori and Dukkeobi," in which a fake seer is asked to reveal what is inside a stone box, which turns out to be a toad.

5 The prominence of analogous scripts in neighboring countries, especially China and Japan, has probably contributed to the great box-office success the film enjoyed across the region. In the first half of the twentieth century, "Buffalo Boy and Weaving Maid" was designated one of China's "Four Great Folktales" and has thus been an object of extensive commentary and retelling (Idema 2012, 33–34). Conversely, the richness of allusion to local/regional tales could not be reproduced in the 2008 American remake.

6 For a straightforward retelling in English, see Riordan (1994).

16

STICK BECOMING CROCODILE

African Fairy-Tale Film

Jessica Tiffin

> In Africa there is a proverb that says that no matter how long a stick remains in the water, it will never become a crocodile. So for me, I remain who I am, and I try to move forward while remaining what I am.
>
> (Mansour Sora Wade, in Itela [2002])

What is "African fairy-tale film"? The category cannot be explored without being problematized, not only because of the size and diversity of the continent, but because of its colonial legacy. What is "African"? How do the technologies and processes of film production, with their strong association with western power and viewpoints, transform the continent's folklore? Do African fairy-tale films comprise only indigenous African traditions, or the patchwork of indigenous traditions juxtaposed and overlaid with western patterns imported and still celebrated by its colonizers? Do they encompass only cinema produced from within Africa? Can we ignore the important western cinematic productions that seek to represent and enshrine a mythologized sense of Africa through traditional magical narratives? And what does "fairy tale" mean in the African context? Does the term even apply, given its association with western and particularly French traditions, and its reliance on a highly specific history of translation into the written word even before it is adapted into film? Fairy tale in the African context comprises a set of shifting categories in which the term must be understood as a broad and complex invocation of folklore and the mythological, and in which oral traditions are more central than they are in many parts of the west.

Folkloric cinema in Africa cannot really be considered in any unified sense. Africa's indigenous cultures and languages represent a bewildering multiplicity of folkloric, oral, and written traditions even without taking into account its place in an increasingly interconnected and globalized world, and its dynamic and ongoing engagement with other cultures' ideas and traditions, as well as with the comparatively new paradigm of film. This cinematic landscape's vastness has necessitated some artificial narrowing of focus for the purposes of this discussion; I have chosen not to attempt to trace African cinema's engagement with non-African magical or fairy-tale traditions, but rather to explore some aspects of the interaction between indigenous African folkloric narrative and the cinematic medium. This follows a broad trend in critical engagement with fairy-tale cinema, which traditionally traces the tale's transmutation into the new medium, and thus relies heavily on the cinematic artifact's connections to its oral or written precursors. I do not limit the discussion solely to direct re-tellings, however; Jack Zipes's useful discussion of fairy-tale adaptation stresses the diffuse and multivalent processes of influence. An originating fairy tale offers "more a notion than anything else, somewhat like a meme carried about in our brains," but acknowledges that filmmakers must "know some variant or variants of a fairy tale either after having re-read it, heard it, seen it in a book, viewed it as a film, or having recalled it from their childhood memories" (2011, 8).

In this notion of influence, particularly as heritage and memory, Zipes's point is especially important for my purposes. In many ways the position from which I explore the bewildering dimensions of the African fairy-tale film shadows something of the contradictions inherent in the category itself. I am a White African, raised in an English-speaking culture, and the tales of my heritage and memory are those of the western tradition; such sense as I have of African folkloric traditions is minor and fragmentary. Like the cinematic tradition itself, I bring to the project a different vocabulary and idiom. While Black African filmmakers are certainly able to wrest the mechanisms of cinematic production to their own purposes, re-defining and appropriating visual and narrative codes, as a critic responding to African folkloric cinema, I am isolated from it in a way that I am not from film versions of "Cinderella" or "Beauty and the Beast" produced within western cinema. I cannot, in fact, understand African folkloric films in the same way, with the same experience of affinity and familiarity or even *ownership*, as a Black African may do—or, equally, in the same way that I enjoy films based on the western tales with which I grew up. The cultural productions of African folklore do not speak, in Zipes's terms, to any "meme carried about in [my] brain" (2011), but rather relegate me to a more external viewpoint from which I recognize fairy-tale patterns either by their most basic traits, or by my necessarily anthropological readings in the continent's collected folklore. Like film technology itself, no matter how firmly I reside in Africa, my origins, and many of my cultural influences, are western.

In short, in addition to the disparity and shifting categories of African film and folklore, no consideration of African cinema can ignore the continent's colonial history. Issues of power and place equally underlie the identity, collection, and dissemination of the continent's folklore, and the western origin and, frequently, ownership and control of the expensive technologies of film. This complicated ideological landscape tends to essentialize the issues at hand. It is fatally easy to equate the fairy tale in any sense with orality, tradition, and heritage, and thus with the past, while film equally easily maps onto notions of the modern and forward-looking. Produced within the context of the historically vexed relationship between African and western cultures, African film has reason to be self-conscious about folkloric elements which might seem to deny the modern identity signaled by film technologies, or to falsely and dangerously conflate African identity with the pre-literate. The tendency for western views to mythologize Africa, exoticizing it and associating it with the primitive and anti-modern (or, as in the case of films such as Disney's *The Lion King* [1994], erasing its people in favor of its landscapes and wild animals), in some ways works against the self-conscious exploration of folkloric traces by African filmmakers themselves. This is, perhaps, one thread of influence in the comparative dearth of contemporary African fairy-tale films that, in the vein of Disney's *Beauty and the Beast* (1991) or a fairy-tale pastiche like *Shrek* (2001), explicitly and specifically celebrate fairy-tale traditions.

Nonetheless, even in its narrowed form, this is no straightforward project. The presence in African cinema of indigenous folkloric or fairy-tale elements is often difficult to trace owing to the breadth of possible references they represent, and the unevenness with which African folkloric texts are both collected and critically explored. Stephen Belcher notes that "the collection and study of African folktales has lagged behind other parts of the world, in part because of the very challenges of the material" (2008, 12). Indeed, the diversity of African cinematic styles encompasses the full range from the broadly popular—whether the westernized commercial films of South Africa or the grassroots video productions of Nigeria or Ghana—to the self-consciously artistic and political productions whose project, rather than being primarily entertainment, is to confront and explore African history and identity in explicit rather than implicit terms.

Despite these complexities, however, Africa's rich folkloric traditions can be and have been tapped for cinematic purposes; they offer, in many ways, a powerful tool in the postcolonial landscape. Their essentialist narratives are a potential reserve of cultural identity and purpose along the lines noted by Lúcia Nagib in discussing the films of Idrissa Ouédraogo, which, she argues, reflect an African sense in which "tradition usually takes on a predominantly positive and strongly active role, in so far as it is a factor for resisting the political and cultural domination of the colonizer" (Nagib 2001, 100). While wholesale fairy-tale adaptations are rare, folkloric traces are a fascinating thread across the varying expressions of African cinema. These traces can be discerned in the representation within African film of oral traditions and magical elements, as well as a broader sense of village culture and custom which bears some resemblance to fairy-tale texture. Despite the breadth and disparity of African cinematic culture, it is possible to trace some common themes and issues in the development of a fairy-tale film tradition, and their implication in particular examples of African folkloric cinema.

Folktale, Film, and Colonialism

The cinematic fairy tale relies on a highly technological medium and, as such, is an even more extreme manifestation of the process by which oral folkloric narratives become literary narratives—by which, in some formulations, folklore becomes fairy tale. Despite the power film has to reproduce some aspects of oral storytelling, it relies as much as do literary fairy tales on the processes and accesses of the written word. In film, as a post-literate art form, the fairy tale's identity is inextricable from the written. This process of mediation is common to almost any folkloric tradition; in nineteenth-century Germany, for example, the work of the Brothers Grimm elided the authentic folkloric voice with their selections and excisions, overlaying bourgeois values onto the tales not only via their own edits, but through the distancing created by their middle-class sources who repeated the peasant tales told to them by their servants (Zipes 1987, xxiv).

The Brothers Grimm, however, were Germans collecting German folklore in their mother tongue and were party to all the implications of identification and ownership inherent in that relationship, and in their effective project of creating a German fairy-tale heritage in a new form. In Africa the complex processes by which the folktale is recorded, translated, and transmitted in written form are particularly close to the surface. The inevitable adaptation, contamination, and re-shaping which attend the collection of any folklore in any context are in the case of the African folktale unavoidably infused with the unequal power structures of the colonial process, with the persistent danger of appropriation, usurpation, and objectification. The earliest written collections of the African tale were in the colonial languages—English, French, German—and collected by White colonial writers. Even now anthropological collections of tales reflect White names as well as the increasing numbers of folklorists collecting tales in their own languages and cultures. To the dilution and transformation represented by the efforts of the Brothers Grimm and other western tale-tellers, Africa's folkloric tradition adds issues of language, power, and culture which are inextricable from the colonial process.

Partially because of the colonial history of the continent and its problematization of notions of ownership and heritage, the interactions between the folkloric body of tale and literary or cinematic re-tellings take very different forms in African and western contexts. Literary versions of folklore may dilute and reshape the tales, but equally those literary versions also enable and disseminate a strong fairy-tale tradition. Contemporary western fairy-tale films rely intrinsically on the written fairy tale because without the shared heritage of retold tales which originated in the work of Charles Perrault and the Brothers Grimm, there would be no basis for the comfortable, pervasive recognition which is the basis for elaboration and play. In transmuting folkloric forms, the literary fairy tale nods to its oral roots in its construction of voice and viewpoint, and in its association with reading aloud to children. While its partial mirror of oral transmission cannot replicate all the functions of orality, in an age of mass media and technological enablement it is also an opportunity for a wider audience than the traditional fireside circle of listeners. Likewise, while literary redefinition of the tale impedes some of the instantaneous flexibility and adaptability of the oral, it also enshrines and proliferates standardized versions, which further foster recognition and identification.

The same process cannot be traced to an equal extent in African fairy tales. The diversity of the continent's languages and cultures operates against any standardized experience of a narrative heritage such as that which characterizes the western corpus. In addition, African tale traditions generally lack any figures comparable in impact and scope to writers such as Perrault or the Brothers Grimm, whose specific fairy-tale collections have achieved a broad popularity that gives western fairy tale a tendency to cultural flattening and cross-pollination. While numerous collections of indigenous African folklore exist, these are for the most part either specialized anthropological texts, or are recorded by fundamentally colonial voices and intended for a westernized gaze, often that of children. Thus, as a White African child, I had a sense of African tales created by collections such as Geraldine Elliot's beast fables in *The Long Grass Whispers* (1939) and others; however, those are Ngoni tales from Malawi. I grew up in Zimbabwe without a strong or specific sense of local Shona or Ndebele tradition, and few of my contemporaries share my experience of reading Elliot. Nor does the reading of such collections give me any sense whatsoever of a Black African's experience of folklore, whether Shona or Ndebele or the Xhosa or Zulu of my current South African environment. Filmmakers in Africa who wish to produce fairy-tale films must thus speak either to a small and specific subset of their audience to invoke the sense of heritage and comfortable recognition engendered by a western cinematic version of "Beauty and the Beast"; or they must present their tale as a decontextualized, partially denatured artifact to be consumed by an outsider gaze.

The outsider perspective is exacerbated by the nature of film production in Africa as much as by the inherent difficulties of a diverse and fragmented body of folktales. While the burgeoning industry has increasingly developed infrastructure, expertise, and its own idioms and characteristics, even with the continent's postcolonial re-shaping, the colonial legacy and associations of film still remain and are exacerbated by the domination of the global film market by Hollywood and other western consumerist productions. Manthia Diawara identifies the roots of African cinema in "Bantu film," the colonial legacy of British and French units that made "educational" and propaganda films designed to impart the western culture that was deemed superior to the African (1992, 1–5). An even stronger association exists specifically with the fairy-tale film. Because film has historically been associated with African folklore firmly in the ethnographic sense, the medium threatens to once again enshrine Africa as an object of study. Philip M. Peek and Kwesi Yankah's *African Folklore: An Encyclopedia* devotes its film entry entirely to ethnographic records of folklore and makes no attempt to acknowledge or trace the presence of folkloric elements in narrative film (Colleyn 2009, 125–34). Peek and Yankah's oversight emphasizes the too-easy assumption that African folktale film records specimens rather than, as is permitted in other cultures, operating as a living tradition expressing itself in new media.

The notion of insider versus outsider perspectives is thus central to the development of the fairy-tale film in Africa. A striking illustration of the inherent problems of colonial and postcolonial pressures can be found in the film which most easily invokes the African fairy tale to the casual viewer, namely Michel Ocelot's *Kirikou et la Sorcière* (1998). Although Ocelot lived in Africa as a child, he is also a French filmmaker. The film, while deliberately synthesizing and simulating Africanness in every way possible, is very much the product of a western gaze, produced entirely in Europe, and with only its voice acting and music recorded in Senegal. Ocelot himself attributes his inspiration for the film to a West African folktale from a collection by François-Victor Equilbecq, a French colonial writer. Terry Staples comments that the film's narrative "invokes the West African oral tradition as filtered through an early twentieth-century colonial folktale and refracts it through the lens of a late twentieth-century European animator" (2008b, 544).

The tale itself is a striking example of magical narrative, employing all of the sparse textures and ritual repetitions associated with fairy-tale texture. The central character is a trickster archetype in the Tom Thumb mold; the magical, capable child undertakes fantastic quests and overcomes dangers and monsters to restore his community. The film's opening sequence, with Kirikou as a child in the womb calling out to his mother with a demand to be born, is both remarkable and unfamiliar to a western gaze. In its unfamiliarity it signals Africanness as powerfully as does the film's visual insistence on bare-breasted African women, and with as much of a troubling tendency to conflate Africa with bodily earthiness, and to hint at the disturbing slippages of the abject.

According to Ocelot himself, the opening sequence adheres most closely to the originating folktale; however, subsequent developments in the plot make radical changes. Most notably, Ocelot retains Kirikou as a hyper-efficient miniature child-person rather than, as Ecquilbecq's version does, growing him into normal adulthood almost immediately. The film reshapes the narrative to give it a diminutive hero familiar from western tales such as "Tom Thumb"; a romantic outcome; and a reconciliatory dénouement which, in its reconfiguration of evil as suffering, presents something of a cliché of western post-Freudian liberalism. Ocelot reports his fascination with the "very African" elements of the story's start, but contends that "after that start the original story was just mediocre. The storyteller forgot about the baby. The hero was big and tall, full of magical powers, and he just killed the sorceress" (Ghibliworld 2014). His comments suggest the same kind of entitlement to African heritage as European fairy-tale filmmakers feel towards their own traditions. To an even greater degree, Ocelot suggests that appropriation is external, entitled, judgmental—not just a creative experimentation morphing forms of the fairy tale, but also a correction.

The film's visual style heavily underlines its African setting in its insistence on landscape and cultural detail, with continual focus on the recognizable signifiers of African huts, women with bundles on their heads, and a meticulous and beautiful rendering of African vegetation. The simplicity and flatness of the film's art is attractive and appropriate to the stylization of the fairy tale, but its look is not entirely African; Ocelot was influenced both by Rousseau and by Egyptian art. The Egyptian elements in the visual framing and in details such as the grandfather's clothing and headdress represent a blurring of cultural otherness which weakens the film's brandishing of authenticity; it also irresistibly recalls Edward Said's (1978) definitions of orientalism and its conflation of "Other" cultures as a seamless and denatured unity. The film, overall, thus encapsulates one extreme of the particular dangers inherent in the exploration of African fairy tales through the cinematic medium, which are an important context to expressions of African fairy-tale film that originate within the continent itself.

Film, Orality, and Folktale in Africa

To some degree, Africa's colonial history problematizes the exploration of orality in African cultures which is an important aspect of any discussion of African film, particularly that which deals explicitly with folktale. Walter Ong identifies electronic media as "secondary orality," which "has striking resemblances to the old in its participatory mystique, its concentration on the present moment, and even its use of formulas" (1999, 69). Not only does film reproduce voice and gesture, its meaning is intensified by its group audience and its function as a shared experience, and the compressed narratives and emblematic visual language of cinema are an excellent fit with the structures and symbols of folklore. Oral traditions are still stronger in Africa than in many other parts of the world, so that African films speak to an awareness embodied in still-vital figures such as praise singers or the griot, the multivalent historian/commentator/praise singer of West Africa. The vivid reality of oral traditions and their natural dialogue with film can be seen in cultural loci such as the Tanzanian live translations and re-narrations of Nigerian films for local audiences reported by Matthias Krings, in which narrators are "adapting the stories to a local hermeneutic framework" and subjecting them to "a profound practice of re-mediation" (2013, 8). Anny Wynchank's discussion of the African filmmaker as a continuation of the griot tradition notes precisely this process of transfiguration, and the essential differences as well as the similarities between the processes of oral transmission and those of film (1994, 12–14).

In a postcolonial setting, however, an awareness of oral tradition can be a pitfall as much as it can access a repository of cultural identity and heritage. Rooted in a pre-literate and pre-technological past, oral narrative could be seen as regressive in an Africa still struggling to overcome perceptions of primitivism in order to defend its place in contemporary global culture. In addition, resistance to colonial occupation has a strong correlation with socially realist forms of cultural expression. In literature as well as film, the use of magical motifs and structures could be seen as a betrayal of the political struggle rooted in contemporary postcolonial experience. While African authors and filmmakers certainly employ fantastic and mythic motifs, these tend to be subordinated to realist narratives, and there are few examples of purely fantastic texts that access a separate, otherworldly, fairy-tale realm. Films which focus in particular on African village life, and which thus re-create something of the essentialist texture of the fairy tale, also run the risk of erasing Africa's complex modern identity in favor of stereotypes of the primitive.

This awareness has provided a thread of contention in the development of African films, particularly given the direction provided by founding figures of African cinematic identity. Diawara discusses difficulties of producing a new tradition of African cinema in the wake of, for example, Ousemane Sembène's formative social realism, his "naturalistic and documentary approach to creating fiction out of reality" (2010, 95). In abandoning Sembène's realism for the magical frameworks of oral tradition, Diawara argues, the fear is that:

> African cinema will lose its edge and identity. . . . Filmmakers who ignored this criticism by attempting to create new cinemas, albeit based on traditional sources and forms of storytelling, were considered assimilated and purveyors of exotic and stereotypical images of Africa . . . "calabash cinema", a cinema made for tourists, depicting an a-historical Africa, with beautiful images of primitive-looking peoples.
>
> (2010, 96)

Once again, folkloric traditions in Africa are associated perhaps unavoidably with the objectifying outsider perspective of the colonizer.

Regardless of these concerns, African filmmakers have produced some powerful cinematic works that rely to a large extent on a narrative framework originating in oral and folkloric culture, and that deliberately invoke such traditions in the stripped-down visual and narrative textures of their films. Sembène himself uses folkloric traditions even while he subordinates them to contemporary political realities; in *Xala* (1974), a trickster figure is the source of the curse of impotence afflicting a corrupt businessman. Thomas J. Lynn's analysis of the film suggests that Sembène self-consciously acts as the griot in his filmmaking, both speaking for and commenting on his society; the film "honours aspects of African tradition, including its communal strength, while cautioning against a blind embrace of the pre-colonial heritage" (2003, 184). The modern urban setting and concern with the corruption of the middle-class elite works against the potentially magical element of the curse, however, which is given a psychological rather than a magical explanation. Thus, while Sembène clearly admits the validity of the folkloric, he negates its potentially mythic qualities, specifically denying those aspects of its expression that could be seen as primitive superstition. A similar contrast of superstition with modernity can be found in Idrissa Ouédraogo's *Yaaba* (1987).

While its village setting renders it more timeless than *Xala* and more open to interpretation as a fable, its witch figure is interrogated rather than being naturalized as part of a mythic landscape.

A closer adherence to fairy-tale texture and symbol is found in Mansour Sora Wade's *The Price of Forgiveness* (2001), which relies on folktale for narrative shape and impetus in developing its pre-modern West African fishing village setting, depicted with a stark cinematic beauty. Its elements are familiar from almost any folkloric tradition: the inexplicable fog which shrouds the village; the powerful father buried beneath the sacred tree; the sacrifice of the tree to provide wood for the canoe in which the hero sets out to right the supernatural wrong; and the jealousy and treachery occasioned by the attempt to win a bride. The film's deliberate pacing and lingering focus on iconic, essentialized images underline its mythic qualities, and Wade's use of vivid color verges on the symbolic.

The generic folktale both structures and pervades the story. The hero Mbanick clearly rescues and renews his community through both bravery and the proper fairy-tale recognition of and respect for the structures of supernatural power, but mythic narratives also underpin his strength and that of his rival Yatma. Shadow-puppet micro-narratives explain the differences in their respective powers, Mbanick's in his ancestor who battled the great shark who is Lord of the Sea, Yatma's in his descent from the lineage of a savannah hunter who survived an encounter with a lion. The film stresses its own connections with orality throughout, framing itself as the retrospective narrative of the village's griot who participates in the story as a child. The origin tales are told in the context of the village, accepted as a natural form of validation of identity as well as being a narrative competition in the same way as the proverb game played by the elders. The film's cinematography lingers frequently on faces, emphasizing the importance of the audience, the circle of watchers whose witnessing confirms the narrative's importance. The director's visual style entails, he says in a director's statement for Film Fest Amiens, "a painstaking observation of reality. . . . My concern was to show ordinary life and the supernatural existing together, without ostentation in a very simple manner, as it was the case in my childhood" (n.d.) (see Figure 16.1).

FIGURE 16.1 The hero Mbanick cuts down the tree that marks his father's grave; in a canoe made from its wood he will travel to confront the Lord of the Sea and free his village, *The Price of Forgiveness*/Ndeysaan (2001).

Wade's film provides an immersive mythic dimension to the social and individual interactions of its protagonists. Its fairy-tale elements transcend the specific, reflecting to some extent the filmmaker's own multiculturalism, a result of his education and partial residence in France. The film is based on the novel by Mbissane Ngom, and is thus rooted in the Lebou ethnic identity and mythology common to both the writer and filmmaker, but the simplicity and universality of its folkloric elements remain accessible outside that cultural context. Wade's project allows him to celebrate and preserve oral traditions while accessing both an insider and an outsider view; unlike Ocelot, he can state that "I remain profoundly anchored in my Culture, and I recognize its value," while also being aware that "it's necessary to remain rooted in one's Culture while being open to others, and it's that which constitutes richness. . . . Whatever one's traditional culture, that culture's tales can have a universal reach" (quoted in Itela 2002). This mature, confident claim of heritage assumes without question the validity and status of African folkloric traditions against those of any other culture, and goes some way towards denying fears of African folkloric film as regressive or objectifying.

A very different expression of confidence in orality and local tradition can be found in the video film industry of Ghana and Nigeria. The so-called "Ghallywood" and "Nollywood" industries are an energetic answer both to the problems of reconciling oral heritage with the contemporary, and to the traditional elitism of film and its association with expensive western technologies. These low-budget straight-to-video productions, originally distributed for home viewing on VHS cassette, represent a grassroots appropriation of technology which essentially subverts both African auteur cinema and—like the Bollywood productions that give rise to the nicknames—western cinema as a whole. These films have a particularly strong folkloric element in the directness with which they arise from Ghanaian or Nigerian cultural experiences and desires, and in their identity as a communal effort rather than the outcome of a monolithic corporate process. This links the films to a communal sense of performance which is particularly culturally resonant in some African cultures, and which infuses some examples of African film outside the straight-to-video film industry. Ouédraogo's *Yaaba*, for example, while a successful and award-winning film in the auteur tradition, was still shot on an extremely small budget and using his relatives as actors.

While the productions of Nigerian and Ghanaian local cinema are generally contemporary in setting, they offer an entirely matter-of-fact inclusion of supernatural elements, what Krings and Onookome Okome define as a "representational regime" which includes "lengthy depictions of witchcraft and magic," and which offers an explicit challenge to the traditions of African political cinema (2013, 2). These magical elements reinforce the folkloric tendency of some of their plots, which tend to show an interest in slightly archetypal notions of good and evil, and to focus on familiar fairy-tale elements such as tricksters, marriages, or the pursuit of wealth and material success. The moralistic elements are not solely folkloric, however, and evince some of the cross-cultural aspects of folklore in Africa in their reliance on Christian values and symbols. Birgit Meyer notes the "distinctive, recurring" feature of Ghanaian video film in "the emphasis put on the visualization of otherwise invisible occult forces and the fact that their narrative is usually placed in the framework of the Christian dualism of God and the Devil." She explains that, "these preferences do not primarily and necessarily reflect the convictions of the filmmakers but spectators' expectations" (2003, 201).

This statement underlines an aspect of African fairy-tale film which is particularly important in distinguishing it from other cultures' magical film traditions, namely the presence of the magical as a living rather than fictional element in many African cultures. This widespread belief perhaps accounts for the comparative dearth of secondary-world fairy-tale films in the vein of, for example, *Stardust* (2007) or *Enchanted* (2007) in the African cinematic corpus; the folkloric in Africa tends to be closer to the real. In my South African context, for example, plotlines based on tokoloshe, the mischievous spirits of Zulu mythology, occasionally find their way into television soap operas, along similar lines to their appearance in Gavin Hood's *A Reasonable Man* (1999). The tokoloshe in Hood's film reflects the trickle of real-world news reports in which tokoloshe activity is claimed as part of a criminal defense or as the root of a social upheaval. Where filmmakers like Sembène feel impelled to deny the reality of the supernatural, Nollywood films cheerfully embody it by portraying the co-existence of contemporary and folkloric elements. As a result, filmmakers are able to create a more textured composite of African identity, encouraging, in Krings and Okome's formulation, "their viewers to imagine what it means to be modern in an African way" (2013, 5). At the same time, Nigerian videos can be controversial, with their formulaic supernatural elements seen as sensationalist or regressive by critics, even while the films themselves are enthusiastically consumed by their local audiences. Nollywood films uniquely embody the conflict between the traditional and the modern as much as do the less popular and more overtly political films of African folkloric cinema.

African Beast Fable as Popular Film

The beast fable has a particular association with Africa, not only because of its importance in the continent's oral traditions, but because of the tendency for the western gaze to embody the tourist position, constructing and consuming the continent as "wild" and "primitive" to obstruct or entirely elide a sense of its people. I have referred above to Elliot's beast fables, which I read as a child. Like many other collections of African folklore packaged for children, these encapsulate the winsome, moralistic tales that most reassuringly and conveniently erase Africa's human inhabitants who were displaced or otherwise affected by colonialism. The magical framework allows the relocation of voice from people to animals, which in western hands appears to give voice to an empty continent in a way that validates the western appropriation of it. African filmmakers have explored and adapted African animal tales into film, and Wade's early short films *Little Bird* (Picc Mi 1992) and *Fary, the Donkey* (Fary, L'Anesse 1987) are good examples of this vein. However, the strong association between beast fable and commercial film, and between commercial film and the western film industry, makes for particular pitfalls in more mainstream animal-tale adaptations.

The western fairy-tale film shows, of course, an especially strong thread not only of beast fable, but of large-budget animated animal tales; examples range from Disney's 1973 *Robin Hood* to *The Lion King* and the contemporary setting of recent financial successes such as the *Madagascar* franchise (beginning in 2005) and its numerous imitators. These are often comedies, gaining some of their comic effects from the enjoyable clash between the animal identity and its contemporary voice, as much as from the particular appropriateness of animation's exaggerated and playful flexibility to depictions of animal bodies. In the African context, this trend has influenced another aspect of African filmmaking which is both extremely westernized and highly commercial, namely the mainstream productions of the South African film industry.

The beast fable in South African film is interesting for the way in which it arises from and relies on a particularly South African tradition of comedic cinema. South Africa has a comparatively long history of commercial film production in the western mode, producing numerous successful comedic films on local themes as well as more serious and globally-relevant works such as Gavin Hood's Oscar-winning *Tsotsi* (2005), or Neill Blomkamp's *District 9* (2009). The earliest versions of the South African comedic film tradition spoke largely to a White South African audience, often with a strong Afrikaans flavor; later films, for example 2009's *White Wedding*, have a more multicultural and representative address. The industry nonetheless continues to reflect something of the legacy of apartheid, and of the colonial associations of film, with control of the industry's finance and technology still residing at least partially in the hands of White Africans.

The tendency for White control to warp film production overly towards western production tropes and assumptions is exacerbated by South Africa's growing popularity as a location for the shooting of American films, which make use of the country's scenery and climate as much as the comparatively low production costs. Thus, while South African film is developing its own contemporary and hybrid identity which encompasses aspects of multiculturalism and the synthesis of indigenous with western traditions, its more commercial productions nonetheless tend to exhibit a dichotomous perspective in their simultaneous insider and outsider gaze on African narratives. For this reason, South African production of folkloric texts forms an important contrast to the output of Black African filmmakers like Sembène or Wade.

Perhaps the most striking example of the outsider gaze on African beast fable is, of course, Disney's *The Lion King*, which, to a lesser extent than Ocelot's *Kirikou*, lays claim to Africanness through its savannah landscapes, carefully differentiated and recognizable animal species, and the occasional use of African voices in Elton John's soundtrack. While the animal tale presents a birthright plot and various trickster and monster archetypes, it makes no attempt at representing African folklore, and the plot is drawn as much from *Hamlet* and the Old Testament as from anything else. Most notably, the Africa represented in the film is mythologized in exclusively beast-fable terms in an animal kingdom that denies and excludes the existence of actual people.

The Lion King is an important comparative text when looking at South African versions of animated beast fable, because of both the parallels and the differences. The South African version of, perhaps, Pixar is Triggerfish Animation Studios, which started in advertising animation and produced short segments for *Sesame Street* before becoming the producers of full-length animated films with magical/mythic themes, such as *Adventures in Zambezia* (2012) and *Khumba* (2013). The latter film, an African beast fable focusing on a young zebra separated from his herd, bears immediate comparison with *The Lion King*, although its influences are likely to also include the more contemporary comedic animals of *Madagascar* and its ilk. While being entirely made in South Africa, *Khumba* is the work of a predominantly White-owned and -staffed company, and is clearly aimed at overseas as much as African markets, with a partially American voice-cast full of well-known actors in addition to local voice talent. The mix of voice actors enables the film to mine the broad cross-cultural appeal of the beast fable, universalizing its fable for international consumption via the American accents of the main characters, while still retaining broad South African comedic appeal by linking accents to animal identities (gemsbok are African whereas springbok are, predictably, Afrikaans, and given to outbreaks of rugby).

Khumba's plot occupies a carefully measured space between *The Lion King* and *Madagascar*. While the film's plot focuses entirely on the animal characters, with no actual humans depicted, it also moves through an African landscape that features obvious traces of human civilization: roads, fences, borehole pumps, and deserted farms. While beautiful landscapes abound, the flat-topped hills peculiar to the Karoo desert are given equal iconic space to that occupied by the classic African borehole windmill; in other words, the mythic animal realm being constructed relies on images of Africa as an agricultural as much as a tourist space. This recoups, to some extent, the erasure of humanity performed by *The Lion King*, and aligns the film far more with the contemporary world as a frame for animal fables that characterizes films such as *Madagascar*.

Unlike those of *The Lion King*, *Khumba*'s wildlife landscapes are loosely tied to an ecological motif, even though this motif is a backdrop to its more stereotypical message, the western media cliché of the hero's desire to belong and his journey towards identity and to an embrace of difference. The extremely topical African issue of drought underlies the film, as the zebra herd follows Khumba in search of water; however, that potential ecological message is secondary to the film's central plot, which relies on animal guides, mythology, and mystical elements of prophecy as the hero's worth is tested (see Figure 16.2). The tourist gaze on the animals themselves is, interestingly,

FIGURE 16.2 Khumba's mother tells the story of the zebra hero who became striped after finding the sacred water hole. The misty, monochromatic animation style for its mythic sequences sets them apart from the bright, clean lines of the conventional animation, *Khumba* (2013).

demonized, with the artificiality of game reserves and animals on display mocked in wholesale fashion, presented only as alarmingly predatory and featureless tourist Land Rovers.

Khumba grapples, surprisingly, with some similar issues to indigenous Black African films. Rather than explicitly exploring African folktale, *Khumba* invents its own mythologies, but its use of the narrative framework of myth and fable raises the same questions posed at the outset of this chapter: what is mythic Africa? How does it interact with the world at large, and how does it retain both its individuality and its integrity in the face of the numerous ideas of mythic Africa constructed outside the continent? How can the modern technologies of film, and Africa's place in the global contemporary, be reconciled with the backward-looking aspects of the folkloric? In the idiom of the quotation from Wade which provides the epigraph for this chapter, how does the stick move forward while remaining a stick and not trying to be a crocodile? The most interesting aspect of African folkloric filmmaking is that these questions are still being asked across a multiplicity of expressions, and will continue to be asked, indefinitely, as their answers continue to evolve.

17

AUSTRALIAN FAIRY-TALE FILMS

Elizabeth Bullen and Naarah Sawers

Australia has a short history of fairy tales and an even shorter history of fairy-tale film. This is not because the country lacks a tradition of oral storytelling. Indeed, Australia has a rich history of stories that have been recorded, collected, and retold. However, the very existence of Australian fairy tales is deeply complicated by the country's history of colonization. The difficulty pertains to the appropriation of the ancient stories of the land's original custodians, and to the role of traditional tales brought by those who have arrived in Australia since it was claimed as a British colony. Like the convicts and settlers who brought stories to Australia, the fairy tales of the northern hemisphere did not easily take root in the antipodes. Early Australian tales were often derivative of European narratives, and reflect an ambivalence about homeland, home, and national identity.

These complex affairs also manifest in the history of Australian cinema. Around the time the technological novelty of moving pictures transformed into a film industry, the Australian colonies federated to form a nation (1901). The country's first feature film, *The Story of the Kelly Gang* (1906)—also the world's first dramatic feature-length film—recounts the exploits of the bushranger outlaw and subsequent folk-hero, Ned Kelly. Like the next three feature films produced in Australia in the early 1900s, its subject matter reflects a nascent nationalism. Indeed, national identity continued to influence the movies that were made and continue to be made in the country, not least in the context of its actual and perceived subordination to the British empire and American cultural imperialism, respectively. Given this situation, and the absence of an indigenous fairy-tale tradition, the comparative scarcity of Australian fairy-tale films is understandable. Consequently, the movies we detail in this chapter were made in the 1970s and afterward.

Our account of the literary and cinematic genealogy of Australian fairy-tale films begins earlier. In this chapter's first section, we explain why we do not include Aboriginal narratives and, therefore, why we focus on the European fairy-tale tradition's influence in regard to the Australian fairy-tale literature of the 1890s and the films we later discuss. We draw attention to the recurring trope of the "lost child" as a signifier of the anxieties of colonial identity. The centrality of national identity in Australian cinema, complicated by the fluctuating fortunes of the domestic film industry, has also had an impact on the production of fairy-tale films in Australia. We outline these matters in the second section, where we survey a range of fairy-tale films made since the 1970s, asking what makes a fairy-tale film Australian. Finally, we present three studies based on what we identify as the dominant and emergent features of Australian fairy-tale films. Our aim is to be representative, not comprehensive, and to focus on films that are distinctively Australian in flavor. The first study returns to the lost-child figure. The second discusses revisionist fairy-tale films, focusing on how an Australian cultural disposition inflects the "happily ever after" ending. The last study addresses recent developmental short films, which we suggest may herald the birth of uniquely Australian fairy tales.

The Landscape of the Australian Literary Fairy Tale

Definitions of fairy tales are varied and porous, but they usually acknowledge an antecedent in oral storytelling and the way that "the characters, settings, and motifs are combined and varied according to specific functions to induce *wonder*" (Zipes 2000, xviii). However, the European trajectory from the wonder tale to the fairy-tale film does not easily translate to the Australian context. When the final volume of Charles-Joseph Mayer's *Cabinet des Fées* (1785–1789) was published, culminating in a collection that, according to Jack Zipes, "paved the way for the institution of the fairy tale in other countries" (2000, xxiv), the colony of Australia was just one year old. It would be more than a century before the first domestic fairy-tale collections were published. Maurice Saxby refers to these early compilations as "so-called fairy tales" because they were "consciously contrived" from European tales and "not linked to a folk tradition" (1969, 46). Thus, Australian fairy tales cannot, as Rebecca-Anne C. Do Rozario reiterates, "be categorized or interpreted with quite the same tools as developed for those tales that evolved from oral or older literary backgrounds" (2011, 23). These viewpoints seem to ignore Aboriginal oral traditions, which might otherwise appear to be a source of uniquely Australian wonder tales. We begin by explaining why traditional Indigenous stories cannot be defined as fairy tales, which will thereby clarify the particular Australian fairy-tale tradition that informs the majority of the films we discuss later in this chapter.

According to Clare Bradford (2001), a mistake "non-indigenous critics and commentators sometimes" make is to "read indigenous texts as though they are, or should be, produced within Western traditions of textuality" (131). Imposing terms such as "folktales" or "fairy tales" onto Indigenous stories means reading them through generic conventions that are western in their origins. Traditional Australian Aboriginal narratives belong to a still-living culture and offer a conduit for transmitting sacred and cultural knowledge and law. They are not fairy tales, and they should not be read according to humanist, Jungian, or poststructuralist models (Bradford 2011a). Nevertheless, they have a history of being drawn upon to define and authenticate an Australian fairy-tale or folktale tradition, Katie Langloh Parker's *Australian Legendary Tales* (1897) and *More Australian Legendary Tales* (1898) being cases in point. Parker's collections recorded the stories of the Yularoi people in New South Wales and were re-published six times, the last in 1978. As Bradford argues, "the history of colonization is littered with instances of appropriation of [traditional Indigenous] stories and the time of such practices is now over" (2007, 51). It is necessary, therefore, to locate the fairy-tale antecedents to Australian fairy-tale film in relation to processes of colonization and the sense of national identity that emerged from it.

Referring to colonial literature for children, Bradford explains "that it seeks to position non-Indigenous readers as young Australians at home in their world, while simultaneously managing the colonial past and its sorry stories of violence and dispossession" (2011b, 122). She argues that Australian fairy tales, and the fairies they "introduced into the Australian landscape," were designed to "reassure readers about their status as inheritors of the ancient (European) traditions of fantasy transposed into a new land" (2011b, 117). The European fairy-tale tradition, in particular the Brothers Grimm, strongly influenced Australian writers of the mid- to late nineteenth century. However, if they "naturalised the Germanic material earnestly," they often did so "incongruously" (Pierce 1999, xv). The initial result, Saxby judges, was that a host of "pale imitations of the traditional fairy story, arose in what was, at first, alien ground" (1969, 44). Subsequently, it would be "the uniqueness of the Australian landscape and its flora and fauna—from the European perspective—[that] allowed the actual environment to fulfill the role of a fairy realm," even though "the fairies themselves emigrated from England" (Do Rozario 2011, 14). Some of the most popular titles of the period include Atha Westbury's *Australian Fairy Tales* (1897), Jessie Whitfield's *The Spirit of the Bush Fire and Other Australian Fairy Tales* (1898), Ethel Pedley's *Dot and the Kangaroo* (1899), and Olga Ernst's *Fairy Tales from the Land of Wattle* (1904). Ida Outhwaite's *Elves and Fairies* (1916), in which the fairies wear fashionable clothes, attend dinner parties, and dance to jazz, exemplifies attempts to normalize and domesticate the Australian landscape (Bradford 2011b, 120).

The land of Australia, however, was not originally so hospitable to the colonists. Peter Pierce identifies a darker subtext to colonial fairy tales, in which the bush is menacing, particularly to the child who wanders away from home. In his study of the lost-child figure in Australian culture, Pierce argues that stories of lost children in Australian literary fairy tales are not cautionary. Although their prevalence reflects the numerous actual cases of lost children in colonial history, it also indicates a peculiarly national anxiety:

> The forlorn girls and boys, bereft, disoriented and crying in a wilderness that is indifferent, if not actively hostile to them, stand also for the older generation, that of their parents. Symbolically, the lost child represents the anxieties of European settlers because of the ties with home which they have cut in coming to Australia, whether or not they journeyed here by choice. The figure of the child stands in part for the apprehensions of adults about having sought to settle in a place where they might never be at peace.
>
> (1999, xii)

For White settlers, the bush was analogous to the forest or wood in European fairy tales like "Little Red Riding Hood," and British folktales like "The Lost Child" and "Babes in the Wood."

Pierce takes the example of *The Australian Babes in the Woods* (1866), written in verse and based on the true story of the three Duff children, who in 1864 survived nine days lost in the bush. Signaling that the happy ending to their story is atypical, Pierce also argues that allusions to European narratives—not only "Babes in the Wood," but the Grimm brothers' "Hansel and Gretel," "The Lost Son," and "The Changeling"—are incongruous because these older tales "involve children who are stolen or abandoned, rather than lost" (1999, 17). During the colonial period of Australian history, the trackless bush's dangers were not those presented by the human and magical denizens of the European forest. Rather, the bush was initially the site, not of the uncanny or of metaphorical threats to the civilizing process to which Zipes (2011) links the mature fairy-tale tradition of the old world, but of literal threats to the process of colonizing a country. To the extent that fairy-tale literature and film "unsettle us by showing what we lack" (Zipes 2011, 1), an abiding lack of home—represented by the lost child—has continued to inform the Australian cultural consciousness, its literature and film. Indeed, that lack has shaped the development of Australian national cinema and the domestic film industry in ways that have influenced its fairy-tale films.

Between Empires: Australian Cinema and the Film Industry

If Australia's colonial history circumscribed the growth of a national fairy-tale tradition, the nation's relationship to empire also militated against a convention of Australian fairy-tale films. According to Benito Cao, "one of the most popular and influential formulations of Australia is that of a nation caught between empires, namely the British Empire and the American Empire," and it is "one that resonates in particular throughout the history of cinema in Australia" (2012, 240–41). In spite of the nationalism of the early feature films that followed Federation, Australia remained part of the British empire and Australians continued to understand themselves as British. As a result, the myth of national identity co-existed with the myths of British-ness and Britain as "home" in post-Federation Australia (Meaney 2001, 80). The enduring tension between national pride and cultural cringe has also informed Australian cinema, including the way it has sought to situate itself, not only in relation to its historical political subordination to Britain, but to the commercial imperialism of the American film industry. Together, these factors have variously influenced the quantity—and quality—of the fairy-tale films produced in Australia. Indeed, they have created contexts in which it becomes important to ask what makes an Australian fairy-tale film *Australian*.

During the first decade of the twentieth century, "Australia was one of the few nations in the world to have an active and prolific feature film industry" (National Film and Sound Archive [NFSA] 2014a). Over the course of the 1920s, however, the industry grew moribund and "by the end of the Second World War Australia had lost its last feature production company. For the next twenty years almost without exception, Australia was a cheap location for foreign productions" (Turner 2012, 187). Between 1940 and 1969, just twenty-three feature films were produced: eight in the 1940s, nine in the 1950s, and six in the 1960s (NFSA 2014b, c, d). The first identifiably Australian fairy-tale film was not produced until 1976.

The Australian film industry revived in the 1970s as a result of a series of federal government cultural policy initiatives, including a combination of public investment and generous tax incentives for private investors. To be eligible, productions were "required to demonstrate 'significant Australian content,' to be evident in crew composition, subject-matter and setting" (Verhoeven 2010, 137). The New Wave in Australian cinema included Ozploitation low-budget genre films: comedies, horror, and action. Cao (2012) argues that the comedies of the 1970s reject Britishness and "became a national catharsis that served to purge the stereotypical vices of the old empire . . . from the perceived virtues of the new nation (vibrant innocence, genuine informality and social equality)" (243). These are qualities we identify in a number of the fairy-tale films addressed in detail below.

The Australian Film Commission did not consider genre films a "worthy investment"; they were not films "we could be proud of" (Dermody and Jacka 1988, 31) and in some respects this continues to be the case. They have been historically regarded as the province of Hollywood, "which has always been interested in developing and refining specific film genres" (Mayer 1999, 178). Disney's long history, and near monopoly over fairy-tale films for children in the twentieth century, is a pertinent example. As a platform for the "representation and preservation of Australian culture, character and identity" (Maher 1999, 13), then, 1970s cinema came to be dominated by stories of nation: colonial, convict, and war narratives and adaptations of Australian novels. This nationalist agenda created an oppositional relationship between culture and commercialism, cultural specificity and universal themes, allegedly authentic national realisms and genre formulas, and art-house aesthetics and popular entertainment. These binaries play a role in determining what constitutes Australian fairy-tale films in this chapter and in the context of this book's international scope. In the absence of a national fairy-tale tradition, they also explain why we could locate only two films with fairy-tale elements in the 1970s, *Oz—A Rock 'n' Roll Road Movie* (1976) and *Dot and the Kangaroo* (1977). Both are specifically Australian in content and were part-funded by the Australian Film Commission.

Surveying the Australian cinema revival from the vantage point of the early 1990s, Graeme Turner identifies a number of formal elements of Australian literature that he uses to characterize the nation's cinema. Although the Australian film industry has become increasingly internationalized, we think Turner's observations help not only to explain the lack of a tradition of fairy-tale films in the country, but also to identify the distinguishing features of those that have been produced. These characteristics manifest as a preference for the "real" over the "imaginary," "history" over "fiction," "formal shapelessness" over "plot," and a "natural" ending over "narratively-motivated closure" (Turner 1993, 103, 104). In sum, Turner identifies the previous preference in Australian film for the historical saga and social realism as symptomatic of "a disavowal of the agency of the individual [and] in its place, the admission of nature or of the power of the social structure in determining individual experience" (1993, 104). Consequently, the impulse towards transcendence that Zipes (2011) identifies in the fairy-tale genre and fairy-tale film is frequently undercut by an Australian cultural disposition, as we will discuss below.

Of course, "Australian directors and Australian-based productions do not just tell stories set in [or about] Australia" (O'Regan 1995). Likewise, foreign investment and the outsourcing of cheap studio facilities have created what Tom O'Regan (1995), describes as "an emerging fuzziness around just what is and is not an Australian film." As Leonie Rutherford explains, "unlike Britain or the United States," the Australian film industry "cannot finance production costs primarily from its domestic exhibition, distribution and merchandising deals," and has often relied on "presales to the US market [or] international coproduction deals" (2003, 256). Many of the fairy-tale films made in Australia in the 1980s and 1990s fall into this category. Made for an international market, they frequently reflect allegedly universal themes rather than a distinctly Australian sensibility.

A case in point is the series of low-budget animated fairy-tale films made for television and video by Burbank Animation Studios, known as Burbank Films Australia until 1991. The studio adapted three literary fairy tales in the 1980s: *Alice through the Looking Glass* (1987), *Alice in Wonderland* (1988), and *Peter Pan* (1988). Subsequently, its catalogue of 50-minute fairy-tale films was extended to include such literary fairy-tale adaptations as *The Emperor's New Clothes* (1991) and *Thumbelina* (1993), among others. Further titles in this suite include *Cinderella* (1996) and *Hansel and Gretel* (1997), "commissioned by Anchor Bay Entertainment, Inc. of Troy, Michigan" (Profile n.d.). We note that the stepmother and stepsisters in Burbank's *Cinderella* are named The Dame, Nellie, and Melba, an allusion to the famous early-twentieth-century Australian soprano. We also note that *Alice through the Looking Glass* includes voice characterizations by American comedians, Phyllis Diller and Jonathan Winter, signifying that it was made for an international, not domestic audience. Adrian Martin asks, "where do we draw the borders around 'Australia'—and do we need to? This is not only a question of the inevitable, unstoppable increase in international co-production. It is a question of self-defined cultural identity, and its impacts on the films we make" (1994, 15). More than two decades later, Martin's observations remain relevant, not least in terms of the Australian fairy-tale film.

Films made in Australia are not necessarily, or only ambiguously, Australian. For instance, *Don't be Afraid of the Dark* (2011), with a screenplay by Guillermo del Toro that draws on fairy tales like his earlier feature, *Pan's Labyrinth* (2006), was filmed in Australia. It stars American actor Katie Holmes and Australian Guy Pearce, but has a predominantly local supporting cast and crew. Yet listings for the film's country of origin sometimes includes Australia, and sometimes not. For instance, the Internet Movie Database [henceforth IMDb] lists the United States, Australia, and Mexico whereas the AllMovie database lists only the United States. Brisbane-born P. J. Hogan directed and co-wrote the screenplay (with American, Michael Goldenberg) for the 2003 *Peter Pan*. It, too, was filmed in Australia, but has a British and American cast, and an American production company, Revolution Studios in cooperation with Universal. The IMDb classifies it as Australian, but *The New York Times* (Scott 2003) lists its country of origin as the United States. Finally, the country of origin of *Beauty and the Beast* (2009), also filmed on the Gold Coast, is identified as United States/Australia (Greenhill and Rudy 2014, 399) and Australia/Canada on IMDb.

According to Ben Goldsmith, "International production confounds and complicates the questions that [Thomas] Elsaesser . . . identifies as lying at the heart of the national cinema project: 'What is typical or specific about a nation's cinema?' and 'what is the function of cinema in articulating nationhood and fostering a sense of belonging?'" (2010, 200). These questions lead him to argue that:

> Hollywood is now well and truly a part not only of Australian screen culture, but also of Australian national cinema. The number of Hollywood productions made in Australia, or with Australian cast and crew, is now so large as to defy any neat separation between local/ national and the international/Hollywood. They are no longer different from Australian cinema; they are part of it.
>
> (2010, 206)

In contrast, Mark David Ryan (2012) suggests that "The most successful Australian movies of all time at the local box-office have traded upon Australianness in the marketplace: distinctively Australian characters, cultural themes, cinematic tropes, *mise-en-scène* and so on (for example, *Crocodile Dundee* [1986], *The Adventures of Priscilla, Queen of the Desert* [1994], *Muriel's Wedding* [1994])" (150). At stake is the tension between traditions for telling a nation's stories and "universal modes of story-telling" (Ryan 2012, 150), such as the fairy tale. Exploring this issue and others, we present three studies of fairy-tale films that reflect various stages in the evolution of the Australian fairy tale, and trace their literary, cinematic, and nationalist influences.

The Lost Child Comes Home: Fairy-Tale Films for Children

Australian writer Carmel Bird, whose fiction is influenced by fairy tales, states that "the stories that resonate and lodge in a culture are, after all, the expression of desires" (2013b, 16). The story of the lost child, she speculates, "must be a narrative that is lodged in the heart and imagination, nightmare and dream, of all human beings. In Australia the nightmare became reality. The child is the future, and if the child goes, there can be no future" (Bird 2013a). Though lost children are evident in the allusions to European narratives in the early literary fairy tales, the lost child in Australian fiction and film also betrays a national anxiety. If this disquiet manifests ambivalence towards the future, it also signifies a similar attitude to the past, and not only in terms of colonial history. Given that its majority, non-Indigenous, population is either immigrant or descended from immigrants, Australia could be regarded as a "country of lost children" (Pierce 1999). The lost child is also a recurring trope in the nation's cinema; indeed, an apt metaphor for the Australian film industry itself, given its location on the margin of the filmmaking centers of the northern hemisphere. Two films featuring a lost child, Yoram Gross's *Dot and the Kangaroo* (1977) and Bill Kroyer's *FernGully: The Last Rainforest* (1992), reveal Australian anxieties about home and homeland, land and identity, in the second half of the twentieth century, but they also differ. Gross's film is a product of the Australian film revival; *FernGully* is an Australian-American co-production.

Dot and *FernGully*, both based on Australian novels, point to a broader preoccupation with place evident in film adaptations of, and allusions to, American and English literary fairy tales made in Australia. The first Australian fairy-tale film was *Oz—A Rock 'n' Roll Road Movie* (1976). Aimed at a teen audience, it simultaneously references L. Frank Baum's *The Wonderful Wizard of Oz* (1900)—Dorothy's realization that "There is no place like home," made memorable in the 1939 film—and the colloquial name for Australia, Oz. There are similar resonances between "Never Never," a term for the Australian Outback, and the island of "Neverland, where the lost children are" (Barrie 1911). Three versions of *Peter Pan* have been made in Australia—Burbank Studios' animated version (1988); Hogan's live action adaptation (2003); and Disney's *Return to Never Land* (2002). Burbank also adapted Lewis Carroll's Alice stories, the first of which, *Alice's Adventures in Wonderland*, links Wonderland to the antipodes. When Alice falls down the rabbit-hole, she wonders if she will "fall right through the earth" to "The Antipathies, I think . . . but I shall have to ask them what the name of the country is, you know. Please, Ma'am, is this New Zealand or Australia?" (Carroll 1865). Unlike the fantasy realms of Carroll, Baum, and J. M. Barrie, however, the wonderland in *Dot* and *FernGully* is not elsewhere, but the homeland of the lost child protagonist. In this regard, these films' conservation message demonstrates Australia's evolving relationship to the land as home.

Polish-Australian Gross's animated feature, *Dot and the Kangaroo* (1977), based on Pedley's 1899 novel of the same name, reflects its colonial origins and its debt to tales like Carroll's *Alice*. In the novel, the bush's treachery and Dot's fear of it is intensified by her recollection of the search for a neighbor's child, and the fact that she "never saw that little boy again, although he had been found." When Dot realizes she is lost, she weeps with "loneliness and fear . . . and with her little hands covering her eyes so as not to see the cruel wild bush in which she was lost"; once in the company of Kangaroo, she sees the bush with new eyes and thinks "they must be in fairyland; it was so beautiful" (Pedley 1899). As Ulla Rahbek argues, "The fairytale aspect of the story is there from the very beginning: like Little Red Riding Hood, Dot has strayed further into the bush while picking flowers, and just as happened to Alice in Wonderland, she is distracted by a hare (not a white rabbit)" (2007).

The same fairy-tale intertexts are evident in Gross's film, although "Hansel and Gretel" is evoked by the image of Dot weeping under a tree during the opening credits. Flashback scenes reference "Little Red Riding Hood" through the warnings of Dot's mother. However, Gross changes the novel's direct allusion to *Alice*, when Dot chases a marsupial hopping mouse and falls down a steep hill into a gully or ravine. When Kangaroo finds her, she feeds the girl berries so that she can understand animal speech. Having lost her own baby joey, Kangaroo sets out to help Dot find her way back to her parents. Along the way they meet a variety of animals who assist them, and Dot learns about their bush home and the threat of (White and Indigenous) hunters. These encounters include song and dance routines, reflecting the conventions of twentieth-century American animation.

Stylistically, however, *Dot and the Kangaroo* differs from typical 1970s American animated features. As Figure 17.1 demonstrates, the animals "are not caricatures, but stylized" (Lynch 1999).

FIGURE 17.1 From *Dot and the Kangaroo* (1977).

Kangaroo is not given "human characteristics, dressed up like say, Mickey Mouse was" (Lynch 1999) or, indeed, those in Carroll's *Alice* stories. The native animals that populate this bush are wondrous enough, even if the song sung by the *Ornithorhynchus paradoxus*, the platypus, resembles Carroll's nonsense verses. More significantly, the animated human and animal characters are super-imposed on a live-action background of Australian bushland. Although this was a cost-saving measure, Rutherford (2003) argues that "the language of animation [in the film] reinforces an aesthetics of place which challenges" the conventions of orthodox animation (255). By contrast, *FernGully* is typical of the "character- and conflict-based narratives" that dominate orthodox or industrial cel-animation (Rutherford 2003, 255).

FernGully is a modern fairy-tale film that addresses environmental anxieties about deforestation, in which fairies and elves occupy the roles of the native animals in *Dot and the Kangaroo*. Sixteen-year-old Zak, who works for the logging company, gets lost when a brunette Tinker Bell, Crysta, accidentally shrinks him to fairy size. He enters a rainforest wonderland where the fairies no longer believe in "human tales." Like Dot, he learns about the impact of human—indeed, his own—actions on the natural world, and helps defeat the evil spirit of destruction, Hexxus, which occupies the machine being used to level the forest. Directed by Kroyer, the screenplay was co-written by Bill Cox and Diana Young, who wrote the 1991 novel on which it is based. The film reveals numerous traces of its American co-production. Although the animators had "visited an Australian rain forest, taken photographs, and created detailed sketches" (Murphy 1993, 32), Cox's prior association with Disney is evidenced by "the presence of many of the typical visual tropes, musical numbers and plot motifs of Disney films of the era in spite of the story's distinctly Australian origins" (Smith and Parsons 2012, 27). The use of Hollywood conventions rather than characteristically Australian storytelling elements described earlier, and an American voice cast, including Robin Williams and Christian Slater, instead of voice actors with Australian accents, indicates that the film targets an international rather than a domestic Australian audience.

In fact, the film is very faithful to the novel, which, like *Dot*, reverses the site and source of danger from the trackless bush in early fairy tales to the civilizing process. However, the climax of the film version underscores the ethos of individualism Rutherford (2003) identifies in orthodox animation. It devotes much more screen time to Zak's role in saving the forest and less to the role of Crysta and the other fairies who, in the novel, choose to fight Hexxus rather than leave their home. The novel makes the assertion that "power is generous. It grows when it is shared" (Young 1991, 112). When Crysta draws on her inner power to deliver the magic seed to Hexxus and destroy him, "hundreds of fairies suddenly appeared and fluttered around her" (122). This manifestation does not occur in the film, which configures the human teenager as the hero and concludes when he leaves FernGully with the intention of ensuring no one tries to destroy the rainforest again, rather than the fairy celebration that takes place in the novel. Its closure is narratively motivated, unlike the natural ending of *Dot and the Kangaroo*, which simply concludes with the lost child's return home. Nevertheless, both films reflect a shift away from colonial attitudes to the land, which is no longer an alien object to be feared, domesticated, or destroyed; instead, they promote a recognition of land as home.

Re-visioning Cultural Identity, Agency, and the Fairy-Tale Ending

In their allusion to traditional and literary fairy tales, the source novels of *Dot and the Kangaroo* and *FernGully* appropriate and domesticate fairy-tale motifs and localize their universal themes, though Kroyer's film version reverses this tendency. The films appropriate the fairy-tale genre and the conventions of the fairy-tale film as a means to reflect on home and identity, but do not resist the fundamental values of the narratives from which they borrow. Two other films reference, modernize, and revise the classic fairy tales "Cinderella" and "Sleeping Beauty." Hogan's *Muriel's Wedding* (1994) and Julia Leigh's *Sleeping Beauty* (2011) explore the "possibilities of estranging ourselves from designated roles and the conventional patterns" (Zipes 2010, xii) in ways that reflect the Australian cultural disposition and a further stage in the progression of its fairy-tale film. Both loosely reproduce the features of Australian film identified by Turner (1993), repudiating individual agency in their social realism and refusing the traditional fairy-tale ending.

Muriel's Wedding asserts itself as contemporary suburban Australiana through the characters and mise-en-scène it constructs, and the irony and kitsch humor it lends to themes of loss and disappointment. From the Bushell's teabag Muriel's mother uses to make tea in the microwave and the iconic Hills Hoist rotary washing line in the backyard, to its broad Australian accents, the film leaves no doubt about setting. The movie's overt cultural positioning locates it within the tradition of Ozploitation films, but without the cultural cringe. Muriel, the eldest of five children in the Heslop family, lives in the fictional suburb, Porpoise Spit. Though ordinary, the family is dysfunctional. Muriel's mother is emotionally absent, her depression implicitly linked to the verbal abuse from her husband, Bill. Indeed, he also constantly belittles Muriel so that, to escape the reality of her life, she listens to ABBA songs and, in spite of her parents' unhappy marriage, constructs a fairy-tale fantasy about her own wedding. In the film's opening scenes, set during the wedding of her high school classmate, Tania, Muriel fights off all contenders to catch the wedding bouquet. Muriel, thrilled to have caught the bouquet and all it symbolizes, is forced by Tania and her friends, loosely representing the "the ugly stepsisters," to re-throw it so that one of their group receives it. Like Cinderella, Muriel is the poor relation.

In spite of her social status, Muriel seeks independence and finds temporary happiness when she moves to Sydney with her old school friend, Rhonda. Muriel's confidence grows so significantly during this time that she forgets her fantasy of a spectacular wedding. Her tenuous sense of self-worth is fragile, however. When a tumor in Rhonda's spine leaves her paraplegic, Muriel reverts to wedding fantasies and ABBA songs. She responds to a singles advertisement for an Australian wife, resulting in her marriage to a South African swimmer looking for citizenship. For Muriel, the wedding represents social acceptance, indeed, fulfills her belief that she will finally "become the object of admiration and envy for her beauty and attractiveness" (Valentine 2007, 578). Weddings also implicate a multitude of social, economic, and gendered power relations that function to sustain hierarchical powers. The fairy-tale ending, the promise of true love, and social mobility reinforced in American adaptations of "Cinderella" especially, are finally rejected in *Muriel's Wedding*.

When Muriel leaves her marriage and overcomes her desire for acceptance from the "ugly stepsisters" in Porpoise Spit, the audience is positioned to celebrate. She realizes that happiness comes from self-acceptance, not social conformity. Furthermore, stirred by her mother's suicide, Muriel's understanding involves looking beyond the fairy tale to her real situation. She returns home to collect Rhonda so they can move back to Sydney. In the final scene, the two leave Porpoise Spit in a taxi. The camera pans from each young woman's face as they look at each other with pure joy, ready to start their life together. In this conclusion, the film offers its biggest challenge to ideologies underpinning conservative fairy tales as it privileges the women's relationship over a heterosexual institution of marriage, resisting the conventional representation of female friendships "as phases on a maturational journey toward a normal heterosexual resolution" (McInally 2006, 93). The film's end, which transforms female friendship into a source of empowerment, is revisionist.

Though transgressive, the conclusion to *Muriel's Wedding* is happy. The same cannot be said of Julia Leigh's *Sleeping Beauty* (2011). Leigh's film makes the Charles Perrault version nearly unrecognizable, using the motif of a sleeping beauty to critique gendered and sexual power relations. Like *Muriel's Wedding*, *Sleeping Beauty* is a revisionist fairy tale, in which the female protagonist is simultaneously object and subject, passive and active, agential and acted-upon. The publicity poster shows a semi-naked young woman posing with her back to the camera, her face turned so that she looks directly at the viewer over her shoulder. She is both observed and observer. Lucy is a university student living in Melbourne, employed in a range of menial jobs. She has few friends except a depressed alcoholic named Birdman, and she struggles to pay the rent. Lucy answers a local magazine advertisement and is subsequently employed as a "sleeping beauty." In this role, she agrees to be drugged and lie naked in a bedchamber in order to service male fantasies of female passivity.

Kyra Clarke's analysis argues that the sleeping beauty motif is further complicated in Leigh's film by Lucy's passivity in other areas of her life. Although she conforms to western ideals of femininity with her youth, alabaster skin, slim figure, and long hair, she is emotionally unavailable or detached in ways that contravene expectations about femininity. Clarke writes that "she may be perceived to passively 'sleep' through the film" (2014, 3) and that the social expectation for "coherence and consistency around representations of girls [is] unapparent" (2014, 2). Lucy manifests the "sexual and moral ambiguity" that Pauline Greenhill and Sidney Eve Matrix observe as a "standard feature of fairy[-]tale films for adults" (2010, 9). On the one hand, she is amoral and shameless; on the other, she is vulnerable. Without family or friends, she is at least metaphorically homeless, and her vulnerability is at its greatest when she waits unconscious in the bedchamber for the clients.

In the concluding scenes, Lucy wakes next to the dead body of an old man who has chosen to die lying beside her. Prince Charming is a corpse. Lucy screams in horror, but the camera immediately cuts to a scene of Lucy and the client resting peacefully in bed. The scene is a recording made on a camera Lucy had hidden in the bedchamber. The footage emphasizes the ambiguity of Lucy's character as both agential and acted-upon. Unlike *Muriel's Wedding*, where audiences' sympathies are unquestionably tied to the awkward protagonist, the ambiguity associated with Lucy's character confronts and disconcerts the viewing audience. As Clarke writes, "Lucy is penetrated and impenetrable, in control and powerless, perceived by the chamber scene men as virgin and slut. Indeed, the way in which her naked body is interpreted by these men identifies the multiple and varying expectations that surround young women" (2014, 10).

Muriel's Wedding and *Sleeping Beauty* are important indications of Australia's changing sensibility, especially if as Greenhill and Matrix (2010) suggest, "the mirror of fairy-tale film reflects not so much what its audience members actually are but how they see themselves and their potential to develop (or, likewise, to regress)" (17). Lucy is trapped in, and as oblivious as a sleeper to, a structural system that is beyond her making. Muriel is caught in the fairy-tale fantasy of living happily ever after, the reality of which is foregrounded by Muriel's mother's suicide. Turner argues that "while conventional notions of the 'Australian' type are represented through signifiers of individuality and independence, Australian novels and films find little difficulty in enclosing such notions within narratives that demonstrate the individual's powerlessness in order to enforce their acceptance of external determining structures" (1993, 104). *Muriel's Wedding* and *Sleeping Beauty* show the limits of individual power, but in so doing, these revisionist fairy-tale films encourage the interrogation of social structures. Similarly, they dispense with concepts of an Australian identity as subordinate to British and American culture.

Short Tales: Australian Developmental Films

In the absence of an indigenous fairy-tale tradition, we suggest that different "tools" are needed not only to interpret Australian fairy tales (Do Rozario 2011), but also to create them. Ironically, this creativity is an outcome of the small size and fluctuating commercial viability of the Australian film industry. Here, we explore short films as representative of the contemporary Australian fairy-tale film. These films create the wonder expected of fairy tales; they project both "pleasure in the fantastic, [and] curiosity about the real" (Warner 1999, xx). They are neither adaptations of European tales (and rarely allude to them), nor overtly Australian in setting. Rather, an Australian sensibility emerges through their mode of production, which supports the tales' simultaneously resistant and transcendent messages. We focus on Isabel Peppard's *Butterflies* (2013) and Nicholas Verso's *Hugo* (2008), which typify a groundswell of recent Australian fairy-tale short films.

Simon Sellars (2010) suggests that the Academy Award success of Adam Elliot's *Harvie Krumpet* (2003) "seemed to galvanise the rest of the country's animators," but in truth "there was always great work being produced." *Butterflies* and *Hugo* belong to the new landscape of Australian fairy-tale film that includes: *A Cautionary Tail* (2013), about a little girl born with a tail; *The Bronze Mirror* (2007), an adaptation of a Korean folktale; *The Goat That Ate Time* (2007), about a timepiece-consuming goat; *Souvenir* (2011), about a little girl who grows up with a bag that gets filled with disappointments and one souvenir; *Zero* (2011), about a little boy called Zero who makes something out of nothing; and Andrew Ruhemann and Shaun Tan's *The Lost Thing* (2010), which we discuss in the conclusion.

As Sellars (2010) notes, it is often difficult to identify what is distinctly Australian about these tales, except for the mode of their production. In her analysis of Australian animation aesthetics, Rutherford (2003) distinguishes between the extremes of orthodox animation, described earlier, and experimental animation, which "tends towards 'Abstraction,' rather than configuration" (253). Rutherford argues that a developmental animation aesthetic, in contrast, "works within the context of realist space" while also "attempting to subvert it" (2003, 254). The developmental animation forms of the Australian short fairy-tale films achieve art-house aesthetics and critical success to blend social realism with the transcendent aspects of the fairy-tale genre.

The Gothic film *Butterflies* uses stop-motion silicone figurines to tell the tale of a young artist, Claire. Figure 17.2 shows an opening scene from the film, where she exchanges her drawings for money at the train station in a beggarly fashion. She says she "always manages to scrape by, and

FIGURE 17.2 From *Butterflies* (2013).

every day I think of new things to draw." Her creative impulse is embodied in the "butterfly": a baby-like, nude, and chubby figure. With lips too large for its alien-like face, it is an ugly, yet heavenly creature. The butterfly sickens, its body visibly disintegrating, when Claire's creativity is stultified as she begins work on a production line for greeting cards. The factory is grey and gloomy, and as the year passes, her capacity to compose her own drawings dissipates. The protagonist enters a horrific fantasy-realm, described by the director as a "psychological landscape" where she sees "the grotesque embodiments of her co-workers trapped in personal purgatory after giving up on their creative practice" (quoted in Mitchell 2013). In a Faustian moment, her employer, Dalton Hearst, tells her to "pay up," by giving him the butterfly. Frightened, she falls down a hole where she is faced with a vision of herself manically drawing greeting cards, the skin falling from her face symbolizing the disintegration of her dreams. Reviving from her horror-fantasy, Claire shuts down the production line and draws a picture for her own pleasure. The butterfly's health returns; pulsating and inelegant (but beautiful), it directs her to the door, and they leave the factory.

The film's opposition to commercialization is clear, and the mode of animation is in itself a form of resistance that contributes to its fairy-tale characteristics. This twelve-minute film took three years to make. The short film is unlike traditional animation, which "privileges story elements and renders invisible its aesthetic achievement and the conditions of its making" (Rutherford 2003, 258). The mode of storytelling in *Butterflies* is also its mode of production, especially when the silicone figurines are made to disintegrate as though flesh is melting. Producer and co-author, Warwick Burton, also notes resonances between the form and fairy-tale effect. He says, "the 'handmade' nature of stop motion also probably lends to its ability to tell 'fairy tales' that seems somehow imbued with 'history'" and, furthermore, that the "process of bringing inanimate objects to life, giving them emotions is, itself 'magic'" (quoted in Mitchell 2013).

Verso's short live-action film *Hugo* uses in-camera effects and puppeteers, and like *Butterflies*, it was also constrained by its budget. It tells the story of a lonely young schoolgirl, Desma, who is participating in a science competition at her boarding school. When her arch rival, Celestine, disturbs her, Desma loses the moth that was to be the object of her science project. She desperately searches in the dark garden for another, but finds "Moth-boy" instead. Believing she has discovered a new species, she takes him back to her room, confident that he will win her the competition. Trapped in the bedroom, Moth-boy becomes ill. Desma eventually relinquishes her desire to win the competition and her hatred of her rival in order to save him with Celestine's help. Like *Butterflies*, the mode of production contributes meaning to the story. For instance, Moth-boy's slimy emergence from his cocoon, his handmade wings, and deteriorating body give the film a sometimes-amateur horror style. The "Peter Pan" conclusion, in which in-camera effects depict Moth-boy flying out the window and becoming a tiny silhouette against the moon, provides a fantastic, fairy-tale ending.

The blurring and blending of boundaries in both films underwrite their critiques of Australian society. Like the butterfly in *Butterflies*, Moth-boy becomes ill when forced into unnatural and enclosed environments, literally and metaphorically. Moth-boy's deteriorating health is linked to Desma's competitiveness; her need to win means that she recognizes him as an insect, and is blind to his magic and beauty. In *Butterflies*, the factory floor symbolizes the effects of commercialization on artists aspiring to be creative and innovative. These critiques exemplify why these films are so important in their conceptual effects and their modes of production. Despite small, often unreliable budgets, Australian filmmakers manage to produce short tales that are fresh, contemporary, and fairy-tale sized.

Wonder and Hope in the Search for Belonging and Home

"So you want to hear a story?" Thus begins *The Lost Thing* (2010), the Academy Award-winning short animated film adapted from Tan's picture book of the same title. Like Desma in *Hugo*, the young protagonist and first-person narrator of *The Lost Thing* is preoccupied with putting things in their place. Living in a world of uniformity, bureaucracy, monotony, and homogeneity, he is collecting and classifying bottle-tops when he sees something extraordinary; a strange-looking "thing" on the beach. They play together for hours and finally the boy realizes it is lost. First, he takes it to his friend, Pete, who determines that the lost thing "didn't belong anywhere." He takes it home for the night, and then to the "Federal Department of Odds and Ends." A strange creature advises him not to leave the Lost Thing at the Department, which is a place for "forgetting, leaving things behind," and gives them a card. The boy and the lost thing follow the arrow on the card until they "find what seemed to be the right place, in a dark little gap off some anonymous little street. The kind of place you'd never know existed unless you were actually looking for it." They discover a utopian sunlit wonderland that is full of color and other hybrid things. This is where the pair say goodbye. The lost thing remains and the boy returns to his own toneless, dull world of numbers, signs, rules, and straight lines.

We tell the tale of *The Lost Thing* by way of conclusion to our chapter because it encapsulates the preoccupations and progression in understandings of identity and place in the Australian fairy-tale films we have discussed, from the little White girl, Dot, lost in a land so different to the homeland of her settler parents, to Tan's lost thing that cannot find a place in a world of sameness. Fairy tales are, as Zipes argues, about home and transformation, and we are drawn to them because they provide "the general parameters for helping us understand how our longing for home . . . is discomforting *and* comforting" (2011, 4). The Australian fairy-tale films in the 1970s reiterated colonial anxieties, reflected in the image of the lost child, but they also asserted national identity through the representation of Australia's unique flora and fauna, and a conservationist message that signified progress towards an understanding of Australia as home. The revisionist fairy-tale films articulated an acceptance of cultural and national identity. *Muriel's Wedding* and *Sleeping Beauty* privilege local realisms in respect to the wish fulfillment that typifies the closure of many film versions of "Cinderella" and "Sleeping Beauty." Most recently, the short film form has extended the definition of Australian fairy tales by shrugging off the need for clichéd signifiers of cultural identity. The short films we describe in this chapter ask more complex questions about who Australians were, have become, and can be. These films critique social practices, the loss of innocence and uniqueness, but are often hopeful about the potential for a positive transformation through wonder.

The Lost Thing is a story about searching for a place to belong. The hope it offers may seem confined to the semi-utopian space available to those who do not belong, but in fact the film cautions the viewer about losing his or her sense of wonder. In its concluding scene, the narrator says: "I still think about that lost thing from time to time, especially when I see something out of the corner of my eye that doesn't quite fit." The lost thing he spies represents identity as hybrid, composite, and unique, and only out-of-place in the context of established structures of place, being, and belonging. As the product of possibly the youngest nation represented in this book, albeit with the oldest living culture on earth, fairy-tale films like *The Lost Thing* demonstrate that Australians' desire for a home, a place to belong, is a work-in-progress, but one which the cinematic trajectory from *Dot and the Kangaroo* to the short fairy-tale film contributes to finding and defining.

18

FAIRY-TALE FILMS IN CANADA/ CANADIAN FAIRY-TALE FILMS

Pauline Greenhill and Steven Kohm

Made in Canada?

From a ridiculous pastiche to a brutal depiction of maternal filicide and its aftermath, from light-hearted animated works for children to serious explorations of law and justice, from blockbuster features to National Film Board (NFB) productions, fairy-tale films made in Canada defy easy categorization. Nevertheless, this chapter locates some common themes and areas of interest, as first steps toward recognizing Canadian contributions to international fairy-tale cinema. We must, however, begin with some caveats. The overwhelming majority of films screened, rented, and/or purchased in Canada are created and produced in the US with American crews and American movie stars. Though we have no specific numbers for fairy-tale films in particular, "statistics show that from 2001 to 2009[,] . . . Hollywood blockbusters dominated 89% of the Canadian box office" (Telefilm 2011, 5); Canadian films had between 2.8 and 4.2 percent. For physical media, between 2006 and 2010, Canadian feature films had between 1.0 and 1.5 percent of sales, and between 1.8 and 2.9 percent of rentals (De Rosa 2012, 45). We expect statistics for online rentals and purchases are comparable, given the extent to which Canada lives in the US's geographical and cultural shadow.

Canadian cinema history follows endeavors to ensure Canadian participation in the making and viewing of audiovisual media in this country. As such, Canadian cinema's political economy moves through "a variety of funding structures: private sector investment, corporate sponsorship and direct investment from the Canadian state" (Gittings 2002, 77). For example, the NFB's establishment in 1939 reflected the intention to focus on national interests and representation of Canada and Canadians internally and abroad that continues today. NFB productions include several fairy-tale shorts, animated and live action, discussed below. The Canadian Film Development Corporation (CFDC), constituted in 1967 to invest in Canadian films, also saw some success. But by the 1970s "although Canadian features were now being produced thanks to CFDC moneys, these films were not seen by the Canadian public because of the US monopoly on theatrical distribution in Canada" (Gittings 2002, 95).

Tax-shelter programs encouraged Canadian productions of generic, Hollywood-type films beginning in the 1970s. However, these initiatives also helped "to develop a cadre of skilled technicians and crews as well as establishing the careers of producers" (Gittings 2002, 97). The CFDC, renamed Telefilm Canada in 1984, recognized that circulation remained a problem so the Feature

Film Distribution Fund was established in 1988. By the mid 1990s, Canada had "a thriving independent production industry" (99) with co-production "used to circumvent the US monopoly on distribution and [to] gain access to new markets for Canadian films" (99–100). However, with bigger budgets came "compromises that could dilute the Canadianness of a production" (100). Canadian film scholar Christopher Gittings notes director Atom Egoyan's *The Sweet Hereafter* (1997, drawing on "The Pied Piper of Hamelin"), discussed below, as an example of a Canadian success; it was an Oscar-nominated film and was "awarded prizes at Cannes" (101). Nevertheless, simply being made in Canada by no means guarantees that a film will reflect Canadian ideas, practices, or values.

Film scholar Jerry White notes some specifics of Canadian film practice, by which he refers to home-grown films, rather than productions transplanted because of financial advantages. Documentary "crosses linguistic and national divides" and "fiction films . . . are heavily influenced by documentary film practice" (4) as "attempts to sustain the production of low-budget but still semicommercial fiction film . . . depended on public subsidy to be produced, but . . . have helped to build a small, reasonably secure local film culture" (5). He concludes, nevertheless, that "Canadian films are, to a great extent, foreign films in their own country" (6).[1]

To summarize the issue bluntly: defining "Canadian films" is a minefield. Being made in Canada does not guarantee any sociocultural reference to the country and its people. Financial incentives usually require Canadian locations and employees, rather than specifying that the film be about Canada and/or Canadians (the latter highly disputed in any case, given the country's social, cultural, ethnic, regional, linguistic, and other diversity). Nevertheless, (co-)production in Canada generally guarantees the presence of Canadian talent behind and on the screen. Monty Python alum Terry Gilliam's UK/Canadian co-production *Tideland* (2005) offers a case in point. An "Alice in Wonderland"-themed film, it was made in Saskatchewan with support from the currently defunct Saskatchewan Film Employment Tax Credit (see Gilliam n.d.; SaskFilm 2008).[2] Though the story, by American writer Mitch Cullin, makes no reference to Canada, filming in the distinctively beautiful Qu'Appelle Valley localizes the work there, if only for those who recognize the location. Canadian actors, including young Jodelle Ferland in the lead role, surround American star Jeff Bridges.

On the basis of Canadian production, we thus claim two of Nick Willing's[3] television specials, *Alice* (2009, "Alice in Wonderland") and *Tin Man* (2007, "The Wizard of Oz"), as well as Hallmark Entertainment's[4] *Snow White: The Fairest of Them All* (2001, co-production with Germany/US) and *Snow Queen* (2002, co-production with US); as well as *The Snow Queen* (2005, co-production with UK), the latter two based on the Hans Christian Andersen story. All include excellent Canadian actors among their international casts. However, on the same basis Canada must also sadly take at least partial responsibility for several features that are, at best, mixed successes. They include the Australian/Canadian co-production *Beauty and the Beast* (2009) and the US/Canadian co-productions *Mirror, Mirror* (2012, "Snow White") and *Red Riding Hood* (2011).

A Few Acres of Snow?

The latter three films in particular illustrate the problem of what makes a Canadian film, since other than the presence of snow scenes in *Beauty*, *Mirror*, and *Red*,[5] it is unlikely that anyone would associate them with the country—though the international folktale type index reports French Canadian versions of "Beauty and the Beast" and "Snow White" (Uther 2004, 252, 384). Voltaire's mid-eighteenth-century dismissal of Canada as "a few acres of snow" remains a stereotypical view. It has also perhaps consciously or unconsciously led Canadian and international filmmakers working in

Canada to represent ice and snow in their live-action fairy-tale films, to locate live-action films with "snow" in their titles in Canada, and/or to produce Christmas (generally a snowy time of year in most regions of Canada) cinema, video, and TV movies and specials in this country.[6]

Most of the latter works were created in English. French and English are Canada's official languages; English linguistically dominates outside Quebec. In 2011, French was the first official language spoken by 23.2 percent of the population, while English was the first official language spoken by 75 percent (Statistics Canada 2014).[7] French-language fairy-tale feature films offer a mixed bag, including the pastiche *Alice's Odyssey* (L'Odyssée d'Alice Tremblay 2002), the harrowing *Le Piège d'Issoudun* (The Juniper Tree 2003), both discussed below, and *Le poil de la bête* (2010, a vaguely "Red Riding Hood"-themed werewolf story, set in seventeenth-century New France). Original fairy-tale films[8] in French include *Babine* (2008) and *Ésimésac* (2012) (discussed below), both based on narratives by storyteller, writer, and actor Fred Pellerin, set in his natal village of Saint-Élie-de-Caxton, Quebec. These have English counterparts in two versions of English Quebecer Mordecai Richler's *Jacob Two-Two Meets the Hooded Fang* (1978 and 1999).[9]

Many NFB fairy-tale shorts are produced in one language; now most are also available in the other, like *Bonifacio in Summertime* (L'été de Boniface 2011). Conventional adaptations available only in English include *Little Red Riding Hood* (1969), narrated and illustrated with colorful, minimalist animation, and *The North Wind and the Sun: A Fable by Aesop* (1972). The live-action *The Bear and the Mouse* (1966) is a somewhat contrived version of the fable "The Lion and the Mouse," set in colonial times, complete with French Canadian habitant and First Nations hunter.

However, more recent NFB shorts deal with the need for intelligibility in French and English by being wordless and conveying story through music, sound effects, and visuals. The results can thus be understood regardless of language, though some knowledge of the related narratives and cultural contexts benefits comprehension. Ishu Patel's beautiful, stylized *Paradise* (1984), for example, depicts a bird living in a golden cage in a palace. It performs for the emperor, transforming in color and form including transbiologically into a flower and a partly human creature. A blackbird covets the same powers, costumes itself, and breaks into the palace, only to be captured and caged. Left outside and accidentally freed, the blackbird sees other colorful birds but no longer seeks to emulate them. Evelyn Lambart's animated *The Lion and the Mouse* (1976) offers a more generic setting than the earlier live-action version. Her *The Town Mouse and the Country Mouse* (1980) similarly uses stylized, colorful visuals, but no twists on the story.

Two other NFB wordless shorts riff more playfully on familiar fairy tales. The Oscar-nominated *The Tender Tale of Cinderella Penguin* (1981) presents the entire cast of characters as penguins, and the glass slipper as a white flipper. The parodic *Sleeping Betty* (Isabelle au bois dormant 2007) shows palace personnel (including a goat in a suit, Queen Victoria, Henry VIII, a jester, and a many-eyed monster with an elephant's trunk) observing the king and queen weeping beside their sleeping daughter's bed. The king eventually telephones a prince who looks suspiciously like England's Prince Charles, who sets out on horseback. In the meantime, the palace folk try several methods to wake the girl, unsuccessfully. The prince encounters a moose-headed dragon breathing fire; his horse boxes it into submission. A witch transforms the princess into various objects. The prince finally arrives, and he and the horse both kiss the princess but fail to waken her. Her alarm clock sounds, and she wakes up to shut it off.

As elsewhere, in Canada children's television has long offered a consistent venue for fairy-tale content (see Greenhill and Rudy 2014). Both English and French TV have presented anthology programming including fairy tales. In English, *Story Theatre*, a version of the Broadway play, "featured farcical recreations of fairy tales and fables from Aesop and the Brothers Grimm. The stories were acted out by a cast of noted actors . . . who on the show, traveled as a group, performing their stories throughout the countryside" (TVarchive.ca 2013). Filmed in British Columbia for the commercial CTV network, its 26 episodes each included between one and four tales. Like Jim Henson's anthology *The StoryTeller* (see Rudy 2014), it incorporated less well-known fairy-tale fare like "The Mouse, the Bird, and the Sausage," "Bearskin," "Clever Elsie" and "Clever Gretel" (see Bacchilega 2012), and "The Robber Bridegroom," rather than the usual suspects.

Fanfreluche (1968–1971), another anthology series, made in Quebec by Radio-Canada (French CBC) began as ten episodes in another Radio-Canada show, *The Surprise Box* (La Boîte à surprise), in which living doll Fanfreluche told stories. A further 36 episodes featured the eponymous doll, notable for physically entering the story to fix endings she disliked. The fairy tales narrated included well-known literary stories like "Pinocchio" and "Alice in Wonderland" and traditional ones like "Little Red Riding Hood" and "Hansel and Gretel," but also less well-known examples like "The Brave Little Tailor," as well as legends like "Rose Latulippe," and mash-ups like "Pinocchio chez Hansel et Gretel" (Pinocchio at Hansel and Gretel's House) (Fanfreluche [série télévisée] 2015).

Iniminimagimo, another Quebec production, had 200 15-minute live-action episodes (1987–1990), comprised mainly of international fairy tales. In the 1991 *Hungry as a Wolf* (Une faim de loup), Marie, a Little Red Riding Hood figure, and friendly wolf Simon had adventures together. *La princesse astronaute* (1993–1996), a live-action series, mixed a fairy-tale topology with voyages to outer space. Princess Noémie, of the kingdom of Dragonville, sought to understand the mystery behind her mother's death from a rain of heavy objects from the skies. She gets help from her friends, Tout-feu-tout-flamme the dragon and Vladimir, her childhood friend who wants to become a knight.

For many from Quebec (the Canadian province with the largest numerical and proportional first-language Francophone population, with 72.8 percent speaking only French at home [Statistics Canada 2014]), the series *Tales for All* (Contes pour tous) has been a significant source for fantasy and fairy-tale films, though the majority had other themes and genres. Beginning in 1971 with *The Christmas Martian* (Le martien de Noël), and continuing to 2009, producer Rock Demers's company Productions La Fête (Festival Productions, Tales for All 2009) has made over twenty films in this generally family-friendly series, in French and English. *The Peanut Butter Solution* (Opération beurre de pinottes 1985) has a boy with Rapunzel-like preternatural hair growth; *Tadpole and the Whale* (La grenouille et la baleine 1988) is about a girl who, like Andersen's Little Mermaid, has a supernatural relationship with the sea and sea creatures. Original *Contes* films set in fairy-tale worlds include *The Great Land of Small* (C'est parce qu'on est petit qu'on peut pas être grand 1987). Many *Contes* were international co-productions, like *Bye Bye Red Riding Hood* (Bye bye chaperon rouge 1989) with Hungary; and the original fairy-tale film *The Flying Sneaker* (Motýlí cas/Danger pleine lune 1990) with Czechoslovakia, in Czech.

Like the latter works, many of those fairy-tale films that Canadians would identify as speaking to their own identities and sensibilities have paradoxically transnational links (as do the fairy tales on which they are based). Such cinema includes Egyptian-born Armenian-Canadian director Egoyan's two fairy-tale films: one based on American writer Russell Banks's novel *The Sweet Hereafter*, and the other on Irish writer William Trevor's novel *Felicia's Journey* (1999, a "Bluebeard" tale). Also relevant to the experiences of Canadians, issues of language and narrative genre become salient. People who know little about Aboriginal and First Nations cultures may wrongly identify those groups' narratives as fairy tales. In fact, though some are presented primarily as entertainment, many others offer traditional wisdom about cultural knowledge from appropriate behavior to the creation of the world and the beings in it. Thus, for example, *Atanarjuat: The Fast Runner* (2001) in the Inuktitut language, based on a legend from Igloolik, Nunavut, concerns "the danger of setting personal desire above the needs of the group" (IsumaTV 2007). It lacks the wonder tale's magical elements but includes preternatural phenomena like a shamanic curse. Further, the story of *The Cave* (ʔeʔanx 2009), about a man who traverses a magical portal but finds on his return that his apparently short experience in a supernatural place has actually taken many years, may seem fantastical to European audiences, but is described as a true Tsilhqot'in (First Nation) story (*ʔeʔanx* 2013). And a film like the short *River* (2008), with giant sturgeons turning human, may remind some of Andersen's "The Little Mermaid," but alludes more to First Nations cultures.[10]

Raven Tales (2004–2010), an anthology series created for television with extensive participation by Aboriginal Canadians at all levels of production, offers a particularly compelling example of the use of First Nations culture. Primarily for children, in English (often a lingua franca for First Nation, Métis, and Inuit people), and organized around the antics of the Northwest Coast trickster Raven, its episodes focus on a variety of traditional narratives from across native North American cultures. The compelling, colorful CGI animation presents the traditional characters in styles that represent those of their cultural origins. Thus, Raven, Frog, and Eagle are rendered in Northwest Coast style, Coyote in Southwestern, and so on. The stories remain in keeping with traditional trickster stories, with extensive humor and even slapstick, but reworked and "spic[ed] up" (Ginsburg 2008, 138) to contain elements that may remind many viewers of traditional fairy-tale motifs.

Thus, in episode 7, "Child of Tears," Igis and Q'os want a child, but have failed to conceive—a familiar opening to fairy tales like "Snow White." Frog tells a weeping Igis to visit Dzunukwa. This forest witch wets mud with Igis's tears to create "Snot Boy," or Klundux. As in fairy tales, the magical boy's creator gives his mother an interdiction; should he ever call to Dzunukwa in sadness, she will take not only Klundux but all the village's children. Predictably—again as in fairy tales—the interdiction is violated. The children honor the promise, but Klundux leaves a snot trail (not unlike Hansel's trails of rocks and breadcrumbs) for the parents to follow. They find the children happily playing and learning about the forest at Dzunukwa's hut, and strike a deal with her, that the kids will visit her in the summer, but stay in the village the rest of the year. The latter type of compromise is more common in European mythology than in fairy tales (see also Hearne 2008; Kisin 2011).

Faced with numerous definitional and stylistic quandaries, seeking to cover the field initially without making judgments, we searched IMDb for works linked with their designations "fairy tale" and "Canada." Supplemented from our own knowledge and suggestions from friends and colleagues, the results included Canadian locations of production, (fictional) settings, and/or filmmakers. In collating Canadian fairy-tale film qualities, we hesitate to resort to Katherine Monk's sardonic "Canadian checklists"—for example, she describes *The Sweet Hereafter* as sharing with other films from Canada: "Internal demons; Outsider stance; Silence does all the talking; Empty landscape; Fractured narrative; Broken time; Missing people/dead children; Weird/dysfunctional sex" (2001, 339). Nevertheless, we see neorealist works and inventive animations; English, French, and language-free films; snow and ice; the road and household alike as confining spaces, and sometimes actual imprisonment; embedded storytelling (see Bacchilega 2013, 73–108); doubled roles; family drama; preternaturally mature women and immature men; and moves from urban to rural (more significant and central than vice versa) in Canadian fairy-tale films. They are also primarily stories of White-identified settler culture; primary characters of color or actors of color are exceedingly rare. To show how these characteristics manifest in very different films, we turn now to neorealist features using traditional fairy tales to explore harms (a general term which may include non-criminalized as well as criminalized behaviors—see for example Ferrell 2013) against children, and fantasies of Canada and/as other worlds.

The Highway/Road is a Dangerous Place

Children in peril are a common feature of many traditional fairy tales. Modern filmic adaptations, especially live-action, often depict young people facing a variety of serious harms, including mental and physical abuse, neglect, abandonment, murder, and even cannibalism, at the hands of the adults around them (see e.g. Zipes 2011, 193–223). Some movies explore crimes (murder, physical and sexual abuse); others criminal forms of neglect. Yet other harms fall short of criminal offences, raising difficult philosophical questions about blame, retribution, and the nature of justice itself (see for example Kohm and Greenhill 2013; Greenhill and Kohm 2013). Canadian fairy-tale crime films trouble and problematize issues around harms to children,[11] adapting fairy-tale plots, themes, and characters to provide rich cultural texts through which to explore Canadian sensibilities toward crime, harm, and justice (see Kohm, Bookman, and Greenhill, forthcoming). We examine in depth three such works: *The Sweet Hereafter*, *Le Piège d'Issoudun*, and *H & G* (2013, "Hansel and Gretel").

Hereafter reimagines Banks's 1991 novel as a Canadian tale, set in the mountainous interior of British Columbia in the aftermath of a tragic school bus accident on a snowy, icy road that kills many of the children of the town of Sam Dent. Diverging from the book, Egoyan weaves his story around a partial narration of *The Pied Piper of Hamelin* (Browning 1888, see Zipes 2011, 217–18). This addition was in part why Banks declared Egoyan's work a rare instance where the film adaptation was better than the original book (DVD commentary). The film explores the difficulty of assigning blame in the aftermath of tragedy as well as child sexual abuse. Metaphorically, it also looks at various ways fathers negotiate the sometimes fractured and dysfunctional relationships with their children (see for example Sarat 2000; LeBel 2006; Baiada 2011). Indeed, law itself becomes a patriarch(y) unable to protect its most vulnerable subjects (Sarat 2000). The film's critical acclaim and nomination for two Academy Awards make it an unusual achievement for an independent Canadian production.

Hereafter centers on the quest of lawyer Mitchell Stevens to recruit grieving parents for a class-action lawsuit against the local government or the bus manufacturer because he assumes they have deep pockets and some measure of responsibility for the tragedy. The pending lawsuit brings out the worst in some townsfolk, but most simply search for meaning in the accident's wake. A few sign on, but some refuse and attempt to dissuade the others from pursuing civil legal justice. As Stevens attempts to put together his case, the film provides glimpses into his own personal family tragedy. He, too, has lost a child; his daughter Zoe is a drug addict living on the streets of a large unnamed city. They interact throughout the film in short and often desperate telephone conversations. Their relationship, marked by anger and distrust, seems broken beyond repair. Indeed, Zoe is past saving; she has contracted HIV, and her father can do nothing but promise to send money.

His anger and helplessness seem only to fuel his vengeful drive to sue the parties he believes are responsible for the deaths of the town's children. In the end, however, Stevens fails to realize justice through the lawsuit because his star witness and the lone child survivor of the accident, Nicole Burnell, uses her deposition to achieve a measure of justice from her sexually abusive father Sam by casting blame for the accident on the bus driver and thus quashing the multi-million dollar lawsuit. As Paul A. LeBel puts it, "the effort to translate the grief of the community of Sam Dent into monetary relief for the loss of its children has been overpowered by the vengeance exacted by its most wounded survivor" (2006, 675).

Le Piège d'Issoudun (Juniper Tree), by director Micheline Lanctôt, deals with the crime of maternal filicide (see also Greenhill 2014 and forthcoming). Like *Hereafter*, it pivots around representations of child victims, but it differs from Egoyan's film in questioning the (legal) responsibility of mothers who kill while impugning the criminal justice system's response to such tragedies. While the French title plays on words—*piège* means "trap" but also "exit," and Issoudun is a Montreal suburb (much of the film takes place at the Issoudun exit of the Trans-Canada Highway)—the English title identifies it as an adaptation of the traditional fairy tale "The Juniper Tree."

Issoudun chronicles an encounter between Esther (Sylvie Drapeau),[12] a distraught mother who has just drowned her two children in their backyard swimming pool and is attempting to commit suicide by recklessly driving her car on a busy highway, and Laurier (Frédéric De Grandpré), a sympathetic Quebec Provincial Police officer, just finishing his shift and anxious to pick up his own two children from school. The main action takes place along the snowy highway and in Esther's car as the pair drive back to Montreal where Laurier discovers the horrible truth waiting there. Intercut into this action is an onstage performance of "The Juniper Tree" with the father and stepmother portrayed by De Grandpré and Drapeau. The film uses the traditional tale's narrative to explore Esther's horrific act and contemplate issues of criminal responsibility and justice.

H & G is a modern-day retelling of "Hansel and Gretel" by director Danishka Esterhazy. The film deals with "the cyclical nature of abuse and neglect" (Norris 2013, 8) and centrally concerns children who are at best victims of a neglectful single mother, or at worst in grave danger of physical harm at the hands of several adult strangers they encounter on a rural pig farm. Loving but negligent mother Krysstal seems more focused on her new romantic relationship with Garry than on the care of her two young children Harley, six, and Gemma, eight. After a night of drinking and partying, the couple argue while the children sleep in the backseat of Garry's car. Garry angrily ejects Krysstal beside a rural highway and speeds away, forgetting that the two kids are still in the car. He abandons them further down the road, leaving Gemma to care for her little brother alone in the woods. The children are taken in by a young pig farmer, Brenden, who provides food, shelter, and importantly, more attention than their irresponsible mother. Unable to reach Krysstal by phone (left in Garry's car), the two children settle into life on the farm. However, their respite is disrupted when Brenden's hard-drinking brother shows up and a loud drinking party ensues. The children become fearful of a drunk and potentially violent Brenden, and flee back to the highway where a kindly Aboriginal woman offers assistance.

While the three films otherwise differ in many respects, more than just the central issue of harm to children links them. Their use of traditional tales assists in disrupting and problematizing issues related to criminal or civil responsibility, crime, and justice. The films sometimes invert expectations by using character and role reversals to highlight important themes around these issues. For example, *H & G* "firmly establishes, prior to the children's abandonment, a role reversal" (Norris 2013, 8). In the earliest scenes, Gemma looks after her younger brother. Even before the primary caretaker role is thrust upon her in the woods, Gemma wakes up well before her mother and ensures Harley receives breakfast. Later at the farm, the girl becomes upset when Brenden bathes her brother, stating "That's my job!" Gemma, though a mere child herself, appears to be the only responsible member of the young family and acts as a voice of maturity and reason, rescuing her mother from sticky situations, and Harley and herself during the chaos on the pig farm.

In *Hereafter*, 15-year-old Nicole cares for the twin children of Billy Ansel, a respected business owner and widower. Nicole babysits while Billy goes to the bar and ultimately to a motel to engage in an affair with a married woman. Thus, Nicole, like Gemma in *H & G*, is propelled into a position of responsibility while the town's adults engage in selfish, morally questionable acts. Billy gives Nicole his dead wife's clothing, further symbolizing the girl's role reversal from child to wife/mother. Also, Egoyan shows Nicole and her father engaged in an incestuous sexual relationship prior to the accident. The interaction demonstrating this disturbing role reversal for Nicole as well as Sam is presented in a dream-like manner, suggesting a blurring of abuse and romance. According to Egoyan, this relationship confuses many viewers, who mistake their sexual intimacy for that of an older boyfriend and girlfriend: "it places the viewer in a very, very provocative place because you're not sure what it is you're seeing. The whole film has set up this relationship as being one that's quite confusing. . . . I've found, interestingly enough, that some people can watch the film and still not quite understand what is happening" (DVD Special Feature *Before and After Hereafter*). Esther and Laurier's interactions in *Issoudun* are similarly ambiguous, oscillating between police officer and detainee, confessor and lover, and mother and son. In particular, the intercut scenes from the theatrical enactment further complicate their roles, suggesting Esther as both wife and (step) mother to Laurier.

These three films are distinctly marked as *Canadian*. *H & G* contains myriad aural and visual cues establishing its setting in Winnipeg, Manitoba. Notably, Krysstal and Garry's drive to the fateful party that precipitates the children's roadside abandonment takes them through central Winnipeg, including the city's notorious skid row and prostitution stroll. A very urban sounding hip-hop song emanating from the car stereo bleats out the refrain "Winnipeg City" as the car passes the architecturally distinctive Aboriginal cultural center, Thunderbird House. Curiously, though the film presents these markers of place, it includes only one Aboriginal character—the final rescuer. The dearth of Aboriginal figures in particular may be read in the sense contemplated by cultural criminologist Nicole Rafter's comment that in crime films "what is not said is easily as important, ideologically, as what is said" (2006, 9), particularly given one filmic subtext. The pig farm setting and insinuations of violence, drinking parties, and exploited women mean that Canadian audiences often read in the context of notorious Canadian serial killer Robert (Willie) Pickton's activities on his own pig farm in Port Coquitlam, British Columbia. Most of his victims were Aboriginal women (see Cameron 2011).

The locations of the drive through Winnipeg foreshadow links to Pickton's abuse and mass murder of street-involved women from Vancouver's skid row, and Canadian missing and murdered Aboriginal women in general (see Jiwani and Young 2006). When the car stops at an intersection, the children look out the window at a teenage female street prostitute. The camera lingers long enough to suggest that this is an important detail to keep in mind. When at the film's climax the children witness Brenden violently stopping a young woman from leaving the farm, and then see something undisclosed but clearly disturbing inside a large freezer, Canadian audiences recall the horror perpetrated by Pickton, including rumors of human flesh being fed to pigs and/or ground up and mixed with pork (see Figure 18.1).

Monk notes, "The secular bent of the film, the visual importance of the snow-covered landscape and the dominance of guilt imagery make *The Sweet Hereafter* a decidedly Canadian film"

FIGURE 18.1 What does Gemma see in the freezer? *H & G* (2013).

(2001, 35). While the novel is set in the Appalachians of New York State near Lake Placid, the film uses the snowy mountains of the interior of British Columbia. In both film and novel, Sam Dent is inhabited by simple, salt-of-the-earth rural people who live in poverty even though they reside in a physically beautiful location, experienced by wealthier city dwellers as a site of outdoor recreation. As big-shot civil litigator Stevens wryly notes in the book, "most of the people who live here year round are castoffs, tossed out into the back forty and made to forage in the woods for their sustenance and shelter" (Banks 1991, 95). A number of subtle clues mark the film's location as distinctly *Canadian*:[13] the ubiquitous Beautiful British Columbia license plates; the Royal Canadian Legion insignia on the jacket of Abbott Driscoll; the embroidered Canadian flag adorning the snowsuit of Mason Ansel, one of Billy Ansel's twin children killed in the school bus accident; and the distinct Hudson's Bay Company blanket draped over the seat of Ansel's truck and later used to cover the bodies of dead children.

This last signifier of Canada links *Hereafter* with *H & G*, wherein an identical Hudson's Bay blanket is offered to the two children when they are left alone to spend the evening in Garry's car. And as with *H & G*, music adds Canadian flavor; *Hereafter* features two versions of "Courage (for Hugh MacLennan)" by the popular 1990s Canadian band The Tragically Hip, the first a mournful country arrangement sung by Nicole. So while international audiences, particularly those familiar with the American novel, may not necessarily read the film as Canadian, it is clearly marked for those in the know.

Issoudun, a product of the vibrant Québécois film culture, is unabashedly *French*-Canadian. The setting along the Trans-Canada Highway (marked as Quebec Autoroute 20 in that province) further marks it as Canadian. This busy stretch of road linking Quebec's two major cities, Montreal and Quebec, places the action at the province's heart. When Laurier pulls Esther's car over, his vehicle and uniform clearly locate him as a Quebec Provincial Police officer (Sûreté du Québec or SQ). There is no mistaking the setting as anything other than Quebec/Canada, nor is there any effort to obscure the location for international audiences.

Fairy-Tale Themes and Criminal Scenes

Egoyan's linking "The Pied Piper of Hamelin" to his film makes significant allusions to harms to children. Browning's poem concerns townspeople who enter into an agreement with a mysterious stranger, promising him a significant sum to drive away the rats which plague their community. The Piper does so, spiriting the animals away with his magical pipes, but the town reneges on the agreement. Angry and wanting to punish Hamelin for breaking its promise, the Piper plays the same instrument to lead all the children, save one disabled boy who cannot keep up, out of town and into the side of a mountain. The remaining child sadly reflects on the loss of his friends who he believes have been led to a "joyous land." However, it seems more likely that these children have met with a more tragic fate.

The film uses Nicole's interactions with Billy Ansel's children before the accident to insert her partial narration of *The Pied Piper of Hamelin* in a way that provides some clarity to the film's moral message.[14] The telling foreshadows the loss of nearly all the town's children, but more importantly, it suggests a motive for the vengeance that Nicole will ultimately visit upon her father. Mason asks Nicole why the Piper took all the children away when he could have presumably used his magic powers to simply make the townspeople pay. Nicole responds thoughtfully: "Because he wanted them to be punished." Mason counters: "Was he mean?" Nicole replies: "No, not mean. Just very, very angry." For Melanie Boyd, this idea amounts to the Piper's "ethics of vengeance" (2007, 283), justifying Nicole's actions that punish her father and derail the lawsuit at the film's end. Tellingly, as in *H & G*, the central girls have grown up well before reaching adulthood, and most of the male adults have not grown up at all.

The Pied Piper narrative brings the theme of lost children and childhood. Nicole is clearly one such child, robbed of her childhood and innocence by her father's actions. Zoe is another child, lost in a world of drug addiction and death while her father channels his sadness into the rage he directs in the lawsuit. Of course, all the young victims of the bus accident are lost too, their fate paralleling that of the children of Hamelin, swallowed up by the mountainside both literally and figuratively, when their school bus plunges into the icy waters of the flooded sandpit.

The film also suggests a number of potential Pied Piper figures. Just as Hamelin's Piper leads the children into the mountain, bus driver Delores Driscoll describes the morning of the accident as if she was "clearing the hillside of its children" like they were "berries waiting to be plucked." Of course, Delores is an unwitting Piper figure. The town owes her no unpaid debt, and she harbors no anger toward her neighbors. Thus, other characters may offer more suitable Pipers, like Stevens who gleefully attempts to gather up all the parents in the hope that he will reap large profits from this work. And like the Pied Piper, Stevens is denied his payday in the end. However, for many scholars who have analyzed the film, Sam Burnell most closely resembles the Pied Piper (Boyd 2007; Dillon 2003; Landwehr 2008; Secchi 2011). Though he also offers a counterpart to the greedy Hamelin mayor and council who cause suffering with their mindless quest for profit, and while Sam enchants only one child—his own—toward a sinister fate of sexual abuse, his visual representation deliberately coincides with Nicole's repeated narration of the tale to make perfectly clear Egoyan's intentional linking of the abusive father to its eponymous figure. However, while Nicole mirrors the child left behind in the traditional tale and her father, the Piper, at the film's end, she becomes Piper as she exacts vengeance for her loss.

H & G uses aspects of the plot and imagery of "Hansel and Gretel" to drive the story of neglected and imperiled children. Director Esterhazy deliberately diverged from the best-known versions of this tale in that she sought to create more sympathetic female characters to counter its evil stepmother and witch. Krysstal is described in the script as "early 20's, pretty, an exhausted young mother" (Norris 2013, 8). The film indeed complicates the sympathetic father and evil stepmother, instead constructing more complex parental figures in the neglectful but loving single mother and the sometimes nice but sometimes mean boyfriend. Gone is the concerted plan to abandon the children. Also gone is the old witch, replaced by the mostly kind young male farmer Brenden, who provides the kids with food and shelter.

Harley appears preoccupied with food and eating throughout the film. The first morning alone in the woods, the boy is delighted to learn that berries can be had in abundance for free. Gemma, on the other hand, seems more concerned that Harley be fed than with her own needs. She prepares his breakfast in the first scenes. She tells Brenden that Harley is hungry the second day on the farm. Also, Gemma attempts to regulate her brother's consumption by urging him to eat his bread crusts and discourages further eating when he complains of hunger in the evening. There is no apparent plan to fatten up Harley for literal consumption by a witch figure. Instead, Gemma discovers clues that lead the audience to believe Brenden's (or perhaps his brother Willie's) appetite might be pedophilic rather than cannibalistic. Nevertheless, the links the film draws to the Pickton murders could be read as implying the latter possibility. Could human remains be stored in the freezer for consumption? What sort of bones does Harley discover in a bucket near the freezer? Why is there a pile of expended shotgun shell casings near the shed? While many aspects of the film are shrouded in ambiguity, the theme of hunger ties the adaptation firmly to the traditional tale, including the children's longing for love, protection, and understanding.

Issoudun differs significantly from the other two films in its literal double engagement with a fairy tale. Rather than simply embedding characters (often instantiating multiple fairy-tale roles), plots, and themes of "The Juniper Tree" in a resituated adaptation to modern context, the film juxtaposes a staged theatrical enactment alongside a modern tale addressing parallel themes and characters. As noted above, through use of the same actors in the theatrical performance and modern-day story taking place along the Trans-Canada highway, the film blurs the characters and repositions them with respect to each other. Police officer Laurier (whose name denotes a tree, linking to the fairy tale's juniper) is in turns positioned as a father figure to Esther—such as when he scolds her for acting up ("You're worse than a kid. I can't leave you alone for one second without you messing up! Get a hold of yourself, miss. You're a big girl now!"); a lover or spouse—as he and Esther kiss and she pulls at his clothing; and as a son (or stepson)—reinforced by the film's climax when he chokes her to death, linking to the fairy-tale resolution when the bird (reincarnated stepson) drops a millstone on the murderous stepmother's head.

Throughout the scenes between Esther and Laurier, the sounds and images of birds and trees link to the traditional tale and suggest how the present-day story of a maternal filicide intersects with its plots, themes, and imagery. One scene in particular illuminates Esther's crime and links to "The Juniper Tree." While stopped at a roadside rest area, Esther tries to explain the source of her malaise: "I was a happy child . . . I was a gifted child, with a brilliant future, thought I could do anything." She describes "having it all"—a great career, a husband, and children. Happiness to Esther, however, was "heavy," and becoming a mother compounded her fragile mental state: "As soon as I started having children, I stopped living. I started to be afraid that something would happen to them. Understand?" Linking to the fairy tale, this scene's images of crows picking at a garbage can symbolize Esther's guilt. Like the bird in "The Juniper Tree," the crows recall Esther's terrible deeds.

As an explanation for why women kill their children, Esther's commentary on the heaviness of happiness appears to many viewers unsatisfactory (see Greenhill 2014). Further, it fails to reproduce the dominant explanations of crime found in most mainstream Hollywood films about women who kill. Instead of locating obvious mental illness, bad biology, greed, or adverse environments (see for example Rafter 2006, 61–85), the film forces its audience to confront the possibility that women may kill sometimes because they cannot cope with conventionally defined success including motherhood itself, and with the stresses and pressures of everyday life. So while Esther lives in an affluent suburb in a large home with a swimming pool, and has a husband and a professional career, she is still driven to murder by anxiety, including her fears for her children themselves (see Figure 18.2).

FIGURE 18.2 Esther's vision of her children's bodies on her car windshield, *Juniper Tree*/Le Piège d'Issoudun (2003).

These three Canadian films, centrally concerned with the problematic of justice, all tend to reach rather similar ambivalent conclusions. In *Hereafter*, the lawsuit fails as a mechanism to produce justice for any of the lost children. The only measure of justice achieved for one lost child comes specifically because the lawsuit is undermined by perjured testimony. In *H & G*, the children face peril not only at the hands of a possible pedophile and murderer on a rural pig farm, but also from neglect by a young though well-meaning mother wholly unprepared for the responsibility of parenthood. So while the children care for themselves through their ordeal in the woods, the film reaches an ambivalent conclusion when Gemma is finally able to ask an adult stranger for help. Perhaps this development might signal a change to their circumstances as children in peril, or perhaps it may only lead to a new fraught chapter in their young lives. It is unclear that these children will find safety in the care of any adults. Finally, *Issoudun* offers the unsettling conclusion that crime may not be readily explicable by the conventional theories of mainstream criminology. The sources of the traditional tale provide popular cultural points of reference with which to grapple with these issues. In addition, the films offer a uniquely Canadian perspective on children in peril, one that goes beyond the boundaries of mainstream Hollywood cinema.

Fantasy Worlds; Canada is no Fantasy

The latter three films instantiate characteristics of Canadian fairy-tale films enumerated above: the claustrophobic road, car, and household; storytelling (in *Issoudun*'s case, story theater); family drama including preternaturally mature girls and/or men who have failed to grow up; urban to rural focus shift; snow or ice (in *H & G*, the pivotal freezer); doubled roles; and Euro North American White predominance. But these qualities also pervade films about otherworldly places that are simultaneously here and not-here, Canada and not-Canada.

Willing's TV specials, *Alice* and *Tin Man*, implicate fairy tales' serious side especially as explorations of flaws, even rifts, within families. The title character in *Alice* has been forced to grow up because of her father's mysterious disappearance.[15] Though she contemplates committing to a relationship with Jack, he is kidnapped by a mysterious figure. Alice seeks Jack, falling through a looking glass into a dystopian magical realist world of sometimes literally compressing spaces, but also sudden drop-offs. Various characters recognize her name. One asks if she is "The Alice? The Alice of legend?" and implications of the embedded story abound, including a wealth of clever allusions and quotations, and a shot of an *Alice's Adventures in Wonderland* book near the film's end. Alice meets several boy-men, including her eventual co-rescuer/rescuee Hatter (though other/worldly wise, the character is played by the decidedly boyish-looking Andrew Lee Potts). Her quest takes her to meet characters from the Lewis Carroll stories, beginning in urban landscapes but moving into snow-covered mountains and woods. She is sometimes literally confined and imprisoned. Ultimately, Alice's father, implicated in Wonderland's evil, dies taking a bullet meant for her, but she rescues Jack, Hatter, and the other prisoners. Actors of color play only very minor roles.

The earlier *Tin Man* (see Zipes 2011, 292–94), though an American production, was filmed in British Columbia and features a significant number of Canadian actors. Like *Alice*, it offers a young woman (named DG) who seeks her family, including an absent father, through a magical dystopia, the O[outer] Z[one], which she accesses via tornado. Her helpers Glitch, Wyatt Cain, and Raw, like their counterparts the Scarecrow, Tin Man, and Cowardly Lion, have deficits of brain, heart, and courage, and DG helps them all gain what they have lost. She ultimately seeks and rescues two women: her sister Azkadellia whose body and mind have been possessed by an evil witch, and her imprisoned mother. Releasing her father Adamo turns out to be a less crucial act. Though DG's story begins, as might be expected, on a farm and in a rural village, the O.Z. is primarily rural and Azkadellia's castle more steampunk than modern. The idyllic surroundings of the palace in which DG and Azkadellia grew up has been transformed into the barren, snow-covered Ice Mountain.

The narrative has many twists and turns, including DG's imprisonment, but eventually reveals that Azkadellia's possession is DG's fault, making it her responsibility to deliver her sister and the O.Z. The sole major characters portrayed by actors of color are transbiological: the sometimes-human, sometimes-dog Toto and the lion-like Raw.[16]

Both specials offer family dramas. DG needs to repair her relationships with her sister and mother; romantic partnership is not her goal in *Tin Man*. In *Alice*, the heterosexual payoff in the doubled role of Hatter and a rescuing construction worker comes after their friendship. Alice and Hatter have been partners and equals, and the implication is that they will remain so as lovers. Relationships take another direction in Denise Filiatrault's farcical musical *Alice's Odyssey*. It features a stable of actors well known in French Canada, including Filiatrault's daughter Sophie Lorain as Alice, comedian and soap opera star Marc Labrèche as the Wolf, pop singer Mitsou as Little Red Riding Hood (and a daycare teacher), and Martin Drainville as Prince Ludovic. Loosely structured as an Alice in Wonderland/Cinderella story, its characters also include the Fairy Godmother (Pierrette Robitaille), Aurora (Myriam Poirier), Snow White, Scheherazade, and Santa Claus—all White-identified.

Having turned down her friend Audrey's (Poirier) offer of a blind date because she has a crush on her foreman (Marc Béland), single mother Alice is sarcastic about infomercials as "tales" (lies), yet becomes dewy-eyed about sentimental pop songs. After reading her daughter fairy tales at bedtime, she crosses a magic portal from her urban Montreal townhouse to a very rural field and woods. Clad in her pink cloud pajamas and rabbit slippers, Alice searches for the way home. In a house in the woods, Granny and the Wolf watch an infomercial about how to cook humans with maple syrup—the first of many parodies of that TV genre. Red Riding Hood resists Alice's attempts to save her from the Wolf, with all the sexualized connotations of consumption played up. A habitant arrives, singing the traditional song "Les Raftmen" (rendered in English subtitles as Monty Python's "I'm a Lumberjack") to rescue Red. Alice meets Ludovic, a Prince Charming in training. Witch Carabosse (Robitaille) knows Alice can find the escape route from the magical land. Looking for the map that will lead her out, Alice encounters womanizer Prince William (Béland). Ludovic saves Alice from William's attempted rape. After an interlude with the "well-adjusted" Snow White, who has left her Prince and is in a consensual polyamorous relationship with the seven dwarfs, an inexplicable, narratively unmotivated basketball game between the dwarfs and a team of tall Black men intervenes; only the White-identified dwarves score.

Ludovic and Alice arrive on the boundary of Winter (with snow, ice, and Santa Claus), near the desert where Scheherazade offers to "unveil . . . the pleasures of the Orient" for the "gorgeous Snowman" Santa. Ludovic and Alice arrive at Aurora's castle where she is mistaken for a fool, and there's some homophobic shtick between Ludovic and a baker. Carabosse takes Alice prisoner, and threatens her with the terrible fate of being an infomercial product demonstrator. Ludovic arrives with the Fairy Godmother and seven dwarfs, who rescue Alice. Crossing a bridge, Alice loses one of her bunny slippers. They reach the portal, but Carabosse zaps Alice. Ludovic kisses her; she awakens and he transforms into a handsome prince in white and gold clothing. He kisses the witch who turns into a frog. Alice expresses regret at leaving Ludovic behind, then awakes in her daughter's bed. The doorbell rings. It's Louis (Drainville), Alice's blind date. He brings the missing bunny slipper which he places on Alice's foot. She kisses him; he kisses her back.

As in *Issoudun*, *Alice's Odyssey* conveys its fairy-tale and real-life plots by literal role doubling of significant characters. Their characters overlap and extend their real-life personas, particularly Prince William, who is even more of a jerk and poser than Alice's supervisor. That Alice's landlady is also Carabosse *and* the Fairy Godmother may suggest Filiatrault's ambivalence about older women. Overall she offers a Second Wave feminist parable about the need for women to be powerful, in control, even the aggressor in their relationships with men, but a heterosexual partnering is offered as the ideal, confirmed by the saccharine (English!) song that Alice listens to (sung by a woman) early in the film, also the first song of the credits (sung by a man).

Babine and *Ésimésac* are magic realist fantasies, filmed in moody sepia colors, and named for their extraordinary male main characters. Babine (Vincent-Guillaume Otis) is the Witch's son and village idiot in Saint-Élie-de-Caxton. His mother sends him to collect icicles, when the church catches fire, killing the old priest, Father Time. The new priest dislikes Babine, accusing him of responsibility for the fire, imprisoning him, coercing him into confessing, and sentencing him to hang. Babine's friend Toussaint Brodeur (Luc Picard)[17] sabotages the rope, freeing the boy. The priest again accuses and sentences Babine to death, but Toussaint helps him escape. Babine follows a circus that features a beautiful dark-haired woman and a giant bull. He obtains what he thinks is a lock of the woman's hair, and returns home to use his mother's spell book to try to summon her. But the hair comes from the bull, which arrives instead. It rampages through Saint-Élie-de-Caxton, terrifying the priest who runs away. Babine plays a song that makes the sun set and the bull magically leaps into the sun. Babine is again sentenced to die, but Toussaint lets him select the manner and he chooses "death by time." The scene moves to the present day, where Babine is buried just before his 276th birthday. The actors from the fantasy are the mourners, in contemporary clothing—including Otis.

Ésimésac Gélinas, whose mother carried him for a preternaturally long time, though only two years old, looks like an adult and is magically strong, but lacks a shadow. The setting for *Ésimésac* is later than *Babine*'s; hard times have fallen on Saint-Élie-de-Caxton. The Gélinas family subsists on hot water, stale bread, and salt. Only the blacksmith Riopel has money, making bomb casings. His daughter Anna Domini, with Ésimésac and his sister Marie, rally the village to plant a community vegetable garden. But their attention is diverted when Riopel bargains with the railroader to supply cheap rails, to bring the station and thus prosperity to Saint-Élie-de-Caxton. Ésimésac gets a shadow from the Witch; it retrieves a missing petal for Anna Domini, who has been keeping the village awake weeping for her lost love. In return, Ésimésac persuades the villagers to work for the railway without payment until the station comes. Marie falls ill. Ésimésac learns what Riopel has known for some time; the station will go to the town of Charette instead. In winter, famine becomes desperate; eventually the village unites at Christmas mass. Ésimésac takes the dying Marie to the tracks, and the village, with Marie transformed into an angel with wings, collectively halts the train. With Ésimésac, they turn the train on its side and remove the food.

Ésimésac pivots around two young but unusually mature female characters—Anna and Marie. Both it and *Babine* have abnormally young or immature males (Babine is intellectually challenged; though Ésimésac appears to be around twenty, he is actually only two). All characters are White-identified Quebecois. The narratives extensively employ quotations from traditional songs and sayings, sometimes parodied to fit the circumstances. Saint-Élie-de-Caxton's isolation and confined space is an advantage; even the *possibility* of a railway station brings selfishness and capitalist mentality. The greatest dangers, like the bull, come from outside, brought unwittingly by characters serving their self-interest. These films offer parables about relationships with greater powers (the English language and the rest of Canada as bull/ies, duplicitous railroaders). Yet the community does not just survive, it flourishes through their collective strength and wisdom. Like in *Alice* and *Tin Man*, family (and its extension in community) in *Ésimésac* needs mature men transformed and rescued by younger women; in contrast, Babine, who cannot grow up, by implication keeps Saint-Élie-de-Caxton unsullied.

Canadian Fairy-Tale Films

In seeking to recognize Canadian fairy-tale films, we have identified common themes and areas of interest. Despite the difficulty of clearly defining Canadian film, our inclusion of movies set in Canada as well as those filmed in Canada both by foreign and domestic filmmakers has led to some telling conclusions. Apparently disparate qualities include neorealist style and content; snowy and icy visual representations; figurative and literal confinement on the road or in the household; characters' multiplied and/or shifting roles; preternaturally mature young women and immature adult men; narratives that move from urban to rural settings; and a preponderance of White settler characters and a general invisibility of Indigenous or racialized minority figures. We located these signifiers of Canadian fairy-tale films when closely examining otherwise very disparate works: those that centrally focus on harms to children and those that take place in otherworldly fantasy settings. Whether a neorealist fairy-tale adaptation set in modern (sub)urban Montreal or a tale of pure fantasy set in the O.Z., Canadian fairy-tale films share aesthetic, cultural, and artistic features that mark them as unique cinematic works reflecting national sensibilities about key socio-political, cultural, and natural aspects of Canada. While no doubt international audiences read these films differently, Canadians may identify with many of the subtle features we note above. Thus, the adaptation of fairy-tale plots, themes, and characters in these works can reinforce, disrupt, or potentially reimagine the cultural image of Canada and what it means to be Canadian.

Notes

1 Further exploration of this paradox is beyond the scope of the present work, but for more information see Beard and White (2002), Clandfield (1987), Leach (2006), Melnyk (2004), Monk (2001), Morris (1978), Pendakur (1990), Pike (2012), Spencer and Ayscough (2003), and White (2006).

2 In addition to the many feature films co-produced in Canada, successful children's TV co-productions with fairy-tale themes and/or episodes include: with US participation, Muppet-creator Jim Henson's *Hey Cinderella!* (1969); as well as *Cyberchase* (2002–), *Dora the Explorer* (2000–), and *Super Why!* (2007–2012; see Brodie and McDavid 2014); with France, *Léa et Gaspard/Zoe & Charlie* (1994–); and with the Netherlands, Germany, and Italy, *Mia and Me* (2011–2012).

3 English director, writer, and producer Willing has created a number of features, television films, and mini-series based on literary fairy tales and aspects of traditional culture.

4 This generally family-oriented American television production company's films and specials often use traditional international fairy tales, literary fairy tales, and fantasy/wonder themes.

5 Ironically, the difficulties of filming in winter and on real snow mean that cinematic snow scenes often feature fake snow or are created using visual effects.

6 Christmas television productions include *Alice* (December 6–7, 2009); *Care Bears Nutcracker Suite* (drawing on the Pyotr Ilyich Tchaikovsky Christmas fairy-tale ballet, December 10, 1988); *I Was A Rat* (based on Philip Pullman's children's novel, with a "Cinderella" sub-plot, November 1, 2001); *Jacob Two-Two Meets the Hooded Fang* (based on Canadian writer Mordecai Richler's novel of the same name, December 1978); *Little Claus & Big Claus* (based on the Andersen story, December 26, 2005); *Rumpelstiltskin* (December 14, 1985); *Snow Queen* (December 8, 2002); *The Snow Queen* (December 24, 2005); *Tin Man* (December 2–4, 2007); and *The Trial of Red Riding Hood* (December 1992); as well as numerous National Ballet of Canada and Canadian Broadcasting Company (CBC) specials (Haase 2000, 516).

7 The balance of 1.8 percent comprises those who could not conduct a conversation in either English or French.

8 We use the term "original fairy-tale film" to refer to cinema that has no direct counterpart in traditional or well-known literary fairy tales.

9 *The Marsh* (2006), *Deeply* (2000), and the American-Canadian co-production *Nervosa* (2005) all deal with authors of children's books.

10 Legend-themed works are not exclusively about First Nations: see for example the Canadian-German co-productions *Deeply*, primarily filmed in Nova Scotia, and *The Marsh*.

11 In addition to the three detailed here, Canadian fairy-tale and folklore films dealing with crimes include: *Atanarjuat*, *Beauty and the Beast*, *Felicia's Journey*, *The Marsh* (supernatural legend), *Le poil de la bête*, *River*, and *The Trial of Red Riding Hood*. Harms to young people are found in *Babine*, *Deeply*, *Ésimésac*, *Jacob Two-Two Meets the Hooded Fang*, *Jacob Two Two Meets the Hooded Fang*, *The Old Woman in the Woods*, *The Snow Queen* (Esterhazy), and *Tideland*.

12 Here and henceforth, we give the actors' names when they are relevant, specifically in role-doubling.

13 Nevertheless, changes to obscure the Canadian setting may have been deliberate attempts to facilitate marketing in the United States (see Gray 2010, 65–70). For example, the bus's speed is expressed in miles rather than kilometers per hour (LeBel 2006, 676) and the more American-sounding "National Weather Bureau" is used instead of "Environment Canada" during the deposition.

14 The embedded narrations in *H & G* are much more rudimentary and fragmented, including Harley's and Gemma's play where the boy dramatizes "The monster ate the princess."

15 In *Tideland*, the young Alice character even prepares needles for her addict father.

16 In contrast, the made-in-Toronto *Beauty and the Beast* (2012–) television show's extensively multiracial, multiethnic cast demonstrates the profoundly unnecessary Whiteness of most North American fairy-tale adaptations.

17 In a further role multiplication, Picard is also the two films' director.

19

THE FAIRY-TALE FILM IN LATIN AMERICA

Laura Hubner

Any investigation of the fairy-tale film in Latin America inevitably entails confronting the dynamic relationship between the fairy tale as a rich, shape-shifting form and the multiple layers, distinctive inputs, and influences of Latin American cinema itself. While Latin American film-making is clearly amorphous and diverse, the political manifestos of the 1960s, calling for a "truth" in filmmaking that aimed to move away from colonial myth-making in relation to representation, narrative structures, and processes of storytelling, have had a lasting influence, resonating with many Latin American filmmakers today. Because of this stimulus, this chapter mainly explores the fairy tale's function in contemporary Latin American cinema. A key interest is how representations of the historically specific, such as the communities of impoverished Colombian young people living on the streets or enduring harsh working conditions, in films such as *The Rose Seller* (La vendedora de rosas, dir. Víctor Gaviria, 1998) and *Maria Full of Grace* (María, llena eres de gracia, dir. Joshua Marston, 2004), adapt fairy-tale forms and motifs to inject more perennial or universal themes and values.

Fairy tales are fantastical forms that emerge and evolve at specific points of history to confront allegorically territories that are difficult or dangerous to address head-on or have been made invisible or taboo, such as abuse within the home, or rivalries and conflicts across boundaries. Bearing this in mind, I examine the extent to which these stories' meanings and structures are regenerated or subverted in specific films, and also consider the complexities and tensions already thriving within the fairy tale. The fairy tale in this context helps to bring a universal appeal or understanding, but also more complex effects, in the sense that the conscious application of familiarity these stories generate can help to reflect back on the devastating reality or historical situation, where there is limited (hope for) change. This intricacy relates to another key focus of this chapter—the interrelation between fantasy and reality in the films explored, both in the way that "realist" representations are interjected momentarily with fantastical visions, and how fantastical and real worlds are heavily interwoven, for example in *Pan's Labyrinth* (El laberinto del fauno 2006) by Mexican director Guillermo del Toro. Drawing on thematic structures in the latter work, the chapter concludes by exploring the current trend of emphasising—particularly in the face of ongoing adversity or entropy—the importance of the internal journey or return, linked allegorically to a national return, to a lost or forgotten identity, in films as diverse as the short *The Saci* (O Saci 2009) from the recent Brazilian animation series "I swear I saw it" and the feature *La jaula de oro* (The Golden Dream, dir. Diego Quemada-Díez, 2013).

The importance of asserting a distinctive voice in Latin American filmmaking might be traced back in part to the need to redress the early predominance of external imports and influences from Europe and the United States. The first films exhibited in Latin America were those of the Lumière brothers in Rio de Janeiro, Montevideo, and Buenos Aires in July 1896, followed by their screenings in Mexico City, Guatemala, Maracaibo, and Lima. As Roy Armes argues, while these displays were celebrated as a badge of progress, "film was essentially just one more product marketed to European-oriented consumers for the greater profit of European manufacturers" (1987, 165).[1] Local film production included a brief "golden age" in Brazil before 1911, creating largely documentaries, though often from the viewpoint of the aristocracy, and thus clearly distinct from Brazil's later anti-colonial drive for a new cinema, or *cinema novo*, in the 1960s.[2] While a great number of documentaries and newsreels were also filmed during the early years of the Mexican Revolution (1910–1913), the continuing presence of locally produced melodramas, and the opportunity for local productions and their wider distribution were radically reduced when Latin America became part of Hollywood's expansive hold on the international marketplace, coinciding with World War I. With the coming of sound, Hollywood continued to dominate by adapting cinema theaters to receive the new technology. Although there were distinctive local productions, popularized (particularly in Brazil, Argentina, and Mexico) with the proliferation of *chanchadas* or musical comedies, tango films, and the *comedias rancheras* (a genre exported from Mexico to other Latin American countries), these generally did not manage to attract international distribution.

In the radical manifestos of the 1960s, Latin American filmmakers and theoreticians called for a new cinema: "Theirs would be a lucid, critical realist, popular, anti-imperialist, revolutionary cinema which would break with neo-colonialist attitudes and the monopolistic practices of North American companies. No aesthetic formulae were laid down: flexibility would be needed to adapt to different social situations" (King 1990, 66). While aiming to unite Latin American dreams, the manifestos also sought to break down barriers and boundaries, mostly upholding "Pan-American," international aspirations that might be seen as part of the endeavor to challenge colonial myth-building of a North and South divide. Aesthetics and style went hand-in-hand with politics and ideology; the move towards de-colonialization led to a rejection of Hollywood strategies of conventional editing, staged studio sets, and professional acting techniques. The established genres of locally produced cinema also came under attack from some spheres, as perhaps pandering to popular interests in the wrong sense, for example the Brazilian *chanchada* (even if only partially based on the Hollywood musical) was "memorably dismissed by [Brazilian director] Glauber Rocha" (Hart 2004, 8). While flexibility was a key element, much of the new cinema aimed to combine low budgets with a freedom of expression, capturing the everyday, on the streets and *favelas*. The early years of New Latin American Cinema were stimulated by a belief in post-World War II Italian neorealism in particular, while the French New Wave and British documentary school also proved inspirational. However, as B. Ruby Rich has insightfully summarized, "A cinema of necessity, it was different things in different countries: in Cuba, an 'imperfect cinema'; in Brazil, an 'aesthetics of hunger'; in Argentina, a 'third cinema'" (1997, 277).

Within this radically diverse film history, and bearing in mind the limited availability of much locally produced early cinema, fairy-tale film appearances are rare, but not impossible to find. On the one hand, classical fairy-tale elements are unexpectedly evident amidst the intricate plotlines of the locally produced melodramas of the 1930s and 1940s. For example, there are strong undercurrents of "Cinderella," "Little Red Riding Hood," "Rapunzel," and "Snow White" in *Enchanting Kisses* (Besos Brujos, dir. José Agustín Ferreyra, Argentina, 1937), where the working-class heroine singer, Marga Lucena, is kidnapped halfway through the film by jealous landowner Don Sebastián and entrapped in a cottage in the middle of a forest, then rescued by her prince-like aristocrat Alberto. Through her own initiative (as is so often the case in folktale and oral fairy-tale traditions), she manages to fool her entrapper, thus bringing about her own rescue in a romantic reunion with Alberto. On the other hand, *Modern Bluebeard* (El moderno Barba Azul, dir. Jaime Salvador, 1946), which might sound like safe territory as a straightforward fairy-tale adaptation, is a science fiction comedy, starring Buster Keaton, bearing scarcely a resemblance to Charles Perrault's 1697 "Bluebeard." Also known as *Boom in the Moon*, it centers on an American soldier (Keaton) escaping from an airplane crash over the Pacific Ocean, and being mistaken for the serial killer called Bluebeard when he washes ashore in a Mexican fishing village, thinking he is in Japan. The amusement revolves around multiple forms of mistaken identity and comedy scenes such as Keaton trying Mexican food.

Diversity and experimentation were common during the 1960s, as evident in the distinctive Latin American flair in Roberto Rodríguez's live-action Mexican films *Little Red Riding Hood* (La Caperucita Roja 1960), *Little Red Riding Hood and her Friends* (Caperucita y sus Tres Amigos 1961), and *Little Red Riding Hood and Tom Thumb against the Monsters* (Caperucita y Pulgarcito contra los Monstruos 1962). The films depict the young heroine saving the wolf and demonstrating that good Christian charity can conquer evil and rescue the community. As Jack Zipes observes, while these films continue a "'homey' and conservative tendency" evident in many postwar European film adaptations of the tale, they nevertheless "represent unique experiments in recreating a classical European tale for Mexican children with a focus on community" (2011, 145). In the films' emphasis upon Red Riding Hood's endeavor to forgive and to show good faith in making the wolf a valuable citizen, the focus moves away (refreshingly) from the moral quandary of the female straying from the path. Furthermore, their Gothic horror array of miscellaneous monsters, including skeletons, a vampire, a man-eating plant, a robot, and an ogre, give the films an idiosyncratic edge.

Within the context of Brazil's *cinema novo*, *Black God, White Devil* (Deus e o Diabo na Terra do Sol, dir. Glauber Rocha, 1963) explores and destabilizes deep-seated folkloric traditions in its representation of the exiled outcast cowboy, Manuel, who undergoes three rites of passage. His individual rebellion challenges classical Hollywood westerns by providing a political motivation (rather than natural etiology) for violence—having been demeaned and tricked by the powerful landowner. As Ivana Bentes argues, by creating a story about transformation for Latin America as a whole, Rocha "tries to construct a new national mythology 'on the margins of a nation' and invent a 'people', calling attention to the different forms of identity and belonging created by mystic experience, by communities, gangs and groups formed by the disinherited and outcasts of a nation" (2003, 96–97). In this sense, the folkloric capacities of cinema as myth-maker are explored, with violence foregrounded as an indication of change, as Rocha would outline in his "An Aesthetic of Hunger" manifesto in 1965: "Only when confronted with violence does the colonizer understand, through horror, the strength of the culture he exploits" (1997, 60).

The publication in Chile in 1971 of *Para Leer al Pato Donald* (*How to Read Donald Duck*), written by Ariel Dorfman and Armand Mattelart (translated into English 1975, updated 1991), also played a key role in confronting the need to dismantle capitalist traditions.[3] The book scrutinizes the Walt Disney comic books featuring Donald Duck, together with Scrooge McDuck's global searches for treasure, and can be seen as part of a broader political critique of the Disney myth, an attempt to de-naturalize US corporate exploitation of Latin American countries:

> When something is *said* about the child/noble savage, it is really the Third World one is *thinking* about. The hegemony which we have detected between the child-adults who arrive with their civilization and technology, and the child-noble savages who accept this alien territory and surrender their riches, stands revealed as an exact replica of the relations between metropolis and satellite, between empire and colony, between master and slave.
>
> (Dorfman and Mattelart 1991, 48–49)

Thus, the book's central concern is unmasking fairy tales or myths masquerading as accepted truths.

Despite her caution about forcing links between the vast assortment that encompasses the generalizing term "Latin American cinema," Deborah Shaw traces important political connections between them: "Many films released from the end of the 1990s to the present have managed to retain a social conscience, so characteristic of New Latin American cinema of the 1960s and 1970s" (2007, 4). When cinema and fairy tale come together, the latter can sometimes become like a magical agent, providing anchorage and a stable frame or structure, bringing either vibrancy or fatality to the film by stretching the specific to the universal in complex, paradoxical ways. While this ambiguity is relevant to all films that adapt or draw on fairy-tale narratives, motifs, or themes, what is particularly intriguing is the way the collectivist or "realist" modes of expression, evident in some Latin American filmmaking, synchronize or collide with fairy-tale elements; we see the two not only pulling against each other but also creating a lively dialectic where new meanings are formed. This uniqueness helps to reflect back on the fairy tale's structural frameworks more universally and on broader thematic and ideological concerns as fairy tales shift within different contexts.

The Rose Seller (La vendedora de rosas, Colombia, 1998) highlights the latter functions, but also opens up much broader questions concerning the rich and complex political or social responsibilities of cinema and fairy tales. With a realist rigor that is ardently political, *The Rose Seller* follows, over a period from Christmas Eve through to Christmas Day morning, the interwoven lives of young people living on the streets of Colombia's second city, Medellín, a place that has undergone extreme social and economic change since the 1980s. Gaviria's "authentic" methodology of filming on location, and employing only non-professional actors direct from the streets of Medellín to convey the characters' plights and experiences, and encouraging them to develop the script throughout the filming stages, is a crucial aspect of *The Rose Seller*'s identity. However, it also reworks Hans Christian Andersen's "The Little Match Girl." Afraid to go home on New Year's Eve, to face a beating from her father for not selling any matches all day, Andersen's little match girl dies on the streets, frozen and alone. Projecting the full white blaze of matches on the wall of a house, she joins the vision of her deceased grandmother and ascends to heaven with her. The girl's body is discovered the next morning, no one knowing "what lovely things she had seen, and how gloriously she had flown with her grandmother into her own New Year" (Andersen 1986, 64). It is fascinating how *The Rose Seller* incorporates Andersen's story of individual pain and magical faith or transcendence into a film so strongly associated with the concept of realism and a collectivism of storytelling rooted in specific political and ethical concerns that stem from the manifestos of Latin America's *novo cinema*.

The Rose Seller portrays young girls (children and teenagers) selling roses to survive on the streets. The context of the trilogy is the violent restructuring created by the expanding cocaine trade, as Geoffrey Kantaris observes:

> The rise of a drugs mafia almost overnight pulled the city, together with its large marginalised population of migrant refugees from political violence in the countryside, into the swirling vortex of a globalized trade capable of destabilizing all of the basic social structures of the nation from street level all the way to the upper echelons of power.
>
> (2010, 35)[4]

Poverty and chaos fuel the young rose sellers' lives, and sounds echoing those of their glue sniffing frame the film score. The young lives revolve around trade and survival, with boys entering into violent drug gangs and girls objectified by the males they associate with, against the backdrop of family abandonment and abuse within the homes they have left. As the girls face the prospect of selling or withholding sexual favors and negotiating prostitution as a minute-to-minute reality, using initiative is often a fight for survival, running alongside a need for intimacy and love. Moments of extreme kindness and practical help are notable, such as the deep humanity Mónica shows Andrea in offering her the chance to stay with her at the rooming house, and the way the girls look out for each other, even as each must fight for her own survival. These moments are often transitory but indelibly striking and powerful. As in many Latin American films, violence is a key part of the narrative, but here it is not shown graphically. Its random practice and lethal effects are noted in passing, such as when two of the gang members murder the wrong man (a homeless drunk on a park bench), mistaken for the rapist who has been pursuing Andrea. He is quickly forgotten by the gang members and the narrative moves swiftly on, instilling the need to keep moving to survive on the streets.

Gaviria states that he continues the New Latin American Cinema directors' neorealist tradition, in which he feels they reveal "principles that are politically important" (Gaviria, Driver, and Tweddell 2008, 240).[5] Gaviria stresses the filmmaker's moral responsibility, in contrast to what he perceives as the mask (untruths) of Hollywood, to listen and give attention to the people's voice. Using non-professional actors, including drug traffickers, street kids, and *pistolocos*[6] in a collective sense, "the script is not an enunciation of the writer, the script writer or the movie maker: it is a collective voice. . . . These movies are not adaptations of books, but rather the product of many voices" (Gaviria, Driver, and Tweddell 2008, 248). Thus this *process* of collecting stories—via Gaviria's "methodology" of "the collective enunciation" (249)—rather than working on a pre-existing script or from books, is crucial to the filmmaking jigsaw, affecting also the way the stories have multiple threads, scenes, situations, characters, and actions.[7]

The multitextured narrative incorporates many protagonists and interwoven stories. As J. Anthony Abbott argues, despite the themes of drug addiction and violence the film shares with mainstream filmmaking, its characterization is not dominated by Hollywood's "good-guy/bad-guy dualisms" (2005, 133). Furthermore, he interprets the film's cobweb narrative strands as key to conveying the interwoven complexities, transience, and difficulties of life: "the threads of this film are somewhat disconnected, leading to a scattered plot, but these separations mirror the disaffected nature of the friendships among the characters" (134). I suggest that *The Rose Seller* maintains openness, while at the same time drawing on some of the major structural and thematic elements of "The Little Match Girl." Much can be gained by looking at how the film moves away from or elusively evades the fairy tale just as it embraces or interweaves it, and how as the narrative moves towards its end the two become more deeply enmeshed.

The narrative's multidirectional fluidity is conveyed stylistically from the film's opening shot. Opening halfway into the non-diegetic musical score, the first shot tilts down and pans to the left along the river away from the city edge, moving in closer to the water. With a dissolve to a long shot towards the city from the opposite direction, the camera tracks parallel with the riverside back towards the city to the right, and then pans back again, surveying the direction it has come from, as the music fades. A cut to a dusk-purple sky follows, as the camera pans through a full rotation towards the right, across, and close to the houses of the city's peripheries as various diegetic noises invade the visual frame: continued banging, yelling, swearing, and hitting, and gradually the tinny sounds of faint pop music. The first encounter with Andrea, the 10-year-old girl who leaves home, is her mother's shouting curse, "Little bitch," accusing her of breaking her tape recorder. The camera continues to pan to the right, sweeping across the front of the houses, and as a young child's legs dangle over the window frame, we hear a baby crying. Andrea herself leaves by climbing out of the ground-floor window, running off down the alleyway as the camera watches, now static for a moment. Thus movement, volatility, and eclectic sounds mark the frenetic life of the city's outskirts.

Parallels between Andrea's and Mónica's lives help to provide the tapestry of "real" life narratives, and draw attention to links with Andersen's fairy tale. Near the beginning of Andrea's journey, once fleeing her home, upon seeing the Madonna statue at the bridge, she blesses herself with the sign of the cross, highlighting the importance of faith in the young children's lives. The gesture and its subject also link her with Mónica, who later in the film has visions seemingly triggered by deep inhalations of glue, of the statue coming alive as her grandmother and beckoning her to rejoin her in death. The cut goes from Andrea's blessing herself to the first ground-level straight-on shot of Mónica coming around the corner, with the flowertips of the roses hanging downwards just visible at the top of the frame. Later, cross-cutting continues to interweave the girls' lives, between Mónica trying on her grandmother's oversized shoes (recalling the match girl's outsized slippers that fall from her feet, leaving her barefoot and freezing) and Andrea fetching shoes from under her mother's bed (on which her lazy stepfather reclines). The cross-cutting continues to the point of Mónica falling asleep on the bed and dreaming of pouring her grandmother's chocolate, only to be awoken by a man touching her legs, whose harassment we learn is the cause of her continued absence.

Although Mónica becomes the protagonist in the final shots, and reviewers certainly understand her as the main character, the film significantly begins with Andrea, and through its course traces the lives of many young people as they encounter each other, and as their paths interweave. Indeed, when Andrea returns to her mother towards the end, for a moment we are led to believe that *The Rose Seller* twists Andersen's tale, with this young girl reversing her fate. However, hauntingly we know that other girls remain on the streets. And when Mónica returns to the home from which she had run away after her grandmother's death, the film's story begins to consolidate, to fuse with Andersen's, heartbreakingly. After making her way across the river on stepping-stones, carrying her shoes, wearing an oversized red tunic jacket (reminiscent also of "Little Red Riding Hood"), she then loses her shoes, crawling along a muddy bank, becoming barefoot as the match girl does. Links with "The Little Match Girl" are thus accelerated, bringing the multiple narratives towards a more controlled finale, like the inevitable snapping of an elastic band; Mónica will receive the fate of the little match girl. It is only a matter of time.

The fairy tale provides a stable frame or structure. It also gives value to and enhances the people's stories and elevates the characters to heroes. Nevertheless, in line with its collective credentials, *The Rose Seller* refuses to offer false solutions for the children and teenagers in this situation. Rather, the focus becomes the need for a larger, sociological change: "What we need to do is to make sure countries don't lead people to live these experiences, because afterwards there is no path of return" (Gaviria, Driver, and Tweddell 2008, 252).[8] Amanda Clinton sees this call for involvement in political and social change as crucial. She asserts that people must see the film despite it being uneasy to watch: "None of us can ignore these children any longer" (1998, 186). An awareness of class and inequality runs through the film, drawing on contrasts evident in Andersen's tale, such as that between the little match girl's cold, dark plight and the lights in every window and the smell of roasting goose drifting down the street.

Similarly, in *The Rose Seller*, Mónica briefly pauses from her flight to look at a Christmas snow-scene in a shop window, and then turns to watch fleetingly (there is no time to linger) a mother pulling two children, their fate seemingly more fortunate than her own, along on a sledge. The moment is observed with a subtlety that avoids heavy-handedness. The film's twists on other fairy tales hint at issues of home abuse that often underline these stories. For example, when Andrea holds the broom, shouting at her stepfather for being lazy, she subverts the traditional innocent persecuted Cinderella heroine. Later, when she makes up with her mother, her plea, "I need to be loved wholeheartedly" cuts to the core of the abandonment. Her sister is glimpsed just to the side, hinting at the sibling rivalry between them, also at the heart of many fairy tales. These elements are seen in passing and are not over-dramatized.

The final scenes of *The Rose Seller* show an increased adherence to "The Little Match Girl" but also some key revisions. Mónica returns to the rubble-filled yard behind her previous home that had been her grandmother's room before the authorities demolished it, leaving it exposed and in ruin. As she crouches down, her red jacket so large it envelopes her to the feet, we see both her fragile size and her adeptness at pouring glue into the black bag, held tight at the top, twisting the bottle top swiftly a couple of times to avoid drips. Cross-cutting between Mónica and Zarco follows, as he flees his own gang who have become his enemies. We witness his anger at Mónica giving him the child's watch she adored, but that he sees no value in; their interaction will mean she gets caught up in the violent encounter that will inevitably lead to the terrible mishap of her death.

Mónica stands, unable to stop inhaling the glue, holding out for the apparitions it brings, and there is a cut to her dream, bathed in deep red. To swathes of pipe sounds, we see the grandmother and other family members preparing food. The scene is heavenly but at the same time claustrophobic and horrific with its red glow, and no diegetic sound. As Mónica makes her way through the white figures (she is the only one in red), she remains unseen. The experience is muted, as if she is willing it, but she is the ghost at the party, and the dream turns to a nightmare when the roasted meat seems to come alive and move towards her. As she flinches, with a cut back to the reality of the yard, she is depicted brushing the sparks from the sparkler she holds, shouting, "Get that off me!" The little match girl's fantasy of the roast goose seeming to appear "nearer and nearer—she could almost touch it" (Andersen 1986, 63) is here Gothicized. The magical agent has an ominous shadow in the film as well, as Mónica's visions are driven by drug-induced desperation.

Anxious to return to the vision, Mónica relights the sparkler, recalling the little match girl hastening to light each match from the box. The sparkler also recalls the falling star in Andersen's tale, as the fireworks do later at the moment of Mónica's death. Thus, the fairy tale's natural image of the falling star linked to the match girl's ascension to heaven is here given a modern, if not overtly synthetic quality. A life is over in a flash, but the wonder in the child's mind perseveres. Mónica's words to her grandmother, "You're going to take me with you," directly echoing the fairy tale, are overlaid with the low-angled shot of Zarco kicking her, brutally, and a brief observation of the knife he holds. The sparkler hangs in the sky as if suspended, followed by a shot of Mónica smiling, looking towards her grandmother, who stands with arms open wide smiling, mirroring the statue on the bridge earlier, whose hands projected festive, electric fairy lights.

The incorporation of these key fairy-tale elements provides a sense of familiarity and hints towards an uplifting Catholic transcendence, inspired to some degree by the intelligent design underlining Andersen's tale whereupon the match girl finds happiness in heaven. However, the Gothic visions and brutality destabilize this design. The incorporation of the fairy tale also casts an increasing shadow of inevitability across the film that is particularly harrowing to witness. Mónica's inhalation of glue holds the vision (like the one on the bridge earlier) until, once ablaze with life, she is suddenly lifeless and cold. Added to this is the myth that surrounds the film itself, with the knowledge that many of the destitute adolescents featured in it are dead.[9]

When young children playing the next morning find Mónica, an extreme low-angled shot looks up at them, wearing their smart Christmas clothes; the girl carries sweets in a gift bag, a marked contrast to the black glue bag earlier held by Mónica. The children look down towards Mónica's dead body, shown from an extreme high angle to capture their viewpoint. She lies on the ground on her back in her red jacket, spread doll-like diagonally across the frame, one knee bent to the side. As the camera tracks downwards, a tiny red gash becomes apparent on the side of her mouth; it is the only sign of the violence committed (see Figure 19.1).

The shot resembles the first of Ofelia as she lies dying at the beginning of *Pan's Labyrinth* (2006) when, as the film reverses, blood trickles back up her nose (see Figure 19.2). This image of Ofelia repeats at the film's end, during a cyclical return to the beginning. As I explore below, *Pan's Labyrinth* experiments with a new way of representing fantasy and real worlds and also draws on the concept of a transcendent ending.

FIGURE 19.1 Mónica dead, *The Rose Seller* (1998).

FIGURE 19.2 Ofelia moments before death, *Pan's Labyrinth* (2006).

The Rose Seller ends with a slow dissolve from the shot of Mónica's body lying on the ground to the full moon to the right of the frame, with white words positioned on the left against a black background, stating that 150 years ago, Hans C. Andersen wrote a tale "about the very same girls 'The Little Match Girl.'"[10] This direct citation gives the film an authorial heritage set specifically in Denmark, in the mid nineteenth century, but also universalizes it, for home and international audiences alike. The use of Andersen's tale works in complex, contradictory ways. While the realist film techniques clearly provide a sense of authenticity, the association with the fairy tale helps to stretch the particular to a more timeless, enduring realm. The political edge given by the specific actuality of drug trafficking, drug use, homelessness, and prostitution in Medellín is thus also given a universal value. Its allusion to the fairy tale evokes the memory of childhood, giving it a primal quality. It mirrors the return to Mónica's childhood, reviving (if only momentarily) the magic of the tale's final ascendance, and the importance of the girl's belief in the vision she sees. On the one hand, it might seem like the ending offers an avoidance strategy or a compromise between the realist style and the magic moment of restoration, with the fairy tale stepping in to provide a formulaic ending to appease mainstream audiences. On the other hand, the stark reality is that nothing has changed; there is no social answer to the situation at the time of making the film. This second reading suggests that such a conscious recourse to the fairy-tale solution means that the fairy tale is also destabilized to some degree by its implementation.

Significantly, the rose—an international symbol of love and romance—is again used as a motif in *Maria Full of Grace* (María, llena eres de gracia, 2004), functioning as a commercial product governing the lives of the underprivileged. At the start of the film, María works long hours under terrible conditions and severe regulations in a profit-driven factory de-thorning and packaging roses. Like many of *The Rose Seller*'s characters, María shares a crowded home, in this instance with her grandmother, mother, and older sister, a single mother. After quitting her job, following an argument with her manager, she takes on the dangerous but relatively well-paid job offered by a stranger at a dance, to become a drug mule in Bogotá. While the film centers on Colombian drug subculture, as Aldona Bialowas Pobutsky (2010, 27) illustrates, fairy-tale motifs and plot-lines are evident, specifically from "Cinderella," such as the bullying mother and sister, the escape (here, to earn money by smuggling drugs), the "fitting" that brings about her liberation (here, by swallowing a large cocaine pellet while pregnant, rather than fitting into a slipper) and the happy ending.[11]

In some respects we might draw parallels with *The Rose Seller*, because of the way that *Maria Full of Grace* seems to draw on fairy-tale characteristics, even if less overtly or consciously, to provide a sense of familiarity to the subject matter for international audiences. However, clear distinctions can be made. *The Rose Seller* overtly uses the fairy tale not only to give familiarity and some order to the narrative, but also to emphasize a certain inevitable, fatal circularity to the individual's circumstances, making the film's appeal for specific, local change in society at this point in history all the more poignant. In contrast, the wider appeal caused by "Cinderella" tropes and narrative elements in *Maria Full of Grace*, as Pobutsky argues, "opens the possibility that the presence of such a highly popular motif complies with universal tastes while obscuring, albeit inadvertently, the ideology that courses through the film" (2010, 31). I would suggest in addition that the unconscious or less explicit use of the fairy tale makes it perhaps more powerfully ideological.

Pobutsky argues that the film can be read in the context of the north seeing southern countries as an intriguing but alien, dangerous, or even criminal "Other." She sees it as refreshing compared to other Colombian films made at this time focusing on drug-related issues, in the sense that it does not celebrate the underworld of production or narco-trafficking or exalt violence. But she also notes that its "patent ideological framework" is reactionary, endorsing the myth of American colonial supremacy, when María decides to remain in the US to have her baby, rather than returning to Colombia: "By rejecting what the film presents as stagnation, chaos, and corruption in Colombia, to, instead, take advantage of the land of opportunities in Queens, New York, María subscribes to the imperial discourse of the desirable metropolis to which all the neo-colonial subjects should aspire" (Pobutsky 2010, 37).

Disregarding the restrictions on immigration from the south at the time the film was made, the film depicts North America as a haven. This ideology is underlined by her friend's sister, who has moved to North America and is herself about to have a baby, saying that where they have come from is no place to raise a child. She tells of the joy she felt at being able to send her first wage packets home. As in *The Rose Seller*, the maternal role is seen as fundamental in providing the foundations of a stable existence. María's decision not to return to Colombia is effected when she accidentally pulls out her next pre-natal appointment card at the airport, cementing the notion that her baby will get better care if she stays. When this reading is aligned with the film's fairy-tale framework, María's role as central hero becomes clearer. Through using initiative, she becomes the chosen one amongst her companions to find a better future. In this sense, as Pobutsky suggests, the film reinforces discourses so strongly fought against in the Third Cinema movement of the 1960s, which called for rejecting the straitjackets of neo-colonial domination (2010, 38).

Although there are potentially radical or even controversial elements in the film, these extend only so far. The allusion to the Virgin Mary, via the film's title, the protagonist's name, and the central narrative of finding a safe place to have her baby, is taken to the extreme in the film's marketing, with posters and DVD covers projecting the close-up image of María's face looking up receiving the drug pellet as though receiving the Holy Communion. However, any hint at provocation or sacrilege is eradicated by the film's earnest sympathy for María on a deeply human level. Indeed, such prolonged empathy with young female drug smugglers is in itself progressive. However, the same degree of earnestness is applied to María's first signs of warming to the US after her arrival. In a montage of shots of the region that suggest a cosmopolitan paradise, depicted over an extended piece of guitar music, María takes a moment to peruse shop windows, including a store rich with Catholic iconography, and to buy a freshly made snack that she settles down to eat in the public square. It is at this point that she catches sight of the pre-natal center—the moment that transforms her own and her unborn baby's life. The brief glimpse at the start of this interlude sequence of the man preparing roses in front of a flower shop gives just a momentary nod to her old life, as the colorful flowers are displayed here in the full light of day, in contrast to those in the Colombian factory. This contrast thus gives a positive spin on her new surroundings, rather than offering a direct critique of North America's complicity in the sweatshop trade she has left behind. It upholds the fantasy of an improved life in the US.

In *Pan's Labyrinth* (El laberinto del fauno, 2006), the fantasy or visionary world (evident on a more secondary or subjective level in *The Rose Seller*) is elevated in relation to its "real" counterpart. Scenes within a woodland setting depicting Fascist atrocities in 1944, five years after the end of the Spanish Civil War, are juxtaposed with the fantasies or dream-world visions associated with the young heroine, Ofelia. Within this context, *Pan's Labyrinth*, similar to del Toro's earlier film, *The Devil's Backbone* (El espinazo del diablo 2001), investigates with intricate intimacy the role of the child in overcoming fear and making difficult decisions through a rite-of-passage journey between childhood and adulthood, navigating between "civilized" and less clearly signposted pathways. While a profound terror resides in *The Devil's Backbone* with its unrestrained massacre of so many children at a deserted orphanage during the Spanish Civil War, both films center on the child visionary, brave enough to enter into the dark abyss, willing to risk death in order to save the lives of others.

The intricate intertwining of the fantasy and real worlds in *Pan's Labyrinth* makes it a key film for investigating the specific, but diverse, function of the fairy tale on screen. The film's two-dimensional villain, Captain Vidal of Spain's Civil Guard, is posted in a remote wooded hamlet in the north of Spain near the French frontier, instructed to extinguish from the area the last remaining (Republican) *maquis* who continue to resist Franco's regime. The head-on, close-up representations of painfully brutal acts, filmed with a graphic (and aurally disturbing) level of detail, illustrate the carnage caused by Franco's control, and make the film groundbreaking for its time. While we might assume that the fantasy world is the place to look for fairy-tale traits, the "real" world has a more conventional fairy-tale framework, and in this sense, certain fairy-tale tropes are adopted to convey more provocative subject matter. Although there is some fluidity between the two worlds, the more rigid, simple character types inhabit the real world, where extreme good is opposed to extreme evil as it is in the classical fairy tale, while more ambiguous characters thrive in the realm of fantasy.

The allegorical, fairy-tale framework permits an allusion to the unspoken activities of fathers and forefathers throughout this historical period. Evil practices are transferred onto the stepfather, rather than being associated with the natural father. Ofelia's good (anti-Fascist) natural father is dead, meaning that cruelty is external to her bloodline; good and evil remain separate, intact, and uncomplicated. In this way, fatherless and then orphaned when her mother dies in childbirth, Ofelia steps into the shoes of the fairy-tale hero. The transfer of wickedness onto the stepparent draws on classical fairy-tale civilizing traditions, as Maria Tatar (2003, 37) has demonstrated in her research of the Grimm brothers' multiple revisions of *Children's and Household Tales* (1812–1857). The way to make a mother's abusive actions more bearable for readers was to turn her into a step-mother.[12] Although on one level, *Pan's Labyrinth* civilizes history by transferring the cruelty onto the two-dimensional, villainous stepfather, seeming to overlook notions of a more complex or conscience-wracked father, it nevertheless opens the way allegorically to the possibility of a world where the father is fearful or regrettable, a notion which remains taboo. This move thus offers testament to the fairy tale's long-held capacity to make allegorical reference to issues that are otherwise unspeakable.

One of the most stimulating aspects of *Pan's Labyrinth* is that the imaginary world associated with Ofelia is as dark as the real one. Indeed the fantasy world contains ambiguous, shadowy qualities that are lacking in its real counterpart. Beyond this, Ofelia, like Lewis Carroll's Alice, is unfazed in her monstrous wonderland, such as when she encounters face-to-face visions of the faun biting off raw flesh. His ambiguous features[13] make the reactions and choices Ofelia has to make in response to his tasks all the more challenging, obscuring the true pathway. It is never confirmed explicitly whether her decisions are morally correct. Furthermore, her encounter with diverse Gothic and grotesque embodiments of aging and decay in the scenes awakened by Ofelia's imagination give depth to her character and visionary capabilities. We might recall the Gothicization of the fantasy momentarily glimpsed at the end of *The Rose Seller*, when as the roasted meat seems to come alive, the vision becomes nightmarish, casting a shadow across secure affinities with the concept of pure transcendence that ends Andersen's fairy tale.

Pan's Labyrinth also reinforces fairy-tale traditions of wonder surrounding the female body, such as the use of the uterine imagery to frame the fantasy world. The film's red on white pays homage to classical fairy-tale conventions, such as the three drops of blood on the snow/milk in "Snow White" and the pricking of the finger in "Sleeping Beauty," symbolizing emerging womanhood, sexuality, or the loss of innocence. The connections' distinct brutality also link childbirth with death, for example when the red ink blotches filling the pages of Ofelia's fairy-tale book like blood on cloth are followed by the shot of her mother bent double, blood spilling around her white skirts below the waist. Close to the film's end, in the moment that returns to the opening shot, when blood flowed back into her nostrils reversing time, Ofelia's body glows white in the full moon light, blood floating from her nose.[14] A slow dissolve through a golden light marks her transcendence into her father's realm, to join the family where, wearing ruby-red boots that offer a tougher version of Dorothy's slippers, she enters his womblike red-gold palace. The thematic use of red and white demonstrates some dependence on essentialist imagery surrounding the mystique of the female body in transition. Nevertheless, the film also resists nature and biology when Ofelia tells Mercedes that she will never have a baby, and the two form a resilient alliance. As Paul Julian Smith argues, if "horror comes from knowing both sides of the story, then those two sides (victim and heroine) are distributed by del Toro to his twin active female protagonists" (2014, 75). Mercedes survives, having slashed Vidal's face as swiftly as gutting a pig.

The film's closing raises Mercedes, her brother, and his companions to heroic levels, and Ofelia's final transcendence validates her decision to become involved, indicating how individual choices lead to collective enterprise. Ofelia disobeys throughout the film, defying Vidal and refusing to call him "Father," venturing into the woods, returning to the labyrinth, and stealing her baby brother. She also disobeys the faun by not handing over the baby. Biology and the (male) bloodline are also undercut at the end. When Vidal, facing death, orders Mercedes to tell his son the time of his death, she rejects the command, stating that his child won't even know his name. As Mar Diestro-Dópido notes, "This line clearly alludes to the fact that around 30,000 children of 'Reds' killed or imprisoned were adopted by Franco supporters. With no knowledge of their past, they became the other disappeared, living for years under identities far removed from their real ones" (2013, 77). Thus, again, the film goes some way in making the invisible visible. Ofelia's new birth at the end comes as a result of pain—the male voiceover preaches the Catholic law that an individual must suffer pain to achieve transcendence. *Pan's Labyrinth* also offers a cyclical return to the fantasy realm of the father, relating to Mexican mythology of death as a cyclical process. As in *The Rose Seller*, though, the historical actuality is not resolved. The true horror of Franco's regime remains.

While Vidal is concerned with obeying orders and wanting to bestow his identity through the male lineage, Ofelia, whose choices guide the film's moral core, learns to disobey and to retrace her path to rediscover something she has lost. There are parallels allegorically with the country's own absent identity, as del Toro suggests: "The essential conundrum of the princess is that she does not remember that she is one. And the pre-Celtic and pagan ancient myths remind us who we are. . . . I love the idea of a primal myth that shakes everyone into remembering who they really are" (Diestro-Dópido 2013, 84–85).

Latin American folktales are diverse and amorphous. However, the moral theme of relocating the right path via a return to the true self that has been forgotten or lost can be seen in some of the recent incarnations of Brazilian folktales (*folclore*) in the series of short-film animations sponsored by the Rio de Janeiro City Council, called "Juro que vi" ("I swear I saw it"). The films were produced with the participation of students, around seven to thirteen years old, from the city's Municipal Elementary schools. Stories of local legendary and folkloric characters are depicted with a contemporary theme, and linked to present-day global concerns such as animal rights, the environment, or prejudice. The series was shown at international festivals and on various educational television channels, winning several national awards, such as the Grand Cinema Award of Brazil (2010) for the Best Short Film Animation.

The Saci (O Saci), a film of about thirteen minutes produced in 2009 and directed by Humberto Avelar, encapsulates the concept of returning to the beginning to rediscover or remember something that has been neglected, as its opening voiceover announces: "This story takes place in Minas Gerais[15] where a man built paths searching for something long forgotten, that one day someone would help him to find it."[16] In the first few scenes of this film that contains no dialogue apart from the opening and closing voiceover narration, we see the rich plantation-owner parade his lands, arrogantly burning down trees to create grazing land, thus ruining the environment, and strutting with his stick that hosts a small artificial horse-head. Puffed up with so much pride and anger that even his horses stand to attention in his stable, he is suddenly visited by Saci, who in accordance with the folktale appears from thin air in a mini-whirlwind, creating havoc.

Saci, also known as Saci Pererê, is a well-known figure of Brazilian folklore. A pesky (and in more overtly racist versions of the story more ominously troublesome) mixed-race or Black boy with one leg who goes about carrying out pranks and mischiefs, he sports a red hat that gives him the power to appear and disappear at will. Anything that goes wrong inside or outside the home (burnt soup, escaped farm animals) can be blamed on Saci. If caught by a sieve or in a net, he can be harnessed in a glass bottle, and called upon to grant wishes by his new master, his magic stolen by the captor donning his hat, which reportedly leaves a lingering bad odor on the person.

The tale has a rich tapestry of variants and origins common to Latin American countries fusing African-American folklore with fairy tales brought by Portuguese, Spanish, and other European settlers and eastern fairy tales brought through trading routes, within a frame of Indigenous folklore. Some stories associated with Saci recall the Indigenous character "Yaci" or "Yaci-Yateré," a one-legged child whistling across forests at night (Giese 1963, 160). Clearly the concept of imprisoning in a corked bottle a supernatural spirit who is forced to grant wishes in return for his freedom echoes Aladdin's genie, from the tale added to *One Thousand and One Nights*. Christian elements are added, for example, when Saci, confronted by a cross, flees: "He is frightened by symbols of Catholicism, the religion that predominated in Brazil, which equated him with the devil" (Dietrich 2010, 146). Tales of Saci abound in Brazil and have been traced in more recent history to the popular children's book *O Saci*, written by Monteiro Lobato and published in 1932. In the 1960s, leading Brazilian cartoonist Ziraldo brought this character further fame in his comic *Turma do Pererê*. There are Brazilian songs, video games, and television programs about Saci and, since 2005, October 31 is dedicated to him ("The Day of the Saci"), bestowing a local spirit on the increasingly popular Anglo-Celtic Halloween.

In Avelar's animation, after wreaking havoc in the stable and farmhouse kitchen, Saci finds old pictures of the plantation-owner, first as a young man grimacing with the hard work he has endured to achieve his current status, and finally as a little boy delighted with his new toy—a miniature automated rocking horse, from which the head had been removed and attached to the stick shown in the opening scenes. When the plantation-owner is stuck in the middle of a burning field, and is forced to liberate Saci from the bottle in which he has trapped him, Saci removes the head from the staff and returns it to the rocking horse, restoring the plantation-owner to his childhood body, repositioned in the current day, joyously cherishing the toy. Catholic or redemptive rain transforms dry sands to green pastures, trees, and flowers. Towards the end of the film, Saci encourages the boy to look at old photographs of himself watering flowers, hugging trees, and letting a bird free from a cage, reinvigorating the tale with a contemporary environmental theme. The voiceover narration concludes, "If you lose track of your path, there is always a way to find your place again. You will just have to search for it deep inside you, retell your own story. Go back to the beginning and transform yourself." To these words, in a near-reflexive reference to animation filmmaking (perhaps the director's own childhood passion) we see the boy astride his saddle, with Saci riding bare-back, galloping, free-spirited, and laughing. A final photograph shows the plantation-owner restored as a happy man, in the middle of his healthy family of three generations—children, wife, and parents, with Saci on his shoulder.

While like most tales of Saci, avoiding stereotype is difficult where race is so obvious within its representation, Avelar's short film achieves a degree of ambivalence that challenges some of the usual "Othering." To some extent, Saci remains essentially the wild figure from the jungle, and his role in unlocking the plantation-owner's soul makes him secondary rather than the central hero. However, it is Saci who leads the man towards the right path; the supernatural figure has wisdom in addition to the usual agility, mischief, and magical power. Traditionally, stories of Saci convey a warning to listeners and audiences. The message here is instead about internal transformation, thus throwing new fairy-tale ingredients into the mix. Moreover, as in *Pan's Labyrinth*, the need for individual return is linked to the nation's collective need to reclaim its path.

I close with *La jaula de oro* (2013), released with the English-language title *The Golden Dream*. The film centers on child migrants, and focuses on three teenagers from the slums of Guatemala— Juan, Sara (dressed as a boy), and Samuel—who set out to travel to the United States in the hope of finding an improved life. On their journey through Mexico, they meet Chauk, an Indigenous Tzotzil from Chiapas unable to speak Spanish, who joins them on their journey. Samuel decides to return, but the other three head out along the railroad tracks to take freight trains across the borders. Only Juan makes it to the final destination. The film is neither an adaptation nor a reworking of a fairy tale, but rather destabilizes the ideological fabric upon which some are based. It is useful here for the way it subverts established myths, in keeping with other Latin American films explored in this chapter and holding true to the manifestos of the 1960s. Motivated by a mission to tell a collectivist story, constructed from the director's conversations with around 600 migrants crossing on the train to the US, the film forms something of a "collectivist testimony" in an attempt to break down the construct of barriers and borders across north/south, rich/poor, languages, and nationalities (Quemada-Díez 2013).[17] This testimony concentrates on the four children, whereupon the realist process is given a dramatic structure; the main character, Juan, undergoes "the journey of the hero" to gain a sense of learning and internal growth.

Inspired by his experiences of working as a clapper loader on Ken Loach's *Land and Freedom* in 1995, Diego Quemada-Díez (2013) revealed the script step by step as they filmed to allow the non-professional actors to adapt it as they went (like the working style adopted in *The Rose Seller*). Influenced also by Italian neorealism and the British documentary school, *The Golden Dream* is shot on Super 16, rather than digital, depicting real migrants often at the characters' eye-level viewpoint. Similar to *The Rose Seller*, the camera does not dwell on the sudden, harrowing tragedies that occur throughout.

As in *The Rose Seller* and *Pan's Labyrinth*, the external journey does not end well. The American dream collapses as Juan, who had believed in western materialist or capitalist dreams, ends up in a meat-processing factory under dire working conditions. The film expresses the migrant's situation, that fifteen million in the US do not have documents and can be deported any minute, and that many are homeless, in jail, or dehumanised (Quemada-Díez 2013). The original title *La jaula de oro*, "The Cage of Gold," refers to the Mexican song of the same title, by Los Tigres Del Norte, which refutes the dream that the US streets are paved with gold, telling instead of the desperate situation faced by many migrants, who experience loss of heritage, limited job opportunities, and difficulty returning home. The film also articulates postcolonial issues in the conflict between Juan and Chauk and the question of original territory and ownership challenged in *Black God, White Devil*.

The Golden Dream shakes up traditional modes of representation. The external journey does not have a happy ending, because the US situation remains: sending weapons to Central America, channeling drug gangs, and creating trading policies that limit national production. Like *O Saci*, the film to some degree conforms to an essentialist, stereotypical representation in that Chauk, its Indigenous soul, is the secondary character and not the hero, which echoes the limitations observed earlier in *How to Read Donald Duck*. However, Juan is moved to an internal transformation via his encounter with Chauk, undergoing many trials along the way towards learning the meaning of brotherhood, and is thus "thrown back into his journey, into his path" (Quemada-Díez 2013). The final, uplifting shot of Juan looking up in the snow both refers back to Chauk's dream and raises the individual journey to a collective potential, in memory of the migrants.

To conclude, this chapter has provided a critical analysis of a few significant examples of contemporary cinema with respect to the rich and dynamic relationship between the fairy-tale film and Latin America. As it traverses relatively new territory within a limited space, it suggests areas for investigation based on shared themes and concerns, spreading breadcrumbs to indicate pathways that may yet be further developed. The idiosyncratic historical frameworks of Latin America, together with its countries' distinctive spiritual and religious inheritances, can be seen to interplay with the specific manifestos that transformed its cinema in the 1960s, and that continue to resonate today. The fairy tale can provide a stable frame to help universalize the specific, and its interaction with Latin American cinema helps to both reinforce and subvert underlying myths that have been taken as natural, reshaping them in line with contemporary trends and values. The films this chapter addresses use folkloric and fairy-tale narratives and motifs to test the bounds of fantasy and reality as they interweave and collide. And it is often in the face of harrowing actuality or uncompromising history that the films also articulate—often through the perspective of the child—a need to return to an identity or internal pathway, both on an individual and a collective level, that has been long overlooked or forgotten.

Notes

1 The Lumières and Edison exhibitions continued across Venezuela, Argentina, Brazil, Cuba, Mexico, and Uruguay during the late 1890s, Chile in 1902, and Colombia in 1905 (see Armes 1987, 164–65).
2 For one of the first main studies of the "golden age" (*bela época*) of Brazilian silent cinema see Araújo (1976), focusing mainly on the years 1908–1911. More recently, the wider period 1896–1916 was explored by de Melo Souza (2004). For an insightful analysis of *cinema novo*, see Nagib (2007).
3 The first (1975) English version of *How to Read Donald Duck* translated by American art historian David Kunzle, who wrote an important introduction, triggered a strong reception.
4 As Kantaris highlights, a similar transition occurred a few years on in Brazil (Rio de Janeiro and São Paulo) after global drug trading seeped into international markets, intensifying violent ghettoization (2010, 33).
5 During the interview Gaviria cites neorealist screenwriter and theorist Cesare Zavattini (Gaviria, Driver, and Tweddell 2008, 246) on the importance of depicting the "here and now" and a diversity of lives, because Cuban film director, screenwriter, and advocate of "imperfect cinema," Julio García Espinosa, had invited Zavattini to work with him in the 1960s (Elena and López 2003, 5).
6 *Pistolocos* are "young assassins who are paid to kill and generally carry out their assignments from the back of a motorbike" (Gaviria, Driver, and Tweddell 2008, 253).
7 Gaviria undertook a rigorous two-year period of investigation, followed by twelve weeks in pre-production and sixteen weeks shooting.
8 A radical and powerfully feminist revision of "Little Red Riding Hood," the Colombian animation short *Red* (dir. Carlo Guillot and Jorge Jaramillo, 2012) challenges this notion of going beyond the point of return. When Red violently attacks the wolf and tears stream down her cheeks, expectations that she feels regret for her actions are confounded when she pulls her grandmother from the wolf's belly, and dons the red cloak.
9 Moreover, the extreme close-up on Mónica's anguished eyes in this sequence is a heart-rending technique, with the potential to unsettle any audiences aware that the actress, Leidy ("Lady") Tabares, has only just been released from prison following a long sentence.
10 The titles of the tale and film, "La Vendedora de Cerillas" and "La Vendedora de Rosas," are closer in Spanish than in English.
11 A "Cinderella" structure is also evident in the extremely successful film *Like Water for Chocolate* (Como agua para chocolate, dir. Alfonso Arau, Mexico, 1992), adapted from Laura Esquivel's best-selling novel, and achieving international popular (if not critical) acclaim, taking nearly 20 million dollars when it was released in the US in 1993, becoming the country's biggest-selling foreign film that year (Finnegan 1999, 311). Similar to Cinderella, the younger sister, Tita, is required to look after her mother, while her two sisters are allowed to leave home.
12 The stepmother is more prevalent in fairy tales than the stepfather, but other examples of splitting the father to create the good, natural (dead) father and the wicked stepfather include William Shakespeare's *Hamlet* and Ingmar Bergman's *Fanny and Alexander* (1982).
13 Although the name seems to have been brought in to supply a marketable English title, del Toro often clarifies that the faun is not Pan, whose name conjures up misleading connotations of danger (see, for example, Del Toro 2007).

14 While so far I have not found direct mention of the similarities between these shots and the ending of *The Rose Seller*, del Toro has stated that Ofelia's transcendence to heaven as a reward for disobedience stems from Andersen's "The Little Match Girl" (interviewed in Diestro-Dópido 2013, 84).

15 Minas Gerais is a state in Brazil, famous for its mineral resources.

16 I am extremely grateful to Nicholas Kucker Triana for translating the voiceover dialogues at the film's start and end, and helping to unlock the story's meanings and wider contexts.

17 Quemada-Díez (2013) reportedly saw over 6,000 children in nine months (3,000 in the Guatemalan slums and 3,000 in the mountains of Mexico). This dedication to "authenticity" is reminiscent of the "methodology" used in *The Rose Seller*.

20

BEYOND DISNEY IN THE TWENTY-FIRST CENTURY

Changing Aspects of Fairy-Tale Films in the American Film Industry

Jack Zipes

Actually, we can never get "beyond" the Disney production of fairy-tale films in the twenty-first century. That is, we can never get beyond notions of the well-made conventional fairy-tale film with its stereotypical characters and beyond the commercial exploitation of oral and literary fairy tales and marketing that panders to the lowest common denominator among viewers—and we must bear in mind that children are not the lowest because they are too intelligent to take Disney fluff, conventionality, and slapstick seriously. The lowest common denominator is constituted by the marketers themselves. In fact the American production of fairy-tale films continues to be market-driven, and great marketing efforts have been made in recent years to produce spectacular blockbusters like *Frozen* (2013), *Maleficent* (2014), *Into the Woods* (2014), and *Cinderella* (2015). But these hugely successful feature-length fairy-tale films are not necessarily indicative of the strength and extent of Disney's influence. Rather, the success of these films is merely a reflection of Disney's skillful marketing stratagems, supported by an intricate network, which includes the merchandising of fairy-tale films made for television, for the after-market home DVD market, for theme parks and stores, and occasionally for the cinema. Let us briefly consider what I call "the annihilation and rebirth of Tinker Bell."

Tinker Bell, as we all know, became famous in J.M. Barrie's 1904 play when she almost dies accidentally from poison. It is only when Peter asks the audience whether they believe in fairies that she will revive from the poison. Generally speaking, even today, audiences will reply with a resounding "yes!" So, Tinker Bell continues to exist in books, comics, graphic novels, films, and on stage usually as a tiny fluttering mischievous fairy with wings. She is Peter's constant companion, too tiny to become his lover, but certainly devoted to him and anxious to keep him in Neverland. Her traditional image and role in Barrie's play has generally been protected somewhat by British copyright laws up to 2008, when the rights owned by the Great Ormond Street Hospital in London expired. As soon as this occurred, the Disney Toon Studios, part of the Disney Fairies Franchise, jumped and quickly produced a computer-animated film series beginning with *Tinker Bell* in 2008 and ending with *Legend of the Never Beast* in 2015. To say the least, Tinker Bell has never been the same after 2008, that is, the same Tinker Bell she was in Barrie' s play: she has been annihilated and reborn as a Barbie-like doll and making millions of dollars for the Disney Studios.

In what is considered to be a prequel to the "Peter Pan" story, Tinker Bell is born from a baby's laugh in the animated film *Tinker Bell* (2008), and a wind carries her as a seed to Pixie Hollow on the island of Never Land, where in a ceremony supervised by the queen of the fairies, she sprouts or is "hatched," so to speak. All of a sudden, Tinker Bell is a petite talking teenager, beautifully formed with wings, as are all the multiethnic fairies. From her birth onward, her mission and meaning in life will be to make and fix things. (For children watching her, she will repeat that she was born from a baby's laugh, as if that were the "normal" way babies are born.) In all seven films, there is a conventional plot mixed with music: Tinker Bell will cause trouble, or she will encounter trouble with her beautiful friends, who are similar to all the multiethnic Disney princesses ever created. Then she will find a way to repair things so that there is a happy ending. The films are well-made, predictable, and harmless so that parents will be encouraged to buy them for their children. Boys will not be especially attracted to the films, but there is a video game and other paraphernalia that they might appreciate. At any rate, girls are the target customers.

These films are pure commodities spread throughout the world as are the other Disney prequel "Cinderella" and "Little Mermaid" films.[1] Their stories are stunningly inane, but it is not the inanity of the Disney fairy-tale films that marks them as characteristically "American" fairy-tale films. It is the corporation's enormous capacity to brand the "normal" fairy tale as Disney-made, to utilize art as efficiently as possible in ways that repeat the same storylines with music and bombastic technical effects and then to capitalize production through massive distribution to gain large profits. Given the growth and development of the Disney Studios with all its international franchises, the American fairy-tale film à la Disney will remain dominant in cinemas, homes, schools, and cultural centers for many years to come.

Given the domination of Disney Studios, which bought an important competitor, Pixar Animation Studios, in 2006, acquired the rights to distribute Ghibli animated Japanese films at the beginning of the twenty-first century, including the important Hayao Miyazaki fairy-tale films, and established in 2006 the Walt Disney Company CIS in Moscow, one of its many international divisions, most of the exceptional American fairy-tale films have been produced either under the shadow of Disney or on the margins of the American film industry. Indeed, exceptions and experiments are generally to be found outside the United States. I have already alluded to some of the exceptional foreign fairy-tale films in Chapter 1, and all the chapters in this book indicate that there is immense experimentation of cinematic fairy-tale films in other countries that enhance the general public's understanding of oral and literary tales. However, in the United States, experimentation in the shadow of the Disney corporation is rare, and the major spectacular American fairy-tale films have been disappointing.

For instance, the tsunami wave, which still keeps rising and receding, brought with it fairy-tale films that are primarily produced for the sake of the spectacle; these productions have little to do with serious and artful interpretation and creation of fairy-tale films. If we were to closely examine several of the live-action films produced in the past five years, *Red Riding Hood* (2011), *Beastly* (2011), *Dorothy and the Witches of Oz* (2011), *Mirror, Mirror* (2012), *Oz the Great and Powerful* (2013), *Jack the Giant Slayer* (2013), *Snow White and the Huntsman* (2012), and *Hansel & Gretel: Witch Hunters* (2013), we would find a certain homogenization despite the fact that the storylines are different and produced for the most part by studios other than Disney.

The similarities of production are more important than the differences: (1) Exorbitant sums of money are spent on publicity and trailers so that the films, all based on well-known fairy tales, need only to be hyped because they claim to be unique approaches to so-called classics. However, the paratexts of the films diminish the alleged uniqueness because they all rely on the same sensational claims. (2) Along with the huge production and publicity costs, film studios hire celebrity actors who must sell films with poor scripts and try to have "fun" in roles that make them look ludicrous. Commercial success of the films does not depend on the quality or artistic merit of the interpretation but on the performance of celebrities and flashy special effects. (3) The ideology of most of the films is questionable because many depend heavily on special effects to increase spectacle for the sale of spectacle.

Moreover, many of the conflicts pit women against women, that is, young beautiful virgins against experienced and smart but villainous women, who seek absolute power to dominate a realm. This is the case in *Mirror, Mirror, Dorothy and the Witches of Oz, Oz the Great and Powerful, Snow White and the Huntsman*, and *Hansel & Gretel: Witch Hunters*. The implicit message in these films is that young women must learn how to use weapons to defend themselves and defeat their female adversaries. In fact, they must often be trained by men to slay and kill. In short, in order to become a "true" woman in today's world, a woman must become a man. That is, she must evince qualities that are generally attributed to maleness. The overall gesture in the films to demonstrate female strength and to defend women's rights ironically leads to a perversion of feminism.

This perversion can also be seen in the TV fairy-tale film series, *Once Upon a Time* (2011–), *Grimm* (2011–), and *Beauty and the Beast* (2012–), which are laughable and stereotypical adaptations of classical fairy tales, even though they are set in the contemporary world and are "modernized." (4) Weapons, those wonderful phallic toys, are highly significant in almost all the contemporary fairy-tale films whether they are simply magic wands, bows and arrows, brooms, swords, intricate machine guns, electronic guns, knives, or clubs. The National Rifle Association would certainly applaud these fairy-tale films and might offer them a seal of good housekeeping if it awarded them. (5) While all of these films have either medieval or otherworldly settings, the sets tend to resemble contrived cardboard posters in my opinion, especially those in *Red Riding Hood* and *Hansel & Gretel: Witch Hunters*, as though inviting tourists to pay a visit to some fairy-tale theme park. (6) As adaptations of well-known fairy tales, these films do not enhance our understanding of what we already know about the tales, nor do they stimulate viewers to reflect more about them, or return to them to explore aspects that they had previously overlooked. Instead, they trivialize the contents so that the films primarily provide entertainment with happy endings even if some of them contain atrocious violence. What might be made relevant to social and political conflicts and problems through new interpretations of the fairy tales is made irrelevant.

If there has been any innovation in American fairy-tale films since the turn of the century, then it has been in the field of animation. The first *Shrek* (2001) film, based loosely on William Steig's delightful picture book, jolted the Disney Corporation in more ways than one. The superb digital artistry and witty original screenplay made previous Disney animated films look antiquated. However, none of the "Shrek" sequels ever matched the original film's irreverent and maverick charm.

Sequels almost inevitably lead to stale repetition. This can be seen in the case of *Hoodwinked* (2005), a computer-animated film, which endeavored to transform the tale of "Little Red Riding Hood" into an intriguing mystery and failed completely. This version dumbed down the classical tale and, in my opinion, did not deserve a sequel. Nevertheless, the Weinstein Company produced *Hoodwinked Too! Hood vs. Evil*, in 2011, to recreate not only the stupidity of the first film but also the meaninglessness of fairy-tale adaptations, even comic animations, when they fail to explore the deeper implications of traditional storytelling. Tex Avery, who produced multiple brilliant "Red Riding Hood" cartoons in the 1930s and 1940s, would surely be mortified by the *Hoodwinked* films if he were still alive today!

The case of *How to Train Your Dragon* (2010) is somewhat different. Based on the book series of the same name by Cressida Cowell, *How to Train Your Dragon* was the first computer-animated version of a fairy tale produced by DreamWorks, and it was visually stunning. Not only are the flight scenes of the multicolored diverse dragons portrayed vividly in the sky over grandiose landscapes, but the clash between the militaristic Viking father Stoick the Vast and his pacifist teenage son Hiccup are touching. In addition, their differences concerning war have clear parallels with debates about contemporary social and political issues in America. It is also clear that "Otherness" is a major theme, for at first, the dragons are viewed as predatory creatures that have to be destroyed. Once Hiccup reveals to his father that the dragons themselves are being oppressed by the enormous dragon Red Death, the war against the dragons turns into a battle against the "dictator" Red Death. The film that concludes with its protagonists moving towards peace and communal living with the amazing dragons raises important political questions.

Unfortunately, the film's first sequel of more to come, is, I believe, a dismal disappointment because it delights more in war than peace. *How to Train Your Dragon 2* depicts and indulges itself in continual battle scenes propelled by new digital technology. Despite the declared allegiance of Hiccup and his long-lost mother to saving dragons, somewhat like animal rights' activists, and maintaining peace between humans and dragons, they are drawn into one battle after another. As a result, the peaceful conclusion with the sentimental mother–son reunion appears contrived, especially after viewers have spent the duration of the film presumably delighting in one battle scene after another. The sequel not only loses the charm of the first film, but also undermines its pacifist intentions.

Yet, it is not always a sequel that undermines an original film or departs from the intentions of the filmmakers. For instance, the Disney/Pixar corporation caused the Academy Award winner, Brenda Chapman, co-director of the innovative animated film *Brave* (2012), to explode when she learned that Merida, the courageous wily heroine, whom she had created, had been changed after the film's first run into one of the Disney princess dolls. According to the report by the *Marin Independent Journal,*

> Disney crowned Merida its 11th princess on Saturday, but ignited a firestorm of protest with a corporate makeover of Chapman's original rendering of the character giving her a Barbie doll waist, sultry eyes and transforming her wild red locks into glamorous flowing tresses. The new image takes away Merida's trusty bow and arrow, a symbol of her strength and independence, and turns her from a girl to a young woman dressed in an off-the-shoulder version of the provocative, glitzy gown she hated in the movie.
>
> "I think it's atrocious what they have done to Merida," Chapman fumed. "When little girls say they like it because it's more sparkly, that's all fine and good but subconsciously, they are soaking in the sexy 'come hither' look and the skinny aspect of the new version. It's horrible! Merida was created to break that mold—to give young girls a better, stronger role model, a more attainable role model, something of substance, not just a pretty face that waits around for romance."
>
> (Liberatore 2013)

Brave is indeed a feminist fairy-tale film, and the fact that it was made by the Pixar Studio distinguishes it from the typical Disney animated films of this period such as *The Princess and the Frog* (2009) and *Tangled* (2010) with their "Barbie" princesses. *Brave* is a carnivalesque version of "King Thrushbeard," which can be compared to *The Taming of the Shrew*. This play and similar stories were perhaps some of the most sexist told throughout the Renaissance period and in the following centuries. The tale generally concerns an arrogant princess who demeans and insults her suitors. Because of her pride, her father banishes her from his kingdom. Sometimes he makes a pact to humiliate his daughter with one of the insulted princes, who disguises himself as a commoner (baker, cook, beggar, performer); alternatively, the insulted prince charms her with extraordinary gifts, sleeps with her, and makes her pregnant. The prince takes her to his own kingdom and compels her to work, often scolding her and beating her. Once she is sufficiently punished, the "commoner" reveals his true identity as prince, and they marry, for she is indeed "fit" to become a queen.

In *Brave*, Chapman and Mark Andrews turn the tale of "King Thrushbeard" upside down. As daughter of the Scottish King Fergus, Merida, who has grown up in the Highlands as an independent young woman, who can shoot a bow and arrow with the very best archers, refuses to follow tradition and marry a prince from another Scottish clan. In an archery contest with various princes, she wins and rejects all her suitors. This decision leads to an argument with her mother Elinor, who wants her to wed a prince chosen for her, and Merida resorts to a witch for her help. She receives a magic cake, which she offers her mother as a gesture of reconciliation, but the cake turns Elinor into a black bear. Merida is sorry and wants to redeem herself. She learns from the witch that only if she can mend the bond torn by pride can she save her mother and return her to her human form. As a bear, Elinor realizes that she was mistaken in wanting her daughter to enter into an arranged marriage and ends up encouraging Merida to remain independent. After a series of mishaps in which another ferocious bear almost kills Merida, Elinor saves her daughter, and Merida mends a tapestry that brings about the re-transformation of Elinor into a human. There is no wedding at the end of this film, but all the clans reaffirm their allegiance to one another. Mother and daughter are reunited with stronger bonds.

Though Chapman, the first female director of animated films at Pixar and screenplay writer, was ironically taken off the film she created because of creative disagreements,[2] her basic "feminist" message comes through. It is not a didactic film by any means. At times comic, it is one of the few fairy-tale films that has explored mother/daughter relationships with tenderness and compassion. In the majority of fairy-tale films mothers are depicted as vicious stepmothers or pushy caregivers. *Brave* breaks with conventional fairy-tale films to show how digital animation can be used artfully to speak to complex familial and social relations.

There are other exceptional American fairy-tale films, which have been produced in the shadow of Disney studios or on the margins of the American film industry. Three of them are worth discussing at length because they are diverse adaptations of oral and literary tales and novels: Tim Burton's unusual animated transformation of a folktale, *Corpse Bride* (2005); Joe Wright's re-vision of the oral and literary tale of "Little Red Riding Hood" as a dark spy mystery in *Hanna* (2011); and Peter Jackson's brilliant adaptation of J.R.R. Tolkien's simple fairy-tale novel, *The Hobbit*, into a fairy-tale epic consisting of three fascinating adventure films, *The Hobbit: An Unexpected Journey* (2012), *The Hobbit: The Desolation of Smaug* (2013), and *The Hobbit: The Battle of the Five Armies* (2014).

Burton has always been one of Hollywood's most provocative filmmakers.[3] Early in his career he made two very weird, short animated films, *Hansel and Gretel* (1982) and *Aladdin and his Wonderful Lamp* (1986), that indicate how he was to approach his later feature-length fairy-tale films *Sleepy Hollow* (1999), *Corpse Bride* (2005), and *Alice in Wonderland* (2010). Burton's fondness for combining animation with live-action filmmaking and projecting bizarre images can be seen in *Hansel and Gretel*, which begins with brightly painted toys running amuck and a gigantic fish swallowing a smaller one. We soon learn that these speckled and brightly colored automatons and clock have been created by a poor Japanese toymaker. But what is the strangest of all is Burton's Japanese cast, unusual for a German tale, with a grotesque stepmother played by a male actor, who also assumes the role of the witch.[4] Burton is intent—even though the short film was intended for family viewers—on queering the fairy tale and bringing out the chilling dark side of the Grimms' story.

Like the children's book author whom he greatly admires, Roald Dahl, Burton constantly seeks to upset conventional expectations and to focus on the gruesome and ridiculous aspects of storytelling. In *Hansel and Gretel*, everything is disproportionate and exaggerated. Nobody fits into traditional roles. The children eat green mush at a table much too large for them. They are taken through wallpapered woods painted green, and their cottage is an obvious artifice as are many of the other sets with live actors, who do not seem to mind such artificiality. A toy duck eats the stones that the children leave behind them so that they cannot find their way home. (In the

Grimms' version, a duck ferries them home to their father.) This toy transforms into a robot that leads them to the witch's cottage, which is, with all its contents, made entirely of gingerbread and candy. The witch sports a crooked, peppermint candy, red and white nose and is obviously a cross-dressed clown, who pretends at first to be kind. After the children eat candy, she leads them to their marshmallow beds. Immediately thereafter, the children's beds come to life, and red and white peppermint candy arms try to strangle them. A slimy gingerbread man demands that Hansel eat him.

The witch yells at the children in the same voice as the stepmother and ends up challenging them to a kung fu battle. The children manage to trick her into plunging through a cardboard silhouette oven into a fire. Thereafter, the house melts, and the duck emerges from the melted candy and carries them through the painted woods to their cardboard home where their father greets them. He tells them that they do not have to worry anymore because their stepmother is gone, and he will prepare a spaghetti dinner for them. When the children ask how they will live without money, the duck begins to spew coins out of its mouth. In the final shots, the father and children float into the air with coins bouncing all around them.

Burton makes a mockery out of the traditional fairy tale of "Hansel and Gretel," turning it into a haunting nightmare that estranges viewers, which is one of the reasons that Disney Studios shelved the film at that time. The actors keep straight faces in absurd costumes and settings that make it seem as if proper children are playing in a proper nursery room. They are not upset or disturbed by anything that happens around them. But, as Burton is wont to do, he unveils that nasty things are connected to sweets and charming objects, and that poverty and cannibalism lurk beneath proper outward appearances.

In his other important mock fairy-tale film, *Aladdin and his Wonderful Lamp*, Burton had to temper his outlandish and provocative style so prominent in *Hansel and Gretel* because he directed the film for Shelley Duvall's TV series *Faerie Tale Theatre*, which basically upholds good clean fun and propriety. Nevertheless, he relied on many of the same techniques from *Hansel and Gretel*, mixing animated settings and characters with real-life places and people, while turning Hollywood stereotypes of oriental characters into caricatures, queering the male characters, and mocking racial prejudice. The major protagonist of the film is not Aladdin—who is more or less an ignorant likeable dolt—but the genie, who narrates the film and interacts with all the characters. The great actor James Earl Jones plays the role of the genie. While he is supposed to be the slave to whoever owns the magic lamp, he constantly laughs and speaks with a boisterous voice, disobeying or resisting the masters of the lamp.

The entire slave/master relationship is turned on its head. Once the genie enters the scene, the film becomes a hilarious rendition of the *Arabian Nights*. As in *Hansel and Gretel* the actors play their roles with straight faces as if magic lamps, transformations, and flights were normal occurrences. In this carnivalesque fairy-tale film, however, there are no Gothic or macabre features. Darkness and horror were to occur in Burton's other fantasy films that followed *Aladdin and his Wonderful Lamp* such as *Edward Scissorhands* (1990) and *James and the Giant Peach* (1996).

By the time Burton produced *Sleepy Hollow* in 1999, he was already at the height of his craft; it was clear that Washington Irving's legend in his hands would be transformed into some kind of horror hybrid fairy tale. Indeed, it was, and it was also a critique of the vapid Disney animated musical film, *The Legend of Sleepy Hollow*, narrated and in part sung by Bing Crosby.[5] The Disney 1949 production made it seem that it was the authentic adaptation of Irving's tale, the sanctified cinematic version, but it is one-dimensional and totally predictable. Ichabod Crane is portrayed as a conniving loathsome schoolmaster, who deserves to be frightened out of his wits. This is basically the plot. There is no thought given to explore the local color and roots of American folklore or to develop the character of Ichabod, to show the problematic aspects of school teaching at the beginning of the nineteenth century and to recall the deeper meaning of the headless horseman.

In contrast, Burton's unusual adaptation sets the tale first about 1799 in New York City where crime is rampant and severely punished. Ichabod Crane is a moralistic New York detective, who believes, despite all evidence to the contrary, that everything in the world can be rationally explained and social justice can be achieved. Because of his idealistic viewpoint, a cruel arrogant judge who cannot tolerate Ichabod's moral stance sends him upstate to Sleepy Hollow to find out who has been chopping off heads in this provincial town. Ichabod's mission is actually a fairy-tale quest, and like most of Burton's heroes, even Alice, he is an anti-hero. That is, he is a geek: un-heroic, more a dreamer than a practical detective, afraid of blood and gore, awkward and yet intelligent and loveable. He is the bumbling young man of fairy tales, who sets out in search of adventures that bring out qualities that he never realized he possessed. Moreover, he is suffering from early childhood trauma that causes him to be anxious: his father, a stern, religious man, killed his mother who was suspected of being a witch, and Ichabod's dreams about this murder haunt him.

To Burton, the filmmaker/outsider, who always pursues out-of-the-box ideas and sometimes erroneously wanders inside into the big studios such as Disney, it is always important that the bizarre anti-hero of his films triumphs against the establishment. Despite all his lust for comic slashing of heads by the headless horseman, Burton unabashedly changes Irving's legend into a serious, moral fairy-tale film with Ichabod, the unassuming little hero, returning from his quest with his sweetheart and loyal assistant, having learned that there are many mysteries he will never be able to solve through scientific means.

In many respects, Burton's *Corpse Bride*, directed with Mike Johnson, continues to explore Burton's predisposition and fondness for portraying "meek geeks," who manage to survive in a world filled with greedy and mercenary people. This marvelously stop-motion digital animated musical,[6] which thrives on the Brechtian estrangement effect and has echoes of Kurt Weil's music from Bertolt Brecht's *The Three-Penny Opera*, casts a poetic son named Victor, clumsy, shy, and modest, into the role of a clumsy bridegroom. When he runs into the woods because he cannot meet a finicky clergyman's expectations of properly reciting the marriage vows to the charming demure Victoria in a dress rehearsal, he accidentally places the wedding ring on a dead bride named Emily, who drags him into the underworld, where he encounters exotic but friendly and talented dead people who know how to sing and enjoy their dead afterlife. One of the amusing characters is his faithful dead dog, who welcomes him with joy. Once Victor is wedded to Emily, he is desperate to return to the real world because of his unfaltering love for Victoria.

To add to his dilemma, there is a subplot about class struggle situated in Victorian England: Victor's parents want him to marry Victoria so they can move up the social register, while Victoria's snobby parents are only willing to approve of the marriage because they are impoverished and need money to save their family's noble name. Ironically, only Victor and Emily demonstrate true nobility—Victor, when he is willing to die for Emily's sake, and Emily, when she refuses to let Victor die because he is devoted to Victoria. In the end of this warm-hearted fairy-tale film, which takes place in a church, the class conflict is resolved when Victor duels with the snickering evil Lord Barkis, who had been Emily's former fiancé and murderer. During the duel, Emily dupes the villain into drinking poison, and as she leaves the church to return to the dead, she is transformed into hundreds of butterflies that fly off into the moonlight. So the film ends as it began when Victor in his study sets a butterfly free from a glass jar so that it can fly through the window into nature.

Burton allegedly based his film on a nineteenth-century Russian folktale,[7] which he heard from his friend Joe Raft, and it is clear that whatever story he heard, it stemmed from the categorical tale type ATU 365, "The Dead Bridegroom Carries off His Bride" (Uther 2004, 229). Generally speaking, this tale, which is several hundred years old with numerous oral and literary variants, involves a young woman who mourns for her bridegroom when he does not return from war. She employs some kind of magic, often a ring or potion, to bring him back to life. One evening he appears on a horse and invites her to ride behind him. When he asks her twice whether she is afraid, she replies no. But after they arrive at a graveyard and he asks a third time, she realizes he is dead and wants to pull her into an open grave. He tears her dress as she tries to escape, and she either manages to free herself or is pulled into the grave where she is torn to pieces or danced to death. This tale type was made famous by the German poet Gottfried August Bürger, who published the ballad, "Leonore," in 1774. In this romantic version, Leonore is more or less punished because she accuses God for being unfair and taking away her fiancé William. One night a mysterious stranger looking like William appears and carries her off on horseback to her grave.

Burton reverses the typical plot of this fairy tale and endows it with a more poignant secular meaning concerned with the freedom of choice within the limitations of social class. Whether he knew about "Leonore" or other oral or written narratives is irrelevant. The tale he heard became his own, Johnson's, and the screenplay writers of the film's, not to mention the animators'. The puppetry, stop-motion animation, and gear mechanism that propelled the puppets, produced outside of America, gave Burton's original interpretation of the tale an extraordinary effect that distanced itself from the sleeker digital animation that has become institutionalized in America. In short, *Corpse Bride* introduced an unusual method and approach to American fairy-tale animation that has yet to be matched.

Joe Wright's film *Hanna* also introduced an innovative approach to the cinematic adaptation of fairy tales that has scarcely been attempted in the US. Though Wright is a British director and most of the leading actors in Hanna are not American, the film was co-produced by an American company and involves a critique of the CIA. It is therefore more of a "globalized" fairy-tale film than an exclusively American product. More important than identifying the nationality of the film, however, is Wright's intricate mixing and adaptation of fairy-tale motifs, which he weaves throughout this spy thriller to demonstrate the cynicism that pervades American intelligence organizations. In the insightful chapter, "Fairy-Tale Remix in Film," in her book *Fairy Tales Transformed?* Cristina Bacchilega comments:

> In approaching how fairy-tale elements mix with other genres in contemporary films, what concerns me is the social significance of this generic complexity, its sociohistorical conditions, and its hierarchical interplay or economy. Most of all, by asking specific questions of these genre remixes, I seek to account for filmic uses of the fairy tale's story powers in ways that attune us to divergent effects, histories, and investments. How do the reality effects produced by generic incongruities match up with the fantasies that support everyday worlds? How are conditions and effects of hybridizing the fairy tale different from those of creolizing it on the big screen? And how do these generic economies call to specific audiences?
>
> (2013, 113)

Certainly, *Hanna* is a compelling example of a remix that blends fairy-tale motifs, characters, and settings to reform a tale such as "Little Red Riding Hood" so that it calls to question generic hierarchy and the sociohistorical conditions of surveillance throughout the world. At the same time, Wright's fascinating fairy-tale crime film also demonstrates how trivial American TV fairy-tale crime films such as *Grimm* and the animated *Hoodwinked* films are by comparison. Unlike the bland happy endings of the episodes in the "buddy-cop" *Grimm* and the mock detective *Hoodwinked* films, the startling open ending of *Hanna* stuns viewers and gives audiences pause for thought. This is because Wright's attitude toward fairy tales is unconventional. As he has stated in an interview with John Hiscock, "Fairy tales. . . are never happy, sweet stories. They're moral stories about overcoming the dark side and the bad. I find it ironic that happy endings now are called fairytale endings because there's nothing happy about most fairytale endings" (2011). Whether this is true is irrelevant because it is Wright's opinion that counts and that he shares with other filmmakers such as Tim Burton and Peter Jackson. In particular, it is the moral allegiance with nerds, freaks, outsiders, and little people that lends substance to the hybridization and cinematic adaptations of fairy tales and tempers the dark aspects of the films themselves.

In *Hanna*, we are dealing with a young teenager who calls herself a freak, and indeed, she is sort of freakish because she has been raised since age two by an ex-CIA operative, her father Erik, to be an assassin. The reason he does this is because he wants to take revenge on Marissa, a CIA agent, who killed Hanna's mother. It was this murder that caused Erik to leave the CIA and take Hanna to a hut in northern Finland, to teach her to speak several languages, to use all kinds of weapons including her bare hands to kill adversaries, and to use her brilliant mind to make her way through the world. So, while the film is indeed a spy thriller about a freakish teenager, who travels from Finland, to Morocco, Spain, and Germany in pursuit of a witchlike CIA agent, it is also a fairy-tale film of how an innocent young girl sets out from the provincial wilderness to the sinister city of Berlin, somewhat like Red Riding Hood setting out on her way to grandma's house that has become dangerous.

In one of the initial scenes of the film Hanna is shown reading a blood-stained book of the Grimms' fairy tales in German that has the signature of Johanna Zadek on it and is open to a page with illustrations of Red Riding Hood and the wolf. This signatory scene marks the fairy-tale path that Hanna will take. Once she leaves the hut in the woods, she will be pursued by wolves headed by a red-haired "witch," and along the way she will fight off predators until she lands in the dilapidated fairy-tale theme park in Berlin (see Figure 20.1). Her grandmother has been killed as has her father, her protector or huntsman, two characters from "Little Red Riding Hood," and she must save herself by shooting Marissa in the heart just as she had shot and killed a reindeer in the opening scene of the film. Whether Hanna will continue to survive in a brutal "civilized" world or return to the northern woods of Finland is an open question. She is alone in the end, simply on her own.

Wright has not adapted a particular fairy tale for this film. Rather he has created a collage in which Hanna, the film's naïve but highly intelligent and gifted protagonist, becomes entangled. There are even echoes of *Alice in Wonderland* in Wright's film, for Hanna has not had any contact with the real world outside of Finland since she was two years old. In many respects, for Hanna, the real world is a wonderland. She is just as much amazed by simple things such as electricity, television, fans, and machines of all sorts as people are amazed by her skills, particularly her skills as assassin. However, Hanna does not want to murder unless provoked. She wants and needs a friend.

FIGURE 20.1 At the fairy-tale theme park, Marissa (left) approaches Hanna (right), *Hanna* (2011).

FIGURE 20.2 Bilbo Baggins (right) joins Gandalf and the dwarfs on their journey, *The Hobbit: An Unexpected Journey* (2012).

And this is why Wright's ending is somewhat frightening. His fairy-tale film mix is a validation of his opinion of how fairy tales should end: Hanna is friendless in an unfriendly world.

This is not how Peter Jackson's three epic films about J.R.R. Tolkien's *The Hobbit* end. The films and Tolkien's fairy-tale novel are all about peace, community, and friendship without which evil cannot be conquered. In this regard, despite the fact that Jackson immensely expands and embellishes Tolkien's short novel, he remains very true to the author's vision. So, let us briefly review the major features of Tolkien's work, which appeared first in 1937 and was revised in 1951 and 1966.[8]

The plot of *The Hobbit* follows the pattern of numerous folk and fairy tales. Bilbo Baggins, a small, unassuming, almost nondescript person, is chosen by a wizard named Gandalf for an adventure because he will make for a good burglar. Though averse to leaving his home, Baggins accepts the challenge (see Figure 20.2). He travels with thirteen rugged dwarfs and has numerous hair-raising encounters with trolls, goblins, Wargs, and spiders, who represent the evil forces in Middle Earth. After showing that he is courageous and cunning by surviving these encounters, he helps the dwarfs regain their treasure-hoard from the dragon Smaug, who is killed by a great archer named Bard while attacking a nearby Lake-town of Men. Since the dwarfs want to keep the entire hoard for themselves, they must now contend with the elves and men who lay claim to some part of it. While they quarrel, the goblins and Wargs appear and seek to annihilate the dwarfs, elves, and the men of Lake-town. As a result, the Battle of Five Armies erupts into savage warfare, and, while Bilbo plays it safe by vanishing from sight thanks to his magic ring, the elves, dwarfs and men (aided by the eagles) defeat the forces of evil. Bilbo then returns home to his snug hobbit-hole, somewhat of a hero, but now regarded as not quite respectable and a little queer by other hobbits, who generally never dare to undertake such dangerous adventures. While Bilbo learns from the wizard Gandalf that he has played a hand in helping fulfill a messianic prophesy, the wizard reminds him to keep things in their proper perspective: "You don't really suppose, do you, that all of your adventures and escapes were managed by mere luck, just for your sole benefit? You are a very fine person, Mr. Baggins, and I am very fond of you; but you are only quite a little fellow in a wide world after all!" (Tolkien 1966, 317).

A little fellow to be sure, but a giant in potential and deeds. Like all "little fellows," Bilbo possesses vital powers which can contribute to the defeat of oppressors and the making of a new world. These powers are within him and must be brought out through "magic" (transformation) and shared communally to realize a common project with other beings. A hobbit is a forbear or descendant of all little fellow heroes—David, Tom Thumb, the brave little tailor, the persecuted maiden, the youngest son, the dumb fool—all those who do combat to right wrongs and create a just society in fairy tales. In *The Hobbit* there is an important twist in the pattern at the beginning of the narrative, and this distinguishes it from most tales about "little fellows." Traditionally, the little hero is fearless, accepts a challenge or banishment, and welcomes the chance to prove himself. Not Bilbo. He is perfectly content to rest in his pleasant hobbit-hole and must be prodded to go on an adventure. Tolkien's description of Bilbo (and all hobbits for that matter) is extremely significant, for it is quite clear that he is depicting the masses of "nondescript" people in the world. Bilbo is an unlikely hero: fifty years old, portly, unassuming, a creature of routine, nothing attractive or alluring about him. In other words, Bilbo is the ideal passive consumer and bachelor, who would probably like to sit in front of his TV set every evening, smoke a cigar, drink a beer, munch on chips, and have his fantasies played out for him on an electronic screen. But Bilbo, like all small people, has a spark within him which, when touched, can cause a chain reaction and explosion of his latent powers.

As Tolkien describes, "although he looked and behaved like a second edition of his solid and comfortable father," Bilbo "got something a bit queer in his makeup from the Took side, something that only awaited to come out" (1966, 11). The Took side was his mother's family, which was known to be adventurous, and indeed, there is something "Tookish" about Bilbo. After a visit by Gandalf, the wizard, who is renowned for sending people on "mad adventures," it is apparent that trouble is brewing. Gandalf is preparing Bilbo for an adventure of his own. This adventure begins in May, for it is the time of rebirth for Bilbo, who gradually sheds his provincial habits to learn about himself and the necessity for brotherhood in the struggle against the evil forces who take the shape of trolls, Gollum, wolves, and goblins. In the initial encounters against trolls and goblins, Bilbo shows that he is no hero in the usual sense, for he is scared. He is just plain ordinary and wonders why he ever left his hobbit-hole. However, soon thereafter he discovers the magic ring that has the power to make him invisible.[9] This discovery signifies the self-discovery of invisible latent powers, which are gradually emerging in Bilbo's character as he faces challenge after challenge.

As a symbol of transformation, the ring endows Bilbo with the power to perform in a way that he himself and the dwarfs never thought possible. Before dying, Thorin, king of the dwarfs, acknowledges this when he blesses Bilbo: "There is more in you of good than you know, child of the kindly West. Some courage and some wisdom, blended in measure. If more of us valued food and cheer and song above hoarded gold, it would be a merrier world" (Tolkien 1966, 301). There is a secure sense of home at the end of *The Hobbit*. Though Bilbo is considered somewhat strange by the other hobbits, he regains his place in society with a more profound understanding of his powers and the knowledge of how to cope with the divisive forces in the world. He has also learned how to work with and trust other creatures and knows the necessity of brotherhood for maintaining peace. A small fellow at the beginning of the tale, he wins the respect of elves, dwarfs, men, and a wizard and becomes a bigger "man" than hobbits generally are.

Jackson's cinematic portrayal of Bilbo, based on his collaboration with Fran Walsh, Philippa Boyens, and Guillermo del Toro, follows Tolkien's premise that small "queer" men can become big stalwart heroes, and for the most part, though the three epic films added new elements and made slight changes, they remain faithful to Tolkien's plot, which Tolkien himself had changed somewhat in two later revised editions of his novel to accord with his trilogy, *The Lord of the Rings*, which was published in 1954/1955. If there are problems with Jackson's cinematic adaptation of *The Hobbit*, they derive more from Jackson's desire to make a spectacle out of a simple fairy-tale novel that calls for subtle condensation rather than blatant expansion.

Having had great success with his cinematic production of *The Lord of the Rings*, Jackson made, in my opinion, a grave error when he essentially tried to repeat his accomplishments and connect

The Hobbit as prequel to *The Lord of the Rings*. Consequently, in all three lavish films there are incessant battle scenes with deus ex machina rescues, breathtaking views of natural landscapes, elaborate sets, frightening automated beasts and cute animals, tender love scenes, and comic escapades. Nor should we forget Jackson's addition of attractive women to provide a bit of glamour and romance, something that would have upset Tolkien because he believed that war was men's business. In short, the special effects offset the serious pacifist message of the three *Hobbit* films, for each one of them wallows in relentless fight after fight and war. This is a common problem in many films that speak out against violence by depicting extensive conflicts to awe audiences, such as in *How to Train your Dragon 2*. If Jackson had compressed the three screenplays into a more intense portrayal of a misfit hobbit drawn unexpectedly into war, his adaptation might have made a more innovative contribution to adaptations of literary fairy tales.

That being said, Jackson's films are interesting examples of how blockbusters, designed more for profit and celebrity, can still retain essential elements of a literary text and transform major themes into compelling stories that subvert conventional notions of geeks, women, and war. It is clear that Jackson and the writers of the screenplay have taken Tolkien's anti-war message seriously and employ a naïve young man, apolitical, tidy, and provincial, who morphs and matures through battles and war, to expose the disasters of war caused by greed and lust for power. Moreover, Jackson's addition of women who are independent and rebellious and conspicuously absent from Tolkien's novel provides a greater understanding of social relations.

Yet, the three films are basically about male camaraderie, pride, and aggression as central themes. War is the last resort of the dwarfs, elves, and humans, who basically want peace and to dwell in harmonious societies. As Jackson shows, keeping in mind Tolkien's own experiences in World War I and his critique of war, fairy-tale films involve position-taking and can address contemporary issues about evil and wars even if they are spectacles. More than ever before in the history of fairy-tale films, fairy tales are being adapted to speak to the dark and "grim" aspects in society, and in these films, as in oral and literary stories, we find moral counter-worlds proposing social changes for resolution that are difficult for us to realize in our contemporary one. Even though Bilbo Baggins learns in the third film of the trilogy that war has no victors, and no victories bring peace, he will never be the same good-natured hobbit upon his return home that he was when he left. Nor is there any indication that he will endeavor to work toward a different world.

In fact, home as a utopian goal will remain beyond his reach forever, just as Jackson's three spectacles do nothing to reveal how the resolution of conflicts might lead to pacifism and alternative worlds without violence. As Inkoo Kang has written in his review of *The Hobbit: Battle of the Five Armies*:

> When J.R.R. Tolkien's son accused Peter Jackson of missing the point of the Middle-earth books two years ago, he was far from alone in his distaste for the director's emphasis on spectacle above all else. If such disapproval bothers Jackson, the action auteur doesn't let it show. In fact, *The Hobbit: The Battle of the Five Armies*, which caps the trilogy, finds Jackson doubling down against his detractors by inserting a 45-minute battle sequence into his adaptation of the anti-war children's book. (2014)

I began this chapter by stating that we can really never get beyond the Disney production of spectacular fairy-tale films, and I did not make this statement because I am pessimistic about the future of American fairy-tale films. There is a dialectic here worth exploring because the Disney corporation is so dependent on audience reaction and reception of its fairy-tale films that Disney must go beyond the well-made Disney fairy-tale film to succeed on the global market.

Two cases in point are *Maleficent* (2014), which subverts the Disney animated *Sleeping Beauty* of 1959, and *Into the Woods* (2014), an adaptation of the 1987 musical, which domesticates this dark play. To begin with *Maleficent*: there are still many clichés in this contemporary film such as the message that only true love can save persecuted people from an evil curse and change the world (a point echoed in *Frozen*). The live-action film minimizes Disney's conventional "special effects for the sake of special effects" and takes a remarkable feminist approach to re-interpreting the tale of "Sleeping Beauty," whether it be the Charles Perrault, Grimm, or Disney version. The tale is told by an elderly narrator who turns out to be the "sleeping princess" Aurora and wants to set historical records straight. Maleficent, the so-called evil thirteenth fairy, is actually queen of the Moors, an idyllic, green and peaceful natural realm, and she was at one time in love with a remarkable peasant named Stefan. However, his ambition and greed led him to separate from Maleficent, to betray, and to rape her so that he could become king of a militaristic realm. Indeed, Aurora as narrator reveals that it is her father who is a viper—power-hungry and greedy. She explains how Maleficent regretted cursing her at birth and how she protected her from her father. In a terrifying battle at the end of the film, King Stefan falls off a tower as he attempts to murder Maleficent. His death enables the two kingdoms, the idyllic Moors and the hostile, aggressive realm under King Stefan's rule, to unite under Aurora, who will undoubtedly bring about a more just world with a prince named Philip at her side and Maleficent as her beneficent "fairy godmother."

Now this happy ending may seem somewhat kitschy and stereotypically "Disney," but this is a film to be taken seriously because it raises controversial issues in fairy tales that the Disney studios generally avoid. In this case, there are two, if not more, themes, in the film that indicate how it moves beyond the "well-made" Disney film: the rape scene and the projection of an alternative "green" world of social justice, one that is ruled by a woman. In an interview with the actress Angelina Jolie, who plays the part of Maleficent, she was asked about the scene in which her magnificent wings are ripped off her, i.e. raped, by Stefan, and she replies that she and the screenplay writer Linda Wolverton asked themselves what could make a woman become so dark and lose all sense of her maternity, her womanhood, and her softness that she would want to curse a baby and challenge another kingdom:

> Something would have to be so violent and aggressive and so of course for us, we were very conscious . . . that it was a metaphor for rape. . . . And then at a certain point, the question of the story is "what would bring her back [from wanting to harm Aurora and Stefan]?" And again it is an extreme Disney, fun version of it, but at the core it is abuse, and how the abused then have a choice of abusing others or overcoming and remaining loving, open people.
>
> (Holmes 2014)[10]

By overcoming abuse and confronting tyranny, *Maleficent* lays the groundwork for a different kind of society that will combine a cultivation of nature and the environment with a more democratic approach to government. Rarely has any Disney fairy-tale film, animated or live-action, addressed these themes with the sensitivity that *Maleficent* delivers so effectively.

In contrast, the Disney version of *Into the Woods* shows a lack of sensitivity with regard to some of the urgent problems at the core of the original musical. Something wooden and mechanical about the cinematic adaptation makes it seem as though none of the characters or themes of the tales are relevant anymore. There is, in fact, nothing alive or lively in the film. As Judith Flanders writes in the *Times Literary Supplement*, by the second part of the film,

> the characters mostly run about in a tizzy, shouting at each other as they attempt to defeat the giant's widow, who is looking for revenge on Jack. And so our empathy fades, the characters

not having done enough in the first part to carry us past this hurry-scurry. Prince Charming (Chris Pine) is a boy-band parody, a walking advertisement for hair product and North American dentistry (indeed he and Cinderella could do their bit for the environment by lighting their palace by the gleam of their pearly whites), while little Cinders is so whiny and nasal that his abandonment of her seems rational. Red Riding Hood, who should be flatly, slyly comic, is merely aggressive. By the second hour, I longed for Johnny Depp to return and swallow them all whole.

(2015, 18)

It seems that director (Rob Marshall), playwright (James Lapine), and composer (Stephen Sondheim) just want to bring off a "well-made" play that will comply with Disney standards and entertain family audiences. This is made clear in an interview with James Lapine, who rewrote his play for a PG family screen audience (Pietzman 2014). The film's dark parody of fairy tales is not related to the social issues of our times but is rather turned into an obligatorily sentimental story about human failings with a pale rosy ending.

Into the Woods, musical and film, combines four different fairy tales, "Jack and the Beanstalk," "Little Red Riding Hood," "Rapunzel," and "Cinderella," in a most innovative way to focus on the danger of wishes. In this respect the storyline based on the saying, "be careful for what you wish for," is highly critical of classical fairy tales, somewhat pessimistic about human relations and compassion, and results in a tragi-comic view of life. As an American play first produced during the Ronald Reagan era, *Into the Woods,* the play, suggests that there was indeed very little hope for the wishes of common American people and for social justice at that time. Indeed, the government offered its own theater of farce and deception. There was nothing authentic to be found in the social consciousness of ruling American elites and in the new laws that were to benefit the rich. In this regard, Stephen Sondheim and James Lapine indicated that the mindlessly idealistic interpretation of fairy tales was an embarrassment in those dark days—just as it remains today.

Whether or not they intended such a critique, they offered a perspective on American life that resonated with the public: be careful for what you wish for. Wolves were still raping young girls in the forest; princes were still callous and sexist; young women were still witches, bitches, or persecuted victims; and money or gold could not bring happiness. Lapine and Sondheim invented an ironic narrator who explained why all this was so, even "once upon a time," and they employed an amusing estrangement effect by having him tell the tales, intervene in the action, and speak to the audience until he is thrown to the giant to be killed because the characters want to tell their own story and determine their own destinies. So, the ending for the survivors who manage to kill the revengeful female giant is bittersweet. They had gone into the woods to learn about themselves and the world, and they return to their village without having their wishes fulfilled. And it is really unclear as to whether their experiences have taught them anything more than to have compassion for their suffering companions.

The result is the same in the film, but the narrator and parody are missing, as is the zest of the characters eager to have their dreams fulfilled. Additionally, it is disturbing to watch a film in which the voices of the actors recorded in a studio are not synchronized when they mouth the words of the songs in the woods. Moreover, many of the sexual gags such as the wolf's penis apparent to everyone and the bawdy elements of the princes' songs about their agony have been virtually eliminated. Little Jack has been woefully miscast as a very young boy while the character was much older and funnier in the play. Finally, even the American actors speak with a British accent. The American vernacular worked well in the play. Just because there are princes in the play, does not mean they must be British!

LIST OF CONTRIBUTORS

Cristina Bacchilega (Professor of English, University of Hawai'i at Mānoa) teaches fairy tales and their adaptations, folklore and literature, and cultural studies. She is the author of *Postmodern Fairy Tales: Gender and Narrative Strategies* (1997), *Legendary Hawai'i and the Politics of Place: Tradition, Translation, and Tourism* (2007), and *Fairy Tales Transformed? 21st-Century Adaptations and the Politics of Wonder* (2013); co-editor of *Angela Carter and the Fairy Tale* (2001) and co-editor of *Marvels & Tales: Journal of Fairy-Tale Studies*. Her recent contributions to fairy-tale studies appear in the journal *Narrative Culture* (2015), *The Cambridge Companion to the Fairy Tale* (2015), *Channeling Wonder: Fairy Tales on Television* (2014), *Marvelous Transformations: An Anthology of Fairy Tales and Contemporary Critical Perspectives* (2012), and *Transgressive Tales: Queering the Grimms* (2012).

Marina Balina is Isaac Funk Professor of Russian Studies at Illinois Wesleyan University, USA. She is the author, editor, and co-editor of numerous volumes, including most recently *Russian Children's Literature and Culture* (with Larissa Rudova, 2008), *Petrified Utopia: Happiness Soviet Style* (with Evgeny Dobrenko, 2009), *The Cambridge Companion to Twentieth Century Russian Literature* (with Evgeny Dobrenko, 2011), *Constructing Childhood: Literature, History, Anthropology* (2011, in Russian) and *To Kill Charskaia: Politics and Aesthetics in Soviet Children's Literature of the 1920s and 1930s* (2012, in Russian). Her main area of investigation is children's literature in Soviet Russia, its historical development, and its theoretical originality. In addition to her work in children's literature, her scholarly interests include the hybrid nature of life-writing in Soviet and post-Soviet Russia (autobiography, memoir, diary, and travelogue) and she has published widely on this subject.

Birgit Beumers is Professor in Film Studies at Aberystwyth University, Wales, UK. After completing her DPhil at St. Antony's College, Oxford, she specialised on Russian theater and cinema, as well as Soviet cultural history. Her publications include *A History of Russian Cinema* (2009) and, with Mark Lipovetsky, *Performing Violence* (2009). She has edited a number of volumes, including *Alexander Shiryaev, Master of Movement* (2009, with D. Robinson and V. Bocharov), *Directory of World Cinema: Russia* (2010), and *The Cinema of Alexander Sokurov* (2011, with Nancy Condee). She is editor of the online journal *KinoKultura* and of the scholarly journal *Studies in Russian and Soviet Cinema*. She is currently writing a book on early Soviet animation, and working on contemporary Russian and Central Asian cinema.

Lauren Bosc is a recent graduate of the Master of Arts in Cultural Studies, Texts and Cultures program at the University of Winnipeg. An interdisciplinary scholar, her research interests span from fairy-tale studies to fat studies, where she is particularly interested in how the representation of the body in television and film is (mis)interpreted by those who choose to consume it. She currently works as research coordinator in the Department of Women's and Gender Studies at the University of Winnipeg.

Elizabeth Bullen is senior lecturer at Deakin University, Melbourne, Australia, where she teaches literary studies and children's literature. An interdisciplinary scholar, her research typically synthesizes literary studies, sociology, and cultural studies theory and perspectives. Her books include *Consuming Children: Education, Entertainment, Advertising* (2001, co-written with Kenway) and *Haunting the Knowledge Economy* (2006, co-written with Kenway, Fahy, and Robb). She has published articles in *Media Culture Society, International Research in Children's Literature, Gender and Education, Children's Literature, Discourse, Children's Literature in Education, Journal of Youth Studies,* and *Theory and Research in Education.* The edited collections in which her research appears include *Contemporary Children's Literature and Film: Engaging with Theory* (2011), *Living and Learning in the Shadow of the "Shopocalypse": Towards a Critical Pedagogy of Consumption* (2010), and *Handbook of Children, Media and Culture* (2008). Her current research focuses on girlhood, class, and consumerism.

Justyna Deszcz-Tryhubczak is Assistant Professor of Literature and Director of the Center for Young People's Literature and Culture at the Department of English Studies, University of Wrocław, Poland, where she teaches courses on children's literature and film. A Kosciuszko Scholar (2012), she published a monograph on Salman Rushdie, *Rushdie in Wonderland: "Fairytaleness" in Salman Rushdie's Fiction* (2004). She has also published articles on Salman Rushdie, Angela Carter, fairy tales, and YA fantasy, for example in *Folklore* and *Marvels & Tales.* She co-edited *Towards or Back to Human Values? Spiritual and Moral Dimensions of Contemporary Fantasy* (2006), *Considering Fantasy: Ethical, Didactic and Therapeutic Aspects of Fantasy in Literature and Film* (2007), and *Relevant across Cultures: Visions of Connectedness and Earth Citizenship in Modern Fantasy for Young Readers* (2009). Her research interests include children's literature and culture, utopianism, ecocriticism, and intermediality.

Anne E. Duggan is Professor of French and Chair of Classical and Modern Languages, Literatures, and Cultures at Wayne State University, Detroit, Michigan. She is author of *Salonnières, Furies, and Fairies: The Politics of Gender and Cultural Change in Absolutist France* (2005), and *Queer Enchantments: Gender, Sexuality, and Class in the Fairy-Tale Cinema of Jacques Demy* (2013; French translation 2015). She is co-editor of *Folktales and Fairy Tales: Traditions and Texts from around the World* (2015) and of *Marvels & Tales: Journal of Fairy-Tale Studies.*

Pauline Greenhill is Professor of Women's and Gender Studies at the University of Winnipeg, Manitoba, Canada. Her recent books are *Channeling Wonder: Fairy Tales on Television* (co-edited with Jill Terry Rudy, 2014), *Unsettling Assumptions: Tradition, Gender, Drag* (co-edited with Diane Tye, 2014), *Transgressive Tales: Queering the Grimms* (co-edited with Kay Turner, 2012), *Fairy Tale Films: Visions of Ambiguity* (co-edited with Sidney Eve Matrix, 2010), and *Make the Night Hideous: Four English Canadian Charivaris, 1881–1940* (2010). She has published in *Atlantis, Canadian Journal of Women and the Law, Canadian Woman Studies, Ethnologies, Fabula, The Folklore Historian, Journal of American Folklore, Journal of Canadian Studies, Journal of Folklore Research, Journal of Ritual Studies, Marvels & Tales, Manitoba History, parallax, Signs,* and *Western Folklore,* among others. In addition to her research on queer and trans fairy tales and fairy-tale films, she is exploring ethnic drag and masquerade in western Canada.

Peter Hames studied international relations at Keele University before taking his PhD in Film Studies at the Slade School of Fine Art, University College, London. He lectured in film and media studies at Staffordshire University until 1998 where he is currently Visiting Professor in Film Studies. He has been a programme advisor to the London Film Festival since 1990 and has contributed to many journals including *Sight and Sound, Studies in Eastern European Cinema, Kinoeye,* and *KinoKultura.* His books include *The Czechoslovak New Wave* (2005), *Czech and Slovak Cinema: Theme and Tradition* (2009), *Best of Slovak Film 1921–1991* (2013) and, as editor, *The Cinema of Central Europe* (2004), *The Cinema of Jan Švankmajer: Dark Alchemy* (2008), and *Cinemas in Transition in Central and Eastern Europe after 1989* (with Catherine Portuges, 2013).

Laura Hubner is Senior Lecturer in Film and Media at the University of Winchester, UK, and she is currently working on a book about fairy-tale and Gothic horror. She is author of *The Films of Ingmar Bergman: Illusions of Light and Darkness* (2007), editor of *Valuing Films: Shifting Perceptions of Worth* (2011), and co-editor of *Framing Film: Cinema and the Visual Arts* (2012) and *The Zombie Renaissance in Popular Culture* (2014).

Steven Kohm is Associate Professor of Criminal Justice at the University of Winnipeg, Manitoba, Canada. His research interests include reality TV and crime, popular criminology and film, and fairy-tale-themed crime films. His research on crime in popular culture appears in such international journals as *Theoretical Criminology, Crime Media Culture,* and *Canadian Journal of Criminology and Criminal Justice.* He is editor of *The Annual Review of Interdisciplinary Justice Research* and a founding member of the Centre for Interdisciplinary Justice Studies at the University of Winnipeg.

Sung-Ae Lee is a lecturer in the Department of International Studies at Macquarie University, Australia, where she teaches mainly Asian cinema and culture. Her major research focus is on fiction, film, and television drama of East Asia, with particular attention to Korea. Her research centers on relationships between cultural ideologies in Asian societies and representational strategies. She has published on fairy tale and folktale in *International Research in Children's Literature* and *Asian Ethnology,* and in *Grimms' Tales Around the Globe* (2014). She is interested in cognitive and imagological approaches to adaptation studies, Asian popular culture, Asian cinema, the impact of colonization in Asia, trauma studies, fiction and film produced in the aftermath of the Korean War, and the literature and popular media of the Korean diaspora.

Jing Li is Assistant Professor of Chinese at Gettysburg College, Pennsylvania, USA. Her research focuses on Chinese folk narrative, festival, women's folklore, touristic dance performance, ethnic tourism in southwest China, and China's Intangible Cultural Heritage movement. Her publications include encyclopedia entries on Chinese tales and book reviews on English-language anthologies of Chinese folk narrative. She has published articles in *Modern China, Asian Ethnicity, Journal of Tourism and Cultural Change, Asia Pacific Journal of Tourism Research, Indian Folklife,* 民俗研究, *Folklore Studies,* and 中国民间文学论坛, *Tribune of Folk Literature.* She is currently co-editing a special journal issue on "New Themes and Perspectives in Contemporary Chinese Folklore Studies."

Kendra Magnus-Johnston (nee Magnusson) is an interdisciplinary studies doctoral student at the University of Manitoba. She holds a master's degree in cultural studies and an undergraduate degree in rhetoric and communications from the University of Winnipeg. Her research has appeared in academic journals, such as *Marvels & Tales* and *Children's Literature Association Quarterly*; edited collections, such as Pauline Greenhill and Jill Terry Rudy's *Channeling Wonder*; and encyclopedias, such as Jack Zipes's *The Oxford Companion to Fairy Tales*. Her research focuses on areas related to folk practice, paratextuality, and fairy-tale studies. She participates in the Fairy-Tale Films Research Group, funded by the Social Sciences and Humanities Research Council of Canada (SSHRC), Principal Investigator Pauline Greenhill, and was awarded an SSHRC doctoral fellowship in 2011 to investigate artistic engagement with urban space in her hometown, Winnipeg, Manitoba.

Sadhana Naithani is Professor of Literature and Folklore at the Centre of German Studies, Jawaharlal Nehru University, New Delhi. Her PhD dissertation in the field of German folksongs was researched under the guidance of Professor Lutz Rohrich at the German Folksong Archive, Freiburg. Her publications in this field include *In Quest of Indian Folktales: Pandit Ram Gharib Chaube and William Crooke* (2006), *The Story-Time of the British Empire: Colonial and Postcolonial Folkloristics* (2010), and *Folklore Theory in Post-War Germany* (2014). She has written on folklore in political propaganda, on the theme of nation in Bollywood films, on the musical folk culture and the form of Bollywood films, and on films based on folktales and fairy tales. She is a member of the Executive Committee of the International Society for Folk Narrative Research.

Susan Napier is Professor of Japanese Studies at Tufts University. Her recent books include *From Impressionism to Anime: Japan as Fantasy and Fan Culture in the Mind of the West, Anime from* Akira *to* Howl's Moving Castle (2007), and *The Fantastic in Modern Japanese Literature* (2005). Her numerous scholarly articles range from discussions of the animated media to an analysis of the *Harry Potter* series as part of the British fantasy tradition. Besides teaching Japan-related courses on literature, gender, and popular culture, she also teaches "Fantasy in World Culture," and "The Cinema of Apocalypse." She also blogs frequently for *The Huffington Post*.

Elisabeth Oxfeldt holds a PhD from the University of California at Berkeley. She is currently Professor of Scandinavian Literature at the University of Oslo, Norway. Her books include *Romanen, nasjonen og verden. Nordisk litteratur i et postnasjonalt perspektiv* (The Novel, the Nation, and the World. Scandinavian Literature from a Postnational Perspective, 2012), *Knut Hamsun: Transgression and Worlding* (co-edited with Dingstad et al., 2011), *Journeys from Scandinavia. Travelogues of Africa, Asia, and South America, 1840–2000* (2010), *H.C. Andersens eventyr på film* (Hans Christian Andersen's Fairy Tales on Film, 2009), *H.C. Andersen—eventyr, kunst og modernitet* (Hans Christian Andersen—Fairy Tales, Art, and Modernity, 2006—editor), and *Nordic Orientalism. Paris and the Cosmopolitan Imagination 1800–1900* (2005). She has published in *Edda*, *Agora*, *Kritik*, *Spring*, and *Animation Journal*, among others. She is currently writing about graphic novels and is always interested in postcolonial studies.

Marek Oziewicz is the Marguerite Henry Professor of Children's and Young Adult Literature at the University of Minnesota—Twin Cities. A firm believer in the power of stories to nurture empathy, the human potential, and understanding across cultures, he has co-edited five collections of essays and published over fifty book chapters and articles in journals such as *International Research in Children's Literature*, *Journal of the Fantastic in the Arts*, *The Lion and the Unicorn*, *Mythlore*, *Children's Literature in Education*, *Extrapolation*, and others. His book *One Earth, One People* (McFarland 2008) won the 2010 Mythopoeic Scholarship Award in Myth and Fantasy Studies. His two most recent books are *Crime and the Fantastic* (WVT 2014, co-edited with Daniel D. Hade) and *Justice in Young Adult Speculative Fiction: A Cognitive Reading* (Routledge 2015). His research interests include speculative fiction and literature-based cognitive modeling for moral education, global citizenship, environmental awareness, and justice literacy. His current projects involve a study of a subgenre of historical fiction dubbed Bloodlands fiction and a series of interviews with authors of children's literature about narrative representations of justice and nonviolence.

Sofia Samatar is Assistant Professor of Literature and Writing at California State University Channel Islands. A scholar of African and Arabic literature, she has published articles in *Research in African Literatures* and *At the Crossroads: Readings of the Postcolonial and the Global in African Literature and Visual Art* (2014), edited by Ghirmai Negash. In addition to her scholarship, she writes fiction and poetry. Her debut novel *A Stranger in Olondria* (2013) won the William L. Crawford Fantasy Award, the British Fantasy Award, and the World Fantasy Award.

Naarah Sawers is a Research Fellow in the Centre for Research in Educational Futures and Innovation, Deakin University, Melbourne, Australia. Her research spans the interdisciplinary intersection between children's and adult literatures, and employs new approaches to analyzing literary fiction, including new science studies, socio-political ethics, feminist philosophies, and cultural theory. Her most recent book is *Critical Fictions: Science, Feminism, and Corporeal Subjectivity* (2008). She has written for the edited collection *Fairy Tale Films: Visions of Ambiguity* (2010) and published in *Children's Literature in Education*, *Children's Literature Association Quarterly*, *Papers: Explorations into Children's Literature*, and *Continuum: Journal of Media and Cultural Studies*.

Jessica Tiffin holds a doctoral degree from the University of Cape Town, where she is Coordinator of Undergraduate Studies for the Faculty of Humanities. Her book *Marvelous Geometry: Narrative and Metafiction in Modern Fairy Tale* (2009) argues for the inherent self-consciousness of the fairy-tale form across a wide range of contemporary literary, popular, and cinematic texts. Her recent articles and conference papers have included explorations of the fairy-tale work of Tanith Lee, Edith Nesbit, and Catherynne M. Valente, and of the pedagogic implications of the *Harry Potter* series. In addition to fairy-tale literature and film, her research and teaching interests include popular narrative, fantasy and science fiction, the Gothic, children's literature, Victorian non-realist fiction, and internet culture.

Paul Wells is Director of the Animation Academy, Loughborough University, UK. He has written widely in the field of animation studies, including *Understanding Animation* (1998), *Animation: Genre and Authorship* (2002), *Halas & Batchelor: An Animated History* (2006), *Re-imagining Animation* (with Johnny Hardstaff) (2008), *The Animated Bestiary* (2009), and *Animation, Sport and Culture* (2014). He is also an established writer and director for radio, TV, film, and theater, recently writing and directing *An Animated Utopia: The Life and Achievement of John Halas* (UK, 2012), and *The Oil Kid* (Norway, 2013), and conducting workshops and consultancies worldwide, based on his book, *Scriptwriting* (2007). He is Chair of the Association of British Animation Collections (ABAC).

Jack Zipes is professor emeritus of German and Comparative Literature at the University of Minnesota. In addition to his scholarly work, he is an active storyteller in public schools and has worked with children's theaters in Europe and the United States. Some of his major publications include *Breaking the Magic Spell: Radical Theories of Folk and Fairy Tales* (1979), *Fairy Tales and the Art of Subversion* (rev. ed. 2006), *The Brothers Grimm: From Enchanted Forests to the Modern World* (1988), *Hans Christian Andersen: The Misunderstood Storyteller* (2005), and *Why Fairy Tales Stick: The Evolution and Relevance of a Genre* (2006). He has also edited *The Oxford Companion to Fairy Tales* (2000), *The Great Fairy Tale Tradition* (2001), and *The Golden Age of Folk and Fairy Tales: From the Brothers Grimms to Andrew Lang* (2013). Most recently he has published *The Enchanted Screen: The Unknown History of Fairy-Tale Films* (2010), *The Irresistible Fairy Tale: The Cultural and Social History of a Genre* (2012), and *Grimm Legacies: The Magic Power of the Grimms' Folk and Fairy Tales* (2014).

FILMOGRAPHY

7 Dwarfs—Men Alone in the Woods (7 Zwerge—Männer allein im Wald). 2004. Dir. Sven Unterwaldt. Germany.

7 Dwarfs—The Woods Are Not Enough (7 Zwerge—Der Wald ist nicht genug). 2006. Dir. Sven Unterwaldt. Germany.

1001 Nights (1001 nuits). 1990. Dir. Philippe de Broca. France.

1001 Nights (Pohádky tisíce a jedné noci). 1974. Dir. Karel Zeman. Czechoslovakia.

1942: A Love Story. 1994. Dir. Vidhu Vinod Chopra. India.

Aandhi. 1975. Dir. Gulzar. India.

About a Sheep and a Goat (Pro barana i kozla). 2004. Dir. Natal'ia Berezovaia and Elena Komarova. Russia.

About Ivan the Fool (Pro Ivana-duraka). 2003. Dir. Mikhail Aldashin. Russia.

Adventures in Zambezia. 2012. Dir. Wayne Thornley. South Africa.

The Adventures of Alenushka and Erema (Prikliucheniia Alenushki i Eremy). 2008. Dir. Georgii Gitis. Russia.

The Adventures of the Blue Knight (Przygody Błękitnego Rycerzyka). 1963–1965. TV. Dir. Stanisław Dulz, Alfred Ledwig, Leszek Lorek, Lechosław Marszałek, Władysław Nehrebecki, and Edward Wator. Poland.

The Adventures of Buratino (Prikliucheniia Buratino). 1976. TV. Created by Leonid Nechaev. USSR.

The Adventures of Colargol the Bear (Przygody Misia Colargola). 1967–1974. TV. Dir. Teresa Badzian, Lucjan Dembiński, Krustyna Dobrowolska, Anna Harda, Janina Hartwig, Eugeniusz Ignaciuk, Marian Kiełbaszczak, Jadwiga Kudrzycka, Edward Sturlis, Tadeusz Wilkosz, and Dariusz Zawilski. Poland.

The Adventures of Filemon the Cat (Przygody kota Filemona). 1977–1981. TV. Dir. Ludwik Kronic, Alina Kotowska, Wacław Fedak, Ireneusz Czesny, Ryszard Szymczak, Andrzej Piliczewski, and Zbigniew Czernelecki. Poland.

The Adventures of Hansel and Gretel (Przygody Jasia i Małgosi). 1983. Dir. Zofia Oraczewska. Poland.

The Adventures of the Little Red Riding Hood (Przygody Czerwonego Kapturka). 1983. Dir. Zofia Oraczewska. Poland.

The Adventures of Pinocchio (Le avventure di Pinocchio). 1972. Dir. Luigi Comencini. Italy/France/West Germany.

The Adventures of Prince Achmed (Die Abenteuer des Prinzen Achmed). 1926. Dir. Lotte Reiniger and Carl Koch. Germany.

The Adventures of Priscilla, Queen of the Desert. 1994. Dir. Stephen Elliot. Australia.

Aladdin and his Wonderful Lamp. 1986. Dir. Tim Burton. United States.

Aladdin and the Magical Lamp (Aladdin et la lampe magique). 1970. Dir. Jean Image. France.

Alesha Popovich and Tugarin the Serpent (Alesha Popovich i Tugarin zmei). 2004. Dir. Konstantin Bronzit. Russia.

Alexander Nevsky. 1938. Dir. Sergei Eisenstein. USSR.

Ali Baba and the Forty Thieves (Ali Baba et les quarante voleurs). 1902. Dir. Ferdinand Zecca. France.

Ali Baba and the Forty Thieves (Ali Baba et les quarante voleurs). 1954. Dir. Jacques Becker. France.

Ali Baba and the Forty Thieves (Ali Baba et les quarante voleurs). 2007. Dir. Pierre Aknine. France.

Ali Baba and the Sacred Crown (Le Sette Fatiche di Ali Baba). 1962. Dir. Emimmo Salvi. Italy.

Ali Baba and the Seven Saracens (Sindbad contro i sette saraceni). 1964. Dir. Emimmo Salvi. Italy.

Alibaba and the Forty Thieves (Alibaba aur 40 chor/Priklyucheniya Ali-Baby i soroka razboinikov). 1980. Dir. Latif Faiziyev and Umesh Mehra. India/USSR.

Alice (Něco z Alenky). 1988. Dir. Jan Švankmajer. Switzerland/Germany/United Kingdom.

Alice. 2009. TV. Dir. Nick Willing. Canada/United Kingdom.

Alice in Wonderland. 1951. Dir. Clyde Geronimi, Wilfred Jackson, and Hamilton Luske. United States.

Alice in Wonderland. 1988. Dir. Rich Trueblood. Australia.

Alice in Wonderland. 2010. Dir. Tim Burton. United States.

Alice through the Looking Glass. 1987. Dir. Andrea Bresciani and Richard Slapczynski. Australia/Italy.

Alice's Odyssey (L'odyssée d'Alice Tremblay). 2002. Dir. Denise Filiatrault. Canada.

Allegro non troppo. 1976. Dir. Bruno Bozzetto. Italy.

Amadeus. 1984. Dir. Miloš Forman. United States.

Anand Math. 1952. Dir. Hemen Gupta. India.

Andersen: A Life without Love (Andersen: Zhizn bez lyubvi). 2006. Dir. Eldar Ryazanov. Russia.

Animal Farm. 1954. Dir. Joy Batchelor and John Halas. United Kingdom.

Animaland Series. 1946. Dir. David Hand/Various. United Kingdom.

Animated Matches Playing Cricket. 1899. Dir. Arthur Melbourne Cooper. United Kingdom.

Animated Matches Playing Volleyball. 1899. Dir. Arthur Melbourne Cooper. United Kingdom.

Arang. 2006. Dir. Ahn Sang-Hoon. South Korea.

As Dreamers Do: The Amazing Life of Walt Disney. 2014. Dir. Logan Sekulow. United States.

Ashima (Ashima 阿诗玛). 1964. Dir. Liu Qiong. China.

The Ashlad and His Good Helpers (Askeladden og de gode hjelperne). 1961. Dir. Ivo Caprino. Norway.

The Ashlad and the Hungry Troll (Gutten som kappåt med trollet). 1967. Dir. Ivo Caprino. Norway.

Astro Boy. 1963–1966. TV. Dir. Osamu Tezuka. Japan.

Atanarjuat: The Fast Runner. 2001. Dir. Zacharias Kunuk. Canada.

Le Avventure di Pinocchio. 1947. Dir. Giannetto Guardone. Italy.

Awaara. 1951. Dir. Raj Kapoor. India.

Azur and Asmar: The Princes' Quest (Azur et Asmar). 2006. Dir. Michel Ocelot. France/Belgium/Spain/Italy.

Baba Yaga from 8 a.m. to 3 p.m. (Baba Jaga od 8.00 do 15.00). 1984. Dir. Leszek Komorowski. Poland.

Babine. 2008. Dir. Luc Picard. Canada.

Babka Ezhka and Others (Babka Ezhka i drugie). 2007. Dir. Valerii Ugarov. Russia.

Ballad of a Soldier (Ballada o soldate). 1959. Dir. Grigorii Chukhrai. USSR.

The Band Concert. 1935. Dir. Wilfred Jackson. United States.

Bandini. 1963. Dir. Bimal Roy. India.

Baron Münchhausen (Baron Prášil). 1961. Dir. Karel Zeman. Czechoslovakia.

Báthory. 2008. Dir. Juraj Jakubisko. Slovakia/Hungary/Czech Republic/United Kingdom.

Battle of Myung-Ryang (Myung-Ryang). 2014. Dir. Kim Han-Min. South Korea.

The Bear and the Mouse. 1966. Dir. F.W. Remmler and Ingrid Remmler. Canada.

Bearskin (Der Bärenhäuter). 1986. Dir. Walter Beck. East Germany.

The Beast and the Beauty (Yasu wa Minyeo). 2005. Dir. Lee Gye-Byeok. South Korea.

Beastly. 2011. Dir. Daniel Barnz. United States.

Beautiful Lukanida (Прекрасная Люканида). 1912. Władysław Starewicz. Russia.

Beautiful Vasilisa (Vasilisa prekrasnaia). 1939. Dir. Aleksandr Rou. USSR.

Beauty and the Beast (La Belle et la Bête). 1946. Dir. Jean Cocteau. France.

Beauty and the Beast (Panna a netvor). 1978. Dir. Juraj Herz. Czechoslovakia.

Beauty and the Beast. 1991. Dir. Gary Trousdale and Kirk Wise. United States.

Beauty and the Beast. 2009. Dir. David Lister. Australia/Canada/United States.

Beauty and the Beast. 2012–. TV. Created by Ron Koslow. United States.

Beauty and the Beast (La Belle et la Bête). 2014. Dir. Christophe Gans. France.

Becoming Jane. 2007. Dir. Julian Jarrold. United Kingdom/Ireland.

Bedtime Story (Dobranocka). 1997. Dir. Daniel Szczechura. Poland.

Bellerofon (Bellerofon). 1959. Dir. Edward Sturlis. Poland.

Betaab. 1983. Dir. Rahul Rawail. India.

Bhavni Bhavai. 1980. Dir. Ketan Mehta. India.

Bheja Fry. 2007. Dir. Sagar Ballary. India.

The Bicycle Thief. 1948. Dir. Vittorio De Sica. Italy.

The Big Animal (Duże zwierzę). 2000. Dir. Jerzy Stuhr. Poland.

The Big Cockerel (Bol'shoi petukh). 2004. Dir. Aleksandr Tatarskii. Russia.

The Birth of the Robot. 1936. Dir. Len Lye. United Kingdom.

Black God, White Devil (Deus e o Diabo na Terra do Sol). 1963. Dir. Glauber Rocha. Brazil.

Blancanieves. 2012. Dir. Pablo Berger. Spain.

The Bloody Lady (Krvavá pani). 1980. Dir. Viktor Kubal. Czechoslovakia.

The Blue Light (Das blaue Licht). 1976. Dir. Iris Gusner. East Germany.

Bluebeard (Barbe bleue). 1951. Dir. Christian-Jaque. France/Switzerland/Germany.

Bluebeard. 1972. Dir. Edward Dmytryk. France/Italy.

Bluebeard (Barbe bleue). 2009. Dir. Catherine Breillat. France.

Bluebeard's Last Wife (La dernière femme de Barbe bleue). 1996. Dir. Alexander Bubnov. France/Ukraine.

Bobby. 1973. Dir. Raj Kapoor. India.

Bombay. 1995. Dir. Mani Ratnam. India.

Bonifacio in Summertime (L'été de Boniface). 2011. Dir. Pierre-Luc Granjon, Antoine Lanciaux. Canada.

Border. 1997. Dir. Jyoti Prakash (J.P.) Dutta. India.

A Bouquet aka *Wild Flowers* (Kytice). 2000. Dir. F.A. Brabec. Czech Republic.

The Boxtrolls. 2014. Dir. Graham Annable and Anthony Stacchi. United States.

The Boy Who Went Out to Learn about Fear (Von einem, der auszog, um fas Fürchten zu lernen). 1935. Dir. the Diehl Brothers. Germany.

Brave. 2012. Dir. Mark Andrews and Brenda Chapman. United States.

The Brave Little Tailor (Das tapfere Schneiderlein). 1941. Dir. Hubert Schonger. Germany.

The Brave Little Tailor (Das tapfere Schneiderlein). 1956. Dir. Helmut Spieß. East Germany.

Bread Crumbs. 2011. Dir. Mike Nichols. United States.

Bread, Love, and Dreams (Amore, pane e fantasia). 1953. Dir. Luigi Comencini. Italy.

The Bremen Town Musicians (Die Bremer Stadtmusikanten). 1935. Dir. the Diehl Brothers. Germany.

Briar Rose (Dornröschen). 1917. Dir. Paul Leni. Germany.

Briar Rose (Dornröschen). 1936. Dir. Alf Zengerling. Germany.

Briar Rose (Dornröschen). 1943. Dir. the Diehl Brothers. Germany.

Briar Rose (Dornröschen). 1955. Dir. Fritz Genschow. West Germany.

Britain's Effort. 1917. Dir. Lancelot Speed. United Kingdom.

The Bronze Mirror. 2007. Dir. S. Danta. Australia.

Brother and Ugly Duck (Oppa wa Miun Ori). 2013. Dir. Shin Hyun-Soo. South Korea.

The Brothers Grimm. 2005. Dir. Terry Gilliam. United States.

The Brothers Lionheart (Bröderna Lejonhjärta). 1977. Dir. Olle Hellbom. Sweden.

Bulandra and the Devil (Bulandra i diabeł). 1959. Dir. Jerzy Ziztman. Poland.

Bully Boy. 1914. Dir. Lancelot Speed. United Kingdom.

The Burial of a Potato (Pogrzeb kartofla). 1990. Dir. Jan Jakub Kolski. Poland.

Butterflies. 2013. Dir. Isabel Peppard. Australia.

Bye Bye Red Riding Hood (Bye bye chaperon rouge). 1989. Dir. Márta Mészáros. Canada/Hungary.

Cabiria. 1914. Dir. Giovanni Pastrone. Italy.

Cain the 18th (Kain XVIII). 1963. Dir. Nadezhda Kosheverova and Mikhail Shapiro. USSR.

Camera Makes Whoopee. 1935. Dir. Norman McLaren. United Kingdom.

Canterbury Road. 1949. Dir. Henry Stringer. United Kingdom.

A Canterbury Tale. 1944. Dir. Michael Powell and Emeric Pressburger. United Kingdom.

The Canterbury Tales (I racconti di Canterbury). 1972. Dir. Pier Paolo Pasolini. Italy/France.

Caprino's Wonderful World (Caprinos eventyrlige verden). 2005. Dir. Ivo Caprino. Norway.

Car Fairy Tales (Autopohádky). 2011. Dir. Jakub Kohák, Libor Pixa, Břetislav Pojar, František Váša, and Michal Žabka. Czech Republic.

Care Bears Nutcracker Suite. 1988. Dir. Laura Shepherd and Joseph Sherman. Canada.

Carmen. 1933. Dir. Lotte Reiniger. Germany.

Cassandra Cat/When the Cat Comes (Až přijde kocour). 1963. Dir. Vojtěch Jasný. Czechoslovakia.

The Cathedral (Katedra). 2002. Dir. Tomasz Bagiński. Poland.

A Cautionary Tail. 2013. Dir. Erica Harrison. Australia.

Chandni. 1989. Dir. Yash Chopra. India.

Chennai Express. 2013. Dir. Rohit Shetty. India.

A Chinese Fairy Story (Qian Nü You Hun 倩女幽魂). 2011. Dir. Ye Weixin. China.

Chinkoroheibei and the Treasure Box (Chinkoroheibei to tamakebako). 1936. Dir. Noburo Ofuji. Japan.

Christmas at the Castle (Jul på slottet). 1986. TV. Dir. Finn Henriksen. Denmark.

A Christmas Dream (Vánoční sen). 1945. Dir. Bořivoj Zeman and Karel Zeman. Czechoslovakia.

Christmas Eve in Blue Mountain (Julenatt i Blåfjell). 2009. Dir. Roar Uthaug and Katarina Launing. Norway.

Christmas Eve in the Forest (Wigilia w lesie). 1996. Dir. Stanisław Lenartowicz. Poland.

Christmas in Blue Mountain (Jul i Blåfjell). 1999. TV. Dir. Torunn Calmeyer Ringen. Norway.

The Christmas Martian (Le martien de Noël). 1971. Dir. Bernard Gosselin. Canada.

Chunhyang. 1961. Dir. Hong Seong-Gi. South Korea.

Chunhyang. 2000. Dir. Im Kwon-Taek. South Korea.

Chunhyangjeon. 1923. Dir. Hayakawa Matsujiro. Korea.

Chunhyangjeon. 1935. Dir. Lee Myeong-U. Korea.

Chunhyangjeon. 1955. Dir. Lee Gyu-Hwan. South Korea.

Cinderella (Aschenputtel). 1931. Dir. Alf Zengerling. Germany.

Cinderella. 1950. Dir. Wilfred Jackson, Clyde Geronimi, and Hamilton Luske. United States.

Cinderella (Aschenputtel). 1955. Dir. Fritz Genschow. Germany.

Cinderella. 1996. Dir. Richard Slapczynski. Australia.

Cinderella. 2006. Dir. Man-Dae Bong. South Korea.

Cinderella (Kopciuszek). 2006–2007. TV. Dir. Jerzy Łukaszewicz. Poland.

Cinderella. 2015. Dir. Kenneth Branagh. United States.

Cinderella 3D (Cinderella au Far West). 2012. Dir. Pascal Hérold. France.

Cinderella II: Dreams Come True. 2002. Dir. John Kafka. United States.

Cinderella III: A Twist in Time. 2007. Dir. Frank Nissen. United States.

City of Brass. 2002. Dir. Hisham M. Bizri. United States.

Cleopatra: Queen of Sex (Kureopatora). 1970. Dir. Osamu Tezuka and Eiichi Yamamoto. Japan.

Clod Hans (Klods Hans). 1999. Dir. Mihail Badica. Denmark.

Clod-Hans (Klods-Hans). 2004. Dir. Jørgen Lerdam. Denmark/United Kingdom.

Clorofilla dal cielo blu. 1984. Dir. J. Victor Tognola. Italy/Switzerland.

The Clown and His Donkey. 1910. Directed Charles Armstrong. United Kingdom.

Colargol and the Magic Suitcase (Colargol i cudowna walizka). 1979. Dir. Tadeusz Wilkosz, Eugeniusz Ignaciuk, Jadwiga Kudrzycka, Janina Hartwig, Marian Kiełbaszczak, Dariusz Zawilski, and Lucjan Dembiński. Poland.

Colargol Conquers Outer Space (Colargol zdobywcą kosmosu). 1978. Dir. Tadeusz Wilkosz, Eugeniusz Ignaciuk, Jadwiga Kudrzycka, Janina Hartwig, Marian Kiełbaszczak, and Dariusz Zawilski. Poland.

Colargol in the Wild West (Colargol na Dzikim Zachodzie). 1976. Dir. Tadeusz Wilkosz, Euganiusz Ignaciuk, Jadwiga Kudrzycka, Janina Hartwig, Marian Kiełbaszczak, Lucjan Dembiński, Dariusz Zawilski, and Edward Sturlis. Poland.

A Colour Box. 1935. Dir. Len Lye. United Kingdom.

The Comb. 1990. Dir. Timothy Quay and Stephen Quay. United Kingdom.

Company. 2002. Dir. Ram Gopal Varma. India.

The Company of Wolves. 1984. Dir. Neil Jordan. United Kingdom.

Conquering the Jun Mountain (Ding Junshan 定军山). 1905. Dir. Ren Jingtai. China.

Conversation with a Man from the Wardrobe (Rozmowa z człowiekiem z szafy). 1993. Dir. Mariusz Grzegorzek. Poland.

Cornwall. 1949. Dir. Henry Stringer. United Kingdom.

Corpse Bride. 2005. Dir. Mike Johnson and Tim Burton. United Kingdom/United States.

Countess Dracula. 1970. Dir. Peter Sasdy. United Kingdom.

The Cranes are Flying (Letiat' zhuravli). 1957. Dir. Mikhail Kalatozov. USSR.

Criminal Lovers (Les amants criminels). 1999. Dir. François Ozon. France.

Crocodile Dundee. 1986. Dir. Peter Faiman. Australia.

Cyberchase. 2002–. TV. Canada.

Daddy's Little Bit of Dresden China. 1988. Dir. Karen Watson. United Kingdom.

Damon. 1958. Dir. Edward Sturlis. Poland.

Danae. 1969. Dir. Edward Sturlis. Poland.

Danemon Ban-The Monster Exterminator (Danemon Ban-shojoji no tanuki-bayashi). 1935. Dir. Yoshitaro Kataoka. Japan.

Dante's Inferno (Inferno). 1911. Dir. Francesco Bertolini and Adolfo Padovan. Italy.

The Decameron (Il Decameron). 1971. Dir. Pier Paolo Pasolini. Italy/France/West Germany.

Deeply. 2000. Dir. Sheri Elwood. Canada/Germany.

Deewaar. 1975. Dir. Yash Chopra. India.

Delightful Girl Chunhyang (Koegeol Chunhyang). 2005. Dir. Jeon Ki-Sang and Ji Byung-Hyun. South Korea.

The Devil's Backbone (El espinazo del diablo). 2001. Dir. Guillermo del Toro. Spain/Mexico/Argentina.

The Devil's Bride (Čertova nevěsta). 2011. Dir. Zdeněk Troška. Czech Republic.

Devon Whey! 1949. Dir. Henry Stringer. United Kingdom.

Die Nibelungen: Kriemhilds Rache. 1924. Dir. Fritz Lang. Germany.

District 9. 2009. Dir. Neill Bloomkamp. South Africa.

Dobrynia Nikitich and Gorynych the Dragon (Dobrynia Nikitich i zmei Gorynych). 2006. Dir. Il'ia Maksimov. Russia.

La dolce vita. 1960. Dir. Federico Fellini. Italy.

The Doll (Die Puppe). 1919. Dir. Ernst Lubitsch. Germany.

Donkey Skin (Peau d'âne). 1970. Dir. Jacques Demy. France.

Don't be Afraid of the Dark. 2011. Dir. Troy Nixey. United States.

Dora the Explorer. 2000–. TV. Created by Chris Gifford, Eric Weiner, and Valerie Walsh. Canada/United States.

Dorothy and the Witches of Oz. 2011. Dir. Leigh Scott. United States.

Dot and the Kangaroo. 1977. Dir. Yoram Gross. Australia.

Down to the Cellar (Do pivnice aka Do sklepa). 1982. Dir. Jan Švankmajer. Czechoslovakia.

The Dragon Ring (Desideria e l'anello del drago). 1994. Dir. Lamberto Bava. Italy.

Dreams (Yume). 1990. Dir. Akira Kurosawa. Japan.

Dreams of Toyland. 1908. Dir. Arthur Melbourne Cooper. United Kingdom.

Duchess Anna's Ring (Pierścień Księżnej Anny). 1970. Dir. Maria Kaniewska. Poland.

Dunia: There and Back (Dunia: tam i z powrotem). 2003. Dir. Joanna Jasińska-Koronkiewicz. Poland.

The Earth Trembles (La terra trema). 1948. Dir. Luchino Visconti. Italy.

Eden. 2002. Dir. Andrzej Czeczot. Poland.

Edward Scissorhands. 1990. Dir. Tim Burton. United States.

The Emperor's New Clothes. 1991. Dir. Richard Slapczynski. Australia.

The Emperor's New Clothes (Kejserens nye klæder). 2004. Dir. Jørgen Lerdam. Denmark/United Kingdom.

The Emperor's Nightingale (Císařův slavík). 1948. Dir. Jiří Trnka. Czechoslovakia.

Enchanted. 2007. Dir. Kevin Lima. United States.

The Enchanted Little Cloth (Der verzauberte Tuch). 1948. Dir. Hubert Schonger. Germany.

The Enchanted Pencil (Zaczarowany ołówek). 1963–1977. TV. Dir. Ireneusz Czesny and Ryszard Szymczak. Poland.

The Enchanted Princess (Die verzauberte Prinzessin). 1940. Dir. Alf Zengerling. Germany.

The Enchanted Toymaker/Toy Maker and Good Fairy. 1904. Dir. Arthur Melbourne Cooper. United Kingdom.

Enchanting Kisses/Bewitching Kisses (Besos Brujos). 1937. Dir. José Agustín Ferreyra. Argentina.

Ésimésac. 2012. Dir. Luc Picard. Canada.

Ever After: A Cinderella Story. 1998. Dir. Andy Tennant. United States

The Everyday Miracle (Obyknovennoe chudo). 1978. Dir. Mark Zakharov. USSR.

The Expedition of Professor Gąbka (Wyprawa Profesora Gąbki). 1978–1980. TV. Dir. Adam Hajduk and Zdzisław Kudła. Poland.

Faerie Tale Theatre. 1982–1987. TV. Dir. Various. United States.

Fairy Story. 1968. Dir. Tony Cattaneo. United Kingdom.

Fairy Tale. 1967. Dir. Dick Horn and Elizabeth Horn. United Kingdom.

A Fairy Tale (Bajka). 1968. Dir. Ryszard Kuziemski. Poland.

The Fairy Tale about the Princess, Who Absolutely Wanted to Appear in a Fairy Tale (Das Märchen von der Prinzessin, die unbedingt in einem Märchen vorkommen wollte). 2013. Dir. Steffen Zacke. Germany.

The Fairy Tale about Three Dragons (Bajka o trzech smokach). 1987. Dir. Krzysztof Kowalski. Poland.

Fairy Tales and Fairy Quarrels (Baśnie i waśnie). 1964. TV. Dir. Bogdan Nowicki. Poland.

FairyTale: A True Story. 1997. Dir. Charles Sturridge. United Kingdom.

The Fairytaler (Der var engang . . .). 2004. TV. Dir. Jørgen Lerdam. Denmark/United Kingdom.

Fanaa. 2006. Dir. Kunal Kohli. India.

Fanfreluche. 1968–1971. TV. Created by Kim Yaroshevskaya. Canada.

Fanny and Alexander (Fanny och Alexander). 1982. Dir. Ingmar Bergman. Sweden/France/West Germany.

Fantasia. 1940. Dir. Norman Ferguson, James Algar, Samuel Armstrong, Ford Beebe Jr., Jim Handley, T. Hee, Wilfred Jackson, Hamilton Luske, Bill Roberts, Paul Satterfield, and Ben Sharpsteen. United States.

Fantastic Planet (La Planète sauvage). 1973. Dir. René Laloux. France.

Father Frost and the Grey Wolf (Ded Moroz i sery volk). 1937. Dir. Ol'ga Khodataeva. USSR.

Fary, the Donkey (Fary, L'Anesse). 1987. Dir. Mansour Sora Wade. Senegal.

Felicia's Journey. 1999. Dir. Atom Egoyan. Canada/United Kingdom.

FernGully: The Last Rainforest. 1992. Dir. Bill Kroyer. Australia/United States.

Fimfárum/Jan Werich's Fimfárum (Fimfárum Jana Wericha). 2002. Dir. Aurel Klimt and Vlasta Pospíšilová. Czech Republic.

Fimfárum 2. 2006. Dir. Jan Balej, Aurel Klimt, Břetislav Pojar, and Vlasta Pospíšilová. Czech Republic.

Fimfárum Third Time Lucky 3D (Fimfárum do třetice všeho dobrého 3D). 2011. Dir. Kristina Dufková, Vlasta Pospíšilová, and David Súkup. Czech Republic.

Finding Neverland. 2004. Dir. Marc Forster. United States.

Finding the Milu King: The Magic Reel (Milu Wang 麋鹿王). 2009. Dir. Guo Weijiao. China.

The Firebird (Pták Ohnivák). 1997. Dir. Václav Vorlíček. Czech Republic/Germany.

The Fisherman and his Wife (Der Fischer und seine Frau). 2005. Dir. Doris Dörrie. Germany.

The Fisherman and the Fish (Skazka o rybake i rybke). 1937. Dir. Aleksandr Ptushko. USSR.

The Flax (Len). 2005. Dir. Joanna Jasińska-Koronkiewicz. Poland.

The Flower of the Arabian Nights (Il fiore delle mille e una note). 1974. Dir. Pier Paolo Pasolini. France/Italy.

The Flying Sneaker (Danger Pleine Lune, Motýlí čas). 1990. Dir. Břetislav Pojar. Canada/Czechoslovakia.

Fool Ondal and Princess Pyeonggang (Babo Ondal gwa Pyeonggang Gongju). 1961. Dir. Lee Gyu-Ung. South Korea.

Four Tank-Men and a Dog (Czterej pancerni i pies). 1966–70. TV. Dir. Konrad Nałęcki. Poland.

Fourteen Fairy Tales from the Kingdom of Lailonia of Leszek Kołakowski (Czternaście bajek z Królestwa Lailonii Leszka Kołakowskiego). 1997–2011. TV. Dir. Maciej Wojtyszko, Jacek Adamaczak, Jacek

Kasprzycki, Krzysztof Kiwerski, Hieronim Neumann, Marek Serafiński, Piotr Muszalski, Paweł Walicki, Łukasz Słuszkiewicz, Zbigniew Kotecki, Tamara Sorbian, and Marek Luzar. Poland.

The Fox and the Hare (Lisa i zaiats). 1973. Dir. Iurii Norshtein. USSR.

Fox Hunt. 1936. Dir. Anthony Gross. United Kingdom.

Fox Leon (Lis Leon). 1981–1993. TV. Dir. Romuald Kłys. Poland.

The Fox Spirit Romance (Hu Yuan 狐缘). 1986. Dir. Sun Yuanxun. China.

The Fox's Widow (Reveenka). 1962. Dir. Ivo Caprino. Norway.

Freeway II: Confessions of a Trickbaby. 1999. Dir. Matthew Bright. United States.

French's Contemptible Little Army. 1914. Dir. Lancelot Speed. United Kingdom.

Fritz the Cat. 1972. Dir. Ralph Bakshi. United States.

The Frog King (Der Froschkönig). 1940. Dir. Alf Zengerling. Germany.

The Frog King (Žabi král). 1990. Dir. Juraj Herz. Czechoslovakia/Germany.

The Frog Princess (Tsarevna-Liagushka). 1954. Dir. Mikhail Tsekhanovskii. USSR.

Frozen. 2013. Dir. Chris Buck and Jennifer Lee. United States.

Les Funerailles. 1932. Dir. Anthony Gross. United Kingdom.

La gabbianella e il gatto. 1998. Dir. Enzo D'Alò. Italy.

The Galoshes of Happiness (Galoše šťastia). 1986. Dir. Juraj Herz. Czechoslovakia/Germany.

Ganga Jumna. 1961. Dir. Nitin Bose. India.

Gangs of Waseypur. 2012. Dir. Anurag Kashyap. India.

Geese-Swans (Gusi-lebedi). 1949. Dir. Aleksandra Snezhko-Blotskaia. USSR.

Gerusalem Delivered (Gerusalemme Liberata). 1918. Dir. Enrico Guazzoni. Italy.

Ghost in the Shell (Kokakukidotai). 1995. Dir. Mamoru Oshii. Japan.

Ghost in the Shell II: Innocence (Inosensu). 2004. Dir. Mamoru Oshii. Japan.

Ghost Sisters (Gui Mei 鬼妹). 1985. Dir. Sun Yuanxun. China.

A Girl From Hunan (Xiangü Xiaoxiao 湘女潇潇). 1986. Dir. Xie Fei and Wu Lan. China.

Girl on a Broom (Dívka na koštěti). 1971. Dir. Václav Vorlíček. Czechoslovakia.

Go There, Don't Know Where (Podi tuda, ne znaiu kuda). 1966. Dir. Ivan Ivanov-Vano. USSR.

The Goat That Ate Time. 2007. Dir. Lucinda Schreiber. Australia.

The Golden Dream (La jaula de oro). 2013. Dir. Diego Quemada-Díez. Guatemala/Spain/Mexico.

The Golden Fern (Zlaté kapradí). 1963. Dir. Jiří Weiss. Czechoslovakia.

The Golden Goose (Die goldene Gans). 1953. Dir. Walter Oehmichen and Hubert Schonger. Germany.

The Golden Key (Zolotoi kliuchik). 1939. Dir. Aleksandr Ptushko. USSR.

The Golem (Golem). 1979. Dir. Piotr Szulkin. Poland.

The Golem (Golem). Unfinished. Dir. Jiří Barta. Czech Republic.

Gomorrah (Gomorra). 2008. Dir. Matteo Garrone. Italy.

Good Woman (Liangjia Funü 良家妇女). 1985. Dir. Huang Jianzhong. China.

Le Grand Melies. 1952. Dir. Georges Franju. France.

The Grasshopper and the Ant. 1954. Dir. Lotte Reiniger. United Kingdom.

The Great Land of Small (C'est parce qu'on est petit qu'on peut pas être grand). 1987. Dir. Vojtěch Jasný. Canada.

Great Story of Janghwa and Hongryeon (Dae Janghwa Hongryeonjeon). 1962. Dir. Jeong Chang-Hwa. South Korea.

The Great Yokai War (Yokai daisensou). 2005. Dir. Takashi Miike. Japan.

Grey Wolf and Little Red Riding Hood (Seryi Volk & Krasnaya Shapochka). 1990. Dir. Garri Bardin. Russia.

Grimm. 2011–. TV. Created by Stephen Carpenter, David Greenwalt and Jim Kouf. United States.

Grimm's Snow White. 2012. Dir. Rachel Goldberg. United States.

Gritta from Rats at Home with Us (Gritta von Rattenzuhausebeiuns). 1985. Dir. Jürgen Brauer. East Germany.

Groundhog Day. 1993. Dir. Harold Ramis. United States.

Gumiho. 1994. Dir. Park Heon-Su. South Korea.

Gumiho. 2009. Dir. Shin Hyun-Soo. South Korea.

Gwen, or the Book of Sand (Gwen, ou le livre de sable). 1985. Dir. Jean-François Laguionie. France.

H & G. 2013. Dir. Danishka Esterhazy. Canada.

H.C. Andersen's The Long Shadow (H.C. Andersen og den skæve skygge). 1998. Dir. Jannik Hastrup. Denmark/Norway/Sweden.

The Handsome Indifferent One (Le Bel Indifférent). 1957. Dir. Jacques Demy. France.

Hanna. 2011. Dir. Joe Wright. United States.

Hans Christian Andersen. 1952. Dir. Charles Vidor. United States.

Hans Christian Andersen: My Life as a Fairytale. 2003. Dir. Philip Saville. United States.

Hans Trutz in the Land of Cockaigne (Hans Trutz im Schlaraffenland). 1917. Dir. Paul Wegener. Germany.

Hansel and Gretel. 1953. Dir. Lotte Reiniger. United Kingdom.

Hansel and Gretel. 1982. Dir. Tim Burton. United States.

Hansel & Gretel. 1997. Dir. Richard Slapczynski. Australia.

Hansel & Gretel (Henjel gwa Geuretel). 2007. Dir. Pil-Sung Yim. South Korea.

Hansel & Gretel Get Baked. 2013. Dir. Duane Journey. United States.

Hansel & Gretel: Warriors of Witchcraft. 2013. Dir. David De Coteau. United States.

Hansel & Gretel: Witch Hunters. 2013. Dir. Tommy Wirkola. United States.

Happy Days of the Moomins (Szczęśliwe dni Muminków). 1983. Dir. Lucjan Dembiński, Krystyna Kulczycka, Dariusz Zawilski, and Jadwiga Kudrzycka. Poland.

Harvie Krumpet. 2003. Dir. Adam Elliot. Australia.

The Heavenly Match (Tianxian Pei 天仙配). 1955. Dir. Shi Hui. China.

Hell Unlimited. 1936. Dir. Norman McLaren. United Kingdom.

Helluva Good Luck (Z pekla štěstí). 1999. Dir. Zdeněk Troška. Czech Republic.

Helluva Good Luck 2 (Z pekla štěstí 2). 2001. Dir. Zdeněk Troška. Czech Republic.

The Herdsman (Mu Ma Ren 牧马人). 1982. Dir. Xie Jin. China.

The Heron and the Crane (Tsaplia i zhuravl'). 1974. Dir. Iurii Norshtein. USSR.

Hey Cinderella! 1969. TV. Dir. Jim Henson. Canada/United States.

Hibiscus Town (Furong Zhen 芙蓉镇). 1986. Dir. Xie Jin. China.

The History of Cinema Theater in Popielavy (Historia kina w Popielawach). 1998. Dir. Jan Jakub Kolski. Poland.

The Hobbit: An Unexpected Journey. 2012. Dir. Peter Jackson. United States/New Zealand.

The Hobbit: The Battle of the Five Armies. 2014. Dir. Peter Jackson. United States/New Zealand.

The Hobbit: The Desolation of Smaug. 2013. Dir. Peter Jackson. United States/New Zealand.

Hoodwinked. 2005. Dir. Cory Edwards, Todd Edwards, and Tony Leach. United States.

Hoodwinked Too! Hood vs. Evil. 2011. Dir. Mike Disa. United States.

The Hour of the Crimson Rose (Godzina pąsowej róży). 1963. Dir. Halina Bielińska. Poland.

The Hours. 2002. Dir. Stephen Daldry. United States.

The House, That Was Built by Swift (Dom, kotoryi postroil Swift). 1982. Dir. Mark Zakharov. USSR.

How I Unleashed World War II: Escape (Jak rozpętałem II Wojnę Światową: Ucieczka). Part 1. 1969. Dir. Tadeusz Chmielewski. Poland.

How I Unleashed World War II: To Arms (Jak rozpętałem II Wojnę Światową: Za bronią). Part 2. 1969. Dir. Tadeusz Chmielewski. Poland.

How I Unleashed World War II: Among my Own (Jak rozpętałem II Wojnę Światową: Wśród swoich). Part 3. 1969. Dir. Tadeusz Chmielewski. Poland.

How Six Made their Way through the World (Sechse kommen durch die Welt). 1972. Dir. Rainer Simon. East Germany.

How to Catch the Firebird's Feather (Kak poimat' pero zhar ptitsy). 2013. Dir. Viacheslav Plotnikov. Russia.

How to Marry a King (Wie man einen König heiratet). 1969. Dir. Rainer Simon. East Germany.

How to Train Your Dragon. 2010. Dir. Dean DeBlois and Chris Sanders. United States.

How to Train Your Dragon 2. 2014. Dir. Dean DeBlois. United States.

How to Wake Up A Princess (Jak se budí princezny). 1977. Dir. Václav Vorlíček. Czechoslovakia.

Howl's Moving Castle. 2004. Dir. Hayao Miyazaki. Japan.

The HPO — Heavenly Post Office. 1938. Dir. Lotte Reiniger. United Kingdom.

Hua Mulan (Hua Mulan 花木兰). 1956. Dir. Liu Guoquan and Zhang Xinshi. China.

Hua Mulan (Hua Mulan 花木兰). 2009. Dir. Ma Chucheng. China.

Hua Mulan Joins the Army or *Maiden in Armor* (Hua Mulan Congjun 花木兰从军). 1927. Dir. Li Pingqian. China.

Hugo. 2008. Dir. Nicholas Verso. Australia.

Hugo. 2011. Dir. Martin Scorsese. United States.

Hum Hindustani. 1960. Dir. Ram Mukherjee. India.

The Humpbacked Horse (Konek-Gorbunok). 1947. Dir. Ivan Ivanov-Vano. USSR.

The Humpbacked Horse (Konek-Gorbunok). 1975. Dir. Ivan Ivanov-Vano and Boris Butakov. USSR.

Hunger (Sult). 1966. Dir. Henning Carlsen. Denmark/Norway/Sweden.

Hungry as a Wolf (Une faim de loup). 1991. Dir. Michel Bériault. Canada.

I am Curious (*Blue*) (Jag är nyfiken—en film i blått). 1968. Dir. Vilgot Sjöman. Sweden.

I am Curious (*Yellow*) (Jag är nyfiken—en film i gult). 1967. Dir. Vilgot Sjöman. Sweden.

I Was A Rat. 2001. Dir. Laurie Lynd. Canada/United Kingdom.

Ilya Muromets. 1956. Dir. Aleksandr Ptushko. USSR.

Ilya Muromets and Robber-Nightingale (Il'ia Muromets i Solovei-razboinik). 2007. Dir. Vladimir Toropchin. Russia.

In Abstentia. 2000. Dir. Timothy Quay and Stephen Quay. United Kingdom.

In the Attic—Who Has a Birthday Today? (Na pude aneb Kdo má dneska narozeniny?). 2009. Dir. Jiří Barta. Czech Republic/Japan/France/Slovakia.

In the Land of Oz the Wizard (W krainie czarnoksiężnika Oza). 1983–1989. TV. Dir. Janusz Galewicz. Poland.

In This Very Moment (Milchwald). 2003. Dir. Christoph Hochhäusler. Germany.

In Times of King Krakus (Za króla Krakusa). 1947. Dir. Zenon Wasilewski. Poland.

The Incredibly Sad Princess (Šileně smutná princezna). 1968. Dir. Bořivoj Zeman. Czechoslovakia.

An Indian Fantasy. 1951. Dir. Anthony Gross. United Kingdom.

Iniminimagimo. 1987–1990. TV. Dir. Albert Girard, Jean-Louis Boudou, Monique Brossard and Michel F. Gelinas. Canada.

Inside an Old Grave (Gu Mu Huang Zhai 古墓荒斋). 1991. Dir. Xie Tieli. China.

Inside the Green Book: The Life and Films of Geoff Dunbar. 2011. Dir. Paul Wells.

Into the Woods. 2014. Dir. Rob Marshall. United States.

Inuyasha. 2000–2004. TV. Created by Rumiko Takahashi. Japan.

An Invention for Destruction (Vynález skázy). 1958. Dir. Karel Zeman. Czechoslovakia.

Invincible Lee Pyeonggang (Cheonhamujeok I Pyeonggang). 2009. Dir. Lee Jung-Seob. South Korea.

Iron Jack (Der Eisenhans). 1988. Dir. Karl-Heinz Lotz. East Germany.

The Italian Key. 2011. Dir. Rosa Karo. Finland/United States/Italy/United Kingdom.

Ivashka and Baba Yaga. 1938. Dir. Valentina and Zinaida Brumberg. USSR.

Iznogoud. 2005. Dir. Patrick Braoudé. France.

Jabberwocky (Žvahlav aneb šatičky Slaměného Huberta). 1971. Dir. Jan Švankmajer. Czechoslovakia.

Jacek and Placek (Jacek i Placek). 1984–1989. TV. Dir. Leszek Gałysz. Poland.

Jacek and Placek (Jacek i Placek). 1992. Dir. Leszek Gałysz. Poland.

Jack and the Beanstalk. 1955. Dir. Lotte Reiniger. United Kingdom.

Jack and the Cuckoo-Clock Heart (Jack et la mécanique due coeur). 2013. Dir. Stéphane Berla and Mathias Malzieu. France.

Jack in the Land of Fairy Tales (Jacek w krainie baśni). 1964. Dir. Stefan Szwakopf. Poland.

Jack the Giant Slayer. 2013. Dir. Bryan Singer. United States.

Jacob Two-Two Meets the Hooded Fang. 1978. Dir. Theodore J. Flicker. Canada.

Jacob Two Two Meets the Hooded Fang. 1999. Dir. George Bloomfield. Canada/United States.

Jai Santoshi Maa. 1975. Dir. Vijay Sharma. India.

James and the Giant Peach. 1996. Dir. Tim Burton. United States.

Janghwa Hongryeonjeon. 1924. Dir. Kim Yeong-Hwan. Korea.

Janghwa Hongryeonjeon. 1936. Dir. Lee Myeong-U. Korea.

Janghwa Hongryeonjeon. 1956. Dir. Jeong Chang-Hwa. South Korea.

Janghwa Hongryeonjeon. 1972. Dir. Lee Yu-Seop. South Korea.

Jasminum. 2006. Dir. Jan Jakub Kolski. Poland.

Jin-Roh: The Wolf Brigade. 1999. Dir. Hiroyuki Okiura. Japan.

Johnnie the Aquarius (Jańcio Wodnik). 1993. Dir. Jan Jakub Kolski. Poland.

Johnny the Giant Killer (Jeannot l'intrépide). 1950. Dir. Jean Image. France.

Joie de Vivre/La Joie de Vivre. 1934. Dir. Anthony Gross. United Kingdom.

Jolly Devil's Friend (Przyjaciel wesołego diabła). 1986. Dir. Jerzy Łukaszewicz. Poland.

Une Journée en Afrique. 1932. Dir. Anthony Gross. United Kingdom.

Journey to the Christmas Star (Reisen til julestjernen). 1976. Dir. Ola Solum. Norway.

Journey to the Christmas Star (Reisen til julestjernen). 2012. Dir. Nils Gaup. Norway.

Juniper Tree (Le Piège d'Issoudun). 2003. Dir. Micheline Lanctôt. Canada.

Jurko the Brigand (Zbojník Jurko). 1967. Dir. Viktor Kubal. Czechoslovakia.

Kahani. 2012. Dir. Sujoy Ghosh. India.

Kalevala (Kalewala). 1983–1986. TV. Dir. Stanisław Lenartowicz. Poland/Finland.

Kama Sutra Rides Again. 1972. Dir. Bob Godfrey. United Kingdom.

Karius and Baktus (Karius og Baktus). 1954. Dir. Ivo Caprino. Norway.

Kashchei the Immortal (Kashchei Bessmertnyi). 1944. Dir. Aleksandr Rou. USSR.

Kashmir ki Kali. 1964. Dir. Shakti Samanta. India.

Khal Nayak. 1993. Dir. Subhash Ghai. India.

Khumba. 2013. Dir. Anthony Silverston. South Africa.

The Kidnapping of Baltazar Gąbka series (Porwanie Baltazara Gąbki). 1969–1970. TV. Dir. Józef Byrdy, Stanisław Dulz, Alfred Ledwig, Wadysaw Nehrebecki, Wacaw Wajser, Edward Wtor, and Bronisaw Zeman. Poland.

The Kidnapping in Tiutiurlistan (Porwanie w Tiutiurlistanie). 1986. Dir. Zdzisław Kudła. Poland.

Kimsobo the Traveler (Kimsobo podróżnik). 1953. Dir. Władysław Nehrebecki. Poland.

The King and the Mockingbird (Le roi et l'oiseau). 1980. Dir. Paul Grimault. France.

King Blackbird (Kráľ Drozdia brada). 1984. Dir. Miloslav Luther. Czechoslovakia/West Germany.

King Lávra (Král Lávra). 1950. Dir. Karel Zeman. Czechoslovakia.

King Matt the First (Król Maciuś I). 1957. Dir. Wanda Jakubowska. Poland.

King Matt the First (Król Maciuś I). 2007. Dir. Andrzej Bogusz. Poland.

King Thrushbeard (König Drosselbart). 1954. Dir. Herbert Fredersdorf. Germany.

King Ubu (Ubu Król). 2003. Dir. Piotr Szulkin. Poland.

The King's Breakfast. 1936 Dir. Lotte Reiniger and Martin Battersby. United Kingdom.

Kingsize. 1987. Dir. Juliusz Machulski. Poland.

Kirikou and the Men and Women (Kirikou et les hommes et les femmes). 2012. Dir. Michel Ocelot. France.

Kirkou and the Sorceress (Kirikou et la sorcière). 1998. Dir. Michel Ocelot. France/Belgium/Luxembourg.

Kirikou and the Wild Beasts (Kirikou et les bêtes sauvages). 2006. Dir. Michel Ocelot. France.

Kolya (Kolja). 1996. Dir. Jan Svěrák. Czech Republic/United Kingdom/France.

Konopielka. 1981. Dir. Witold Leszczyński. Poland.

Kooky (Kuky se vrací). 2010. Dir. Jan Svěrák. Czech Republic/Denmark.

Krabat. 1978. See *The Sorcerer's Apprentice.*

Krabat. 2008. Dir. Marco Kreuzpaintner. Germany.

Kwaidan. 1964. Dir. Masaki Kobayashi. Japan.

Labyrinth. 1986. Dir. Jim Henson. United Kingdom/United States.

The Lady in the Painting (Hua Zhong Ren 画中人). 1958. Dir. Wang Bin. China.

Lady Winter (Perinbaba). 1985. Dir. Juraj Jakubisko. Czechoslovakia/West Germany/Italy/Austria.

Land and Freedom. 1995. Dir. Ken Loach. United Kingdom/Spain/Germany/Italy.

Language of Love (Ur kärlekens språk). 1969. Dir. Torgny Wickman. Sweden.

Last Days of Pompeii (Gli ultimi giorni di Pompei). 1908. Dir. Arturo Ambrosio and Luigi Maggi. Italy.

Léa et Gaspard/Zoe & Charlie. 1994–. TV. Dir. Gilles Gay, Alain Jaspard, and Louis Duquet. France/Canada.

The Legend of Sleepy Hollow. 1949. Dir. Jack Kinney and Claude Geronimi. United States.

Legend of the Never Beast. 2015. Dir. Steve Loter. United States.

Let's Love Monsters (Kochajmy straszydła). 1970. TV. Dir. Stefan Szwakopf, Alina Maliszewska, Zofia Oraczewska, Krzysztof Dębowski, Ryszard Słapczyński, and Roman Huszczo. Poland.

Liang Shanbo and Zhu Yingtai (Liang Shanbo and Zhu Yingtai 梁山伯与祝英台). 1953. Dir. Sang Hu and Huang Sha. China.

Life Is Beautiful (La vita è bella). 1997. Dir. Roberto Benigni. Italy.

The Life of Matthew (Żywot Mateusza). 1967. Dir. Witold Leszczyński. Poland.

Like Water for Chocolate (Como agua para chocolate). 1992. Dir. Alfonso Arau. Mexico.

Lilet Never Happened. 2012. Dir. Jacco Groen. Netherlands/United Kingdom/Philippines.

The Lion and the Mouse. 1976. Dir. Evelyn Lambart. Canada.

The Lion King. 1994. Dir. Roger Allers and Rob Minkoff. United States.

Little Bird (Picc Mi). 1992. Dir. Mansour Sora Wade. Senegal.

Little Black Riding Hood (Czarny Kapturek). 1983. Dir. Piotr Dumała. Poland.

Little Brother and Little Sister (Brüderchen und Schwesterchen). 1953. Dir. Walter Oehmichen and Hubert Schonger. Germany.

The Little Chimney Sweep. 1955. Dir. Lotte Reiniger. United Kingdom.

Little Claus & Big Claus. 2005. TV. Dir. James Ricker. Canada.

Little Frick and the Fiddle (Veslefrikk med fela). 1952. Dir. Ivo Caprino. Norway.

Little from the Fish Shop (Mála z rybárny). 2015. Dir. Jan Balej. Czech Republic/Slovak Republic/France.

Little Long-Nose (Karlik nos). 2003. Dir. Il'ia Maksimov. Russia.

The Little Mermaid (Rusalochka). 1968. Dir. Ivan Aksenchuk. USSR.

The Little Mermaid. 1989. Dir. Ron Clements and John Musker. United States.

The Little Mermaid (Den lille havfrue). 2004. Dir. Jørgen Lerdam. Denmark/United Kingdom.

The Little Mermaid II: The Return to the Sea. 2000. Dir. Jim Kamerud and Brian Smith. United States.

The Little Mermaid III: Ariel's Beginning. 2008. Dir. Peggy Holmes. United States.

Little Muck (Der kleine Muck). 1944. Dir. Franz Fiedler. Germany.

Little Otik (Otesánek). 2000. Dir. Jan Švankmajer. Czech Republic/United Kingdom/Japan.

The Little Parade (La Petite Parade). 1928. Dir. Władysław Starewicz. France.

Little Red Cap (Rotkäppchen). 1953. Dir. Fritz Genschow. Germany.

Little Red Cap (Rotkäppchen). 1954. Dir. Walter Janssen. Germany.

Little Red Cap (Rotkäppchen). 1962. Dir. Götz Friedrich. East Germany.

Little Red Cap and the Wolf (Rotkäppchen und der Wolf). 1937. Dir. Fritz Genschow. Germany.

Little Red Riding Hood (La Caperucita Roja). 1960. Dir. Roberto Rodríguez. Mexico.

Little Red Riding Hood. 1969. Dir. Rhoda Leyer. Canada.

Little Red Riding Hood and her Friends (Caperucita y sus Tres Amigos). 1961. Dir. Roberto Rodríguez. Mexico.

Little Red Riding Hood and Tom Thumb against the Monsters (Caperucita y Pulgarcito contra los Monstruos). 1962. Dir. Roberto Rodríguez. Mexico.

Little Thumbling (Le Petit Poucet). 1972. Dir. Michel Boisrond. France.

Little Thumbling (Le Petit Poucet). 2001. Dir. Olivier Dahan. France.

The Lost Boys. 1978. TV. Dir. Rodney Bennett. United Kingdom.

The Lost Shadow (Der verlorene Schatten). 1920. Dir. Paul Wegener. Germany.

The Lost Shoe (Der verlorene Schuh). 1923. Dir. Ludwig Berger. Germany.

The Lost Thing. 2010. Dir. Andrew Ruhemann and Shaun Tan. Australia.

The Lost Town of Świteź (Świteź). 2010. Dir. Kamil Polak. Poland.

Louisiana (Louisiane). 1984. Dir. Philippe de Broca and Jacques Demy. France.

Love Story on Lushan Mountain (Lushan Lian 庐山恋). 1980. Dir. Huang Zumo. China.

The Loveliest Riddle (Nekrásnější hádanka). 2008. Dir. Zdeněk Troška. Czech Republic.

Lucanus Cervus (Жук-олень). 1910. Dir. Władysław Starewicz. Russia.

Maachis. 1996. Dir. Gulzar. India.

Maciste. 1915. Dir. Luigi Romano Borgnetto and Vincenzo Denizot. Italy.

Madagascar. 2005. Dir. Eric Darnell and Tom McGrath. United States.

Madame Perrault's Bluebeard. 2011. Dir. A.J. Bond. Canada.

The Magic Aster (Malan Hua 马兰花). 2009. Dir. Yao Guanghua. China.

The Magic Book (Kouzelný měšec). 1996. Dir. Václav Vorlíček. Germany/Czech Republic.

The Magic Flute (Il flauto magico). 1978. Dir. Giulio Gianini and Emanuele Luzzati. Italy.

The Magic Little Bell (Chudesnyi kolokol'chik). 1949. Dir. Valentina and Zinaida Brumberg. USSR.

The Magic Lotus Lantern (Bao Lian Deng 宝莲灯). 1999. Dir. Chang Guangxi. China.

The Magic Playground (Zaczarowane podwórko). 1974. Dir. Maria Kaniewska. Poland.

Magic Tree (Magiczne drzewo). 2003–2006. TV. Dir. Andrzej Maleszka. Poland.

The Magic Tree: The Red Chair (Magiczne drzewo: czerwone krzesło). 2009. Dir. Andrzej Maleszka. Poland.

The Magical Flute (La flûte magique). 1946. Dir. Paul Grimault. France.

Magical Gifts (Czarodziejskie dary). 1956. Dir. Zenon Wasilewski. Poland.

Mahuliena: The Golden Princess (Mahuliena, zlatá panna). 1986. Dir. Miloslav Luther. Czechoslovakia/West Germany.

Main Hoon Na. 2004. Dir. Farah Khan. India.

Maleficent. 2014. Dir. Robert Stromberg. United States.

Mangal Pandey: The Rising. 2005. Dir. Ketan Mehta. India.

Märchenperlen. 2005–. TV. Dir. Various. Germany/Austria/Finland.

Maria Full of Grace (María, llena eres de gracia). 2004. Dir. Joshua Marston. Colombia/United States/Ecuador.

The Marsh. 2006. Dir. Jordan Barker. Canada/United States.

Mary and the Gnomes (Marysia i krasnoludki). 1960. Dir. Jerzy Szeski and Konrad Paradowski. Poland.

Maska. 2010. Dir. Timothy Quay and Stephen Quay. Poland.

Master Twardowski (Pan Twardowski). 1921. Dir. Wiktor Biegański. Poland.

Master Twardowski (Pan Twardowski). 1936. Dir. Henryk Szaro. Poland.

Master Twardowski (Pan Twardowski). 1995. Dir. Krzysztof Gradowski. Poland.

Matches Appeal/Matches: An Appeal. 1899. Dir. Arthur Melbourne Cooper. United Kingdom.

May (Máj). 2008. Dir. F.A. Brabec. Czech Republic.

May Night (Maiskaia noch'). 1952. Dir. Aleksandr Rou. USSR.

Meanies (Zlydni). 2005. Dir. Stepan Koval' and Aleksandr Tatarskii. Russia.

Mergen. 2013. Dir. Andrei Kuznetsov. Russia.

The Mermaid (Rusalka). 2007. Dir. Anna Melikian. Russia.

Metropolis. 1927. Dir. Fritz Lang. Germany.

Mia and Me. 2011–2012. TV. Dir. Various. Netherlands/Germany/Italy/Canada.

Michałkowice Tale (Opowieść Michałkowicka). 1954. Dir. Zenon Wasilewski. Poland.

Mickey Mouse Monopoly: Disney, Childhood & Corporate Power. 2002. Dir. Miguel Picker and Chyng Sun. United States.

A Midsummer Night's Dream (Sen noci svatojánské). 1959. Dir. Jiří Trnka. Czechoslovakia.

Mikola and Mikolko (Mikola a Mikolko). 1988. Dir. Dušan Trančik. Czechoslovakia/West Germany.

Milenka. 2001. Dir. Joanna Jasińska-Koronkiewicz. Poland.

Miracle in Milan (Miracolo a Milano). 1951. Dir. Vittorio De Sica. Italy.

Miraculous Place (Cudowne miejsce). 1994. Dir. Jan Jakub Kolski. Poland.

Mirror, Mirror. 2012. Dir. Tarsem Singh. Canada/United States.

Miss Austen Regrets. 2008. Dir. Jeremy Lovering. United States/United Kingdom.

Modern Bluebeard/Boom in the Moon (El moderno Barba Azul). 1946. Dir. Jaime Salvador. Mexico.

A Modern Cinderella (Cenerentola). 1913. Dir. Eleuterio Rodolfi. Italy.

Momo. 1986. Dir. Johannes Schaaf. West Germany/Italy.

Momotaro's Divine Warriors of the Sea (Momotaro no umi o shimpei). 1945. Dir. Mitsuyo Seo. Japan.

Momotaro's Sea Eagle (Momotaro no umiwashi). 1942. Dir. Mitsuyo Seo. Japan.

A Monkey's Tale (Château des singes). 1999. Dir. Jean-François Laguionie. France/United Kingdom/Germany/Hungary.

The Moomin Stories (Opowiadania Muminków). 1977–1982. TV. Dir. Lucjan Dembiński, Krystyna Kulczycka, Dariusz Zawilski, and Jadwiga Kudrzycka. Poland.

The Moomins and the Comet Chase (Mumiki w pogoni za kometą). 2010. Dir. Maria Lindberg. Poland/Austria/United Kingdom.

The Moomins' Summer (Lato muminków). 2008. Dir. Maria Lindberg. Austria/Poland/Finland.

More than a Miracle (C'era una volta). 1967. Dir. Francesco Rosi. France/Italy.

Mother Holle (Frau Holle). 1947. Dir. Hubert Schonger. Germany.

Mother India. 1957. Dir. Mehboob Khan. India.

Mr. Asquith and the Clown. 1911. Dir. Charles Armstrong. United Kingdom.

Mr. Blot's Academy (Akademia Pana Kleksa). 1983, two parts. Dir. Krzysztof Gradowski. Poland.

Mr. Blot in Space (Pan Kleks w kosmosie). 1988. Dir. Krzysztof Gradowski. Poland.

Mr. Blot's Triumph (Triumf Pana Kleksa). 2001. Dir. Krzysztof Gradowski. Poland.

Mr. Blot's Voyages (Podróże Pana Kleksa). 1985. Dir. Krzysztof Gradowski. Poland.

Mr. Feather Dreams (Pan Piórko śni). 1949. Dir. Zenon Wasilewski. Poland.

Mughal-e-Azam. 1960. Dir. Karimuddin (K.) Asif. India.

Mulan. 1998. Dir. Tony Bancroft and Barry Cook. United States.

Mulan Joins the Army (Mulan Congjun 木兰从军). 1928. Dir. Hou Yao, China.

Mulan Joins the Army (Mulan Congjun 木兰从军). 1939. Dir. Bu Wanchang. China.

Muriel's Wedding. 1994. Dir. P. J. Hogan. Australia/France.

Musical Paintbox Series. 1946. Dir. Henry Springer/Various. United Kingdom.

My Girlfriend is a Gumiho (Nae Yeojachinguneun Gumiho). 2010. Dir. Boo Sung-Chul. South Korea.

My Neighbor Totoro (Tonari no Totoro). 1988. Dir. Hayao Miyazaki. Japan.

My Sassy Girl (Yeopgijeogin Geunyeo). 2001. Dir. Kwak Jae-Yong. South Korea.

The Mystery of Sagala (Tajemnica Sagali). 1996. TV. Dir. Jerzy Łukaszewicz. Poland.

The Mystery of the Fern (Tajemnica kwiatu paproci). 2004. Dir. Tadeusz Wilkosz. Poland.

Neecha Nagar. 1946. Dir. Chetan Anand. India.

The NeverEnding Story (Die unendliche Geschichte). 1984. Dir. Wolfgang Petersen. West Germany/United States.

Neverwas. 2005. Dir. Joshua Michael Stern. Canada/United States.

New Adventures of Babka Ezhka (Novye prikliucheniia Babki Ezhki). 2007. Dir. Nikolai Titov and Oktiabrina Potapova. Russia.

The New Gulliver (Novyi Gulliver). 1935. Dir. Aleksandr Ptushko. USSR.

New Robin Hood (Nowy Robin Hood). 1983. Dir. Alina Maliszewska. Poland.

Nina's Heavenly Delights. 2006. Dir. Pratibha Parmar. United Kingdom.

Noah's Ark. 1906. Dir. Arthur Melbourne Cooper. United Kingdom.

The Nonexistent Knight (Il cavaliere inesistente). 1969. Dir. Pino Zac. Italy.

The North Wind and the Sun. 1972. Dir. Rhoda Leyer, Les Drew and Jacques Avoine. Canada.

The Nutcracker (Dziadek do orzechów). 1967. Dir. Halina Bielińska. Poland.

The Nutcracker (Shchelkunchik). 2003. Dir. Tat'iana Il'ina. Russia.

O-bi, O-ba: The End of Civilization (O-bi, O-ba: koniec cywilizacji). 1984. Dir. Piotr Szulkin. Poland.

"Oh"Phelia. 1919. Dir. Anson Dyer. United Kingdom.

Old Czech Legends (Staré pověsti české). 1953. Dir. Jiří Trnka. Czechoslovakia.

The Old Woman in the Woods. 2012. Dir. Caroline Coutts. Canada.

On the Pike's Command (Po shchuch'emu veleniiu). 1938. Dir. Aleksandr Rou. USSR.

Once Upon a Brothers Grimm. 1977. Dir. Norman Campbell. United States.

Once Upon a Time . . . (V nekotorom tsarstve). 1957. Dir. Ivan Ivanov-Vano. USSR.

Once Upon a Time. 2011–. TV. Dir. Various. United States.

Once Upon a Time There Was a King (Byl jednou jeden kraal . . .). 1954. Dir. Bořivoj Zeman. Czechoslovakia.

Once Upon a Time There Was a Little Pig (Była sobie świnka mała). 1960. Dir. Zenon Wasilewski. Poland.

Ondraszek. 1959. Dir. Wacław Kondek. Poland.

Orpheus and Eurydice (Orfeusz i Eurydyka). 1961. Dir. Edward Sturlis. Poland.

Oseam. 2003. Dir. Sung Baek-Yeop. South Korea.

Othello. 1920. Dir. Anson Dyer. United Kingdom.

Oz—A Rock 'n' Roll Road Movie. 1976. Dir. Chris Löfvén. Australia.

Oz the Great and Powerful. 2013. Dir. Sam Raimi. United States.

Paheli. 2005. Dir. Amol Palekar. India.

Paint Me a Fairy Tale (Namaluj mi bajkę). In production. TV. Dir. Joanna Jasińska-Koronkiewicz. Poland.

Painted Skin (Hua Pi 画皮). 2008. Dir. Chen Jiashang. China.

Painted Skin (Hua Pi). 1965. Dir. Pao Fang. Hong Kong.

The Painting (Le Tableau). 2011. Dir. Jean-François Laguionie. France.

The Palace of the Thousand and One Nights (Le Palais des mille et une nuits). 1905. Dir. Georges Méliès. France.

Pan's Labyrinth (El laberinto del fauno). 2006. Dir. Guillermo del Toro. Spain/Mexico/United States.

Papageno. 1935. Dir. Lotte Reiniger. Germany.

Paradise. 1984. Dir. Ishu Patel. Canada.

ParaNorman. 2012. Dir. Sam Fell and Chris Butler. United States.

Parking. 1982. Dir. Jacques Demy. France.

Pathfinder (Ofelaš; Veiviseren). 1987. Dir. Nils Gaup. Norway.

The Peanut Butter Solution (Opération beurre de pinottes). 1985. Dir. Michael Rubbo. Canada.

Peculiar Penguins. 1934. Dir. Wilfred Jackson. United States.

Penelope. 2006. Dir. Mark Palansky. United States/United Kingdom.

Peter Pan. 1988. Dir. Roz Phillips. Australia.

Peter Pan. 2003. Dir. P. J. Hogan. Australia/United Kingdom/United States.

The Phantom Museum/The Phantom Museum: Random Forays Into the Vaults of Sir Henry Wellcome's Medical Collection. 2003. Dir. Timothy Quay and Stephen Quay. United Kingdom.

The Pied Piper (Der Rattenfänger). 1919. Dir. Paul Wegener. Germany.

The Pied Piper (Krysař). 1986. Dir. Jiří Barta. Czechoslovakia/West Germany.

Pinchcliffe Grand Prix (Flåklypa Grand Prix). 1975. Dir. Ivo Caprino. Norway.

Pinocchio. 1911. Dir. Giulio Antamoro. Italy.

Pinocchio. 1940. Dir. Norman Ferguson, T. Hee, Wilfred Jackson, Jack Kinney, Hamilton Luske, Bill Roberts, and Ben Sharpsteen. United States.

Pinocchio (Un burattino di nome Pinocchio). 1972. Dir. Giuliano Cenci. Italy.

Pinocchio. 2002. Dir. Roberto Benigni. Germany/France/Italy/United States.

Pinocchio. 2008. Dir. Alberto Sironi. Italy/United Kingdom.

Pinocchio. 2012. Dir. Enzo D'Alò. Belgium/France/Italy/Luxemburg.

The Plate Player (Grający z talerza). 1995. Dir. Jan Jakub Kolski. Poland.

Le poil de la bête. 2010. Dir. Philippe Gagnon. Canada.

The Polar Bear King (Kvitebjørn Kong Valemon). 1991. Dir. Ola Solum. Germany/Norway/Sweden.

Polish Fairy Tales and Folk Stories (Baśnie i bajki polskie). 2002–2005, 2007–2009. TV. Dir. Zbigniew Kotecki, Artur Wrotniewski, Witold Giersz, Jacek Adamczak, Andrzej Kukuła, Robert Turło, and Jacek Kasprzycki. Poland.

Ponpoko (Heisei gassen tanuki ponpoko). 1994. Dir. Isao Takahata. Japan.

Ponyo. 2008. Dir. Hayao Miyazaki. Japan.

Porco Rosso (Kurenai buta). 1992. Dir. Hayao Miyazaki. Japan.

The Post (Pochta). 1929. Dir. Mikhail Tsekhanovskii. USSR.

The Posthumous Boy (Pograbek). 1992. Dir. Jan Jakub Kolski. Poland.

The Price of Forgiveness (Ndeysaan). 2001. Dir. Mansour Sora Wade. Senegal.

The Prince and the Evening Star (Princ a Večernice). 1978. Dir. Václav Vorlíček. Czechoslovakia.

Prince Ivan and the Grey Wolf (Ivan tsarevich and seryi volk). 2011. Dir. Vladimir Toropchin. Russia.

Prince Ivan and the Grey Wolf 2 (Ivan tsarevich and seryi volk 2). 2013. Dir. Vladimir Toropchin. Russia.

Prince Yeonsan (Yeonsangun). 1961. Dir. Shin Sang-Ok. South Korea.

Princes et princesses. 2000. Dir. Michel Ocelot. France.

The Princess and the Frog. 2009. Dir. Ron Clements and John Musker. United States.

The Princess and the Pauper (La principessa e il povero). 1997. Dir. Lamberto Bava. Italy/Germany.

The Princess and the Swineherd (Die Prinzessin und der Schweinehirt). 1953. Dir. Herbert Fredersdorf. Germany.

La princesse astronaute. 1993–1996. TV. Dir. Various. Canada.

Princess Cinderella (Cenerentola e il signor Bonaventura). 1941. Dir. Sergio Tofano. Italy.

Princess from the Mill (Princezna ze mlejna). 1994. Dir. Zdeněk Troška. Czech Republic.

Princess from the Mill 2 (Princezna ze mlejna 2). 2000. Dir. Zdeněk Troška. Czech Republic.

Princess Goldenhair (Zlatovláska). Forthcoming. Dir. Václav Vorlíček. Czech Republic.

Princess Iron Fan (Tieshan Gongzhu 铁扇公主). 1941. Dir. Wan Laiming and Wan Guchan. China.

Princess Jasna and the Flying Cobbler (O princezně Jasněnce a létajícím ševci). 1987. Dir. Zdeněk Troška. Czechoslovakia.

The Princess on the Pea (Die Prinzessin auf der Erbse). 1953. Dir. Alf Zengerling. Germany.

Princesse Shéhérazade. 1996. TV. Dir. Philippe Mest. France.

Princess Snow White (Baekseol Gongju). 1964. Dir. Park Gu. South Korea.

The Princess with the Golden Star (Princezna se zlatou hvězdou). 1959. Dir. Martin Frič. Czechoslovakia.

Prometheus (Prometeusz). 1985. Dir. Kzysztof Raynoch. Poland.

The Proud Princess (Pyšná princezna). 1952. Dir. Bořivoj Zeman. Czechoslovakia.

Pulcinella e il pesce magico. 1981. Dir. Emanuele Luzzati and Giulio Gianini. Italy.

Puss in Boots (Der gestiefelte Kater). 1935. Dir. Alf Zengerling. Germany.

Puss in Boots (Der gestiefelte Kater). 1940. Dir. the Diehl Brothers. Germany.

Puss in Boots (Der gestiefelte Kater). 1955. Dir. Herbert Fredersdorf. Germany.

Puss in Boots (Kot v sapogakh). 1995. Dir. Garri Bardin. Russia.

Puss in Boots. 2011. Dir. Chris Miller. United States.

Pyza's Travels (Wędrówki Pyzy). 1977–1983. TV. Dir. Piotr Paweł Lutczyn, Jan Siupik, and Stefan Szwakopf. Poland.

Queen. 2014. Dir. Vikas Bahl. India.

Queen of the Lake (Jezerní královna). 1998. Dir. Václav Vorlíček. Czech Republic/Germany.

Radúz and Mahulena (Radúz a Mahulena). 1970. Dir. Petr Weigl. Czechoslovakia.

Rainbow Dance. 1936. Dir. Len Lye. United Kingdom.

Raja Harishchandra. 1913. Dir. (Dadasaheb) Dhundiraj Govind Phalke. India.

Ranma 1/2. 1989–1992. TV. Created by Rumiko Takahashi. Japan.

Rashomon. 1950. Dir. Akira Kurosawa. Japan.

Raven Tales. 2004–2010. TV. Dir. Caleb Hystad, Vincent Smith, Chris Kientz, Jeremy Klem, and Karl Bossler. Canada

——. *The Child of Tears.* 2006. Season 1, Episode 7.

Reality. 2012. Dir. Matteo Garrone. Italy/France.

A Reasonable Man. 1999. Dir. Gavin Hood. South Africa.

Red. 2012. Dir. Carlo Guillot and Jorge Jaramillo. Colombia.

Red: Werewolf Hunter. 2010. Dir. Sheldon Wilson. United States.

The Red Detachment of Women (Hongse Niangzijun 红色娘子军). 1960. Dir. Xie Jin. China.

Red Riding Hood. 2003. Dir. Giacomo Cimini. Italy.

Red Riding Hood. 2011. Dir. Catherine Hardwicke. Canada/United States.

Red Riding Hood (Krasnaia shapochka). 1937. Dir. Valentina and Zinaida Brumberg. USSR.

Red Riding Hood/Little Red Riding Hood. 1922. Dir. Anson Dyer. United Kingdom.

The Red Shoes. 1948. Dir. Michael Powell and Emeric Pressburger. United Kingdom.

The Red Shoes. 2005. Dir. Yong-gyun Kim. South Korea.

Rehearsals for Extinct Anatomies. 1987. Dir. Timothy Quay and Stephen Quay. United Kingdom.

Reksio (Reksio). 1967–1990. TV. Dir. Lechosław Marszałek, Józef Cwietnia, and Ryszard Lepióra. Poland.

The Reluctant Dragon. 1941. Dir. Alfred Werker and Hamilton Luske. United States.

Requiem. 2001. Dir. Witold Leszczyński. Poland.

Return of the Gumiho (Gumihoui Gwihwan). 2008. Dir. Kwak Jung-Hwan. South Korea.

Return to Never Land. 2002. Dir. Robin Budd and Donovan Cook. Australia/Canada/United States.

The Return to the Wicker Bay (Powrot do wiklinowej zatoki). 1995. TV. Dir. Wiesław Zięba. Poland.

Revolutionary Girl Utena (Shojo Kakumei Utena). 1997. TV. Dir. Kunihiko Ikuhara. Japan.

Revolutionary Girl Utena. 1999. Dir. Kunihiko Ikuhara. Japan.

The Ring and the Rose (Pierścień i Róża). 1986. TV. Dir. Jerzy Gruza. Poland.

River. 2008. Dir. Jennifer Moore. Canada.

The Road Home (Wo de Fuqin Muqin 我的父亲母亲). 1999. Dir. Zhang Yimou. China.

Robin Hood. 1973. Dir. Wolfgang Reitherman. United States.

The Romance of West Chamber (Xixiangji 西厢记). 1927. Dir. Hou Yao. China.

Rome, Open City (Roma città aperta). 1945. Dir. Roberto Rossellini. Italy.

Romeo and Juliet (Romeo e Giulietta). 1908. Dir. Mario Caserini. Italy.

Ronia the Robber's Daughter (Ronja Rövardotter). 1984. Dir. Tage Danielsson. Sweden.

The Rose Seller (La vendedora de rosas). 1998. Dir. Víctor Gaviria. Colombia.

Rübezahl's Wedding (Rübezahls Hochzeit). 1916. Dir. Paul Wegener. Germany.

Rumpelstiltskin (Rumpelstilzchen). 1955. Dir. Herbert Fredersdorf. Germany.

Rumpelstiltskin. 1960. Dir. Christoph Engel. Germany.

Rumpelstiltskin. 1985. Dir. Pino Van Lamsweerde. Canada.

Running Man (Reoningmaen). 2010. Dir. Im Hyung-Taek. South Korea.

Rupert and the Frog Song. 1982. Dir. Geoff Dunbar. United Kingdom.

Rusalka. 1977. Dir. Petr Weigl. Czechoslovakia.

Ruslan and Ludmila. 1972. Dir. Aleksandr Ptushko. USSR.

The Sabre from the Commander (Szabla od komendanta). 1995. Dir. Jan Jakub Kolski. Poland.

The Saci (O Saci). 2009. Dir. Humberto Avelar. Brazil.

Sadko. 1952. Dir. Aleksandr Ptushko. USSR.

Sailor Moon (Seera Muun). 1992–1997. TV. Dir. Junichi Sato, Kunihiko Ikuhara, and Takuya Igarashi. Japan.

Sailor Moon S The Movie: Hearts on Ice. 1994. Dir. Hiroki Shibata. Japan.

Salt More than Gold (Soľ nad zlato). 1983. Dir. Martin Hollý. Czechoslovakia/West Germany.

The Samoyed Boy (Samoedskii mal'chik). 1928. Dir. Ol'ga Khodataeva, with Zinaida Brumberg, Valentina Brumberg, and Nikolai Khodataev. USSR.

Sampo. 1959. Dir. Aleksandr Ptushko. USSR.

Saturday Mountain (Sobotnia góra). 2012. Dir. Marta Filipiak. Poland.

Saving Mr. Banks. 2013. Dir. John Lee Hancock. United States.

Saxana and the Lexikon (Saxána a Lexikon kouzel). 2011. Dir. Václav Vorlíček. Czech Republic/ Slovak Republic/Germany.

Scandal in Sorrento (Pane, amore e . . .). 1955. Dir. Dino Risi. Italy.

The Scarecrow (L'Epouvantail). 1942. Dir. Paul Grimault. France.

Scheherazade, Tell Me a Story (Eḥkī yā Shahrazād). 2009. Dir. Yousry Nasrallah. Egypt.

Sea Dreams. 1914. Dir. Lancelot Speed. United Kingdom.

Sechs auf einen Streich. 2008–. TV. Germany.

The Secret of Kells. 2009. Dir. Tomm Moore and Nora Twomey. Ireland/France/Belgium.

The Secret of the Marabut's Code (Tajemnica szyfru Marabuta). 1976–1979. TV. Dir. Maciej Wojtyszko. Poland.

The Secrets of the Wicker Bay (Tajemnice wiklinowej zatoki). 1984–1988. TV. Dir. Wiesław Zięba. Poland.

The Selfish Giant. 2013. Dir. Clio Barnard. United Kingdom.

Senka, the African Boy (Sen'ka Afrikanets). 1927. Dir. Iurii Merkulov, Daniil Cherkes and Ivan Ivanov-Vano. USSR.

Seong Chunhyang. 1961. Dir. Shin Sang-Ok. South Korea.

The Seven Deadly Sins (Les Sept péchés capitaux). 1962. Dir. Philippe de Broca, Claude Chabrol, Jacques Demy, Sylvain Dhomme, Max Douy, Jean-Luc Godard, Edouard Molinaro, and Roger Vadim. France/Italy.

Seven with One Blow (Sedem jednou ranou). 1989. Dir. Dušan Trančík. Czechoslovakia/West Germany.

The Seven Ravens (Die sieben Raben). 1937. Dir. the Diehl Brothers. Germany.

Seven Ravens (Sedmeru krkavců). 2015. Dir. Alice Nellis. Czech Republic/Slovak Republic.

The Seventh Dwarf (Der siebte Zwerg). 2014. Dir. Boris Aljinovic and Harald Siepermann. Germany.

The Seventh Master of the House (Sjuende far i huset). 1966. Dir. Ivo Caprino. Norway.

The Shadow (Ten'). 1971. Dir. Nadezhda Kosheverova. USSR.

Shaheed. 1965. Dir. S. Ram Sharma. India.

Shéhérazade. 1963. Dir. Pierre Gaspard-Huit. France.

Shéhérazade. 1995. Dir. Florence Miailhe. France.

She Sees Dwarfs Everywhere! (Elle voit des nains partout!). 1982. Dir. Jean-Claude Sussfeld. France.

Shimcheong. 1937. Dir. An Seog-Yeong. Korea.

Shimcheongjeon. 1925. Dir. Lee Gyeong-Son. Korea.

Shimcheongjeon. 1956. Dir. Lee Gyu-Hwan. South Korea.

Shoebox (Shoebox Zoo). 2004–. TV. Dir. Justin Molotnikov, James Henry, Francis Damberger, and Grant Harvey. United Kingdom/Canada.

Sholay. 1975. Dir. Ramesh Sippy. India.

Shree 420. 1955. Dir. Raj Kapoor. India.

Shrek. 2001. Dir. Andrew Adamson and Vicky Jenson. United States.

Shrek 2. 2004. Dir. Andrew Adamson, Kelly Asbury, and Conrad Vernon. United States.

Shrek Forever After. 2010. Dir. Mike Mitchell. United States.

Shrek the Third. 2007. Dir. Chris Miller and Raman Hui. United States.

The Silences of the Palace (Ṣamt al-Quṣūr). 1994. Dir. Moufida Tlatli. France/Tunisia.

Silly Symphonies. 1929–1939. Dir. Walt Disney, Burt Gillet, David Hand, Wilfred Jackson, Ben Sharpsteen, and Ub Iwerks. United States.

SimsalaGrimm. 1999–2010. TV. Created by Claus Clausen, André Sikojev, and Stefan Beiten. Germany.

Sinderella. 1972. Dir. Ron Inkpen. United Kingdom.

The Singing Princess (La rosa di Bagdad). 1949. Dir. Anton Gino Domeneghini. Italy.

The Singing Ringing Tree (Das singende, klingende Bäumchen). 1957. Dir. Helmut Spieß. East Germany.

Sister Alenushka and Brother Ivanushka (Sestritsa Alenushka and bratets Ivanushka). 1953. Dir. Ol'ga Khodataeva. USSR.

Sitcom. 1998. Dir. François Ozon. France.

Sketches of Scotland. 1948. Dir. Henry Stringer. United Kingdom.

Sleeping Beauty. 1959. Dir. Walt Disney, Clyde Geronimi, Les Clark, Eric Larson, and Wolfgang Reighterman. United States.

Sleeping Beauty. 2011. Dir. Julia Leigh. Australia.

Sleeping Beauty (La bella addormentata). 1942. Dir. Luigi Chiarini. Italy.

The Sleeping Beauty (La belle endormie). 2010. Dir. Catherine Breillat. France.

Sleeping Betty (Isabelle au bois dormant). 2007. Dir. Claude Cloutier. Canada.

Sleepless. 1914. Dir. Lancelot Speed. United Kingdom.

Sleepy Hollow. 1999. Dir. Tim Burton. United States.

Slumdog Millionaire. 2008. Dir. Danny Boyle and Loveleen Tandan. United Kingdom/India.

The Snow Queen (Snedronningen). 2000. Dir. Jacob Jørgensen and Kristof Kuncewicz. Denmark.

Snow Queen. 2002. TV. Dir. David Wu. Canada/United States/Germany.

The Snow Queen. 2005. Dir. Danishka Esterhazy. Canada.

The Snow Queen. 2005. TV. Dir. Julian Gibbs. Canada/United Kingdom.

Snow Queen (Snezhnaia koroleva). 2012. Dir. Maksim Sveshnikov and Vladlen Barbe. Russia.

Snow White (Schneewittchen). 1928. Dir. Alf Zengerling. Germany.

Snow White (Snegurochka). 1952. Dir. Ivan Ivanov-Vano. USSR.

Snow White (Schneewittchen). 1955. Dir. Erich Kobler. Germany.

Snow White (Schneewittchen). 1959. Dir. Fritz Genschow. Germany.

Snow White (Schneewittchen). 1961. Dir. Gottfried Kolditz. East Germany.

Snow White: A Deadly Summer. 2012. Dir. David DeCoteau. United States.

Snow White: The Fairest of Them All. 2001. Dir. Caroline Thompson. Canada/Germany/United States.

Snow White: The Sequel. 2007. Dir. Picha. Belgium/France/United Kingdom/Poland.

Snow White & Co. (Biancaneve & Co.). 1982. Dir. Mario Bianchi. Italy.

Snow White and the Huntsman. 2012. Dir. Rupert Sanders. United States.

Snow White and Rose Red (Schneeweißchen und Rosenrot). 1938. Dir. Hubert Schonger. Germany.

Snow White and Rose Red (Schneeweißchen und Rosenrot). 1954. Dir. Fritz Genschow. Germany.

Snow White and Rose Red (Schneeweißchen und Rosenrot). 1955. Dir. Erich Kobler. Germany.

Snow White and the Seven Dwarfs. 1937. Dir. William Cottrell, David Hand, Wilfred Jackson, Larry Morey, Perce Pearce, and Ben Sharpsteen. United States.

The Snowman. 1982. Dir. Dianne Jackson and Jimmy T. Murakami. United Kingdom.

Song of the Sea. 2014. Dir. Tomm Moore. Ireland.

The Sorcerer's Apprentice (Čarodějův učeň aka Krabat). 1978. Dir. Karel Zeman. Czechoslovakia/West Germany.

Souvenir. 2011. Dir. Xiaoxue "Snow" Zheng. Australia.

Spear of the Sun (Słoneczna włócznia). 1999. TV. Dir. Jerzy Łukaszewicz. Poland.

Spirited Away (Sen to Chihiro no kamikakushi). 2001. Dir. Hayao Miyazaki. Japan.

Splinter (Drzazga). 2006. Dir. Wojtek Wawszczyk. Poland.

The Sporting Mice. 1909. Dir. Charles Armstrong. United Kingdom.

The Stain. 1992. Dir. Marjut Rimminen and Christine Roche. United Kingdom.

The Star (Gwiazda). 1984. Dir. Witold Giersz. Poland.

The Star Coins (Die Sterntaler). 1940. Dir. Hubert Schonger. Germany.

Stardust. 2007. Dir. Matthew Vaughn. United Kingdom/United States.

The Steadfast Tin Soldier (Den standhaftige tinsoldat). 1955. Dir. Ivo Caprino. Norway.

Stick, Start Beating! (Obušku, z pytle ven!). 1955. Dir. Jaromír Pleskot. Czechoslovakia.

Stille Nacht. 1988–2001. Dir. Timothy Quay and Stephen Quay. United Kingdom/Canada/United States.

The Stone Flower (Kamennyi tsvetok). 1946. Dir. Aleksandr Ptushko. USSR.

The Story of the Kelly Gang. 1906. Dir. Charles Tait. Australia.

The Story of Little Mook (Die Geschichte vom kleinen Muck). 1953. Dir. Wolfgang Staudte. East Germany.

The Story of Liu Bao Village (Liu Bao de Gushi 柳堡的故事). 1957. Dir. Wang Ping. China.

The StoryTeller. 1987–1989. TV. Dir. Various. United Kingdom.

Story Theatre. 1971–1972. TV. Created by Paul Sills. Canada.

Strange Magic. 2015. Dir. Gary Rydstrom. United States.

The Strange Adventures of Matołek the Billy-Goat (Dziwne przygody Koziołka Matołka). (1969–1971). TV. Dir. Roman Huszczo, Piotr Lutczyn, Alina Maliszewska, Bogdan Nowicki, Leonard Pulchny, Ryszard Słapczyński, Piotr Szpakowicz, and Stefan Szwakopf. Poland.

The Strange World of Filemon the Cat (Dziwny świat kota Filemona). 1972–1981. TV. Dir. Ludwik Kronic, Alina Kotowska, Wacław Fedak, Ireneusz Czesny, and Ryszard Szymczak. Poland.

Street of Crocodiles. 1986. Dir. Timothy Quay and Stephen Quay. United Kingdom.

The Strike (Stachka). 1924. Dir. Sergei Eisenstein. USSR.

Sumurun. 1920. Dir. Ernst Lubitisch. Germany.

Super Why! 2007–2012. TV. Created by Angela Santomero. Canada/United States.

The Surprise Box (La Boîte à surprise). 1956–1972. TV. Canada.

Suspiria. 1977. Dir. Dario Argento. Italy.

The Sweet Hereafter. 1997. Dir. Atom Egoyan. Canada.

Table Be Covered (Tischlein, deck dich). 1936. Dir. the Diehl Brothers. Germany.

Table Be Covered (Tischlein, deck dich). 1956. Dir. Fritz Genschow. Germany.

Tadpole and the Whale (La grenouille et la baleine). 1988. Dir. Jean-Claude Lord. Canada.

The Taking of Rome (La presa di Roma). 1905. Dir. Filoteo Alberini. Italy.

The Tale of the Dead Princess and the Seven Knights (Skazka o mertvoi tsarevne i semi bogatyriakh). 1951. Dir. Ivan Ivanov-Vano. USSR.

The Tale of the Fisherman and the Fish (Skazka o rybake i rybke). 1937. Dir. Aleksandr Ptushko. USSR.

The Tale of the Fisherman and the Fish (Skazka o rybake i rybke). 1950. Dir. Mikhail Tsekhanovskii. USSR.

The Tale of the Fox (Le Roman de Renard). 1930. Dir. Władysław Starewicz. France.

Tale of the Golden Cockerel (Skazka o zolotom petushke). 1967. Dir. Aleksandra Snezhko-Blotskaia. USSR.

The Tale of the Pope and His Worker Balda (Skazka o pope i ego rabotnike Balde). 1936. Dir. Mikhail Tsekhanovskii. USSR.

The Tale of the Princess Kaguya (Kaguyahime monogatari). 2013. Dir. Isao Takahata. Japan.

The Tale of Tales. 2015. Dir. Matteo Garrone. Italy/France/United Kingdom.

The Tale of Tsar Saltan (Skazka o tsare Saltane). 1943. Dir. Valentina and Zinaida Brumberg. USSR.

The Tale of the Tsar Saltan (Skazka o tsare Saltane). 1966. Dir. Aleksandr Ptushko. USSR.

A Tale of Two Sisters (Janghwa, Hongryeon). 2003. Dir. Kim Jee-woon. South Korea.

Tales for All (Contes pour tous). 1971–2009. Film series. Canada.

Tales of the Night (Les contes de la nuit). 2011. Dir. Michel Ocelot. France.

Tangled. 2010. Dir. Nathan Greno and Byron Howard. United States.

Teddy Floppy Ear (Miś Uszatek). 1975–1987. TV. Dir. Lucjan Dembiński, Marian Kiełbaszczak, Dariusz Zawilski, Eugeniusz Ignaciuk, Jadwiga Kudrzycka, Eugenusz Strus, Teresa Puchowska-Sturlis, Janusz Galewicz, Krystyna Kulczycka, and Lanina Hartwig. Poland.

The Tender Tale of Cinderella Penguin. 1981. Dir. Janet Perlman. Canada.

Teorema. 1968. Dir. Pier Paolo Pasolini. Italy.

That Very Münchausen (Tot samyi Miunkhgauzen). 1973. Dir. Mark Zakharov. USSR.

The Thief of Bagdad. 1924. Dir. Raoul Walsh. United States.

The Thief of Bagdad. 1940. Dir. Ludwig Berger, Michael Powell, and Tim Whelan. United States.

The Thief of Baghdad Castle (Baguda-jō no tōzoku). 1926. Dir. Ōfuji Noburō. Japan.

Third Sister Liu (Liu Sanjie 刘三姐). 1960. Dir. Su Li. China.

The Thirteenth Year. 1999. Dir. Duwayne Dunham. United States.

Thomas the Falconer (Sokoliar Tomáš). 2000. Dir. Václav Vorlíček. Czech Republic/Slovak Republic/Poland/Hungary/Germany/France.

A Thousand and One Nights (Binbir Gece). 2006–2009. TV. Dir. Kudret Sabanci. Turkey.

Thousand and One Nights (Mille et une nuits). 1993. TV. Dir. René Huchez and Bahram Rohani. France.

A Thousand and One Nights (Senya ichiya monotagari). 1969. Dir. Eiichi Yamamoto. Japan.

The Thousand-Year-Old Fox (Cheonnyeonho). 1969. Dir. Shin Sang-Ok. South Korea.

Three Brothers (Tři bratři). 2014. Dir. Jan Svěrák. Czech Republic/Denmark.

Three Fat Men (Tri tolstiaka). 1966. Dir. Aleksei Batalov. USSR.

The Three Golden Hairs of Old Man Know-All (Tři zlaté vlasy děda Vševěda). 1963. Dir. Jan Valášek. Czechoslovakia.

Three Knights on Distant Shores (Tri bogatyria na dal'nikh beregakh). 2012. Dir. Konstantin Feoktistov. Russia.

Three Knights and the Queen of Shamakhan (Tri bogatyria i Shamakhanskaia tsaritsa). 2010. Dir. Sergei Glezin. Russia.

Three Little Pigs. 1933. Dir. Burt Gillett. United States.

The Three Little Pigs/Three Little Pigs. 1922. Dir. Anson Dyer. United Kingdom.

Three Nuts for Cinderella aka *Three Wishes for Cinderella* (Tři oříšky pro Popelku). 1973. Dir. Václav Vorlíček. Czechoslovakia/East Germany.

The Three Wishes. 1953. Dir. Lotte Reiniger. United Kingdom.

Thumbelina. 1993. Dir. Richard Slapczynski. Australia.

Thumbelina (Diuimovochka). 1964. Dir. Leonid Amalrik. USSR.

Tideland. 2005. Dir. Terry Gilliam. Canada/United Kingdom.

The Tin Drum (Die Blechtrommel). 1979. Dir. Volker Schlöndorff. West Germany/France/Poland.

Tin Man. 2007. Dir. Nick Willing. United States.

The Tinderbox (Das Feuerzeug). 1959. Dir. Siegfried Hartmann. East Germany.

The Tinderbox (Fyrtøjet). 1946. Dir. Svend Methling. Denmark.

The Tinderbox (Fyrtøjet). 1993. TV. Dir. Mihail Badica. Denmark.

Tinker Bell. 2008. Dir. Bradley Raymond. United States.

Tinker Bell and the Great Fairy Rescue. 2010. Dir. Bradley Raymond. United States.

Tinker Bell and the Lost Treasure. 2009. Dir. Klay Hall. United States.

Tired Death (Der Müde Tod). 1921. Dir. Fritz Lang. Germany.

Tomcat and Fox (Kot i lisa). 2004. Dir. Konstantin Bronzit. Russia.

The Town Mouse and the Country Mouse (Le rat de maison et le rat des champs). 1980. Dir. Evelyn Lambart. Canada.

Toys in the Attic. See *In the Attic – Who Has a Birthday Today?*

The Transformation Machine (Maszyna zmian). 1995–1996. TV. Dir. Andrzej Maleszka. Poland.

Trap for Cinderella. 2013. Dir. Iain Softley. United Kingdom.

The Treasure of Count Chamaré (Poklad hraběte Chamaré). 1984. Dir. Zdeněk Troška. Czechoslovakia.

The Trial of Red Riding Hood. 1992. TV. Dir. Eric Till. Canada.

The Troll Hunter (Trolljegeren). 2010. Dir. André Øvrelid. Norway.

Tsar Saltan (Skazka o tsare Saltane). 1943. Dir. Valentina and Zinaida Brumberg. USSR.

Tsar Saltan (Skazka o tsare Saltane). 1984. Dir. Ivan Ivanov-Vano. USSR.

Tsotsi. 2005. Dir. Gavin Hood. South Africa.

Tuesday. 2001. Dir. Geoff Dunbar. United Kingdom.

The Turning Table (La Table tournante). 1988. Dir. Paul Grimault and Jacques Demy. France.

Twelve Months (Dvenadtsat' mesiatsev). 1956. Dir. Ivan Ivanov-Vano. USSR.

The Two Who Stole the Moon (O dwóch takich co ukradli Księżyc). 1962. Dir. Jan Batory. Poland.

Tytus, Romek and A'Tomek Among Dream Thieves (Tytus, Romek i A'Tomek wśród złodziei marzeń). 2002. Dir. Leszek Gałysz. Poland.

The U-Tube. 1917. Dir. Lancelot Speed. United Kingdom.

Ugetsu. 1953. Dir. Kenzo Mizoguchi. Japan.

The Ugly Duckling (Den grimme ælling). 2004. Dir. Jørgen Lerdam. Denmark/United Kingdom.

The Ugly Duckling (Gadkii utenok). 1956. Dir. Vladimir Degtiarev. USSR.

The Ugly Duckling (Gadkii utenok). 2010. Dir. Garri Bardin. Russia.

The Ugly Duckling (Miun Orisaekki). 2012. Dir. Kwak Kyung-Taek. South Korea.

The Unnameable Little Broom. 1985. Dir. Timothy Quay and Stephen Quay, Keith Griffiths. United Kingdom.

Urusei Yatsura. 1981–1986. TV. Created by Rumiko Takahashi. Japan.

Urusei Yatsura: Beautiful Dreamer (Urusei yatsura biyoochifuru doriima). 1984. Dir. Mamoru Oshii. Japan.

Valerie and Her Week of Wonders (Valerie a týden divů). 1970. Dir. Jaromil Jireš. Czechoslovakia.

Ventures into Fairy Tales (Podróże do bajek). 1989–1993. TV. Dir. Aleksandra Magnuszewska-Oczko. Poland.

Visiting the Fairy Tale (V gostiakh u skazki). 1976–1995. TV. Created by Gosteleradio. USSR.

The Voice of the Nightingale (Les voix du rossignol). 1923. Dir. Władysław Starewicz. France.

Votes for Women: A Caricature. 1909. Dir. Charles Armstrong. United Kingdom.

Wales. 1948. Dir. Henry Stringer. United Kingdom.

Walt before Mickey. 2014. Dir. Khoa Le. United States.

The War of the Worlds: Next Century (Wojna światów: następne stulecie). 1981. Dir. Piotr Szulkin. Poland.

The Warsaw Uprising. 2014. Dir. Jan Komasa. Poland.

The Waterbabies/A Fairy Tale for a Land Baby. 1978. Dir. Lionel Jeffries. United Kingdom.

Waxworks (Das Wachsfigurenkabinett). 1924. Dir. Leo Birinsky and Paul Leni. Germany.

The Wet Fairy Tale (Mokra bajeczka). 2006. Dir. Wojciech Gierłowski. Poland.

Whisper of the Heart (Mimi o sumaseba). 1995. Dir. Yoshifumi Kondo. Japan.

White Wedding. 2009. Dir. Jann Turner. South Africa.

Who's Afraid of the Devil? (Wer reißt denn gleich vorm Teufel aus). 1977. Dir. Egon Schlegel. East Germany.

Who's Afraid of the Wolf? (Kdopak by se vlka bál). 2008. Dir. Maria Procházková. Czech Republic.

The Wild Swans (De vilde svaner). 2009. Dir. Ghita Nørby and Peter Flinth. Denmark.

Wild Swans (Dikie lebedi). 1962. Dir. Mikhail Tsekhanovskii. USSR.

Winter in Moominland (Zima w Dolinie Muminków). 1986. Dir. Lucjan Dembiński, Dariusz Zawilski, Krystyna Kulczycka, and Jadwiga Kudrzycka. Poland.

Winter in the Wicker Bay (Zima w wiklinowej zatoce). 1998. TV. Dir. Wiesław Zięba. Poland.

The Wizard of Oz. 1939. Dir. Victor Fleming. United States.

The Wolf and the Seven Goats (Volk i semero kozliat). 1938. Dir. Sarra Mokil. USSR.

The Wolf and the Seven Kids (Der Wolf und die sieben jungen Geisslein). 1939. Dir. the Diehl Brothers. Germany.

Woman Demon Human (Ren Gui Qing 人鬼情). 1987. Dir. Huang Shuqin. China.

Woman in the Dunes (Suna no onna). 1964. Dir. Hiroshi Teshigahara. Japan.

The Wonderful Adventures of Nils (Nils Holgerssons underbara resa). 2011. Dir. Dirk Regel. Sweden/ Germany.

The Wonderful World of the Brothers Grimm. 1962. Dir. Henry Levin and George Pal. United States.

The Wooden Rider (Drewniany jeździec). 1964. Dir. Zenon Wasilewski. Poland.

Xala. 1974. Dir. Ousmane Sembène. Senegal.

Yaaba (Grand'Mère). 1987. Dir. Idrissa Ouédraogo. Burkina Faso/Switzerland.

The Yellow Submarine. 1968. Dir. George Dunning. United Kingdom/United States.

Yeonsan the Tyrant (Pokgun Yeonsan). 1962. Dir. Shin Sang-Ok. South Korea.

Yeoubi, the Five-Tailed Fox (Cheonnyeonyeou Yeoubi). 2007. Dir. Lee Sung-Gang. South Korea.

Yorkshire Ditty. 1949. Dir. Henry Stringer. United Kingdom.

Young Andersen (Unge Andersen). 2005. Dir. Rumle Hammerlich. Denmark.

Zero. 2011. Dir. Christopher Kezelos. Australia.

Zhikharka. 2006. Dir. Oleg Uzhinov. Russia.

?e?anx (The Cave). 2009. Dir. Helen Haig-Brown. Canada.

REFERENCES

Aalen, Kristin. 2012. "Feiende flott fantasy-eventyr." *Stavanger Aftenblad*, November 8.

Abbott, J. Anthony. 2005. "Review: *La Vendedora de Rosas* (The Rose Seller) and *Ratas, Ratones, Rateros* (Rodents)." *Journal of Latin American Geography* 4 (2): 133–37.

Abel, Richard. 1998. *The Ciné Goes to Town: French Cinema, 1896–1914.* Berkeley: University of California Press.

———. 1999. *The Red Rooster Scare: Making Cinema American, 1900–1910.* Berkeley: University of California Press.

Adorno, Theodor. 2002. *The Culture Industry: Selected Essays on Mass Culture.* New York: Routledge.

Afanas'ev, Aleksandr. 1984. *Narodnye russkie skazki.* Moscow: Nauka.

AFP. 2013. "In India, Less Prudish Censors for Cut-Up Bollywood." *Newsweek Online*, May 5. Online. Available HTTP: <http://newsweekpakistan.com/in-india-less-prudish-censors-for-cut-up-bollywood/>.

Agger, Gunhild. 2013. "Danish TV Christmas Calendars: Folklore, Myth and Cultural History." *Journal of Scandinavian Cinema* 3 (3): 267–80.

Aguilar, Carlos. 2014. "'Song of the Sea' is a Blissfully Beautiful Journey into Irish Folklore." *Toronto Review,* September 7. Online. Available HTTP: <http://blogs.indiewire.com/sydneylevine/toronto-review-song-of-the-sea-is-a-blissfully-beautiful-journey-into-irish-folklore-20140907>.

Allen, Joseph. 1996. "Dressing and Undressing the Chinese Woman Warrior." *Position* 4 (2): 343–69.

Andersen, Hans Christian. 1835. "Den lille Idas Blomster." In *Eventyr, fortalte for Børn. Første Samling. Første Hefte*, 45. Copenhagen: C.A. Reitzel.

———. 1837. "Keiserens nye Klæder." In *Eventyr, fortalte for Børn. Første Samling. Tredie Hefte*, 52. Copenhagen: C.A. Reitzel.

———. 1838. "Den standhaftige Tinsoldat." In *Eventyr, fortalte for Børn. Ny Samling. Første Hefte*, 14. Copenhagen: C.A. Reitzel.

———. 1842. "Ole Lukoie." In *Eventyr, fortalte for Børn. Ny Samling. Tredie Hefte*, 1. Copenhagen: C.A. Reitzel.

———. 1843. "Nattergalen." In *Nye Eventyr*, 7. Copenhagen: C.A. Reitzel.

———. 1847. "The Story of a Mother." In *A Christmas Greeting to my English Friends.* London: Richard Bentley.

———. 1848. "Hørren blev trykt for første gang i Den nye Børneven." In *Ilustreret Tidsskrift for Børn*, 5–11. Copenhagen: Chr. Steen & Søns Forlag.

———. 1852. "Det er ganske vist!" In *Historier. Første Samling*, 43. Copenhagen: C.A. Reitzel.

———. 1861. "Hvad Fatter gjør, det er altid det Rigtige." In *Nye Eventyr og Historier. Anden Række. Første Samling*, 23. Copenhagen: C.A. Reitzel.

———. 1986. "The Little Match Girl." In *The Flying Trunk and Other Stories from Andersen*, retold by Naomi Lewis, 61–64. London: Guild Publishing.

———. 2000. *Snedronningen. Et eventyr af H.C. Andersen*, decoupage art by Queen Margrethe II. Copenhagen: JJ Film and Gads Forlag.

——. 2003. *Andersen. Eventyr og historier.* Copenhagen: Det Danske Sprog- og Litteraturselskab and Gyldendalske Boghandel, Nordisk Forlag.

——. 2003. "Historien om en Moder." In *Andersen. Eventyr og historier*, Vol. I. Copenhagen: Det Danske Sprog- og Litteraturselskab and Gyldendalske Boghandel, Nordisk Forlag.

——. 2007. *The Annotated Hans Christian Andersen*, edited and annotated by Maria Tatar. Translated by Maria Tatar and Julie K. Allen. New York: W.W. Norton and Co.

——. 2009. *De vilde svaner. Et eventyr af H.C. Andersen.* Decoupage art by Queen Margrethe II. Copenhagen: Kristeligt Dagblads Forlag and JJ Film.

Andersen, Jens. 2005. *Hans Christian Andersen: A New Life*, translated by Tiina Nunnally. New York: Overlook Press.

Antunes, Luis Rocha. 2013. "Thematic Segmentation and Acting Style in *Journey to the Christmas Star.*" *Journal of Scandinavian Cinema* 3 (3): 241–51.

Apostolou, Fotini. 2009. "Cultural Translations: Transcending Boundaries in Michel Ocelot's Animated Film *Azur et Asmar* (2006)." *Communication, Politics & Culture* 42 (1): 96–117.

Araújo, Vicente de Paula. 1976. *A bela época do cinema brasileiro.* São Paulo: Perspectiva.

Armata, Jerzy. 2008. "1981–1990: Przerwana dekada." In *Polski Film Animowany*, edited by Marcin Giżycki and Bogusław Zmudzinski, 78–93. Warszawa: Polskie Wydawnictwo Audiowizualne.

Armes, Roy. 1987. *Third World Film Making and the West.* Berkeley: University of California Press.

Asbjørnsen, Peter Christen and Jørgen Moe. 2002. *Norske folkeeventyr.* Oslo: Kagge.

Author of "Little Jessie". 1866. *The Australian Babes in the Woods: A True Story Told in Rhyme for the Young.* London: Griffith & Farran.

Bacchilega, Cristina. 2012. "Whetting Her Appetite: What's a 'Clever' Woman To Do in the Grimms' Collection?" In *Transgressive Tales: Queering the Grimms*, edited by Kay Turner and Pauline Greenhill, 27–47. Detroit: Wayne State University Press.

——. 2013. *Fairy Tales Transformed? Twenty-First-Century Adaptations and the Politics of Wonder.* Detroit: Wayne State University Press.

Bacchilega, Cristina and John Rieder. 2014. "The Fairy Tale and the Commercial in *Carosello* and *Fractured Fairy Tales.*" In *Channelling Wonder: Fairy Tales on Television*, edited by Pauline Greenhill and Jill Rudy, 336–59. Detroit: Wayne State University Press.

Bagrov, Petr. 2005. "Svinarka i pastukh, Ot Gansa Khristiana k Khristianu Gansu," *Seans* 25/26. Online. Available HTTP: <http://seance.ru/n/25–26/andersen/svinarka-i-pastuh/>.

Bahadur, Nina. 2014. "Angelina Jolie: 'Maleficent' Scene Is A 'Metaphor for Rape.'" *The Huffington Post*, June 11. Online. Available HTTP: <www.huffingtonpost.com/2014/06/011/angelina-jolie-maleficent-rape-scne_n_5485633.html>.

Bahadur, Satish. 2014. "The Language of Cinema." *YouTube*, June 19. Online. Available HTTP: <http://www.youtube.com/watch?v=tQh5V8U_ctI>.

Bahadur, Satish and Shyamla Vanarase. 2011. *A Textual Study of the Apu Trilogy.* New Delhi: Vani Prakashan.

Baiada, Christa. 2011. "Where Have All the Good Men Gone?: Afflicted Fathers and Endangered Daughters in Russell Banks's *The Sweet Hereafter.*" *The Journal of Men's Studies* 19 (3): 191–208.

Balina, Marina. 2009. "Sowjetische Magie: die subversive Macht des Märchens." In *Filme der Kindheit/Kindheit im Film*, edited by Christine Goelz, Karin Hoff, and Anja Tippner, 183–99. Frankfurt am Main: Kulturwissenschaftliche Beiträge, Band 66.

Banks, Russell. 1991. *The Sweet Hereafter.* Toronto: Vintage Canada.

Bao, Yuheng and Ma Lin. 2009. "Heshi Cai Buzai Handan Xuebu: Ping Guoqing Xianji Donghua Dapian *Malan Hua* (No More 'Learning To Walk in Handan': A Review on Animation Megaproduction *Malan Flower* Produced for the 50th Anniversary of the State)." *Dianying Pingjie (Movie Review)* 24: 35–36, 48.

Barlow, Tani. 1994. "Theorizing Woman: Funü, Guojia, Jiating." In *Body, Subject, and Power in China*, edited by Angela Zito and Tani Barlow, 253–90. Chicago: University of Chicago Press.

Barr, Allan. 1989. "Disarming Intruders: Alien Women in *Liaozhai Zhiyi.*" *Harvard Journal of Asiatic Studies* 49 (2): 501–17.

Barrie, James M. 1911. *Peter Pan and Wendy.* London: Hodder & Stoughton.

——. (1911) 2012. *Peter Pan [Peter Pan and Wendy].* Project Gutenberg. Online. Available HTTP: <http://www.gutenberg.org/files/16/16-h/16-h.htm>.

——. 1928. *Peter Pan, or, The Boy Who Would Not Grow Up.* New York: Charles Scribner's Sons.

Barsch, Achim and Peter Seibert, eds. 2007. *Märchen und Medien.* Baltmannsweiler: Schneider erlag Hohengehren.

Barthes, Roland. 1973. *Mythologies*, translated by Annette Lavers. London: Granada.

Bascom, William. 1965. "The Forms of Folklore: Prose Narrative." *Journal of American Folklore* 78: 3–20.

Basile, Giambattista. 2007. *The Tale of Tales, or Entertainment for Little Ones*, translated by Nancy L. Canepa. Detroit: Wayne State University Press.

Bastian, Ulrike. 1981. *Die "Kinder- und Hausmärchen" der Brüder Grimm in der literaturpädagogischen Diskussion des 19. und 20. Jahrhunderts*. Frankfurt am Main: Haag & Herchen.

Baum, L. Frank. (1900) 2008. *The Wonderful Wizard of Oz*. Project Gutenberg. Online. Available HTTP: <http://www.gutenberg.org/files/55/55-h/55-h.htm>.

Bauman, Zygmunt. 2005. *Liquid Life*. London: Polity Press.

Beard, William and Jerry White, eds. 2002. *North of Everything: English-Canadian Cinema Since 1980*. Edmonton: University of Alberta Press.

——. 2002a. "Introduction." In *North of Everything: English-Canadian Cinema Since 1980*, edited by William Beard and Jerry White, xvii–xxiii. Edmonton: University of Alberta Press.

Beckman, Karen. 2012. "Mixing Memory and Desire: Animation, Documentary and the Sexual Event." In *Animating the Unconscious: Desire, Sexuality, and Animation*, edited by Jayne Pilling, 187–92. New York: Columbia University Press.

Belcher, Stephen. 2008. "African Tales." In *The Greenwood Encyclopedia of Folktales and Fairy Tales*, Vol. 1, edited by Donald Haase, 12–20. Westport: Greenwood.

Bell, Florence Eveleen Eleanore Olliffe. 1896. *Fairy Tale Plays and How to Act Them*. London: Longmans, Green & Co. Ltd.

Bendazzi, Giannalberto. 2008. "Przedmowa I." In *Polski Film Animowany*, edited by Marcin Giżycki, and Bogusław Zmudzinski, 6–7. Warszawa: Polskie Wydawnictwo Audiowizualne.

Bennung, Isa. 1975. *Das deutsche Märchen als Kinderliteratur: Eine Untersuchung von den Anfängen bis zur Entwicklung in der DDR*. PhD dissertation. Halle: Martin-Luther-Universität.

Bentes, Ivana. 2003. "Deus E O Diabo Na Terra Do Sol/Black God, White Devil." In *The Cinema of Latin America*, edited by Alberto Elena and Marina Díaz López, 89–97. London: Wallflower Press.

Berg, A. Scott. 1990. *Goldwyn: A Biography*. New York: Ballantine Books.

Berry, Chris and Mary Farquhar. 2006. *China on Screen: Cinema and Nation*. New York: Columbia University Press.

Berthomé, Jean-Pierre. 1996. *Jacques Demy et les racines du rêve*. Nantes: L'Atalante.

Bettelheim, Bruno. 1976. *The Uses of Enchantment*. New York: Alfred Knopf.

Beumers, Birgit. 1999. "Cinemarket, or the Russian Film Industry in 'Mission Possible'." *Europe-Asia Studies* 51 (5): 871–96.

——. 2014. "Folklore and New Russian Animation." *KinoKultura* 43. Online. Available HTTP: <http://www.kinokultura.com/2014/issue43.shtml>.

Beumers, Birgit, Nikolai Izvolov, Natalia Miloserdova, and Natalia Riabchikova. 2009. "Margarita Barskaia and the Emergence of Soviet Children's Cinema." *Studies in Russian and Soviet Cinema* 3 (2): 229–62.

Bingham, Dennis. 2010. *Whose Lives are they Anyway? The Biopic as Contemporary Film Genre*. New Brunswick, NJ: Rutgers University Press.

Bird, Carmel. 2013a. "Dreaming the Place." In *Griffith REVIEW Special Issue: Once Upon a Time in OZ*, edited by Julianne Schultz, n.p. South Brisbane, QLD: Text Publishing Company Online. Available HTTP: <https://griffithreview.com/articles/dreaming-the-place/>.

——. 2013b. "Metaphors of Fairy Tales in Australian Culture." In *Griffith REVIEW Special Issue: Once upon a time in OZ*, edited by Julianne Schultz, 15–31. South Brisbane, QLD: Text Publishing Company.

Birkin, Andrew. 2003. *J.M. Barrie & the Lost Boys*. New Haven, CT: Yale University Press.

Bizri, Hisham M. 2003. "The Art of Masking Reality in Digital Film." *Leonardo* 36 (1): 7–11.

Blissett, William. 1959. "The Despots of the Rings." *South Atlantic Quarterly* 58: 448–56.

Boettger, Gerhard. 1948. "Das Gute und Böse im Märchen." *Lehrerrundbrief* 3: 290–91.

Bogatyrev, Petr and Roman Jakobson. 1966. "Die Folklore als eine besondere Form des Schaffens." In *Selected Writings, Vol. IV: "Slavic Epic Studies,"* edited by Roman Jakobson, 1–15. The Hague: De Gruyter-Mouton.

Bolte, Johannes and Jiří Polívka. 1913–1932. *Anmerkungen zu den Kinder- und Hausmärchen der Brüder Grimm* (*Notes to the Tales of the Brothers Grimm*). 5 vols. Leipzig: Dieterich.

Bondanella, Peter. 2009. *A History of Italian Cinema*. New York: Continuum.

Bordwell, David. 2012. "The Wayward Charms of Cinerama." *David Bordwell's Website on Cinema*, September 26. Online. Available HTTP: <http://www.davidbordwell.net/blog/2012/09/26/the-wayward-charms-of-cinerama/>.

Bose, Derek. 2005. *Bollywood Uncensored: What You Don't See on Screen and Why.* New Delhi: Rupa & Co.

Boyd, Melanie. 2007. "To Blame Her Sadness: Representing Incest in Atom Egoyan's *The Sweet Hereafter.*" In *Image and Territory: Essays on Atom Egoyan*, edited by Monique Tschofen, 284–93. Waterloo, ON: Wilfrid Laurier University Press.

Bradfer, Fabienne. 2001. "Nouveau film 'Le Petit Poucet,' d'Olivier Dahan, sort en salle mercredi. Des Poucets perdus partout dans le monde." *Le soir*, October 24: 26.

Bradford, Clare. 2001. *Reading Race: Aboriginality in Australian Children's Literature.* Melbourne: Melbourne University Press.

——. 2007. *Unsettling Narratives: Postcolonial Readings of Children's Literature.* Waterloo, ON: Wilfrid Laurier University Press.

——. 2011a. "Reading Indigeneity: Ethics of Interpretation and Representation." In *Handbook of Research on Children's and Young Adult Literature*, edited by Shelby A Wolf, Karen Coats, Patricia Enciso, and Christine A Jenkins, 238–52. New York: Routledge.

——. 2011b. "The Return of the Fairy: Australian Medievalist Fantasy for the Young." *Australian Literary Studies* 26 (4): 117–35.

Braester, Yomi. 2011. "Contemporary Mainstream PRC Cinema." In *The Chinese Cinema Book*, edited by Song Hwee Lim and Julian Ward, 176–84. London: Palgrave Macmillan BFI.

Bredsdorff, Elias. 1975. *Hans Christian Andersen: The Story of His Life and Work, 1805–75.* New York: Charles Scribner's Sons.

Březan, Jurij. 1976. *Krabat oder Die Verwandlung der Welt* (*Krabat or the Transformation of the World*). Germany: Neues Leuben.

——. 1993. *Krabat oder Die Bewahrung der Welt* (*Krabat or The Preservation of the World*). Bautzen: Domowina.

Brodie, Ian and Jodi McDavid. 2014. "Who's Got the Power? *Super Why!*, Viewer Agency, and Traditional Narrative." In *Channeling Wonder: Fairy Tales on Television*, edited by Pauline Greenhill and Jill Terry Rudy, 25–42. Detroit: Wayne State University Press.

Brook, Tom. 2011. "Indian Film's Love Affair with Fantasy." *BBC News Online*, December 2. Online. Available HTTP: <http://www.bbc.co.uk/news/world-radio-and-tv-15820462>.

Brooker, Will. 2013. "Condemned to Life on the Scrapheap." *Times Higher Education*, October 24. Online. Available HTTP: <http://timeshigher education.co.uk/features/culture/review-the-selfish-giant/2008286. article>.

Browning, Robert. 1888. *The Pied Piper of Hamelin.* London: Frederick Warne and Co., Ltd.

Brunetta, Gian Piero. 2003. *The History of Italian Cinema.* Princeton: Princeton University Press.

Bryant, Sylvia. 1989. "Re-Construction Oedipus through 'Beauty and the Beast.'" *Criticism* 31 (4): 439–53.

Brzechwa, Jan. 1946. *Akademia pana Kleksa* [Mr. Blot's Academy]. Warszawa: Czytelnik.

——. 1961. *Podróże Pana Kleksa* [Mr. Blot's Travels]. Warszawa: Czytelnik.

——. 1965. *Tryumf pana Kleksa* [Mr. Blot's Triumph]. Warszawa: Czytelnik.

Bukker, Igor. 2011. "Every Soviet Citizen Dreamed of Bollywood." *Pravda.ru*, January 27. Online. Available HTTP: <http://english.pravda.ru/society/showbiz/27–01–2011/116686-bollywood-0/>.

Bulgakova, Oksana. 2002. "Sovetskie krasavitsy v stalinskom kino." In *Sovetskoe bogatstvo: stat'i o kul'ture, literature i kino*, edited by M. Balina, E. Dobrenko, and Iu. Murashov, 391–412. St. Petersburg: Akademicheskii proekt.

Bullaro, Grace R. 2003. "Roberto Benigni's *Life Is Beautiful* and the Protection of Innocence: Fable, Fairy Tale, or Just Excuses?" *Post Script* 15 (3): 13–26.

Burkley, Melissa, Edward Burkley, S. Paul Stermer, Angela Andrade, Angela C. Bell, and Jessica Curtis. 2014. "The Ugly Duckling Effect: Examining Fixed versus Malleable Beliefs about Beauty." *Social Cognition* 32 (5): 466–83.

Cahill, Susan. 2010. "Through the Looking Glass: Fairy-tale Cinema and the Spectacle of Femininity in *Stardust* and *The Brothers Grimm.*" *Marvels & Tales* 24 (1): 57–67.

Calvino, Italo. 1962. *The Nonexistent Knight,* with *The Cloven Viscount*, translated by Archibald Colquhoun. New York: Random House.

Cameron, Stevie. 2011. *On the Farm: Robert William Pickton and the Tragic Story of Vancouver's Missing Women.* Toronto: Random House.

Canziani, Estella. 1914. "The Piper of Dreams." Birmingham: Birmingham Museum and Art Gallery.

Cao, Benito. 2012. "Beyond Empire: Australian Cinematic Identity in the Twenty-first Century." *Studies in Australasian Cinema* 6 (3): 239–50.

Čapek, Karel. 1932. *Devatero pohádek a ještě jedna od Josefa Čapka jako přívažek* (*Nine Fairy Stories*). Prague: Fr. Borový-Aventinum.

——. 1990. *Nine Fairy Tales and One More Thrown in for Good Measure*, illustrated by Josef Čapek. Translated by Dagmar Herrmann. Evanston: Northwestern University Press.

Cardinal, Roger. 1989. *The Landscape Vision of Paul Nash*. London: Reaktion Books.

Cardwell, Douglas. 1983. "The Well-Made Play of Eugène Scribe." *The French Review* 56 (6): 876–84.

Carroll, Lewis. 1876. *The Hunting of the Snark*. London: Macmillan.

——. (1865) 2012. *Alice's Adventures in Wonderland*. Project Gutenberg. Online. Available HTTP: <http://www.gutenberg.org/files/11/11-h/11-h.htm>.

Carter, Angela. 1988. "Alice." *City Limits*, October 20.

——. 1993. *American Ghosts and Old World Wonders*. London: Chatto and Windus.

Carter, Lin. 1969. *Tolkien: A Look Behind* The Lord of the Rings. New York: Ballantine.

Cavallaro, Dani. 2011. *The Fairy Tale and Anime: Traditional Themes, Images and Symbols at Play on Screen*. Jefferson, NC: McFarland.

Central Board of Film Certification. 2010. "About CBFC." Ministry of Information and Broadcasting, Government of India. http://cbfcindia.gov.in/.

Chakravarty, Sumita S. 1993. *National Identity in Indian Popular Cinema, 1947–1987*. Austin: University of Texas Press.

Chang, Justin. 2015. "'Strange Magic' Review: George Lucas' Animated Fairy Tale." *Variety*, January 21. Online. Available HTTP: <http://variety.com/2015/film/reviews/film-review-strange-magic-1201410499/>.

Chapman, Brenda. 2012. "How Can Women Gain Influence in Hollywood? Stand Up for Yourself and Mentor Others." *New York Times*, August 14. Online. Available HTTP: <www.nytimes.com/roomfordebate/2012/08/14/how-can-women-gain-influence-in-Hollywood/Stand-up-for-yourself-and-mentor-others>.

Chen, Huangmei. 1989. *Dangdai Zhongguo Dianying* (*Contemporary Chinese Cinema*), Vol 1. Beijing: Zhongguo Shehui Kexue Chubanshe (Chinese Social Sciences Press).

Chen, Xiaoyun. 2004. *Zhongguo Dangdai Dianying* (*Contemporary Chinese Cinema*). Hangzhou: Zhejiang Daxue Chubanshe (Zhejiang University Press).

Chen, Yanrong. 2012. *Xiyouji Yingshi Gaibian Yanjiu* (*On the Filmic and TV Adaptations of Xiyouji*). MA thesis. Shanghai: East China Normal University.

Cho, Insoo. 2008. "*Midnight Rendezvous*: Ardent Love and Heartache of Separation." *Koreana* 22 (3): 50–53.

Choi, JungBong. 2011. "National Cinema: An Anachronistic Delirium?" *Journal of Korean Studies* 16 (2): 173–91.

Chowdhury, Debasish Roy. 2008. "China's Bollywood Love Affair." *Asia Times Online*, January 19. Online. Available HTTP: <http://www.atimes.com/atimes/China/JA19Ad01.html>.

Chraïbi, Aboubakr. 2004. "Galland's 'Ali Baba' and Other Arabic Versions." *Marvels & Tales* 18 (2): 159–69.

Chujo, Shohei. 2013. "Yakudo suru sukechi o kyooraku suru." *Eureka* 45 (17): 71–82.

Clandfield, David. 1987. *Canadian Film*. Toronto: Oxford University Press.

Clark, Ken. 1987. "GBA – A Great British Achievement." *Animator* 19: 25–27.

Clark, Paul. 1987. "Ethnic Minorities in Chinese Films: Cinema and the Exotic." *East-West Film Journal* 1 (2): 15–31.

——. 1991. "Two Hundred Flowers on China's Screens." In *Perspective on Chinese Cinema*, edited by Chris Berry, 40–61. London: BFI Publishing.

Clarke, Kyra. 2014. "Surrendering Expectations of the Girl in Julia Leigh's *Sleeping Beauty*." *Studies in Australasian Cinema* 8 (1): 2–15.

Clement, Jennifer and Christian B. Long. 2012. "*Hugo*, Remediation and the Cinema of Attractions, or, The Adaptation of Hugo Cabret." *Senses of Cinema* 63. Online. Available HTTP: <http://sensesofcinema.com/2012/feature-articles/hugo-remediation-and-the-cinema-of-attractions-or-the-adaptation-of-hugo-cabret/#b10>.

Clinton, Amanda. 1998. "Review: *La vendedora de rosas* by Víctor Gaviria." *Chasqui: revista de literatura latinoamericana* 27 (2): 185–86.

Colleyn, Jean-Paul. 2009. "Films on African Folklore." In *African Folklore: An Encyclopedia,* edited by Philip M. Peek and Kwesi Yankah, 125–34. Abingdon: Routledge.

Collodi, Carlo. 2002. *The Adventures of Pinocchio. Story of a Puppet*, translated by Nancy Canepa. South Royalton, VT: Steerforth Italia.

Crafton, Donald. 1990. *Emile Cohl, Caricature, and Film*. Princeton: Princeton University Press.

——. 1993. *Before Mickey: The Animated Film 1898–1928*. Chicago: University of Chicago Press.

Cui, Shuqin. 2003. *Women Through the Lens: Gender and Nation in a Century of Chinese Cinema*. Honolulu: University of Hawaii Press.

Cummins, June. 1995. "Romancing the Plot: The Real Beast of Disney's *Beauty and the Beast.*" *Children's Literature* 20 (1): 22–28.

Custen, George Frederick. 1992. *Bio/pics: How Hollywood Constructed Public History*. New Brunswick, NJ: Rutgers University Press.

Dadd, Richard. 1855–1864. *The Fairy-Feller's Master-Stroke*. London: Tate Britain.

Das Gupta, Chidananda. 1991. *The Painted Face: Studies in India's Popular Cinema*. New Delhi: Roli Books.

Dai, Jinghua. 2004. *Dianying Piping (Film Criticism)*. Beijing: Peking University Press.

Dargis, Manohla. 2012. "Intricate and Odd, With Little Child's Play." *The New York Times*, September 6. Online. Available HTTP: <http://www.nytimes.com/2012/09/07/movies/toys-in-the-attic-directed-by-jiri-barta.html?_r=0>.

De Berti, Raffaele. 2004. "Italy and America: Pinocchio's First Cinematic Trip." In *A Companion to Literature and Film*, edited by Robert Stam and Alessandra Raengo, 112–26. Malden: Blackwell.

De Melo Souza, José Inácio. 2004. *Imagens do passado: São Paulo e Rio de Janeiro nos primórdios do cinema*. São Paulo: Senac.

De la Motte Fouqué, Friedrich. 1811. "Undine: eine Erzählung." *Die Jahreszeiten* 1: 1–189.

De Rosa, Maria. 2012. *The Canadian Feature Film Distribution Sector in Review: Trends, Policies and Market Developments*. Online. Available HTTP: <http://www.omdc.on.ca/Assets/Research/Research+Reports/The+Canadian+Feature+Film+Distribution+Sector/The+Canadian+Feature+Film+Distribution+Sector+in+Review+Trends$!2c+Policies+and+Market+Developments.pdf>.

Debruge, Peter. 2014. "Film Review:'Jack and the Cuckoo-Clock Heart.'" *Variety*, March 16. Online. Available HTTP: <http://variety.com/2014/film/reviews/film-review-jack-and-the-cuckoo-clock-heart-1201135842>.

Del Toro, Guillermo. 2007. "The Power of Myth." Disc 2. *Pan's Labyrinth*, 2 Disc DVD set. Spain/Mexico/USA: Optimum Home Entertainment.

Deng, Wenhe. 2011. "Xin Shiji Zhongguo Dalu Langman Aiqing Dianying Paoxi (Analysis on the Mainland Romance Films of the New Century)." *Dongnan Chuanbo (Southeast Communication Studies)* 9: 98–100.

Dermody, Susan and Elizabeth Jacka. 1988. *The Screening of Australia: Anatomy of a National Cinema,* Vol 2. Sydney: Currency Press.

Desai, Meghnad. 2005. *Nehru's Hero Dilip Kumar: In the Life of India*. New Delhi: Roli Books Pvt. Ltd.

Desowitz, Bill. 2005. "'Corpse Bride': Stop Motion Goes Digital." *Animation World Network*, September 16. Online. Available HTTP:<http://www.awn.com/vfxworld/corpse-bride-stop-stop-motion-goes-digital>.

Diawara, Manthia. 1992. *African Cinema: Politics and Culture*. Bloomington: Indiana University Press.

——. 2010. *African Film: New Forms of Aesthetics and Politics*. Munich: Prestel Verlag.

Diestro-Dópido, Mar. 2013. *Pan's Labyrinth*. London: Palgrave Macmillan.

Dietrich, Elise. 2010. "'Turma do Pererê': Representations of Race in a Brazilian Children's Comic." *Afro-Hispanic Review: The African Diaspora In Brazil* 29 (2): 143–60.

Dillon, Steven. 2003. "Lyricism and accident in *The Sweet Hereafter.*" *Literature Film Quarterly* 31 (3): 227–30.

Djebar, Assia. [1987] 1989. *A Sister to Scheherazade*, translated by Dorothy S. Blair. London: Quartet.

Do Rozario, Rebecca-Anne C. 2011. "Australia's Fairy Tales Illustrated in Print: Instances of Indigeneity: Colonization and Suburbanization." *Marvels & Tales* 25 (1): 13–32.

Dobrenko, Evgenii. 1997. *Formovka sovetskogo chitatelia*. St. Petersburg: Akademicheskii proekt.

Dorfman, Ariel and Armand Mattelart. 1991. *How to Read Donald Duck: Imperialist Ideology in the Disney Comic*, translation and introduction by David Kunzle. New York: International General.

Douglas, Kate. 2010. *Contesting Childhood Autobiography, Trauma, and Memory*. New Brunswick, NJ: Rutgers University Press.

Dower, John. 1986. *War Without Mercy: Race and Power in the Pacific War*. New York: Pantheon Books.

Drascek, Daniel. 2001. "'SimsalaGrimm': Zur Adaption und Modernisierung der Märchenwelt." *Schweizerisches Archiv für Volkskunde* 97: 79–89.

Drda, Jan. 1958. *České pohádky* (Czech Fairy Tales), illustrated by Josef Lada. Prague: Československý spisovatel.

Dreyer, Carl Theodor. 1964. *Om Filmen: Artikler og Interviews*. 2nd ed. Copenhagen: Gyldendal.

Du, Binbin. 2011. "Dangxia Guochan Aiqing Dianying 'Aiqing Benwei' de Shenmei Queshi (The Missing of the Ontological Aesthetics of 'Love' in the Current Mainland Romance Films)." *Chuangzuo yu Pinglun (Writing and Review)* 5: 108–10, 123.

Duggan, Anne E. 2013. *Queer Enchantments: Gender, Sexuality, and Class in the Fairy-Tale Cinema of Jacques Demy*. Detroit: Wayne State University Press.

——. Forthcoming. "Binary Outlaws: Queering the Classical Tale in François Ozon's *Criminal Lovers* and Catherine Breillat's *Sleeping Beauty*." In *New Approaches to Teaching Folk and Fairy Tales*, edited by Christa Jones and Claudia Schwabe. Logan: Utah State University Press.

Dupuy, Coralline. 2007. "'Why Don't You Remember? Are You Crazy?' Korean Gothic and Psychosis in *A Tale of Two Sisters*." *The Irish Journal of Gothic and Horror Studies* 3: n.p.

Dvořák, Antonín. 1899. *The Devil and Kate*. Opera. Prague, Czechoslovakia.

——. 1900. *Rusalka*. Opera. Prague, Czechoslovakia.

Dwyer, Rachel. 2004. "Yeh shaadi nahin ho sakti! ('This wedding cannot happen!'): Romance and Marriage in Contemporary Hindi Cinema." In *(Un)tying the Knot: Ideal and Reality in Asian Marriage,* edited by Gavin W. Jones and Kamalini Ramdas, 59–90. Singapore: Asia Research Institute, National University of Singapore.

——. 2014. *Bollywood's India: Hindi Cinema as a Guide to Contemporary India*. London: Reaktion Books.

Ebert, Roger. 1993. "My Neighbor Totoro Movie Review (1993)." *RogerEbert.com*. Online. Available HTTP: <http://www.rogerebert.com/reviews/great-movie-my-neighbor-totoro-1993>.

Effenberger, Vratislav. (1972) 2008. "Žvahlav/Jabberwocky." In *The Cinema of Jan Švankmajer: Dark Alchemy*. 2nd ed, edited by Peter Hames. London: Wallflower Press.

Eldridge, David. 2006. *Hollywood's History Films*. London: I.B. Tauris.

Elena, Alberto and Marina Díaz López. 2003. "Introduction." In *The Cinema of Latin America*, edited by Alberto Elena and Marina Díaz López, 1–12. London: Wallflower Press.

Elias, Norbert. 1978. *The Civilizing Process: The History of Manners*, translated by Edmund Jephcott. New York: Urizen.

Elliott, Geraldine. 1939. *The Long Grass Whispers*. London: Routledge.

Endler, Cornelia. 2006. *Es war einmal . . . im Dritten Reich: Die Märchenfilmproduktion für den nationalsozialistischen Unterricht*. Frankfurt am Main: Peter Lang.

Erben, Karel Jaromír. 1853. *Kytice z pověstí národních (A Bouquet of Folk Legends)*. Prague: J. Pospíšil.

——. 2012. *A Bouquet of Czech Folktales*, translated by Marcela Malek Sulak. Prague: Twisted Spoon Press.

——. 2013. *Kytice*. Czech and English bilingual edition. Translated by Susan Reynolds. London: Jantar Publishing.

Ernst, Olga. 1904. *Fairy Tales from the Land of Wattle*, illustrations by Dorothy Ashley. Melbourne: McCarron, Bird & Co.

Ershov, Petr. 2011. *Konek-Gorbunok*. Moscow: AST-Press.

Everett-Millais, John. 1852. *Ophelia*. London: Tate Britain.

Eynat-Confino, Irène. 2008. *On the Uses of the Fantastic in Modern Theatre: Cocteau, Oedipus, and the Monster*. New York: Palgrave.

"Fakta—Blånissene." 2009. *Dagbladet*, November 17.

Fanfreluche (série télévisée). 2015. *Wikipedia*. Online. Available HTTP: <http://fr.wikipedia.org/wiki/Fanfreluche_%28s%C3%A9rie_t%C3%A9l%C3%A9vis%C3%A9e%29>.

Ferrell, Jeff. 2013. "Tangled Up in Green: Cultural Criminology and Green Criminology." In *Routledge International Handbook of Green Criminology*, edited by Nigel South and Avi Brisman, 349–64. New York: Routledge.

Figal, Gerald. 1999. *Civilization and Monsters*. Durham, NC: Duke University Press.

Finnegan, N. 1999. "At Boiling Point: 'Like Water for Chocolate' and the Boundaries of Mexican Identity." *Bulletin of Latin American Research* 18 (3): 311–26.

Fischlin, Daniel. 1998. "Queer Margins: Cocteau, *La Belle et la bête*, and the Jewish Differend." *Textual Practice* 12 (1): 69–88.

Flanders, Judith. 2015. "After Happy Ever After." *Times Literary Supplement*, January 23.

Fleming Jr., Mike. 2014. "Warner Bros, 3 Arts Set Script-Ment for 7-film Arabian Nights Franchise." *Deadline Hollywood*, July 23. Online. Available HTTP: <http://deadline.com/2014/07/warner-bros-arabian-nights-808677/>.

Foster, Michael Dylan. 2009. *Pandemonium and Parade: Japanese Monsters and the Culture of Yokai*. Berkeley: University of California Press.

Foucault, Michel. 1979. "What is an Author?" *The Foucault Reader*, edited by Paul Rabinow, 101–20. New York: Pantheon.

France, Anatole. (1909) 1991. "Seven Wives of Bluebeard." *Spells of Enchantment: The Wondrous Fairy Tales of Western Culture*, edited by Jack Zipes, 566–82. New York: Viking Penguin.

Frank, Arthur W. 2010. *Letting Stories Breathe: A Socio-Narratology*. Chicago: University of Chicago Press.

Franz, Kurt, Jürgen Janning, Claudia Maria Pecher, and Karin Richter, eds. 2011. *Faszinierende Märchenwelt: Das Märchen in Illustration, Theater und Film*. Baltmannsweiler: Schneider Verlag Hohengehren.

Franz, Kurt and Walter Kahn, eds. 2000. *Märchen—Kinder—Medien: Beiträge zur medialen Adaptation von Märchen und zum didaktischen Umgang*. Baltmannsweiler: Schneider Verlag Hohengehren.

Frazer, John. 1979. *Artificially Arranged Scenes: The Films of Georges Méliès*. Boston: G. K. Hall.

Frow, John. 2013. *Genre*. New York: Routledge.

Fu, Poshek. 1998. "Projecting Ambivalence: Chinese Cinema in Semi-occupied Shanghai, 1937–41." In *Wartime Shanghai*, edited by Wen-hsin Yeh, 86–109. London: Routledge.

Fu, Yanzhi and Huang Jinyuan. 2004. "Jianxi Ershi Shiji Bashi Niandai *Liaozhai Zhiyi* Yingshi Gaibian zhong de Daode Xuanlü (Analysis on the Moral Theme in the Cinematic Adaptations of *Liaozhai Zhiyi* in the 1980s)." *Pu Songling Yanjiu (Pu Songling Studies)* 2: 94–101.

Ganti, Tejaswini. 2012. *Producing Bollywood: Inside the Contemporary Film Industry*. Durham, NC: Duke University Press.

Garcia, Maria. 2011. "Rewriting Fairy Tales, Revising Female Identity. An Interview with Catherine Breillat." *Cineaste* 32–35.

Gauch, Suzanne. 2007. *Liberating Shahrazad: Feminism, Postcolonialism, and Islam*. Minneapolis: University of Minnesota Press.

Gaviria, Víctor, Alice Driver, and Joshua Jennings Tweddell. 2008. "Cinematic Realism and the Restoration of Everyday Life. An Interview with Víctor Gaviria." *Arizona Journal of Hispanic Cultural Studies* 12: 237–54.

Geer, Jennifer. 2007. "J.M. Barrie Gets the Miramax Treatment: Finding (and Marketing) Neverland." *Children's Literature Association Quarterly* 32 (3): 193–212.

Genette, Gérard. 1997a. *Palimpsests: Literature in the Second Degree*, translated by Channa Newman and Claude Doubinsky. Lincoln: University of Nebraska Press.

——. 1997b. *Paratexts: Thresholds of Interpretation*, translated by Jane E. Lewin. Cambridge: Cambridge University Press.

Ghibliworld.com. 2014. "This is Animation: An Extensive Personal Interview with Michel Ocelot." Ghibli World. Online. Available HTTP: <http://www.ghibliworld.com/michel_ocelot_interview.html>.

Giera, Joachim. 2003. "Mit Aschenputtel durch die Zeiten: Märchen aus dem DEFA-Trickfilmstudio." In *Die Trick-Fabrik: DEFA-Animationsfilme 1955–1990*, edited by Ralf Schenk and Sabine Scholze, 225–62. Berlin: Bertz.

Giese, Wilhelm. 1963. "Review of *Folklore del Paraguay* by Paulo de Carvalho Neto." *Zeitschrift für Ethnologie* 88 (1): 159–60.

Giesen, Rolf and J.P. Storm. 2012. *Animation under the Swastika: A History of Trickfilm in Nazi Germany, 1933–1945*. Jefferson, NC: McFarland.

Gifford, Denis. 1987. *British Animated Films, 1895–1985: A Filmography*. London: McFarland & Co.

Gilliam, Terry. n.d. "My Saskatchewan includes the Film and Television Industry." SMPIA Saskatchewan Media Production Industry Association. Online. Available HTTP: <http://www.filmtvsask.com/index. php/terry-gilliam-director/>.

Ginsburg, Faye. 2008. "Rethinking the Digital Age." In *The Media and Social Theory*, edited by David Hesmondhalgh and Jason Toynbee, 127–44. London: Routledge.

Ginzburg, Semen. 1957. *Risovannyi i kukol'nyi fil'm*. Moskva: Iskusstvo.

Gittings, Christopher E. 2002. *Canadian National Cinema: Ideology, Difference and Representation*. London: Routledge.

Giżycki, Marcin. 2008a. "Przed 1945: Prekursorzy i pionierzy." In *Polski Film Animowany*, edited by Marcin Giżycki and Bogusław Zmudzinski, 12–27. Warszawa: Polskie Wydawnictwo Audiowizualne.

——. 2008b. "1946–1960: Socrealizm i odwilż." In *Polski Film Animowany*, edited by Marcin Giżycki and Bogusław Zmudzinski. 28–39. Warszawa: Polskie Wydawnictwo Audiowizualne.

Gladfelder, Hal. 2013. "Franju, Georges." In *The Concise Routledge Encyclopedia of the Documentary Film*, edited by Ian Aitken, 272–75. New York: Routledge.

Goldsmith, Ben. 2010. "Outward-Looking Australian Cinema." *Studies in Australasian Cinema* 4 (3): 199–214.

Gong, W. 1947. "Vorschule der Grausamkeit?" *Der Tagesspiegel* February 7: 1.

Gopal, Sangita and Sujata Moorti. 2008. *Global Bollywood: Travels of Hindi Song and Dance*. Minneapolis: University of Minnesota Press.

Gradowski, Krzysztof. 1986. Untitled press note. *Sprawy i Ludzie* 48, November 15.

Grahame, Kenneth. 1908. *The Wind in the Willows*. London: Methuen.

Granet-Abisset, Anne-Marie. 2010. "The French Experience: STO, a Memory to Collect, a History to Write." In *Hitler's Slaves: Life Stories of Forced Labourers in Nazi-Ocupied Europe*, edited by Alexander von Plato, Almut Leh, and Christoph Thonfeld, 113–23. Oxford: Berghahn.

Grant, John. 1993. *Encyclopaedia of Walt Disney's Animated Characters*. New York: Hyperion.

——. 2001. *Masters of Animation*. New York: Watson-Guptill Publications.

Gray, Jonathan. 2010. *Show Sold Separately: Promos, Spoilers, and other Media Paratexts*. New York: New York University Press.

Greenhill, Pauline. 2014. "*Le Piège d'Issoudun*: Motherhood in Crisis." *Narrative Culture* 1 (1): 49–70.

——. 2015. "'The Snow Queen': Queer Coding in Male Directors' Films." *Marvels & Tales* 29 (1): 110–34.

——. Forthcoming. "*Le piège d'Issoudun*: Motherhood and Murder in a Fairy-Tale Film." In *Screening Justice in Canada: Canadian Crime Films and Society*, edited by Steven Kohm, Sonia Bookman, and Pauline Greenhill. Winnipeg: Fernwood.

Greenhill, Pauline and Steven Kohm. 2013. "*Hoodwinked!* and *Jin-Roh: The Wolf Brigade*: Animated "Little Red Riding Hood" Films and the Rashômon Effect." *Marvels & Tales* 27 (1): 89–108.

Greenhill, Pauline and Sidney Eve Matrix. 2010. "Envisioning Ambiguity: Fairy Tale Films." In *Fairy Tale Films: Visions of Ambiguity*, edited by Pauline Greenhill and Sidney Eve Matrix, 1–22. Logan: Utah State University Press.

Greenhill, Pauline and Sidney Eve Matrix, eds. 2010. *Fairy Tale Films: Visions of Ambiguity*. Logan: Utah State University Press.

Greenhill, Pauline and Jill Terry Rudy, eds. 2014. *Channeling Wonder: Fairy Tales on Television*. Detroit: Wayne State University Press.

Grimm, Jacob and Wilhelm Grimm. (1812) 2014. "Gen den Fischer und siine Fru." In *The Original Folk and Fairy Tales of the Brothers Grimm*, translated and edited by Jack Zipes, 56–62. Princeton: Princeton University Press.

——. 2012. *The Annotated Brothers Grimm: The Bicentennial Edition*, edited and translated by Maria Tatar. New York: W.W. Norton & Company.

Gross, Mary. 1992. *Anthony Gross*, edited by Peter Gross. London: Scolar Press.

Gunning, Tom. 1986. "The Cinema of Attractions: Early Film, Its Spectator and the Avant-Garde." *Wide Angle* 8 (3/4): 63–70.

Günsberg, Maggie. 2005. *Italian Cinema: Gender and Genre*. Basingstoke UK: Palgrave MacMillan.

Haase, Donald. 1998. "Overcoming the Present: Children and the Fairy Tale in Exile, War, and the Holocaust." In *Mit den Augen eines Kindes: Children in the Holocaust, Children in Exile, and Children under Fascism*, edited by Viktoria Hertling, 86–99. Amsterdam: Rodopi.

——. 2000. "Television and Fairy Tales." In *The Oxford Companion to Fairy Tales: The Western Fairy Tale Tradition from Medieval to Modern*, edited by Jack Zipes, 513–18. New York: Oxford University Press.

——, ed. 2004. *Fairy Tales and Feminism: New Approaches*. Detroit: Wayne State University Press.

——. 2006. "Hypertextual Gutenberg. The Textual and Hypertextual Life of Folktales and Fairy Tales in English-Language Popular Print Editions." *Fabula* 47 (3–4): 222–30.

Haddad, Joumana. (2010) 2011. *I Killed Scheherazade: Confessions of an Angry Arab Woman*. Chicago: Chicago Review Press.

Haddawy, Husain, Muhsin Mahdi, and Daniel Heller-Roazen. 2010. *The Arabian Nights*. New York: W.W. Norton & Co.

Hain, Mark. 2007. "Explicit Ambiguity: Sexual Identity, Hitchcockian Criticism, and the Films of François Ozon." *Quarterly Review of Film Studies* 24 (3): 277–88.

Halas, John. 1989. "Animation and Art." *Animator* 25: 21.

Halperin, David M. 1995. *Saint Foucault: Towards a Gay Hagiography*. London: Oxford University Press.

Haltof, Marek. 2002. *Polish National Cinema*. New York: Berghahn Books.

——. 2007. *Historical Dictionary of Polish Cinema*. Lanham, MD: Scarecrow Press.

Hames, Peter. 2008. *The Cinema of Jan Švankmajer: Dark Alchemy*, 2nd ed. London, Wallflower Press.

——. 2014. "Jánošík: The Cross-Border Hero." In *Postcolonial Approaches to Eastern European Cinema: Portraying Neighbours On-Screen*, edited by Ewa Mazierska, Lars Kristensen, and Eva Näripea, 115–45. London: I.B. Tauris.

Han, Heung-Sub. 2007. "Traditional Korean Music: Its Genres and Aesthetics." *Korea Journal* 47 (3): 76–103.

Han, Jong-Woo. 2013. *Power, Place, and State-Society Relations in Korea: Neo-Confucian and Geomantic Reconstruction of Developmental State and Democratization.* Lanham, MD: Lexington Books.

Han, Tingting. 2012. *Zhongguo Zhuliu Shangye Dianying de Shixue Yanjiu (The Historical Research of China's Mainstream Commercial Films).* Beijing: Zhongguo Shuji Chubenshe (China Book Press).

Haney, Jack, ed. and trans. 2001. *Russian Wondertales. I. Tales of Heroes and Villains.* Armonk, NY: M.E. Sharpe.

Haraway, Donna. 1988. "Situated Knowledges: The Science Question in Feminism and the Privilege of Partial Perspective." *Feminist Studies* 14 (3): 575–99.

Hariharan, Githa. 1999. *When Dreams Travel.* London: Picador.

Harries, Elizabeth Wanning. 2008. "Literary Fairy Tale." In *The Greenwood Encyclopedia of Folktales and Fairy Tales,* edited by Donald Haase, 578–83. Westport, CT: Greenwood.

Harris, Kristine. 2012. "Modern Mulans: Reimagining the Mulan Legend in Chinese Film, 1920s–60s." In *The New Woman International: Representations in Photography and Film From the 1870s through the 1960s,* edited by Elizabeth Otto and Vanessa Rocco, 309–330. Ann Arbor: University of Michigan Press.

Hart, Stephen. 2004. *A Companion to Latin American Film.* New York: Tamesis.

Hay, Rebecca and Christa Baxter. 2014. "Happily Never After: The Commodification and Critique in ABC's *Once Upon a Time.*" In *Channeling Wonder: Fairy Tales on Television,* edited by Pauline Greenhill and Jill Terry Rudy, 316–35. Detroit: Wayne State University Press.

Hayward, Susan. 1993. *French National Cinema.* London: Routledge.

——. 1996. "La Belle et la Bête." *History Today* 46 (7): 43–48.

——. 2010. *French Costume Drama of the 1950s: Fashioning Politics in Film.* Chicago: Intellect.

hdturg. 2011. "Hans Christian Andersen Trailer 1952." *Youtube,* November 14. Online. Available HTTP: <https://www.youtube.com/watch?v=8xW9BpS1bN4>.

He, Tianjie. 2004. "*Liaozhai Zhiyi* Qingai Gushi yu Nüquan Yishi (Love Story and Feminist Consciousness in *Liaozhai Zhiyi*)." *Wenxue Pinglun (Literary Review)* 5: 150–55.

Hearn, Lafcadio. 2004. *Kwaidan.* New York: Cosimo Publishing.

Hearne, Betsy. 1989. *Beauty and the Beast: Visions and Revisions of an Old Tale.* Chicago: University of Chicago Press.

Hearne, Joanna. 2008. "Indigenous Animation: Educational Programming, Narrative Interventions, and Children's Cultures." In *Global Indigenous Media: Cultures, Poetics, and Politics,* edited by Pamela Wilson and Michelle Stewart, 89–108. Durham, NC: Duke University Press.

Heidtmann, Horst. 2000. "Wilhelm, Jacob und Simsala Grimm: Medienadaptionen von Volksmärchen." Presentation at the "Fairy Tales in the Modern Media Symposium," Volkach am Main in Germany, May 8–9.

——. 2007. "Von Dornröschen bis Shrek." In *Märchen und Medien,* edited by Achim Barsch and Peter Seibert, 90–107. Baltmannsweiler: Schneider Verlag Hohengehren.

Heiduschke, Sebastian. 2013. "GDR Cinema as Commodity: Marketing DEFA Films since Unification." *German Studies Review* 36 (1): 65.

Hellman, Ben. 2013. *Fairy Tales and True Stories: The History of Russian Literature for Children and Young People (1574–2010).* Amsterdam: Brill.

Herman, David. 2002. *Story Logic: Problems and Possibilities of Narrative.* Lincoln, NB: University of Nebraska Press.

Hetzel, Andreas. 2004. "Die Fremdheit der Kultur. Differenztheoretische Perspektiven." *KulturPoetik* 4 (2): 235–44.

Hipkins, Danielle. 2008. "Why Italian Film Studies Needs a Second Take on Gender." *Italian Studies* 63 (2): 213–34.

Hiscock, John. 2011. "Joe Wright Interview on Hanna." *Telegraph,* April 22. Online. Available HTTP: <http://www.telegraph.co.uk/culture/film/filmmakersonfilm/8467169/Joe-Wright-interview-on-Hanna.html>.

Hoffmann, E.T.A. 1816. "Nußknacker und Mausekönig." In *Kinder Märchen,* edited by Karl Wilhelm Contessa, Friedrich de la Motte Fouqué and E.T.A. Hoffmann. Berlin.

Höfig, Willi. 2008. "Die stumme Märchenfrau: Märchen und Sage im Stummfilm: Beispiele und theoretische Überlegungen der Zeit." In *Erzählkulturen im Medienwandel,* edited by Christoph Schmitt, 87–108. Münster: Waxmann.

Holdaway, Dom. 2012. "'L'esperienza del passato': Situating Crisis in Italian Film History." *Italian Studies* 67 (2): 267–82.

Holland, Rupert, S. 1919. *King Arthur and the Knights of the Round Table.* London: Kingsman & Co.

Holmes, Sally. 2014. "Angelina Jolie Says Violent *Malificent* Scene Was a Metaphor for Rape." *Elle*, July 12. Online. Available HTTP: <www.elle.com/news/culture/angelina-jolie-malificent-scene-metaphor-for-rape>.

Hrubín, František. 1960. *Špalíček pohádek (A Bundle of Tales)*. Prague: SNDK.

Hu, Ke. 1996. "Cong Duo Jiaodu Lijie Zhongguo Wusheng Dianying (Understand Chinese Silent Films from Multiple Perspectives)." *Dangdai Dianying (Contemporary Cinema)* 5: 51–59.

Hürlimann, Bettina. 1967. *Three Centuries of Children's Books in Europe*, translated by Brian W. Alderson. London: Oxford University Press.

Hutcheon, Linda. 2006. *A Theory of Adaptation*. New York: Routledge.

Ianovskaia, Esfir'. 1926. *Nuzhna li skazka proletarskomu rebenku*. Moscow: Gosizdat.

Idema, Wilt L. 2012. "Old Tales for New Times: Some Comments on the Cultural Translation of China's Four Great Folktales in the Twentieth Century." *Taiwan Journal of East Asian Studies* 9 (1): 25–46.

Ince, Kate. 2005. *Georges Franju*. Manchester: Manchester University Press.

Ipsen, Carl. 2006. *Italy in the Age of Pinocchio: Children and Danger in the Liberal Era*. New York: Palgrave Macmillan.

Isuma TV. 2007. *Atanarjuat: The Fast Runner*. Online. Available HTTP: <http://www.isuma.tv/en/atanarjuat>.

Itela, Albertine. 2002. "Interview with Mansour Sora Wade." *Cascade Festival of African Films 14*, translated by Michael Dembrow. Online. Available HTTP: <http://spot.pcc.edu/~mdembrow/wadeinterview.htm>.

Ivy, Marilyn. 1995. *Discourses of the Vanishing: Modernity, Phantasm, Japan*. Chicago: University of Chicago Press.

Jackson, Julian. 2001. *France: The Dark Years, 1940–44*. Oxford: Oxford University Press.

Jagose, Annamarie. 1996. *Queer Theory: An Introduction*. New York: New York University Press.

Januszewska, Hanna. 1956. *Pyza na polskich dróżkach*. Warszawa: Nasza Księgarnia.

Jiang, Yuqin. 2010. "Jiedu 2009nian Ban Dianying *Hua Mulan* de Minzu Zhuyi (On Nationalism in 2009 Film *Hua Mulan*)." *Dianying Wenxue (Cinema Literature)* 5: 13–15.

Jirásek, Alois. 1894. *Staré pověsti české* (Old Czech Legends), illustrated by Mikoláš Aleš. Prague: Vilímek.

Jireš, Jaromil. 1970. Statement in "Valerie and a Week of Wonders: A New Film by Director Jaromil Jireš." *Československý Film/The Czechoslovak Film* 70: 3.

Jiwani, Yasmin and Mary Lynn Young. 2006. "Missing and Murdered Women: Reproducing Marginality in News Discourse." *Canadian Journal of Communication* 31 (4): 895–917.

Jörg, Holger. 1994. *Die sagen- und märchenhafte Leinwand: Erzählstoffe, Motive und narrative Strukturen der Volksprosa im "klassischen" deutschen Stummfilm (1910–1930)*. Sinzheim: Pro-Universitate-Verlag.

Joshi, Lalit Mohan, ed. 2002. *Bollywood: Popular Indian Cinema*. London: Dakini.

Kafka, Franz. 2009 (1915). *The Metamorphosis and Other Stories*. Oxford: Oxford University Press.

Kahlo, Gerhard. 1954. *Die Wahrheit des Märchens: grundsätzliche Betrachtung*. Halle: Niemeyer.

Kang, Inkoo. 2014. "'The Hobbit: Battle of the Five Armies' Review: Martin Freeman and Company End Trilogy, Provide Fan Service." *The Wrap*, December 1. Online. Available HTTP: <http://www.thewrap.com/the-hobbit-the-battle-of-the-five-armies-review-martin-freeman-ian-mckellen-cate-blanchett/>.

Kannapin, Detlef. 2002. "Is There a Specific DEFA Aesthetik?" Translated by Barton Byg. In *Moving Images of East Germany: Past and Future of DEFA Film*, edited by Barton Byg and Betheny Moore, 16–38. Washington, DC: American Institute for Contemporary German Studies.

Kantaris, Geoffrey. 2010. "Drugs and assassins in the city of flows." In *Globalization, Violence, and the Visual Culture of Cities*, edited by Christoph Lindner, 32–48. Abingdon, Oxon: Routledge.

Kaur, Raminder and Ajay J. Sinha, eds. 2005. *Bollyworld: Popular Indian Cinema Through a Transnational Lens*. London: Sage Publications.

Kawai, Hayao. 1996. *The Japanese Psyche: Major Motifs in the Fairy Tales of Japan*. Woodstock, CT: Spring Publications.

Kazmi, Fareed. 1999. *The Politics of India's Conventional Cinema: Imaging a Universe, Subverting a Multiverse*. New Delhi, Thousand Oaks, Calif.: Sage Publications.

——. 2010. *Sex in Cinema: A History of Female Sexuality in Indian Films*. Allahabad: Rupa Publications.

Ke, Qianting. 2012. "Xingbie, Jiaguo, Zhanzheng: Mulan Chuanshuo de Xiandaihua yu Shijuehua: Gender, Family/State, and War: The Modernization and Visualization of Mulan Legends." *Huadong Shifan Daxue Xuebao (Journal of South China Normal Univeristy, Social Science Edition)* 3: 12–18.

Kennedy, Philip F. and Marina Warner, eds. 2013. *Scheherazade's Children: Global Encounters with* The Arabian Nights. New York: New York University Press.

Kervorkian, Martin. 2003. "'You Must Never Move the Body!' Burying Irving's Text in *Sleepy Hollow*." *Literature/Film Quarterly* 31 (1): 27–32.

Kielland, Aksel. 2012. "Disneyfiseringen av den norske kulturarven." *Bergens Tidende*, November 8.

Kilito, Abdelfattah. 2010. "The Eye and the Needle." Translated by Zachary E. Woolfe. In *The Arabian Nights*, translated by Husain Haddawy, edited by Muhsin Mahdi and Daniel Heller-Roazen, 500–504. New York: W.W. Norton & Co.

Kim, Hyang-I and Choe Jeong-In (Illustrator). 2009. *Gyeonu and Jiknyeo* (Gyeonu wa Jiknyeo). Seoul: Biryongso.

Kim, Seung-Hee and Choi Jung-In (Illustrator). 2006. *Princess Bari* (Bari Gongju). Seoul: Biryongso.

Kim, Sooni and Lee Jong-Mi (Illustrator). 2010. *The Heavenly Maiden and the Woodcutter*. Seoul: Borim.

Kim, Sung-Moon. 2014. "The Way to Become a Female Sage: Im Yunjidang's Confucian Feminism." *Journal of the History of Ideas* 75 (3): 395–416.

Kim, Taeyon. 2003. "Neo-Confucian Body Techniques: Women's Bodies in Korea's Consumer Society." *Body and Society* 9 (2): 97–113.

Kimura, Saeko. 2013. "Zense no kioku (Memories of a Former World)." *Eureka* 45 (17): 100–105.

King, John. 1990. *Magical Reels: A History of Cinema in Latin America*. London: Verso.

King, Randall. 2012. "Bollywood Ending." *Winnipeg Free Press*, March 31. Online. Available HTTP: <http://www.winnipegfreepress.com/special/ourcityourworld/southAsia/bollywood-ending-145317795.html>.

Kingsley, Charles. 1863. *The Waterbabies, A Fairy Tale for a Land Baby*. London: Macmillan.

Kipling, Rudyard. 1906. *Puck of Pook's Hill*. Ware: Wordsworth's Classics.

Kishore, Vikrant, Amit Sarwal, and Parichay Patra. 2014. *Bollywood and its Other(s): Towards New Configurations*. London: Palgrave Macmillan.

Kisin, Eugenia. 2011. "Ravens and Film: Stories of Continuity and Mediation." *Visual Anthropology Review* 27 (2): 131–40.

Kitson, Clare. 2005. *Yuri Norstein and Tale of Tales: An Animator's Journey*. Eastleigh: John Libbey and Indiana University Press.

Ko, Dorothy, JaHyun Kim Haboush, and Joan R. Piggott, eds. 2003. *Women and Confucian Cultures in Premodern China, Korea, and Japan*. Berkeley: University of California Press.

Kocialek, Anneliese. 1955. *Die Bedeutung der Volksmärchen für Unterricht und Erziehung in der Unterstufe der deutschen demokratischen Schule*. PhD dissertation. Berlin: Humboldt-Universität.

Kohm, Steven, Sonia Bookman, and Pauline Greenhill, eds. Forthcoming. *Screening Justice in Canada: Canadian Crime Films and Society*. Winnipeg: Fernwood.

Kohm, Steven and Pauline Greenhill. 2013. "'This is the North, where we do what we want': Popular Green Criminology and 'Little Red Riding Hood' Films." In *Routledge International Handbook of Green Criminology*, edited by Nigel South and Avi Brisman, 365–378. New York: Routledge.

Kołakowski, Leszek. 1963. *13 bajek z królestwa Lailonii dla dużych i małych*. Warszawa: Czytelnik.

König, Ingelore, Dieter Wiedemann, and Lothar Wolf, eds. 1996. *Zwischen Marx und Muck: DEFA-Filme für Kinder*. Berlin: Henschel.

——. 1998. *Märchen: Arbeiten mit DEFA-Kinderfilmen*. Munich: KoPäd.

Konopnicka, Maria. 1896. *O krasnoludkach i sierotce Marysi*. Warszawa: n.p.

Korczak, Janusz. 1922. *Król Maciuś Pierwszy* [King Matt the First]. Warszawa: Towarzystwo Naukowe.

Kornacki, Krzysztof. 2012. "Dorosłe dzieci mają żal: O pewnej tendencji młodego kina polskiego." *Studia Filmoznawcze* 33: 145–61.

Körner, Jan. 2009. "Dronningen flopper." *Ekstra Bladet*, October 18.

Kovalova, Anna. 2012. "Nikolai Erdman and the Poetics of Children's Film Scripts." *Studies in Russian and Soviet Cinema* 6 (2): 163–75.

Koven, Mikel. 2008. *Film, Folklore, and Urban Legends*. Lanham, MD: Scarecrow Press.

Kraszewski, Józef Ignacy. 1840. *Mistrz Twardowski: powieść z podań gminnych*. Vilnius: Józef Zawadzki.

Krings, Matthias. 2013. "*Karishika* with Kiswahili Flavor: A Nollywood Film Retold by a Tanzanian Video Narrator." In *Global Nollywood: The Transnational Dimensions of an African Video Film Industry*, edited by Matthias Krings and Onookome Okome, 306–26. Bloomington: Indiana University Press.

Krings, Matthias and Onookome Okome. 2013. "Nollywood and its Diaspora: An Introduction." In *Global Nollywood: The Transnational Dimensions of an African Video Film Industry*, edited by Matthias Krings and Onookome Okome, 1–24. Bloomington: Indiana University Press.

Krüger, Maria. 1960. *Godzina pąsowej róży: powieść dla dziewcząt*. Warszawa: Iskry.

Kulås, Guri. 2012. "Ustø tradisjonsøving." *Klassekampen*, November 8.

Kursor. 1988. "W Kinie Kleksów." *Kino* 1: 15–16.

Kuti, Elizabeth. 2013. "Scheherazade, *Bluebeard*, and Theatrical Curiosity." In *Scheherazade's Children: Global Encounters with* The Arabian Nights, edited by Philip F. Kennedy and Marina Warner, 322–46. New York: New York University Press.

La Fontaine, Jean. 1668. *Fables choisies, mises en vers par M. de La Fontaine*. Paris: Cl. Barbin.

Lada, Josef. 1939. *Nezbedné pohádky* (*Topsy-turvy Tales*). Prague: Albatros.

Lagerlöf, Selma. 1996. *Nils Holgerssons underbara resa genom Sverige* (*The Wonderful Adventures of Nils* [1906–1907]). Stockholm: Albert Bonniers förlag.

Lamarre, Thomas. 2008. "Speciesism Part 1: Translating Races into Animals in Wartime Animation." *Mechademia* 3: 75–95.

——. 2009. *The Anime Machine: A Media Theory of Animation*. Minneapolis: University of Minnesota Press.

Landwehr, Margarete Johanna. 2008. "Egoyan's Film Adaptation of Banks's *The Sweet Hereafter*: The Pied Piper as Trauma Narrative and *Mise-en-abyme*." *Literature/Film Quarterly* 36 (3): 215–22.

Lang, Andrew. 1890. *The Red Fairy Book*. London: Kingsman & Co.

Langfeldt, Johannes. 1940. "Märchen und Pädagogik." *Pädagogische Rundschau* 2: 521–25.

Larzul, Sylvette. 2004. "Further Considerations on Galland's *Mille et une Nuits*: A Study of the Tales Told by Hanna." *Marvels & Tales* 18 (2): 258–71.

Lavignette-Ammoun, Céline and Kim Dong-Seong (Illustrator). 2011. *Les étoiles amoureuses* (*Gyeonu and Jiknyeo*), translated by Lee Gyeong-Hye. Seoul: Hyeon Books.

Laws, Maury, Jules Bass, Danny Kaye, and H. C. Andersen. 1960. *The Enchanted World of Danny Kaye*. Rankin-Bass Production.

Leach, Jim. 2006. *Film in Canada*. Don Mills, ON: Oxford University Press.

Lear, David, ed. 2013. "Urashima Taro" in *The Tale of the Bamboo Cutter and Other Fantastic Stories*. Los Angeles: Firestone Books.

LeBel, Paul A. 2006. "Giving Voice to Anger: The Role of the Lawyer in *The Sweet Hereafter* (1997)." In *Screening Justice—The Cinema of Law: Significant Films of Law, Order and Social Justice*, edited by Rennard Strickland, Teree E. Foster, and Taunya Lovell Banks, 657–77. Buffalo, NY: William S. Hein & Company.

Lee, Hyangjin. 2005. "Chunhyang: Marketing an Old Tradition in New Korean Cinema." In *New Korean Cinema*, edited by Chi-Yun Shin and Julian Stringer, 63–78. New York: New York University Press.

Lee, Hyo-Won. 2014. "2014 South Korean Box Office: *Roaring Currents* (*Battle of Myung-Ryang*) Takes All-Time Record, Stellar Year for Hollywood." *The Hollywood Reporter*, December 21. Online. Available HTTP: <http://www.hollywoodreporter.com/news/2014-south-korean-box-office-759768>.

Lee, Sung-Ae. 2011. "Lures and Horrors of Alterity: Adapting Korean Tales of Fox Spirits." *International Research in Children's Literature* 4 (2): 135–50.

——. 2014. "Fairy-Tale Scripts and Intercultural Conceptual Blending in Modern Korean Film and Television Drama." In *Grimms' Tales Around the Globe: The Dynamics of Their International Reception*, edited by Vanessa Joosen and Gillian Lathey, 275–93. Detroit: Wayne State University Press.

Lee, Young-Il and Choe Young-Chol. 1998. *The History of Korean Cinema*. Seoul: Jimoondang Publishing.

Lenartz, Werner. 1948. "Von der erzieherischen Kraft des Märchens." *Pädagogische Rundschau* 2: 330–36.

Leprince de Beaumont, Jeanne-Marie. 1758. "La Belle et La Bête." *Magasin de Jeunes Dames*: n.p.

——. (1756) 1989. "Beauty and the Beast." *Beauties, Beasts and Enchantment: Classic French Fairy Tales*, translated by Jack Zipes, 233–45. New York: New American Library.

Leszenko, Włodzimierz and Władysław Zaszyński. 1971. *Katalog Filmów dla Dzieci i Młodzieży*. Warszawa: Centrala Filmów Oświatowych Filmos.

Leyda, Jay, ed. 1986. *Eisenstein on Disney*. Calcutta: Seagull Books.

Lezubski, Kirstian. 2014. "The Power to Revolutionize the World, or Absolute Gender Apocalypse? Queering the New Fairy-Tale Feminine in *Revolutionary Girl Utena*." In *Channeling Wonder: Fairy Tales on Television*, edited by Pauline Greenhill and Jill Terry Rudy, 163–85. Detroit: Wayne State University Press.

Li, Aifen. 2010. "Chuantong Minjian Gushi zai Xiandai Yingshiju zhong de Zai Chuangzuo: yi *Bao Lian Deng* weili (The Rewriting of Traditional Folktales in Modern Films and TV Shows: The Case of Magic Lotus Lantern Tales)." MA thesis. Yunnan, China: Yunnan University.

Li, Chunfang. 2008. "Zeren Fengxian Chengquan: Dianying *Hua Pi* duiyu Ai de Xiandai Quanshi (Responsibility, Devotion, Compassion: The Modern Interpretation of Love in *Painted Skin*)." *Dianying Wenxue* (*Cinema Literature*) 12: 92–93.

Li, Daoxin. 2007. *Zhongguo Dianying Piping Shi (History of Chinese Film Criticism, 1897–2000)*. Beijing: Peking University Press.

Li, Jing. 2008. "Chinese Tales." In *The Greenwood Encyclopedia of Folktales and Fairy Tales*, Vol. 1, edited by Donald Haase, 194–200. Westport, CT: Greenwood Press.

Li, Shaobai, ed. 2006. *Zhongguo Dianying Shi (History of Chinese Cinema)*. Beijing: Gaodeng Jiaoyu Chubanshe (Higher Education Press).

Liberatore, Paul. 2013. "'Brave' Creator Blasts Disney for 'Blatant' Sexism' in Princess Makeover." *Marin Independent Journal*, November 5. Online. Available HTTP: <http://www.marinij.com/millvalley/ci_23224741/brave-creator-blasts-disney-blatant-sexism-princess-makeover>.

Lichtner, Giacomo. 2012. "The Age of Innocence? Child Narratives and Italian Holocaust Films." *Modern Italy* 17 (2): 197–208.

Lim, Song Hwee and Julian Ward. 2011. "The Coming of Age of Chinese Cinema Studies." In *The Chinese Cinema Book*, edited by Song Hwee Lim and Julian Ward, 1–5. London: Palgrave Macmillan BFI.

Lindgren, Astrid. 1973. *Bröderna Lejonhjärta*. Stockholm: Rabén & Sjögren.

———. 1981. *Ronja Rövardotter*. Stockholm: Rabén & Sjögren.

Lipovetskii, Mark. 2003. "Utopiia svobodnoj marionetki, ili kak sdelan arkhetip." *Novoe literaturnoe obozrenie* 60: 252–68.

Lipovetsky [Lipovetskii], Mark. 2010. *Charms of Cynical Reason: Trickster in Soviet and Post-Soviet Culture*. Boston: Academic Studies Press.

Lismoen, Kjetil. 2012. "En forbausende gammelmodig tilnærming." *Aftenposten*, Nov. 8.

Liu, Lydia. 1991. "The Female Tradition in Modern Chinese Literature: Negotiating Feminisms Across East/West Boundaries." *Genders* 12: 22–44.

Lobato, Monteiro and José Bento. 1977. *O Saci*. 29th ed. São Paulo: Editora Brasiliense.

Lochner, Jim. 2010. "The Wonderful World of the Brothers Grimm: Supplemental Liner Notes." *Film Score Monthly* 13 (4): 1–13.

Loesser, Frank, Danny Kaye, Jane Wyman, and Gordon Jenkins. 1952. *Hans Christian Andersen*. Sound Recording. New York: Decca Records.

Lundell, Michael James. 2013. "Pasolini's Splendid Infidelities: Un/Faithful Film Versions of *The Thousand and One Nights*." *Adaptation* 6 (1): 120–27.

Luo, Hui. 2009. "The Ghost of *Liaozhai*: Pu Songling's Ghostlore and its History of Reception." PhD dissertation. Toronto: University of Toronto Press.

Lüthi, Max. 1976. *Once Upon A Time: On the Nature of Fairy-Tales*. Bloomington: Indiana University Press.

———. (1982) 1986. *The European Folktale: Form and Nature*, translated by John D. Niles. Bloomington: Indiana University Press.

Lynch, Stephen. 1999. "Marsupial Madness: The Success of Yoram Gross." *Animation World Magazine*, October 1. Online. Available HTTP: <http://www.awn.com/animationworld/marsupial-madness-success-yoram-gross>.

Lynn, Thomas J. 2003. "Politics, Plunder, and Postcolonial Tricksters: Ousmane Sembène's *Xala*." *International Journal of Film Studies* 6 (3): 183–96.

Ma, Ruifang. 2000. "*Liaozhai Zhiyi* de Nanquan Huayu he Qingai Wutuobang (Patriarchal Discourse and Love Utopia in *Liaozhai Zhiyi*)." *Wen Shi Zhe (Journal of Literature, History and Philosophy)* 4: 73–79.

Macnab, Geoffrey. 1993. *J. Arthur Rank and the British Film Industry*. New York: Routledge.

Magnus-Johnston, Kendra. 2013. "'Reeling In' Grimm Masculinities: Hucksters, Cross-Dressers, and Ninnies." *Marvels & Tales* 27 (1): 65–88.

———. Forthcoming. "Monkey King Films." In *Folktales and Fairy Tales: Traditions and Texts from around the World, Revised and Expanded*. Santa Barbara, CA: ABC-Clio.

Maher, Sean. 1999. *The Internationalisation of Australian Film and Television through the 1990s*. Woolloomooloo, NSW: Australian Film Commission.

Maier, Sarah E. 2007. "From *Peter Pan* to *Finding Neverland*: A Visual Biomythography of James M. Barrie." In *Fantasy Fiction into Film: Essays*, edited by Leslie Stratyner and James R. Keller, 150–62. Jefferson: McFarland.

Makdisi, Saree and Felicity A. Nussbaum. 2008. *The Arabian Nights in Historical Context: Between East and West*. Oxford: Oxford University Press.

Makuszyński, Kornel. 1928. *O dwóch takich, co ukradli księżyc* [The Two Who Stole the Moon]. Warszawa: Gebethner i Wolff.

——. 1930. *Przyjaciel wesołego diabła: powieść dla młodzieży*. Warszawa: Gebethner i Wolff.

Makuszyński, Kornel and Marian Walentynowicz. 1932. *120 przygód Koziołka Matołka*. Warszawa: Gebethner i Wolff.

Malthête, Jacques and Laurent Mannoni, eds. 2002. *Méliès: Magie et cinéma*. Paris: Paris Musées.

Malý, Jakub. 1838. *Národní české pohádky a pověsti (Czech National Folktales and Legends)*. Prague: Špinka.

Manai, Franco. 2009. "The Movie *Pinocchio* by Roberto Benigni and its Reception in the United States." *Studies in European Cinema* 6 (2–3): 153–63.

Manovich, Lev. 2001. *The Language of New Media*. Cambridge: MIT Press.

Mantel, Hilary. 2005. *Great Fairytales: Wicked Parents*. London: Oxford University Press.

Marchese, Pasquale. 1983. *Bibiografia pinocchiesca*. Firenze: La Stamperia.

Marcus, Millicent. 1986. *Italian Film in the Light of Neorealism*. Princeton: Princeton University Press.

Marks, Louis. 2004. "Introduction." In *The Lost Boys*, by Andrew Birkin. Screenplay. London: BBC Publications. Online. Available HTTP: <http://www.jmbarrie.co.uk/abpage/TLB%20SCRIPTS/TLB.htm>.

Martin, Adrian. 1994. "Ghosts . . . of a National Cinema." *Cinema Papers* 97 (8): 14–15.

Martin, François. 2003. *Ladislas Starewitch: 1882–1965*. Paris: L'Harmattan.

Martin-Jones, David. 2009. *Scotland: Global Cinema: Genres, Modes and Identities*. Edinburgh: Edinburgh University Press.

Mason, Peter. 1998. *Infelicities: Representations of the Exotic*. Baltimore: Johns Hopkins University Press.

Mayer, Charles-Joseph, chevalier de. 1785–1789. *Le Cabinet des Fées; Ou Collection Choisie des Contes des Fées, et Autres Contes Merveilleux*. 41 vols. Amsterdam.

Mayer, G. 1999. "Genre, post-World War II." In *The Oxford Companion to Australian Film*, edited by Brian McFarlane, Geoff Mayer, and Ina Bertrand, 177–80. Oxford: Oxford University Press.

Mayorov, Nikolai. 2012. "Soviet Colours." *Studies in Russian & Soviet Cinema* 6 (2): 241–55.

Mazzarella, William. 2010. "'A Different Kind of Flesh': Public Obscenity, Globalization, and the Mumbai Dance Bar Ban." Academia.edu. Online. Available HTTP: <https://www.academia.edu/367951/_A_Different_Kind_of_Flesh_Public_Obscenity_ Globalization_and_the_Mumbai_Dance_Bar_Ban>.

McInally, Kate. 2006. "Reading Girls' Desire in *Touching Earth Lightly*." *CREArTA, Special Issue: Imagining Childhood* 6: 93–102.

McRoy, Jay, ed. 2005. *Japanese Horror Cinema*. Honolulu: University of Hawai'i Press.

Meaney, Neville. 2001. "Britishness and Australian Identity: The Problem of Nationalism in Australian History and Historiography." *Australian Historical Studies* 32 (116): 76–90.

Mehta, Rini Bhattacharya and Rajeshwai V. Pandharipande, eds. 2011. *Bollywood and Globalization: Indian Popular Cinema, Nation and Diaspora*. London: Anthem Press.

Melnyk, George. 2004. *One Hundred Years of Canadian Cinema*. Toronto: University of Toronto Press.

Mernissi, Fatema. 1995. *Dreams of Trespass: Tales of a Harem Girlhood*. Cambridge, MA: Perseus Books.

Meyer, Birgit. 2003. "Ghanaian Popular Cinema and the Magic In and Of Film." In *Magic and Modernity: Interfaces of Revelation and Concealment*, edited by Birgit Meyer and Peter Pels, 200–22. Stanford: Stanford University Press.

Mickiewicz, Adam. 1822. "Świteź." In *Ballady i romanse*. Vilnius: Józef Zawadzki.

Mikkelsen, Svend-Vilhelm. 2014. "Historien om julekalendere." Juleweb. Online. Available HTTP: <http://www.juleweb.dk/historien_om_julekalenderne_04.htm>.

Mitchell, B. 2013. "*Butterflies*—Q&A with Warwick Burton and Isabel Peppard." *Skwigly*, June 5. Online. Available HTTP: <http://www.skwigly.co.uk/butterflies/>.

Miyao, Daisuke. 2007. "Thieves of Baghdad: Transnational Networks of Cinema and Anime in the 1920s." *Mechademia* 2: 83–102.

Moen, Kristian. 2013. *Film and Fairy Tales: The Birth of Modern Fantasy*. London: I.B. Tauris.

Monk, Katherine. 2001. *Weird Sex & Snowshoes and Other Canadian Film Phenomena*. Vancouver: Raincoast Books.

Morcom, Anna. 2007. *Hindi Film Songs and the Cinema*. London: Ashgate Publishing Ltd.

Morris, Jeremy. 2009. "Babka Ezhka and Others." *KinoKultura* 23. Online. Available HTTP: <http://www.kinokultura.com/2009/23r-babka.shtml>. Accessed July 20, 2014.

Morris, Peter. 1978. *Embattled Shadows: A History of Canadian Cinema, 1895–1939*. Montreal: McGill-Queen's University Press.

Mortensen, Klaus P. 2003. "H.C. Andersens eventyr og historier". In *Andersen, H.C. Andersens samlede værker*, Vol. 1. Copenhagen: Det Danske Sprog- og Litteraturselskab and Gyldendalske Boghandel, Nordisk Forlag.

Müller, Kathrin. 2006. "Formulas and Formulaic Pictures: Elements of Oral Literature in the *Thousand and One Nights*." In *The Arabian Nights and Orientalism: Perspectives from East and West*, edited by Yuriko Yamanaka and Tetsuo Nishio, 47–67. London: I.B. Tauris.

Murphy, Tony P. 1993. "The Portrayal of the Environment and Development in Two Commercial Movies." *The Journal of Environmental Education* 25 (1): 30–36.

Murray, Simone. 2012. *The Adaptation Industry: The Cultural Economy of Contemporary Literary Adaptation*. New York: Routledge.

Nafisi, Azar. 1997. "Imagination as Subversion: Narrative as a Tool of Civic Awareness." In *Muslim Women and the Politics of Participation: Implementing the Beijing Platform*, edited by Erika Friedl, 58–71. Syracuse, NY: Syracuse University Press.

Nagib, Lúcia. 2001. "Ouédraogo and the Aesthetics of Silence." In *African Oral Literature: Functions in Contemporary Contexts*, edited by Russel H Kaschula, 100–111. Cape Town: New Africa Books.

———. 2007. *Brazil on Screen: Cinema Novo, New Cinema, Utopia*. London: I.B. Taurus.

Nairn, Tom. 1997. *Faces of Nationalism: Janus Revisited*. London: Verso.

Napier, Susan. 1996. *The Fantastic in Modern Japanese Literature: The Subversion of Modernity*. London: Routledge.

———. 2005. *Anime from Akira to Howl's Moving Castle: Experiencing Japanese Animation*. New York: Palgrave.

National Film and Sound Archive. 2014a. Golden Summer. Online. Available HTTP: <http://nfsa.gov.au/calendar/?type=cinemas-golden-summer>.

National Film and Sound Archive. 2014b. Australian Screen: 1940s. Online. Available HTTP: <http://aso.gov.au/titles/decades/1940s/?page=1&order=chrono>.

National Film and Sound Archive. 2014c. Australian Screen: 1950s. Online. Available HTTP: <http://aso.gov.au/titles/decades/1950s/?page=3&order=chrono>.

National Film and Sound Archive. 2014d. Australian Screen: 1960s. Online. Available HTTP: <http://aso.gov.au/titles/decades/1960s/?page=3&order=chrono>.

Němcová, Božena. 1855. *Babička (Grandmother)*. Prague: J. Pospíšil.

———. (1892) 1999. *The Grandmother: A Story of Country Life in Bohemia*, translated by Frances Gregor. Prague: One Third Publishing.

Neupert, Richard. 2011. *French Animation History*. Oxford: Wiley-Blackwell.

Nishio, Tetsuo. 2006. "The *Arabian Nights* and Orientalism from a Japanese Perspective." In *The Arabian Nights and Orientalism: Perspectives from East and West*, edited by Yuriko Yamanaka and Tetsuo Nishio, 154–67. London: I.B. Tauris.

Niü, Lülin. 2010. "*Hua Mulan*: Yichang wei Aiqing er Jiangou de Zhanzheng (*Hua Mulan*: A War Constructed for Love)." *Dianying Wenxue (Cinema Literature)* 9: 68–69.

Norris, Allison. 2013. "Where Are All the Grown-Ups?: Three Films That Understand Why Hansel and Gretel Must Save Themselves." Paper presented at the Folklore Studies Association of Canada Annual Conference, June 18, Corner Brook, Newfoundland.

O, Jeong-Hi and Jang Seon-Hwan (Illustrator). 2011. *The Woodcutter and the Heavenly Maiden*. Seoul: Biryongso.

O'Leary, Alan and Catherine O'Rawe. 2011. "Against Realism: On a 'Certain Tendency' in Italian Film Criticism." *Journal of Modern Italian Studies* 16 (1): 107–28.

O'Regan, Tom. 1995. "Beyond 'Australian' Film? Australian Cinema in the 1990s." Perth: Centre for Research in Culture & Communication, Murdoch University. Online. Available HTTP: <http://wwwmcc.murdoch.edu.au/ReadingRoom/film/1990s.html>.

Ocelot, Michel. n.d. "Director's Notes." *Kirikou et la Sorciere*. Online. Available HTTP: <http://www.kirikou.net/teachers.html>.

Oinas, Felix J. 1978. "The Political Uses and Themes of Folklore in the Soviet Union." In *Folklore, Nationalism and Politics*, edited by Felix J. Oinas, 77–97. Columbus, OH: Slavica.

Oita, Haruhiko. 2014. "Taketorimonogatari o yomitoku: Tanjyoo kara *Kaguyahime no monogatari* (Reading *The Tale of the Old Bamboo Cutter*: From Inception to *The Tale of Princess Kaguya*)." *Bijutsu techo* 1: 74–78.

Ong, Walter. 1999. "Orality, Literacy and Modern Media." In *Communication in History: Technology, Culture, Society*, edited by David Crowley and Paul Heyer, 60–67. New York: Longman.

Oring, Elliott. 1986. "Folk Narratives." In *Folk Groups and Folklore Genres: An Introduction*, edited by Elliott Oring, 121–46. Logan: Utah State University Press.

Oscarson, Christopher. 2009. "*Nils Holgersson*, Empty Maps and the Entangled Bird's-Eye View of Sweden." *Edda* 109 (2): 99–117.

Ostrovskii, Aleksandr. 2013. *Snegurochka*. Moscow: Detskaia Literatura.

Ouhiba, Insaf. 2012. "Jacques Becker." In *Dictionnaire des orientalistes de langue française*, edited by François Pouillon, 75–76. Paris: Karthala.

Outhwaite, Ida Rentoul. 1916. *Elves & Fairies of Ida Rentoul Outhwaite*, stories and verses by Annie R. Rentoul, edited by Grenbry Outhwaite, illustrated by I.R. Outhwaite. Sydney: Lothian Book Publishing.

Oxfeldt, Elisabeth. 2006. "Life and Death in *The Little Mermaid*: Three Contemporary Adaptations of Hans Christian Andersen's Fairy Tale." *Animation Journal*: 4–25.

——. 2009. *H.C. Andersens eventyr på film*. Odense: Syddansk universitetsforlag.

Oziewicz, Marek. 2011. "Dwarf Resistance in Communist Poland." *Journal of the Fantastic in the Arts* 22 (3): 363–76.

——. 2012. "The First Polish Story Combo: Andrew Maleszka's *The Magic Tree*." *Studia Filmoznawcze* 33: 29–41.

Pagaczewski, Stanisław. 1966. *Porwanie Baltazara Gąbki*. Kraków: Wydawnictwo Literackie.

Pang, Laikwan. 2011. "The Making of a National Cinema: Shanghai Films of the 1930s." In *The Chinese Cinema Book*, edited by Song Hwee Lim and Julian Ward, 56–64. London: Palgrave Macmillan BFI.

Paramonova, Kira. 1979. *Aleksandr Rou*. Moscow: Iskusstvo.

Parker, Katie Langloh. 1897. *Australian Legendary Tales: Folk-lore of the Noongahburrahs as Told to the Piccaninnies*. 2nd ed., introduction by Andrew Lang. London: David Nutt.

——. 1898. *More Australian Legendary Tales*, introduction by Andrew Lang. London: David Nutt.

Pedley, Ethel C. (1899) 2006. *Dot and the Kangaroo*. Project Gutenberg. Online. Available HTTP: <http://www.gutenberg.org/files/18891/18891-h/18891-h.htm>.

Peirse, Alison and James Byrne. 2013. "Creepy Liver-Eating Fox Ladies: The Thousand Year Old Fox and Korea's *Gumiho*." In *Korean Horror Cinema*, edited by Alison Peirse and Daniel Martin, 35–47. Edinburgh: Edinburgh University Press.

Pendakur, Manjunath. 1990. *Canadian Dreams and American Control: The Political Economy of the Canadian Film Industry*. Toronto: Garamond Press.

Peng, Xiaobo. 2010. "Nüxing Zhuyi Shijiao xia de Hua Mulan yu Guojia: Ping Ma Chucheng Dianying *Hua Mulan* (Hua Mulan and the State in Feminist Lens: Review on Ma Chucheng's Film *Hua Mulan*)." *Dianying Pingjie* (*Cinema Review*) 3: 35, 37.

Petzet, Wolfgang. 1947. "Verteidigung des Märchens gegen seine Verleumder." *Prisma* 1: 3–11.

Pickowicz, Paul. 2012. *China on Film: A Century of Exploration, Confrontation, and Controversy*. Lanham, MD: Rowman & Littlefield.

Pierce, Peter. 1999. *The Country of Lost Children: An Australian Anxiety*. Cambridge: Cambridge University Press.

Pietzman, Lewis. 2014. "Behind the Changes That Brought 'Into the Woods' from Stage to Screen." *BuzzFeed*, December 5. Online. Available HTTP: <http://www.buzzfeed.com/louispeitzman/behind-the-changes-that-brought-into-the-woods-from-stage-to#.uml40akQJn>.

Pike, David L. 2012. *Canadian Cinema Since the 1980s: At the Heart of the World*. Toronto: University of Toronto Press.

Pinto, Jerry. 2006. *Helen: The Life and Times of an H-Bomb*. New Delhi: Penguin Books.

Pobutsky, Aldona Bialowas. 2010. "*María llena eres de gracia*: Fairy Tale, Drug Culture, and the American Dream." *Hispanófila* 160 (1): 27–41.

Polaschek, Bronwyn. 2013. *The Postfeminist Biopic: Narrating the Lives of Plath, Kahlo, Woolf and Austen*. New York: Palgrave Macmillan.

Pontieri Hlavacek, Laura. 2011. "Garri Bardin: The Ugly Duckling (Gadkii utenok, 2010)." *KinoKultura* 32. Online. Available HTTP: <http://www.kinokultura.com/2011/32r-gadkiiutenok.shtml>.

Pontieri, Laura. 2012. *Soviet Animation and the Thaw of the 1960s: Not Only for Children*. Eastleigh: John Libbey.

Potter, Beatrix. 1902. *The Tale of Peter Rabbit*. London: Frederick Warne & Co.

Power, Natsu Onoda. 2009. *God of Comics: Osamu Tezuka and the Creation of Post-World War II Manga*. Jackson: University Press of Mississippi.

Prabhakar, Anu. 2012. "Has Bollywood Breached the Great Wall?" DNA: Diligent Media Coporation Ltd., April 22. Online. Available HTTP: <http://www.dnaindia.com/entertainment/report-has-bollywood-breached-the-great-wall-1678982>.

Pranshu. 2014. "A Complete List of Bollywood (Indian) Movies copied from Hollywood: Plain Plagiarism." HubPages.com. Online. Available HTTP: <http://pranshu.hubpages.com/hub/a-complete-list-of-bollywood-movies-copied-from-hollywood-plain-plagiarism>.

Prasad, M. Madhava. 1998. *Ideology of the Hindi Film: A Historical Construction*. Delhi, New York: Oxford University Press.

Preußler, Otfried. 1952. *Die kleine Hexe*. Stuttgart: Thienemann.

——. 1971. *Krabat*, translated by Anthea Bell as *The Satanic Mill*. London: Abelard-Schuman.

Profile. n.d. *Burbank Animation Studios*. Online. Available HTTP: <http://www.burbankanimation.com/pages/profile.html>.

Prokhorov, Aleksandr. 2008. "Tri Buratino: Evolutsiia sovetskogo kinogeroia." In *Veselye chelovechki: kul'turnye geroi sovetskogo detstva*, edited by I. Kukulin, M. Lipovetskii, and M. Maiofis, 153–81. Moscow: NLO.

Propp, Vladimir I. 1968. *Morphology of the Folktale*. Austin: University of Texas Press.

PTI. 2013. "Bollywood's 'Raj' in Russia Continues." *The Times of India Online*, September 22. Online. Available HTTP: <http://timesofindia.indiatimes.com/nri/cinema/Bollywoods-Raj-in-Russia-continues/articleshow/22887005.cms>.

Punathambekar, Aswin. 2013. *From Bombay to Bollywood: The Making of a Global Media Industry*. New York: New York University Press.

Pushkin, Aleksandr. 1990. *The Golden Cockerel and Other Tales*. London: Doubleday.

Qin, Liyan. 2012. "The Intertwinement of Chinese Film and Literature: Choices and Strategies in Adaptations." In *A Companion to Chinese Cinema*, edited by Yingjin Zhang, 361–76. London: Blackwell.

Queen Margrethe II. 2009. "Introduction to: Hans Christian Andersen." *De vilde svaner. Et eventyr af H.C. Andersen*, decoupage art by Queen Margrethe II. Copenhagen: Kristeligt Dagblads Forlag and JJ Film.

Quemada-Díez, Diego. 2013. "Interview with Director." *The Golden Dream*. Dir. Diego Quemada-Díez. Guatemala/Spain/Mexico: Peccadillo Pictures.

Radner, Joan Newlon, ed. 1993. *Feminist Messages: Coding in Women's Folk Culture*. Champaign: University of Illinois Press.

Rafferty, Terence. 1994. "Review of *Dreams*." In *Perspectives on Akira Kurosawa*, edited by James Goodwin, 218–21. New York: Macmillan.

Rafter, Nicole. 2006. *Shots in the Mirror: Crime Films and Society*. New York: Oxford University Press.

Rahbek, Ulla. 2007. "Revisiting *Dot and the Kangaroo*: Finding a Way in the Australian Bush." *Australian Humanities Review* 41: n.p. Online. Available HTTP: <http://www.australianhumanitiesreview.org/archive/Issue-February-2007/EcoRahbek.html>.

Rao, Shuguang et al. 2013. *Zhongguo Leixing Dianying: Lishi, Xianzhuang, Weilai (Chinese Genre Films: History, Current Development, and Future)*. Beijing: Zhongguo Dianying Chubanshe (China Film Press).

Ray, Brian. 2010. "Tim Burton and the Idea of Fairy Tales." In *Fairy Tale Films: Visions of Ambiguity*, edited by Pauline Greenhill and Sidney Eve Matrix 198–218. Logan: Utah State University Press.

Rayns, Tony. 1991. "Breakthroughs and Setbacks: The Origins of the New CHN Cinema." In *Perspective on Chinese Cinema*, edited by Chris Berry, 104–13. London: BFI Publishing.

Reed, B. 1914. "An Interview with the Inventor of the 'Bully Boy' cartoons." *The Bioscope*, 497–99.

Rees, Ellen. 2011. "Trolls, Monster Masts, and National Neurosis: André Øverlid's *The Troll Hunter*." *Scandinavica* 50 (2): 52–62.

Rège, Philippe. 2010. *Encyclopedia of French Film Directors*, Vol. 1. Lanham, MD: Scarecrow Press.

Rehman, Asha'ar. 2014. "Indian Films Still Rule." *DAWN*, January 5. Online. Available HTTP: <http://www.dawn.com/news/1078424>.

Reingold, Jennifer. 2014. "Disney CEO Iger: Frozen has Restored our Mojo." *Fortune*, January 13. Online. Available HTTP: <http://fortune.com/2014/01/13/disney-ceo-iger-frozen-has-restored-our-mojo>.

Rich, B. Ruby. 1997. "An/Other View of New Latin American Cinema." In *New Latin American Cinema: Theory, Practices, and Transcontinental Articulations*, Vol. 1, edited by Michael T. Martin, 273–97. Detroit: Wayne State University Press.

Riordan, James. 1994. *Korean Folk-Tales*. Oxford: Oxford University Press.

Rocha, Glauber. 1997. "An Esthetic of Hunger." Translated by Randal Johnson and Burnes Hollyman. In *New Latin American Cinema Volume One: Theory Practices, and Transcontinental Articulations*, edited by Michael T. Martin, 59–61. Detroit: Wayne State University Press.

Roffat, Sébastien. 2014. *Histoire du dessin animé français. Entre 1936 et 1940. Une politique culturelle d'Etat?* Paris: L'Harmattan.

Röhrich, Lutz. 1956. *Märchen und Wirklichkeit, eine volkskundliche Untersuchung*. Wiesbaden: F. Steiner

——. 1991. *Folktale and Reality*. Bloomington: Indiana University Press.

Rollberg, Peter. 2009. *Historical Dictionary of Russian and Soviet Cinema*. Lanham, MD: Scarecrow Press.

Rosen, Stanley. 2002. "The Wolf at the Door: Hollywood and the Film Market in China from 1994–2000." In *Southern California in the World and the World in Southern California*, edited by Eric Heikkila and Rafael Pizarro, 49–78. Westport, CT: Greenwood.

Rosenbaum, Jonathan. (1970) 2008. DVD cover of *Valerie and Her Week of Wonders*. London: Second Run DVD.

Rudy, Jill Terry. 2014. "Things Jim Henson Showed Us: Intermediality and the Artistic Making of Jim Henson's *The StoryTeller*." In *Channeling Wonder: Fairy Tales on Television*, edited by Pauline Greenhill and Jill Terry Rudy, 82–99. Detroit: Wayne State University Press.

Rutherford, Leonie. 2003. "Australian Animation Aesthetics." *The Lion and the Unicorn* 27 (2): 251–67.

Ryan, Mark David. 2012. "A Silver Bullet for Australian Cinema? Genre Movies and the Audience Debate." *Studies in Australasian Cinema* 6 (2): 141–57.

Rybnikov, Nikolai. 1928. *Skazka i rebenok. Sbornik stat'ei*. Moscow and Leningrad: Gosizdat.

Sabry, Somaya Sami. 2011. "Performing Sheherazade: Arab-American Women's Contestations of Identity." *Alif: Journal of Contemporary Poetics* 31: 196–219.

Sæverås, Nils Olav. 2012. "Smakfull juleoppdatering." *Bergensavisen*, November 8.

Said, Edward. (1978) 2003. *Orientalism*. London: Penguin.

Salam, Ziya Us. 2013. "'Our Cinema will Emerge Stronger'- Mahesh Bhatt." *Fisheye Network*, October 4. Online. Available HTTP: <http://www.fisheyenetwork.com/press.html?id=143#.U-49nkvGGBJ>.

Salazkina, Masha. 2010. "Soviet-Indian Coproductions: Alibaba as Political Allegory." *Cinema Journal* 49 (4): 71–89.

Salisbury, Mark. 1995. *Burton on Burton*. London: Faber and Faber.

San, Gege. 2009. "Ma Chucheng: Dui Yi Yuchun Yanji Mei Xinxin, Ganhan Baizhi Pianchou Gao (Ma Chucheng: No Confidence in Li YuChun's Performance and Sighed at the High Remuneration for Baizhi)." Xinmin.cn. Online. Available HTTP: <http://news.xinmin.cn/rollnews/2009/08/13/2372077.html>.

Sanghi, Anuraag. 2012. "Bollywood in Russia." 2ndlook, January 29. Online. Available HTTP: <http://2ndlook.wordpress.com/2012/01/29/bollywood-in-russia/>.

Sarat, Austin. 2000. "Imagining the Law of the Father: Loss, Dread, and Mourning in *The Sweet Hereafter*." *Law & Society Review* 34 (1): 3–46.

SaskFilm. 2008. "Policy Manual." The Saskatchewan Film Employment Tax Credit Program. Online: <http://www.saskfilm.com/docs/assets9SFETC_Policy_Manual_Oct_08.pdf>.

Sato, Tadao. 2008. *Kenzo Mizoguchi and the Art of Japanese Cinema*. Oxford: Berg.

Savage, Mark. 2011. "Can Martin Scorsese's Hugo save 3D?" *BBC News*, December 2. Online. Available HTTP: <http://www.bbc.co.uk/news/entertainment-arts-15967276>.

Saxby, H.M. 1969. *A History of Australian Children's Literature, 1814–1941*. Sydney: Wentworth Books.

Scheib, Richard. 2012. "The Ugly Duckling (Gadkiy Utyonok)." *Moria: Science Fiction, Horror and Fantasy Film Review*. Online. Available HTTP: <http://moria.co.nz/fantasy/ugly-duckling-2010.htm>.

Schenk, Ralf and Sabine Scholze, eds. 2003. *Die Trick-Fabrik: DEFA-Animationsfilme 1955–1990*. Berlin: Bertz-Verlag.

Schepelern, Peter. 2004. "Billedbog med billeder." In *H.C. Andersen på film—et undervisningsmateriale*. Copenhagen: Det Danske Filminstitut.

Schilt, Thibaut. 2011. *François Ozon*. Urbana: University of Illinois Press.

Schlesinger, Ron. 2010. *Rotkäppchen im Dritten Reich: Die deutsche Märchenfilmproduktion zwischen 1933 und 1945*. Krumbach: Frick, DEFA-Stiftung.

Schmitt, Christoph. 1993. *Adaptionen klassischer Märchen im Kinder- und Familienfernsehen: Eine volkskundlich-filmwissenschaftliche Dokumentation und genrespezifische Analyse der in den achtziger Jahren von den westdeutschen Fernsehanstalten gesendeten Märchenadaptionen mit einer Statistik aller Ausstrahlungen seit 1954*. Frankfurt am Main: Haag & Herchen.

——. 1994. "...so leben sie noch heute: Märchen Adaptionen in Film und Fernsehen." In *Unterhaltung, Werbung und Zielgruppenprogramme*, edited by Hans Dieter Erlinger, Hans-Friedrich Foltin, and Muni Schoemann, 405–37. Munich: Wolfgang Fink.

Schmitt, Christoph, ed. 2008. *Erzählkulturen im Medienwandel*. Münster: Waxmann.

Schwabe, Claudia. 2014. "Getting Real with Fairy Tales: Magic Realism in *Grimm* and *Once Upon a Time*." In *Channeling Wonder: Fairy Tales on Television*, edited by Pauline Greenhill and Jill Terry Rudy, 294–315. Detroit: Wayne State University Press.

Scott, A.O. 2003. "Review Summary: Peter Pan (2003)." *The New York Times*. Online. Available HTTP: <http://www.nytimes.com/movies/movie/285317/Peter-Pan/overview>.

Secchi, Cesare. 2011. "*The Sweet Hereafter* by Atom Egoyan: Extreme Loss and Psychic Survival." *The International Journal of Psychoanalysis* 92: 1631–40.

Sellars, Simon. 2010. "Hiding in Plain Sight." *Overland* 198: n.p. Online. Available HTTP: <http://overland.org.au/previous-issues/issue-198/feature-simon-sellars/>.

Selznick, Brian. 2007. *The Invention of Hugo Cabret: A Novel in Words and Pictures.* New York: Scholastic Press.

Seong, Seok-Jae and Kim Se-Hyeon (Illustrator). 2012. *Story of the Wise Princess Pyeonggang and the Brave Ondal the Fool* (Pyeonggang Gongju wa Babo Ondal). Seoul: Biryongso.

Shakespeare, William. 2005. *Hamlet*, edited by Ann Thompson and Neil Taylor. London: The Arden Shakespeare.

Shaw, Deborah. 2007. "Latin American Cinema Today: A Qualified Success Story." In *Contemporary Latin American Cinema: Breaking into the Global Market*, edited by Deborah Shaw, 1–10. New York: Rowman & Littlefield Publishers, Inc.

Sheaffer-Jones, Caroline. 2002. "Fixing the Gaze: Jean Cocteau's *La Belle et la Bête*." *Romanic Review* 93 (3): 361–74.

Shen, Qinna. 2015. *The Politics of Magic: DEFA Fairy-Tale Films.* Detroit: Wayne State University Press.

Sheridan, Simon. 2004. *The A–Z of Classic Children's Television.* London: Reynolds & Hearn Ltd.

Shi, Hui. 1957. "*Tianxianpei* de Daoyin Shouji (The Director's Notes on *The Heavenly Match*)." *Zhongguo Dianying* (*Chinese Cinema*) 5: 24–27.

Shikibu, Murasaki. 1978. *The Tale of Genji*, translated by Edwin Seidensticker. New York: Penguin Classics.

Shimizu, Tomoko. 2001. "Ghibli monstazu to kankaku no toporoji (Ghibli Monsters: The Topology of Sensation)." In *Miyazaki no Sekai*, no editor, 110–15. Tokyo: Takeshobo.

Shirane, Haruo. 2013. *Japan and the Culture of the Four Seasons: Nature, Literature and the Arts.* New York: Columbia University Press.

Short, Sue. 2014. *Fairy Tale and Film: Old Tales with a New Spin.* Basingstoke: Palgrave Macmillan.

"SimsalaGrimm [Documentation]." 2000. *Märchenspiegel* 11 (1): 33–48.

Sirivlia, Natal'ia. 1997. "'Kashchei Bessmertnyi' i 'Nibelungi'." *Iskusstvo kino* 3. Online: <http://kinoart.ru/archive/1997/03/n3-article>.

Skotte, Kim. 2000. "Snedronningen. En digital teaterfortælling." *Politiken*, April 4.

Smith, Kevin Paul. 2007. *The Postmodern Fairy Tale: Folkloric Intertexts in Contemporary Fiction.* New York: Palgrave Macmillan.

Smith, Michael G. 1997. "Cinema for the 'Soviet East': National Fact and Revolutionary Fiction in Early Azerbaijani Film." *Slavic Review* 56 (4): 645–78.

Smith, Michelle J. and Elizabeth Parsons. 2012. "Animating Child Activism: Environmentalism and Class Politics in Ghibli's *Princess Mononoke* (1997) and Fox's *FernGully* (1992)." *Continuum: Journal of Media & Cultural Studies* 26 (1): 25–37.

Smith, Paul Julian. 2014. *Mexican Screen Fiction.* Malden, USA: Polity Press.

Sokolianskii, Ivan, Aleksandr Popov, and Aleksandr Zaluzhnyi, eds. 1928. *My protiv skazki.* Kharkov: n.p.

Sorlin, Pierre. 1995. "Popular Films or Industrial Byproduct? The Italian Melodramas of the 1950s." *Historical Journal of Film, Radio & Television* 15 (3): 349–59.

"South and Southeast Asian Cinema: A Selected Bibliography/Videography of Materials in the UC Berkeley." 1996. Berkeley Library. Online. Available HTTP: <http://www.lib.berkeley.edu/MRC/AsianBib.html>.

Spence, Lewis. 1946. *British Fairy Origins.* Wellingborough: Aquarian Press Ltd.

Spencer, Michael with Suzan Ayscough. 2003. *Hollywood North: Creating the Canadian Motion Picture Industry.* Montreal: Cantos Original Publishing.

Srinivas, Lakshmi. 2005. "Communicating Globalization in Bombay Cinema." *Comparative American Studies* 3 (3): 319–44.

Stanton, Stephen. 1957. "'Bertrand et Raton': A Well-Made Play." *The Tulane Drama Review* 2 (1): 58–70.

Staples, Terry. 2008a. "Andersen, Hans Christian, in Biopics." *The Greenwood Encyclopedia of Folktales and Fairy Tales*, edited by Donald Haase, 36–38. Westport, CT: Greenwood Press.

——. 2008b. "Kirikou et la sorcière." *Greenwood Encyclopaedia of Folktales and Fairy Tales*, Vol. 2, edited by Donald Haase, 544–45. Westport: Greenwood.

Statistics Canada. 2014. "Linguistic Characteristics of Canadians." 2014. *Statistics Canada.* January 14. Online. Available HTTP: <http://www12.statcan.gc.ca/census-recensement/2011/as-sa/98–314-x/98–314-x2011001-eng.cfm>.

Steig, William. 1990. *Shrek!* New York: Farrar, Straus and Giroux.

Steinitz, Wolfgang. 1951. "Das deutsche Volksmärchen: Ein wichtiger Teil nationalen Kulturerbes." *Neues Deutschland*, November 17.

Steinkjer, Mode. 2012. "Fører eventyrtradisjonen videre." *Dagsavisen*, November 7.

Stephens, John. 2011. "Schemas and Scripts: Cognitive Instruments and the Representation of Cultural Diversity in Children's Literature." In *Contemporary Children's Literature and Film*, edited by Kerry Mallan and Clare Bradford, 12–35. London: Palgrave Macmillan.

Stewart-Steinberg, Suzanne. 2007. *The Pinocchio Effect: On Making Italians (1860–1920)*. Chicago: University of Chicago Press.

Stites, Richard. 1990. "Stalinism and the Restructuring of Revolutionary Utopianism." In *The Culture of the Stalin Period*, edited by Hans Günther, 78–94. New York: St. Martin Press.

Straßer, Susanne. 2010. *Das Märchen von der Prinzessin, die unbedingt in einem Märchen vorkommen wollte*. Rostock: Hinstorff.

Sun, Caihui. 2014. "Xi Shiji Zhongguo Aiqing Dianying zhong de Aiqingguan de Liubian (The Perceptive Transformation of Love in Chinese Romance Films of the New Century)." *Dangdai Dianying* (*Contemporary Cinema*) 5: 163–66.

Švankmajerová, Eva. 2004. *Otesánek*. Prague: Arbor Vitae.

Taboulay, Camille. 1996. *Le cinéma enchanté de Jacques Demy*. Paris: Cahiers du Cinéma.

Tales for All. 2009. *Productions La Fête*. La Fête. Online. Available HTTP: <http://www.lafete.com/en/productions_contes_contes_tous.html>.

Tan, Chunfa. 1995. "Changqi Bei Wudu Bei Lengluo de Yiye: Zaoqi de Zhongguo Dianying (A Long Misunderstood and Long Neglected Chapter: Early Chinese Cinema)." *Dangdai Dianying* (*Contemporary Cinema*) 2: 13–20.

Tan, Shaun. 2000. *The Lost Thing*. Melbourne: Lothian Books.

Tarakhovskaia, Elizaveta. 1965. *Stikhi i skazki*. Moscow: Detskaia literatura.

Tatar, Maria, ed. 1999. *The Classic Fairy Tales*. New York: W. W. Norton and Company.

Tatar, Maria. 2003. *The Hard Facts of the Grimms' Fairy Tales*. Princeton: Princeton University Press.

——. 2004. *Secrets Beyond the Door: The Story of Bluebeard and His Wives*. Princeton: Princeton University Press.

Taylor, John Russell. 1967. *The Rise and Fall of the Well-Made Play*. London: Methuen.

Telefilm Canada. 2011. "Fostering Cultural Success: Telefilm Canada's Corporate Plan 2011–2012–2014–2015." Telefilm Canada. Online. Available HTTP: <http://www.telefilm.ca/document/en/01/17/Telefilm-Canada-corporate-plan-2011–2014.pdf>.

Teo, Stephen. 2013. "The Opera Film in Chinese Cinema: Cultural Nationalism and Cinematic Form." In *The Oxford Handbook of Chinese Cinemas*, edited by Carlos Rojas and Eileen Cheng-yin Chow, 209–24. Oxford: Oxford University Press.

Thackeray, William Makepeace. 1854. *The Rose and the Ring; or, the History of Prince Giglio and Prince Bulbo: A Fire-side Pantomime for Great and Small Children*. London: Bradbury and Evans.

Thirard, Marie-Agnès. 2008. "Du Petit Poucet à l'enfant-Océan." *D'un conte à l'autre, d'une génération à l'autre*, edited by Catherine d'Humières, 73–88. Clermont-Ferrand: Presses universitaires Blaise Pascal.

Thomas, Kristin. 2011. "Hugo: Scorsese's Birthday Present to Georges Méliès." *David Bordwell's Website on Cinema*, December 7. Online. Available HTTP: <http://www.davidbordwell.net/blog/2011/12/07/hugo-scorseses-birthday-present-to-georges-melies/>.

Thomas, Rosie. 2013. "Thieves of the Orient: The *Arabian Nights* in Early Indian Cinema." In *Scheherazade's Children: Global Encounters with* The Arabian Nights, edited by Philip F. Kennedy and Marina Warner, 362–93. New York: New York University Press.

Tian, Youying. 2009. "Shenti de Yinyu: *Hua Pi* zhong de Nüxing Xingxiang (The Metaphor of Body: Female Images in *Painted Skin*)." *Dianying Wenxue* (*Cinema Literature*) 14: 44–45, 49.

Tiffin, Jessica. 2009. *Marvellous Geometry: Narrative and Metafiction in Modern Fairy Tale*. Detroit: Wayne State University Press.

Tofano, Sergio. 1917–1943. "Il signor Bonaventura." *Il corriere dei piccoli*. Italy.

Tolkien, J. R. R. 1954–1955. *The Lord of the Rings*. London: Allen & Unwin.

——. 1966. *The Hobbit or There and Back Again*. 3rd ed. New York: Ballantine.

Tolstaia, Elena. 1997. "Buratino i podteksty Alekseia Tolstogo." *Izvestiia Akademii Nauk* 56 (2): 30–41.

Tolstoi, Aleksei. 1960. "Zolotoi kliuchik, ili prikliucheniia Buratino." In *Sobranie sochinenii* Vol. 10, 180–259. Moscow: Khudozhestvennaia literatura.

——. 1984. *Russkie narodnye skazki v obrabotke A. N. Tolstogo*. Moscow: Pravda.

Tourtel, Mary. 1928–1936. *Rupert Bear Little Library*. London: Sampson Low.

Trevor, William. 1994. *Felicia's Journey*. Toronto: A.A. Knopf Canada.

Turner, Graeme. 1993. "The Genres are American: Australian Narrative, Australian Film and the Problem of Genre." *Literature Film Quarterly* 21 (2): 102–11.

———. 2012. *Film as Social Practice*. Trowbridge, Wiltshire: Routledge.

Turner, Kay and Pauline Greenhill, eds. 2012. *Transgressive Tales: Queering the Grimms*. Detroit: Wayne State University Press.

TVarchive.ca. 2013. "Story Theatre (Series) (1971–1972)." TV Archive Canada. Online. Available HTTP: <http://www.tvarchive.ca/database/18607/story_theatre/details/>.

Ueda, Akinari. 2008. *Tales of Moonlight and Rain*. New York: Columbia University Press.

Ury, Marian. 1993. *Tales of Time Now Past (Konjaku monogatari): Sixty-two Tales from a Medieval Japanese Collection*. Ann Arbor: University of Michigan Press.

Uther, Hans-Jörg. 2004. *The Types of International Folktales: A Classification and Bibliography*. 3 vols. Helsinki: Academia Scientiarum Fennica.

Valentine, Marguerite. 2007. "Analyzing *Muriel's Wedding* with Reference to Cinderella." *British Journal of Psychotherapy* 23 (4): 575–86.

van Geldern, James and Richard Stites, eds. 1995. *Mass Culture in Soviet Russia*. Bloomington: Indiana University Press.

Vasudevan, Ravi. 1989. "The Melodramatic Mode and the Commercial Hindi Cinema: Notes on Film History, Narrative and Performance in the 1950s." *Screen* 30 (3): 29–50.

———. 2000. "National Pasts and Futures: Indian Cinema." *Screen* 41 (1): 119–25.

Verhoeven, Deb. 2010. "Film, Video, DVD and Online Delivery." In *The Media and Communications in Australia*. 3rd ed, edited by Stuart Cunningham and Graeme Turner, 133–54. Crow's Nest, NSW: Allen & Unwin.

Verne, Jules. 1873. *Around the World in Eighty Days*. Paris: Pierre Jules Etzel.

Vesaas, Tarjei. 1957. *The Birds*. Oslo: Gyldendal.

Vignaux, Valérie. 2000. *Jacques Becker, ou l'exercice de la liberté*. Liège: Editions du Céfal.

Vimenet, Pascal. 1985. "La capture du mouvement." *Cahiers du cinéma* 375: 46–54.

Vivarelli, Nick. 2014. "Cannes: Italo Auteur Matteo Garrone Talks About His 'Tale of Tales.'" *Variety*, May 15. Online. Available HTTP: <http://variety.com/2014/film/news/italo-auteur-matteo-garrone-talks-about-his-tale-of-tales-ecxlusive-1201181531/>.

Wade, Mansour Sora. n.d. "Director's statement: *Ndeysaan / The Price of Forgiveness*." Film Fest Amiens. <http://www.filmfestamiens.org/archives/cinemasacp/filmsen/pardon.html>.

Wajda, Katarzyna. 2004. "Jan Jakub Kolski: 'Dobijam się o osobowość.'" In *Autorzy Kina Polskiego*, Vol. 1, edited by Grażyna Stachówna and Joanna Wojnicka, 197–214. Kraków: Rabid.

Wan, Laiming. 1981. "Donghua yishu shengya wushiwu nian (Fifty-five years of Activity in the Art of Animation." *Yingju Meishu (Film Theater Fine Arts)* 1: 20.

Wang, Gang. 2009. "Lüelun Guochan Donghua Dianying *Malan Hua* Minzu Fengge de De yu Shi (On the Strength and Weakness of the Using of National Style in Domestic Animation Film *Malan Flower*)." *Dianying Pingjie (Movie Review)* 20: 29–30.

Wang, Wei. 2014. "Xi Dushi Aiqing Dianying de Leixinghua Fenxi (Analysis on the Genres of New Urban Romance Films)." *Dianying Xinzuo (New Works in Cinema)* 2: 96–99.

Wardetzsky, Kristin. 2014. "'Mit Überraschung bemerkt man die Verwandtschaft mit den Märchen anderer weit entfernter Völker': Zum Anmerkungsband der KHM." *Märchenspiegel* 25 (3): 20–29.

Warner, Marina. 1999. *From the Beast to the Blonde: On Fairy Tales and their Tellers*. New York: Noonday Press.

———. 2005. *Great Fairytales: Beastly Tales*. London: Oxford University Press.

———. 2006. *Phantasmagoria*. London: Oxford University Press.

———. 2012. *Stranger Magic: Charmed States and the* Arabian Nights. Cambridge, MA: Belknap Press of Harvard University Press.

Weintraub, Richard M. 1988. "In Indian Films, Fantasy's the Thing." *Washington Post*, October 24.

Wells, H.G. 1901. *The First Men in the Moon*. London: Newnes.

Wells, Paul. 1998. *Understanding Animation*. New York: Routledge.

———. 2009. *The Animated Bestiary: Animals, Cartoons, Culture*. New Brunswick, NJ: Rutgers University Press.

———. 2014. *Animation, Sport and Culture*. New York: Palgrave Macmillan.

Werich, Jan. 1960. *Fimfárum*. Prague: Československý spisovatel.

Westbury, Atha. 1897. *Australian Fairy Tales*. London: Ward, Lock.

White, Jerry. 2006. *The Cinema of Canada*. London: Wallflower Press.

Whitfield, Jessie. 1898. *The Spirit of the Bush Fire*. Sydney: Angus & Robertson.

Whitley, David. 2012. *The Idea of Nature in Disney Animation: From* Snow White *to* WALL-E, 2nd ed. Farnham, Surrey: Ashgate.

Wiesner, David. 1991. *Tuesday*. New York: Clarion Books.

Wikipedia. n.d. "List of Bollywood Films." *Wikipedia: The Free Encyclopedia*. Online. Available HTTP: <http://en.wikipedia.org/wiki/List_of_Bollywood_films>.

Wilkie, Christine. 1999. "Relating Texts: Intertextuality." In *Understanding Children's Literature*, edited by Peter Hunt, 130–37. New York: Routledge.

Willemen, Paul. 2006. "The National Revisited." In *Theorizing National Cinema*, edited by Valentina Vitali and Paul Willemen, 29–43. London: BFI Publishing.

Willsey, Kristiana. 2014. "New Fairy Tales Are Old Again: *Grimm* and the Brothers Grimm." In *Channeling Wonder: Fairy Tales on Television*, edited by Pauline Greenhill and Jill Terry Rudy, 210–28. Detroit: Wayne State University Press.

Woeller, Waltraut. 1955. *Der soziale Gehalt und die soziale Funktion der deutschen Volksmärchen*. Berlin: Habilitations-Schrift der Humboldt-Universität zu Berlin.

Wood, Naomi. 2006. "The Ugly Duckling's Legacy: Adulteration, Contemporary Fantasy, and the Dark." *Marvels & Tales* 20 (2): 193–207.

Wu, Cheng'en. 1980 (1592?). *Xiyouji* (*Journey to the West*). Beijing: Renmin Wenxue Chubanshe (People's Literature Press).

Wu, Rongsheng. 2008. "Zhongguo Aiqing Dianying Zhuti de Xushi Bianqian (The Transformation of the Narrative Mode of Chinese Romance Films)." *Xiandai Chuanbo* (*Modern Communication Studies*) 3: 139–40.

Wullschlager, Jackie. 2000. *Hans Christian Andersen: The Life of a Storyteller*. London: Allen Lane/Penguin.

Wynchank, Anny. 1994. "The Cineaste as a Modern Griot in West Africa." In *Oral Tradition and its Transmission: The Many Forms of Message*, edited by Edgard Ienaert, Meg Cowper-Lewis, and Nigel Bell, 12–26. Durban: Campbell Collections and Centre for Oral Studies, University of Natal.

Xu, Dajun. 2003. "Nanquan Yishi Shiye zhong de Nüxing: *Liaozhai Zhiyi* Zhong Nüxing Xingxiang Saomiao (Women in the Patriarchal Discourse: Female Images in *Liaozhai Zhiyi*)." *Pu Songling Yanjiu* (*Pu Songling Studies*) 3: 68–75.

Yamanaka, Yuriko. 2013. "The *Arabian Nights* in Traditional Japanese Performing Arts." In *Scheherazade's Children: Global Encounters with* The Arabian Nights, edited by Philip F. Kennedy and Marina Warner, 274–81. New York: New York University Press.

Yang, Lin. 1986. "Cong Minjian Zouxiang Yinmu (From Folklore to the Silver Screen)." *Minzu Yishu* (*Ethnic Arts*) 4: 71–81.

Yang, Xiaolin. 2009. "*Malan Hua*: Pimei Disini Jingdian Donghua de Feifan zhi Zuo (*Malan Flower*: The Extraordinary Work that Is Comparable with Disney's Classical Productions)." *Dianying Wenxue* (*Cinema Literature*) 21: 37–39.

Yao, Guanghua. 2009. "Xinling zhi Hua: Yingyuan Gonghuapian *Malan Hua* Daoyan Chuangzuotan (The Flower of Soul: The Director's Discussion on the Making of the Animation Film *Malan Flower*)." *Dianying XianZuo* (*New Works in Cinema*) 5: 28–30.

Yoshimoto, Mitsuhiro. 2000. *Kurosawa*. Durham, NC: Duke University Press.

Young, Deborah and Phil Gallo. 1996. "Local Films Still India's Sacred Cash Cow." *Variety* 362 (4): 169–70.

Young, Diana. 1991. *FernGully*. Sydney: Ashton Scholastic.

Yu, Eun-Sil and Hong Seon-Ju (Illustrator). 2010. *Shimcheongjeon*. Seoul: Biryongso.

ZDYYZ (Zhongguo Dianying Yishu Yanjiu Zhongxin, China Film Art Research Center), ed. 1995. *Zhongguo Dianying Tuzhi* (*Illustrated Annals of Chinese Films*). Guangxi: Zhuhai chubanshe.

ZDZ (zhongguo dianying ziliao guan, China Film Archive), ed. 1996. *Zhongguo Wusheng Dianying* (*Chinese Silent Cinema*). Beijing: Zhongguo Dianying Chubanshe (China Film Press).

Zeitlin, Judith. 1997. "Embodying the Disembodied: Representations of Ghosts and the Feminine." In *Writing Women in Later Imperial China*, edited by Ellen Widmer and Kong-I Sun Chang, 242–63. Stanford: Stanford University Press.

———. 2010. "Operatic Ghosts on Screen: *The Case of a Test of Love* (1958)." *Opera Quarterly* 26: 220–55.

Zeyer, Julius. 1898. Radúz and Mahulena. Play. Prague, Czechoslovakia.

Zhang, Jing. 2014. *Wei Wancheng de Xushi: Zhongguo Dangdai Dainying Xushi Fengge Yanjiu* (*Unfinished Narrative: A Study on the Narrative Styles of Contemporary Chinese Cinema*). Beijing: Zhongguo Chuanmei Daxue Chubanshe (The Chinese University of Mass Media Press).

Zhang, Jiyue. 2014. *Xin Zhongguo Geming Ticai Dianying zhong de Nüxing Yuyan* (*The Cinematic Narrations on Women in PRC's Revolution Films*). Beijing: Zhongguo Shehui Kexue Chubanshe (Chinese Social Sciences Press).

Zhang, Yingjin. 2004. *Chinese National Cinema.* New York and London: Routledge.

———. 2011. "National Cinema as Translocal Practice: Reflections on Chinese Film Historiography." In *The Chinese Cinema Book*, edited by Song Hwee Lim and Julian Ward, 17–25. London: Palgrave Macmillan/BFI.

Zheng, Tianjian. 1960. "Guanyu *Liu Sanjie* de Chuangzuo (On the Creation of *Third Sister Liu*)." *Juben* (*Screenplay*) Z1: 91–96.

Zhu, Mingjie. 2007. "Zhengjiu Muqin de Gezhe: Donghuapian *Bao Lian Deng* Jiedu (The Mother-rescuing Tale: Analysis on Animation Film *Magic Lotus Lantern*)." *Dianying Wenxue* (*Cinema Literature*) 16: 17–18.

Zhu, Ying. 2003. *Chinese Cinema During the Era of Reform: The Ingenuity of the System.* Westport, CT: Praeger.

Zipes, Jack. 1982. "Grimms in Farbe und Bild: Der deutsche Märchenfilm im Zeitalter der Kulturindustrie." In *Aufbruch zum neuen bundesdeutschen Kinderfilm*, edited by Wolfgang Schneider, 212–24. Hardebek: Eulenhof-Verlag.

———. 1983. *Fairy Tales and the Art of Subversion.* London: Heinemann.

———. 1994. *Fairy Tale as Myth / Myth as Fairy Tale.* Lexington: University Press of Kentucky.

———. 1996. "Towards a Theory of Fairy-Tale Film: The Case of *Pinocchio*." *The Lion and the Unicorn* 20 (1): 1–24.

———. 1997. *Happily Ever After: Fairy Tales, Children and the Culture Industry.* New York: Routledge.

———. 2000. Introduction to *The Oxford Companion to Fairy Tales*, edited by Jack Zipes, xv–xxxii. Oxford: Oxford University Press.

———. 2002. *Breaking the Magic Spell: Radical Theories of Folk and Fairy Tales.* Lexington: University Press of Kentucky.

———. 2005. *Hans Christian Andersen: The Misunderstood Storyteller.* New York: Routledge.

———. 2006a. *Fairy Tales and the Art of Subversion: The Classical Genre for Children and the Process of Civilization.* 2nd ed. New York: Routledge.

———. 2006b. *Why Fairy Tales Stick: The Evolution and Relevance of a Genre.* New York: Routledge.

———. 2007. *When Dreams Came True: Classical Fairy Tales and their Tradition.* New York: Routledge.

———. 2008. *Relentless Progress: The Reconfiguration of Children's Literature, Fairy Tales, and Storytelling.* Hoboken: Taylor and Francis.

———. 2010. Foreword to *Fairy Tale Film: Visions of Ambiguity*, edited by Pauline Greenhill and Sidney Eve Matrix, ix–xii. Logan: Utah State University Press.

———. 2011. *The Enchanted Screen: The Unknown History of Fairy-Tale Films.* New York: Routledge.

———. 2012. *The Irresistible Fairy Tale: The Cultural and Social History of a Genre.* Princeton: Princeton University Press.

Zipes, Jack, ed. and trans. 1987. *The Complete Fairy Tales of the Brothers Grimm.* New York: Bantam.

Zipes, Jack, Pauline Greenhill, and Kendra Magnus-Johnston. n.d. *International Fairy-Tale Filmography.* Online. Available HTTP: <http://iftf.uwinnipeg.ca/>.

Zŏng, In-Sŏb. 1982. *Folk Tales from Korea.* 3rd ed. Seoul: Hollym.

Żukrowski, Wojciech. 1946. *Porwanie w Tiutiurlistanie.* Kraków: Wydawnictwo Księgarni Stefana Kamińskiego.

Ɂeɂanx (*The Cave*). 2013. "National Museum of the American Indian." Film Catalog. Online. Available HTTP: <http://filmcatalog.nmai.si.edu/title/2892/>.

INDEX